CRIMINAL JUSTICE ACT 2003

CRIMINAL JUSTICE ACT 2003

A Guide to the New Law

Andrew Keogh

The Law Society

Reprinted twice in 2005

ISBN 1–85328–877–2

Published in 2004 by the Law Society
113 Chancery Lane, London WC2A 1PL

Typeset by J&L Composition, Filey, North Yorkshire
Printed by Antony Rowe, Chippenham, Wiltshire

CONTENTS

PREFACE

The Act which is reproduced in the appendix to this book bears little resemblance to the Bill presented to Parliament, now over a year ago. It is correct to say that the resulting piece of legislation is improved in a large number of respects through the hard work, skill and extensive life experience of dozens of parliamentarians who contributed to its final form. Despite all of this effort, practitioners and judges will find it no easier to either ascertain what the law says or fathom out what it means in practice. Once again we have a substantial piece of legislation that seeks to achieve its aims largely as a result of amending large numbers of other Acts of Parliament. The result is chaos, and I join an ever increasing number of lawyers who call on Parliament to desist in this practice and instead work towards an entirely codified and consolidated base for our criminal laws on procedure and sentencing.

The Act will clearly have a great impact, but perhaps not quite how you may have at first thought. Practitioners will be little troubled by judge-only trial, if at all. Retrial for offenders as a result of the abolition of the double-jeopardy provisions will no doubt fail to excite any public anger and all the erudite and passionate debate had in Parliament will soon fade to be a distant memory.

The real impact will be in relation to the interpretation of the provisions on character evidence, and the ability to use evidence of propensity to support a conviction. Immense changes have been made in relation to hearsay evidence that will sweep away centuries of English jurisprudence and replace it by an overriding 'interests of justice test', something that sounds tempting, but raises the question: 'who's justice?'. Sentencing provisions will seek to implement a new and effective regime for short and long term prisoners alike, with immense changes to procedures in the lower courts. Inevitably, implementation will be a slow and painful process over many years.

Whether all of these changes, and some are unarguably for the better, will result in a modern justice system, better able to protect the rights of *all* citizens and redress any perceived imbalance in those rights remains to be seen; if the Act fails it certainly will not be for want of trying on the Government's part.

I have tried to produce a book that introduces the reader to the more important parts of the Act, and explain the effect those provisions will have. Inevitably a book on an Act such as this can only ever be an introduction, and the reader will have to grapple with the Act itself to unravel its intricacies and finer points, for that reason I make no apology in providing a copy of the full text to the Act in the appendix.

I am grateful to the many people who have assisted me with this endeavour and commented upon my work as it has progressed; any errors of course remain mine alone. This book is dedicated to my wonderful wife, Roiseen, who once again has been a source of unstinting support.

Andrew Keogh
Manchester, December 2003

TABLE OF CASES

TABLE OF STATUTES

TABLE OF SECONDARY AND EUROPEAN LEGISLATION

1 INTRODUCTION TO THE ACT

1.1 INTRODUCTION

The Criminal Justice Bill, introduced into the House of Commons on 21 November 2002, formed part of the Government's overall package to reform the criminal justice system in England and Wales, and was to 'ensure that criminal trials are run more efficiently and to reduce the scope for abuse of the system', in addition to providing a sentencing framework 'which is clearer and more flexible than the current one'. As well as proposing legislation to meet these wide-ranging aims the bill also suggested change to a number of ancillary areas, not least policing.

The resulting Criminal Justice Act 2003 (the Act) is the seventeenth piece of criminal justice legislation in six years, and was one of six proposed Acts affecting criminal justice announced in the November 2002 Queen's Speech; unlike many other pieces of legislation this Act has been based on detailed and thorough research conducted by Sir Robin Auld in his *Review of the Criminal Courts of England and Wales* (2001) and John Halliday's *Making Punishment Work: Report of a Review of the Sentencing Framework of England and Wales* (2001). In addition to these two major reports it is right to acknowledge the important part played by the Law Commission in the framing of this legislation, notably through the reports it delivered on hearsay (LC 245), double jeopardy (LC 267) and bad character (LC 273).

Much of the Act is uncontroversial and makes many commonsense and practical changes to the way in which the criminal justice system works; the passage of the Act was however dogged with debate on the more contentious topics of double jeopardy, bad character and jury trial, the scene having been set by Matthias Kelly's inaugural speech on taking up Chairmanship of the Bar Council:

> Indeed, as things stand with the Bill, the Government is neither tough on crime nor tough on the causes of crime, to borrow an expression. It is tough on people's basic rights. Tough on the right to a jury trial in a serious case. Tough on the right to a fair trial. And tough on the presumption of innocence. Tampering with the scales of justice will never solve the crime problem. It will make it easier to convict the wrong person of an offence. We are working closely with Justice, Liberty, the Legal Action Group and the Law Society in lobbying for changes to the Bill. We have already lined

up a powerful coalition in the House of Commons against the Government's proposals. The All-party Home Affairs Select Committee. The Conservative and Liberal Democrat frontbenches. There will be an intense battle in the Lords as well. And the Home Secretary should not waste his breath on lectures about it being his democratic duty to strip away people's rights. The public did not vote to abolish jury trial and to create miscarriages of justice. Democracy is a borrowed book in the hands of the politician. It is not the Home Secretary's right to tear out its pages.

Despite tough opposition the Bill survived largely intact with the more controversial provisions still in place save for the flagship proposals in relation to jury trial, which while enacted in part are unlikely ever to be implemented.

The purpose of this book is to provide the practitioner with an overview of the main provisions with an analysis of how they will impact on practice. The Act reforms large swathes of criminal legislation, and it will be necessary in order to fully understand the impact of this legislation to spend time studying the detailed amendments made to existing law – regrettably there is no easy way out, and once again a major piece of legislation has assisted only in adding to the considerable burden placed on lawyers and judges in interpreting and understanding substantial reforms to the criminal process. There can be no stronger argument for the consolidation and codification of our criminal laws into structured and logical criminal codes than this Act. Schedule 3 of the Act in particular is a fine example of how not to amend existing laws.

1.1.1 Composition of the Act

The Act itself is composed of 14 parts comprising 339 sections supplemented by 38 Schedules, which break down into 11 discrete subject areas:

Police powers, Bail, Disclosure, Allocation on offences, Trial on indictment without jury, Prosecution appeals, Evidence of bad character, Retrial for serious offences, Hearsay evidence, Sentencing and Miscellaneous provisions.

1.1.2 Implementation and resources

The following provisions came into force when Royal Assent was given on 20 November 2003:

Sections 168(1) and (2), 183(8), 307(1) to (3), (5) and (6), 330, 331(1) to (5), 334, 335, 336, 337, 338, 339. The repeal in Part 9 of Schedule 37 of section 81(2) and (3) of the Countryside and Rights of Way Act 2000 (and section 332 so far as relating to that appeal), and paragraphs 1 and 6 of Schedule 38 (and section 333(6) so far as relating to that appeal).

The following provisions came into force on 18 December 2003:

Chapter 7 of Part 12 (and Schedules 21 and 22); section 303(b)(i) and (ii); paragraphs 42, 43(3), 66, 83(1) to (3), 84 and 109(2), (3)(b), (4) and (5) of Schedule 32 (and section 304 so far as relating to that part of that Schedule).

Other parts of the Act will come into force on days to be appointed by the Home Secretary, where concrete indications have been given of those dates I have incorporated them into the text. Some parts of the Act have potentially huge public spending implications, and it is likely that the Act will only come fully into force sometime in 2005, possibly even later.

To be able to understand this Act fully and argue its provisions, particularly at appellate level, it is vital that practitioners have access to the reports on which much of the Act is based, and other works which have commented in detail on its scope and potential to operate in practice.

Links to such reports and a free updating service which will keep readers abreast of developments in relation to this Act, and in particular commencement orders, can be accessed via the CrimeLine website. For resources and to register for free updating visit the website (**www.cja2003.com**).

2 POLICE POWERS AND CHARGING REFORMS

2.1 INTRODUCTION

The Act brings in major changes to the processes under which the police deal with suspects, from the point of suspicion right through to disposal by way of caution or charging. Practitioners will note that some of the changes go hand in hand with the amended Police and Criminal Evidence Act 1984 (PACE 1984) Codes of Practice that were brought in to force on 1 April 2003, and simply seek to streamline police procedures to achieve an objective of freeing police from unnecessary paperwork.

Key Changes:

- Amendment to powers of stop and search, including greater role for support staff under supervision.
- New powers of arrest for passport offences, certain class C drug offences (now to include cannabis), and offences under section 174 of the Road Traffic Act 1988.
- Street bail – new initiative to streamline processing of certain prisoners, significant advantages for police and potentially defence lawyers.
- New 36-hour detention limit for all arrestable offences.
- Detention for up to 14 days for those suspected of terrorism.
- Telephone reviews of suspects.
- Extension of power to fingerprint and take non-intimate samples without consent.
- Extension of drug testing to under 18-year-olds.
- Conditional cautioning.
- New system for charging of suspects, with greater involvement for Crown Prosecution Service and greater use of guidelines.
- New methods of instituting proceedings.

2.2 STOP AND SEARCH

Section 1 of PACE 1984 allows a constable to detain and search any person or vehicle and anything which is in or on a vehicle for the purposes of ascertaining whether there are any stolen or prohibited articles. Prohibited articles are defined as articles made or adapted for use in the course of or in connection with an offence listed under section 1(8), or intended by the person having it with him for such use by him or by some other person.

The effect of section 1 of this Act is to add the offences under section 1 of the Criminal Damage Act 1971 (destroying or damaging property) to the list of offences under section 1(8) of PACE 1984.

This section has widespread police support and will allow the search for articles such as spray paint cans and the like, and may even extend to the searching of suspected bill posters. Home Office guidance, which was unpublished at the time of writing, recognises that this provision represents a major extension to the existing powers of stop and search, and that searches based on up-to-date and accurate intelligence are most likely to be effective, lawful and secure public confidence. It is essential that all stop and search powers are used fairly, objectively and without any bias against ethnic or other groups within the community. Since the exercise of these powers may bring officers into greater contact with juveniles, officers should be fully aware of and ready to take account of the special needs of juveniles and other vulnerable groups.

2.2.1 Commencement

This provision came into force on 20 January 2004.

2.3 WARRANTS TO ENTER AND SEARCH

Section 16(2) of PACE 1984 allows for a warrant authorising 'persons to accompany any constable who is executing it', it does not however provide for the person to carry out any search and seizure, and the role is thought to be limited to observing and advising. The lack of clarity in PACE for the role of those accompanying officers, is now remedied by section 2 of this Act which provides that persons authorised to accompany officers on a search shall have the same powers as the constable in respect of (a) the execution of the warrant, and (b) the seizure of anything to which the warrant relate. This is achieved by the addition of a section 16(2A) in PACE 1984.

2.3.1 Presence of constable

Section 2 of the Act also inserts a section 16(2B) into PACE 1984, which states 'But he may exercise those powers only in the company, and under the supervision, of a constable'.

The purpose of the amendment is to allow other professionals to have an effective role in what are increasingly complex search operations. One major area of activity at the present time is in relation to computer seizures, and it could be questioned how effectively, if at all, a constable could supervise a computer technician carrying out complex searches of electronic hardware.

The term 'in the company [of a constable]' is designed to ensure that the supervising constable is on the premises with the authorised person (House of Lords, *Hansard*, 29 October 2003, col. 308).

The supervising officer must, wherever practicable, identify any accompanying persons to the occupier of premises at the start of the search and explain why they are there and their role in the process.

Accountability rests with the supervising officer, but police civilian staff exercising a search role under supervision will need to be aware that they fall under the wider police disciplinary rules as of 1 April 2004 and therefore face serious sanction for improper or unlawful use of these powers unless they can show that responsibility lay solely with the supervising officer. It is essential therefore that full training for all officers and civilian staff is provided.

It should be noted that there are powers in sections 38–47 of the Police Reform Act 2002 and Schedule 4 Part 2 of the same Act, to allow for police civilian staff to undertake some search duties independently. These provisions are not yet in force.

2.3.2 Human Rights Act compatibility

Unlike the authorisation and training of support officers under sections 38–47 of the Police Reform Act 2002, there is no statutory control of those non-police staff that will accompany officers, and now conduct searches under their supervision. Absent an authorisation process and code of practice, it can be questioned whether the involvement of non-police staff in the search process may fall foul of Article 8 of the European Convention of Human Rights. The case of *Funke v. France* (1993) 16 EHRR 297 was mentioned in parliamentary debates, and there is certainly an argument that the new procedures under this Act may well give rise to Article 8 points.

2.3.3 Commencement

This provision came into force on 20 January 2004.

2.4 POWERS OF ARREST

Section 3 of the Act creates makes the following offences arrestable offences:

■ An offence under section 36 of the Criminal Justice Act 1925 (untrue statement for procuring a passport).

- An offence under section 5(2) of the Misuse of Drugs Act 1971 (having possession of a controlled drug) in respect of cannabis or cannabis resin only.
- An offence under section 174 of the Road Traffic Act 1988 (false statements and withholding material information).

The Association of Chief Police Officers is to issue guidance on when the power of arrest in relation to the possession of cannabis or cannabis resin should be exercised. It is expected that the power will only be used in exceptional circumstances where the law is being openly flouted. An example given by the Home Office is where a person smokes cannabis in front of a police officer.

2.4.1 Commencement

An offence under section 5(2) of the Misuse of Drugs Act 1971 will become an arrestable offence on 29 January 2004, the two other offences are expected to become arrestable offences by the end of January 2004 but no date had been set at the time of writing.

2.5 STREET BAIL

Section 4 of the Act allows police officers, as an alternative to taking them to a police station following arrest, to bail the detained person to attend at a police station at a later date. It has been estimated that if 10 per cent of arrests were managed by way of street bail, it would lead to 390,000 police patrol hours being saved, which is the equivalent to having almost 200 additional police officers.

2.5.1 Key benefits

The new provisions are achieved by amending section 30 of PACE 1984 and by the addition of sections 30A, 30B, 30C and 30D to PACE 1984.

Benefits to police	*Benefits to suspects*
Reduce the amount of time travelling to and from the station. Better plan the investigation and work caseload. Spend less time waiting at the police station to progress the investigation. Ensure appropriate representation on answering bail.	Reduce the need to travel to a police station. Avoid spending time in detention while awaiting representation, etc. Ensure that time spent in detention is focused on the investigation and not awaiting representation.
Benefits to legal representatives, parents and appropriate adults	*Benefits to the community*
Ability to plan and prepare for attendance.	Increased police presence on the street. More officers' time spent patrolling than dealing with 'bureaucratic' delays.

2.5.2   When the power can be exercised

The following rules apply to the grant of bail:

- A constable must arrest a person for an offence or take a person into custody after having been arrested for an offence by a person other than the constable (for example a store detective).
- The person must not be at a police station.
- He must be bailed with a requirement to attend at *any* police station at a later date or time.
- No other requirements can be imposed on his bail.

2.5.3   Alleged offences not suited to the grant of street bail

The Act is silent as to when the powers are to be used. There is no presumption in favour of police bail, and the Bail Act 1976 has no application to bail in these circumstances (PACE 1984, s.30C(3)). The Police Bureaucracy Task force, which argued strongly for police bail, suggested that street bail would not be appropriate in the following circumstances:

- serious criminality;
- immediate evidence-gathering required away from the scene;
- accomplices adrift;
- risk of immediate re-offending or vulnerable victim;
- offender drunk, intoxicated or violent;
- vulnerable offender (e.g. mental health problems);
- previous offending history indicates that bail not suitable;
- offender not likely to surrender for other reasons (e.g. foreign visitor);
- offender unwilling to engage, preferring arrest and custody;
- offender's identity is unconfirmed.

The four key considerations:

- the nature of the offence;
- the ability to progress the investigation at the station if not bailed;
- confidence in the suspect answering bail; and
- the level of awareness and understanding of the procedure by the suspect.

Guidance to be issued emphasises that street bail must be used fairly, objectively and without any bias against ethnic or other groups within the community.

2.5.4   Bail notices

Section 30B of PACE 1984 provides that a written bail notice must be given to the detainee before release, stating the offence for which he was arrested (PACE 1984, s.30B(2)(a)), the ground on which he was arrested (PACE 1984, s.30B(2)(b)), and that he is required to attend a police station. A draft notice is reproduced below in Figure 2.1.

Notice to arrested person granted bail
in accordance with section 30A
Police and Criminal Evidence Act 1984

A. TO: (details of person granted bail)

Surname: ....

Forenames: ....

Age: ...... Date of birth ..... /...... /...... M/F ID Code .... SDE Code ....

Address: ....

....

B. CIRCUMSTANCES OF ARREST

On .... day (date) .... /.......... /.......... at (time 24hrs) ....

At (place) ....

You were arrested/taken into custody after your arrest by someone other than a constable by (*officer arresting/taking into custody*)

Name .... Rank .... No. ....

Stn/Branch ....

For Offence ....

When committed ....

Where committed ....

Grounds for arrest ....

....

....

C. DETAILS OF BAIL REQUIREMENT TO ATTEND POLICE
STATION (*complete/delete 1, 2 or 3 as applicable, invite person to sign at 4*)

IMPORTANT: You will be liable to arrest if you do not attend the above police station as required by this notice or by any further notice which you are given.

continued

Figure 2.1 Draft street bail notice

1* **You are required to attend:**

.... police station

Address: ....

on .... day (date) .... /............ /.............. at (time 24hrs) ....

unless you are later given notice in writing that:

(a) you are required to attend a *different* police station *and/or* to attend at a *different* time; or

(b) that you are *no longer* required to attend a police station

2. **You will be given a notice in writing within (X) days of the name and address of the police station and date and time that you are required to attend.**

3. **If you are under 17, you must provide the name, address and, if possible, a contact telephone number of your parent, guardian or other carer. The officer will discuss with you making contact with the person named**

Name ....

Address ....

.... Tel no ....

Status: (Parent/guardian/other (describe)) ....

If in the care of the local authority, state which one ....

4. **Signature of person bailed:**

....

D. OFFICER GRANTING BAIL

On .... day (date) .... /............ /............ at (time 24hrs) ....

At (place) ....

I granted bail to the person named above. I am satisfied that he/she understood the explanation I gave him/her of the bail requirement and gave them this notice.

Signature ....

Name .... Rank .... No. ....

Stn/Branch ....

Contact telephone number: ....

Please read the information on the back of this notice.

Figure 2.1 *continued*

Back of Notice given to arrested person

The Police and Criminal Evidence Act 1984 (PACE) gives a police officer power to grant bail to someone arrested for an offence which requires them to attend a police station at a later date rather than taking them to a police station immediately after arrest.

Attending the police station will provide you with the opportunity to give your version of events. As indicated below, you will have support and professional advice available to you at the police station when you answer bail.

This notice explains the bail requirement.

IF YOU ARE 16 OR UNDER:

1. Please show this notice to your parent/guardian or other person or local authority representative responsible for looking after you.
2. The police will contact your parent/ guardian or other person responsible for looking after you by telephone to inform them that you have been arrested and street bail granted. If in care, contact will be made with the relevant local authority.
3. A copy of this notice will also be sent to the person you have named as being responsible for looking after you. They will also be asked to come to the station with you. <u>Tell the constable if you think that there are reasons why this form should not be sent to them.</u>
4. When you attend the police station you will be entitled to have your parent/guardian or another adult present to help and support you. The police will be required to contact this adult but to avoid delay, you can make your own arrangements for an adult to come with you to the police station.

RIGHTS AND ENTITLEMENTS AT THE POLICE STATION

1. When you attend the police station you will be entitled to free, independent legal advice. If you prefer a solicitor of your own you can make your own arrangements for them to come to, or meet you at, the station.
2. Full details of all your rights and entitlements when you attend the police station are set out in the Codes of Practice issued under the Police and Criminal Evidence Act 1984 (PACE) and you have a right to consult the Codes.
3. Copies of the Codes are kept at all police stations for the public to refer to at any time.

2.5.5   Requirement to attend at a police station

The notice need not specify the time and police station to be attended (PACE 1984, s.30B(4)), but in those circumstances he must subsequently be given a further written notice with those details (PACE 1984, s.30B(5)). Further written notices may alter the police station to be attended and the time, such changes not limited in number (PACE 1984, s.30B(6), (7)).

The requirements allow for considerable flexibility, and it will be possible, for example, to bail persons arrested for alleged football offences at away games to be bailed to their local police station for investigation there at a more appropriate time. It would be unlikely that any date for answering bail would be greater than six weeks unless there are exceptional local circumstances, and consideration of shorter bail dates for juveniles should be considered.

Persons bailed to attend a police station which is not a designated police station must, on their surrender there, be released or taken to a designated police station not more than six hours after their arrival (PACE 1984, s.30C(2)).

2.5.6   Change of bail status

Bail under this section can be cancelled by written notice (PACE 1984, s.30C(1)), and persons can be re-arrested without warrant if new evidence justifying a further arrest has come to light since his release (PACE 1984, s.30C(4)).

2.5.7   Special considerations for juvenile suspects released on bail

Proposed guidance states that in the case of a juvenile, telephone contact should be made as soon as possible with the parent, guardian or other carer in order to notify them of the following information:

- that the juvenile has been arrested;
- of the offence;
- that bail has been granted;
- that the offender has a copy of the bail notice; and
- that a further copy of the bail notice will be forwarded to them setting out the reporting requirements.

2.5.8   Failure to answer police bail

A person who fails to surrender to bail may be arrested without warrant and taken to any police station as soon as practicable after arrest. The provisions of sections 30 and 31 of PACE 1984, shall apply to an arrest for breach of police bail (PACE 1984, s.30D(4)).

2.5.9   Implementation

These provisions came into force on 20 January 2004.

2.6   SUSPECT'S PROPERTY AT THE POLICE STATION

At the present time there is a requirement under section 54 of PACE 1984 to record each item of property held by a suspect when detained at a police station. The process can often be time-consuming, and was heavily criticised by the police during the review of PACE. Section 8 of this Act removes the need to record property, whether as part of the custody record or otherwise. However, there is still a duty on the custody officer to ascertain the property that the suspect has with him.

Property will be retained in secure bags, but despite the wholesale repeal of the recording provisions the Government envisages that 'it will still be necessary to make records, not least to ensure against claims that property has been mishandled or removed'.

2.6.1   How records are made

How those records are made is now within the judgement of the police and the following guidance will be issued to police:

- Consider the circumstances of the case. Property that is or may be the proceeds of crime or may have evidential value should be carefully recorded.
- Consider the nature and volume of the property. Drugs, money and property of significant value, such as jewellery, should always be specifically recorded. A bulk of low value items may not warrant detailed recording.
- Any request of the detained person. The detained person should be asked whether he wants any particular item recording, and where reasonable and practicable the request should be granted.
- Facilities for securing property. Police should consider the use of large sealable bags or containers. By then only allowing the seal to be broken in the detainee's presence, the security of property can be maintained until the detainee's release.

2.7   LIMITS ON PERIOD OF DETENTION WITHOUT CHARGE

Changes to the periods under which suspects can be held without charge have been amended by the Act in relation to arrestable offences and terrorism offences.

2.7.1   Arrestable offences

Section 7 of the Act amends section 42(1)(b) of PACE to allow for detention of up to 36 hours for all arrestable offences. Previously only those detained for serious arrestable offences qualified. This extension of time has serious constitutional implications, and it should be remembered that when the Philips Commission (1981, Cmnd 8092) reported its findings, it was of the view that no detention beyond 24 hours should be sanctioned without a court process or independent visitation. The Philips report was only partially enacted in relation to that suggestion, but nonetheless it is important to recognise how far away from the founding principles of PACE we appear to be moving. Recent evidence (Home Office Research Series 185 (1998)) would tend to suggest that the case for change has not been made out, with typical detention times being much less than the present maximums.

Definition of arrestable offence

An arrestable offence is defined (see PACE 1984, s.24) as any offence for which the sentence is fixed by law, any offence for which a sentence of imprisonment of five years or more may be imposed on a person of 21 years of age or over, or, any offence specifically listed in Schedule 1A to PACE 1984.

Conditions

An officer of the rank of superintendent or above must have reasonable grounds for believing that the detention of that person without charge is necessary to secure or preserve evidence relating to an offence for which he is under arrest or to obtain such evidence by questioning him; and that the investigation is being conducted diligently and expeditiously. It will be incumbent on solicitors advising at the police station to monitor closely the progress being made during an investigation to ensure that the police do not try to take advantage of the increased powers of detention.

Implementation

This provision came into force on 20 January 2004.

2.7.2   Terrorism offences

Section 306 of the Act amends Schedule 8 to the Terrorism Act 2000, with the overall effect that persons suspected of offences of terrorism having been arrested under the Terrorism Act 2000, can now be detained for a total of 14 days without charge. An extension of a warrant of detention beyond seven days can only be granted if seven days has already been allowed. By way of example:

Suspect detained for 4 days: First application must not exceed 3 days. Subsequent application for a further 7 days can later be made. The subsequent application can be made before the expiry of the original extension (so on day 6 an application can be made for extension up to maximum of 14 days from time of detention).

Grounds

The existing grounds in paragraph 32 of Schedule 8 to the Terrorism Act 2000 apply equally to the extended periods of detention:

32. – (1) A judicial authority may issue a warrant of further detention only if satisfied that –

  (a) there are reasonable grounds for believing that the further detention of the person to whom the application relates is necessary to obtain relevant evidence whether by questioning him or otherwise or to preserve relevant evidence, and

  (b) the investigation in connection with which the person is detained is being conducted diligently and expeditiously.

  (2) In sub-paragraph (1) 'relevant evidence' means, in relation to the person to whom the application relates, evidence which –

  (a) relates to his commission of an offence under any of the provisions mentioned in section 40(1)(a), or

  (b) indicates that he is a person falling within section 40(1)(b).

Enhanced power – used sparingly

It is expected that these enhanced powers will be used only sparingly. For the Government's justification for these powers and an informative background to how they are used in practice see House of Lords report stage, *Hansard*, 11 November 2003, col. 1301 (links to all Parliamentary debates can be found at **www.cja2003.com**).

2.8 POLICE DETENTION – TELEPHONE REVIEWS

Section 6 of the Act amends section 40A of PACE 1984 to provide for reviews of detention to be conducted by telephone. Reviews which are of the kind authorised by regulations under section 45A to be carried out using video-conferencing facilities must not be conducted by telephone if it is reasonably practicable to carry it out via the video-conferencing facilities.

At the time of writing, video-conferencing facilities were subject to a pilot scheme in Alton and Winchester (North Walls) police stations in Hampshire (The Police and Criminal Evidence Act 1984 (Remote Reviews of Detention) (Specified Police Stations) Regulations 2003, SI 2003/2397).

2.8.1   Considerations

The decision as to whether to carry out a telephone or face to face review must always take full account of the needs of the person in custody. The benefits of carrying out a review in person should always be considered, based on the individual circumstances of each case with specific additional consideration if the person is:

- a juvenile; or
- mentally vulnerable; or
- has been subject to medical attention for other than routine minor ailments; or
- there are presentational or community issues around the person's detention.

A telephone review can be terminated at any stage in order to continue the review in person.

2.8.2   Commencement

This provision came into force on 20 January 2004.

2.9   TAKING FINGERPRINTS WITHOUT CONSENT

Section 9 of the Act significantly amends Section 61 of PACE 1984, to allow for the taking of fingerprints without consent, of any person who is detained following arrest for a recordable offence, or of any person charged with a recordable offence or notified that he will be reported for such an offence, provided always that he has not had fingerprints taken earlier in the course of the investigation. The Government's justification for this power was given during debate:

> It is important for the police to [take fingerprints] quickly in order to prevent persons evading justice by giving the police false identity and for the police to be aware of anyone who may pose a risk to themselves or to others.

2.9.1   Human rights considerations

At the time of writing the case of R (Marper) v. Chief Constable of South Yorkshire [2003] 1 All ER 148, was awaiting hearing in the House of Lords in relation to the retention of samples and fingerprints.

2.9.2   Implementation

These provisions are expected to come into force in spring 2004.

2.10   TAKING NON-INTIMATE SAMPLES WITHOUT CONSENT

Section 10 of the Act, by way of amendment to section 63 of PACE 1984, allows non-intimate samples to be taken without consent if a person is in police detention following arrest for a recordable offence and he has not had a non-intimate sample of the same type and from the same part of his body taken in the course of the investigation (of the offence). If a sample had been taken but proved insufficient, a further sample can be taken.

2.10.1   Section 63 of PACE 1984

The Act retains the other powers to take samples in section 63 of PACE 1984, although minor amendments are made to the wording.

The reasoning behind this power was expressed by the Government as:

> [the taking of samples] will potentially allow for more crimes to be resolved and at an earlier stage, with corresponding savings in police time and cost but, just as importantly will save from misery those who have continued offences visited upon them by people who are not so identified.

2.10.2   Human rights considerations

See paragraph 2.9.1 above.

2.10.3   Commencement

These provisions are expected to come in to force in spring 2004.

2.11   DRUG TESTING FOR UNDER 18-YEAR-OLDS

Section 5 of the Act amends sections 38 and 63B of PACE 1984, to allow for the testing of persons aged between 14 and 18 years, for the presence of Class-A drugs. Section 63B of PACE 1984 presently only applies to those aged 18 or above. There is provision in section 63B(6A) for the Secretary of State to vary the age requirement should evidence emerge (which is not available now) to indicate widespread drug misuse in a lower age group.

2.11.1   Conditions

Before such a sample can be taken the following conditions must be met:

(1) That the person concerned has been charged with a trigger offence; or that the person concerned has been charged with an offence and a police officer of at least the rank of inspector, who has reasonable grounds for suspecting

that the misuse by that person of any specified Class-A drug caused or contributed to the offence, has authorised the sample to be taken;

(2) That the person has attained the age of 14 years;

(3) That a police officer has requested the person concerned to give a sample, and has warned the person that refusal without good cause may render him liable to prosecution; and

(4) In the case of a person who has not at the time of the request attained 17 years, has made the request, and given the warning, in the presence of an appropriate adult.

Continued detention

A custody officer may authorise continued detention for up to six hours from the time of charge to enable a sample to be taken.

Specified Class-A drugs	Trigger offences
Class-A drugs are defined in the Misuse of Drugs Act 1971, specified by the Secretary of State (in SI 2001/1816) as:	Theft, robbery, aggravated burglary, taking a motor vehicle or other conveyance without authority, aggravated vehicle taking, obtaining by deception, going equipped or stealing, etc.
Cocaine, its salts and any preparation or other product containing cocaine or its salts.	Sections 4, 5(2) and 5(3) Misuse of Drugs Act 1971 if committed in respect of a specified Class-A drug.
Diamorphine, its salts and any preparation or other product containing diamorphine or its salts.	

2.11.2   Refusal

A person who refuses, without good cause, to give a sample is guilty of an offence punishable on summary conviction to imprisonment for a term not exceeding three months, or to a fine not exceeding level 4 on the standard scale, or both.

2.11.3   Use of samples

Information obtained from a sample may be disclosed:

(1) For the purpose of informing decisions about bail.

(2) Where a person is detained or otherwise remanded, or has been granted bail, for the purpose of informing any decision about his supervision.

(3) Where the person is convicted of an offence, for the purpose of informing any decision about the appropriate sentence to be passed by a court and any decision about his supervision or release.

(4) For the purpose of ensuring that appropriate advice and treatment is made available to the person concerned.

Samples may not be used for identification purposes.

2.11.4 Commencement

These provisions are expected to come into force in summer 2004 and will initially apply in pilot areas only.

2.12 CONDITIONAL CAUTIONS

Cautions are widely administered, particularly in relation to first-time adult offenders. The new scheme allows for conditions to be attached to a caution, with a prosecution following if the conditions are breached. The idea of a conditional caution is not new and was raised by the Runciman Commission inquiry in its 1993 report and more recently by Lord Justice Auld. It is beyond doubt, following the decision in *Omar v. Chief Constable of Bedfordshire Constabulary* [2002] EWHC 3060 Admin., that the proposed scheme is compatible with principles of autrefois convict (see paragraphs 41–46 of that judgment). This new scheme of cautioning will be implemented following the publication of extensive guidance on how the scheme might work. Conditional cautions are expected to quickly become a large and important part of the diversionary process, aimed at removing non-violent offenders from the court system wherever possible. Practitioners should be alert to these new provisions and any guidance issued, and ensure that in appropriate cases enquiry is made of the police as to whether such a disposal might be appropriate. It ought to be remembered that following the case of *R (on the application of F) v. Crown Prosecution Service and another*, DC, unreported, 12 December 2003, cautions will only exceptionally be available once an offender has been charged. It is therefore important to consider, at an early stage at the police station, whether an admission in interview might be appropriate.

2.12.1 Types of condition

Only conditions that have either or both of the following objectives can be imposed: (a) facilitating the rehabilitation of the offender; (b) ensuring that he makes reparation for the offence (s.22(3)).

Reparative solutions are expected to play a big part in this new scheme, the Government has outlined the way in which the scheme might work:

> We also believe that conditional cautioning could be used to deliver more sophisticated restorative justice solutions. That is potentially very exciting, as it would involve bringing victims and offenders into direct or indirect contact, where they want that, to discuss the crime and its effects, leading to outcome agreements in which the parties agree what the offender will do in response to the crime. The Government have recently produced a strategy document on that matter. It is a very interesting area that is not without its issues for some people. I have seen it in operation personally and have seen how beneficial it can be, but I also recognise that one must overcome certain hurdles. The outcomes might be compensation, reparation, rehabilitative activities or a formal apology. The evidence certainly shows that restorative justice can reduce reoffending and improve victim satisfaction with the criminal justice system. Conditional cautioning offers a potential way in which to

deal with the problem, but it cannot be done without training. We would clearly have to assess the results before we could recommend the approach on any great scale. We intend to test that use of conditional cautioning in two pilot areas, where we provide funding to train officers in using restorative processes. Those pilots would start when the general scheme is implemented and would be evaluated after a year of operation. That gives more of the flesh on how we would like to proceed.

2.12.2   Age restrictions

Conditional cautions can only be given to those aged 18 or over (s.22(1)).

2.12.3   Authorised persons

The Act speaks of authorised persons in respect to the conditional cautioning regime. An authorised person is a constable, an investigating officer, or a person authorised by a relevant prosecutor for the purposes of section 22 of the Act.

There is nothing in the Act to remove the existing system of cautioning, and it is assumed that the Code of Practice, to be issued under section 25 of the Act will detail the circumstances in which an unconditional caution might be administered.

A key difference of the conditional caution is the approval of the relevant prosecutor before such a caution can be issued.

2.12.4   The five requirements

The following requirements must be met before a conditional caution can be administered (s.23):

(1) The authorised person must have evidence that the offender has committed an offence.
(2) The relevant prosecutor (see s.27) must decide that there is sufficient evidence to charge the offender with the offence, and that a conditional caution should be given to the offender in respect of that offence.
(3) The offender must admit that he committed the offence.
(4) The authorised person must explain the effect of the conditional caution to the offender and warn him that failure to comply with any of the conditions attached to the caution may result in his being prosecuted for the offence.
(5) The offender must sign a document which contains details of the offence, an admission by him that he committed the offence, his consent to being given the conditional caution and the conditions attached to the caution.

2.12.5   Conditions that can be attached

The Act provides for a code of practice which will outline the mechanics of the conditional caution, along with a list of the conditions that may be attached to such cautions and the length of time for which such conditions may have effect (s.25).

2.12.6   Failure to comply with conditions

An offender who fails, without reasonable excuse to comply with any of the conditions attached to the conditional caution may have criminal proceedings instituted against him for the offence in question (s.24(1)). Police will be able to use discretion in deciding whether or not to prosecute, it having been recognised that if it were the policy that every breach, however trivial, automatically resulted in prosecution, it would be unduly restrictive in that genuine reasons for non compliance could not be taken into consideration. The document signed by the offender is admissible in such proceedings (s.24(2)). A prosecution brings to an end the conditional caution (s.24(3)).

2.12.7   Escaping prosecution for summary only offences

It would appear that an offender who is conditionally cautioned for an offence of common assault (for example) can break the terms of his conditional caution after a period of six months have elapsed from the date of the offence (not the date of caution) and escape prosecution, as any proceedings would be time-barred. This lacuna operates in respect of most summary-only offences, unless section 24(1) of the Act is interpreted in such a way as to override other time bar provisions.

2.12.8   Implementation

These provisions are expected to be piloted beginning April 2004.

2.13   CHARGING SUSPECTS

Part 4 of the Act introduces a new method of charging suspects, which replaces the current system of charging and the laying of an information. The requirement to substantiate certain matters on oath is removed, and a comprehensive system of procedure for dealing with the charging of persons at the police station is introduced.

2.13.1   Procedures for charging or releasing those in police detention

Schedule 2 of the Act makes provision in relation to the charging or release of persons in police detention. Section 37 of PACE 1984 is amended to reflect the new procedure.

Table 2.1 provides an overview of the provisions.

Table 2.1   Options available to custody officer – DPP may issue guidance as to how this discretion is to be exercised

Charge with an offence	Release without charge and without bail	Release without charge but with bail	Release without charge and on bail for the purpose of enabling the DPP to make a decision under section 37B
The police still retain the right to charge a suspect with any appropriate offence. Upon charge, a decision is taken either to bail the suspect to court, or to keep him in custody and produce before the next available court.	This brings the investigation to an end, although the suspect may be later arrested if new evidence comes to light.	This is to allow for the release of the suspect on bail while the police undertake further enquiries.	This option is wider than the present 'advice file' procedure and is designed to ensure that the charge (if there is to be one) is right first time. Note: Conditional bail can be imposed

Options open to DPP when case referred:

(1) Insufficient evidence to charge (notice given to suspect).
(2) Sufficient evidence to charge but decision made not to charge (public interest grounds) (notice given to suspect).
(3) Sufficient evidence to charge, but caution appropriate (police *must* caution, unless not possible) (notice to be given to suspect).
(4) Charge with offence, either by virtue of provisions under section 29 of CJA 2003 or by police on answering police bail.

Code of practice

For the purposes of enabling custody officers to decide how to proceed under section 37 of PACE 1984, the Director of Public Prosecutions (DPP) may issue guidance to custody officers. Such guidance may make provision for different cases, circumstances or areas. The guidance may have the effect of ensuring that all decisions in particularly sensitive cases, such as those involving the death of a person, be referred to the DPP.

Options available to a custody officer

These include the following:

(1) If there is insufficient evidence to charge a suspect, the officer may decide to refuse charge. A refusal of charge will release the suspect from any obligation to return to the station on bail, and effectively brings the investigation to an end at that stage. The investigation may well be resurrected at a later date (PACE 1984, s.37(7)(c)).

(2) The police may decide there is insufficient evidence to charge, but wish to continue with the investigation. The suspect can be released on bail, but without charge, for this purpose (PACE 1984, s.37(7)(b)). The bail must be unconditional.

(3) Charge the suspect if there is sufficient evidence (PACE 1984, s.37(7)(d)).

(4) Refer the file to the Director of Public Prosecutions, to decide whether there is sufficient evidence to charge (PACE 1984, s.37(7)(a)).

Consulting with the DPP

A file is to be sent to the DPP as soon as is practicable (PACE 1984, s.37B(1)), in order that a decision can be taken as to what action, if any, is to be taken against the offender.

The DPP has the following options:

(1) Decide that there is insufficient evidence to charge, or that there is sufficient evidence to charge the person with an offence, but that he should not be charged with an offence or given a caution. The latter option allows the DPP to decide not to take any further action on public interest grounds. In the event that the DPP decides on any of these options a custody officer shall give the suspect notice in writing that he is not to be prosecuted (PACE 1984, s.37B(5)).

(2) Decide that the suspect should be charged or cautioned with an offence, and for what offence (PACE 1984, s.37B(3)). Once the decision is made the police must charge or caution as advised. This brings to an end the current practice whereby police occasionally refuse to caution a suspect even when advised to do so by the Crown Prosecution Service (CPS), very often leading to no action at all being taken by the prosecution as it is then felt not to be in the public interest to continue with a prosecution.

Cautioning

Cautioning includes a conditional caution under the 2003 Act and a warning or reprimand under section 65 of the Crime and Disorder Act 1998 (PACE 1984, s.37B(9)).

In the event that it proves not to be possible to give the offender a caution, he shall instead be charged with the offence (PACE 1984, s.37B(7)).

Charging

If a decision is taken by the DPP to charge the offender, this can occur either when the offender returns to the police station to answer his bail, or alternatively in accordance with section 29 of the Act, by the issuing of a written charge and requisition (PACE 1984, s.37B(8)).

Bail

The Act makes provision for the bailing of suspects under the above procedures by inserting sections 37C and 37D of PACE 1984. If a suspect is released on bail pending consultation with the prosecution he may be made subject to conditional bail and arrested for any breach of that bail. On being arrested he may be further released (with or without bail conditions or bail) or charged with an offence. The DPP may issue guidance as to how a person should be dealt with under this provision. It is anticipated that the police may be able to seek a more urgent decision from the CPS in such cases. During debate on the Act it was proposed that a time limit should be fixed in relation to such bail, but that argument was rejected by the Government which made passing reference to a five-week period being sufficient in most cases. In rejecting amendments to the Act the Government argued:

> That does not mean that the period for which suspects should be bailed, whether on conditions or not, should be unreasonably long, but the appropriate place to make that clear is in the guidance and instructions which will be issued by the Director of Public Prosecutions and by ACPO . . . rather than in the Bill. I emphasise that it would be open to a suspect to apply to a magistrates' court for conditional bail to be varied or discharged. Legal aid will be made available for that purpose.
>
> (House of Lords Committee Stage, *Hansard*, 14 July 2003, col. 684)

At the time of writing no amendments had been made to allow for legal aid to be granted in such cases, nor for such applications to be covered by a duty solicitor at court.

Implementation

These provisions are expected to come into force in spring 2004.

2.14 · NEW METHOD OF INSTITUTING PROCEEDINGS

Section 29 of the Act introduces the concept of a 'written charge' and 'requisition'. A written charge is precisely what it says it is, and must be accompanied by a requisition which requires a person to appear before a magistrates' court to answer the written charge (s.29(2)). Copies of both documents must be served on both the accused and the court. The power to issue a charge and requisition rests with a public prosecutor (see s.29(5)). It is anticipated that prosecutors will use this procedure when considering cases referred under section 37B of PACE 1984 as an alternative to having the suspect return to the police station to be charged in the traditional way.

Once this section is implemented, public prosecutors will have no power to apply for a summons under section 1 of the Magistrates' Courts Act 1980 (section 29(4)), although the power to lay an information for the purposes of obtaining a warrant under section 1 is retained (s.30(4)(a)), as are the powers under section 1 in respect of persons who are not public prosecutors (s.30(4)(b)).

2.14.1   Charging of persons in custody

Nothing in section 29 takes away any power to charge a person with an offence while he is in custody (s.30(4)(c)).

2.14.2   Definition of public prosecutor

Section 29(5) defines a public prosecutor as:

(1) a police force or a person authorised by a police force to institute criminal proceedings;
(2) the Director of the Serious Fraud Office or a person authorised by him to institute criminal proceedings;
(3) the Director of Public Prosecutions or a person authorised by him to institute criminal proceedings;
(4) the Attorney General or a person authorised by him to institute criminal proceedings;
(5) a Secretary of State or a person authorised by a Secretary of State to institute criminal proceedings;
(6) the Commissioners of Inland Revenue or a person authorised by them to institute criminal proceedings;
(7) the Commissioners of Customs and Excise or a person authorised by them to institute criminal proceedings;
(8) a person specified in an order made by the Secretary of State for the purposes of this section or a person authorised by such a person to institute criminal proceedings.

2.14.3   Rules

Rule-making powers under section 144 of the Magistrates' Courts Act 1980 may be used to provide for the form, content, recording, authentication and service of written charges or requisitions; and such other provision in relation to the same as appears to the Lord Chancellor to be necessary or expedient (s.30).

2.15   REMOVAL OF REQUIREMENT TO SUBSTANTIATE INFORMATION ON OATH

Section 31 removes the requirement under sections 1(3) and 13 of the Magistrates' Courts Act 1980 to substantiate those applications (for warrants) on oath. This is a welcome development as the current practice adds nothing at all to the efficacy of the proceedings.

2.16   POLICE AND CRIMINAL EVIDENCE ACT – AMENDING THE CODES OF PRACTICE

Section 11 of the Act provides for the issuing and amendment of the Codes of Practice authorised pursuant to sections 60, 60A, 66 or 113 of PACE 1984.

A code may be made, or revised, so as to apply:

(a) only in relation to one or more specified areas;
(b) have effect only for a specified period;
(c) apply only in relation to specified offences or descriptions of offender.

Any code, or revised code, must be laid before Parliament and approved by a resolution of each House.

2.16.1   Duty to consult

The Secretary of State must consult persons whom he considers to represent the interests of police authorities, persons whom he considers to represent the interests of chief officers of police, the General Council of the Bar, the Law Society of England and Wales, the Institute of Legal Executives and such other persons as he thinks fit (s.11(4)(f)). Different provisions apply in relation to Armed Service codes of practice under section 113 of PACE 1984.

3 PROVISIONS RELATING TO BAIL

Key changes:

- Presumption against bail where an adult offender commits offence while on bail or absconds.
- New jurisdiction of Crown Court to consider appeals in relation to conditional bail.
- Removal of High Court jurisdiction in relation to bail.
- Extension of prosecution power to appeal grant of bail by magistrates' court.
- Restrictions on the grant of bail to drug users.

3.1 OVERVIEW

Part 2 of the Act makes substantial amendment to the Bail Act 1976, largely in order to make it compliant with the European Convention of Human Rights (ECHR). Changes are made to the grant of conditional bail, the ability to use the fact that an offence has been committed while on bail as a ground in itself for refusing bail and tightening up the procedures to be followed when a defendant commits a breach of bail conditions or fails to surrender to bail.

The jurisdiction of the High Court is severely curtailed by the new Act, and the prosecution are given extended powers to appeal the grant of bail.

To deal with the causal link between drug addiction and offending, the Act introduces a reverse burden for certain offenders to show that 'there is no significant risk of his committing an offence while on bail', before bail can be granted. It is highly likely that this latter provision will meet with argument under article 5 of the ECHR.

3.2   CONDITIONS OF BAIL

Section 13 of the Act amends the Bail Act 1976 to allow for conditional bail to be imposed, with such requirements as appear to the court to be necessary for 'his own protection or, if he is a child or young person, for his own welfare or in his own interests'.

The same amendment has been made to section 3A(5) of the Bail Act 1976, to allow for such conditions in respect to police bail post charge.

Prior to this amendment there was no power to impose conditions for this reason, although a remand into custody was possible.

Police bail prior to charge can be made subject to conditions in cases where the file is referred to the prosecution for a decision to be made on charge. Section 47 of PACE 1984 has been amended to give effect to this change, and regard should be had to the procedure for applying to vary the conditions of bail, which is not under section 43B of the Magistrates' Courts Act 1980, but by way of a new procedure under section 47(1E) of PACE 1984.

3.3   BAIL FOLLOWING A BREACH OF BAIL

There is no presumption in favour of bail for a defendant arrested and brought before the court who is found to be in breach of his existing bail conditions. The Act (s.13(4)) changes the current situation by stipulating that a defendant need not be granted bail if –

(a) having been released on bail in or in connection with the proceedings for the offence, he has been arrested in pursuance of section 7 of the Bail Act; and
(b) the court is satisfied that there are substantial grounds for believing that the defendant, if released on bail (whether subject to conditions or not) would fail to surrender to custody, commit an offence on bail or interfere with witnesses or otherwise obstruct the course of justice (whether in relation to himself or any other person).

3.3.1   Nature of the breach

In many cases the nature of the breach may in itself make a finding in relation to the grounds for refusing bail much more likely, for example an arrest in the vicinity of a complainant's address in breach of an exclusion. The Act gives statutory effect to the practice already adopted following *R (on the application of the DPP) v. Havering Magistrates Court* [2001] 2 Cr App R 2, DC.

3.4 BAIL FOR AN OFFENCE ALLEGEDLY COMMITTED WHILE ON BAIL

The Bail Act 1976 states that a defendant need not be granted bail if he is accused of an indictable-only offence, or an offence triable either way, if it appears to the court that he was on bail in criminal proceedings on the date of the offence. This existing provision has been criticised as not being compliant with the ECHR, but it is unlikely that the new proposals will convince critics, since there is a clear presumption against bail in the case of adults allegedly offending while subject to bail.

3.4.1 Defendants aged 18 or over

Section 14 of the Act introduces a new paragraph 2A of Part 1 of Schedule 1 to the Bail Act 1976, which provides that where it appears a defendant who is aged 18 or over, was on bail in criminal proceedings on the date of the new offence, *he may not be granted bail* unless the court is satisfied that there is no significant risk of his committing an offence while on bail, whether subject to conditions or not.

3.4.2 Is the burden on the defendant?

There is clearly a reverse burden on defendants to satisfy the court that there is no risk of offending while on bail. Reverse burdens are not necessarily in conflict with the ECHR, but the point is at least arguable, and will no doubt be litigated very shortly after the commencement of this section.

3.4.3 Defendants under 18 years of age

For offenders under the age of 18 a new Section 9AA is inserted into the Bail Act 1976 and provides that for the purpose of deciding whether there are substantial grounds for believing that a defendant (aged under 18), if released on bail (whether subject to conditions or not), would commit an offence while on bail, the court shall give *particular weight* to the fact that the defendant was on bail in criminal proceedings on the date of the offence.

3.5 ABSCONDING WHILE ON BAIL

An offender, aged 18 or over, who fails without reasonable excuse to surrender to his bail, or having a reasonable excuse thereafter fails to surrender as soon as reasonably practicable thereafter, *may not be granted bail*, unless the court is satisfied that there is no significant risk that, if released on bail (whether subject to conditions or not), he would fail to surrender to custody (s.15). For the purpose of this section a failure of the court to provide a copy of the bail record shall not constitute a reasonable cause for his failure to surrender to custody.

3.5.1   Offenders under 18 years of age (s.15(2)).

Where an offender under 18 years of age fails to surrender to his bail, the court, when deciding whether there are substantial grounds for believing the defendant would fail to appear, shall give particular weight to the fact that the offender previously failed to surrender without reasonable excuse, or having reasonable excuse failed to surrender as soon as reasonably practicable thereafter. For the purpose of this section a failure of the court to provide a copy of the bail record shall not constitute a reasonable cause for his failure to surrender to custody.

3.5.2   Limitation period on Bail Act charges

Previously, in respect of police bail, an information needed to have been laid within six months of the failing to surrender to custody. Frequently, this was not done, and offenders escaped conviction. Under the new provision, if information was not laid within six months of the date of the Bail Act offence, it can be laid within three months following the defendant's subsequent surrender to custody, arrest or otherwise being brought before the court in connection with the offence (s.15(3)).

3.6   APPEALS TO THE CROWN COURT IN RESPECT OF BAIL

Section 16 of the Act prescribes the circumstances in which a defendant, granted bail by a magistrates' court can appeal to the Crown Court. Previously, appeals in respect to conditional bail lay only to the High Court.

Appeals can only be made in relation to the following conditions (s.16(3)):

- that the person concerned resides away from a particular place or area;
- that the person concerned resides at a particular place other than a bail hostel;
- that a surety (or sureties), or security be provided;
- that the person concerned remains indoors between certain hours;
- that the person be subject to electronic monitoring of a bail condition under section 3(6ZAA) of the Bail Act 1976;
- that the person concerned makes no contact with another person.

3.6.1   Conditions must be satisfied

Before an appeal can be made, one of the following conditions must be satisfied:

(1) That an application under section 3(8)(a) of the Bail Act 1976 has been made and determined prior to the appeal. An application under section 3(8), to vary bail conditions must be made to the court that imposed the conditions, save where there has been a committal for trial or sentence (when the

application should be made to the Crown Court – rendering the appeal unnecessary in any event), or;

(2) An application under section 3(8)(b) or 5B(1) of the Bail Act 1976 has been made and determined prior to the appeal. These sections deal with appeals by constables and prosecutors in respect to varying bail conditions imposed on the accused.

3.6.2   Powers of the Crown Court on appeal

The Crown Court may vary the conditions of bail, but may not remove bail altogether, so defendants need not be at risk when asking for bail conditions to be varied, of being remanded into custody (s.16(7)).

3.6.3   Further appeals

Further appeals are allowed, but must follow from a further application made and determined under section 3(8)(a) of the Bail Act 1976, i.e. an application to the justices to vary the conditions (s.16(8)).

3.7   HIGH COURT JURISDICTION IN RELATION TO BAIL

3.7.1   Magistrates' court proceedings

Save for a limited jurisdiction retained following an application to state a case for the consideration of the High Court, the inherent power of the High Court to entertain an application for bail, or to vary bail, from the magistrates' court is abolished (s.17(1),(2)). This is so even where the Crown Court has refused to vary bail under section 16 of the Act.

3.7.2   Crown Court proceedings

Once section 17 is implemented there will be no right of appeal to the High Court following a refusal of bail in the Crown Court, or a refusal in the Crown Court to vary the conditions of bail. This restriction covers the denial of bail in respect to those facing retrial, under section 88 or 89 of the Criminal Justice Act 2003.

3.7.3   Retained jurisdiction

The High Court retains all other powers in relation to bail, including those in respect of judicial review, habeas corpus and any other prerogative remedy (s.17(6)).

3.8   PROSECUTION APPEALS AGAINST THE GRANT OF BAIL

At present the Bail (Amendment) Act 1993 allows prosecutors to appeal the grant of bail, where it had been opposed, in relation to offences carrying a sentence of imprisonment of five years or more.

Section 18 of the Act, enables prosecutors to appeal the grant of bail in respect to all imprisonable offences.

Practitioners will note that the power is sparingly used at present, and internal procedures at the CPS require consideration to be given in advance to such applications, by prosecutors of appropriate seniority.

This amendment flows from the Auld report, which the Government cited with approval in Committee. The approach to the new power was outlined by Home Office Minister Hilary Benn:

> Sir Robin referred to the sorts of offences, not especially serious in themselves, that, if repeated, can affect the quality of life of large numbers of people, and give rise to a concern about the inability of the criminal justice system to prevent the commission of offences on bail . . . It would not be usual for the prosecution to appeal against a grant of bail for a defendant charged with a minor offence. However, there will occasionally be circumstances in which it is appropriate to challenge a decision to grant bail – even for those offences punishable by less than two years imprisonment.

3.9   DRUG USERS – RESTRICTIONS ON BAIL

This is one of the more contentious provisions in the Act, likely to have a significant impact on the operation of the courts in relation to bail applications in most areas. The apparent need for the provision is emphasised in the Government's White Paper, *Criminal Justice: The Way Ahead*, where it was said 'drug-addicted defendants can be extremely prolific in their offending. Offenders using heroin or crack cocaine are estimated to commit property offences at twice the rate of offenders who do not use drugs'.

Section 19 provides that where the three conditions below are satisfied, an offender aged 18 or over may not be granted bail unless the court is satisfied that there is no significant risk of his committing an offence while on bail (whether subject to conditions or not):

(1) There is drug test evidence that the person has a specified Class-A drug in his body. The test will be under section 63B of the Police and Criminal Evidence Act 1984 or section 161 of the Criminal Justice Act 2003 (pre-sentence drug testing);

(2) The court is satisfied that there are substantial grounds for believing that the misuse of a specified Class-A drug caused or contributed to that offence, or

(even if it did not) the offence was motivated wholly or partly by his intended misuse of such a drug, or the offence is one under section 5(2) or (3) of the Misuse of Drugs Act 1971; and

(3) The person does not agree to undergo an assessment as to his dependency upon or propensity to misuse specified Class-A drugs or, has undergone such an assessment but does not agree to participate in any follow-up offered. When considering subsequent applications for bail the court must consider whether this condition remains satisfied.

3.9.1   Specified Class-A drugs

A specified Class-A drug is given the same meaning as in Part 3 of the Criminal Justice and Court Services Act 2000, namely:

(a) cocaine, its salts and any preparation or other product containing cocaine or its salts; and

(b) diamorphine, its salts and any preparation or other product containing diamorphine or its salts.

3.9.2   Mandatory conditions for assessment and follow-up

If the court grants bail it shall impose as a condition of that bail that the defendant both undergo the relevant assessment and participate in any relevant follow-up proposed to him or, if a relevant assessment has been carried out, that the defendant participate in the relevant follow-up.

3.9.3   Refusal of bail

The fact that an offender has allegedly committed an offence linked to Class-A drug misuse and is willing to be assessed and treated, does not mean that he must be granted bail; it is clear that these provisions are primarily aimed at addressing re-offending while on bail, as opposed to failing to surrender or interference with witnesses/obstructing justice.

3.9.4   Nexus between drug dependency and offending

Drug users will not always commit offences as a direct result of drug misuse, and it will be important not to allow this section to be used in respect of such offenders where no link is shown. If a court is satisfied that there is no significant risk of a person offending while on bail, the fact that a defendant may have refused drug treatment will be of little if any relevance. This section is primarily aimed at acquisitive offending behaviour.

3.9.5   Availability

These provisions are expected to be rolled out in pilot areas; no court may order an assessment or follow-up unless previously notified by the Secretary of State that the programmes are available. It follows that bail cannot be withheld simply because a defendant refused treatment that was not in fact available.

3.9.6   Human rights considerations

While detention of drug addicts may be justified under article 5(1)(e) of the ECHR, it is arguable that this does not extend to detention of those awaiting trial, and the reverse burden imposed may offend article 5(3). These views are shared by Liberty and the Law Commission.

The Government answered the human rights objections in this way:

> I turn now to the human rights issues, which comprise the second point made by the noble Baroness. I am aware of the two points raised by Liberty. I do not accept them. First, I address the proposition that the clause does not fit into one of the permitted exceptions under Article 5(1)(c) of the ECHR. The exception under Article 5 to which this does relate is that which refers to detention considered reasonably necessary to prevent a person committing an offence. We have in fact amended this approach in line with the report of the Law Commission, to which the noble Baroness referred, in order to make it clear that it focuses on the likelihood of further offences being committed, which is a permitted exception. The issue is not simply the fact of drug use; it is the fact of drug use which leads to further offences being likely. That is why there is the exception to which I drew attention before.
>
> So, there being a link between drug addiction and re-offending, which I suggest that all those involved in the criminal justice system and noble Lords in this House would accept without hesitation, we can focus on the perfectly proper exception: whether further offences are likely to be committed.
>
> The other point raised by Liberty relates to Article 8 of the convention, covering the right to private and family life. I understand that that is in the context of a defendant being required to undergo a drug test to obtain bail. As noble Lords will know, Article 8 is one of those which is subject to limitations. Put broadly, those limitations are appropriate in a democratic society for the protection of the rights of others or other perfectly proper purposes. I have no doubt that the requirement that a person should submit to a drug test in order to be in a certain position so far as bail is concerned is a proper requirement, justified under Article 8(2).
>
> Perhaps I may repeat what I said in Committee: these provisions are justified by the need to balance the protections of society against the risk of re-offending, with appropriate incentives for treatment for those who can benefit from it.
>
> (House of Lords, *Hansard*, 29 October 2003, col. 334)

4 ALLOCATION AND TRANSFER OF OFFENCES

4.1 INTRODUCTION

Section 41 and Schedule 3 of the Criminal Justice Act 2003 (the Act) make substantial changes to the way cases are allocated between courts. The Act amends the sending, plea before venue, mode of trial and committal procedures significantly. Similar changes are made to the procedures in the youth court.

Key changes:

- Committal and transfer proceedings abolished. All cases not suitable for summary trial to be sent under section 51 of the Crime and Disorder Act 1998 (CDA 1998).
- Committal proceedings abolished in relation to youths, with homicide and grave crime cases being sent under section 51A of CDA 1998.
- New notice procedure for serious or complex fraud cases, and some cases involving children.
- New venue procedure for adults, with possibility of magistrates indicating whether a custodial or non-custodial sentence will follow if a guilty plea is entered.
- New powers to commit for sentence. Separate power for committal of 'dangerous adult and youth offenders', and youths who wish to plead guilty to grave crimes at the youth court.
- No power to commit adult for sentence following plea before venue when indication of sentence given (certain exceptions).
- No power to commit for sentence if offence suitable for summary trial (certain exceptions).

4.2   CASES TO BE SENT TO THE CROWN COURT

4.2.1   Adults

An adult who appears or is brought before the magistrates' court must have his case sent to the Crown Court forthwith if the following conditions are satisfied:

(1) The offence is triable only on indictment (other than one in respect to which notice has been given under section 51B or 51C of the CDA 1998). This is largely an existing provision.

(2) The offence is triable either way but the court is required to proceed to send the case by virtue of sections 20(9)(b), 21, 23(4) or (5) or 25(2D) of the Magistrates' Courts Act 1980 (MCA 1980);

(3) That the offence is one in respect of which notice has been given under sections 51B or 51C of the CDA 1998.

(4) That the offence is an either-way offence, and he is jointly charged with a youth who has been sent (or is to be sent) to the Crown Court in respect to that matter, or that matter is related to an offence already sent in respect to the youth (see sections 51A(6)(b) and (7) of the CDA 1998).

(5) That the offence is a related summary or either-way offence (punishable by imprisonment or disqualification in the case of summary offences). If another adult appears jointly charged or with a related offence, he shall also be sent for trial.

Sending in relation to these matters is discretionary or mandatory dependent upon the timing of the appearance before the court.

Key differences

Paragraph number (2) above relates to offences in respect of which:

(1) The defendant, having been asked to elect summary trial or trial on indictment, has chosen trial on indictment, or his consent to summary trial has not been signified by the person representing him (MCA 1980, ss.20(9)(b) and 23(4)).

(2) The court has decided are not suitable for summary trial (MCA 1980, ss.21 or 23(5)).

(3) The court makes a decision to change from summary trial to (what would have been) committal proceedings (MCA 1980, s.25).

These changes have the effect of abolishing committal proceedings and ensuring that once a decision is made that summary trial is either unsuitable or not desired the offence is sent to the Crown Court.

Paragraph number (3) above relates to offences in respect of which:

(1) A notice has been given in respect to a serious fraud case (CDA 1998, s.51B).

(2) A notice has been given in respect to certain cases involving children (CDA 1998, s.51C). The offences concerned are listed in s.51C(3) and apply in

relation to children under 17 years of age (or who gave a video-taped interview while under that age).

These changes largely mirror the old provisions under the Criminal Justice Act 1991 (child offences) and Criminal Justice Act 1987 (fraud cases).

4.2.2 Youths

Prior to this Act youths were only sent for trial under the provisions of section 51 of the CDA 1998 in relation to offences with which they were jointly charged with an adult. This Act makes a number of key changes and enacts a section 51A of the CDA 1998. Offences will be sent forthwith for trial in the following instances:

(1) The offence is one of homicide (CDA 1998, s.51A(12)).
(2) The offence is one that would attract a minimum sentence under section 51A of the Firearms Act 1968 (see section 287 of the Act for the relevant criteria).
(3) The offence is one that falls within section 91(1) of the Powers of Criminal Courts (Sentencing) Act 2000 (PCC(S)A 2000) and which might merit a sentence under section 91 of that Act (so called grave crimes). If the offence also falls within number (5) below, it should be sent as such.
(4) The offence is one in respect of which a notice has been given under sections 51B or 51C of the CDA 1998 (serious or complex fraud, and child cases).
(5) The offence is a specified offence within the meaning of section 224 of the Act and it appears to the court that if he is found guilty of the offence the criteria for the imposition of a sentence under sections 226(3) or 228(2) of the Act would be met.
(6) Where the offence is a related indictable or summary offence to an offence already sent (must carry imprisonment or disqualification). It does not matter whether the appearance in relation to the related offence is at the same time as the original offence is sent (see CDA 1998, s.51A(5)).
(7) Where the youth is jointly charged with an adult and the adult's case is sent for trial (CDA 1998, s.51(7)). Related offences can also be sent.

4.2.3 Notice procedure for fraud and child cases

Sections 51B and 51C of the CDA 1998 detail the relevant provisions, and are set out in Schedule 3 to the Act. The provisions are almost identical to those that they replace, the main difference being that the cases are no longer transferred, but sent, under the procedures outlined above.

4.2.4 Reporting rules

A new section 52A of the CDA 1998 sets out the rules for the reporting of allocation or sending proceedings. The section merely consolidates existing rules taking into account the new procedures.

4.3   NEW VENUE AND MODE OF TRIAL PROCEDURE FOR ADULTS

Before a magistrates' court embarks on deciding whether to accept jurisdiction for an either-way offence it will not only hear representations about the offence, as now, but will also be informed of the accused's antecedent history if he has one. A court will also have to have full regard to any allocation or sentencing guidelines.

It will be important for courts to be fully appraised of the facts of the case, since if they accept jurisdiction there will be only limited opportunity to thereafter commit for sentence. See Chapter 10 for changes to sentencing powers.

4.3.1   Defendant's right

The new procedure allows for a defendant to ask for an indication of sentence before deciding on whether to be tried summarily or on indictment. Magistrates do not have to give such an indication, but if they indicate a non-custodial sentence, and as a consequence the defendant asks for plea before venue to be re-visited, and enters a guilty plea, he must thereafter receive a non-custodial sentence. If an indication is given but a defendant does not change his plea to guilty, that previous indication will not be binding on any sentencing court (MCA 1980, s.20A(3)).

4.3.2   What is the nature of the sentence indication?

The wording of the Act is an indication as to whether 'a custodial sentence or non-custodial sentence would be more likely to be imposed if he were to be tried summarily for the offence and plead guilty' (MCA 1980, s.20(3)).

The fact that a non-custodial sentence may be 'more likely' than a custodial sentence is not quite the same as saying that a custodial sentence will definitely not be imposed, but that is the effect of the section. Section 20A of the MCA 1980 states that where a case is dealt with in accordance with section 20(7) of the MCA 1980 (entry of a guilty plea following a sentence indication), 'no court may impose a custodial sentence for the offence unless such a sentence was indicated . . .'.

4.3.3 Overview

Plea before venue
Offender to indicate plea of guilty,
not guilty (or refusal to enter plea)

──── **Guilty plea indicated** ─┐

NG or NO indication

Court must consider mode of trial decision.
Court can receive representations from
defence and prosecution, and can be
informed of the accused's previous
convictions if any.

Court must decide whether, considering its
sentencing powers and other factors
whether summary trial is appropriate.

Is case suitable for summary trial? ─ **NO** →

Is the court of the opinion that its
sentencing powers are insufficient
(PCC(S)A 2000, s.3), or that the criteria
for the imposition of a sentence under
ss.225(3) or 227(2) of the CJA 2003
would be met (PCC(S)A 2000, s.3A)?

If *yes* commit for sentence under the
relevant power.

If *no* sentence summarily.

Case will be sent to Crown Court
under s.51 of the CDA 1998.

YES

Offender to be asked whether he wishes to be tried summarily or
on indictment. Must be warned that there is a power to commit
for sentence under s.3A of the PCC(S)A 2000.
(Note that if court deem case suitable for summary trial all other
powers of committal save s.4 of the PCC(S)A 2000 are lost.)

Offender may ask for an indication of sentence to be given:
whether a custodial sentence or non-custodial sentence would be
more likely to be imposed if he were tried summarily for the
offence *and* to plead guilty.

Is indication of sentence
asked for and given?

Offender asked whether he wishes to reconsider his
earlier indication of plea. If he does wish to reconsider
and pleads guilty at the (renewed) plea before venue
stage he will be convicted.

── **YES** → **What sentence will he get?**
If the court indicated a non-custodial sentence then
such a sentence must be imposed, *unless* the court
decides to commit for sentence under
s.3A(4) of the PCC(S)A 2000 or s.4.

If no indication asked for, or
court refuses, or offender
having been given an
opportunity to revisit plea
before venue does not
indicate a guilty plea:

**What if having been given an indication he does not
wish to revisit plea before venue or indicates
not guilty?**
This situation will no doubt arise when the indication
given is not favourable. In such circumstances the
procedure below is followed.

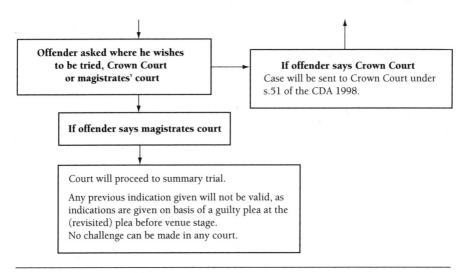

Figure 4.1 Overview of new plea before venue and mode of trial procedure

4.4   COMMITTAL FOR SENTENCE

In relation to offences triable either way an adult is given the option of entering a plea at the plea before venue stage. If a guilty plea is entered, the court must decide whether their sentencing powers are sufficient, or whether the offender should be committed to the Crown Court for sentence. If an offence is deemed suitable for summary trial, the power to later commit for sentence is abolished, save in the case of dangerous offenders, or where an offence is to be sent to the Crown Court and it is appropriate to commit the new offence for sentence alongside.

In the Youth Court, committal for sentence was abolished when the courts' sentencing powers were increased to two years detention and training. An offender did not have the opportunity of pleading guilty in the lower court to a grave crime, and instead had to wait until the case arrived in the Crown Court. Under the new rules a Youth Court will be able to accept a guilty plea in relation to a grave crime, and commit the youth for sentence.

The new procedure will do little to speed up proceedings, as a grave crime would now be sent (as outlined above) to the Crown Court forthwith in any event. It will however allow for sentencing reports to be prepared earlier, and greater credit to be given for a plea at an earlier stage in line with *R v. Rafferty* [1998] 2 Cr App R (s) 450 where it was stated:

> when a defendant pleads guilty before venue at the magistrates' court, the judge at the Crown Court must have regard to the fact that the plea has been made at that early stage. In the usual case therefore a defendant who enters a guilty plea before

venue should be entitled to a greater discount than a person who delays making a plea until he pleads to the indictment . . .

4.4.1 In the Youth Court – grave crimes

A youth appearing in respect of a grave crime can indicate a guilty plea to that offence (MCA 1980, s.24A). If the court is of the opinion that its sentencing powers are not sufficient (i.e. that a sentence under PCC(S)A 2000, section 91(3) is appropriate), it shall commit him for sentence to the Crown Court under PCC(S)A 2000, sections 3B or 3C (for which see below). Related offences can be committed under section 6 of the PCC(S)A 2000.

If he has already been sent for trial on one or more related offences the court may commit him in custody or on bail in respect of the offence. (For example, the youth may indicate a plea to one robbery at plea before venue, but be denying a second robbery. In this situation the second offence would be sent for trial and the first offence would be committed for sentence alongside.) The court may adjourn the decision to commit if they have not yet determined whether to send the second offence (PCC(S)A 2000, s.4A).

4.4.2 In the Youth Court – dangerous young offenders

The Youth Court can commit a youth for sentence following summary trial if, in relation to the offence, it appears to the court that the criteria for the imposition of a sentence under sections 226(3) or 228(2) of the Act would be met (PCC(S)A 2000, s.3C). The committal may be in custody or on bail. Nothing in this section prevents a court from dealing with the case as a grave crime (see above). This power is exercisable at any time, and not limited to a plea at the plea before venue stage.

These provisions relate to sentences for public protection and extended sentences. The relevant criteria are outlined in Chapter 10.

4.4.3 Adult offenders – power to commit at plea before venue stage

The usual powers to commit an adult offender for sentence following a plea of guilty is retained by the court, where that plea is tendered at plea before venue. However, there is one important exception. A committal for sentence cannot follow (unless the offender is a dangerous adult offender – see below) when the plea was entered as a result of having been given an indication of sentence and the offender asking to revisit the plea before venue procedure (MCA 1980, s.20(7)).

4.4.4   Dangerous adult offenders

The court must commit an adult for sentence following conviction on summary trial if, in relation to the offence, it appears to the court that the criteria for the imposition of a sentence under sections 225(3) or 227(2) of the Act would be met (PCC(S)A 2000, s.3A). The committal may be in custody or on bail. This committal power is independent from that in section 3 of the PCC(S)A 2000, in that it allows committal for sentence where a conviction is recorded not only at plea before venue, but at a later stage also. If a court has accepted jurisdiction for an offence, no committal for sentence would be permissible save under this section. It would appear extremely unlikely that the power would be ever used in this way, as one would expect jurisdiction to have been declined in such cases.

These provisions relate to sentences for public protection and extended sentences. The relevant criteria are outlined in Chapter 10.

The fact that the offender may have been given an otherwise binding indication of sentence does not prevent the committal under this power (PCC(S)A 2000, s.3A(4)).

5 DISCLOSURE

Key points:

- New objective duty of disclosure on prosecution, with one single test.
- Duty on defence to provide details of defence witnesses and experts instructed.
- Code of practice on police interviewing of defence witnesses.
- Obligation on defence to update defence case statement.
- Sanctions for certain non-disclosure by defence.

5.1 INTRODUCTION

Part 5 of the Criminal Justice Act 2003 (the Act) provides for a comprehensive overhaul of the present rules of disclosure. Lord Justice Auld commented in his review of the criminal court that 'The 1996 Act has not worked well'; that statement may well be viewed by many as a clear understatement, as the disclosure provisions under the Criminal Procedure and Investigations Act 1996 (CPIA 1996) have come in for widespread criticism from both defence and prosecution lobbies. A major omission in the Act is any attempt to address continuing concerns in relation to ex parte rulings in relation to public interest immunity, a gap all the more wide following the court's ruling in *Edwards and Lewis v. United Kingdom*, *The Times*, 29 July 2003.

The new rules provide for an overhaul of both prosecution and defence disclosure, and defence lawyers who fear that the system is moving away from an adversarial system to an inquisitorial one will find little of comfort in the new rules. It is clear however that the rules are designed with dual aims of more efficient case management and lessening the chances of ambush defences, it is already widely documented that there is little if any evidence to support the notion that there is widespread use of ambush defences, but that argument has not convinced the Government nor perhaps the judiciary (see *R v. Gleeson*, *The Times*, 30 October 2003; *Hughes v. DPP* [2003] EWHC 2470 Admin.). To understand fully the Government's approach on this issue one need look no further than Lord Justice Auld's comments, adopted by Home Office Minister Hilary Benn during the passage of the Bill:

> I can understand why, as a matter of tactics, a defendant might prefer to keep his case close to his chest. But that is not a valid reason for preventing a full and fair hearing on the issues canvassed at the trial. A criminal trial is not a game under which a guilty defendant should be provided with a sporting chance. It is a search for the truth.

5.1.1   Single test for disclosure

Section 32 of the Act introduces a one-stage disclosure test replacing the present system of primary and secondary disclosure. Section 3(1) of the CPIA 1996 is amended to provide for disclosure under the following test:

> The prosecutor must –
>
> (a) disclose to the accused any prosecution material which has not previously been disclosed to the accused and which might reasonably be considered capable of undermining the case for the prosecution against the accused or of assisting the case for the accused, or
> (b) give to the accused a written statement that there is no material of a description mentioned in paragraph (a).

Nature of the test

The key change in this provision is the removal of the subjective 'prosecutor's opinion' found in the old section 3(1)(a) of the CPIA 1996, and the introduction of an objective test for disclosure, albeit one still exercised by the prosecution.

5.1.2   Continuing duty of prosecutor to disclose

Full disclosure is no longer dependent on the service of a defence case statement, a new section 7A of the CPIA 1996, inserted by section 37 of the Act provides that:

> The prosecutor must keep under review the question whether at any given time (and, in particular, following the giving of a defence statement) there is prosecution material which might reasonably be considered capable of undermining the case for the prosecution against the accused or of assisting the case for the accused (CPIA 1996, s.7A(2)).

Timing of disclosure

Material must be disclosed to the accused as 'soon as is reasonably practicable', or within the period described in section 12 of the CPIA 1996 following the service of an initial or updated defence case statement (CPIA 1996, s.7A(3), (5)).

Applications for disclosure

Where an accused has served a defence case statement (but not otherwise), and the prosecution has complied with its duty of disclosure, or purportedly complied, or failed, the accused can if he has reasonable cause to believe that there is prosecution material that is properly disclosable but has not been so disclosed, apply to the court for an order of disclosure (CPIA 1996, s.8).

The requirement to serve a defence statement contradicts the intention of the single test of disclosure detailed above, and in theory means that if a prosecutor fails to disclose any information at all, the defendant could not challenge that failure until he himself served a defence statement. The Home Office Minister was notified of the contradiction when the bill was in committee on 9 January 2003, and undertook to consider the matter further; there has however been no change to the Act as a result.

5.1.3   Defence disclosure

The Act provides for prescribed contents within a defence case statement (CPIA 1996, s.6A), with the Secretary of State able to make regulations to specify the content (CPIA 1996, s.6A(4)).

A defence statement must be in writing and state the following:

- Nature of accused's defence, including any particular defences on which he intends to rely.
- The matters of fact on which he takes issue with the prosecution, and why issue is taken in relation to each matter.
- Any points of law, including any point as to the admissibility of evidence or abuse of process, which he wishes to take, and any authority on which he intends to rely for that purpose.

Alibi

A defence statement that discloses an alibi must give particulars of it (CPIA 1996, s.6A(2)), including:

(a) the name, address and date of birth of any witness the accused believes is able to give evidence in support of the alibi, or as many of those details as are known to the accused when the statement is given;

(b) any information in the accused's possession which might be of material assistance in identifying or finding any such witness in whose case any of the details mentioned in paragraph (a) are not known to the accused when the statement is given.

Service of defence case statement

A defence case statement must be given within the timescales set down under section 12 of the CPIA 1996 on both the court and prosecution. A court may also order, following application by any party or its own motion, the service of the defence case statement on other parties to the proceedings (i.e. co-defendants).

5.1.4   Updated disclosure by accused

New regulations will prescribe a time limit for updated defence disclosure (provided that initial disclosure has been completed within the statutory time limits).

The updated statement must comply with all of the above requirements that apply to the initial defence case statement, but must be updated by reference to the state of affairs at the time when the statement is given (CPIA 1996, s.6B(3)).

Service of updated defence case statement

An updated defence case statement must be given within the timescales set down under section 12 of the CPIA 1996 on both the court and prosecution. A court may also order, following application by any party or its own motion, the service of the updated statement on other parties to the proceedings (i.e. co-defendants). The updated statement must conform to section 6A of the CPIA 1996. As an alternative to an updated defence statement the accused may give a written statement stating that he has no changes to make to the earlier defence statement (CPIA 1996, s.6B).

5.1.5   Notices in relation to defence witnesses

Section 34 of the Act inserts a new section 6C into the CPIA 1996 that provides for the service of a notice on the court and prosecutor (within timescales to be prescribed) indicating whether the accused intends to give or call any evidence at trial, and if so:

(a) giving the name, address and date of birth of each proposed witness (other than the accused himself), or as many of those details as are known to the accused when the notice is given (save where these witnesses are in relation to alibi and the information has already been given);

(b) providing any information in the accused's possession which might be of material assistance in identifying, or finding any proposed witness in whose case any of the details mentioned in paragraph (a) are not known to the accused when the notice is given.

Amended notices

If, following the giving of a notice, the accused:

(a) decides to call a person who is not included in the notice as a proposed witness, or decides not to call a person who is so included; or
(b) discovers any information which he would have had to include in the notice if he had been aware of it when giving the notice.

He must give an appropriately amended notice to the court and the prosecutor.

Code of practice in relation to police interviews of witnesses notified by accused – Section 40 of the Act

Section 40 inserts a new section 21A into the CPIA 1996, providing for the Secretary of State to issue a code of practice in relation to the interviewing of such witnesses, the code will provide an important safeguard against police abuse of requirement to identify defence witnesses, and will in particular contain guidance in relation to the following issues:

(a) information that should be provided to the interviewee and the accused in relation to such an interview;
(b) the notification of the accused's solicitor of such an interview;
(c) the attendance of the interviewee's solicitor at such an interview;
(d) the attendance of the accused's solicitor at such an interview;
(e) the attendance of any other appropriate person at such an interview taking into account the interviewee's age or any disability of the interviewee.

The code will be binding on the police who must have regard to it when interviewing witnesses (CPIA 1996, s.21A(3)).

If the police adopt the practice of interviewing defence witnesses, and the only purpose in reality is to try to collate an account that might be inconsistent with any given in court, it will no doubt become defence practice to likewise seek to interview prosecution witnesses prior to trial. There is nothing in the Law Society code of conduct that would prevent such a course of action, although guidance is given.

5.1.6   Notices in relation to defence experts (s.33)

If the accused instructs a person with a view to his providing any expert opinion for *possible* use as evidence at the trial of the accused, a notice must be served on the court and prosecutor specifying the person's name and address, unless that information has already been given as part of the accused's notification of defence witnesses.

Section 12 of the CPIA 1996 will prescribe time limits for the service of such notices.

Privilege

There is nothing in the Act that alters the rules of privilege in relation to expert witnesses, but defence lawyers may consider it prudent to remind experts of their legal obligations in any standard letter of instruction.

Sanctions

There is no sanction for failing to serve details of defence experts, and in the absence of any professional conduct rules elsewhere it is difficult to see why any defence lawyer would wish to comply with this rule. No prosecution comment is allowed if the defence fail to serve such notices, as confirmed by Lord Goldsmith for the Government during the passage of the Act:

> However, in the case of the notification of defence experts not called as witnesses, the prosecution will not be able to invite the jury to draw an adverse inference or otherwise comment to the jury on either the failure of the defence to comply with this provision or on the fact that an expert has been consulted and not used as a witness.
>
> (House of Lords, *Hansard*, 17 November 2003, col. 1781)

5.1.7   Faults in defence disclosure

The Act inserts by virtue of section 39 a radically different section 11 into CPIA 1996, which provides for the following sanctions following any defence failure to comply with the above rules of defence disclosure.

Failure	Sanction	Notes
In cases under section 5 of the CPIA 1996 (compulsory disclosure in Crown Court):	The court or any other party may make such comment as appears appropriate.	In relation to the failures identified below, the sanction is subject to the relevant proviso: comment may only be made with leave of the court (s.11(6)).
(a) fails to give an initial defence statement,	The court or jury may draw such inferences as appear proper in deciding whether the accused is guilty of the offence concerned.	
(b) gives an initial defence statement out of time,		
(c) fails to give an updated defence statement after being required to do so,		
(d) gives an updated defence statement out of time,	Where an accused calls a witness who he has failed to notify or adequately identify, the court must have regard to whether there is justification for the failure.	
(e) sets out inconsistent defences in his defence statement,		
(f) **At his trial:**		
(i) puts forward a defence which was not mentioned in	Where an accused puts forward a defence different	

Failure	Sanction	Notes
his defence statement or is different from any defence set out in that statement, (ii) relies on a matter which, in breach of the requirements imposed by or under section 6A (contents of defence statement), was not mentioned in his defence statement,* (iii) adduces evidence in support of an alibi, without having given particulars of the alibi in his defence statement, or (iv) calls a witness to give evidence in support of an alibi without having complied with sections 6A(2)(a) or (b) as regards the witness in giving his defence statement.	to that mentioned in the defence statement the court must have regard to the extent of the differences in the defences and to whether there is any justification for it.	
In cases under section 6 of the CPIA 1996 (voluntary disclosure in summary proceedings): (a) gives a voluntary defence case statement out of time, or (b) does any of the things mentioned in paragraphs (c) to (f) above.*	The court or any other party may make such comment as appears appropriate. The court or jury may draw such inferences as appear proper in deciding whether the accused is guilty of the offence concerned. Where the accused calls a witness who he has failed to notify or adequately identify, the court must have regard to whether there is justification for the failure. Where an accused puts forward a defence different to that mentioned in the defence statement the court must have regard	

Failure	Sanction	Notes
	to the extent of the differences in the defences and to whether there is any justification for it.	
In any case: (a) gives a witness notice out of time, or (b) at his trial calls a witness not included, or not adequately identified, in a witness notice.	The court or any other party may make such comment as appears appropriate. The court or jury may draw such inferences as appear proper in deciding whether the accused is guilty of the offence concerned.	Leave of court required to make comment (s.11(7)).

* Comment with leave of court (s.11(6)).

Interpretation

References to defence statement include amended defence statements if applicable to any particular case.

Warning to accused

If it appears to the judge at a pretrial hearing that an accused has failed to comply with defence obligations to disclose, such that there is a possibility of comment being made or inferences being drawn, he shall warn the accused accordingly (CPIA 1996, s.6E(2)).

Proving the defence document

A defence statement given on behalf of an accused by his solicitor shall, unless the contrary is proved, be deemed to be given with the authority of the accused (CPIA 1996, s.6E(1)).

Presumably therefore if counsel drafts a statement and hands it to the court this deeming provision will not be satisfied.

Admissibility of defence disclosure documents

A judge on his own motion, or following application by any party, may direct that the jury be given copies of any defence statement (including an updated defence statement), and if he does so, may direct that it be edited so as not to include references to matters evidence of which would be inadmissible (CPIA 1996, s.6E(4)). Before the statement is made available to the jury the judge must be of the opinion that seeing a copy of the defence statement would help the jury to understand the case or resolve any issue in the case.

It would still be open to the defence to seek to exclude such documents, but applications are unlikely to meet with much success if case law on alibi notices is followed (*R v. Rossborough* (1985) 81 Cr App R 139).

Protection from conviction on sanctions alone

A person shall not be convicted of an offence solely on an inference drawn under section 11(5) of the CPIA 1996. This caveat mirrors the existing law.

5.1.8   Commencement

These provisions are expected to come into force in 2005.

6 TRIALS ON INDICTMENT WITHOUT A JURY

> **Key points:**
> - Trial by judge alone in fraud cases enacted but unlikely to be introduced in its present form.
> - Trial by judge alone in cases where there is risk of jury tampering. High threshold for such cases with only a handful of cases each year likely.

6.1 INTRODUCTION

Part 7 of the Criminal Justice Act 2003 (the Act) provides for trial on indictment, without a jury, in two instances. Applications for trial without jury can be made by the prosecution in relation to certain fraud trials or those trials where there is a danger of jury tampering. In cases where a jury has had to be discharged as a result of jury tampering there is a procedure to allow for the trial to continue without a jury, and with the judge alone.

The Government spoke, during the parliamentary stages of this Act, of the 'serious and persistent problem of jury tampering', and the 'increasingly sophisticated and determined attempts that are made in our courts to interfere with the course of justice by tampering with the jury', but it is anticipated that only a handful of cases a year will qualify for such measures.

Where a trial is conducted or continued without a jury, the court is to have all the powers, authorities and jurisdiction which the court would have had if the trial had been conducted or continued with a jury (including power to determine any question and to make any findings which would be required to be determined or made by a jury) (s.48(3)). If a trial is conducted or continued without a jury, reasons must be given on conviction.

This chapter considers the relevant test in relation to the two forms of non-jury trial before exploring the procedure to be followed and appeal routes open.

These provisions were some of the most hard fought by opposition parties and key parts of the Bill were lost by the Government at the end of the parliamentary session. The provisions in relation to fraud trials are for all intents and purposes obsolete as the Home Secretary gave an undertaking to the House of Commons that they would not be brought into force in the form enacted. The relevant extract from Hansard on this point, from the consideration of Lords amendments on 20 November 2003 is:

> **Mr. Blunkett** First, in moving to a single judge sitting alone we are prepared to have to secure the consent of the Lord Chief Justice. Secondly, we are prepared to agree that we will not implement the proposals set out in clause 42, as amended, while we seek an improved way forward that does not rely on a single judge sitting alone.

> During the debate, proposals in relation to how specialist advice and support might be offered have been made, including measures drawing on a specialist range of expertise for a jury. On Second Reading and again on Report, I said that I was not against looking at such measures, so I find no difficulty tonight in offering the opportunity to the two main Opposition parties working with the Attorney-General, the Serious Fraud Office and the senior judiciary to take a further look at how that might be taken forward. We are able to look at that in relation to the SFO in a way that Roskill could not. In that light, I will not press for implementation of the clause. I am prepared to offer an affirmative resolution, should that be required.

> I am prepared to do that because of two pieces of legislation: the draft Corruption Bill, which we have been scrutinising, and a measure in relation to domestic violence, crime and victims that will be in the Queen's Speech next Wednesday. That, together with the measures on multiple offences that we discussed across the Dispatch Box on Tuesday, will give us the opportunity to secure an improved provision that will provide the safeguards that Members have sought without giving way on the principle that we should not undermine the task of the SFO in bringing criminals to book who are engaged in serious crime, which has eluded many past efforts.

> **Simon Hughes (Southwark, North and Bermondsey):** The Home Secretary knows that his statement on this issue is welcome. Some of us have argued for a long time that for serious fraud cases there should be an alternative to the conventional jury, which keeps the principle of jury trial. I seek a public clarification from him, which I have asked for privately. Is the implication of his remarks that, as a result of the Bill passing into law tonight, there will not be any serious fraud trial by a single judge in England and Wales?

> **Mr. Blunkett:** I am prepared to give that undertaking. It is part of the agreement that we will retain the clause, but move forward towards looking at the alternative solutions that I have mentioned and that could be incorporated in one or other of the two measures that have either been consulted on or will come before the House in the Queen's Speech. That safeguard is appropriate. I give a binding undertaking that we will follow that agreement.

6.2   FRAUD TRIALS

Section 43 provides for judge alone trial in the following circumstances:

(a) one or more defendants stand trial and a notice has been given under section 51B of the Crime and Disorder Act 1998 in respect of the offence(s);

(b) the prosecution applies for a trial without jury;

(c) the judge, with the approval of the Lord Chief Justice (or a judge nominated by him) approves the order.

6.2.1   Conditions

An order for a judge only trial can only be made if the complexity of the trial or the length of trial (or both) is likely to make the trial so burdensome to members of a jury hearing the trial that the interests of justice require that serious consideration should be given to the question of whether the trial should be conducted without a jury.

In deciding whether or not he is satisfied that that condition is fulfilled, the judge must have regard to any steps, provided that such steps would not significantly disadvantage the prosecution, which might reasonably be taken to reduce the complexity or length of the trial.

6.3   TRIALS WHERE DANGER OF JURY TAMPERING

Under section 44 of the Act, the prosecution can apply for a judge alone trial in any case where there is a danger of jury tampering. Provisions in relation to the discharge of a jury if jury tampering is evident during the proceedings are dealt with in paragraph 6.5 below.

A judge may only accede to such an application if satisfied that there is both a real and present danger that jury tampering would take place, and, notwithstanding any steps (including police protection) which might reasonably be taken to prevent tampering, the likelihood that it would take place would be so substantial so as to make it necessary in the interests of justice for the trial to be conducted without a jury.

6.3.1   Evidence of jury tampering

Section 44(6) of the Act gives examples of cases where there may be evidence of a real and present danger that jury tampering would take place:

- In a retrial where the original jury was discharged due to tampering.
- Where jury tampering has taken place in a previous case involving one or more of the defendants.
- In cases where there has been intimidation or attempted intimidation of witnesses (or likely witnesses).

This list is not exhaustive and much will depend on the individual circumstances of the case including the totality of incidents which in themselves are relatively minor but collectively build to form an air of intimidation in the court proceedings to such an extent that the interests of justice can no longer be met.

6.3.2   Threshold – the last resort

Baroness Scotland, during the passage of the Act stated that:

> I emphasise that the clauses are intended as a last resort. Jury protection measures
> will be appropriate and effective in most cases when there is a risk of tampering. I
> also remind the House that the test for jury exclusion in these circumstances is a
> high one, and deliberately so: we anticipate that only a handful of cases each year
> will meet it.
>
> (*Hansard*, 19 November 2003, col. 1962–3)

Evidence must be presented which is both 'firm and substantial', and there is no
question of the prosecution 'simply whispering in the judge's ear'.

It is argued that the comments of the Government during debate make it abun-
dantly clear that such evidence must be subject to defence scrutiny and challenge
and a judge must subject such applications to 'minute scrutiny'.

6.3.3   Questioning the jury

It is proper for the trial judge to question the jury in appropriate cases. The Court
of Appeal in *R v. Blackwell* [1995] 2 Cr App R 625 offered this guidance:

> If there is any realistic suspicion that the Jury or one or more members of it may
> have been approached or tampered with or pressurised, it is the duty of the Judge to
> investigate the matter and probably depending on the circumstances the investiga-
> tion will include questioning of individual jurors or even the Jury as a whole. Any
> such questioning must be directed to the possibility of the Jury's independence hav-
> ing been compromised and not the Jury's deliberations on the issues in the case.
> When the Judge has completed his investigations whether relating to the activities
> of people outside the Jury or the Jury collectively or individually the Judge is in a
> position to make an informed exercise of judicial discretion as to whether or not the
> trial should continue with all twelve jurors or continue after the discharge of an
> individual juror, or the whole Jury may have to be discharged.

6.3.4   Public interest immunity

In England and Wales, issues of public interest immunity are decided by the trial
judge. In many cases tried today the judge is in possession of information that is
prejudicial, but very often not placed before a jury. The effect that such prejudicial information might have on judicial decision making has already been challenged before the European Courts, most recently in *Edwards and Lewis v. United
Kingdom, The Times*, 29 July 2003. It is unlikely that a judge-only trial, where
such potentially prejudicial material is placed before the court, could withstand
an article 6 challenge unless a special counsel procedure is adopted (see: Keogh,
Public Interest Immunity and the Future for Special Counsel, NLJ (2003) vol. 153
No. 7097 pages 1437–8). The Government is however '. . . confident that existing public interest immunity procedures are fair and effective and do not in any
way endanger the rights of defendants' (*Hansard*, 19 November 2003, col. 1966).

6.4   PROCEDURE FOR APPLICATIONS UNDER SECTIONS 43 AND 44

All applications for trial by judge alone *must* be determined at a preliminary hearing within the meaning of the Criminal Justice Act 1987 or the Criminal Procedure and Investigations Act 1996, which have been amended to provide for such eventuality. Both parties are entitled to make representations, and as outlined above, it may be appropriate to hear formal evidence on the matter.

6.4.1   Right of appeal

The prosecution can appeal a judge's refusal to try the case alone, and the defence can appeal a successful prosecution application to have the case so tried.

6.4.2   Issues of fitness to plead

Fitness to plead issues under section 4 and 4A of the Criminal Procedure (Insanity) Act 1964 must continue to be tried by a jury (s.48(6)).

6.5   DISCHARGE OF JURY DUE TO JURY TAMPERING

Section 46 of the Act empowers a judge to discharge a jury due to jury tampering having taken place. Upon discharge the judge must determine whether to continue the trial without a jury, or to order a retrial (either with a jury or without a jury under section 44 of the Act).

6.5.1   Procedure

Where a judge is minded to discharge a jury due to jury tampering he must inform the parties in the case that he is so minded, and state the grounds on which this is based. All parties will be invited to make representations as to the future progress of the case.

6.5.2   Options

The judge has the following options having considered representations:

- Allow the trial to continue as before.
- Allow the trial to continue with jury protection (subject to the existing common law rules).
- Discharge the jury and continue with judge alone, provided that the judge is satisfied that jury tampering has taken place and that it would be fair to the defendant or defendants to continue without a jury. If it is necessary in the interests of justice to terminate the trial the judge must order termination (s.46(3), (4)).

- Discharge the jury, terminating the trial, and order a new trial under section 44 (judge alone), provided that the criteria in that section are likely to be fulfilled (see paragraph 6.3 above).
- Discharge the jury, terminating the trial, and order a retrial with a fresh jury.

6.5.3   Appeals

Appeals lie by virtue of section 47, with leave of the trial judge or Court of Appeal, against a ruling that the trial continue with judge alone (s.46(3), or a retrial should be determined by judge alone (s.46(5)).

The proceedings cannot continue until such appeals have been determined (s.47(3)).

6.6   GIVING OF REASONS

Section 48(5)(a) provides for the giving of reasons at the time of, or as soon as reasonably practicable after, the time of the conviction. For appeal purposes, the reference in section 18(2) of the Criminal Appeal Act 1968 to the date of conviction shall be read as a reference to the date on which the reasons for conviction are given.

7 EVIDENCE OF BAD CHARACTER

Key points:

- Definition of bad character.
- Abolition of many common law and statutory rules.
- More liberal admittance of bad character evidence.

7.1 OVERVIEW

The Criminal Justice Act 2003 (the Act) makes fundamental changes to the admissibility of evidence relating to character in respect to defendants and others. The Act is far-reaching, particularly section 103 which provides for the admissibility of previous convictions in support of propensity to commit like offences and untruthfulness. Common law rules in relation to the admissibility of bad character evidence are abolished save for one exception (s.99(2)). The legislation, and indeed this chapter of this book draw heavily on Law Commission Paper No. 273 which needs to be read in detail to understand fully the rationale behind the new rules. Where appropriate I have extracted whole passages from that paper to illustrate the various concepts being discussed. A copy of the paper is available online (**www.lawcom.gov.uk/files/lc273.pdf**).

In this chapter reference is made to the old rules under section 1(f) (i)–(iii) of the Criminal Evidence Act 1898. I use this reference mainly because this is how the provisions are still referenced, incorrectly, in most legal texts. Paragraph 1(7) of Schedule 4 to the Youth Justice and Criminal Evidence Act 1999 renumbered the 1898 Act, and the corresponding provisions are now sections 1(3)(i)–(iii). This is mentioned as any practitioner looking for a repeal of section 1(f) will not find it in Schedule 37, but will instead see a correct reference to section 1(3).

7.1.1 Definition

Bad character evidence is evidence of, or a disposition towards misconduct; other than evidence which has to do with the alleged facts of the offence with which the defendant is charged or is evidence of misconduct in connection with the investigation or prosecution of that offence. Misconduct is defined as 'the commission of an offence or other reprehensible behaviour' (s.112(1)).

Bad character in relation to the alleged facts offence itself has always been admissible for obvious reasons. The Act provides for different rules in relation to the bad character of defendants, and that of non-defendants. In assessing the probative value of evidence it is assumed to be true, unless there is material to suggest the contrary (s.109).

Apart from evidence of previous convictions, other evidence, amounting to 'reprehensible behaviour' is admissible. The Government stated the following during debate:

> Examples of where it might be appropriate to admit such evidence include circumstances where evidence on a number of charges being tried concurrently is cross-admissible in respect of the other charges. It might also be appropriate to admit evidence relating to charges on which the defendant was acquitted, as I have already cited in the example of R v. Z. It would be unfortunate if an argument were to be accepted that, because a person has not actually been convicted of the offence, it cannot be said that the evidence shows that he has indeed committed such an offence and it is therefore excluded.

7.1.2   Offences committed by children

In relation to a defendant aged over 21 years, evidence of his conviction for an offence committed when under the age of 14 is not admissible unless both of the offences are triable only on indictment and the court is satisfied that the interests of justice require the evidence to be admitted (s.108(2)). The previous partial prohibition on using juvenile convictions under section 16(2) and (3) of the Children and Young Persons Act 1963 is repealed.

7.1.3   Exclusion

In addition to the statutory tests for exclusion that are discussed below, the power to exclude evidence under section 78 of PACE 1984 is not affected by these provisions (House of Lords, *Hansard*, 19 November 2003, col. 1988).

7.1.4   Further protections

The Act provides for the stopping of a case if it is felt by the judge that the evidence is contaminated. These provisions are dealt with in detail below.

7.1.5   Rulings

Section 110 provides for reasons to be given in relation to certain rulings in relation to bad character evidence.

7.2   BAD CHARACTER OF PERSONS OTHER THAN THE DEFENDANT

Leave is required before evidence of bad character can be admitted in the case of a non-defendant, unless all parties consent to the admission of that evidence. The court cannot give leave for the admission of bad character evidence against a person other than the defendant unless the evidence is important explanatory evidence, or has substantial probative value in relation to a matter which is a matter in issue in the proceedings, and is of substantial importance in the context of the case as a whole. The court need not be asked to give leave if all parties agree to the evidence being admissible (s.100(1)(c)).

7.2.1   Evidence with important explanatory value

Evidence falls into this category if the court or jury would find it impossible or difficult properly to understand other evidence in the case, and its value for understanding the case as a whole is substantial (s.100(2)). The evidence is not in itself probative of any fact in issue, but nonetheless is important if the case is to be understood fully in context.

An example of this kind of evidence, used by the Law Commission is:

> Thus, for example, in a case of intra-familial abuse, it was not only abusive behaviour by the defendant on occasions other than that charged which was valuable in explaining the case as a whole to the jury, but also abusive behaviour by other members of the family.

7.2.2   Evidence going to a matter in issue

Evidence in this category must have substantial probative value in relation to the matter in issue and be of substantial importance in the context of the case as a whole.

In assessing probative value the court must have regard to the following factors (and any others it thinks relevant) (s.100(3)):

- The nature and number of events, or other things, to which the evidence relates.
- When those events or things are alleged to have happened, or existed.
- In the case of evidence of misconduct, which is said to have probative value by reason of similarity between that conduct and other alleged misconduct, the nature and extent of the similarities and the dissimilarities between each of the alleged instances of misconduct.
- In the case of misconduct, when it is alleged that the person is also responsible for the offence charged, and the identity of the person responsible for the misconduct is disputed, the extent to which evidence shows or tends to show that the same person was responsible each time.

Substantial probative value

It is clear that past misconduct can be probative of the propensity of persons to act in the same way in the future but the probative value of a single incident for example is capable of being overestimated. The Act therefore imports a 'substantial' test in relation to probative value. Previous misconduct is likely to impact on a witness's general credibility, but since little significance if any can be attached to general credibility, such a route to admissibility needs to be treated with extreme caution. Of more importance is credibility in relation to an issue in the case – for example why a person would lie about a particular incident, as opposed to why they should generally be disbelieved (the boy who cried wolf test).

Steps have been taken in relation to sex cases to limit such questioning (see later), the reasoning for which is outlined above, and explained in the speech of Lord Steyn in Re A [2001] UKHL 25, paragraph 27:

> Nevertheless, it has to be acknowledged that in the criminal courts of our country, as in others, outmoded beliefs about women and sexual matters lingered on. In recent Canadian jurisprudence they have been described as the discredited twin myths, viz 'that unchaste women were more likely to consent to intercourse and in any event, were less worthy of belief': R v. Seaboyer (1991) 83 DLR (4th) 193, 258, 278C per McLachlin J. Such generalised, stereotyped and unfounded prejudices ought to have no place in our legal system. But even in the very recent past such defensive strategies were habitually employed. It resulted in an absurdly low conviction rate in rape cases. It also inflicted unacceptable humiliation on complainants in rape cases.

Questioning of little probative value

Questioning which has little if any probative value, but may have the effect of undermining the case against the accused is the type of questioning that this Act seeks to prevent once and for all. Under the Act, questioning in relation to the following scenario would not be admissible:

> W is a middle-aged woman, who is raped by an acquaintance. D says she consented. The police explain to her that, when she gives evidence, which she must for the prosecution to succeed, she might be asked about a 20-year-old shoplifting conviction. Neither her husband nor her children nor her friends know about this conviction. The fear that it would be mentioned in public is enough to dissuade her from giving evidence.

The prohibition is not about protecting the sensibilities of witnesses per se, but about ensuring that the answer to the question is capable of properly advancing the defence case, and not at the expense of improperly distorting the fact-finding process.

In making the application for leave, an advocate would have to point to the features of the evidence which support the argument that the evidence is substantially relevant – for example, how recent was any alleged misconduct, and how similar to any misconduct alleged in relation to the facts of the offence charged (which may include the giving of false evidence as to those facts).

Required level of relevance

Applying the rigour of requiring the advocate to satisfy the court of the enhanced level of relevance (substantial probative value) would mean that evidence going to the 'specific credibility' of a witness (that is, evidence which suggests that the witness has an incentive to lie *on this occasion*) would be more likely to have the required level of relevance than evidence which merely suggests that the witness *might* lie if he or she *did* have an incentive to do so.

Further examples given by the Law Commission are:

> D is charged with theft. W, who was D's employee at the time of the alleged offence, is a witness who will give incriminating evidence which a jury could hardly accept without convicting D. The bad character evidence in question is the fact (not disputed by the prosecution) that, in her previous job, four years before the time of D's alleged offence, W was dishonest in her expenses claims. D says that the witness is incompetent and therefore mistaken. It is hard to conceive that the evidence would be admissible under the enhanced test.

> Alternatively, D is charged with theft, and wishes to ask W about an allegation that she was dishonest in her previous job. In this example, D's case is that W is lying, not incompetent. The fact that in the relatively recent past she has been guilty of dishonesty at the work place might well surmount the test of enhanced relevance.

> A third variation: D is charged with theft and wishes to ask W about an allegation of dishonesty 10 years previously, or in a non-work context. The court might well take the view that it did not pass the enhanced relevance test.

Substantial importance in the context of the case as a whole

This is the second limb of the admissibility test and is of crucial importance. It may well be that the fact may have substantial relevance to the credibility of a person whose credibility is in issue, and thus to the matter in issue on which she gives evidence, although that matter is not of substantial importance in the context of the case as a whole. If the matter on which she gives evidence is of only marginal relevance to the central issues in the case, then no amount of relevance to her credibility can ever amount to *substantial* importance in the context of the case as a whole. For example, a witness may have an extensive antecedent history, but their evidence may simply be in relation to a matter not in dispute in the case (perhaps producing a video-tape for example). That witness can give evidence safe in the knowledge that their antecedent history is unlikely to be explored.

Sexual offence cases

Nothing in the Act alters the operation of section 41 of the Youth Justice and Criminal Evidence Act 1999. However, once leave is given under section 41 for questions in relation to previous sexual behaviour to be asked, the advocate must then make an application for the evidence to be admissible under section 100 of the Act if the sexual behaviour cited also amounts to bad character (unlikely in most cases unless it could properly be classed as reprehensible behaviour (s.112(1)).

Of course, if leave is refused under section 41 that is the end of the matter.

Is the test Human Rights Act compliant?

The Law Commission, who drafted the sections on which the Act is based, commented:

> It follows, from the decision in A, that a requirement of enhanced relevance for bad character evidence would risk infringing Article 6 *only* if the required level of relevance were set so high that evidence sufficiently probative to be necessary for a fair trial might nevertheless fail to satisfy it. This result could be avoided by formulating the requirement in such a way that it will *inevitably* be satisfied whenever the exclusion of the evidence might render the trial unfair. We therefore do not accept that the introduction of a test of enhanced relevance would necessarily risk infringing Article 6. That risk can be eliminated if the test is properly formulated and applied.

7.3   DEFENDANT'S BAD CHARACTER

Evidence of the defendant's bad character is admissible if and only if (s.101):

- all parties agree to its admissibility;
- the evidence is adduced by the defendant himself or is given in answer to a question asked by him in cross-examination and intended to elicit it;
- evidence with important explanatory value;
- evidence going to a matter in issue between the defendant and prosecution;
- substantial probative value in relation to an important matter in issue between the defendant and a co-defendant;
- evidence to correct false impression;
- attack on another person's character.

7.3.1   Evidence with explanatory value

Evidence falls within this category of admissibility if the court or jury would find it impossible or difficult properly to understand other evidence in the case, and that the value of the evidence for the understanding of the case as a whole is substantial (s.102).

It is disappointing that Parliament rejected clause 7(3) and (4) of the Law Commission's draft bill on character evidence which imported a protection in relation to prejudicial evidence. The Law Commission suggested that explanatory evidence that was prejudicial (and much of it would be) should only be admitted if the interests of justice required its admission having considered the prejudice and the value of the evidence for the understanding of the case as a whole. The

Law Commission stated that this extra safeguard was needed to secure a fair, rational and consistent approach to the inclusion of such evidence.

As this section stands the rule is no different from the old law.

7.3.2   Evidence going to an important matter in issue between defendant and prosecution

Only prosecution evidence can fall within this section (s.103(6)). This section is potentially far-reaching and allows for the admission of bad character evidence to show that the defendant has a propensity to commit offences of the kind with which he is charged and be untruthful. Evidence of similar fact would be admissible under this section, going to prove the core issue(s) between the defendant and prosecution. Evidence of bad character because it is an essential element of the offence with which he is charged will remain admissible (e.g. for an offence under section 21 of the Firearms Act 1968). Evidence under section 27(3) of the Theft Act 1968 is still admissible.

Admission of previous convictions

The reason that this Act goes much further than simply codifying the common law is that it makes both kinds of propensity a fact in issue in *all* cases, thereby opening the door for the admission of previous convictions.

Applications to exclude

The court must not admit evidence under section 101(1)(d) if on a defence application to exclude it appears to the court that the admission of the evidence would have such an adverse effect on the fairness of the proceedings that the court ought not to admit it. The court must have particular regard to the length of time between the matters to which that evidence relates and the matters which form the subject of the offence charged (s.101(4)).

Propensity to commit offences

A propensity to commit offences of the kind with which he is charged can be proved (without prejudice to any other way of doing so) by evidence that he has been convicted of an offence of the same description or category as the one with which he has been charged (s.103(2)). A court can exclude such evidence if satisfied that the length of time since the conviction for the like offence would make it unjust for it to be admitted (s.103(3)).

An offence of the same description is one which would be written in the same terms in a charge or indictment (s.103(4)(a)). Categories of offence are to be defined by order of the Secretary of State (s.103(4)(b)).

Evidence of bad character to support propensity is of no relevance and should not be admitted where such a propensity makes it no more likely that he is guilty of the offence (s.103(1)(a)). An example of this might be where the defendant admits an assault on someone in relation to a murder allegation but argues only that causation is not made out.

Application of the section

It is unclear as to the intended effect of this section as Government ministers were unable to clarify its operation in any meaningful way when pressed. In parliamentary debate it was queried whether it went any further than placing similar-fact evidence on a statutory footing. As outlined above this section does go much further than simply codifying the law in relation to similar fact. The question for judges, who have been educated in a system where evidence of propensity has never been admissible, is how to apply these new principles. If a person has one conviction for burglary would that be admissible on a burglary charge? The following examples illustrate the possible issues.

X has one conviction for burglary. The offence was committed on 1 January 1999

Case 1: X is being tried for a burglary allegedly committed on 10 January 2004. Evidence of propensity unlikely to make it more likely that he is guilty of the offence.

Case 2: X is being tried for a burglary allegedly committed on 2 January 1999 at a location near to the address burgled previously. Evidence of propensity likely to be admitted.

X has 20 convictions for dwelling house burglary

Case 1: X is being tried for a burglary of industrial premises during the course of which specialist equipment is stolen. Defence may well be able to argue that propensity to burgle does not make it more likely that he committed this offence as he has never stolen from non-dwellings and the previous convictions do not show that he is any more likely to be involved in the burglary of premises in order to steal specialist items.

Case 2: X is being tried for a dwelling house burglary allegedly committed two years after his last conviction for burglary. Evidence of propensity likely to be admitted.

Case 3: X is being tried for a dwelling house burglary allegedly committed 10 years after his last conviction for burglary. It is this kind of case that will raise real difficulties for judges, the question of whether the previous cycle of offending has been broken will be open to dispute.

Propensity to be untruthful

The Act makes propensity to be untruthful a fact in issue in all cases. Once again this provision was discussed and rejected by the Law Commission who stated:

> We take the view, however, that the defendant's general propensity to be untruthful is not a matter which it would be fair to allow the prosecution to assert as part of its

case against the defendant. Where the defendant simply denies the truth of some or all of the prosecution's evidence in relation to the offence charged, and makes no attempt to attack anyone *else's* credibility, we think it virtually inconceivable that evidence of the defendant's general untruthfulness could ever have sufficient probative value to outweigh the risk of prejudice.

Convictions for perjury or deception offences

The types of character evidence that might support such propensity would be convictions for perjury or deception offences. A conviction for theft would not necessarily qualify as the act of stealing does not equate to a propensity to tell lies. Query though evidence that a defendant has been convicted of an offence having denied it and given evidence. Such evidence may well be admissible.

If untruthfulness is not to be part of the prosecution case such evidence cannot be admitted. If the defence was one simply of causation, or whether even if the facts were true it would amount to a defence, such evidence will have no relevance (s.103(1)(b)).

It is important to note that there is no 'shield' to lose in relation to this section, the prosecution in all cases can seek to show that a defendant's character is so poor that it is cogent evidence of untruthfulness.

7.4   MATTER IN ISSUE BETWEEN A DEFENDANT AND A CO-DEFENDANT

Evidence in relation to a matter in issue between a defendant and a co-defendant, including propensity to be untruthful is admissible under the Act. Propensity evidence in relation to untruthfulness is only admissible if the nature of his defence is such as to undermine his co-defendant's defence (s.104(1)), but other relevant evidence (such as general propensity does not need such an attack in order to render it admissible). This presents a key departure away from the old system where a co-defendant was protected from evidence relating to propensity if his shield were retained.

Such evidence is only admissible if adduced by the co-defendant or by a witness invited to give that evidence in cross-examination by the co-defendant (s.104(2)). This prevents the prosecution from adducing bad character where the issue is one between co-defendants only. Leave is not required.

7.4.1   Section 1(f)(iii) of the Criminal Evidence Act 1898

This rule is not simply a re-enactment of section 1(f)(iii) of the Criminal Evidence Act 1898, as there are a number of key differences:

(1) The evidence must have *substantial* probative value in relation to an important issue in dispute (s.101(1)(e)). Judges will need to balance very carefully

the previous almost unfettered right to introduce bad character in this scenario against this Act's more restrictive scheme. The enhanced relevance test is discussed at paragraph 7.4.1 above. It ought to be remembered that the issue in dispute will not always be limited to credibility, particularly in many 'cut throat' defence cases, where one party has previous conviction for like offending and the other does not. In such instances propensity (to commit the offence, or an argument that one accused is more likely than another to have committed it) can be very much in issue, as confirmed by the House of Lords in *R v. Randall* [2003] UKHL 69. Practitioners should be aware that save where such propensity is the issue in dispute the co-defendant need *not* have undermined the defendant's case, in terms of the old law there need be no 'loss of shield'.

(2) In the case of evidence relating to propensity to be untruthful, the defendant must have undermined the case of the co-accused (the old shield requirement).

(3) The prosecution cannot avail itself of the section (effectively overruling cases such as *R v. Seigley* (1911) 6 Cr App R 106).

(4) The defendant need not give evidence in order for the evidence to be admitted; the co-defendant would be entitled to adduce the evidence regardless. While it has been argued that since the admission of such evidence is most often to go towards undermining credibility, and that is not in issue where a defendant does not give evidence, that argument was recognised by the Government as being too restrictive in nature. The defendant who does not give evidence will nonetheless put his credibility in issue in relation to out of court statements or by the general nature of his defence.

7.5   EVIDENCE TO CORRECT FALSE IMPRESSION

The prosecution (and only the prosecution (s.105(7)) can adduce evidence of bad character to correct a false impression given by a defendant (s.105). A false impression is defined as an express or implied assertion that is apt to give the court or jury a false or misleading impression about the defendant. The evidence adduced must have probative value in correcting the false assertion.

7.5.1   Making the assertion

The assertion can be made in the proceedings (and is not reliant on the defendant having given evidence of the fact himself), on being questioned under caution before charge or upon being charged (or informed he might be prosecuted for the offence).

Assertions can be made in the proceedings by the defendant, a witness on his behalf, as a result of a question asked by the defendant intended to elicit the answer, or in an out of court statement adduced by the defendant during the proceedings.

An assertion can be made by way of conduct as opposed to evidence. Conduct includes appearance or dress, and would arguably mean that a defendant who turned up to court in a suit could face having evidence of bad character admitted.

7.5.2   Withdrawing the assertion

Section 105(3) allows a defendant to withdraw or disassociate himself from an assertion, and if he does so shall not be treated as having made the assertion. The disassociation may be partial.

7.5.3   Conditions to be satisfied

Before such evidence can be admitted the court must be sure that the evidence of bad character has probative value in correcting the false or misleading impression. The evidence should go no further than that which is necessary to correct the false impression (s.105(6)).

7.5.4   Scope of the section

This provision is similar to section 1(f)(ii) of the Criminal Evidence Act 1898, save that the defendant is not protected from having such evidence adduced by reason of avoiding the witness box.

7.6   ATTACK ON ANOTHER PERSON'S CHARACTER

An attack on another's character can be adduced by the accused or a legal representative appointed under section 38(4) of the Youth Justice and Criminal Evidence Act 1999. Such an attack can also be made when being questioned under caution before charge, or upon being charged or officially warned that he may be prosecuted.

7.6.1   What amounts to an attack on character?

An attack on character is evidence to the effect that the person has committed an offence (which might be alleged to be the charge the defendant is facing) or has behaved, or is disposed to behave in a reprehensible way (s.106(2)).

It does not matter that the person attacked is not a witness in the proceedings; it can be seen that this section goes considerably further than section 1(f)(ii) of the Criminal Evidence Act 1898. Defendants are no longer at liberty to simply attack the character of others, the test in section 100 will still need to be satisfied (see above).

7.6.2   Exclusion of such evidence

The defendant can apply for evidence of his own bad character (admissible as a result of the attack on another) to be excluded under section 101(3) if its admission would have an adverse effect on the fairness of the proceedings.

7.7   STOPPING THE CASE WHERE EVIDENCE CONTAMINATED

A court can order the acquittal of a defendant, or a retrial, if evidence of bad character evidence has been admitted and later found to be contaminated. Only evidence adduced under sections 101(1)(c) to (g) can be excluded under this section, but a judge is not prevented from using any other exclusionary power. The contamination must be such that any resulting conviction would be unsafe given the importance of the contaminated evidence in relation to the case (s.107(1)).

Similar provisions apply in relation to determining whether the defendant did an act or made an omission, in accordance with section 4A(2) of the Criminal Procedure (Insanity) Act 1964.

7.7.1   Meaning of contaminated

A person's evidence can be contaminated in two ways:

(1) Where as a result of an agreement or understanding between the person and one or more others, the evidence is false or misleading in any respect, or is different from what it would otherwise have been. Or
(2) Where as a result of the person being aware of anything alleged by one or more others who are, or could be, witnesses in the proceedings, the evidence is false or misleading in any respect, or is different from what it would otherwise have been.

7.7.2   Collusion

These provisions deal with collusion, which can be a particular feature of sexual offence cases, and general contamination as a result of witnesses being in possession of information they should not be aware.

8 HEARSAY

Key points:

- Overriding discretion to admit hearsay when in the interests of justice to do so.
- Re-enactment of many existing statutory rules, and retention of some common law rules.
- Previous statements no longer admissible just in relation to issue of credibility, but as truth of their contents.
- Multiple hearsay in limited cases.
- Recent complaint evidence extended to all offences, and admissible as truth of the statement.
- Wider use of video-taped evidence in chief.

8.1 INTRODUCTION

The Criminal Justice Act 2003 (the Act) makes radical amendments to the law on hearsay, and seeks to simplify greatly the common law and legislative framework, with some measure of success. An important provision in relation to the admissibility of video-taped interviews for all witnesses in certain circumstances is likely to have far-reaching effects on the conviction rates in such cases. A statement not made in oral evidence in the proceedings will only be admissible in evidence if admitted under the Act, a rule of law preserved by section 118 of the Act, with the agreement of all parties or where a court is satisfied that it is in the interests of justice for it to be admitted.

A major change in relation to the new framework in relation to hearsay evidence is in relation to the admissibility of previous statements, hitherto only going to credibility, but under this Act now able to be admitted as evidence of the truth of its contents.

The Act provides for an extensive framework of court rules that will be needed to regulate the new rules (s.132).

8.1.1   Definition

The Act in this part is concerned with the admissibility of out of court statements and 'matters stated'.

Section 115 provides the definitions of the above terms:

> *Statement* – any representation of fact or opinion made by a person by whatever means, including a sketch, photofit or other pictorial form.

> *Matter stated* – a statement made for the purpose (or one of the purposes) of causing another person to believe the matter or cause another person to act, or a machine to operate on the basis that the matter is as stated.

8.1.2   Capability to make a statement

Under section 123 the court, when considering admitting a statement under section 116, 119 or 120 is empowered to examine the capability of the person concerned to have made the statement that is in issue. A person has the required capability if he is capable of understanding the questions put to him and giving answers that can be understood. The court can in appropriate cases receive expert evidence.

8.1.3   Matters regarding credibility

Section 124 allows for the admission of evidence casting doubt on the credibility of a hearsay statement if such evidence would have been admissible had the maker of the statement given oral evidence of the facts stated. Evidence of previous inconsistent statements is similarly admissible.

8.1.4   Halting a case due to unconvincing evidence

If the case against the defendant is based wholly or partly on a hearsay statement, the judge can stop the case at any time after the close of the prosecution case if the evidence provided by the statement is so unconvincing that, considering its importance to the case against the defendant, his conviction for the offence would be unsafe. The court may either acquit the defendant or order a retrial (s.125). Similar provisions apply in relation to hearings to determine whether a person did the act or omission charged in accordance with section 4A(2) of the Criminal Procedure (Insanity) Act 1964.

8.1.5   General discretion to exclude hearsay statements

A judge may refuse to admit hearsay evidence if satisfied that the case for excluding the statement, taking account of the danger that to admit it would result in an undue waste of time, substantially outweighs the case for admitting it, taking account of the value of the evidence (s.126). The courts' common law powers to exclude evidence are preserved, as is the power under section 78 of PACE 1984.

8.2 ADMISSIBILITY

8.2.1 Overriding discretion to admit hearsay evidence

Hearsay may be admissible under a wide range of existing and new rules which are dealt with in turn below. Aside from the specific rules below, the Act introduces the ability of a court to admit hearsay evidence if it is in the interests of justice for it to be admitted (s.114(1)(d)). This rule will allow the courts to move away from the somewhat rigid framework that has operated in the past (and is still adopted in the new Act), and instead look at any individual case or piece of hearsay evidence and consider whether it ought to be admitted. Section 114(2) details the factors that a court should take into account:

(a) how much probative value the statement has (assuming it to be true) in relation to a matter in issue in the proceedings, or how valuable it is for the understanding of other evidence in the case;
(b) what other evidence has been, or can be, given on the matter or evidence mentioned in paragraph (a);
(c) how important the matter or evidence mentioned in paragraph (a) is in the context of the case as a whole;
(d) the circumstances in which the statement was made;
(e) how reliable the maker of the statement appears to be;
(f) how reliable the evidence of the making of the statement appears to be;
(g) whether oral evidence of the matter stated can be given and, if not, why it cannot;
(h) the amount of difficulty involved in challenging the statement;
(i) the extent to which that difficulty would be likely to prejudice the party facing it.

Section 114 is a potentially exciting development in the law of English evidence, and will allow justice to be achieved free from the constraints of illogical and often contradictory rules of common law, with an emphasis instead on the interests of justice, which after all is what any modern criminal justice system should be primarily concerned.

8.2.2 Admissibility when a witness is unavailable

These provisions (s.116), which mirror section 23 of the Criminal Justice Act 1988, provide that a statement not made in oral evidence will be admissible provided that:

(1) Oral evidence given in the proceedings by the person who made the statement would be admissible as evidence of the matter stated.
(2) The identity of the maker of the statement (the 'relevant person') is established to the court's satisfaction. The identity of the witness is important to the defence, as it allows them in appropriate cases to be able to challenge the absent witness's credibility.

(3) Any of the five conditions details below are satisfied.

The five conditions

(1) That the relevant person is dead.
(2) That the relevant person is unfit to be a witness because of his bodily or mental condition.
(3) That the relevant person is outside the United Kingdom and it is not reasonably practicable to secure his attendance.
(4) That the relevant person cannot be found although such steps as it is reasonably practicable to take to find him have been taken.
(5) That through fear the relevant person does not give (or does not continue to give) oral evidence in the proceedings, either at all or in connection with the subject matter of the statement, and the court gives leave for the statement to be given in evidence. Fear is to be widely construed (s.116(3)), and includes, for example, the fear of the death or injury of another person or of financial loss.

Leave granted

Leave may only be given under ground 5 above, if the court considers that it is in the interests of justice to admit the statement, having regard to the contents of the statement, risk of unfairness to any party in the proceedings by a decision to admit or exclude it, the availability of a special measures direction and any other relevant circumstances. Particular regard should be had to how difficult it will be to challenge the statement if the witness does not give oral evidence (s.116(4)(b)).

Conditions not satisfied

The conditions above are deemed to be not satisfied (where they otherwise would be) if the circumstance described is caused by the person seeking to rely upon the statement in order to prevent them giving evidence (s.116(5)). For example if it were shown that the person seeking to adduce the statement had arranged for a person to be absent, or had placed them in fear, the statement would not be admissible. In the explanatory notes to the original bill it was stated that it was for the opposing party to prove that this is in fact the case – this is not reflected in the Act, and a court can make the finding on its own motion if appropriate evidence is available.

8.2.3   Business and other documents

These provisions, which mirror section 24 of the Criminal Justice Act 1988, provide that a statement not made in oral evidence will be admissible provided that:

(1) oral evidence given in the proceedings would be admissible as evidence of that matter,

(2) all of the following three requirements (along with any additional conditions) are satisfied:

(a) the document or the part containing the statement was created or received by a person in the course of a trade, business, profession or other occupation, or as the holder of a paid or unpaid office,

(b) the person who supplied the information contained in the statement (the relevant person) had or may reasonably be supposed to have had personal knowledge of the matters dealt with, and

(c) each person (if any) through whom the information was supplied from the relevant person to the person mentioned in (a) above received the information in the course of a trade, business, profession or other occupation, or as the holder of a paid or unpaid office.

The person in (a) and (b) above may be the same person (s.117(3)).

Statements prepared for criminal proceedings

If the statement was prepared for the purposes of pending or contemplated criminal proceedings (save for proceedings mentioned in section 117(4)(b)) the statement will not be admissible unless one of the five conditions (s.116(2)) in paragraph 8.2.2 above is satisfied, or the relevant person cannot reasonably be expected to have any recollection of the matters dealt with in the statement, having regard to the length of time since he supplied the statement and all other circumstances.

Power of court to declare statement inadmissible

A hearsay statement will not be admissible if the court is satisfied that the statement's reliability as evidence for the purpose for which it is tendered is doubtful in view of its contents, the source of the information, the way in which or the circumstances in which the information was supplied or received, or the way in which or the circumstances in which the document concerned was created or received (s.117(6), (7)).

8.2.4   Preserved categories of hearsay evidence

Section 118 preserves many of the common law categories of hearsay, such as public information, reputation (subject to the evidence proving or disproving the matter concerned), *res gestae* and confessions. All common law categories of hearsay not preserved by this section are abolished by virtue of section 118(2).

8.2.5   Previous inconsistent statements

Inconsistent statements are admitted pursuant to section 119, with one important change. The previous inconsistent statement will be admissible as evidence of the matter stated, not serving only to undermine credibility as was the case prior to this Act. If the witness does not admit making the previous statement it can be proved in the usual way under sections 3, 4 or 5 of the Criminal Procedure Act 1865. If the previous statement is admitted as an exhibit, it must not accompany the jury when they retire to consider their verdict unless the court considers it appropriate, or all the parties to the proceedings agree that the jury should have the document with them.

8.2.6   Other previous statements of witnesses

Under section 120, other statements made by a witness in proceedings will be admissible as to the truth of their contents (not merely to credibility) in the following circumstances:

(1) A previous statement is used to rebut a suggestion of recent fabrication. Prior to this Act, such statements were only admissible to show consistency and rebut allegations of recent concoction; they were never admissible as evidence of the truth of the facts stated (R v. Benjamin (1913) 8 Cr App R 146).

(2) A previous statement used by a witness to refresh his memory, provided that the witness has been cross-examined on that statement and as a consequence is received in evidence in the proceedings. Section 139 deals with memory refreshing in more detail, and removes some of the more artificial restrictions that have hitherto applied.

(3) Where a witness indicates that to the best of his belief he made the statement to be relied upon and that to the best of his belief it states the truth that statement shall be admissible as to the facts stated in it, in any one of the following three situations:

(a) Where the statement identifies or describes a person, object or place (an example given by the Government during debate on the Act was a vehicle registration plate).

(b) Where the statement was made by the witness when the matters stated were fresh in his memory but he does not remember them, and cannot reasonably be expected to remember them, well enough to give oral evidence of them in the proceedings.

(c) Evidence of recent complaint, admissible prior to the Act in sexual offence cases, is now admissible in respect to all offences under section 120(7). Once again the Act goes much further than common law, and renders the statement admissible as to the truth of its contents, not merely to evidence the consistency of the conduct of the witness with the account being given in court (see R v. Lillyman [1896] 2 QB 167, CCR). For evidence of recent complaint to be admitted the following additional criteria must be met:

(i) the witness claims to be a person against whom an offence has been committed;

(ii) the offence is one to which the proceedings relate;

> (iii) the statement consists of a complaint made by the witness (whether to a person in authority or not) about conduct which would, if proved, constitute the offence or part of the offence;
>
> (iv) the complaint was made as soon as could reasonably be expected after the alleged conduct;
>
> (v) the complaint was not made as a result of a threat or a promise; and
>
> (vi) before the statement is adduced the witness gives oral evidence in connection with its subject matter.

If the previous statement is admitted as an exhibit, it must not accompany the jury when they retire to consider their verdict unless the court considers it appropriate, or all the parties to the proceedings agree that the jury should have the document with them.

8.2.7   Multiple hearsay

A hearsay statement which proves that a previous hearsay statement was made is not admissible unless either of the statements is admissible under section 117, 119 or 120 and all the parties agree to its admissibility or the court is satisfied that the interests of justice require its admissibility. The full test is set out in section 121.

8.2.8   Confession evidence

Section 128 inserts a new section 76A in PACE 1984. The Act allows a defendant to admit a confession of a co-accused with the proviso that confessions made as a consequence of oppression or anything said or done that was likely to render the confession unreliable, shall not be admitted. This section brings the rules for defence and prosecution use of confessions into line, save that a defendant will only have to discharge the standard of proof in relation to oppressive or otherwise unreliable confessions, to the civil standard (balance of probabilities), and whereas the prosecution are obliged to discharge the criminal standard of proof.

8.2.9   Expert evidence

Section 127 provides for the admissibility of statements detailing preparatory work on which an expert bases his own oral evidence. Notice will be given of an intention to rely upon such statements and an application to the court must be made if the maker of the statement is required at court to give oral evidence. The court will consider the factors in section 127(5) in deciding whether that witness should be called to court.

8.2.10   Evidence by video recording

Section 137 provides for the admissibility of video-taped accounts of events in question in relation to a trial (i.e. events central to the case), provided that at the time the video was made those events were fresh in the person's memory. This section applies to indictable only offences and prescribed triable either-way offences. The video will stand as that witness's evidence in chief, provided that the witness's recollection of events is likely to have been significantly better when he made the video and it is in the interests of justice for the recording to be admitted. This section does not apply to defendants, but will apply to other defence witnesses. Defence solicitors will need to start considering how their own witnesses can practically take advantage of this measure, as police video suites are unlikely to be made available to them.

The court can make an order that any part of the video stand as evidence in chief.

Interests of justice test

In determining whether the admission of such evidence is in the interests of justice the court must consider in particular:

(1) Time interval between events and making of video.
(2) Factors affecting reliability of what is said in the video account (for example if the video was made very shortly after the event it could be tainted by grief or anger).
(3) The quality of the recording.
(4) Any view of the witness as to whether his account should be given orally or by way of video.

Risk of prejudice to accused

If the court concludes that admitting *any part* of the video would carry a risk of prejudice to the accused, it should nevertheless go on to consider whether the interests of justice as a whole require it to be admitted in view of the desirability of showing the whole, or substantially the whole, of the recorded video (s.138(3)).

Further evidence in chief

Oral evidence cannot be given to supplement any matter which in the opinion of the court has been adequately dealt with in the video.

8.2.11   Memory refreshing

A witness giving oral evidence, may at any stage in the course of proceedings, refresh his memory from a document. The document must record his recollection of the matter at that earlier time, and his recollection must be likely to be significantly better at that earlier time than at the time of his oral evidence (s.139).

Witnesses who have given an earlier account recorded in sound may similarly refresh their memory from a transcript of the recording. This provision may also apply to a defendant, refreshing memory from an interview summary for example.

This section does not allow a witness to refresh their memory from an earlier video recording, as the definition of document in this part of the Act does not include any recording of sounds or moving images. Sound recordings are catered for separately, as outlined above.

This section ought to bring to an end the growing volume of case law on the subject of memory refreshing. Cases such as *R v. South Ribble Stipendiary Magistrate, ex parte Cochrane* [1996] 2 Cr App R 544 are unlikely to occur again.

9 PROSECUTION APPEALS

Key points:

- Prosecution right of appeal against 'termination rulings' such as no case to answer and a stay of the indictment.
- Prosecution right of appeal against 'evidentiary rulings' that significantly weaken the prosecution case.

9.1 INTRODUCTION

Part 9 of the Criminal Justice Act 2003 (the Act) gives the prosecution the right to appeal to the Court of Appeal certain (termination or de facto termination) rulings by a judge during trial and other rulings in respect to evidence. These provisions only apply in respect of trial on indictment. There are important procedural differences between the two regimes and it is anticipated that the provisions in respect to appeals against evidentiary rulings will only be brought into force once an assessment has been made into the efficacy of appeals for termination rulings.

The first set of appeal provisions in section 58 previously titled 'termination rulings' in the bill; refer to those rulings that have the effect of stopping the case, such as a stay of the indictment or a ruling of no case to answer. The Government during the passage of the Act remarked on the inherent unfairness on the prosecution of being unable to effectively appeal rulings that have the effect of terminating a trial, a problem recently and seriously highlighted in the case of *R v. Van Hoogstraten* [2003] EWCA 3642 Crim. The Government stated that:

> The vast majority of practitioners and commentators who have studied this area are firmly of the opinion that a prosecution appeal against the judge's terminating, or de facto terminating, ruling is just, equitable and long overdue. It is a matter of serious concern that defendants have had a right of appeal against their conviction for almost a century while the prosecution has had no right to challenge a judge ordered acquittal, no matter how manifestly unjust such a ruling may be on rare occasions.

(House of Lords, *Hansard*, 17 November 2003, col. 1782)

9.1.1   Routine evidentiary rulings

The second set of provisions in section 62 refers to more routine evidentiary rulings, such as the exclusion of evidence that can often have an important impact on the running of the prosecution case. An example of such rulings can be found in the Damilola Taylor case, which attracted criticism in the report on the case by Bishop Sentamu, which stated:

> The Panel believes that the current rules of evidence and procedure had a significant effect on the trial of those accused of Damilola's murder, in that the rulings made in favour of the defence not only eroded essential parts of the prosecution case but provided the defence with an opportunity to develop what might have been untenable arguments had the evidence remained available for the Jury to consider. The Panel accepts that judicial rulings are difficult and entirely a matter for the Trial Judge, but considers that the exclusionary rules of evidence may have the effect of preventing critical evidence reaching the Jury, thereby inhibiting its ability to make sound decisions in circumstances where neither the victims of crime nor those responsible for the prosecution of offenders have any remedy. The Panel also believe that the absence of a prosecution right of appeal in trials where evidence qualifies to be considered for exclusion, in some cases, has the effect of affording inferior rights to victims compared to those of an accused.
>
> (The Damilola Taylor Murder Investigation Review, 2002, paragraphs 5.2.22–5.2.24)

9.1.2   Decisions to discharge a jury

No appeal under this part can be made in respect of decisions to discharge a jury, or in relation to matters which are already appealable under other legislation (s.57(2)).

9.1.3   Test to be applied

It is important that the prosecution do not see these provisions as amounting to an automatic appeal route. First, leave is required before a ruling can be appealed, and second, the Court of Appeal is not to become concerned with simply second guessing the trial judge, and can only reverse a ruling where it is satisfied that the ruling was wrong in law, involved an error of law or principle or was not reasonable (s.67).

It is not clear whether the term 'not reasonable' is to import a test of *Wednesbury* reasonableness into the courts' deliberation, and this will no doubt be a source of argument in the future.

9.2 GENERAL APPEAL IN RESPECT TO JUDGES' RULINGS

9.2.1 Rulings that can be appealed

Despite the general heading to section 58, the prosecution can only appeal those rulings which would result in a defendant being acquitted if the appeal did not proceed (s.58(8)). Appeals will therefore be confined to those rulings that have the effect of stopping the prosecution and resulting in an acquittal, effectively rulings of no case to answer, and rulings that have the effect of staying an indictment. It is important to remember that the stay of a case does not of itself lead to an acquittal, the practice adopted in many cases has been to invite the judge to lift the stay in order to offer no evidence and thereby achieve the acquittal. This procedure may seem a nonsense, but it was required under the Attorney General's reference procedure pursuant to section 36(1) of the Criminal Justice Act 1972 (as the prosecution could not appeal unless there had been an acquittal), and can be illustrated in numerous cases (e.g. *Attorney General's Reference (No.1 of 1990)* [1992] 95 Cr App R 296, at 298). A prosecutor must therefore be in a position to tell the judge that he would accept that no evidence should be offered (as a consequence of the stay) should leave of the Court of Appeal be refused, or the appeal abandoned. If the interpretation of 'acquittal' should ever need to be decided in the context of this Act, reference should be made to House of Lords Committee Stage, *Hansard*, 17 July 2003, col. 1014 in support.

9.2.2 Pre-trial rulings

Pre-trial rulings can be appealed.

How many times can the prosecutor appeal?

If a prosecutor has previously informed the court of his intention to appeal a ruling (and regardless of whether the appeal was proceeded with), no further appeal can lie against the same ruling (s.74(3)).

Procedural overview

This is illustrated in Figure 9.1.

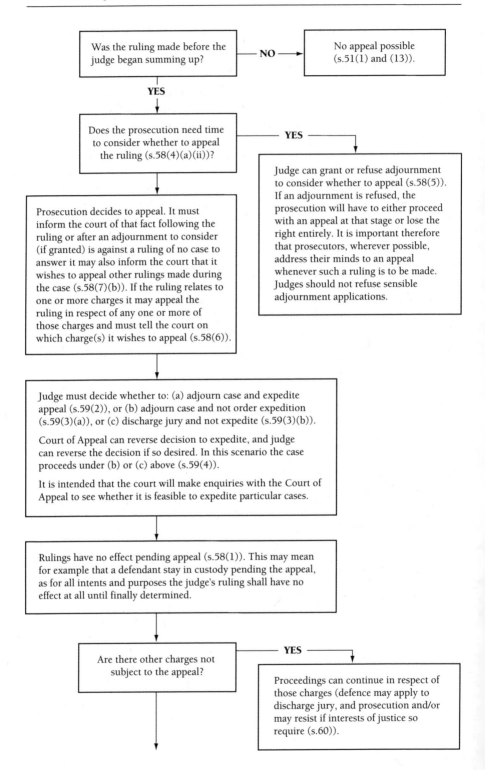

Was the ruling made before the judge began summing up?

NO → No appeal possible (s.51(1) and (13)).

YES

Does the prosecution need time to consider whether to appeal the ruling (s.58(4)(a)(ii))?

YES

Judge can grant or refuse adjournment to consider whether to appeal (s.58(5)). If an adjournment is refused, the prosecution will have to either proceed with an appeal at that stage or lose the right entirely. It is important therefore that prosecutors, wherever possible, address their minds to an appeal whenever such a ruling is to be made. Judges should not refuse sensible adjournment applications.

Prosecution decides to appeal. It must inform the court of that fact following the ruling or after an adjournment to consider (if granted) is against a ruling of no case to answer it may also inform the court that it wishes to appeal other rulings made during the case (s.58(7)(b)). If the ruling relates to one or more charges it may appeal the ruling in respect of any one or more of those charges and must tell the court on which charge(s) it wishes to appeal (s.58(6)).

Judge must decide whether to: (a) adjourn case and expedite appeal (s.59(2)), or (b) adjourn case and not order expedition (s.59(3)(a)), or (c) discharge jury and not expedite (s.59(3)(b)).

Court of Appeal can reverse decision to expedite, and judge can reverse the decision if so desired. In this scenario the case proceeds under (b) or (c) above (s.59(4)).

It is intended that the court will make enquiries with the Court of Appeal to see whether it is feasible to expedite particular cases.

Rulings have no effect pending appeal (s.58(1)). This may mean for example that a defendant stay in custody pending the appeal, as for all intents and purposes the judge's ruling shall have no effect at all until finally determined.

Are there other charges not subject to the appeal?

YES

Proceedings can continue in respect of those charges (defence may apply to discharge jury, and prosecution and/or may resist if interests of justice so require (s.60)).

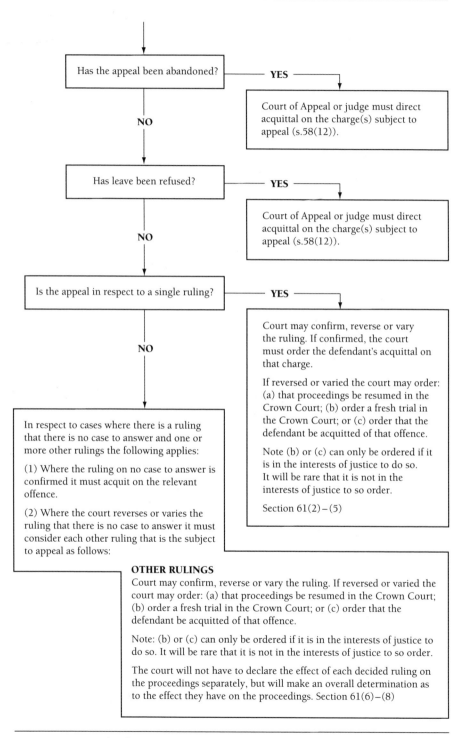

Figure 9.1   Procedural overview

9.2.3   What other rulings may be appealed at the same time as a ruling of no case to answer?

If a ruling of no case to answer is appealed, the prosecution may refer other rulings for appeal at the same time. It is important to note though that in the absence of a no case to answer ruling, no other ruling can be appealed under this section, the prosecution would need to rely upon section 62 in those circumstances. So, if the judge had made evidentiary rulings, and then rules that the indictment should be stayed, only the ruling in relation to the stay can be appealed (s.58(7)(a)). The Act is largely silent on the nature of these rulings, save for a wide definition in section 74(1) which defines a ruling as 'a decision, determination, direction, finding, notice, order, refusal, rejection or requirement'.

This definition would appear to include the types of evidentiary rulings catered for in section 62 of the Act, without the limitations placed on that section in respect of qualifying offences and a requirement that the ruling would have the effect of significantly weakening the prosecution case. This proposition is supported by section 62(11) which states that nothing in this section (relating to appealing evidentiary rulings) 'affects the right of the prosecution to appeal in respect of an evidentiary ruling under section 58'. This would mean therefore that if the judge excluded a certain piece of evidence from the prosecution case, the prosecution could wait to see whether that ruling proved to be potentially fatal to its case; if it were to be fatal; an appeal would lie not only against the termination ruling, but also in respect of the evidentiary ruling.

It is submitted that in those circumstances the Court of Appeal should refuse leave in relation to such rulings unless the criteria in section 63(2), (3) are met.

The rationale behind being able to appeal other rulings alongside a ruling of no case to answer was given by the Government during debate on the Bill:

> a ruling of no case to answer is a special case. It may well be preceded by a number of earlier rulings, each of them incrementally weakening the prosecution case. The effect of some or all of those earlier rulings might contribute significantly to the judge's eventual decision to make the ruling of no case to answer.
>
> For that reason, where the prosecution appeals against a ruling of no case to answer, we consider that it should be able to nominate such earlier rulings as it specifies for the Court of Appeal to review at the same time all as part of the same appeal. It seems to us that it is only sensible and logical that where the prosecution appeals against a ruling of no case to answer there should be arrangements for the Court of Appeal to examine formally those earlier rulings which led up to the eventual ruling of no case. In that way the Court of Appeal will have a better grasp of the case and as a whole will be able to review more effectively the judge's terminating ruling.

(House of Lords, *Hansard*, 30 October 2003, col. 444)

9.2.4   Effect on trial

Once a prosecutor has signified his intention to appeal, a decision must be made as to whether that appeal should be expedited or not. Much will depend on the particular facts of the case, and if a trial has been running for a number of weeks it is unlikely that it would be in the interests of justice to discharge a jury at that point. However, the workload of the Court of Appeal and its ability to make judges available at short notice for such hearings will be severely tested by the operation of this Act, and it remains to be seen whether or not the Court, without a significant increase to its judicial and other resources, will be able to react in the way the Government clearly intended.

Even if a case is expedited, the power to order an adjournment is discetionary (s.59(2)), and he may instead discharge the jury, this may be an option when a defendant has been in custody for an inordinate length of time. A decision to expedite can be reversed by the Court of Appeal. Similarly, a judge may adjourn, as opposed to discharging the jury, when expedition is not ordered – such instances will be rare.

9.2.5   Effect of rulings pending an appeal?

Section 58(11) states that no ruling, nor the consequences of a ruling are to have effect pending the appeal. The section goes further and states that 'the judge may not take any steps in consequence of the ruling, and if he does so, any such steps are to have no effect'. This innocuously worded section is of great practical importance to the prosecution, and will have the effect of ensuring for example, that no defendant is to be released on bail pending the appeal, if that decision flowed from the judge's view that there was no evidence against the defendant. Prosecutors should ensure that if bail applications are made, and they inevitably will be, the effect of this section should be drawn to the trial judge's attention. Since any steps taken are also to have no effect, this may lead to conflict between a purportedly lawful order of the court (for example to release a defendant) and the duty on (say) a prison not to give effect to the order.

9.2.6   What about other charges?

The judge has a discretion (s.60(2)) to continue proceedings in respect to any other charge. In some instances a jury may need to be discharged before this happens. If the appealed matter impacts upon the remaining charge(s), then it would be inappropriate to proceed (similar fact cases for example).

9.2.7   What about co-defendants?

If a co-defendant is on a joint charge, the charge is considered for the purposes of this part of the Act to be two separate charges (s.74(5)). This means that the prosecutor needs to ensure that if a ruling affects both defendants the intention to appeal in respect of both is stated. If a co-defendant is not the subject of an appeal, his case can continue, as outlined in the preceding paragraph.

9.2.8   Leave

It is implicit from the wording of section 58(9)(a) that leave of the Court of Appeal is required. If leave is refused, either the trial judge or the Court of Appeal (it is submitted that it should be the trial judge) should acquit the defendant on the relevant charge. If the Court refused leave on the termination ruling, it is questionable whether the Court would then have jurisdiction to hear argument on any other rulings appealed. If these circumstances arose, the question is once again raised as to whether the tests in section 62 and 63 would need to be met.

9.2.9   Effect of abandonment

If the appeal is abandoned, either the trial judge or the Court of Appeal should acquit the defendant on the relevant charge.

9.2.10   Powers available to the Court of Appeal

The Court may either confirm, reverse or vary any ruling (s.61(1)). The test to be applied is outlined in paragraph 9.1.3 above.

If the Court confirms a ruling resulting in termination (no case to answer, stay of indictment, or other form of directed acquittal), the court must order the defendant's acquittal in respect to that offence. There would be no need to consider any other rulings made, but the Court would presumably have the discretion to do so.

If the ruling is reversed or varies the ruling it must do one of three things:

(1) Order that the proceedings for the offence(s) continue in the Crown Court.
(2) Order a fresh trial take place in the Crown Court.
(3) Order an acquittal.

9.2.11   In interests of justice

The Court shall not order (1) or (2) unless it considers it to be in the interests of justice to do so.

9.2.12   Submission of no case

The situation is the same if an appeal is made against a submission of no case and one or more other rulings. A confirmation of the no case ruling would mean an acquittal, but if the ruling was reversed or varied the court would need to consider all of the rulings together before ordering one of the steps in (1)–(3) above.

9.2.13   Further rights of appeal, costs and reporting restrictions

Appeals from the Court of Appeal lie to the House of Lords (s.68). The Court has power to award costs relating to these appeals (s.69), and the Act lays down a framework for reporting restrictions in relation to appeals under Part 9 of the Act (ss.71, 72).

9.3   APPEALS IN RESPECT OF EVIDENTIARY RULINGS

9.3.1   Rulings that can be appealed

The prosecution can appeal one or more evidentiary rulings made at any time before the opening of the case for the defence (s.62). An evidentiary ruling is defined as a ruling which relates to the admissibility or exclusion of any prosecution evidence (s.62(9)).

A ruling must relate to a qualifying offence as listed in Part 1 of Schedule 4. Provided that the ruling does relate to a qualifying offence, an appeal can be made at the same time in respect of a non-qualifying offence. So for example, if a defendant was charged with theft under section 1 of the Theft Act 1968 the prosecution would have no right to appeal. However, if the defendant were charged with rape and theft, and the ruling related to both charges, the appeal could be in respect to both charges, as rape is a qualifying offence.

Where more than one ruling is appealed, each ruling must relate to at least one qualifying offence. As explained above, provided that each ruling does relate to at least one qualifying offence, the same ruling can also be appealed in relation to non-qualifying offences.

9.3.2   Pre-trial rulings

Pre-trial rulings can be appealed.

9.3.3   How many times can the prosecutor appeal?

If a prosecutor has previously informed the court of his intention to appeal a ruling (and regardless of whether the appeal was proceeded with), no further appeal can lie against the same ruling (s.74(3)).

9.3.4   Procedure

The prosecutor must inform the court that he intends to appeal before the opening of the case for the defence, and must identify the ruling(s) and the qualifying offence(s) to which it applies. The prosecutor may also identify any other offences to which the ruling relates if it his intention to appeal the ruling in respect of that or those offences also (s.62(5)–(7)).

9.3.5   When does the defence case open?

The prosecution must have closed its case, and the earliest of the following events occurs:

(1) Evidence begins to be adduced on behalf of the defendant.
(2) It is indicated that no evidence will be called. Or
(3) A defendant's case is opened as permitted by section 2 of the Criminal Procedure Act 1865 (opening speech).

9.3.6   Effect on trial

Once the prosecutor has properly signified his intention to appeal, the judge must decide whether to expedite the application. If the hearing is to be expedited, the judge may order an adjournment of the case. In the absence of an adjournment the only avenue open to the judge is for the discharge of the jury (if one has been sworn). If the judge refuses to expedite the appeal he may similarly order an adjournment or discharge the jury.

A decision to expedite can be reversed by the judge or the Court of Appeal (s.64(4)), at which point the judge may once again either adjourn the case or discharge the jury pending the outcome of the appeal.

See paragraph 9.2.4 above for relevant considerations in relation to expedition.

9.3.7   What about other charges?

Charges that are not subject to an appeal can continue to be tried (s.65(2)), and consideration will need to be given at that stage to the discharge of the jury and a fresh trial on the remaining charge(s).

9.3.8   What about co-defendants?

See paragraph 9.2.7 above.

9.3.9   Abandonment

The Act is silent on abandonment in relation to appeals under this section, it is expected however that rules made pursuant to section 73 will deal with this and other procedural points.

9.3.10   Leave

Leave may not be given unless the trial judge or the Court of Appeal is satisfied that the evidentiary ruling, or one or more evidentiary rulings taken together, would 'significantly weaken' the prosecution case in relation to the offence or offences which are subject to the appeal (s.63). Quite sensibly, the Act does not seek to define what 'significantly weaken' means.

9.3.11   Powers available to the Court of Appeal

The Court of Appeal may confirm, reverse or vary any ruling to which the appeal relates (s.66). The test to be applied is outlined in paragraph 9.1.3 above.

Upon so ruling, the Court must, in respect of the offence or each offence which is the subject of the appeal, do one of the following (s.66(2)):

(1) Order that proceedings be resumed in the Crown Court.
(2) Order that a fresh trial take place in the Crown Court for that offence.
(3) Order that the defendant be acquitted of that offence, but only if the prosecution has indicated that it does not intend to continue with the prosecution of that offence.

9.3.12   Further rights of appeal, costs and reporting restrictions

See paragraph 9.2.13 above.

10 SENTENCING

Key points:

- New sentencing framework.
- Sentencing guidelines council to advise on sentence and allocation guidelines.
- Increase to magistrates' sentencing powers.
- Constructive short-term sentences of less than 12 months.
- Stringent licence provisions.
- Sentences for dangerous offenders including indeterminate custody.
- Increase in penalty for drugs, firearm and some driving offences, with minimum sentences in some cases.
- Increased scope for use of community sentences, with emphasis on effective enforcement.

10.1 THE SENTENCING FRAMEWORK

10.1.1 Interpretation

For reasons that are not entirely clear, the Criminal Justice Act 2003 (the Act) makes widespread reference to the 'Sentencing Act', this is clarified in section 305 as being a reference to the Powers of Criminal Courts (Sentencing) Act 2000 (PCC(S)A 2000).

10.1.2 The purpose of sentencing

For the first time the purposes of sentencing has been set out in Statute (s.142). This should end the kind of debates that flowed following the Criminal Justice Act 1991, in particular in relation to deterrent sentencing.

Any court dealing with an offender must have regard to the following purposes of sentencing:

- punishment of offenders;
- reduction of crime (including its reduction by deterrence);
- reform and rehabilitation of offenders;
- protection of the public;
- making of reparation by offenders to persons affected by their offences.

The Act does not specify any particular weight to be attached to each provision, and this may lead to considerable legal argument, particularly as to whether non-custodial sentences are appropriate.

Exceptions

The above does not apply to an offender aged under 18 at the time of conviction, offences for which the sentence is fixed by law, offences where a minimum or required sentence is specified or in relation to the making of hospital orders.

10.1.3   Determining the seriousness of the offence

A court must consider (s.143) the offender's culpability in committing the offence and any harm that was caused, was intended to be caused or might foreseeably have been caused. The Act is silent on whether the test of foreseeability is subjective or objective, but it is submitted following the comments of the House of Lords in *R v. G and R* [2003] UKHL 50 that the test should be subjective.

Each previous conviction must, provided the court considers such consideration to be reasonable, be treated as an aggravating factor (s.143(2)). In deciding whether it is reasonable to treat the previous offence as aggravating the court should have particular regard to the nature of the offence and its relevance to the current offence, and the time elapsed since the original offence. The court must treat an offence on bail as an aggravating factor (s.143(3)). Previous convictions relate to those convictions recorded by a court in the United Kingdom, service offences, or, in cases where the court considers it appropriate, convictions by a court outside of the United Kingdom.

10.1.4   Effect of guilty plea

In determining what sentence to pass, the court must take into account, in relation to an offender who has pleaded guilty, the stage in the proceedings at which he indicated his intention to plead guilty and the circumstances in which the indication was given (s.144).

A guilty plea allows a sentence under section 110 or 111 of the PCC(S)A 2000 to be mitigated by up to 20 per cent.

10.1.5   Racial or religious aggravation

Racially or religiously aggravated offences in relation to assault, criminal damage, and other offences are created by virtue of sections 29 to 32 of the Crime and Disorder Act 1998 (CDA 1998).

Section 145 of the Act provides that where an offence (other than one under sections 28–32 of the CDA 1998) is found to be racially or religiously aggravated, within the meaning of section 28 of the CDA 1998, the court must treat this fact as an aggravating factor, and state in open court that the offence was so aggravated.

It is submitted that if an offence that could have been charged as aggravated under sections 28–32 of the CDA 1998, is not so charged, then section 145 can still be used, and nothing in section 145(1) acts as a bar to that being the case.

The approach to be adopted in deciding to what degree the offence should be treated as aggravated, is to be found in R v. *Kelly and Donnelly* [2001] Crim LR 411:

(1) Arrive at the appropriate sentence without the element of racial or religious aggravation, but including any other aggravating or mitigating factors.
(2) Enhance that sentence to take account of the racial or religious aggravation. The amount to be added to the sentence would differ according to the circumstances of the individual case, but the following factors ought to be taken into account:

    (a) planning or pattern of racist/religious offending;
    (b) membership of a group promoting such unlawful activity;
    (c) deliberately exposing the victim to offence or humiliation;
    (d) offences within the victim's home;
    (e) particularly vulnerable victims or victim performing public service;
    (f) if the timing of the offence was calculated to maximise harm (e.g. during a religious festival);
    (g) repeated or prolonged expressions of hostility; and
    (h) fear or distress within the community flowing from the offence.

(3) Declare to the court what the appropriate sentence would have been for the offence without the aggravation so that the sentence for the racial or religious element of the offence could be clearly seen.

Prosecutors should ensure that such offences are tried at the correct level, and it is unlikely that aggravated offences would be suitable for summary trial (Magistrates' Association sentencing guidelines support this view).

10.1.6   Offences aggravated by reference to disability or sexual orientation

Section 146 of the Act requires that offences that are motivated by hostility in relation to a person's disability or sexual orientation are to be treated as aggravated. This section would also apply if hostility was demonstrated toward the victim based on disability or sexual orientation. A court is required to state when sentencing that it has treated the above factors as aggravating features of the case.

10.1.7 Reports to be obtained before sentence

Mentally disordered offenders

Unless the court is of the opinion that a report is unnecessary, it must obtain and consider a medical report on the offender before passing a custodial sentence, other than one fixed by law (s.157). A sentence will not be invalidated by failure to obtain and consider such a report, but in such instances any appeal Court should obtain such a report itself.

Pre-sentence reports

Sections 156, 158 and 159 of the Act lay down the requirements for the obtaining and purpose of pre-sentence reports, including the disclosure of the same. Additional provision is made (s.160) for reports in relation to young offenders.

10.1.8 Duties to outline sentence and its effects to defendants

Section 174 of the Act provides that a court must state in open court, and in ordinary language and general terms, the reasons for deciding on the sentence passed. The court must explain to the offender the effects of the sentence, the effects of not complying with court orders that may form part of that sentence. The court must outline the effects of failing to pay any fine ordered and any powers of the court to review a sentence that has been passed. In passing a custodial or community sentence the court must state that the criteria for such sentences have been met, and why. Aggravating and mitigating factors, including a guilty plea must be mentioned during sentence.

In order to greater promote the use and adherence to sentencing guidelines, the court must state its reasons for deciding on a sentence that is of a different kind to, or outside the range of, the guideline sentence.

The duties imposed by section 174 are onerous, and will require greater assistance from prosecution advocates than that often afforded at present. Advocates should have regard to *Attorney General's Reference (No. 7 of 1997)* [1998] 1 Cr App R (S) 268 for guidance as to prosecuting advocate's duty of assistance to the Court. It is now the duty of prosecuting advocates to not only be able to refer judges to key sentencing authorities, but also to be able to provide the judge with a copy (*Attorney General's Reference (No. 52 of 2003)* CA, *The Times*, 12 December 2003).

10.1.9   Sentencing and allocation guidelines

Formation of Sentencing Guidelines Council

The Act provides for the establishing of a Sentencing Guidelines Council (hereinafter the Council), consisting of the Lord Chief Justice, seven additional judicial members and four non-judicial members. Judicial members can be appointed from the ranks of Justice of the Peace, upwards to Lord Justices of Appeal, with a minimum composition comprising at least one lay justice, District Judge (Magistrates' Courts) and a circuit judge.

Non-judicial members must have experience of one or more of the areas of policing, criminal prosecution, criminal defence, the promotion of the welfare of victims of crime and sentencing and the administration of sentences.

The Council was set up following a recommendation in the Halliday Report, to fulfil the recommendation that codified guidelines should be produced for application by all criminal courts, taking account of existing guidelines and the need for their further development and modification in the light of changes resulting from the wider changes to sentencing envisaged by the Halliday Report and largely adopted in the Act. The Council must report on its activities on a yearly basis to the Secretary of State for Home Affairs and the Lord Chancellor, who will lay the report before Parliament.

Sentencing Advisory Panel

The existing Sentencing Advisory Panel (hereinafter the Panel) is retained by the Act.

The Panel can propose that the Council issue a new or revised sentencing or allocation guideline and must be informed of all such proposals to issue or amend guidelines that have been initiated by the Secretary of State or the Council itself. The Panel will continue to consult on such proposals and formulate and communicate its views to the Council, but will no longer report to the Court of Appeal.

The Chairman of the Sentencing Advisory Panel, writing in the 2002/03 annual report commented on the Criminal Justice Bill and the anticipated changes to the Panel's relationship with the Court of Appeal by stating:

> The issuing of sentencing guidelines is not, of course, the end of the story. Guidelines are intended to encourage more consistent sentencing. To do this successfully, they must have the confidence of judges and magistrates who sentence offenders on a day to day basis in the criminal courts. This, I believe, has been achieved through the combination of the Court of Appeal's authority with the Panel's collective expertise and its consultative procedure.

The Panel maintains a comprehensive website (**www.sentencing-advisory-panel. gov.uk**).

Functions of the Council

It is the duty of the Council, either on request from the Secretary of State, or the Sentencing Advisory Panel, to consider formulating sentencing and allocation guidelines. Sentencing guidelines may be general in nature or limited to a particular category of offence or offender (s.170(2)). Allocation guidelines relate to whether an offence is more suitable for summary trial, or trial on indictment, and replace the present National Mode of Trial Guidelines, last issued in 1995 (s.170(1)(b)).

The Council must consult published draft guidelines and consult with the Secretary of State and such other person as the Lord Chancellor (after consultation with the Secretary of State) may direct, and such other persons as the Council considers appropriate.

10.1.10 Overview of formulation of guidelines

These are illustrated in Figure 10.1.

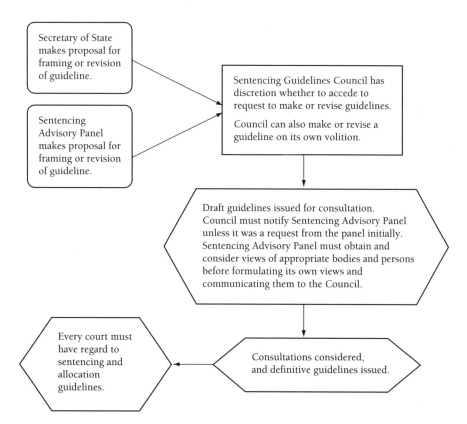

Figure 10.1 Overview of formulation of guidelines

Matters to which the Council must have regard when framing or revising guidelines

The Council must, when considering sentencing guidelines, have regard to the following factors (s.170(5)):

(1) Need to promote consistency in sentencing.
(2) The sentences imposed by courts in England and Wales for offences to which the guidelines relate.
(3) The cost of different sentences and their relative effectiveness in preventing re-offending.
(4) The need to promote public confidence in the criminal justice system.
(5) The views communicated to the Council by the Sentencing Advisory Panel.

When considering allocation guidelines the Council must have regard to:

(1) The need to promote consistency in decisions under section 19 of the Magistrates' Courts Act 1980, relating to the most suitable venue for the trial of an offence.
(2) The views communicated to the Council by the Sentencing Advisory Panel.

Effect of the guidelines

Every court must, in sentencing an offender, have regard to any guidelines which are relevant to the offender's case, and in exercising any other function (e.g. mode of trial decisions) relating to sentencing of offenders, have regard to any guidelines which are relevant to the exercise of the function (s.172).

10.2   FINANCIAL PENALTIES

10.2.1   Financial circumstances order

A court, following conviction, can make a financial circumstances order against an offender, which requires that offender to give to the court a statement of his financial circumstances (s.162). The information to be sought is open to the Court, but is expected to be more detailed than the basic statement of means that is required at present. The court can specify timescales for compliance.

An order can be made in respect of an offender who does not appear before the court (typically motoring cases dealt with in absence).

Offence for failing to comply with a financial circumstances order

Failure to comply with the order, without reasonable excuse, is an offence punishable with a fine not exceeding level 3 on the standard scale (s.162(4)).

Offence of giving false information in relation to a financial circumstances order

Any person who makes a statement which he knows to be false, or recklessly furnishes a statement which is false in a material particular or knowingly fails to disclose any material fact, commits an offence (s.162(5)).

The offence is punishable with a maximum of 51 weeks imprisonment and/or a fine not exceeding level 4 on the standard scale. Despite being a summary only offence, proceedings can be brought within two years of the offence having been committed or within 6 months from its first discovery by the prosecutor, whichever period expires the earlier.

10.2.2 Crown Court's power to fine

The Crown Court, save when sentencing for an offence where the penalty is fixed by law, where the offender is sentenced under section 110(2) or 111(2) of the PCC(S)A 2000, or a sentence prescribed as life for serious offenders (ss.225–228) has the power (unless prohibited by another enactment) to impose a fine instead of or additional to, another way of dealing with him.

There is nothing in this section that takes away the Court's duty to follow normal sentencing guidelines and any deviance from those guidelines would have to be explained.

10.2.3 Fixing the level of fine

Before fining an individual (but not a company or other entity) a court must enquire into his financial circumstances. Any fine must reflect the seriousness of the offence, taking into account the circumstances of the offence and the financial circumstances of the offender as they appear or are known to the court (s.164). It may be the case that after taking into account the financial circumstances of the offender, the fine is increased or decreased. This power would seem to make allowance for the fact that small fines, while otherwise consistent with the seriousness of the offence, might have a disproportionately small impact on wealthy individuals.

Procedure where the court is not in possession of information relating to means

If an offender is convicted in his absence, or otherwise fails to cooperate with a court's request to furnish financial information, the court can make such determination as it thinks fit in the circumstances (s.164(5)).

10.2.4   Remission of fines

If a court has fixed a financial penalty without enquiring into an offender's means, but subsequently does so enquire, it can remit all or part of the fine (s.165). This power caters for circumstances when the court, appraised of full information, realises that it either would not have fined the offender, or would have fined him a smaller amount.

10.2.5   Fine defaulters – community penalties and driving disqualification

Section 300 allows a magistrates' court to impose an unpaid work or curfew requirement on a person aged 16 or over if they have defaulted on fine repayment. Electronic monitoring of such requirements can additionally be imposed in the same way as they might in respect to a community order. The order can be reduced in whole or part by payment of the financial penalty at any time.

Period of disqualification

Section 301 allows a magistrates' court to impose a period of disqualification (from holding or obtaining a licence), of up to 12 months, on a fine defaulter. Again, the order can be reduced in whole or part by payment of the financial penalty at any time.

10.3   COMMUNITY SENTENCES

10.3.1   Definitions

A community sentence is defined as a sentence which consists of or includes a community order or one or more youth community orders (s.147(1)).

Community order

A community order can be made in respect of a person aged 16 or over convicted of an offence. The order, for a maximum length of three years, comprises one or more of the following requirements:

- an unpaid work requirement (s.199);
- an activity requirement (s.201);
- a programme requirement (s.202);
- a prohibited activity requirement (s.203);
- a curfew requirement (s.204);
- an exclusion requirement (s.205);
- a residence requirement (s.206);
- a mental health treatment requirement (s.207);
- a drug rehabilitation requirement (s.209);

- an alcohol treatment requirement (s.212);
- a supervision requirement (s.213);
- an attendance centre requirement (s.214) (for offenders below 25 years of age).

The specific requirements of these orders are set out below.

Youth community order

This order, for a maximum period of three years comprises one of:

- a curfew order under section 163 of the PCC(S)A 2000;
- an exclusion order under section 40A(1) of the PCC(S)A 2000;
- an attendance centre order as defined by section 163 of the PCC(S)A 2000;
- a supervision order under section 63(1) of the PCC(S)A 2000;
- an action plan order under section 69(1) of the PCC(S)A 2000.

Drug treatment and testing requirement

A drug treatment and testing requirement can be imposed as a requirement of an action plan or supervision order, in accordance with Schedule 24 to the Act. The offender must be aged 14 years or over and consent.

10.3.2   Restrictions on imposing community sentences

Seriousness criteria

A court must not pass a community sentence unless of the opinion that the offence, or the combination of the offence and one or more offences associated with it, was serious enough to warrant such a sentence (s.148(1)).

The community sentence must comprise elements that are suitable for the offender (s.148(2)(a)) and restrictions on liberty imposed must be commensurate with the seriousness of the offence, or the combination of the offence and one or more offences associated with it (s.148(2)(b)).

Community order for persistent offender previously fined

A community sentence can be passed, regardless of the fact that the seriousness criteria are not met, in the following circumstances (s.151):

- person aged 16 years or over convicted of an offence;
- on three or more previous occasions has been convicted by a court in the United Kingdom of an offence committed by him after attaining the age of 16, and has had passed on him a sentence consisting only of a fine; and
- the current offence would not otherwise be serious enough to warrant a community sentence; and

■ having considered the nature of the previous offences and their relevance to the current offence, and the time that has elapsed since the offender's conviction of each of those offences, it is in all of the circumstances in the interests of justice to make such an order.

Effect of previous remand in custody on length of community sentence

The court must have regard to any period served on remand in custody prior to sentence for the offence or any other offence the charge for which was founded on the same facts or evidence (s.149). This section reflects current sentencing practice.

Effect of mandatory sentences

A court cannot pass a community sentence in respect of an offence for which the sentence is fixed by law, where the offender falls to be sentenced under section 51A(2) of the Firearms Act 1968 (required custodial sentence for certain firearms offences), or falls to receive a minimum sentence for a third drug trafficking offence or third burglary (PCC(S)A 2000, ss.110(2) and 111(2)). Nor can a community sentence be imposed where a sentence under sections 225–228 of the Act falls to be imposed.

10.3.3   Requirement for pre-sentence report before passing community sentence

Adults

The court must order and consider a pre-sentence report unless, having consideration to the circumstances of the case, it is of the opinion that a report is unnecessary (s.156).

Youths

Unless the youth falls to be sentenced for an indictable-only offence (whether on its own or in combination with one or more other offences of any description), the court must not dispense with a pre-sentence report unless there exists a previous pre-sentence report which the court has had regard to (s.156). If there is more than one previous report the court must have consider the most recent.

Effect of failure to obtain a pre-sentence report

A sentence is not invalidated by the failure of a court to obtain a pre-sentence report, but a court on appeal should order and consider such a report unless it agrees that such a report was unnecessary or is at the time of the appeal unnecessary. In the case of a youth the appeal court should consider any earlier report.

Disclosure of pre-sentence reports

Section 159 details the parties who must receive any written report. A copy must be given to the offender, his legal representative and the prosecutor. A report in respect to an unrepresented offender should be given to his parent or guardian if present in court.

The report is only to be used for formulating and making representations to the court in relation to its contents.

Other reports, such as those prepared by a member of the youth offending team, must be similarly disclosed if given to a court other than a youth court.

10.3.4   Pre-sentence drug testing

A court can order a convicted offender aged 14 years or over, in respect of whom it is considering passing a community sentence, to provide samples for the purpose of ascertaining whether the offender has any specified Class-A drug in his body (s.161).

If the offender is under 17 years of age such samples must be provided in the presence of an appropriate adult, and the order should reflect this fact.

A failure to comply with such an order, without reasonable excuse is an offence punishable with a fine not exceeding level 4 on the standard scale.

Specified Class-A drugs

These are:

■ cocaine, its salts and any preparation or other product containing cocaine or its salts;
■ diamorphine (commonly known as heroin), its salts and any preparation or other product containing diamorphine or its salts.

10.3.5   Types of community order

Overview

The community sentence can be made up of a combination of different orders, but must consider when combining orders whether the requirements are compatible with each other. Some orders carry an electronic-monitoring requirement, unless exceptions are met. Reference is made to other penalties such as custody plus, this is because these community orders can now be combined with various types of custodial sentence and licence conditions. The following table provides a summary.

Name	Nature of order	Minimum length/hours (no minimum period unless otherwise specified)	Maximum length/hours (note the maximum of 3 years for community orders, unless otherwise specified)	Comments
Unpaid work requirement	Performance of unpaid work.	40 hours.	300 hours. Must be completed within 12 months unless the period is extended.	Court must be satisfied that offender is a suitable person to perform such work. Concurrent orders must not exceed 300 hours. Court may impose electronic monitoring requirement unless prevented from doing so by section 215.
Activity requirement	To present himself to a person at such place and time as specified, and/or participate in specified activities. Such activities to include reparative schemes.	n/a	60 days, comprising attendance and/or activities.	Court must consult officer of local probation board before imposing such a requirement, or in the case of an offender aged under 18 years either an officer of the local probation board or a member of a youth offending team. Following consultation court must be satisfied that it is feasible to ensure compliance with the requirement(s) to be imposed. If the requirement involves the cooperation of a person other than the offender (for example a victim in a reparative scheme), the person concerned must consent before the requirement can be imposed. Court may impose electronic monitoring requirement unless prevented from doing so by section 215

Name	Nature of order	Minimum length/hours (no minimum period unless otherwise specified)	Maximum length/hours (note the maximum of 3 years for community orders, unless otherwise specified)	Comments
Programme requirement	Participation in an accredited programme of activities.	Not specified. This order will generally be in addition to a supervision requirement, and would include courses such as 'Think First' and domestic violence programmes.	Not specified.	If the requirement involves the cooperation of a person other than the offender, the person concerned must consent before the requirement can be imposed Court may impose electronic-monitoring requirement unless prevented from doing so by section 215 Court must consult officer of local probation board before imposing such a requirement, or in the case of an offender aged under 18 years either an officer of the local probation board or a member of a youth offending team. Following consultation court must be satisfied that it is feasible to ensure compliance with the requirement(s) to be imposed.
Prohibited activity requirement	An order refraining the offender from participating in activities specified in the order, on a day or days so specified, or during a period so specified.	Not specified.	Not specified.	An order requiring the offender not to possess, use or carry a firearm (within the meaning of the Firearms Act 1968) can be included in such an order. Court may impose electronic monitoring requirement unless prevented from doing so by section 215

continued

Name	Nature of order	Minimum length/hours (no minimum period unless otherwise specified)	Maximum length/hours (note the maximum of 3 years for community orders, unless otherwise specified)	Comments
				Court must consult officer of local probation board before imposing such a requirement, or in the case of an offender aged under 18 years either an officer of the local probation board or a member of a youth offending team. Following consultation court must be satisfied that it is feasible to ensure compliance with the requirement(s) to be imposed.
Curfew requirement	An order requiring the offender to remain at a place specified in the order.	2 hours per day.	12 hours per day (see additional notes).	The court must also impose an electronic-monitoring requirement unless it is prevented from doing so by section 215 or in the particular circumstances of the case it considers it inappropriate to do so.
				A community order or suspended custody order which imposes a curfew requirement may not specify periods which fall outside the period of 6 months beginning with the day on which the order is made. If imposed as part of a custody plus order the 6-month period starts with the first day of the licence period.
				If the order is made as part of an intermittent custody order, the aggregate number of days on which the offender is subject to the requirement for any part of the day must not exceed 182 days.

Name	Nature of order	Minimum length/hours (no minimum period unless otherwise specified)	Maximum length/hours (note the maximum of 3 years for community orders, unless otherwise specified)	Comments
				The court must obtain and consider information about the place proposed to be specified in the order, including information as to the attitude of persons likely to be affected by the enforced presence there of the offender.
Exclusion requirement	An order prohibiting the offender from entering a place specified in the order.	Not specified.	Not exceeding a 2-year period where the relevant order is a community order.	The court must also impose an electronic-monitoring requirement unless it is prevented from doing so by section 215 or in the particular circumstances of the case it considers it inappropriate to do so.

Exclusions can operate for certain defined periods and may specify different places for different periods or days. |
| Residence requirement | In relation to a community order or a suspended sentence order, means a requirement that, during a period specified, the offender must reside at a particular place. | Not specified. | Not specified. | The court must consider the home surroundings of the offender before making an order.

A court may not specify a hostel or other institution except on the recommendation of an officer of the local probation board.
Court may impose electronic-monitoring requirement unless prevented from doing so by section 215 |

continued

Name	Nature of order	Minimum length/hours (no minimum period unless otherwise specified)	Maximum length/hours (note the maximum of 3 years for community orders, unless otherwise specified)	Comments
Mental health treatment requirement	Order requiring offender to submit to treatment by or under the direction of a registered medical practitioner or a chartered psychologist or both. The order must be made with a view to the improvement of the offender's mental condition.	Not specified.	Not specified.	Court must be satisfied on the evidence of a person approved under section 12 of the Mental Health Act 1983 that the mental condition of the offender is: (a) such as requires and may be susceptible to treatment; but (b) is not such as to warrant the making of a hospital order or guardianship order within the meaning of the Mental Health Act 1983. Court may impose electronic monitoring requirement unless prevented from doing so by section 215.
Drug rehabilitation requirement	An order requiring the offender to submit to treatment, with a view to the reduction or elimination of the offender's dependency on or propensity to misuse drugs, and, for the purpose of ascertaining whether he has drugs in his body may impose a requirement to supply samples for analysis.	Treatment and testing period must be for a minimum of 6 months.	Not specified.	Can only impose the order if satisfied that the offender is dependent on, or has propensity to misuse drugs, and that his dependency or propensity is such as requires and may be susceptible to treatment. Mandatory court review for orders of more that 12 months, otherwise discretionary (s.210). Court may impose electronic-monitoring requirement unless prevented from doing so by section 215.

Name	Nature of order	Minimum length/hours (no minimum period unless otherwise specified)	Maximum length/hours (note the maximum of 3 years for community orders, unless otherwise specified)	Comments
				Court must consult officer of local probation board before imposing such a requirement, or in the case of an offender aged under 18 years either an officer of the local probation board or a member of a youth offending team. Following consultation court must be satisfied that it is feasible to ensure compliance with the requirement(s) to be imposed.
Alcohol treatment requirement	Order requiring offender to submit to treatment, with a view to the reduction or elimination of the offender's dependency on alcohol.	6 months minimum.	Not specified.	Court must be satisfied that the offender is dependent on alcohol, that his dependency is such as requires and may be susceptible to treatment, and, that suitable arrangements have been made, or can be made, for the reception of the offender.

Court may impose electronic-monitoring requirement unless prevented from doing so by section 215. |
| Supervision requirement | Order requiring that the offender attend appointments with the 'responsible officer', in order to promote the offender's rehabilitation. | See notes. | See notes. | The order will apply during the 'relevant period', which is the period that the community order remains in force (i.e. for up to 3 years), or in relation to a custody plus order, the licence period as defined by section 181(3)(b). In relation to an intermittent custody order the period is the licence period specified by section 183(3), and for a suspended sentence order it is |

continued

Name	Nature of order	Minimum length/hours (no minimum period unless otherwise specified)	Maximum length/hours (note the maximum of 3 years for community orders, unless otherwise specified)	Comments
				the supervision period as specified by section 189(1)(a).
				Court may impose electronic-monitoring requirement unless prevented from doing so by section 215.
Attendance centre requirement	Requirement to attend at an attendance centre.	12 hours.	36 hours.	Offender must be under 25 years of age.
			Cannot be required to attend on more than one occasion on any one day.	Court must have regard to whether the centre is reasonably accessible to the offender, having regard to the means of access available to him and any other circumstances.
			Cannot be required to attend for more than 3 hours on any one day.	Court may impose electronic-monitoring requirement unless prevented from doing so by section 215.

Electronic-monitoring

Electronic-monitoring is to ensure compliance with various orders, as outlined above. Any other person, whose cooperation is necessary to make the order work, must consent to the order.

Religious beliefs and other conflicts

A court must ensure as far as practicable that a community order does not conflict with an offender's religious beliefs or schooling (s.217).

10.3.6   Review of community orders

The Secretary of State can, by order, enable or require a court to provide for the review or amendment of community orders, and make provision for the timing and conduct of such reviews and the powers of the court on review (s.178). Such an order from the Secretary of State can have the effect of repealing or amending any provision of Part 12 of the Act.

10.3.7   Breach, revocation and amendment of community orders

Schedule 8 deals with breach, revocation and amendment of community orders, and provides for a warning system in relation to offenders. Generally, unless the breach is serious or cannot be remedied by a warning, a first warning will be given to the offender, outlining the circumstances of the failure to comply with the order and that the failure is unacceptable, and informing the offender that a further failure within 12 months will lead to the offender being brought before the court for breach proceedings.

Effect of previous warning

If a warning has previously been given, and within 12 months of that warning the responsible officer is of the opinion that the offender has since that date failed without reasonable excuse to comply with any of the requirements of the order, the officer must cause court proceedings to be taken in respect to the breach.

Crown Court Orders

Orders made by the Crown Court will be dealt with at first instance by the Crown Court unless the order included a requirement that failure to comply with the order was to be dealt with by the magistrates' court. This power recognises that in many instances the Crown Court will be content for Justices to decide whether a breach should be sent to the Crown Court for re-sentencing, or whether it can be dealt with in the lower court.

Powers of magistrates' court if breach proved

If a person fails, without reasonable excuse, to comply with any of the requirements of the community order, it can be dealt with in any one of the following ways, taking into account beforehand the extent of compliance with the order aside from the breach:

(1) Amending the order to include more onerous requirements.
(2) Where the order is one made by the magistrates' court: by dealing with the offender in any way in which the court could have dealt with him if he had just been convicted of the offence (i.e. re-sentencing). The original order must be revoked.
(3) Where the community order was made by a magistrates' court and the offence was not an offence punishable by imprisonment, the court has the power to impose a term of imprisonment not exceeding 51 weeks, provided the offender is aged 18 or over and has wilfully and persistently failed to comply with the requirements of the order. The original order must be revoked.

If the community order was made by the Crown Court, the magistrates instead of dealing with the offender in one of the three ways specified above, can instead, commit him to the Crown Court to be dealt with, either on bail or in custody. The Crown Court can deal with the offender in any one of the three ways specified above.

Effect of certain breaches

An offender required under a mental health, drug rehabilitation or alcohol treatment requirement to submit to treatment, is not to be treated as having failed to comply with that requirement on the ground only that he had refused to undergo any surgical, electrical or other treatment if, in the opinion of the court, his refusal was reasonable having regard to all of the circumstances.

Revocation of orders

A court can revoke the order, or revoke the order and re-sentence and deal with the offender in any which it could have dealt with him had he just been convicted. Orders can be revoked on the grounds of good progress or satisfactory response to treatment or supervision.

Amendment of orders

Schedule 8, paragraph 16 contains provision for the amendment of orders.

Effect of subsequent conviction

An offender convicted of an offence during the currency of a community order may have his order revoked. On revoking an order the court can go on to re-sentence for the original offence and deal with him in any way it could have when he was first convicted. The provisions for the Crown Court and magistrates' court are the same, and reflect current practice.

10.4   CUSTODIAL PENALTIES

The Act completely overhauls custodial penalties, providing for novel sentencing options in relation to short-term prisoners, and the introduction of intermittent custody as a means of dealing with offenders for whom a prison sentence is called, but would otherwise have particularly counterproductive effects (loss of employment for example). More stringent licensing conditions will become the norm, as will severe sentences for dangerous offenders. Sentencing penalties in relation to firearms offences have been radically altered. All prison sentences of less than 12 months will be either 'custody plus' or 'intermittent custody' orders as outlined below.

A key change is the removal of the maximum penalty of six months' imprisonment for any one offence in the magistrates' court. These provisions do not have effect in the Youth Court.

Key changes:

- Loss of committal for sentence in most cases when magistrates accept jurisdiction.
- Power to sentence up to 12 months' imprisonment in relation to any single either-way offence (not applicable in Youth Court).
- All sentences less than 12 months to be custody plus or intermittent custody (not applicable in Youth Court).

10.5   NEW MAGISTRATES' SENTENCING POWERS

Section 154 of the Act will allow a magistrates' court to impose a sentence of up to 12 months in respect to any one offence (provided of course that it does not exceed the statutory maximum). As a result of this increased sentencing power the magistrates' court will lose its power to commit for sentence having accepted jurisdiction for a case.

Some summary-only offences which previously carried short terms of imprisonment are taken away from the custodial scheme, and only a community penalty can be passed in relation to those offences (see Schedule 25).

Some other summary offences (involving violence, public health, cruelty, etc.), typically those that carried three months' imprisonment (but in some cases only one month), have had their maximum penalties increased to 51 weeks (which will mean a maximum 13-week custodial term under the new scheme detailed below).

All other summary only offences currently carrying a maximum sentence of 6 months' imprisonment, the penalties are raised to 51 weeks (to keep punishment within the new scheme). Consider the following examples:

Example 1
D is charged with the theft from his employer of £20 from a till. Under previous rules the court would not have known about any antecedent history of D, and may well have declined jurisdiction. Under the new rules the court can accept jurisdiction (and it will be able to hear of any antecedent history before doing so), in the knowledge that it can impose custody of up to 12 months for this single offence. The court, having accepted jurisdiction, will not be able to commit D for sentence thereafter.

If the sentence imposed is less that 12 months, it will be expressed as either a custody plus or intermittent custody sentence (for which see below).

Example 2
D is charged with common assault (maximum now 51 weeks). The magistrates wish to imprison him for 32 weeks: this sentence is not available; the court will have to sentence him under the new rules below.

Example 3
D is charged with two offences of common assault, each of which carry 51 weeks' maximum penalty. In order to avoid a custody plus sentence, the magistrates wish to sentence D to 6 months in respect to each offence, to run consecutively. The clerk advises that this is possible since section 133 of the Magistrates' Courts Act 1980 has been amended to provide for consecutive sentences of up to 65 weeks. This sentence is not available, since the two individual sentences are less than 12 months, sentencing falls within section 181 of the Act, and the court will have to impose a custody plus or intermittent custody sentence for D. Note that under the old rules two offences of common assault could only ever have received a sentence of six months' imprisonment, of which only half would have been served (12 weeks), under the new custody plus regime, two summary offences consecutively sentenced can be met with up to 26 weeks' imprisonment which will not be subject to any remission.

10.6   PRISON SENTENCES OF LESS THAN 12 MONTHS

All custodial sentences of less than 12 months, imposed by a magistrates' or Crown Court, will be a 'custody plus order' or 'intermittent custody order'.

10.6.1   Custody plus order

A custody plus order is a term of custody and stringent licence period that must be expressed in weeks. Various parts of a community order can be attached to the licence period to allow for unpaid work and other activities to be completed during the licence period. The order is made up as set out below.

Custodial period	Licence period	Notes
Minimum 2 weeks, maximum 13 weeks in respect of any one offence (for multiple offences that are to be sentenced consecutively see below)	Minimum of 26 weeks	The minimum combined sentence must be 28 weeks. The combined custody and licence period must not exceed 51 weeks in relation to any one offence, nor may it exceed the maximum penalty for the offence in question. Many summary-only offences have been increased to 51 weeks to cater for this new sentence.

Example

A court wishing to impose a custodial sentence of four weeks' duration, and the minimum 26 weeks' licence period would sentence the offender to a custody plus order of 30 weeks.

While many summary only offences now carry 51 weeks' imprisonment, the effect of the custody plus order is that the offender cannot ever serve more than 13 weeks in prison for more than one offence, the same period he would have served when receiving the previous maximum sentence of six months' imprisonment. Prisoners are still eligible for release on licence.

Consecutive sentences

In respect to an offender who falls to be sentenced for more than one offence, and where the court wishes to impose consecutive sentences, the following provisions apply:

Custodial period	Licence period	Notes
Custodial period not to exceed 26 weeks in respect to two or more offences	Licence period must be for a minimum of 26 weeks	The combined custody and licence period cannot exceed 65 weeks

Licence conditions

Save where the court imposes a suspended sentence, it may require the offender to be subject to a licence with one or more requirements attached. Those requirements, which must be compatible with each other, are:

- unpaid work;
- activity;
- programme;
- prohibited activity;
- curfew (with electronic monitoring if appropriate under s.215);
- exclusion (with electronic monitoring if appropriate under s.215);
- supervision;
- attendance centre (for offender under 25 years).

Breach of licence

See paragraph 10.13.10.

10.6.2   Intermittent custody

Intermittent custody allows the offender to serve the custodial element of the sentence over a longer period of time, and not on consecutive days. The effect of this sentence would be to allow those working for example to serve their prison sentence at weekends, allowing them to keep their normal jobs and therefore protect against the wider family losing their home.

Length of order

These are set out below.

Custodial period	Licence period	Notes
14 days minimum, 90 days maximum. (The same applies if sentencing concurrently for offences, i.e. the maximum term for the longest period must not exceed 90 days.) For consecutive sentences see below.	The period required to ensure that the minimum sentence of 28 weeks is served, up to a maximum of 51 weeks. E.g.: if the court imposed a 28 day custodial period (4 weeks) a licence period of at least 24 weeks would be required to ensure a minimum overall sentence of 28 weeks was imposed.	Minimum combined sentence of 28 weeks, maximum of 51 weeks for any one offence, or the longest of any of the offences sentenced concurrently.

Consecutive sentences

These are set out below.

Custodial period	Licence period	Notes
Minimum 14 days for each offence. Maximum consecutive sentence of 180 days.	The period required to ensure that the minimum sentence of 28 weeks is served, up to a maximum of 65 weeks. E.g.: an offender is sentenced to 70 days' custodial period (10 weeks), the licence period would have to be a minimum of 18 weeks.	A court in specifying licence periods may specify: (a) periods of a prescribed duration; (b) periods beginning or ending at prescribed times; or (c) periods including, or not including, specified parts of the week.

Licence conditions

An intermittent custody order can contain the following additional requirements:

- unpaid work;
- activity;
- programme; and
- prohibited activity.

10.6.3 Revocation or amendment of custody plus and intermittent custody orders

Revocation

Schedule 10 provides for the revocation and amendment of the licence conditions attached to these orders, including alterations to the pattern of temporary release in relation to intermittent custody orders.

10.6.4 Suspended sentences

Short-term sentences of between 28 and 51 (65 in relation to consecutively sentenced offences) weeks, which would otherwise be custody plus or intermittent custody sentences, can be suspended (s.189).

The court must specify a supervision period and a operational period (of not less than six months and not exceeding two years). During the supervision period the offender can be made subject to one or more additional requirements. The supervision period must not exceed the operational period of the order, which is the period during which the offender can be re-sentenced for the offence should he commit a further offence in that period. The additional requirements that can be imposed are (s.190):

- unpaid work;
- activity;
- programme;
- prohibited activity;
- curfew (including electronic monitoring, provided not excluded under s.215);
- exclusion (including electronic monitoring, provided not excluded under s.215);
- residence;
- mental health;
- drug rehabilitation;
- alcohol;
- supervision;
- attendance centre (for offenders aged under 25 years).

Effect of suspension

The sentence of imprisonment will not take effect unless either during the supervision period the offender fails to comply with a requirement imposed in the order, or, the offender commits an offence (whether or not punishable with imprisonment) during the operational period of the order.

Review of order

The order can be reviewed at periodic intervals, and the court can order that it be given a report on the offender's progress in complying with the community requirements of the order. Drug rehabilitation requirements are reviewed as part of the provisions under section 210.

The powers of the court on review are specified in section 191.

Breach, revocation or amendment of a suspended sentence order

Schedule 12 details the powers of the court in relation to breach, revocation and amendment.

10.7   ALTERATION OF PENALTIES FOR SUMMARY OFFENCES

The Act changes the maximum sentence for many summary offences from four months or less to one of 51 weeks (Schedule 26). Other offences of five months or less not listed in Schedules 25 or 26 can, by order of the Secretary of State, be punished by up to 51 weeks' imprisonment, and all offences currently carrying six months' maximum imprisonment carry by virtue of section 281(4) and (5) a new maximum of 51 weeks. Like amendments are made to the magistrates' powers when sentencing on summary conviction for either-way offences. Some summary offences, previously punishable with imprisonment are now not so punishable (Schedule 25).

The Act provides for increased penalties for drug-related offences and for certain driving-related offences causing death. Increases in sentence take effect for offences committed after the commencement of the relevant provision.

10.7.1   Increase in maximum term that can be imposed on summary conviction of offence triable either way

A magistrates' court can impose a sentence not exceeding 12 months on any offence triable either way. This is achieved by an amendment to section 32 of the Magistrates' Courts Act 1980, made pursuant to section 282 of the Act. Offences not previously listed in Schedule 1 to the 1980 Act are also brought in line with this provision by virtue of section 282(3).

10.7.2   Powers to alter maximum penalties

Section 283 allows the Secretary of State to make amendments to sentencing powers in certain cases.

10.7.3   Term of detention and training order

A maximum of six months' detention and training can be imposed for a summary offence which in the case of an offender aged 18 or over would carry a maximum sentence of 51 weeks' imprisonment (s.298).

10.8   INCREASED SENTENCES FOR CERTAIN CRIMES

10.8.1   Drug-related offences

Schedule 28 introduces the following changes in relation to Class-C drugs, increasing, in each case, the maximum penalty to 14 years.

Table 10.1   Amendments to sentencing for offences under Misuse of Drugs Act 1971

Section	Offence	Penalty
4(2)	Production, or being concerned in the production, of a controlled drug	14 years
4(3)	Supplying or offering to supply a controlled drug or being concerned in the doing of either activity by another	14 years
5(3)	Having possession of a controlled drug with intent to supply it to another	14 years
8	Being the occupier, or concerned in the management, of premises and permitting or suffering certain activities to take place there	14 years
12(6)	Contravention of direction prohibiting practitioner, etc. from possessing, supplying, etc. controlled drugs	14 years
13(3)	Contravention of direction prohibiting practitioner, etc. from prescribing, supplying, etc. controlled drugs	14 years

Increases in sentence

Increases in sentence take effect for offences committed after the commencement of the relevant provision.

Offences under Customs and Excise Management Act 1971

Penalties listed under paragraph 2(c) of Schedule 1 to this Act are increased from five years to 14 years in relation to Class-C drugs.

Offence under section 19 of the Criminal Justice (International Co-operation) Act 1990

Offences under section 19(4)(c)(ii) in relation to Class-C drugs are now punishable with 14 years.

Increases in sentence

Increases in sentence take effect for offences committed after the commencement of the relevant provision.

10.8.2   Increase for certain driving-related offences causing death

Section 284 imposes the increased penalties as set out in Table 10.2.

Table 10.2   Increased penalties as imposed by section 284

Act	Offence	New penalty
s.12A Theft Act 1968	Aggravated vehicle taking where death is caused. Old penalty: 5 years.	14 years
s.1 Road Traffic Act 1988	Causing death by dangerous driving. Old penalty: 10 years.	14 years
s.3A Road Traffic Act 1988	Causing death by careless driving when under the influence of drink or drugs. Old penalty: 10 years.	14 years

Increases in sentence

Increases in sentence take effect for offences committed after the commencement of the relevant provision.

10.9   DANGEROUS OFFENDERS

10.9.1   Life sentence or imprisonment for public protection for serious offences

A person aged 18 or over, convicted of a serious offence committed after the commencement of this section is liable to be detained either for life (if the offence carries that sentence and the judge feels that a sentence of imprisonment for life is justified), or a period of indeterminate imprisonment for the purpose of public protection. Before invoking this power the court must be of the opinion that there is a significant risk to members of the public of serious harm occasioned by the commission, by him, of further specified offences.

Date of commission of offence

Section 232 states that where an offence is alleged to have been committed over a period of two or more days, it shall be taken to have been committed on the last of those days.

Specified offences

Specified offences are violent or sexual in nature and listed in Schedule 15. The list is extensive.

Serious offence

An offence is a serious offence if it is a specified offence and it would be punishable in the case of a person aged 18 or over, with imprisonment for life, or a determinate period of imprisonment exceeding 10 years. Consider the following examples:

Example 1

The offender is convicted of assault occasioning actual bodily harm and the judge considers that there is a significant risk to members of the public of serious harm occasioned by the commission by him of further specified offences (which need not be the same offence as he was convicted of).

A judge could not impose a life sentence as the maximum period of imprisonment for this offence is five years. Nor could the judge impose an indeterminate sentence for public protection, as the offence must carry 10 years or more for this provision to be invoked.

Example 2

If the offence were one of wounding contrary to section 18 Offences Against the Person Act 1861 (an offence carrying life), the judge would either be able to impose life imprisonment if that were justified, or imprisonment for an indeterminate period if there was a serious risk to the public.

Overview

An overview of adult offenders is illustrated in Figure 10.2.

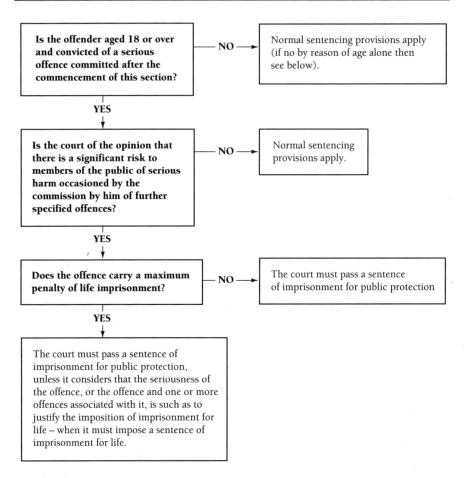

Figure 10.2

Offenders under 18 years

Section 226 mirrors the scheme above, save that before imposing a sentence for public protection the court must first consider whether an extended sentence would be adequate to protect the public. Only if such a sentence would be inadequate should a sentence under this section be imposed. If a court is of the view that a sentence of detention for life should be imposed, it must be imposed (s.226(2)).

Assessment of serious harm ('dangerousness')

See paragraph 10.9.3 below.

What is a sentence of imprisonment for public protection?

A sentence of imprisonment for public protection is a sentence of imprisonment for an indeterminate period. Release from such sentences is governed by the provisions of Chapter 2 of Part 2 of the Crime (Sentences) Act 1997 (which is amended by the Act), and Schedule 18 to the Act. A sentencing judge will, at the time of sentencing, determine the tariff period (to reflect punishment and deterrence, but not the factors in section 142 of the Act) to be served before release can be considered by the parole board.

10.9.2   Extended sentences for certain violent or sexual offences

Offences which are not classified as serious specified offences (because they do not carry a maximum sentence of 10 years or more) are dealt with under section 227.

An extended sentence can be imposed in relation to a person aged 18 years or over, convicted of a specified offence (other than a serious offence), committed after the commencement of this section, provided that the court considers that there is a significant risk to members of the public of serious harm occasioned by the commission by the offender of further specified offences.

Specified offence has the same meaning as outlined in paragraph 10.9.1 above.

Offenders aged less than 18 years

Mirror provisions apply by virtue of section 228, but there is one important difference. In the case of an adult, a serious specified offence must always be dealt with by virtue of section 225. For those under 18 years an extended sentence can be imposed for serious specified offences as an alternative to a detention for public protection, save where detention for life or for public protection is needed.

Effect of extended sentence

The court must pass on the offender an extended term of imprisonment comprising:

The appropriate custodial term for the offence in question (which must be at least 12 months minimum, and not exceed the maximum for the offence in question) and an *extension period* for which the offender is to be subject to a licence, to be of such length as the court considers necessary for the purpose of protecting members of the public from serious harm occasioned by the commission by him of further specified offences.

Maximum length of extension period

The extension period must not exceed five years in the case of a specified violent offence, and eight years in the case of a specified sexual offence.

The aggregate sentence must not exceed the maximum term permitted for the offence. For example, a custodial sentence of three years, followed by an extension period of four years would not be permissible for an offence of assault occasioning actual bodily harm, as the maximum sentence for that offence is five years. The maximum extension period in that instance would be two years.

10.9.3   Assessing dangerousness

A court must determine whether there is a significant risk to members of the public of serious harm occasioned by the commission by him of further such offences (s.229).

In the case of a person aged under 18 or an offender not previously convicted of any relevant offence (i.e. in England a specified offence) the court must take into account all such information as is available to it about the nature and circumstances of the offence, any pattern of behaviour of which the offence forms part and any information about the offender which is before it.

It is questionable as to whether patterns of behaviour are necessarily to be confined to matters recorded as convictions. It is further arguable that this provision violates articles 5 and 6 of the European Convention on Human Rights.

The two strikes presumption

In the case of an offender aged over 18 when the offence was committed, who had previously been convicted of one or more relevant offences (i.e. in England a specified offence) the court must assume that there is a 'significant risk to members of the public of serious harm occasioned by the commission by him of further such offences', unless having taken into consideration all such information as is available to the court about the nature and circumstances of the offence, pattern of behaviour and offender, that it would be unreasonable to conclude that there is such a risk (s.229(3)). It will be clear to practitioners that this provision allows for the repeal of section 109 of the PCC(S)A 2000 (s.303(d)(iv)).

It has been argued by Liberty that the test of 'unreasonable' is a straitjacketing provision which is 'an affront to the role of an independent and skilled judiciary . . . [This] could result in unfairness in individual cases'.

Offences committed prior to the commencement of the Act

While the second offence must have been committed after the commencement of this section, the first offence can pre-date the coming in to force of these provisions, as was the case under section 109 of the PCC(S)A 2000.

10.10   MINIMUM SENTENCES FOR FIREARMS OFFENCES

At section 287 the Act makes substantial changes to the mode of trial and sentencing of certain firearms offences, including minimum terms for some offences committed after the commencement of this section. The minimum sentence must be imposed unless the court is of the opinion that there are exceptional circumstances relating to the offence or to the offender which justify the court not imposing such a sentence. The Secretary of State can, by order, exclude the application of minimum sentences to those under 18 if he so wishes.

10.10.1 Overview of firearms offences

This is set out in Table 10.3.

Table 10.3   Overview of firearms offences

Section of Firearms Act 1968	Offence	Place of trial	Maximum sentence	Minimum sentence
5(1)(a), (ab), (aba), (ac), (ad), (ae), (af) or (c)	Possessing or distributing prohibited weapons or ammunition	On indictment	10 years or a fine or both	In the case of an offender who was aged 18 or over when he committed the offence 5 years In the case of an offender under 18 years at the time of committing the offence but aged at least 16 years, 3 years
5(1)(b)	Possessing or distributing prohibited weapon designed for discharge of a noxious liquid, etc.	(a) summary (b) on indictment	6 months or a fine of the statutory maximum or both 10 years or a fine or both	Not applicable
5(1A)(a)	Possessing or distributing firearm disguised as other object	On indictment	10 years or a fine or both	In the case of an offender who was aged 18 or over when he committed the offence 5 years In the case of an offender under 18 years at the time of committing the offence but aged at least 16 years, 3 years

Table 10.3 *continued*

Section of Firearms Act 1968	Offence	Place of trial	Maximum sentence	Minimum sentence
5(1A)(b), (c), (d), (e), (f) or (g)	Possessing or distributing other prohibited weapons	(a) summary	6 months or a fine of the statutory maximum or both	Not applicable
		(b) on indictment	10 years or a fine or both	

Offences under Customs and Excise Management Act 1979 (CEMA 1979)

Penalties for improper importation of certain firearms under section 50(5A) of the CEMA 1979 are increased from seven years to 10 years, likewise for exportation offences under section 68(4A) and section 170(4A). These penalties take effect for offences committed after the commencement of this section.

10.11   LIFE SENTENCES – MANDATORY MINIMUMS

Key changes:

- Guideline starting points in relation to mandatory life terms.
- Whole life tariff in multiple murders and some child-killing cases.
- Duty to consider sentencing guidelines when fixing tariff.
- Rules for prisoners already subject to tariff set by Secretary of State.

10.11.1   Guideline minimum-term life sentences

Chapter 7 of the Act provides for guideline minimum-term life sentences for offences where the sentence is fixed by law. These provisions came into force on 18 December 2003. Aggravating and mitigating features are indicated, and the court is duty bound to give consideration to Schedule 21 indications and any guidelines relating to offences in general that are not incompatible with Schedule 21 – this prevents the sentencing guidelines council from being able to dictate less serious penalties. It is important to note that the aggravating and mitigating factors may serve to reduce or increase the guideline tariff. The Secretary of State is given a wide ranging power to amend Schedule 21. Important transitional provisions apply which are detailed in paragraph 10.11.4 below.

10.11.2   Prescribed tariffs

The Act prescribes tariffs in terms (Schedule 21) as set out in Table 10.4.

Table 10.4   Prescribed tariffs of the Act

Definition	Examples	Tariff (starting point)
Offence or combination of the offence and one or more offences associated with it, is of an exceptionally high seriousness *and* the offender was aged 21 or over when he committed the offence	Cases that would normally fall within this category: (a) The murder of 2 or more persons, where each murder involves any of the following – (i) a substantial degree of premeditation or planning, (ii) the abduction of the victim, or (iii) sexual or sadistic conduct. (b) The murder of a child involving the abduction of the child or sexual or sadistic motivation. (c) A murder done for the purpose of advancing a political, religious or ideological cause. (d) A murder by an offender previously convicted of murder.	Whole life order (30 years if offender aged under 21)
Cases not falling in the category above, but, in the case of an offender aged 18 or over when he committed the offence, the court considers that the seriousness of the offence (or the combination of the offence and one or more offences associated with it) is particularly high.	(a) The murder of a police or prison officer in the course of his duty. (b) A murder involving the use of a firearm or explosive. (c) A murder done for gain (such as a murder done in the course or furtherance of robbery or burglary, done for payment or done in the expectation of gain as a result of the death). (d) A murder intended to obstruct or interfere with the course of justice. (e) A murder involving sexual or sadistic conduct. (f) The murder of 2 or more persons. (g) A murder that is racially or religiously aggravated or aggravated by sexual orientation. Or (h) A murder falling in the category above, but committed by an offender under 21 years.	30 years

continued

Table 10.4   *continued*

Definition	Examples	Tariff (starting point)
Cases not falling into any of the above categories		15 years for offenders aged 18 or over when offence committed. 12 years for offenders aged under 18 years when offence committed.

Aggravating and mitigating features

Having chosen a starting point, the court should take into account any aggravating or mitigating features, to the extent that it has not allowed for them in its choice of starting point. Detailed consideration of aggravating or mitigating features may result in a minimum term of any length (whatever the starting point), or in the making of a whole life order.

10.11.3   Aggravating/mitigating factors – relevancy

These are as illustrated by Table 10.5.

Table 10.5   Aggravating and mitigating factors and their relevancy

Aggravating factors that **may be relevant**	Mitigating factors that **may be relevant**
Significant degree of planning or premeditation	An intention to cause serious bodily harm rather than to kill
The fact that the victim was particularly vulnerable because of age or disability	Lack of premeditation
Mental or physical suffering inflicted on the victim before death	The fact that the offender suffered from any mental disorder or mental disability which (although not falling within
The abuse of a position of trust	section 2(1) of the Homicide Act 1957),
The use of duress or threats against another person to facilitate the commission of the offence	lowered his degree of culpability
	The fact that the offender was provoked (for example, by prolonged stress) in a way not amounting to a defence of
The fact that the victim was providing a public service or performing a public duty	provocation
	The fact that the offender acted to any
Concealment, destruction or dismemberment of the body	extent in self defence
	A belief by the offender that the murder was an act of mercy
	The age of the offender

Duty to give reasons

The court must state the starting point adopted and the reasons for so choosing, as well as the reasons for departing from any starting point (s.270).

Early release provisions

The court when sentencing an offender under these provisions must state that the early release provisions of section 28(5)–(8) of the Crime (Sentences) Act 1997 are to apply to the offender as soon as the tariff has been served, unless, in the case of an offender aged 21 or over when he committed the offence, the court is of the opinion that (which should be stated), because of the seriousness of the offence and one or more offences associated with it, no order in relation to the early release provisions should be made (s.269(2), (4)).

Appeals

An appeal lies in respect to the length of tariff.

An Attorney General's reference against the tariff period can be made to the Court of Appeal, and the Court, in considering that reference shall make no allowance for the fact that the offender is being sentenced for a second time (s.272).

Life prisoners transferred to England and Wales

The Act makes provision for the imposition of tariff sentences on prisoners transferred to England and Wales. The prisoner's case will be transferred to a single judge of the High Court for determination, with an appeal lying to the Court of Appeal.

10.11.4   Transitional cases

Transitional cases are dealt with under Schedule 22 of the Act, which provides for the following scheme in relation to persons serving a mandatory life sentence before the coming into force of sections 269–277. Juveniles, who already have their terms reviewed by the Lord Chief Justice, do not fall within this scheme. Different schemes apply depending on whether a tariff has already been set by the Home Secretary, or the prisoner is still awaiting a tariff to be set following the Secretary of State's decision to suspend tariff setting following *R v. Anderson* [2002] UKHL 46.

Prisoners subject to existing tariff

Such prisoners have the right to have their tariff reviewed by the High Court, which has the power to affirm or reduce the tariff period, or in the case of a whole-life prisoner order that the early release provisions shall not apply. The court cannot increase the tariff. If a prisoner chooses not to have his tariff reviewed the early release provisions shall apply to the prisoner as soon as he has served the minimum term. If the minimum term has already been served when this provision comes into force, the early release provisions will apply from that date.

The High Court must have regard to the seriousness of the offence (or combination of offences associated with it), having regard to the principles set out in Schedule 21 and any recommendation made to the Secretary of State by the trial judge or the Lord Chief Justice as to the minimum term to be served by the offender before his release on licence. See **www.cja2003.com** for the latest information on this section.

Prisoners awaiting notification

The Secretary of State must refer the cases of all such prisoners to the High Court for their tariffs to be determined. The factors in Schedule 21 must be taken into account, but the court must not set a tariff higher than that which would have been set by the Secretary of State before December 2002. The High Court must not set a whole-life tariff unless it is of the opinion that under the practice followed by the Secretary of State before December 2002, the Secretary of State would have been likely to have set the same.

The above is designed to protect against retrospectivity arguments under article 7 of the ECHR. Quite how this sentencing exercise is going to be achieved is difficult to predict but one can expect practitioners to enter into prolonged analysis of previous decisions of the Home Secretary to try to discern sentencing patterns and trends.

Prisoners sentenced after commencement in respect to murders committed before commencement

In these cases the court must place itself in the position pre-December 2002 and not set a sentence greater than that which would have been imposed by the Secretary of State. The court may not disapply the early release provisions by invoking section 269(4) unless satisfied that the Secretary of State would have been likely to give the prisoner such a notification.

The full provisions are to be found in Schedule 22 paras 9 and 10. Home Office circular 62/2003 deals with these provisions, but was not widely available at the time of writing. A copy of the circular can be found online (**www.cja2003.com**).

Appeals

Both prisoners and the Attorney General can appeal against the tariffs that are set under this Schedule.

10.12   RELEASE ON LICENCE OF FIXED-TERM PRISONERS

Fixed-term prisoners are those serving either a determinate term of imprisonment, or a determinate period of detention under section 91 of the PCC(S)A 2000, or section 228 of the Act.

Key changes:

- Release for sentences of less than 12 months incorporated within those new sentences (see above).
- All prisoners sentenced to 12 months or more eligible for release after half sentence served.
- Home detention curfew scheme can be extended to last 135 days of sentence (by order of Secretary of State).
- Stringent licence conditions, including drugs testing for those over 14 years of age.
- Recall to serve all of remaining sentence if in breach of licence.

10.12.1   Release on licence

Power of judge to recommend licence conditions

A court, when sentencing an offender to a term of imprisonment of 12 months or more may recommend to the Secretary of State that conditions be attached to the offender's licence on his release (s.238(1)). Conditions cannot be attached, under this section, to sentences of detention under section 91 of the PCC(S)A 2000 or section 228 of the Act.

Licence provisions for those serving sentences of 12 months or more

The Act, in sections 244–256 details the wider provisions in relation to the release of prisoners on licence, including release on compassionate grounds (s.248). In relation to sentence of 12 months or more there is a duty to release on licence after half of that sentence has been served. Additional days may have to be served for disciplinary offences (s.257). Release on licence under the general provisions does not apply to those cases set out in section 246(4).

Licence provisions for those serving sentences of less than 12 months

For sentences of less than 12 months the regime described above for custody plus and intermittent custody sentences outlines the requisite custody and licence periods. The licence conditions must satisfy the minimum requirements of section 251(2) of the Act.

Prisoners serving an extended sentence under section 227 or 228 of the Act

Prisoners subject to sentences under section 227 or 228 of the Act will not be eligible for release until the parole board has so directed (s.247(2)). Release may not be ordered unless the parole board is satisfied that it is no longer necessary for the protection of the public that the prisoner should be confined (s.247(3)).

Early release

Early release on compassionate grounds is provided for under section 248. The Secretary of State can also release prisoners during the last 135 days of their sentence (the home detention curfew scheme, currently set at 90 days). A prisoner must have received a custodial sentence of at least six weeks and have served at least four weeks of that sentence before release. Different provisions apply in relation to prisoners serving sentences of intermittent custody. A curfew condition under section 253 can be imposed as part of the early release terms. The curfew must take effect for no less than nine hours daily.

These provisions do not apply to those prisoners serving extended sentences under sections 227 and 228 of the Act, or to a whole range of other situations defined in section 246(4).

Prisoners subject to removal

Prisoners liable to removal from the United Kingdom can be removed early during the 135-day period under the rules prescribed in sections 259–260 of the Act.

Drug testing

Section 266 allows for drug testing of persons aged 14 years or over during a licence period.

Recall

The Secretary of State may recall a prisoner released on licence and revoke that licence. A prisoner returned under this section has the right to apply to the parole board for his release (s.254). If release is not ordered the prisoner will serve the remaining term of his sentence.

Prisoners released early on the home detention curfew scheme (s.246) can similarly be recalled (s.255).

10.13   DEFERRED SENTENCE

Schedule 23 of the Act lays down a framework for the deferment of sentences. A Crown Court or magistrates' court can defer sentence on any offender who consents and undertakes to comply with any conditions of deferment, provided that the court is satisfied, having regard to the nature of the offence and the character and circumstances of the offender, that it would be in the interests of justice to do so.

10.13.1   Purpose of deferment

Deferment is for the purposes of assessing an offender's conduct post conviction, including the making (if appropriate) by him of reparation for his offence, and any change in his circumstances. The court will further be able to assess adherence to any requirements imposed.

10.13.2   Conditions

A wide range of conditions can be imposed, as at present. Paragraph 1A of the Schedule allows for the imposition of a condition of residence during the deferment period, and appoint the probation service to supervise the offender.

10.13.3   Period of deferment

Deferment cannot exceed six months, nor can a sentence be further deferred.

10.13.4   Breach

Paragraphs 1B and 1C deal with breach and convictions during the period of deferment. A magistrates' court, in dealing with an offender for a new offence during a period of deferment may not deal with the deferred sentence if it was passed by a Crown Court. A Crown Court may deal with a sentence deferred by a magistrates' court but may not pass a greater penalty than that which could have been imposed in the lower court.

10.14   DISQUALIFICATION FROM WORKING WITH CHILDREN

Schedule 30 to the Act makes three key amendments to the Criminal Justice and Court Services Act 2000 (hereinafter the 2000 Act) in relation to disqualification orders.

10.14.1   Disqualification orders for offences against children

A new section 29A in the 2000 Act provides for disqualification orders to be made against juveniles and adults sentenced by a Crown Court or Court of Appeal in respect to offences against a child.

If the court is satisfied that the offender is likely to commit a further offence against a child, it must make a disqualification order, and state its reasons for so doing.

10.14.2   Prosecution applications for disqualification orders

A new section 29B of the 2000 Act allows the prosecutor to invite a court to reconsider making a disqualification order *at any time*, if a court at the time of sentencing either did not make an order that it was required to make by law (under s.28(4)), or did not make the declaration required under section 28(6) of the 2000 Act.

10.14.3   Qualifying sentences

Paragraph 3 of Schedule 30 to the Act amends the list of qualifying offences in the 2000 Act. Reference is made to offences under section 198 or 200 of the Criminal Justice Act 2000. It is assumed that these references are in fact incorrect and should relate to sections 226 and 228 of the Act (sections that corresponded to the Bill as printed after amendment on report, on 11 November 2003).

11 RETRIAL FOR SERIOUS OFFENCES

> **Key changes:**
>
> - Retrial of acquitted defendants where new and compelling evidence comes to light after acquittal.

11.1 INTRODUCTION

Part 10 of the Criminal Justice Act 2003 (the Act) allows for an exception to the double-jeopardy rule, and the retrial of acquitted defendants in relation to some serious offences. Important procedural steps have been put in place in relation to the police investigation of persons who are to be the subject of retrial applications. It is anticipated that very few retrials will take place.

11.1.1 Offences that can be retried

Qualifying offences are listed in Part 1 of Schedule 5, and include offences ranging from murder to arson endangering life. The defendant must previously have been acquitted of the offence, either on indictment or as a result of an appeal (s.75(1)). He is deemed to have also been acquitted of any other qualifying offences that he could have been convicted of in the proceedings (as an alternative for example). There can be no retrial of any offence for which the defendant has previously been convicted, and such offences could not be offered as an alternative in any new proceedings. There are also exceptions for offences of which the defendant has been found not guilty by reason of insanity (s.75(2)(b)) or in respect of which he has been found under a disability (s.75(2)(c)).

The Act makes provision for the retrial of offences committed outside of the United Kingdom under section 75(4).

How many times can a person be retried?

A person acquitted after retrial under these provisions cannot be retried again.

Is the Act retrospective?

The Act is retrospective (s.75(6)).

Is the Act Human Rights Act compliant?

The Government believe the provisions in this Act to be compliant with the ECHR, and a declaration to this effect appeared in the original Bill. Lawyers will no doubt seek to challenge these provisions under article 4(1) of the seventh protocol to the convention (not yet ratified by the UK) and article 7 of the convention. A detailed analysis of whether such a challenge is likely to succeed is outside the scope of this book, and readers are referred to the Law Commission paper on the topic as a first port of call (see **www.lawcom.gov.uk/files/cp156.pdf**).

11.1.2   Investigation stages

Save in cases of urgency (s.86) an officer may not arrest, question, undertake certain searches, seize certain items or fingerprint a suspect who is subject to a retrial investigation (even with the suspect's consent) unless the DPP has given his consent for an investigation or certified that the acquittal would not be a bar to retrial. The criteria for consent are to be found in section 85(6).

There is no requirement that the police obtain the DPP's consent in order to undertake investigative steps not listed in section 85(3), such as re-interviewing witnesses.

Sections 87–91 deal with arrest, detention and bail.

11.1.3   Procedure for retrial

Detailed procedures relating to these applications are to be found in section 80 of the Act, and provide for notice, time limits, presence of defendant at any hearing and representation.

How many attempts can be made to retry a defendant?

Only one attempt can be made to retry an acquittal (s.76(5)).

Stage 1 – consent of DPP

The DPP may only consent (s.76(4)) if satisfied that there is evidence in respect of the requirement in section 78 (new and compelling evidence – for which see paragraph 11.1.4 below), it is in the public interests to proceed and any trial would not be inconsistent with the obligations of the UK under article 31 or 34 of the Treaty on European Union to the principle of *ne bis in idem*.

Essentially European treaty may allow a case to be appealed by the prosecution or have it reopened at some later stage. What European treaty law prohibits is the bringing of new proceedings, as distinct to reopening the old – the principle of *ne bis in idem*. The reader is referred to the Law Commission report for a full and detailed discussion of this area of law (**www.lawcom.gov.uk/files/cp156.pdf**).

Stage 2 – Permission of the Court of Appeal

Includes the following steps:

- prosecutor must give notice to the Court of Appeal that he wishes to retry a suspect;
- that notice must be served on the person concerned within two days;
- the application is considered at an oral hearing;
- the person concerned is entitled to be present, even if he is in custody (provided he is in custody in England and Wales);
- he is entitled to be represented at the hearing.

New and compelling evidence

The Court of Appeal must be satisfied that there is new and compelling evidence against the person in respect to the qualifying offence and that it is in the interests of justice for a retrial to be held.

In respect to offences committed outside of the United Kingdom, the court must first consider whether there is a bar to retrial in law, if not it must declare so. If the acquittal in the foreign state is deemed to be a bar to retrial, then it must go on to consider whether to lift that bar. The bar on retrial can only be lifted if the two tests outlined above are met.

11.1.4   What is new and compelling evidence?

New evidence

New evidence is evidence that was not adduced in the original proceedings (including any appeal stage) (s.78). Evidence purposely withheld, with the intention of keeping something back for a later attempt at retrial should the defendant be acquitted, would fall within this definition, and it is for this reason that Lord Goldsmith made the following statement in the House of Lords (*Hansard*, 4 November 2003, Col. 710):

> I can give the House an undertaking, which I have agreed with the Director of Public Prosecutions, that where evidence was not adduced for tactical reasons, it would not be right to use it as a basis for an application under Part 9. I hope that that will give some comfort. It will be reflected in guidance.

> (NB: the provisions fell under Part 9 of the Bill, but are now Part 10 of the Act)

New evidence can relate to a new discovery in relation to a piece of 'old' evidence, this was illustrated by the Government in the following way:

> There will be examples of evidence which had been discovered but the relevance of which only recently came to light – for example, new testing techniques, such as DNA. The provision must allow for DNA testing to constitute 'new' evidence, even when the police may have had the sample for many years.

Compelling evidence

Evidence is compelling if it is reliable, substantial and in the context of the outstanding issues it appears highly probative of the case against the acquitted person (s.78(3)). The outstanding issues are the issues in dispute in the proceedings (including any appeal proceedings) in which the person was acquitted, such as presence at scene, penetration of complainant, etc. The admissibility of the evidence in earlier proceedings is of no relevance to this determination.

11.1.5   Interests of justice

In deciding whether a retrial is in the interests of justice the Court must have regard in particular to the factors outlined in section 79(2):

(a) whether existing circumstances make a fair trial unlikely;
(b) for the purposes of that question and otherwise, the length of time since the qualifying offence was allegedly committed;
(c) whether it is likely that the new evidence would have been adduced in the earlier proceedings against the acquitted person but for a failure by an officer or by a prosecutor to act with due diligence or expedition;
(d) whether, since those proceedings or, if later, since the commencement of this Part, any officer or prosecutor has failed to act with due diligence or expedition.

It will be a matter for the Court of Appeal to decide whether people of good character, having led a law abiding life for 30 years since their original acquittal should be retried for old offences. It may always be in the interests of justice to retry a person for murder, but rarely so in relation to drugs offences after such time. The parliamentary debates during the passage of the Act are littered with dozens of examples of cases that may fall either side of the line, but no discernable principle could be derived from those discussions, leaving it for the Court of Appeal, over time, to form guiding principles.

11.1.6   Right of appeal and reporting restrictions

Section 81 inserts a right of appeal to the House of Lords against a Court of Appeal decision in relation to a retrial. Both prosecution and acquitted person can appeal.

Section 82 of the Act provide for reporting restrictions in respect of retrial if in the opinion of the Court of Appeal publication would give rise to a substantial risk of prejudice to the administration of justice.

11.1.7   Retrial

A person should be arraigned on an indictment in relation to retrial within two months, and may not be arraigned thereafter without leave of the Court of Appeal (s.84(3)).

11.1.8   Further reading

Includes the following:

- *Double Jeopardy*, Law Commission Consultation Paper Nos. 156 and 267;
- The Third Report of the Home Affairs Select Committee (1999–2000), *The Double Jeopardy Rule*, HC 190.

12 MISCELLANEOUS PROVISIONS

Key changes:

- Extension of guilty plea by post procedure.
- Ability to utilise video links outside of court building and petty session area.
- Amendment to powers of Criminal Cases Review Commission.
- Jury service provisions to widen pool of available jurors.
- Individual support orders for youths subject to anti-social behaviour orders.

12.1 INTRODUCTION

In addition to the fundamental overhauls of individual components of the criminal justice system, detailed in earlier chapters, the Criminal Justice Act 2003 (the Act) makes sometimes substantial modification to other important areas of practice.

12.1.1 Non-appearance of accused: plea of guilty by post

Section 308 of the Act removes section 12(1)(a)(i) of the Magistrates' Courts Act 1980. The effect of this is to allow for pleas of guilty by post to be entered in respect of offences that are punishable with imprisonment for periods exceeding three months. The remaining criteria must still be satisfied, namely that the offence is not specified by the Secretary of State as being exempt from the procedure and that the clerk of the court is notified by or on behalf of the prosecutor that the relevant documents have been served on the defendant.

12.1.2 Video links

Section 51 of the Act empowers the court, in most criminal proceedings (including summary trial), to receive the evidence of a witness, other than the defendant, by way of live link. The definition of live link is to be found in section 56(2); it is clear when one considers this definition that this power should not be confused with live links being made available as a special measures provision under the Youth Justice and Criminal Evidence Act 1999.

Applications

Application can be made by any party to the proceedings, or on the court's own motion and may not be granted unless the court is satisfied that it is in the interests of the efficient or effective administration of justice for the evidence to be given through a live link. The effect of the order is that the witness must then only give evidence via the live link unless the order is rescinded.

Factors considered

Section 51(7) sets out some of the factors to be considered when determining the application, but the list is not exhaustive and the court must consider all the circumstances of the case. An order under section 51 can be rescinded later if it appears to be in the interests of justice to do so.

Jury warnings

Section 54 empowers a judge to give a warning to the jury in relation to the weight to be attached to evidence delivered via live link. The Act stipulates that the jury (if so directed) should give the same weight to the evidence as if it had been given by the witness in the courtroom (or other place where the proceedings are held).

Section 55 allows for rule-making powers in respect to applications under sections 51 and 52.

12.1.3   Location of magistrates' court sittings

At any location

Section 53 of the Act allows for the sitting of the magistrates' court at any location so as to give effect to a direction under the sections above. This is to allow for courts to take advantage of live link facilities in other locations when they are not available in the courtroom itself, including locations outside of the court's petty sessional division.

12.1.4   Endangered species

Section 307 gives effect to community legislation protecting species of wild fauna and flora. Breaches of community legislation are punishable with up to five years' imprisonment on indictment. Further information on the European directive can be found online (**http://europa.eu.int/comm/environment/cites/legislation_en.htm**).

Commencement

Section 307(1) to (3), (5) and (6) came into force on Royal Assent (20 November 2003).

12.1.5   Criminal Cases Review Commission

The Act makes two key changes in respect to the remit of the Criminal Cases Review Commission (CCRC), in response to recent case law and concerns voiced elsewhere.

Investigations during leave stage

The Act extends the Court of Appeals authority to order the CCRC to carry out investigation into cases which are at the application for leave stage. Section 313 effectively overturns the Court of Appeal decision in *R v. Shillibier*, *The Times*, 29 October 2003.

Such orders cannot be made by a single judge, notwithstanding the fact that a single judge can ultimately determine the application. The CCRC made representations that these orders should only be made by a full court in order to 'encourage sparing and consistent use'.

Grounds of appeal following a reference by the CCRC

Section 315 of the Act amends section 14 of the Criminal Appeal Act 1995 to provide that an appeal following a reference by the CCRC may not be on any ground which is not related to any reason given by the CCRC for making the reference save with leave of the court. This amendment overrules the finding on this point in *R v. Garner*, CA, unreported, 27 September 2002.

12.1.6   Power to substitute conviction of alternative offence on appeal

Section 316 amends section 3 of the Criminal Appeal Act 1968 so that where an appellant successfully appeals a conviction in respect to an offence to which he pleaded guilty, the Court of Appeal can substitute a conviction for any other offence for which he could have been found guilty at trial. The Court may sentence for the new offence, but cannot pass a sentence of greater severity than that already imposed. This amendment removes the lacuna identified in *R v. Horsman* [1997] 3 All ER 385. Identical provisions are made in respect to Courts-Martial Appeals (s.318).

12.1.7   Appeals against sentence

Section 319 of the Act amends section 10(3) of the Criminal Appeals Act 1968 to allow an offender sentenced following a committal for sentence (or re-sentenced in the ways identified in section 10(2)(b) of the Criminal Appeals Act 1968), to appeal to the Court of Appeal. Prior to this section being implemented only sentences of 6 months' imprisonment or more could be appealed.

Section 319(3) adds a section 11(7) to the Criminal Appeals Act 1968 in order to clarify what sentences are to be treated as having been passed in the same proceedings. The definition covers sentences passed on the same day, and those on different days if the judge states that they are to be treated as substantially one sentence.

12.1.8   Preparatory hearings

The Act makes three key changes to the preparatory hearing regime. Hearings can now be held in relation to cases on the grounds of seriousness alone in non-fraud cases (s.309), and can additionally be ordered in relation to issues of severance or joinder of charges (s.310). Finally, reporting restrictions in relation to these hearing is extended from Great Britain only to include Northern Ireland (s.311). These changes are achieved by amendments to the CJA 1987 and the Criminal Procedure and Investigations Act 1996.

12.1.9   Costs on appeal

Section 312 amends the Prosecution of Offences Act 1985, sections 16(4A) and 18(2) to provide for the award of costs in relation to appeals under section 35(1) of the Criminal Procedure and Investigations Act 1996.

12.1.10   Outraging public decency

This offence is triable only on indictment as it is derived from common law. The offence is frequently charged against homosexual men engaging in sexual activity in public places, and rarely if ever merits being tried in the Crown Court. Section 320 of the Act provides for it to be triable either-way. The provision is not retrospective. This provision came into force 20 January 2004.

12.1.11   Jury service

Section 321 of and Schedule 33 to the Act substantially amends the Juries Act 1974, to widen the categories of person who are eligible for service, and allow for discretionary excusal in certain circumstances. In addition, changes are made to the categories of person ineligible for jury service, so as to bring the Juries Act 1974 in line with recent developments.

The Act opens up jury service for persons who would have otherwise remained ineligible, including police officers, lawyers and the judiciary.

There is a special dispensation for members of the armed forces, with excusal being granted where a commanding officer certifies that it would be prejudicial to the efficiency of the service if that person were to be required to be absent from duty.

All other requests for excusal will be dealt with in accordance with guidelines to be issued by the Lord Chancellor.

The Department for Constitutional Affairs has published a consultation paper in respect to jury summoning, which can be accessed online (**www.dca.gov.uk/ consult/juries/summoning.htm**).

Research on jury composition can be accessed online (**www.kingston.ac.uk/ ~ku00596/elsres01.pdf**) as can the comments of Auld LJ (**www.criminal-courts-review.org.uk/ccr-05.htm#p11**).

12.1.12   Civil proceedings brought by offenders for trespass to the person

Section 329 introduces a leave requirement in respect to civil proceedings arising from an offender's criminal activity. The Act introduces a test of gross disproportionality to such actions when considered in the context of acts of protection of property or person during criminal activity. This section was enacted in response to the civil action launched against the farmer Tony Martin in the high-profile shooting case.

12.1.13   Individual support orders

If a court makes an anti-social behaviour order against a child or young person it must also consider making an individual support order (s.322). A court must first be satisfied that the following individual support conditions are met, and if so *must* make the order:

- that such an order would be desirable in the interests of preventing any repetition of the kind of behaviour which led to the making of the anti-social behaviour order;
- that the defendant is not already subject to such an order; and
- arrangements are in place for such orders.

If the conditions are not met the reasons why must be stated in open court.

Nature of the order

The order will require the offender to comply, for a period not exceeding six months, with the requirements of the order. Requirements to be specified are those that the court considers will be desirable in preventing the kind of behaviour that led to the making of the anti-social behaviour order.

A newly inserted section 1AA of the Crime and Disorder Act 1998 specifies the type of conditions appropriate (s.1AA(6)).

The Act provides for amendment and revocation of such orders. An individual support order will cease to have effect at any time when the anti-social behaviour order ceases.

Breach

Breach, without reasonable excuse is punishable with a fine not exceeding £1,000 for a child over 14 years, and £250 for those below. A referral order may not be made.

12.1.14 Parenting and referral orders

The Act removes the prohibition on making parenting orders alongside referral orders (s.324 and Schedule 34). A court can make a parenting order at the same time as a referral order, or later if a parent is referred to the court following a failure to attend panel meetings.

Appendix
CRIMINAL JUSTICE ACT 2003 (c. 44)

CONTENTS

PART 1   AMENDMENTS OF POLICE AND CRIMINAL EVIDENCE ACT 1984

PART 2   BAIL

PART 3   CONDITIONAL CAUTIONS

PART 4   CHARGING ETC

PART 5   DISCLOSURE

PART 6   ALLOCATION AND SENDING OF OFFENCES

PART 7   TRIALS ON INDICTMENT WITHOUT A JURY

PART 8   LIVE LINKS

PART 9   PROSECUTION APPEALS

Introduction

General right of appeal in respect of rulings

Right of appeal in respect of evidentiary rulings

Miscellaneous and supplemental

PART 10   RETRIAL FOR SERIOUS OFFENCES

Cases that may be retried

Application for retrial

PART 11   EVIDENCE

CHAPTER 1   EVIDENCE OF BAD CHARACTER

General

CHAPTER 2   HEARSAY EVIDENCE

Hearsay: main provisions

Principal categories of admissibility

Supplementary

Miscellaneous

General

CHAPTER 3   MISCELLANEOUS AND SUPPLEMENTAL

PART 12   SENTENCING

CHAPTER 1   GENERAL PROVISIONS ABOUT SENTENCING

Matters to be taken into account in sentencing

General restrictions on community sentences

General restrictions on discretionary custodial sentences

General limit on magistrates' court's power to impose imprisonment

Procedural requirements for imposing community sentences and discretionary custodial sentences

Disclosure of pre-sentence reports etc

Pre-sentence drug testing

Fines

Savings for power to mitigate etc

Sentencing and allocation guidelines

Duty of court to explain sentence

Publication of information by Secretary of State

Interpretation of Chapter

CHAPTER 2   COMMUNITY ORDERS: OFFENDERS AGED 16 OR OVER

CHAPTER 3   PRISON SENTENCES OF LESS THAN 12 MONTHS

Prison sentences of less than twelve months

Intermittent custody

Further provision about custody plus orders and intermittent custody orders

Suspended sentences

Interpretation of Chapter

CHAPTER 4   FURTHER PROVISIONS ABOUT ORDERS UNDER CHAPTERS 2 AND 3

Introductory

Requirements available in case of all offenders

Requirements available only in case of offenders aged under 25

Electronic monitoring

Provisions applying to relevant orders generally

Powers of Secretary of State

CHAPTER 5   DANGEROUS OFFENDERS

CHAPTER 6   RELEASE ON LICENCE

Alteration of penalties for offences

Firearms offences

Offenders transferred to mental hospital

Term of detention and training order

Disqualification from working with children

Fine defaulters

CHAPTER 9   SUPPLEMENTARY

Assessing etc risks posed by sexual or violent offenders

Criminal record certificates

Civil proceedings brought by offenders

PART 14   GENERAL

CRIMINAL JUSTICE ACT 2003

2003 CHAPTER 44

An Act to make provision about criminal justice (including the powers and duties of the police) and about dealing with offenders; to amend the law relating to jury service; to amend Chapter 1 of Part 1 of the Crime and Disorder Act 1998 and Part 5 of the Police Act 1997; to make provision about civil proceedings brought by offenders; and for connected purposes.

[20th November 2003]

BE IT ENACTED by the Queen's most Excellent Majesty, by and with the advice and consent of the Lords Spiritual and Temporal, and Commons, in this present Parliament assembled, and by the authority of the same, as follows: –

PART 1   AMENDMENTS OF POLICE AND CRIMINAL EVIDENCE ACT 1984

1 Extension of powers to stop and search

(1) In this Part, 'the 1984 Act' means the Police and Criminal Evidence Act 1984 (c. 60).

(2) In section 1(8) of the 1984 Act (offences for purpose of definition of prohibited article), at the end of paragraph (d) there is inserted '; and

(e)   offences under section 1 of the Criminal Damage Act 1971 (destroying or damaging property).'

2 Warrants to enter and search

In section 16 of the 1984 Act (execution of warrants), after subsection (2) there is inserted –

'(2A)   A person so authorised has the same powers as the constable whom he accompanies in respect of –

(a)   the execution of the warrant, and
(b)   the seizure of anything to which the warrant relates.

(2B)   But he may exercise those powers only in the company, and under the supervision, of a constable.'

3 Arrestable offences

(1)   Schedule 1A to the 1984 Act (specific offences which are arrestable offences) is amended as follows.
(2)   After paragraph 2 there is inserted –

'Criminal Justice Act 1925

2ZA   An offence under section 36 of the Criminal Justice Act 1925 (untrue statement for procuring a passport).'

(3)   After paragraph 6 there is inserted –

'Misuse of Drugs Act 1971

6A   An offence under section 5(2) of the Misuse of Drugs Act 1971 (having possession of a controlled drug) in respect of cannabis or cannabis resin (within the meaning of that Act).'

(4)   After paragraph 17 there is inserted –

'17A   An offence under section 174 of the Road Traffic Act 1988 (false statements and withholding material information).'

4 Bail elsewhere than at police station

(1)   Section 30 of the 1984 Act (arrest elsewhere than at police station) is amended as follows.
(2)   For subsection (1) there is substituted –

'(1)   Subsection (1A) applies where a person is, at any place other than a police station –

(a)   arrested by a constable for an offence, or
(b)   taken into custody by a constable after being arrested for an offence by a person other than a constable.

(1A)   The person must be taken by a constable to a police station as soon as practicable after the arrest.
(1B)   Subsection (1A) has effect subject to section 30A (release on bail) and subsection (7) (release without bail).'

(3)   In subsection (2) for 'subsection (1)' there is substituted 'subsection (1A)'.
(4)   For subsection (7) there is substituted –

'(7)   A person arrested by a constable at any place other than a police station must be released without bail if the condition in subsection (7A) is satisfied.
(7A)   The condition is that, at any time before the person arrested reaches a police station, a constable is satisfied that there are no grounds for keeping him under arrest or releasing him on bail under section 30A.'

(5)   For subsections (10) and (11) there is substituted –

'(10)   Nothing in subsection (1A) or in section 30A prevents a constable delaying taking a person to a police station or releasing him on bail if the condition in subsection (10A) is satisfied.

(10A)   The condition is that the presence of the person at a place (other than a police station) is necessary in order to carry out such investigations as it is reasonable to carry out immediately.

(11)   Where there is any such delay the reasons for the delay must be recorded when the person first arrives at the police station or (as the case may be) is released on bail.'

(6)   In subsection (12) for 'subsection (1)' there is substituted 'subsection (1A) or section 30A'.

(7)   After section 30 there is inserted –

'30A Bail elsewhere than at police station

(1)   A constable may release on bail a person who is arrested or taken into custody in the circumstances mentioned in section 30(1).

(2)   A person may be released on bail under subsection (1) at any time before he arrives at a police station.

(3)   A person released on bail under subsection (1) must be required to attend a police station.

(4)   No other requirement may be imposed on the person as a condition of bail.

(5)   The police station which the person is required to attend may be any police station.

30B Bail under section 30A: notices

(1)   Where a constable grants bail to a person under section 30A, he must give that person a notice in writing before he is released.

(2)   The notice must state –

(a)   the offence for which he was arrested, and

(b)   the ground on which he was arrested.

(3)   The notice must inform him that he is required to attend a police station.

(4)   It may also specify the police station which he is required to attend and the time when he is required to attend.

(5)   If the notice does not include the information mentioned in subsection (4), the person must subsequently be given a further notice in writing which contains that information.

(6)   The person may be required to attend a different police station from that specified in the notice under subsection (1) or (5) or to attend at a different time.

(7)   He must be given notice in writing of any such change as is mentioned in subsection (6) but more than one such notice may be given to him.

30C Bail under section 30A: supplemental

(1)   A person who has been required to attend a police station is not required to do so if he is given notice in writing that his attendance is no longer required.

(2)   If a person is required to attend a police station which is not a designated police station he must be –

(a)   released, or

(b)   taken to a designated police station,

not more than six hours after his arrival.

(3)   Nothing in the Bail Act 1976 applies in relation to bail under section 30A.

(4)   Nothing in section 30A or 30B or in this section prevents the re-arrest without a warrant of a person released on bail under section 30A if new evidence justifying a further arrest has come to light since his release.

30D Failure to answer to bail under section 30A

(1) A constable may arrest without a warrant a person who –

(a) has been released on bail under section 30A subject to a requirement to attend a specified police station, but

(b) fails to attend the police station at the specified time.

(2) A person arrested under subsection (1) must be taken to a police station (which may be the specified police station or any other police station) as soon as practicable after the arrest.

(3) In subsection (1), "specified" means specified in a notice under subsection (1) or (5) of section 30B or, if notice of change has been given under subsection (7) of that section, in that notice.

(4) For the purposes of –

(a) section 30 (subject to the obligation in subsection (2)), and

(b) section 31,

an arrest under this section is to be treated as an arrest for an offence.'

5 Drug testing for under-eighteens

(1) The 1984 Act is amended as follows.

(2) In section 38 (duties of custody officer after charge) –

(a) in subsection (1) –

(i) for sub-paragraph (iiia) of paragraph (a) there is substituted –

'(iiia) except in a case where (by virtue of subsection (9) of section 63B below) that section does not apply, the custody officer has reasonable grounds for believing that the detention of the person is necessary to enable a sample to be taken from him under that section;',

(ii) in sub-paragraph (i) of paragraph (b), after 'satisfied' there is inserted '(but, in the case of paragraph (a)(iiia) above, only if the arrested juvenile has attained the minimum age)',

(b) in subsection (6A), after the definition of 'local authority accommodation' there is inserted –

'"minimum age" means the age specified in section 63B(3) below;'.

(3) In section 63B (testing for presence of Class A drugs) –

(a) in subsection (3), for '18' there is substituted '14',

(b) after subsection (5) there is inserted –

'(5A) In the case of a person who has not attained the age of 17 –

(a) the making of the request under subsection (4) above;

(b) the giving of the warning and (where applicable) the information under subsection (5) above; and

(c) the taking of the sample,

may not take place except in the presence of an appropriate adult.',

(c) after subsection (6) there is inserted –

'(6A) The Secretary of State may by order made by statutory instrument amend subsection (3) above by substituting for the age for the time being specified a different age specified in the order.

(6B) A statutory instrument containing an order under subsection (6A) above shall not be made unless a draft of the instrument has been laid before, and approved by a resolution of, each House of Parliament.',

(d) after subsection (8) there is inserted –

'(9) In relation to a person who has not attained the age of 18, this section applies only where –

(a)   the relevant chief officer has been notified by the Secretary of State that arrangements for the taking of samples under this section from persons who have not attained the age of 18 have been made for the police area as a whole, or for the particular police station, in which the person is in police detention; and

(b)   the notice has not been withdrawn.

(10) In this section –

"appropriate adult", in relation to a person who has not attained the age of 17, means –

(a)   his parent or guardian or, if he is in the care of a local authority or voluntary organisation, a person representing that authority or organisation; or

(b)   a social worker of a local authority social services department; or

(c)   if no person falling within paragraph (a) or (b) is available, any responsible person aged 18 or over who is not a police officer or a person employed by the police;

"relevant chief officer" means –

(a)   in relation to a police area, the chief officer of police of the police force for that police area; or

(b)   in relation to a police station, the chief officer of police of the police force for the police area in which the police station is situated.'

6 Use of telephones for review of police detention

For section 40A(1) and (2) of the 1984 Act (use of telephone for review under s.40) there is substituted –

'(1) A review under section 40(1)(b) may be carried out by means of a discussion, conducted by telephone, with one or more persons at the police station where the arrested person is held.

(2) But subsection (1) does not apply if –

(a)   the review is of a kind authorised by regulations under section 45A to be carried out using video-conferencing facilities; and

(b)   it is reasonably practicable to carry it out in accordance with those regulations.'

7 Limits on period of detention without charge

In section 42(1) of the 1984 Act (conditions to be satisfied before detention without charge may be extended from 24 to 36 hours), for paragraph (b) there is substituted –

'(b) an offence for which he is under arrest is an arrestable offence; and'.

8 Property of detained persons

(1)   In subsection (1) of section 54 of the 1984 Act (which requires the custody officer at a police station to ascertain and record everything which a detained person has with him), there is omitted 'and record or cause to be recorded'.

(2)   For subsection (2) of that section (record of arrested person to be made as part of custody record) there is substituted –

'(2)   The custody officer may record or cause to be recorded all or any of the things which he ascertains under subsection (1).

(2A) In the case of an arrested person, any such record may be made as part of his custody record.'

9 Taking fingerprints without consent

(1)   Section 61 of the 1984 Act (fingerprinting) is amended as follows.

(2)   For subsections (3) and (4) (taking of fingerprints without appropriate consent) there is substituted –

'(3) The fingerprints of a person detained at a police station may be taken without the appropriate consent if –

    (a)   he is detained in consequence of his arrest for a recordable offence; and

    (b)   he has not had his fingerprints taken in the course of the investigation of the offence by the police.

(4) The fingerprints of a person detained at a police station may be taken without the appropriate consent if –

    (a)   he has been charged with a recordable offence or informed that he will be reported for such an offence; and

    (b)   he has not had his fingerprints taken in the course of the investigation of the offence by the police.'

(3)   In subsection (3A) (disregard of incomplete or unsatisfactory fingerprints) for the words from the beginning to 'subsection (3) above' there is substituted 'Where a person mentioned in paragraph (a) of subsection (3) or (4) has already had his fingerprints taken in the course of the investigation of the offence by the police'.

(4)   In subsection (5) (authorisation to be given or confirmed in writing) for 'subsection (3)(a) or (4A)' there is substituted 'subsection (4A)'.

(5)   In subsection (7) (reasons for taking of fingerprints without consent) for 'subsection (3) or (6)' there is substituted 'subsection (3), (4) or (6)'.

10 Taking non-intimate samples without consent

(1)   Section 63 of the 1984 Act (other samples) is amended as follows.

(2)   After subsection (2) (consent to be given in writing) there is inserted –

'(2A) A non-intimate sample may be taken from a person without the appropriate consent if two conditions are satisfied.

(2B) The first is that the person is in police detention in consequence of his arrest for a recordable offence.

(2C) The second is that –

    (a)   he has not had a non-intimate sample of the same type and from the same part of the body taken in the course of the investigation of the offence by the police, or

    (b)   he has had such a sample taken but it proved insufficient.'

(3)   In subsection (3)(a) (taking of samples without appropriate consent) the words 'is in police detention or' are omitted.

(4)   In subsection (3A) (taking of samples without appropriate consent after charge) for '(whether or not he falls within subsection (3)(a) above)' there is substituted '(whether or not he is in police detention or held in custody by the police on the authority of a court)'.

(5)   In subsection (8A) (reasons for taking of samples without consent) for 'subsection (3A)' there is substituted 'subsection (2A), (3A)'.

11 Codes of practice

(1) In section 67 of the 1984 Act (supplementary provisions about codes), for subsections (1) to (7C) there is substituted –

'(1) In this section, "code" means a code of practice under section 60, 60A or 66.

(2) The Secretary of State may at any time revise the whole or any part of a code.

(3) A code may be made, or revised, so as to –

(a) apply only in relation to one or more specified areas,

(b) have effect only for a specified period,

(c) apply only in relation to specified offences or descriptions of offender.

(4) Before issuing a code, or any revision of a code, the Secretary of State must consult –

(a) persons whom he considers to represent the interests of police authorities,

(b) persons whom he considers to represent the interests of chief officers of police,

(c) the General Council of the Bar,

(d) the Law Society of England and Wales,

(e) the Institute of Legal Executives, and

(f) such other persons as he thinks fit.

(5) A code, or a revision of a code, does not come into operation until the Secretary of State by order so provides.

(6) The power conferred by subsection (5) is exercisable by statutory instrument.

(7) An order bringing a code into operation may not be made unless a draft of the order has been laid before Parliament and approved by a resolution of each House.

(7A) An order bringing a revision of a code into operation must be laid before Parliament if the order has been made without a draft having been so laid and approved by a resolution of each House.

(7B) When an order or draft of an order is laid, the code or revision of a code to which it relates must also be laid.

(7C) No order or draft of an order may be laid until the consultation required by subsection (4) has taken place.

(7D) An order bringing a code, or a revision of a code, into operation may include transitional or saving provisions.'

(2) Section 113 of the 1984 Act (application of Act to armed forces) is amended as follows.

(3) After subsection (3) there is inserted –

'(3A) In subsections (4) to (10), "code" means a code of practice under subsection (3).'

(4) For subsections (5) to (7) there is substituted –

'(5) The Secretary of State may at any time revise the whole or any part of a code.

(6) A code may be made, or revised, so as to –

(a) apply only in relation to one or more specified areas,

(b) have effect only for a specified period,

(c) apply only in relation to specified offences or descriptions of offender.

(7) The Secretary of State must lay a code, or any revision of a code, before Parliament.'

12 Amendments related to Part 1

Schedule 1 (which makes amendments related to the provisions of this Part) has effect.

PART 2   BAIL

13 Grant and conditions of bail

(1) In section 3(6) of the 1976 Act (which sets out cases where bail conditions may be imposed) –

   (a) the words 'to secure that' are omitted,
   (b) the words 'to secure that' are inserted at the beginning of each of paragraphs (a) to (e),
   (c) after paragraph (c) there is inserted –

      '(ca) for his own protection or, if he is a child or young person, for his own welfare or in his own interests,',

   (d) for 'or (c)' there is substituted ', (c) or (ca)'.

(2) In section 3A(5) of the 1976 Act (no conditions may be imposed under section 3(4), (5), (6) or (7) unless necessary for certain purposes) –

   (a) the words 'for the purpose of preventing that person from' are omitted,
   (b) the words 'for the purpose of preventing that person from' are inserted at the beginning of each of paragraphs (a) to (c),
   (c) after paragraph (c) there is inserted 'or
      (d) for that person's own protection or, if he is a child or young person, for his own welfare or in his own interests.'

(3) In paragraph 8(1) of Part 1 of Schedule 1 to the 1976 Act (no conditions may be imposed under section 3(4) to (7) unless necessary to do so for certain purposes) for the words from 'that it is necessary to do so' onwards there is substituted 'that it is necessary to do so –

   (a) for the purpose of preventing the occurrence of any of the events mentioned in paragraph 2(1) of this Part of this Schedule, or
   (b) for the defendant's own protection or, if he is a child or young person, for his own welfare or in his own interests.'

(4) For paragraph 5 of Part 2 of that Schedule (defendant need not be granted bail if having been released on bail he has been arrested in pursuance of section 7) there is substituted –

      '5   The defendant need not be granted bail if –

      (a) having been released on bail in or in connection with the proceedings for the offence, he has been arrested in pursuance of section 7 of this Act; and
      (b) the court is satisfied that there are substantial grounds for believing that the defendant, if released on bail (whether subject to conditions or not) would fail to surrender to custody, commit an offence on bail or interfere with witnesses or otherwise obstruct the course of justice (whether in relation to himself or any other person).'

14 Offences committed on bail

(1) For paragraph 2A of Part 1 of Schedule 1 to the 1976 Act (defendant need not be granted bail where he was on bail on date of offence) there is substituted –

      '2A (1) If the defendant falls within this paragraph he may not be granted bail unless the court is satisfied that there is no significant risk of his committing an offence while on bail (whether subject to conditions or not).
      (2) The defendant falls within this paragraph if –

      (a) he is aged 18 or over, and
      (b) it appears to the court that he was on bail in criminal proceedings on the date of the offence.'

(2)   After paragraph 9 of that Part there is inserted –

'9AA(1)   This paragraph applies if –

    (a)   the defendant is under the age of 18, and

    (b)   it appears to the court that he was on bail in criminal proceedings on the date of the offence.

(2)   In deciding for the purposes of paragraph 2(1) of this Part of this Schedule whether it is satisfied that there are substantial grounds for believing that the defendant, if released on bail (whether subject to conditions or not), would commit an offence while on bail, the court shall give particular weight to the fact that the defendant was on bail in criminal proceedings on the date of the offence.'

15 Absconding by persons released on bail

(1)   For paragraph 6 of Part 1 of Schedule 1 to the 1976 Act (defendant need not be granted bail if having been released on bail he has been arrested in pursuance of section 7) there is substituted –

'6   (1)   If the defendant falls within this paragraph, he may not be granted bail unless the court is satisfied that there is no significant risk that, if released on bail (whether subject to conditions or not), he would fail to surrender to custody.

(2)   Subject to sub-paragraph (3) below, the defendant falls within this paragraph if –

    (a)   he is aged 18 or over, and

    (b)   it appears to the court that, having been released on bail in or in connection with the proceedings for the offence, he failed to surrender to custody.

(3)   Where it appears to the court that the defendant had reasonable cause for his failure to surrender to custody, he does not fall within this paragraph unless it also appears to the court that he failed to surrender to custody at the appointed place as soon as reasonably practicable after the appointed time.

(4)   For the purposes of sub-paragraph (3) above, a failure to give to the defendant a copy of the record of the decision to grant him bail shall not constitute a reasonable cause for his failure to surrender to custody.'

(2)   After paragraph 9AA of that Part (inserted by section 14(2)) there is inserted –

'9AB(1)   Subject to sub-paragraph (2) below, this paragraph applies if –

    (a)   the defendant is under the age of 18, and

    (b)   it appears to the court that, having been released on bail in or in connection with the proceedings for the offence, he failed to surrender to custody.

(2)   Where it appears to the court that the defendant had reasonable cause for his failure to surrender to custody, this paragraph does not apply unless it also appears to the court that he failed to surrender to custody at the appointed place as soon as reasonably practicable after the appointed time.

(3)   In deciding for the purposes of paragraph 2(1) of this Part of this Schedule whether it is satisfied that there are substantial grounds for believing that the defendant, if released on bail (whether subject to conditions or not), would fail to surrender to custody, the court shall give particular weight to –

    (a)   where the defendant did not have reasonable cause for his failure to surrender to custody, the fact that he failed to surrender to custody, or

(b)   where he did have reasonable cause for his failure to surrender to custody, the fact that he failed to surrender to custody at the appointed place as soon as reasonably practicable after the appointed time.

(4)   For the purposes of this paragraph, a failure to give to the defendant a copy of the record of the decision to grant him bail shall not constitute a reasonable cause for his failure to surrender to custody.'

(3)   In section 6 of the 1976 Act (offence of absconding by person released on bail) after subsection (9) there is inserted –

'(10)   Section 127 of the Magistrates' Courts Act 1980 shall not apply in relation to an offence under subsection (1) or (2) above.

(11)   Where a person has been released on bail in criminal proceedings and that bail was granted by a constable, a magistrates' court shall not try that person for an offence under subsection (1) or (2) above in relation to that bail (the "relevant offence") unless either or both of subsections (12) and (13) below applies.

(12)   This subsection applies if an information is laid for the relevant offence within 6 months from the time of the commission of the relevant offence.

(13)   This subsection applies if an information is laid for the relevant offence no later than 3 months from the time of the occurrence of the first of the events mentioned in subsection (14) below to occur after the commission of the relevant offence.

(14)   Those events are –

(a)   the person surrenders to custody at the appointed place;

(b)   the person is arrested, or attends at a police station, in connection with the relevant offence or the offence for which he was granted bail;

(c)   the person appears or is brought before a court in connection with the relevant offence or the offence for which he was granted bail.'

16 Appeal to Crown Court

(1)   This section applies where a magistrates' court grants bail to a person ('the person concerned') on adjourning a case under –

(a)   section 10 of the Magistrates' Courts Act 1980 (c. 43) (adjournment of trial),

(b)   section 17C of that Act (intention as to plea: adjournment),

(c)   section 18 of that Act (initial procedure on information against adult for offence triable either way),

(d)   section 24C of that Act (intention as to plea by child or young person: adjournment),

(e)   section 52(5) of the Crime and Disorder Act 1998 (c. 37) (adjournment of proceedings under section 51 etc), or

(f)   section 11 of the Powers of Criminal Courts (Sentencing) Act 2000 (c. 6) (remand for medical examination).

(2)   Subject to the following provisions of this section, the person concerned may appeal to the Crown Court against any condition of bail falling within subsection (3).

(3)   A condition of bail falls within this subsection if it is a requirement –

(a)   that the person concerned resides away from a particular place or area,

(b)   that the person concerned resides at a particular place other than a bail hostel,

(c)   for the provision of a surety or sureties or the giving of a security,

(d)   that the person concerned remains indoors between certain hours,

(e)   imposed under section 3(6ZAA) of the 1976 Act (requirements with respect to electronic monitoring), or

(f)   that the person concerned makes no contact with another person.

(4)   An appeal under this section may not be brought unless subsection (5) or (6) applies.

(5) This subsection applies if an application to the magistrates' court under section 3(8)(a) of the 1976 Act (application by or on behalf of person granted bail) was made and determined before the appeal was brought.

(6) This subsection applies if an application to the magistrates' court –

    (a) under section 3(8)(b) of the 1976 Act (application by constable or prosecutor), or

    (b) under section 5B(1) of that Act (application by prosecutor),

was made and determined before the appeal was brought.

(7) On an appeal under this section the Crown Court may vary the conditions of bail.

(8) Where the Crown Court determines an appeal under this section, the person concerned may not bring any further appeal under this section in respect of the conditions of bail unless an application or a further application to the magistrates' court under section 3(8)(a) of the 1976 Act is made and determined after the appeal.

17 Appeals to High Court

(1) In section 22(1) of the Criminal Justice Act 1967 (c. 80) (extension of power of High Court to grant, or vary conditions of, bail) –

    (a) after 'Where' there is inserted '(a)', and

    (b) after 'proceedings,', in the second place where it occurs, there is inserted 'and

        (b) it does so where an application to the court to state a case for the opinion of the High Court is made,'.

(2) The inherent power of the High Court to entertain an application in relation to bail where a magistrates' court –

    (a) has granted or withheld bail, or

    (b) has varied the conditions of bail,

is abolished.

(3) The inherent power of the High Court to entertain an application in relation to bail where the Crown Court has determined –

    (a) an application under section 3(8) of the 1976 Act, or

    (b) an application under section 81(1)(a), (b), (c) or (g) of the Supreme Court Act 1981 (c. 54),

is abolished.

(4) The High Court is to have no power to entertain an application in relation to bail where the Crown Court has determined an appeal under section 16 of this Act.

(5) The High Court is to have no power to entertain an application in relation to bail where the Crown Court has granted or withheld bail under section 88 or 89 of this Act.

(6) Nothing in this section affects –

    (a) any other power of the High Court to grant or withhold bail or to vary the conditions of bail, or

    (b) any right of a person to apply for a writ of habeas corpus or any other prerogative remedy.

(7) Any reference in this section to an application in relation to bail is to be read as including –

    (a) an application for bail to be granted,

    (b) an application for bail to be withheld,

    (c) an application for the conditions of bail to be varied.

(8) Any reference in this section to the withholding of bail is to be read as including a reference to the revocation of bail.

18 Appeal by prosecution

(1) Section 1 of the Bail (Amendment) Act 1993 (c. 26) (prosecution right of appeal) is amended as follows.

(2) For subsection (1) (prosecution may appeal to Crown Court judge against bail in case of offence punishable by imprisonment for five years or more etc) there is substituted –

'(1) Where a magistrates' court grants bail to a person who is charged with, or convicted of, an offence punishable by imprisonment, the prosecution may appeal to a judge of the Crown Court against the granting of bail.'

(3) In subsection (10)(a) for 'punishable by a term of imprisonment' there is substituted 'punishable by imprisonment'.

19 Drug users: restriction on bail

(1) The 1976 Act is amended as follows.

(2) In section 3 (general provisions), after subsection (6B) there is inserted –

'(6C) Subsection (6D) below applies where –

    (a)   the court has been notified by the Secretary of State that arrangements for conducting a relevant assessment or, as the case may be, providing relevant follow-up have been made for the petty sessions area in which it appears to the court that the person referred to in subsection (6D) would reside if granted bail; and

    (b)   the notice has not been withdrawn.

(6D) In the case of a person ("P") –

    (a)   in relation to whom paragraphs (a) to (c) of paragraph 6B(1) of Part 1 of Schedule 1 to this Act apply;

    (b)   who, after analysis of the sample referred to in paragraph (b) of that paragraph, has been offered a relevant assessment or, if a relevant assessment has been carried out, has had relevant follow-up proposed to him; and

    (c)   who has agreed to undergo the relevant assessment or, as the case may be, to participate in the relevant follow-up,

the court, if it grants bail, shall impose as a condition of bail that P both undergo the relevant assessment and participate in any relevant follow-up proposed to him or, if a relevant assessment has been carried out, that P participate in the relevant follow-up.

(6E) In subsections (6C) and (6D) above –

    (a)   "relevant assessment" means an assessment conducted by a suitably qualified person of whether P is dependent upon or has a propensity to misuse any specified Class A drugs;

    (b)   "relevant follow-up" means, in a case where the person who conducted the relevant assessment believes P to have such a dependency or propensity, such further assessment, and such assistance or treatment (or both) in connection with the dependency or propensity, as the person who conducted the relevant assessment (or conducts any later assessment) considers to be appropriate in P's case,

and in paragraph (a) above "Class A drug" and "misuse" have the same meaning as in the Misuse of Drugs Act 1971, and "specified" (in relation to a Class A drug) has the same meaning as in Part 3 of the Criminal Justice and Court Services Act 2000.

(6F) In subsection (6E)(a) above, "suitably qualified person" means a person who has such qualifications or experience as are from time to time specified by the Secretary of State for the purposes of this subsection.'

(3) In section 3A(3) (conditions of bail in case of police bail), for ', (6A) and (6B)' there is substituted 'and (6A) to (6F)'.

(4) In Schedule 1 (which contains supplementary provisions about bail), in Part 1 (imprisonable offences) –

(a) after paragraph 6 there is inserted –

'Exception applicable to drug users in certain areas

6A   Subject to paragraph 6C below, a defendant who falls within paragraph 6B below may not be granted bail unless the court is satisfied that there is no significant risk of his committing an offence while on bail (whether subject to conditions or not).

6B (1) A defendant falls within this paragraph if –

    (a) he is aged 18 or over;

    (b) a sample taken –

        (i) under section 63B of the Police and Criminal Evidence Act 1984 (testing for presence of Class A drugs) in connection with the offence; or

        (ii) under section 161 of the Criminal Justice Act 2003 (drug testing after conviction of an offence but before sentence), has revealed the presence in his body of a specified Class A drug;

    (c) either the offence is one under section 5(2) or (3) of the Misuse of Drugs Act 1971 and relates to a specified Class A drug, or the court is satisfied that there are substantial grounds for believing –

        (i) that misuse by him of any specified Class A drug caused or contributed to the offence; or

        (ii) (even if it did not) that the offence was motivated wholly or partly by his intended misuse of such a drug; and

    (d) the condition set out in sub-paragraph (2) below is satisfied or (if the court is considering on a second or subsequent occasion whether or not to grant bail) has been, and continues to be, satisfied.

  (2) The condition referred to is that after the taking and analysis of the sample –

    (a) a relevant assessment has been offered to the defendant but he does not agree to undergo it; or

    (b) he has undergone a relevant assessment, and relevant follow-up has been proposed to him, but he does not agree to participate in it.

  (3) In this paragraph and paragraph 6C below –

    (a) "Class A drug" and "misuse" have the same meaning as in the Misuse of Drugs Act 1971;

    (b) "relevant assessment" and "relevant follow-up" have the meaning given by section 3(6E) of this Act;

    (c) "specified" (in relation to a Class A drug) has the same meaning as in Part 3 of the Criminal Justice and Court Services Act 2000.

6C   Paragraph 6A above does not apply unless –

    (a) the court has been notified by the Secretary of State that arrangements for conducting a relevant assessment or, as the case may be, providing relevant follow-up have been made for the petty sessions area in which it appears to the court that the defendant would reside if granted bail; and

    (b) the notice has not been withdrawn.',

(b) in paragraph 8(1), for '(4) to (7)' there is substituted '(4) to (6B) or (7)'.

20 Supplementary amendments to the Bail Act 1976

(1) In Part 1 of Schedule 1 to the 1976 Act (supplementary provisions relating to bail of defendant accused or convicted of imprisonable offence) the existing text of paragraph 2 is to be sub-paragraph (1) of that paragraph, and after that sub-paragraph (as so re-numbered) there is inserted –

'(2) Where the defendant falls within one or more of paragraphs 2A, 6 and 6B of this Part of this Schedule, this paragraph shall not apply unless –

> (a)   where the defendant falls within paragraph 2A, the court is satisfied as mentioned in sub-paragraph (1) of that paragraph;
>
> (b)   where the defendant falls within paragraph 6, the court is satisfied as mentioned in sub-paragraph (1) of that paragraph;
>
> (c)   where the defendant falls within paragraph 6B, the court is satisfied as mentioned in paragraph 6A of this Part of this Schedule or paragraph 6A does not apply by virtue of paragraph 6C of this Part of this Schedule.'

(2) In paragraph 9 of that Part (matters to be taken into account in making decisions under paragraph 2 or 2A of that Part) for '2 or 2A' there is substituted '2(1), or in deciding whether it is satisfied as mentioned in paragraph 2A(1), 6(1) or 6A,'.

21 Interpretation of Part 2

In this Part –

> 'bail' means bail in criminal proceedings (within the meaning of the 1976 Act),
> 'bail hostel' has the meaning given by section 2(2) of the 1976 Act,
> 'the 1976 Act' means the Bail Act 1976 (c. 63),
> 'vary' has the same meaning as in the 1976 Act.

PART 3   CONDITIONAL CAUTIONS

22 Conditional cautions

(1) An authorised person may give a conditional caution to a person aged 18 or over ('the offender') if each of the five requirements in section 23 is satisfied.

(2) In this Part 'conditional caution' means a caution which is given in respect of an offence committed by the offender and which has conditions attached to it with which the offender must comply.

(3) The conditions which may be attached to such a caution are those which have either or both of the following objects –

> (a)   facilitating the rehabilitation of the offender,
> (b)   ensuring that he makes reparation for the offence.

(4) In this Part 'authorised person' means –

> (a)   a constable,
> (b)   an investigating officer, or
> (c)   a person authorised by a relevant prosecutor for the purposes of this section.

23 The five requirements

(1) The first requirement is that the authorised person has evidence that the offender has committed an offence.

(2) The second requirement is that a relevant prosecutor decides –

> (a)   that there is sufficient evidence to charge the offender with the offence, and
> (b)   that a conditional caution should be given to the offender in respect of the offence.

(3) The third requirement is that the offender admits to the authorised person that he committed the offence.

(4) The fourth requirement is that the authorised person explains the effect of the conditional caution to the offender and warns him that failure to comply with any of the conditions attached to the caution may result in his being prosecuted for the offence.

(5) The fifth requirement is that the offender signs a document which contains –

(a) details of the offence,
(b) an admission by him that he committed the offence,
(c) his consent to being given the conditional caution, and
(d) the conditions attached to the caution.

24 Failure to comply with conditions

(1) If the offender fails, without reasonable excuse, to comply with any of the conditions attached to the conditional caution, criminal proceedings may be instituted against the person for the offence in question.

(2) The document mentioned in section 23(5) is to be admissible in such proceedings.

(3) Where such proceedings are instituted, the conditional caution is to cease to have effect.

25 Code of practice

(1) The Secretary of State must prepare a code of practice in relation to conditional cautions.

(2) The code may, in particular, include provision as to –

(a) the circumstances in which conditional cautions may be given,
(b) the procedure to be followed in connection with the giving of such cautions,
(c) the conditions which may be attached to such cautions and the time for which they may have effect,
(d) the category of constable or investigating officer by whom such cautions may be given,
(e) the persons who may be authorised by a relevant prosecutor for the purposes of section 22,
(f) the form which such cautions are to take and the manner in which they are to be given and recorded,
(g) the places where such cautions may be given, and
(h) the monitoring of compliance with conditions attached to such cautions.

(3) After preparing a draft of the code the Secretary of State –

(a) must publish the draft,
(b) must consider any representations made to him about the draft, and
(c) may amend the draft accordingly,

but he may not publish or amend the draft without the consent of the Attorney General.

(4) After the Secretary of State has proceeded under subsection (3) he must lay the code before each House of Parliament.

(5) When he has done so he may bring the code into force by order.

(6) The Secretary of State may from time to time revise a code of practice brought into force under this section.

(7) Subsections (3) to (6) are to apply (with appropriate modifications) to a revised code as they apply to an original code.

26 Assistance of National Probation Service

(1) Section 1 of the Criminal Justice and Court Services Act 2000 (c. 43) (purposes of Chapter 1) is amended as follows.

(2) After subsection (1) there is inserted –

'(1A) This Chapter also has effect for the purposes of providing for –

    (a)   authorised persons to be given assistance in determining whether con-
ditional cautions should be given and which conditions to attach to
conditional cautions; and

    (b)   the supervision and rehabilitation of persons to whom conditional cautions
are given.'

(3) After subsection (3) there is inserted –

'(4) In this section "authorised person" and "conditional caution" have the same
meaning as in Part 3 of the Criminal Justice Act 2003.'

27 Interpretation of Part 3

In this Part –

'authorised person' has the meaning given by section 22(4),
'conditional caution' has the meaning given by section 22(2),
'investigating officer' means a person designated as an investigating officer under
section 38 of the Police Reform Act 2002 (c. 30),
'the offender' has the meaning given by section 22(1),
'relevant prosecutor' means –

    (a)   the Attorney General,
    (b)   the Director of the Serious Fraud Office,
    (c)   the Director of Public Prosecutions,
    (d)   a Secretary of State,
    (e)   the Commissioners of Inland Revenue,
    (f)   the Commissioners of Customs and Excise, or
    (g)   a person who is specified in an order made by the Secretary of State as being
a relevant prosecutor for the purposes of this Part.

PART 4   CHARGING ETC

28 Charging or release of persons in police detention

Schedule 2 (which makes provision in relation to the charging or release of persons in
police detention) shall have effect.

29 New method of instituting proceedings

(1) A public prosecutor may institute criminal proceedings against a person by issuing a
document (a 'written charge') which charges the person with an offence.

(2) Where a public prosecutor issues a written charge, it must at the same time issue a
document (a 'requisition') which requires the person to appear before a magistrates'
court to answer the written charge.

(3) The written charge and requisition must be served on the person concerned, and a
copy of both must be served on the court named in the requisition.

(4) In consequence of subsections (1) to (3), a public prosecutor is not to have the power
to lay an information for the purpose of obtaining the issue of a summons under
section 1 of the Magistrates' Courts Act 1980 (c. 43).

(5) In this section 'public prosecutor' means –

    (a)   a police force or a person authorised by a police force to institute criminal
proceedings,
    (b)   the Director of the Serious Fraud Office or a person authorised by him to
institute criminal proceedings,
    (c)   the Director of Public Prosecutions or a person authorised by him to institute
criminal proceedings,

(d)   the Attorney General or a person authorised by him to institute criminal proceedings,

(e)   a Secretary of State or a person authorised by a Secretary of State to institute criminal proceedings,

(f)   the Commissioners of Inland Revenue or a person authorised by them to institute criminal proceedings,

(g)   the Commissioners of Customs and Excise or a person authorised by them to institute criminal proceedings, or

(h)   a person specified in an order made by the Secretary of State for the purposes of this section or a person authorised by such a person to institute criminal proceedings.

(6)   In subsection (5) 'police force' has the meaning given by section 3(3) of the Prosecution of Offences Act 1985 (c. 23).

30 Further provision about new method

(1)   Rules under section 144 of the Magistrates' Courts Act 1980 may make –

(a)   provision as to the form, content, recording, authentication and service of written charges or requisitions, and

(b)   such other provision in relation to written charges or requisitions as appears to the Lord Chancellor to be necessary or expedient.

(2)   Without limiting subsection (1), the provision which may be made by virtue of that subsection includes provision –

(a)   which applies (with or without modifications), or which disapplies, the provision of any enactment relating to the service of documents,

(b)   for or in connection with the issue of further requisitions.

(3)   Nothing in subsection (1) or (2) is to be taken as affecting the generality of section 144(1) of that Act.

(4)   Nothing in section 29 affects –

(a)   the power of a public prosecutor to lay an information for the purpose of obtaining the issue of a warrant under section 1 of the Magistrates' Courts Act 1980 (c. 43),

(b)   the power of a person who is not a public prosecutor to lay an information for the purpose of obtaining the issue of a summons or warrant under section 1 of that Act, or

(c)   any power to charge a person with an offence whilst he is in custody.

(5)   Except where the context otherwise requires, in any enactment contained in an Act passed before this Act –

(a)   any reference (however expressed) which is or includes a reference to an information within the meaning of section 1 of the Magistrates' Courts Act 1980 (c.43) (or to the laying of such an information) is to be read as including a reference to a written charge (or to the issue of a written charge),

(b)   any reference (however expressed) which is or includes a reference to a summons under section 1 of the Magistrates' Courts Act 1980 (or to a justice of the peace issuing such a summons) is to be read as including a reference to a requisition (or to a public prosecutor issuing a requisition).

(6)   Subsection (5) does not apply to section 1 of the Magistrates' Courts Act 1980.

(7)   The reference in subsection (5) to an enactment contained in an Act passed before this Act includes a reference to an enactment contained in that Act as a result of an amendment to that Act made by this Act or by any other Act passed in the same Session as this Act.

(8)   In this section 'public prosecutor', 'requisition' and 'written charge' have the same meaning as in section 29.

31 Removal of requirement to substantiate information on oath

(1) In section 1(3) of the Magistrates' Courts Act 1980 (warrant may not be issued unless information substantiated on oath) the words 'and substantiated on oath' are omitted.

(2) In section 13 of that Act (non-appearance of defendant: issue of warrant) in subsection (3)(a) the words 'the information has been substantiated on oath and' are omitted.

(3) For subsection (3A)(a) of that section there is substituted –

'(a) the offence to which the warrant relates is punishable, in the case of a person who has attained the age of 18, with imprisonment, or'.

PART 5   DISCLOSURE

32 Initial duty of disclosure by prosecutor

In the Criminal Procedure and Investigations Act 1996 (c. 25) (in this Part referred to as 'the 1996 Act'), in subsection (1)(a) of section 3 (primary disclosure by prosecutor) –

(a) for 'in the prosecutor's opinion might undermine' there is substituted 'might reasonably be considered capable of undermining';

(b) after 'against the accused' there is inserted 'or of assisting the case for the accused'.

33 Defence disclosure

(1) In section 5 of the 1996 Act (compulsory disclosure by accused), after subsection (5) there is inserted –

'(5A) Where there are other accused in the proceedings and the court so orders, the accused must also give a defence statement to each other accused specified by the court.

(5B) The court may make an order under subsection (5A) either of its own motion or on the application of any party.

(5C) A defence statement that has to be given to the court and the prosecutor (under subsection (5)) must be given during the period which, by virtue of section 12, is the relevant period for this section.

(5D) A defence statement that has to be given to a co-accused (under subsection (5A)) must be given within such period as the court may specify.'

(2) After section 6 of that Act there is inserted –

'6A Contents of defence statement

(1) For the purposes of this Part a defence statement is a written statement –

(a) setting out the nature of the accused's defence, including any particular defences on which he intends to rely,

(b) indicating the matters of fact on which he takes issue with the prosecution,

(c) setting out, in the case of each such matter, why he takes issue with the prosecution, and

(d) indicating any point of law (including any point as to the admissibility of evidence or an abuse of process) which he wishes to take, and any authority on which he intends to rely for that purpose.

(2) A defence statement that discloses an alibi must give particulars of it, including –

(a) the name, address and date of birth of any witness the accused believes is able to give evidence in support of the alibi, or as many of those details as are known to the accused when the statement is given;

(b) any information in the accused's possession which might be of material assistance in identifying or finding any such witness in whose case any of the details mentioned in paragraph (a) are not known to the accused when the statement is given.

(3) For the purposes of this section evidence in support of an alibi is evidence tending to show that by reason of the presence of the accused at a particular place or in a particular area at a particular time he was not, or was unlikely to have been, at the place where the offence is alleged to have been committed at the time of its alleged commission.

(4) The Secretary of State may by regulations make provision as to the details of the matters that, by virtue of subsection (1), are to be included in defence statements.'

(3) After section 6A of that Act (inserted by subsection (2) above) there is inserted –

'6B Updated disclosure by accused

(1) Where the accused has, before the beginning of the relevant period for this section, given a defence statement under section 5 or 6, he must during that period give to the court and the prosecutor either –

(a) a defence statement under this section (an "updated defence statement"), or

(b) a statement of the kind mentioned in subsection (4).

(2) The relevant period for this section is determined under section 12.

(3) An updated defence statement must comply with the requirements imposed by or under section 6A by reference to the state of affairs at the time when the statement is given.

(4) Instead of an updated defence statement, the accused may give a written statement stating that he has no changes to make to the defence statement which was given under section 5 or 6.

(5) Where there are other accused in the proceedings and the court so orders, the accused must also give either an updated defence statement or a statement of the kind mentioned in subsection (4), within such period as may be specified by the court, to each other accused so specified.

(6) The court may make an order under subsection (5) either of its own motion or on the application of any party.'

34 Notification of intention to call defence witnesses

After section 6B of the 1996 Act (inserted by section 33 above) there is inserted –

'6C Notification of intention to call defence witnesses

(1) The accused must give to the court and the prosecutor a notice indicating whether he intends to call any persons (other than himself) as witnesses at his trial and, if so –

(a) giving the name, address and date of birth of each such proposed witness, or as many of those details as are known to the accused when the notice is given;

(b) providing any information in the accused's possession which might be of material assistance in identifying or finding any such proposed witness in whose case any of the details mentioned in paragraph (a) are not known to the accused when the notice is given.

(2) Details do not have to be given under this section to the extent that they have already been given under section 6A(2).

(3) The accused must give a notice under this section during the period which, by virtue of section 12, is the relevant period for this section.

(4) If, following the giving of a notice under this section, the accused –

(a) decides to call a person (other than himself) who is not included in the notice as a proposed witness, or decides not to call a person who is so included, or

(b) discovers any information which, under subsection (1), he would have had to include in the notice if he had been aware of it when giving the notice,

he must give an appropriately amended notice to the court and the prosecutor.'

35 Notification of names of experts instructed by defendant

After section 6C of the 1996 Act (inserted by section 34 above) there is inserted –

'6D Notification of names of experts instructed by accused

(1) If the accused instructs a person with a view to his providing any expert opinion for possible use as evidence at the trial of the accused, he must give to the court and the prosecutor a notice specifying the person's name and address.

(2) A notice does not have to be given under this section specifying the name and address of a person whose name and address have already been given under section 6C.

(3) A notice under this section must be given during the period which, by virtue of section 12, is the relevant period for this section.'

36 Further provisions about defence disclosure

After section 6D of the 1996 Act (inserted by section 35 above) there is inserted –

'6E Disclosure by accused: further provisions

(1) Where an accused's solicitor purports to give on behalf of the accused –

(a) a defence statement under section 5, 6 or 6B, or

(b) a statement of the kind mentioned in section 6B(4),

the statement shall, unless the contrary is proved, be deemed to be given with the authority of the accused.

(2) If it appears to the judge at a pre-trial hearing that an accused has failed to comply fully with section 5, 6B or 6C, so that there is a possibility of comment being made or inferences drawn under section 11(5), he shall warn the accused accordingly.

(3) In subsection (2) "pre-trial hearing" has the same meaning as in Part 4 (see section 39).

(4) The judge in a trial before a judge and jury –

(a) may direct that the jury be given a copy of any defence statement, and

(b) if he does so, may direct that it be edited so as not to include references to matters evidence of which would be inadmissible.

(5) A direction under subsection (4) –

(a) may be made either of the judge's own motion or on the application of any party;

(b) may be made only if the judge is of the opinion that seeing a copy of the defence statement would help the jury to understand the case or to resolve any issue in the case.

(6) The reference in subsection (4) to a defence statement is a reference –

(a) where the accused has given only an initial defence statement (that is, a defence statement given under section 5 or 6), to that statement;

(b) where he has given both an initial defence statement and an updated defence statement (that is, a defence statement given under section 6B), to the updated defence statement;

(c)   where he has given both an initial defence statement and a statement of the kind mentioned in section 6B(4), to the initial defence statement.'

37 Continuing duty of disclosure by prosecutor

Before section 8 of the 1996 Act there is inserted –

'7A Continuing duty of prosecutor to disclose

(1)   This section applies at all times –

    (a)   after the prosecutor has complied with section 3 or purported to comply with it, and

    (b)   before the accused is acquitted or convicted or the prosecutor decides not to proceed with the case concerned.

(2)   The prosecutor must keep under review the question whether at any given time (and, in particular, following the giving of a defence statement) there is prosecution material which –

    (a)   might reasonably be considered capable of undermining the case for the prosecution against the accused or of assisting the case for the accused, and

    (b)   has not been disclosed to the accused.

(3)   If at any time there is any such material as is mentioned in subsection (2) the prosecutor must disclose it to the accused as soon as is reasonably practicable (or within the period mentioned in subsection (5)(a), where that applies).

(4)   In applying subsection (2) by reference to any given time the state of affairs at that time (including the case for the prosecution as it stands at that time) must be taken into account.

(5)   Where the accused gives a defence statement under section 5, 6 or 6B –

    (a)   if as a result of that statement the prosecutor is required by this section to make any disclosure, or further disclosure, he must do so during the period which, by virtue of section 12, is the relevant period for this section;

    (b)   if the prosecutor considers that he is not so required, he must during that period give to the accused a written statement to that effect.

(6)   For the purposes of this section prosecution material is material –

    (a)   which is in the prosecutor's possession and came into his possession in connection with the case for the prosecution against the accused, or

    (b)   which, in pursuance of a code operative under Part 2, he has inspected in connection with the case for the prosecution against the accused.

(7)   Subsections (3) to (5) of section 3 (method by which prosecutor discloses) apply for the purposes of this section as they apply for the purposes of that.

(8)   Material must not be disclosed under this section to the extent that the court, on an application by the prosecutor, concludes it is not in the public interest to disclose it and orders accordingly.

(9)   Material must not be disclosed under this section to the extent that it is material the disclosure of which is prohibited by section 17 of the Regulation of Investigatory Powers Act 2000 (c. 23).'

38 Application by defence for disclosure

In section 8 of the 1996 Act (application by accused for disclosure), for subsections (1) and (2) there is substituted –

'(1)   This section applies where the accused has given a defence statement under section 5, 6 or 6B and the prosecutor has complied with section 7A(5) or has purported to comply with it or has failed to comply with it.

(2)   If the accused has at any time reasonable cause to believe that there is prosecution material which is required by section 7A to be disclosed to him and has not

been, he may apply to the court for an order requiring the prosecutor to disclose it to him.'

39 Faults in defence disclosure

For section 11 of the 1996 Act there is substituted –

'11 Faults in disclosure by accused

(1)   This section applies in the three cases set out in subsections (2), (3) and (4).

(2)   The first case is where section 5 applies and the accused –

  (a)   fails to give an initial defence statement,

  (b)   gives an initial defence statement but does so after the end of the period which, by virtue of section 12, is the relevant period for section 5,

  (c)   is required by section 6B to give either an updated defence statement or a statement of the kind mentioned in subsection (4) of that section but fails to do so,

  (d)   gives an updated defence statement or a statement of the kind mentioned in section 6B(4) but does so after the end of the period which, by virtue of section 12, is the relevant period for section 6B,

  (e)   sets out inconsistent defences in his defence statement, or

  (f)   at his trial –

    (i)   puts forward a defence which was not mentioned in his defence statement or is different from any defence set out in that statement,

    (ii)   relies on a matter which, in breach of the requirements imposed by or under section 6A, was not mentioned in his defence statement,

    (iii)   adduces evidence in support of an alibi without having given particulars of the alibi in his defence statement, or

    (iv)   calls a witness to give evidence in support of an alibi without having complied with section 6A(2)(a) or (b) as regards the witness in his defence statement.

(3)   The second case is where section 6 applies, the accused gives an initial defence statement, and the accused –

  (a)   gives the initial defence statement after the end of the period which, by virtue of section 12, is the relevant period for section 6, or

  (b)   does any of the things mentioned in paragraphs (c) to (f) of subsection (2).

(4)   The third case is where the accused –

  (a)   gives a witness notice but does so after the end of the period which, by virtue of section 12, is the relevant period for section 6C, or

  (b)   at his trial calls a witness (other than himself) not included, or not adequately identified, in a witness notice.

(5)   Where this section applies –

  (a)   the court or any other party may make such comment as appears appropriate;

  (b)   the court or jury may draw such inferences as appear proper in deciding whether the accused is guilty of the offence concerned.

(6)   Where –

  (a)   this section applies by virtue of subsection (2)(f)(ii) (including that provision as it applies by virtue of subsection (3)(b)), and

  (b)   the matter which was not mentioned is a point of law (including any point as to the admissibility of evidence or an abuse of process) or an authority,

  comment by another party under subsection (5)(a) may be made only with the leave of the court.

(7) Where this section applies by virtue of subsection (4), comment by another party under subsection (5)(a) may be made only with the leave of the court.

(8) Where the accused puts forward a defence which is different from any defence set out in his defence statement, in doing anything under subsection (5) or in deciding whether to do anything under it the court shall have regard –

(a)   to the extent of the differences in the defences, and
(b)   to whether there is any justification for it.

(9) Where the accused calls a witness whom he has failed to include, or to identify adequately, in a witness notice, in doing anything under subsection (5) or in deciding whether to do anything under it the court shall have regard to whether there is any justification for the failure.

(10) A person shall not be convicted of an offence solely on an inference drawn under subsection (5).

(11) Where the accused has given a statement of the kind mentioned in section 6B(4), then, for the purposes of subsections (2)(f)(ii) and (iv), the question as to whether there has been a breach of the requirements imposed by or under section 6A or a failure to comply with section 6A(2)(a) or (b) shall be determined –

(a)   by reference to the state of affairs at the time when that statement was given, and
(b)   as if the defence statement was given at the same time as that statement.

(12) In this section –

(a)   "initial defence statement" means a defence statement given under section 5 or 6;
(b)   "updated defence statement" means a defence statement given under section 6B;
(c)   a reference simply to an accused's "defence statement" is a reference –
   (i)   where he has given only an initial defence statement, to that statement;
   (ii) where he has given both an initial and an updated defence statement, to the updated defence statement;
   (iii) where he has given both an initial defence statement and a statement of the kind mentioned in section 6B(4), to the initial defence statement;
(d)   a reference to evidence in support of an alibi shall be construed in accordance with section 6A(3);
(e)   "witness notice" means a notice given under section 6C.'

40 Code of practice for police interviews of witnesses notified by accused

In Part 1 of the 1996 Act after section 21 there is inserted –

'21A Code of practice for police interviews of witnesses notified by accused

(1) The Secretary of State shall prepare a code of practice which gives guidance to police officers, and other persons charged with the duty of investigating offences, in relation to the arranging and conducting of interviews of persons –

(a)   particulars of whom are given in a defence statement in accordance with section 6A(2), or
(b)   who are included as proposed witnesses in a notice given under section 6C.

(2) The code must include (in particular) guidance in relation to –

(a)   information that should be provided to the interviewee and the accused in relation to such an interview;

(b) the notification of the accused's solicitor of such an interview;

(c) the attendance of the interviewee's solicitor at such an interview;

(d) the attendance of the accused's solicitor at such an interview;

(e) the attendance of any other appropriate person at such an interview taking into account the interviewee's age or any disability of the interviewee.

(3) Any police officer or other person charged with the duty of investigating offences who arranges or conducts such an interview shall have regard to the code.

(4) In preparing the code, the Secretary of State shall consult –

    (a) to the extent the code applies to England and Wales –

        (i) any person who he considers to represent the interests of chief officers of police;

        (ii) the General Council of the Bar;

        (iii) the Law Society of England and Wales;

        (iv) the Institute of Legal Executives;

    (b) to the extent the code applies to Northern Ireland –

        (i) the Chief Constable of the Police Service of Northern Ireland;

        (ii) the General Council of the Bar of Northern Ireland;

        (iii) the Law Society of Northern Ireland;

    (c) such other persons as he thinks fit.

(5) The code shall not come into operation until the Secretary of State by order so provides.

(6) The Secretary of State may from time to time revise the code and subsections (4) and (5) shall apply to a revised code as they apply to the code as first prepared.

(7) An order bringing the code into operation may not be made unless a draft of the order has been laid before each House of Parliament and approved by a resolution of each House.

(8) An order bringing a revised code into operation shall be laid before each House of Parliament if the order has been made without a draft having been so laid and approved by a resolution of each House.

(9) When an order or a draft of an order is laid in accordance with subsection (7) or (8), the code to which it relates shall also be laid.

(10) No order or draft of an order may be laid until the consultation required by subsection (4) has taken place.

(11) A failure by a person mentioned in subsection (3) to have regard to any provision of a code for the time being in operation by virtue of an order under this section shall not in itself render him liable to any criminal or civil proceedings.

(12) In all criminal and civil proceedings a code in operation at any time by virtue of an order under this section shall be admissible in evidence.

(13) If it appears to a court or tribunal conducting criminal or civil proceedings that –

    (a) any provision of a code in operation at any time by virtue of an order under this section, or

    (b) any failure mentioned in subsection (11),

is relevant to any question arising in the proceedings, the provision or failure shall be taken into account in deciding the question.'

PART 6   ALLOCATION AND SENDING OF OFFENCES

41 Allocation of offences triable either way, and sending cases to Crown Court

Schedule 3 (which makes provision in relation to the allocation and other treatment of offences triable either way, and the sending of cases to the Crown Court) shall have effect.

42 Mode of trial for certain firearms offences: transitory arrangements

(1) The Magistrates' Courts Act 1980 is amended as follows.

(2) In section 24 (summary trial of information against child or young person for indictable offence) –

    (a) in subsection (1), for 'homicide' there is substituted 'one falling within subsection (1B) below',

    (b) in subsection (1A)(a), for 'of homicide' there is substituted 'falling within subsection (1B) below',

    (c) after subsection (1A), there is inserted –

        '(1B) An offence falls within this subsection if –

            (a) it is an offence of homicide; or

            (b) each of the requirements of section 51A(1) of the Firearms Act 1968 would be satisfied with respect to –

                (i)   the offence; and

                (ii) the person charged with it,

            if he were convicted of the offence.'

(3) In section 25 (power to change from summary trial to committal proceedings and vice versa), in subsection (5), for 'homicide' there is substituted 'one falling within section 24(1B) above'.

PART 7   TRIALS ON INDICTMENT WITHOUT A JURY

43 Applications by prosecution for certain fraud cases to be conducted without a jury

(1) This section applies where –

    (a) one or more defendants are to be tried on indictment for one or more offences, and

    (b) notice has been given under section 51B of the Crime and Disorder Act 1998 (c. 37) (notices in serious or complex fraud cases) in respect of that offence or those offences.

(2) The prosecution may apply to a judge of the Crown Court for the trial to be conducted without a jury.

(3) If an application under subsection (2) is made and the judge is satisfied that the condition in subsection (5) is fulfilled, he may make an order that the trial is to be conducted without a jury; but if he is not so satisfied he must refuse the application.

(4) The judge may not make such an order without the approval of the Lord Chief Justice or a judge nominated by him.

(5) The condition is that the complexity of the trial or the length of the trial (or both) is likely to make the trial so burdensome to the members of a jury hearing the trial that the interests of justice require that serious consideration should be given to the question of whether the trial should be conducted without a jury.

(6) In deciding whether or not he is satisfied that that condition is fulfilled, the judge must have regard to any steps which might reasonably be taken to reduce the complexity or length of the trial.

(7)   But a step is not to be regarded as reasonable if it would significantly disadvantage the prosecution.

44 Application by prosecution for trial to be conducted without a jury where danger of jury tampering

(1)   This section applies where one or more defendants are to be tried on indictment for one or more offences.

(2)   The prosecution may apply to a judge of the Crown Court for the trial to be conducted without a jury.

(3)   If an application under subsection (2) is made and the judge is satisfied that both of the following two conditions are fulfilled, he must make an order that the trial is to be conducted without a jury; but if he is not so satisfied he must refuse the application.

(4)   The first condition is that there is evidence of a real and present danger that jury tampering would take place.

(5)   The second condition is that, notwithstanding any steps (including the provision of police protection) which might reasonably be taken to prevent jury tampering, the likelihood that it would take place would be so substantial as to make it necessary in the interests of justice for the trial to be conducted without a jury.

(6)   The following are examples of cases where there may be evidence of a real and present danger that jury tampering would take place –

   (a)   a case where the trial is a retrial and the jury in the previous trial was discharged because jury tampering had taken place,

   (b)   a case where jury tampering has taken place in previous criminal proceedings involving the defendant or any of the defendants,

   (c)   a case where there has been intimidation, or attempted intimidation, of any person who is likely to be a witness in the trial.

45 Procedure for applications under sections 43 and 44

(1)   This section applies –

   (a)   to an application under section 43, and

   (b)   to an application under section 44.

(2)   An application to which this section applies must be determined at a preparatory hearing (within the meaning of the 1987 Act or Part 3 of the 1996 Act).

(3)   The parties to a preparatory hearing at which an application to which this section applies is to be determined must be given an opportunity to make representations with respect to the application.

(4)   In section 7(1) of the 1987 Act (which sets out the purposes of preparatory hearings) for paragraphs (a) to (c) there is substituted –

   '(a)   identifying issues which are likely to be material to the determinations and findings which are likely to be required during the trial,

   (b)   if there is to be a jury, assisting their comprehension of those issues and expediting the proceedings before them,

   (c)   determining an application to which section 45 of the Criminal Justice Act 2003 applies,'.

(5)   In section 9(11) of that Act (appeal to Court of Appeal) after 'above,' there is inserted 'from the refusal by a judge of an application to which section 45 of the Criminal Justice Act 2003 applies or from an order of a judge under section 43 or 44 of that Act which is made on the determination of such an application,'.

(6)   In section 29 of the 1996 Act (power to order preparatory hearing) after subsection (1) there is inserted –

'(1A) A judge of the Crown Court may also order that a preparatory hearing shall be held if an application to which section 45 of the Criminal Justice Act 2003 applies (application for trial without jury) is made.'

(7) In subsection (2) of that section (which sets out the purposes of preparatory hearings) for paragraphs (a) to (c) there is substituted –

'(a) identifying issues which are likely to be material to the determinations and findings which are likely to be required during the trial,
(b) if there is to be a jury, assisting their comprehension of those issues and expediting the proceedings before them,
(c) determining an application to which section 45 of the Criminal Justice Act 2003 applies,'.

(8) In subsections (3) and (4) of that section for 'subsection (1)' there is substituted 'this section'.

(9) In section 35(1) of that Act (appeal to Court of Appeal) after '31(3),' there is inserted 'from the refusal by a judge of an application to which section 45 of the Criminal Justice Act 2003 applies or from an order of a judge under section 43 or 44 of that Act which is made on the determination of such an application,'.

(10) In this section –

'the 1987 Act' means the Criminal Justice Act 1987 (c. 38),
'the 1996 Act' means the Criminal Procedure and Investigations Act 1996 (c. 25).

46 Discharge of jury because of jury tampering

(1) This section applies where –

(a) a judge is minded during a trial on indictment to discharge the jury, and
(b) he is so minded because jury tampering appears to have taken place.

(2) Before taking any steps to discharge the jury, the judge must –

(a) inform the parties that he is minded to discharge the jury,
(b) inform the parties of the grounds on which he is so minded, and
(c) allow the parties an opportunity to make representations.

(3) Where the judge, after considering any such representations, discharges the jury, he may make an order that the trial is to continue without a jury if, but only if, he is satisfied –

(a) that jury tampering has taken place, and
(b) that to continue the trial without a jury would be fair to the defendant or defendants;

but this is subject to subsection (4).

(4) If the judge considers that it is necessary in the interests of justice for the trial to be terminated, he must terminate the trial.

(5) Where the judge terminates the trial under subsection (4), he may make an order that any new trial which is to take place must be conducted without a jury if he is satisfied in respect of the new trial that both of the conditions set out in section 44 are likely to be fulfilled.

(6) Subsection (5) is without prejudice to any other power that the judge may have on terminating the trial.

(7) Subject to subsection (5), nothing in this section affects the application of section 43 or 44 in relation to any new trial which takes place following the termination of the trial.

47 Appeals

(1) An appeal shall lie to the Court of Appeal from an order under section 46(3) or (5).

(2) Such an appeal may be brought only with the leave of the judge or the Court of Appeal.

(3) An order from which an appeal under this section lies is not to take effect –

(a) before the expiration of the period for bringing an appeal under this section, or

(b) if such an appeal is brought, before the appeal is finally disposed of or abandoned.

(4) On the termination of the hearing of an appeal under this section, the Court of Appeal may confirm or revoke the order.

(5) Subject to rules of court made under section 53(1) of the Supreme Court Act 1981 (c. 54) (power by rules to distribute business of Court of Appeal between its civil and criminal divisions) –

(a) the jurisdiction of the Court of Appeal under this section is to be exercised by the criminal division of that court, and

(b) references in this section to the Court of Appeal are to be construed as references to that division.

(6) In section 33(1) of the Criminal Appeal Act 1968 (c. 19) (right of appeal to House of Lords) after '1996' there is inserted 'or section 47 of the Criminal Justice Act 2003'.

(7) In section 36 of that Act (bail on appeal by defendant) after 'hearings)' there is inserted 'or section 47 of the Criminal Justice Act 2003'.

(8) The Secretary of State may make an order containing provision, in relation to proceedings before the Court of Appeal under this section, which corresponds to any provision, in relation to appeals or other proceedings before that court, which is contained in the Criminal Appeal Act 1968 (subject to any specified modifications).

48 Further provision about trials without a jury

(1) The effect of an order under section 43, 44 or 46(5) is that the trial to which the order relates is to be conducted without a jury.

(2) The effect of an order under section 46(3) is that the trial to which the order relates is to be continued without a jury.

(3) Where a trial is conducted or continued without a jury, the court is to have all the powers, authorities and jurisdiction which the court would have had if the trial had been conducted or continued with a jury (including power to determine any question and to make any finding which would be required to be determined or made by a jury).

(4) Except where the context otherwise requires, any reference in an enactment to a jury, the verdict of a jury or the finding of a jury is to be read, in relation to a trial conducted or continued without a jury, as a reference to the court, the verdict of the court or the finding of the court.

(5) Where a trial is conducted or continued without a jury and the court convicts a defendant –

(a) the court must give a judgment which states the reasons for the conviction at, or as soon as reasonably practicable after, the time of the conviction, and

(b) the reference in section 18(2) of the Criminal Appeal Act 1968 (c. 19) (notice of appeal or of application for leave to appeal to be given within 28 days from date of conviction etc) to the date of the conviction is to be read as a reference to the date of the judgment mentioned in paragraph (a).

(6) Nothing in this Part affects –

(a) the requirement under section 4 of the Criminal Procedure (Insanity) Act 1964 (c. 84) that a question of fitness to be tried be determined by a jury, or

(b) the requirement under section 4A of that Act that any question, finding or verdict mentioned in that section be determined, made or returned by a jury.

49 Rules of court

(1) Rules of court may make such provision as appears to the authority making them to be necessary or expedient for the purposes of this Part.

(2) Without limiting subsection (1), rules of court may in particular make provision for time limits within which applications under this Part must be made or within which other things in connection with this Part must be done.

(3) Nothing in this section is to be taken as affecting the generality of any enactment conferring powers to make rules of court.

50 Application of Part 7 to Northern Ireland

(1) In its application to Northern Ireland this Part is to have effect –

    (a) subject to subsection (2), and

    (b) subject to the modifications in subsections (3) to (16).

(2) This Part does not apply in relation to a trial to which section 75 of the Terrorism Act 2000 (c. 11) (trial without jury for certain offences) applies.

(3) For section 45 substitute –

    '45 Procedure for applications under sections 43 and 44

    (1) This section applies –

        (a) to an application under section 43, and

        (b) to an application under section 44.

    (2) An application to which this section applies must be determined –

        (a) at a preparatory hearing (within the meaning of the 1988 Order), or

        (b) at a hearing specified in, or for which provision is made by, Crown Court rules.

    (3) The parties to a hearing mentioned in subsection (2) at which an application to which this section applies is to be determined must be given an opportunity to make representations with respect to the application.

    (4) In Article 6(1) of the 1988 Order (which sets out the purposes of preparatory hearings) for sub-paragraphs (a) to (c) there is substituted –

        "(a) identifying issues which are likely to be material to the determinations and findings which are likely to be required during the trial;

        (b) if there is to be a jury, assisting their comprehension of those issues and expediting the proceedings before them;

        (c) determining an application to which section 45 of the Criminal Justice Act 2003 applies; or".

    (5) In Article 8(11) of the 1988 Order (appeal to Court of Appeal) after "(3)," there is inserted "from the refusal by a judge of an application to which section 45 of the Criminal Justice Act 2003 applies or from an order of a judge under section 43 or 44 of that Act which is made on the determination of such an application,"

    (6) In this section "the 1988 Order" means the Criminal Justice (Serious Fraud) (Northern Ireland) Order 1988.'

(4) For section 47(1) substitute –

    '(1) An appeal shall lie to the Court of Appeal –

        (a) from the refusal by a judge at a hearing mentioned in section 45(2)(b) of an application to which section 45 applies or from an order of a judge at such a hearing under section 43 or 44 which is made on the determination of such an application,

        (b) from an order under section 46(3) or (5).'

(5) In section 47(3) after 'order' insert 'or a refusal of an application'.

(6) In section 47(4) for 'confirm or revoke the order' substitute –

'(a) where the appeal is from an order, confirm or revoke the order, or

(b) where the appeal is from a refusal of an application, confirm the refusal or make the order which is the subject of the application'.

(7) Omit section 47(5).

(8) For section 47(6) substitute –

'(6) In section 31(1) of the Criminal Appeal (Northern Ireland) Act 1980 (right of appeal to House of Lords) after "1988" there is inserted "or section 47 of the Criminal Justice Act 2003".'

(9) For section 47(7) substitute –

'(7) In section 35 of that Act (bail) after 'hearings)' there is inserted 'or section 47 of the Criminal Justice Act 2003'.'

(10) In section 47(8) for 'Criminal Appeal Act 1968' substitute 'Criminal Appeal (Northern Ireland) Act 1980'.

(11) In section 48(4) after 'enactment' insert '(including any provision of Northern Ireland legislation)'.

(12) For section 48(5)(b) substitute –

'(b) the reference in section 16(1) of the Criminal Appeal (Northern Ireland) Act 1980 (c. 47) (notice of appeal or application for leave) to the date of the conviction is to be read as a reference to the date of the judgment mentioned in paragraph (a).'

(13) In section 48(6) –

(a) for 'section 4 of the Criminal Procedure (Insanity) Act 1964 (c. 84)' substitute 'Article 49 of the Mental Health (Northern Ireland) Order 1986',

(b) for 'section 4A of that Act' substitute 'Article 49A of that Order', and

(c) for 'that section' substitute 'that Article'.

(14) After section 48 insert –

'48A Reporting restrictions

(1) Sections 41 and 42 of the Criminal Procedure and Investigations Act 1996 (c. 25) are to apply in relation to –

(a) a hearing of the kind mentioned in section 45(2)(b), and

(b) any appeal or application for leave to appeal relating to such a hearing,

as they apply in relation to a ruling under section 40 of that Act, but subject to the following modifications.

(2) Section 41(2) of that Act is to have effect as if for paragraphs (a) to (d) there were substituted –

"(a) a hearing of the kind mentioned in section 45(2)(b) of the Criminal Justice Act 2003;

(b) any appeal or application for leave to appeal relating to such a hearing."

(3) Section 41(3) of that Act is to have effect as if –

(a) for "(2)" there were substituted "(2)(a) or an application to that judge for leave to appeal to the Court of Appeal", and

(b) after "matter" in the second place where it occurs there were inserted "or application".

(4) Section 41 of that Act is to have effect as if after subsection (3) there were inserted –

"(3A) The Court of Appeal may order that subsection (1) shall not apply, or shall not apply to a specified extent, to a report of –

(a) an appeal to that Court, or

(b) an application to that Court for leave to appeal.

(3B) The House of Lords may order that subsection (1) shall not apply, or shall not apply to a specified extent, to a report of –

(a)   an appeal to that House, or

(b)   an application to that House for leave to appeal."

(5) Section 41(4) of that Act is to have effect as if for "(3) the judge" there were substituted "(3), (3A) or (3B), the judge, the Court of Appeal or the House of Lords".

(6) Section 41(5) of that Act is to have effect as if for "(3) the judge" there were substituted "(3), (3A) or (3B), the judge, the Court of Appeal or the House of Lords".'

(15) For section 49(2) substitute –

'(2) Without limiting subsection (1), rules of court may in particular make provision –

(a)   for time limits within which applications under this Part must be made or within which other things in connection with this Part must be done;

(b)   in relation to hearings of the kind mentioned in section 45(2)(b) and appeals under section 47.'

(16) In section 49(3) –

(a)   after 'section' insert 'or section 45(2)(b)', and

(b)   after 'enactment' insert '(including any provision of Northern Ireland legislation)'.

PART 8   LIVE LINKS

51 Live links in criminal proceedings

(1) A witness (other than the defendant) may, if the court so directs, give evidence through a live link in the following criminal proceedings.

(2) They are –

(a)   a summary trial,

(b)   an appeal to the Crown Court arising out of such a trial,

(c)   a trial on indictment,

(d)   an appeal to the criminal division of the Court of Appeal,

(e)   the hearing of a reference under section 9 or 11 of the Criminal Appeal Act 1995 (c. 35),

(f)   a hearing before a magistrates' court or the Crown Court which is held after the defendant has entered a plea of guilty, and

(g)   a hearing before the Court of Appeal under section 80 of this Act.

(3) A direction may be given under this section –

(a)   on an application by a party to the proceedings, or

(b)   of the court's own motion.

(4) But a direction may not be given under this section unless –

(a)   the court is satisfied that it is in the interests of the efficient or effective administration of justice for the person concerned to give evidence in the proceedings through a live link,

(b)   it has been notified by the Secretary of State that suitable facilities for receiving evidence through a live link are available in the area in which it appears to the court that the proceedings will take place, and

(c)   that notification has not been withdrawn.

(5) The withdrawal of such a notification is not to affect a direction given under this section before that withdrawal.

(6)   In deciding whether to give a direction under this section the court must consider all the circumstances of the case.

(7)   Those circumstances include in particular –

(a)   the availability of the witness,

(b)   the need for the witness to attend in person,

(c)   the importance of the witness's evidence to the proceedings,

(d)   the views of the witness,

(e)   the suitability of the facilities at the place where the witness would give evidence through a live link,

(f)   whether a direction might tend to inhibit any party to the proceedings from effectively testing the witness's evidence.

(8)   The court must state in open court its reasons for refusing an application for a direction under this section and, if it is a magistrates' court, must cause them to be entered in the register of its proceedings.

52 Effect of, and rescission of, direction

(1)   Subsection (2) applies where the court gives a direction under section 51 for a person to give evidence through a live link in particular proceedings.

(2)   The person concerned may not give evidence in those proceedings after the direction is given otherwise than through a live link (but this is subject to the following provisions of this section).

(3)   The court may rescind a direction under section 51 if it appears to the court to be in the interests of justice to do so.

(4)   Where it does so, the person concerned shall cease to be able to give evidence in the proceedings through a live link, but this does not prevent the court from giving a further direction under section 51 in relation to him.

(5)   A direction under section 51 may be rescinded under subsection (3) –

(a)   on an application by a party to the proceedings, or

(b)   of the court's own motion.

(6)   But an application may not be made under subsection (5)(a) unless there has been a material change of circumstances since the direction was given.

(7)   The court must state in open court its reasons –

(a)   for rescinding a direction under section 51, or

(b)   for refusing an application to rescind such a direction,

and, if it is a magistrates' court, must cause them to be entered in the register of its proceedings.

53 Magistrates' courts permitted to sit at other locations

(1)   This section applies where –

(a)   a magistrates' court is minded to give a direction under section 51 for evidence to be given through a live link in proceedings before the court, and

(b)   suitable facilities for receiving such evidence are not available at any petty-sessional court-house in which the court can (apart from subsection (2)) lawfully sit.

(2)   The court may sit for the purposes of the whole or any part of the proceedings at any place at which such facilities are available and which has been appointed for the purposes of this section by the justices acting for the petty sessions area for which the court acts.

(3)   A place appointed under subsection (2) may be outside the petty sessions area for which it is appointed; but (if so) it shall be deemed to be in that area for the purpose of the jurisdiction of the justices acting for that area.

54 Warning to jury

(1) This section applies where, as a result of a direction under section 51, evidence has been given through a live link in proceedings before the Crown Court.

(2) The judge may give the jury (if there is one) such direction as he thinks necessary to ensure that the jury gives the same weight to the evidence as if it had been given by the witness in the courtroom or other place where the proceedings are held.

55 Rules of court

(1) Rules of court may make such provision as appears to the authority making them to be necessary or expedient for the purposes of this Part.

(2) Rules of court may in particular make provision –

(a) as to the procedure to be followed in connection with applications under section 51 or 52, and

(b) as to the arrangements or safeguards to be put in place in connection with the operation of live links.

(3) The provision which may be made by virtue of subsection (2)(a) includes provision –

(a) for uncontested applications to be determined by the court without a hearing,

(b) for preventing the renewal of an unsuccessful application under section 51 unless there has been a material change of circumstances,

(c) for the manner in which confidential or sensitive information is to be treated in connection with an application under section 51 or 52 and in particular as to its being disclosed to, or withheld from, a party to the proceedings.

(4) Nothing in this section is to be taken as affecting the generality of any enactment conferring power to make rules of court.

56 Interpretation of Part 8

(1) In this Part –

'legal representative' means an authorised advocate or authorised litigator (as defined by section 119(1) of the Courts and Legal Services Act 1990 (c. 41)),

'petty-sessional court-house' has the same meaning as in the Magistrates' Courts Act 1980 (c. 43),

'petty sessions area' has the same meaning as in the Justices of the Peace Act 1997 (c. 25),

'rules of court' means Magistrates' Courts Rules, Crown Court Rules or Criminal Appeal Rules,

'witness', in relation to any criminal proceedings, means a person called, or proposed to be called, to give evidence in the proceedings.

(2) In this Part 'live link' means a live television link or other arrangement by which a witness, while at a place in the United Kingdom which is outside the building where the proceedings are being held, is able to see and hear a person at the place where the proceedings are being held and to be seen and heard by the following persons.

(3) They are –

(a) the defendant or defendants,

(b) the judge or justices (or both) and the jury (if there is one),

(c) legal representatives acting in the proceedings, and

(d) any interpreter or other person appointed by the court to assist the witness.

(4) The extent (if any) to which a person is unable to see or hear by reason of any impairment of eyesight or hearing is to be disregarded for the purposes of subsection (2).

(5) Nothing in this Part is to be regarded as affecting any power of a court –

    (a) to make an order, give directions or give leave of any description in relation to any witness (including the defendant or defendants), or

    (b) to exclude evidence at its discretion (whether by preventing questions being put or otherwise).

PART 9   PROSECUTION APPEALS

Introduction

57 Introduction

(1) In relation to a trial on indictment, the prosecution is to have the rights of appeal for which provision is made by this Part.

(2) But the prosecution is to have no right of appeal under this Part in respect of –

    (a) a ruling that a jury be discharged, or

    (b) a ruling from which an appeal lies to the Court of Appeal by virtue of any other enactment.

(3) An appeal under this Part is to lie to the Court of Appeal.

(4) Such an appeal may be brought only with the leave of the judge or the Court of Appeal.

58 General right of appeal in respect of rulings

(1) This section applies where a judge makes a ruling in relation to a trial on indictment at an applicable time and the ruling relates to one or more offences included in the indictment.

(2) The prosecution may appeal in respect of the ruling in accordance with this section.

(3) The ruling is to have no effect whilst the prosecution is able to take any steps under subsection (4).

(4) The prosecution may not appeal in respect of the ruling unless –

    (a) following the making of the ruling, it –

        (i)   informs the court that it intends to appeal, or

        (ii) requests an adjournment to consider whether to appeal, and

    (b) if such an adjournment is granted, it informs the court following the adjournment that it intends to appeal.

(5) If the prosecution requests an adjournment under subsection (4)(a)(ii), the judge may grant such an adjournment.

(6) Where the ruling relates to two or more offences –

    (a) any one or more of those offences may be the subject of the appeal, and

    (b) if the prosecution informs the court in accordance with subsection (4) that it intends to appeal, it must at the same time inform the court of the offence or offences which are the subject of the appeal.

(7) Where –

    (a) the ruling is a ruling that there is no case to answer, and

    (b) the prosecution, at the same time that it informs the court in accordance with subsection (4) that it intends to appeal, nominates one or more other rulings which have been made by a judge in relation to the trial on indictment at an applicable time and which relate to the offence or offences which are the subject of the appeal,

that other ruling, or those other rulings, are also to be treated as the subject of the appeal.

(8) The prosecution may not inform the court in accordance with subsection (4) that it intends to appeal, unless, at or before that time, it informs the court that it agrees that, in respect of the offence or each offence which is the subject of the appeal, the defendant in relation to that offence should be acquitted of that offence if either of the conditions mentioned in subsection (9) is fulfilled.

(9) Those conditions are –

(a) that leave to appeal to the Court of Appeal is not obtained, and

(b) that the appeal is abandoned before it is determined by the Court of Appeal.

(10) If the prosecution informs the court in accordance with subsection (4) that it intends to appeal, the ruling mentioned in subsection (1) is to continue to have no effect in relation to the offence or offences which are the subject of the appeal whilst the appeal is pursued.

(11) If and to the extent that a ruling has no effect in accordance with this section –

(a) any consequences of the ruling are also to have no effect,

(b) the judge may not take any steps in consequence of the ruling, and

(c) if he does so, any such steps are also to have no effect.

(12) Where the prosecution has informed the court of its agreement under subsection (8) and either of the conditions mentioned in subsection (9) is fulfilled, the judge or the Court of Appeal must order that the defendant in relation to the offence or each offence concerned be acquitted of that offence.

(13) In this section 'applicable time', in relation to a trial on indictment, means any time (whether before or after the commencement of the trial) before the start of the judge's summing-up to the jury.

59 Expedited and non-expedited appeals

(1) Where the prosecution informs the court in accordance with section 58(4) that it intends to appeal, the judge must decide whether or not the appeal should be expedited.

(2) If the judge decides that the appeal should be expedited, he may order an adjournment.

(3) If the judge decides that the appeal should not be expedited, he may –

(a) order an adjournment, or

(b) discharge the jury (if one has been sworn).

(4) If he decides that the appeal should be expedited, he or the Court of Appeal may subsequently reverse that decision and, if it is reversed, the judge may act as mentioned in subsection (3)(a) or (b).

60 Continuation of proceedings for offences not affected by ruling

(1) This section applies where the prosecution informs the court in accordance with section 58(4) that it intends to appeal.

(2) Proceedings may be continued in respect of any offence which is not the subject of the appeal.

61 Determination of appeal by Court of Appeal

(1) On an appeal under section 58, the Court of Appeal may confirm, reverse or vary any ruling to which the appeal relates.

(2) Subsections (3) to (5) apply where the appeal relates to a single ruling.

(3) Where the Court of Appeal confirms the ruling, it must, in respect of the offence or each offence which is the subject of the appeal, order that the defendant in relation to that offence be acquitted of that offence.

(4) Where the Court of Appeal reverses or varies the ruling, it must, in respect of the offence or each offence which is the subject of the appeal, do any of the following –

      (a)   order that proceedings for that offence may be resumed in the Crown Court,

      (b)   order that a fresh trial may take place in the Crown Court for that offence,

      (c)   order that the defendant in relation to that offence be acquitted of that offence.

(5)   But the Court of Appeal may not make an order under subsection (4)(a) or (b) in respect of an offence unless it considers it necessary in the interests of justice to do so.

(6)   Subsections (7) and (8) apply where the appeal relates to a ruling that there is no case to answer and one or more other rulings.

(7)   Where the Court of Appeal confirms the ruling that there is no case to answer, it must, in respect of the offence or each offence which is the subject of the appeal, order that the defendant in relation to that offence be acquitted of that offence.

(8)   Where the Court of Appeal reverses or varies the ruling that there is no case to answer, it must in respect of the offence or each offence which is the subject of the appeal, make any of the orders mentioned in subsection (4)(a) to (c) (but subject to subsection (5)).

Right of appeal in respect of evidentiary rulings

62 Right of appeal in respect of evidentiary rulings

(1)   The prosecution may, in accordance with this section and section 63, appeal in respect of –

      (a)   a single qualifying evidentiary ruling, or

      (b)   two or more qualifying evidentiary rulings.

(2)   A 'qualifying evidentiary ruling' is an evidentiary ruling of a judge in relation to a trial on indictment which is made at any time (whether before or after the commencement of the trial) before the opening of the case for the defence.

(3)   The prosecution may not appeal in respect of a single qualifying evidentiary ruling unless the ruling relates to one or more qualifying offences (whether or not it relates to any other offence).

(4)   The prosecution may not appeal in respect of two or more qualifying evidentiary rulings unless each ruling relates to one or more qualifying offences (whether or not it relates to any other offence).

(5)   If the prosecution intends to appeal under this section, it must before the opening of the case for the defence inform the court –

      (a)   of its intention to do so, and

      (b)   of the ruling or rulings to which the appeal relates.

(6)   In respect of the ruling, or each ruling, to which the appeal relates –

      (a)   the qualifying offence, or at least one of the qualifying offences, to which the ruling relates must be the subject of the appeal, and

      (b)   any other offence to which the ruling relates may, but need not, be the subject of the appeal.

(7)   The prosecution must, at the same time that it informs the court in accordance with subsection (5), inform the court of the offence or offences which are the subject of the appeal.

(8)   For the purposes of this section, the case for the defence opens when, after the conclusion of the prosecution evidence, the earliest of the following events occurs –

      (a)   evidence begins to be adduced by or on behalf of a defendant,

      (b)   it is indicated to the court that no evidence will be adduced by or on behalf of a defendant,

      (c)   a defendant's case is opened, as permitted by section 2 of the Criminal Procedure Act 1865 (c. 18).

(9) In this section –

'evidentiary ruling' means a ruling which relates to the admissibility or exclusion of any prosecution evidence,

'qualifying offence' means an offence described in Part 1 of Schedule 4.

(10) The Secretary of State may by order amend that Part by doing any one or more of the following –

(a)   adding a description of offence,

(b)   removing a description of offence for the time being included,

(c)   modifying a description of offence for the time being included.

(11) Nothing in this section affects the right of the prosecution to appeal in respect of an evidentiary ruling under section 58.

63 Condition that evidentiary ruling significantly weakens prosecution case

(1) Leave to appeal may not be given in relation to an appeal under section 62 unless the judge or, as the case may be, the Court of Appeal is satisfied that the relevant condition is fulfilled.

(2) In relation to an appeal in respect of a single qualifying evidentiary ruling, the relevant condition is that the ruling significantly weakens the prosecution's case in relation to the offence or offences which are the subject of the appeal.

(3) In relation to an appeal in respect of two or more qualifying evidentiary rulings, the relevant condition is that the rulings taken together significantly weaken the prosecution's case in relation to the offence or offences which are the subject of the appeal.

64 Expedited and non-expedited appeals

(1) Where the prosecution informs the court in accordance with section 62(5), the judge must decide whether or not the appeal should be expedited.

(2) If the judge decides that the appeal should be expedited, he may order an adjournment.

(3) If the judge decides that the appeal should not be expedited, he may –

(a)   order an adjournment, or

(b)   discharge the jury (if one has been sworn).

(4) If he decides that the appeal should be expedited, he or the Court of Appeal may subsequently reverse that decision and, if it is reversed, the judge may act as mentioned in subsection (3)(a) or (b).

65 Continuation of proceedings for offences not affected by ruling

(1) This section applies where the prosecution informs the court in accordance with section 62(5).

(2) Proceedings may be continued in respect of any offence which is not the subject of the appeal.

66 Determination of appeal by Court of Appeal

(1) On an appeal under section 62, the Court of Appeal may confirm, reverse or vary any ruling to which the appeal relates.

(2) In addition, the Court of Appeal must, in respect of the offence or each offence which is the subject of the appeal, do any of the following –

(a)   order that proceedings for that offence be resumed in the Crown Court,

(b)   order that a fresh trial may take place in the Crown Court for that offence,

(c)   order that the defendant in relation to that offence be acquitted of that offence.

(3) But no order may be made under subsection (2)(c) in respect of an offence unless the prosecution has indicated that it does not intend to continue with the prosecution of that offence.

67 Reversal of rulings

The Court of Appeal may not reverse a ruling on an appeal under this Part unless it is satisfied –

(a) that the ruling was wrong in law,

(b) that the ruling involved an error of law or principle, or

(c) that the ruling was a ruling that it was not reasonable for the judge to have made.

Miscellaneous and supplemental

68 Appeals to the House of Lords

(1) In section 33(1) of the 1968 Act (right of appeal to House of Lords) after 'this Act' there is inserted 'or Part 9 of the Criminal Justice Act 2003'.

(2) In section 36 of the 1968 Act (bail on appeal by defendant) after 'under' there is inserted 'Part 9 of the Criminal Justice Act 2003 or'.

(3) In this Part 'the 1968 Act' means the Criminal Appeal Act 1968 (c. 19).

69 Costs

(1) The Prosecution of Offences Act 1985 (c. 23) is amended as follows.

(2) In section 16(4A) (defence costs on an appeal under section 9(11) of Criminal Justice Act 1987 may be met out of central funds) after 'hearings)' there is inserted 'or under Part 9 of the Criminal Justice Act 2003'.

(3) In section 18 (award of costs against accused) after subsection (2) there is inserted –

'(2A) Where the Court of Appeal reverses or varies a ruling on an appeal under Part 9 of the Criminal Justice Act 2003, it may make such order as to the costs to be paid by the accused, to such person as may be named in the order, as it considers just and reasonable.'

(4) In subsection (6) after 'subsection (2)' there is inserted 'or (2A)'.

70 Effect on time limits in relation to preliminary stages

(1) Section 22 of the Prosecution of Offences Act 1985 (c. 23) (power of Secretary of State to set time limits in relation to preliminary stages of criminal proceedings) is amended as follows.

(2) After subsection (6A) there is inserted –

'(6B) Any period during which proceedings for an offence are adjourned pending the determination of an appeal under Part 9 of the Criminal Justice Act 2003 shall be disregarded, so far as the offence is concerned, for the purposes of the overall time limit and the custody time limit which applies to the stage which the proceedings have reached when they are adjourned.'

71 Restrictions on reporting

(1) Except as provided by this section no publication shall include a report of –

(a) anything done under section 58, 59, 62, 63 or 64,

(b) an appeal under this Part,

(c) an appeal under Part 2 of the 1968 Act in relation to an appeal under this Part, or

(d) an application for leave to appeal in relation to an appeal mentioned in paragraph (b) or (c).

(2) The judge may order that subsection (1) is not to apply, or is not to apply to a specified extent, to a report of –

(a) anything done under section 58, 59, 62, 63 or 64, or

(b) an application to the judge for leave to appeal to the Court of Appeal under this Part.

(3) The Court of Appeal may order that subsection (1) is not to apply, or is not to apply to a specified extent, to a report of –

(a) an appeal to the Court of Appeal under this Part,

(b) an application to that Court for leave to appeal to it under this Part, or

(c) an application to that Court for leave to appeal to the House of Lords under Part 2 of the 1968 Act.

(4) The House of Lords may order that subsection (1) is not to apply, or is not to apply to a specified extent, to a report of –

(a) an appeal to that House under Part 2 of the 1968 Act, or

(b) an application to that House for leave to appeal to it under Part 2 of that Act.

(5) Where there is only one defendant and he objects to the making of an order under subsection (2), (3) or (4) –

(a) the judge, the Court of Appeal or the House of Lords are to make the order if (and only if) satisfied, after hearing the representations of the defendant, that it is in the interests of justice to do so, and

(b) the order (if made) is not to apply to the extent that a report deals with any such objection or representations.

(6) Where there are two or more defendants and one or more of them object to the making of an order under subsection (2), (3) or (4) –

(a) the judge, the Court of Appeal or the House of Lords are to make the order if (and only if) satisfied, after hearing the representations of each of the defendants, that it is in the interests of justice to do so, and

(b) the order (if made) is not to apply to the extent that a report deals with any such objection or representations.

(7) Subsection (1) does not apply to the inclusion in a publication of a report of –

(a) anything done under section 58, 59, 62, 63 or 64,

(b) an appeal under this Part,

(c) an appeal under Part 2 of the 1968 Act in relation to an appeal under this Part, or

(d) an application for leave to appeal in relation to an appeal mentioned in paragraph (b) or (c),

at the conclusion of the trial of the defendant or the last of the defendants to be tried.

(8) Subsection (1) does not apply to a report which contains only one or more of the following matters –

(a) the identity of the court and the name of the judge,

(b) the names, ages, home addresses and occupations of the defendant or defendants and witnesses,

(c) the offence or offences, or a summary of them, with which the defendant or defendants are charged,

(d) the names of counsel and solicitors in the proceedings,

(e) where the proceedings are adjourned, the date and place to which they are adjourned,

(f) any arrangements as to bail,

(g) whether a right to representation funded by the Legal Services Commission as part of the Criminal Defence Service was granted to the defendant or any of the defendants.

(9) The addresses that may be included in a report by virtue of subsection (8) are addresses –

(a) at any relevant time, and

(b) at the time of their inclusion in the publication.

(10) Nothing in this section affects any prohibition or restriction by virtue of any other enactment on the inclusion of any matter in a publication.

(11) In this section –

'programme service' has the same meaning as in the Broadcasting Act 1990 (c. 42),

'publication' includes any speech, writing, relevant programme or other communication in whatever form, which is addressed to the public at large or any section of the public (and for this purpose every relevant programme is to be taken to be so addressed), but does not include an indictment or other document prepared for use in particular legal proceedings,

'relevant time' means a time when events giving rise to the charges to which the proceedings relate are alleged to have occurred,

'relevant programme' means a programme included in a programme service.

72 Offences in connection with reporting

(1) This section applies if a publication includes a report in contravention of section 71.

(2) Where the publication is a newspaper or periodical, any proprietor, editor or publisher of the newspaper or periodical is guilty of an offence.

(3) Where the publication is a relevant programme –

(a) any body corporate or Scottish partnership engaged in providing the programme service in which the programme is included, and

(b) any person having functions in relation to the programme corresponding to those of an editor of a newspaper,

is guilty of an offence.

(4) In the case of any other publication, any person publishing it is guilty of an offence.

(5) If an offence under this section committed by a body corporate is proved –

(a) to have been committed with the consent or connivance of, or

(b) to be attributable to any neglect on the part of,

an officer, the officer as well as the body corporate is guilty of the offence and liable to be proceeded against and punished accordingly.

(6) In subsection (5), 'officer' means a director, manager, secretary or other similar officer of the body, or a person purporting to act in any such capacity.

(7) If the affairs of a body corporate are managed by its members, 'director' in subsection (6) means a member of that body.

(8) Where an offence under this section is committed by a Scottish partnership and is proved to have been committed with the consent or connivance of a partner, he as well as the partnership shall be guilty of the offence and shall be liable to be proceeded against and punished accordingly.

(9) A person guilty of an offence under this section is liable on summary conviction to a fine not exceeding level 5 on the standard scale.

(10) Proceedings for an offence under this section may not be instituted –

(a) in England and Wales otherwise than by or with the consent of the Attorney General, or

(b) in Northern Ireland otherwise than by or with the consent of –

(i) before the relevant date, the Attorney General for Northern Ireland, or

(ii) on or after the relevant date, the Director of Public Prosecutions for Northern Ireland.

(11) In subsection (10) 'the relevant date' means the date on which section 22(1) of the Justice (Northern Ireland) Act 2002 (c. 26) comes into force.

73 Rules of court

(1) Rules of court may make such provision as appears to the authority making them to be necessary or expedient for the purposes of this Part.

(2) Without limiting subsection (1), rules of court may in particular make provision –

    (a) for time limits which are to apply in connection with any provisions of this Part,

    (b) as to procedures to be applied in connection with this Part,

    (c) enabling a single judge of the Court of Appeal to give leave to appeal under this Part or to exercise the power of the Court of Appeal under section 58(12).

(3) Nothing in this section is to be taken as affecting the generality of any enactment conferring powers to make rules of court.

74 Interpretation of Part 9

(1) In this Part –

    'programme service' has the meaning given by section 71(11),

    'publication' has the meaning given by section 71(11),

    'qualifying evidentiary ruling' is to be construed in accordance with section 62(2),

    'the relevant condition' is to be construed in accordance with section 63(2) and (3),

    'relevant programme' has the meaning given by section 71(11),

    'ruling' includes a decision, determination, direction, finding, notice, order, refusal, rejection or requirement,

    'the 1968 Act' means the Criminal Appeal Act 1968 (c. 19).

(2) Any reference in this Part (other than section 73(2)(c)) to a judge is a reference to a judge of the Crown Court.

(3) There is to be no right of appeal under this Part in respect of a ruling in relation to which the prosecution has previously informed the court of its intention to appeal under either section 58(4) or 62(5).

(4) Where a ruling relates to two or more offences but not all of those offences are the subject of an appeal under this Part, nothing in this Part is to be regarded as affecting the ruling so far as it relates to any offence which is not the subject of the appeal.

(5) Where two or more defendants are charged jointly with the same offence, the provisions of this Part are to apply as if the offence, so far as relating to each defendant, were a separate offence (so that, for example, any reference in this Part to a ruling which relates to one or more offences includes a ruling which relates to one or more of those separate offences).

(6) Subject to rules of court made under section 53(1) of the Supreme Court Act 1981 (c. 54) (power by rules to distribute business of Court of Appeal between its civil and criminal divisions) –

    (a) the jurisdiction of the Court of Appeal under this Part is to be exercised by the criminal division of that court, and

    (b) references in this Part to the Court of Appeal are to be construed as references to that division.

PART 10   RETRIAL FOR SERIOUS OFFENCES

Cases that may be retried

75 Cases that may be retried

(1) This Part applies where a person has been acquitted of a qualifying offence in proceedings –

    (a) on indictment in England and Wales,

    (b) on appeal against a conviction, verdict or finding in proceedings on indictment in England and Wales, or

    (c) on appeal from a decision on such an appeal.

(2) A person acquitted of an offence in proceedings mentioned in subsection (1) is treated for the purposes of that subsection as also acquitted of any qualifying offence of which he could have been convicted in the proceedings because of the first-mentioned offence being charged in the indictment, except an offence –

(a) of which he has been convicted,

(b) of which he has been found not guilty by reason of insanity, or

(c) in respect of which, in proceedings where he has been found to be under a disability (as defined by section 4 of the Criminal Procedure (Insanity) Act 1964 (c. 84)), a finding has been made that he did the act or made the omission charged against him.

(3) References in subsections (1) and (2) to a qualifying offence do not include references to an offence which, at the time of the acquittal, was the subject of an order under section 77(1) or (3).

(4) This Part also applies where a person has been acquitted, in proceedings elsewhere than in the United Kingdom, of an offence under the law of the place where the proceedings were held, if the commission of the offence as alleged would have amounted to or included the commission (in the United Kingdom or elsewhere) of a qualifying offence.

(5) Conduct punishable under the law in force elsewhere than in the United Kingdom is an offence under that law for the purposes of subsection (4), however it is described in that law.

(6) This Part applies whether the acquittal was before or after the passing of this Act.

(7) References in this Part to acquittal are to acquittal in circumstances within subsection (1) or (4).

(8) In this Part 'qualifying offence' means an offence listed in Part 1 of Schedule 5.

Application for retrial

76 Application to Court of Appeal

(1) A prosecutor may apply to the Court of Appeal for an order –

(a) quashing a person's acquittal in proceedings within section 75(1), and

(b) ordering him to be retried for the qualifying offence.

(2) A prosecutor may apply to the Court of Appeal, in the case of a person acquitted elsewhere than in the United Kingdom, for –

(a) a determination whether the acquittal is a bar to the person being tried in England and Wales for the qualifying offence, and

(b) if it is, an order that the acquittal is not to be a bar.

(3) A prosecutor may make an application under subsection (1) or (2) only with the written consent of the Director of Public Prosecutions.

(4) The Director of Public Prosecutions may give his consent only if satisfied that –

(a) there is evidence as respects which the requirements of section 78 appear to be met,

(b) it is in the public interest for the application to proceed, and

(c) any trial pursuant to an order on the application would not be inconsistent with obligations of the United Kingdom under Article 31 or 34 of the Treaty on European Union relating to the principle of *ne bis in idem*.

(5) Not more than one application may be made under subsection (1) or (2) in relation to an acquittal.

77 Determination by Court of Appeal

(1) On an application under section 76(1), the Court of Appeal –

   (a) if satisfied that the requirements of sections 78 and 79 are met, must make the order applied for;

   (b) otherwise, must dismiss the application.

(2) Subsections (3) and (4) apply to an application under section 76(2).

(3) Where the Court of Appeal determines that the acquittal is a bar to the person being tried for the qualifying offence, the court –

   (a) if satisfied that the requirements of sections 78 and 79 are met, must make the order applied for;

   (b) otherwise, must make a declaration to the effect that the acquittal is a bar to the person being tried for the offence.

(4) Where the Court of Appeal determines that the acquittal is not a bar to the person being tried for the qualifying offence, it must make a declaration to that effect.

78 New and compelling evidence

(1) The requirements of this section are met if there is new and compelling evidence against the acquitted person in relation to the qualifying offence.

(2) Evidence is new if it was not adduced in the proceedings in which the person was acquitted (nor, if those were appeal proceedings, in earlier proceedings to which the appeal related).

(3) Evidence is compelling if –

   (a) it is reliable,

   (b) it is substantial, and

   (c) in the context of the outstanding issues, it appears highly probative of the case against the acquitted person.

(4) The outstanding issues are the issues in dispute in the proceedings in which the person was acquitted and, if those were appeal proceedings, any other issues remaining in dispute from earlier proceedings to which the appeal related.

(5) For the purposes of this section, it is irrelevant whether any evidence would have been admissible in earlier proceedings against the acquitted person.

79 Interests of justice

(1) The requirements of this section are met if in all the circumstances it is in the interests of justice for the court to make the order under section 77.

(2) That question is to be determined having regard in particular to –

   (a) whether existing circumstances make a fair trial unlikely;

   (b) for the purposes of that question and otherwise, the length of time since the qualifying offence was allegedly committed;

   (c) whether it is likely that the new evidence would have been adduced in the earlier proceedings against the acquitted person but for a failure by an officer or by a prosecutor to act with due diligence or expedition;

   (d) whether, since those proceedings or, if later, since the commencement of this Part, any officer or prosecutor has failed to act with due diligence or expedition.

(3) In subsection (2) references to an officer or prosecutor include references to a person charged with corresponding duties under the law in force elsewhere than in England and Wales.

(4) Where the earlier prosecution was conducted by a person other than a prosecutor, subsection (2)(c) applies in relation to that person as well as in relation to a prosecutor.

80 Procedure and evidence

(1) A prosecutor who wishes to make an application under section 76(1) or (2) must give notice of the application to the Court of Appeal.

(2) Within two days beginning with the day on which any such notice is given, notice of the application must be served by the prosecutor on the person to whom the application relates, charging him with the offence to which it relates or, if he has been charged with it in accordance with section 87(4), stating that he has been so charged.

(3) Subsection (2) applies whether the person to whom the application relates is in the United Kingdom or elsewhere, but the Court of Appeal may, on application by the prosecutor, extend the time for service under that subsection if it considers it necessary to do so because of that person's absence from the United Kingdom.

(4) The Court of Appeal must consider the application at a hearing.

(5) The person to whom the application relates –

(a) is entitled to be present at the hearing, although he may be in custody, unless he is in custody elsewhere than in England and Wales or Northern Ireland, and

(b) is entitled to be represented at the hearing, whether he is present or not.

(6) For the purposes of the application, the Court of Appeal may, if it thinks it necessary or expedient in the interests of justice –

(a) order the production of any document, exhibit or other thing, the production of which appears to the court to be necessary for the determination of the application, and

(b) order any witness who would be a compellable witness in proceedings pursuant to an order or declaration made on the application to attend for examination and be examined before the court.

(7) The Court of Appeal may at one hearing consider more than one application (whether or not relating to the same person), but only if the offences concerned could be tried on the same indictment.

81 Appeals

(1) The Criminal Appeal Act 1968 (c. 19) is amended as follows.

(2) In section 33 (right of appeal to House of Lords), after subsection (1A) there is inserted –

'(1B) An appeal lies to the House of Lords, at the instance of the acquitted person or the prosecutor, from any decision of the Court of Appeal on an application under section 76(1) or (2) of the Criminal Justice Act 2003 (retrial for serious offences).'

(3) At the end of that section there is inserted –

'(4) In relation to an appeal under subsection (1B), references in this Part to a defendant are references to the acquitted person.'

(4) In section 34(2) (extension of time for leave to appeal), after 'defendant' there is inserted 'or, in the case of an appeal under section 33(1B), by the prosecutor'.

(5) In section 38 (presence of defendant at hearing), for 'has been convicted of an offence and' substitute 'has been convicted of an offence, or in whose case an order under section 77 of the Criminal Justice Act 2003 or a declaration under section 77(4) of that Act has been made, and who'.

82 Restrictions on publication in the interests of justice

(1) Where it appears to the Court of Appeal that the inclusion of any matter in a publication would give rise to a substantial risk of prejudice to the administration of justice in a retrial, the court may order that the matter is not to be included in any publication while the order has effect.

(2) In subsection (1) 'retrial' means the trial of an acquitted person for a qualifying offence pursuant to any order made or that may be made under section 77.

(3) The court may make an order under this section only if it appears to it necessary in the interests of justice to do so.

(4) An order under this section may apply to a matter which has been included in a publication published before the order takes effect, but such an order –

    (a)   applies only to the later inclusion of the matter in a publication (whether directly or by inclusion of the earlier publication), and

    (b)   does not otherwise affect the earlier publication.

(5) After notice of an application has been given under section 80(1) relating to the acquitted person and the qualifying offence, the court may make an order under this section only –

    (a)   of its own motion, or

    (b)   on the application of the Director of Public Prosecutions.

(6) Before such notice has been given, an order under this section –

    (a)   may be made only on the application of the Director of Public Prosecutions, and

    (b)   may not be made unless, since the acquittal concerned, an investigation of the commission by the acquitted person of the qualifying offence has been commenced by officers.

(7) The court may at any time, of its own motion or on an application made by the Director of Public Prosecutions or the acquitted person, vary or revoke an order under this section.

(8) Any order made under this section before notice of an application has been given under section 80(1) relating to the acquitted person and the qualifying offence must specify the time when it ceases to have effect.

(9) An order under this section which is made or has effect after such notice has been given ceases to have effect, unless it specifies an earlier time –

    (a)   when there is no longer any step that could be taken which would lead to the acquitted person being tried pursuant to an order made on the application, or

    (b)   if he is tried pursuant to such an order, at the conclusion of the trial.

(10) Nothing in this section affects any prohibition or restriction by virtue of any other enactment on the inclusion of any matter in a publication or any power, under an enactment or otherwise, to impose such a prohibition or restriction.

(11) In this section –

    'programme service' has the same meaning as in the Broadcasting Act 1990 (c. 42),

    'publication' includes any speech, writing, relevant programme or other communication in whatever form, which is addressed to the public at large or any section of the public (and for this purpose every relevant programme is to be taken to be so addressed), but does not include an indictment or other document prepared for use in particular legal proceedings,

    'relevant programme' means a programme included in a programme service.

83 Offences in connection with publication restrictions

(1) This section applies if –

    (a)   an order under section 82 is made, whether in England and Wales or Northern Ireland, and

    (b)   while the order has effect, any matter is included in a publication, in any part of the United Kingdom, in contravention of the order.

(2) Where the publication is a newspaper or periodical, any proprietor, editor or publisher of the newspaper or periodical is guilty of an offence.

(3) Where the publication is a relevant programme –

(a) any body corporate or Scottish partnership engaged in providing the programme service in which the programme is included, and

(b) any person having functions in relation to the programme corresponding to those of an editor of a newspaper,

is guilty of an offence.

(4) In the case of any other publication, any person publishing it is guilty of an offence.

(5) If an offence under this section committed by a body corporate is proved –

(a) to have been committed with the consent or connivance of, or

(b) to be attributable to any neglect on the part of,

an officer, the officer as well as the body corporate is guilty of the offence and liable to be proceeded against and punished accordingly.

(6) In subsection (5), 'officer' means a director, manager, secretary or other similar officer of the body, or a person purporting to act in any such capacity.

(7) If the affairs of a body corporate are managed by its members, 'director' in subsection (6) means a member of that body.

(8) Where an offence under this section is committed by a Scottish partnership and is proved to have been committed with the consent or connivance of a partner, he as well as the partnership shall be guilty of the offence and shall be liable to be proceeded against and punished accordingly.

(9) A person guilty of an offence under this section is liable on summary conviction to a fine not exceeding level 5 on the standard scale.

(10) Proceedings for an offence under this section may not be instituted –

(a) in England and Wales otherwise than by or with the consent of the Attorney General, or

(b) in Northern Ireland otherwise than by or with the consent of –

(i)   before the relevant date, the Attorney General for Northern Ireland, or

(ii) on or after the relevant date, the Director of Public Prosecutions for Northern Ireland.

(11) In subsection (10) 'the relevant date' means the date on which section 22(1) of the Justice (Northern Ireland) Act 2002 (c. 26) comes into force.

Retrial

84 Retrial

(1) Where a person –

(a) is tried pursuant to an order under section 77(1), or

(b) is tried on indictment pursuant to an order under section 77(3),

the trial must be on an indictment preferred by direction of the Court of Appeal.

(2) After the end of 2 months after the date of the order, the person may not be arraigned on an indictment preferred in pursuance of such a direction unless the Court of Appeal gives leave.

(3) The Court of Appeal must not give leave unless satisfied that –

(a) the prosecutor has acted with due expedition, and

(b) there is a good and sufficient cause for trial despite the lapse of time since the order under section 77.

(4) Where the person may not be arraigned without leave, he may apply to the Court of Appeal to set aside the order and –

(a) for any direction required for restoring an earlier judgment and verdict of acquittal of the qualifying offence, or

(b) in the case of a person acquitted elsewhere than in the United Kingdom, for a declaration to the effect that the acquittal is a bar to his being tried for the qualifying offence.

(5) An indictment under subsection (1) may relate to more than one offence, or more than one person, and may relate to an offence which, or a person who, is not the subject of an order or declaration under section 77.

(6) Evidence given at a trial pursuant to an order under section 77(1) or (3) must be given orally if it was given orally at the original trial, unless –

(a) all the parties to the trial agree otherwise,

(b) section 116 applies, or

(c) the witness is unavailable to give evidence, otherwise than as mentioned in subsection (2) of that section, and section 114(1)(d) applies.

(7) At a trial pursuant to an order under section 77(1), paragraph 5 of Schedule 3 to the Crime and Disorder Act 1998 (c. 37) (use of depositions) does not apply to a deposition read as evidence at the original trial.

Investigations

85 Authorisation of investigations

(1) This section applies to the investigation of the commission of a qualifying offence by a person –

(a) acquitted in proceedings within section 75(1) of the qualifying offence, or

(b) acquitted elsewhere than in the United Kingdom of an offence the commission of which as alleged would have amounted to or included the commission (in the United Kingdom or elsewhere) of the qualifying offence.

(2) Subject to section 86, an officer may not do anything within subsection (3) for the purposes of such an investigation unless the Director of Public Prosecutions –

(a) has certified that in his opinion the acquittal would not be a bar to the trial of the acquitted person in England and Wales for the qualifying offence, or

(b) has given his written consent to the investigation (whether before or after the start of the investigation).

(3) The officer may not, either with or without the consent of the acquitted person –

(a) arrest or question him,

(b) search him or premises owned or occupied by him,

(c) search a vehicle owned by him or anything in or on such a vehicle,

(d) seize anything in his possession, or

(e) take his fingerprints or take a sample from him.

(4) The Director of Public Prosecutions may only give his consent on a written application, and such an application may be made only by an officer who –

(a) if he is an officer of the metropolitan police force or the City of London police force, is of the rank of commander or above, or

(b) in any other case, is of the rank of assistant chief constable or above.

(5) An officer may make an application under subsection (4) only if –

(a) he is satisfied that new evidence has been obtained which would be relevant to an application under section 76(1) or (2) in respect of the qualifying offence to which the investigation relates, or

(b) he has reasonable grounds for believing that such new evidence is likely to be obtained as a result of the investigation.

(6) The Director of Public Prosecutions may not give his consent unless satisfied that –

(a) there is, or there is likely as a result of the investigation to be, sufficient new evidence to warrant the conduct of the investigation, and

(b) it is in the public interest for the investigation to proceed.

(7) In giving his consent, the Director of Public Prosecutions may recommend that the investigation be conducted otherwise than by officers of a specified police force or specified team of customs and excise officers.

86 Urgent investigative steps

(1) Section 85 does not prevent an officer from taking any action for the purposes of an investigation if –

(a) the action is necessary as a matter of urgency to prevent the investigation being substantially and irrevocably prejudiced,

(b) the requirements of subsection (2) are met, and

(c) either –

    (i) the action is authorised under subsection (3), or

    (ii) the requirements of subsection (5) are met.

(2) The requirements of this subsection are met if –

(a) there has been no undue delay in applying for consent under section 85(2),

(b) that consent has not been refused, and

(c) taking into account the urgency of the situation, it is not reasonably practicable to obtain that consent before taking the action.

(3) An officer of the rank of superintendent or above may authorise the action if –

(a) he is satisfied that new evidence has been obtained which would be relevant to an application under section 76(1) or (2) in respect of the qualifying offence to which the investigation relates, or

(b) he has reasonable grounds for believing that such new evidence is likely to be obtained as a result of the investigation.

(4) An authorisation under subsection (3) must –

(a) if reasonably practicable, be given in writing;

(b) otherwise, be recorded in writing by the officer giving it as soon as is reasonably practicable.

(5) The requirements of this subsection are met if –

(a) there has been no undue delay in applying for authorisation under subsection (3),

(b) that authorisation has not been refused, and

(c) taking into account the urgency of the situation, it is not reasonably practicable to obtain that authorisation before taking the action.

(6) Where the requirements of subsection (5) are met, the action is nevertheless to be treated as having been unlawful unless, as soon as reasonably practicable after the action is taken, an officer of the rank of superintendent or above certifies in writing that he is satisfied that, when the action was taken –

(a) new evidence had been obtained which would be relevant to an application under section 76(1) or (2) in respect of the qualifying offence to which the investigation relates, or

(b) the officer who took the action had reasonable grounds for believing that such new evidence was likely to be obtained as a result of the investigation.

Arrest, custody and bail

87 Arrest and charge

(1) Where section 85 applies to the investigation of the commission of an offence by any person and no certification has been given under subsection (2) of that section –

   (a) a justice of the peace may issue a warrant to arrest that person for that offence only if satisfied by written information that new evidence has been obtained which would be relevant to an application under section 76(1) or (2) in respect of the commission by that person of that offence, and

   (b) that person may not be arrested for that offence except under a warrant so issued.

(2) Subsection (1) does not affect section 89(3)(b) or 91(3), or any other power to arrest a person, or to issue a warrant for the arrest of a person, otherwise than for an offence.

(3) Part 4 of the 1984 Act (detention) applies as follows where a person –

   (a) is arrested for an offence under a warrant issued in accordance with subsection (1)(a), or

   (b) having been so arrested, is subsequently treated under section 34(7) of that Act as arrested for that offence.

(4) For the purposes of that Part there is sufficient evidence to charge the person with the offence for which he has been arrested if, and only if, an officer of the rank of superintendent or above (who has not been directly involved in the investigation) is of the opinion that the evidence available or known to him is sufficient for the case to be referred to a prosecutor to consider whether consent should be sought for an application in respect of that person under section 76.

(5) For the purposes of that Part it is the duty of the custody officer at each police station where the person is detained to make available or known to an officer at that police station of the rank of superintendent or above any evidence which it appears to him may be relevant to an application under section 76(1) or (2) in respect of the offence for which the person has been arrested, and to do so as soon as practicable –

   (a) after the evidence becomes available or known to him, or

   (b) if later, after he forms that view.

(6) Section 37 of that Act (including any provision of that section as applied by section 40(8) of that Act) has effect subject to the following modifications –

   (a) in subsection (1) –

      (i) for 'determine whether he has before him' there is substituted 'request an officer of the rank of superintendent or above (who has not been directly involved in the investigation) to determine, in accordance with section 87(4) of the Criminal Justice Act 2003, whether there is';

      (ii) for 'him to do so' there is substituted 'that determination to be made';

   (b) in subsection (2) –

      (i) for the words from 'custody officer determines' to 'before him' there is substituted 'officer determines that there is not such sufficient evidence';

      (ii) the word 'custody' is omitted from the second place where it occurs;

   (c) in subsection (3) –

      (i) the word 'custody' is omitted;

      (ii) after 'may' there is inserted 'direct the custody officer to';

   (d) in subsection (7) for the words from 'the custody officer' to the end of that subsection there is substituted 'an officer of the rank of superintendent or above (who has not been directly involved in the investigation) determines, in accordance with section 87(4) of the Criminal Justice Act 2003, that there is sufficient evidence to charge the person arrested with the offence for which he was arrested, the person arrested shall be charged.';

    (e) subsections (7A), (7B) and (8) do not apply;

    (f) after subsection (10) there is inserted –

        '(10A) The officer who is requested by the custody officer to make a determination under subsection (1) above shall make that determination as soon as practicable after the request is made.'.

(7) Section 40 of that Act has effect as if in subsections (8) and (9) of that section after '(6)' there were inserted 'and (10A)'.

(8) Section 42 of that Act has effect as if in subsection (1) of that section for the words from 'who' to 'detained' there were substituted '(who has not been directly involved in the investigation)'.

88 Bail and custody before application

(1) In relation to a person charged in accordance with section 87(4) –

    (a) section 38 of the 1984 Act (including any provision of that section as applied by section 40(10) of that Act) has effect as if, in subsection (1), for 'either on bail or without bail' there were substituted 'on bail',

    (b) section 47(3) of that Act does not apply and references in section 38 of that Act to bail are references to bail subject to a duty to appear before the Crown Court at such place as the custody officer may appoint and at such time, not later than 24 hours after the person is released, as that officer may appoint, and

    (c) section 43B of the Magistrates' Courts Act 1980 (c. 43) does not apply.

(2) Where such a person is, after being charged –

    (a) kept in police detention, or

    (b) detained by a local authority in pursuance of arrangements made under section 38(6) of the 1984 Act,

he must be brought before the Crown Court as soon as practicable and, in any event, not more than 24 hours after he is charged, and section 46 of the 1984 Act does not apply.

(3) For the purpose of calculating the period referred to in subsection (1) or (2), the following are to be disregarded –

    (a) Sunday,

    (b) Christmas Day,

    (c) Good Friday, and

    (d) any day which is a bank holiday under the Banking and Financial Dealings Act 1971 (c. 80) in the part of the United Kingdom where the person is to appear before the Crown Court as mentioned in subsection (1) or, where subsection (2) applies, is for the time being detained.

(4) Where a person appears or is brought before the Crown Court in accordance with subsection (1) or (2), the Crown Court may either –

    (a) grant bail for the person to appear, if notice of an application is served on him under section 80(2), before the Court of Appeal at the hearing of that application, or

    (b) remand the person in custody to be brought before the Crown Court under section 89(2).

(5) If the Crown Court grants bail under subsection (4), it may revoke bail and remand the person in custody as referred to in subsection (4)(b).

(6) In subsection (7) the 'relevant period', in relation to a person granted bail or remanded in custody under subsection (4), means –

    (a) the period of 42 days beginning with the day on which he is granted bail or remanded in custody under that subsection, or

    (b) that period as extended or further extended under subsection (8).

(7) If at the end of the relevant period no notice of an application under section 76(1) or (2) in relation to the person has been given under section 80(1), the person –

    (a) if on bail subject to a duty to appear as mentioned in subsection (4)(a), ceases to be subject to that duty and to any conditions of that bail, and

    (b) if in custody on remand under subsection (4)(b) or (5), must be released immediately without bail.

(8) The Crown Court may, on the application of a prosecutor, extend or further extend the period mentioned in subsection (6)(a) until a specified date, but only if satisfied that –

    (a) the need for the extension is due to some good and sufficient cause, and

    (b) the prosecutor has acted with all due diligence and expedition.

89 Bail and custody before hearing

(1) This section applies where notice of an application is given under section 80(1).

(2) If the person to whom the application relates is in custody under section 88(4)(b) or (5), he must be brought before the Crown Court as soon as practicable and, in any event, within 48 hours after the notice is given.

(3) If that person is not in custody under section 88(4)(b) or (5), the Crown Court may, on application by the prosecutor –

    (a) issue a summons requiring the person to appear before the Court of Appeal at the hearing of the application, or

    (b) issue a warrant for the person's arrest,

and a warrant under paragraph (b) may be issued at any time even though a summons has previously been issued.

(4) Where a summons is issued under subsection (3)(a), the time and place at which the person must appear may be specified either –

    (a) in the summons, or

    (b) in a subsequent direction of the Crown Court.

(5) The time or place specified may be varied from time to time by a direction of the Crown Court.

(6) A person arrested under a warrant under subsection (3)(b) must be brought before the Crown Court as soon as practicable and in any event within 48 hours after his arrest, and section 81(5) of the Supreme Court Act 1981 (c. 54) does not apply.

(7) If a person is brought before the Crown Court under subsection (2) or (6) the court must either –

    (a) remand him in custody to be brought before the Court of Appeal at the hearing of the application, or

    (b) grant bail for him to appear before the Court of Appeal at the hearing.

(8) If bail is granted under subsection (7)(b), the Crown Court may revoke the bail and remand the person in custody as referred to in subsection (7)(a).

(9) For the purpose of calculating the period referred to in subsection (2) or (6), the following are to be disregarded –

    (a) Sunday,

    (b) Christmas Day,

    (c) Good Friday, and

    (d) any day which is a bank holiday under the Banking and Financial Dealings Act 1971 (c. 80) in the part of the United Kingdom where the person is for the time being detained.

90 Bail and custody during and after hearing

(1) The Court of Appeal may, at any adjournment of the hearing of an application under section 76(1) or (2) –

    (a)   remand the person to whom the application relates on bail, or

    (b)   remand him in custody.

(2) At a hearing at which the Court of Appeal –

    (a)   makes an order under section 77,

    (b)   makes a declaration under subsection (4) of that section, or

    (c)   dismisses the application or makes a declaration under subsection (3) of that section, if it also gives the prosecutor leave to appeal against its decision or the prosecutor gives notice that he intends to apply for such leave,

the court may make such order as it sees fit for the custody or bail of the acquitted person pending trial pursuant to the order or declaration, or pending determination of the appeal.

(3) For the purpose of subsection (2), the determination of an appeal is pending –

    (a)   until any application for leave to appeal is disposed of, or the time within which it must be made expires;

    (b)   if leave to appeal is granted, until the appeal is disposed of.

(4) Section 4 of the Bail Act 1976 (c. 63) applies in relation to the grant of bail under this section as if in subsection (2) the reference to the Crown Court included a reference to the Court of Appeal.

(5) The court may at any time, as it sees fit –

    (a)   revoke bail granted under this section and remand the person in custody, or

    (b)   vary an order under subsection (2).

91 Revocation of bail

(1) Where –

    (a)   a court revokes a person's bail under this Part, and

    (b)   that person is not before the court when his bail is revoked,

the court must order him to surrender himself forthwith to the custody of the court.

(2) Where a person surrenders himself into the custody of the court in compliance with an order under subsection (1), the court must remand him in custody.

(3) A person who has been ordered to surrender to custody under subsection (1) may be arrested without a warrant by an officer if he fails without reasonable cause to surrender to custody in accordance with the order.

(4) A person arrested under subsection (3) must be brought as soon as practicable, and, in any event, not more than 24 hours after he is arrested, before the court and the court must remand him in custody.

(5) For the purpose of calculating the period referred to in subsection (4), the following are to be disregarded –

    (a)   Sunday,

    (b)   Christmas Day,

    (c)   Good Friday,

    (d)   any day which is a bank holiday under the Banking and Financial Dealings Act 1971 (c. 80) in the part of the United Kingdom where the person is for the time being detained.

Part 10: supplementary

92 Functions of the DPP

(1) Section 1(7) of the Prosecution of Offences Act 1985 (c. 23) (DPP's functions exercisable by Crown Prosecutor) does not apply to the provisions of this Part other than section 85(2)(a).

(2) In the absence of the Director of Public Prosecutions, his functions under those provisions may be exercised by a person authorised by him.

(3) An authorisation under subsection (2) –

(a) may relate to a specified person or to persons of a specified description, and

(b) may be general or relate to a specified function or specified circumstances.

93 Rules of court

(1) Rules of court may make such provision as appears to the authority making them to be necessary or expedient for the purposes of this Part.

(2) Without limiting subsection (1), rules of court may in particular make provision as to procedures to be applied in connection with sections 76 to 82, 84 and 88 to 90.

(3) Nothing in this section is to be taken as affecting the generality of any enactment conferring power to make rules of court.

94 Armed Forces: Part 10

(1) Section 31 of the Armed Forces Act 2001 (c. 19) (provision in consequence of enactments relating to criminal justice) applies to an enactment contained in this Part so far as relating to matters not specified in subsection (2) of that section as it applies to a criminal justice enactment.

(2) The power under that section to make provision equivalent to that made in relation to qualifying offences by an enactment contained in this Part (with or without modifications) includes power to make such provision in relation to such service offences as the Secretary of State thinks fit.

(3) In subsection (2) 'service offence' means an offence under the Army Act 1955 (3 & 4 Eliz. 2 c. 18), the Air Force Act 1955 (3 & 4 Eliz. 2 c. 19) or the Naval Discipline Act 1957 (c. 53).

95 Interpretation of Part 10

(1) In this Part –

'the 1984 Act' means the Police and Criminal Evidence Act 1984 (c. 60),

'acquittal' and related expressions are to be read in accordance with section 75(7),

'customs and excise officer' means an officer as defined by section 1(1) of the Customs and Excise Management Act 1979 (c. 2), or a person to whom section 8(2) of that Act applies,

'new evidence' is to be read in accordance with section 78(2),

'officer', except in section 83, means an officer of a police force or a customs and excise officer,

'police force' has the meaning given by section 3(3) of the Prosecution of Offences Act 1985 (c. 23),

'prosecutor' means an individual or body charged with duties to conduct criminal prosecutions,

'qualifying offence' has the meaning given by section 75(8).

(2) Subject to rules of court made under section 53(1) of the Supreme Court Act 1981 (c. 54) (power by rules to distribute business of Court of Appeal between its civil and criminal divisions) –

(a) the jurisdiction of the Court of Appeal under this Part is to be exercised by the criminal division of that court, and

    (b) references in this Part to the Court of Appeal are to be construed as references to that division.

(3) References in this Part to an officer of a specified rank or above are, in the case of a customs and excise officer, references to an officer of such description as –

    (a) appears to the Commissioners of Customs and Excise to comprise officers of equivalent rank or above, and

    (b) is specified by the Commissioners for the purposes of the provision concerned.

96 Application of Part 10 to Northern Ireland

(1) In its application to Northern Ireland this Part is to have effect subject to the modifications in this section.

(2) In sections 75(1)(a) and (b), 76(2)(a), 79(3) and 85(2)(a) for 'England and Wales' substitute 'Northern Ireland'.

(3) For section 75(2)(c) substitute –

    '(c) in respect of which, in proceedings where he has been found to be unfit to be tried in accordance with Article 49 of the Mental Health (Northern Ireland) Order 1986 (S.I. 1986/595 (N.I. 4)), a finding has been made that he did the act or made the omission charged against him.'

(4) In section 75(8) for 'Part 1' substitute 'Part 2'.

(5) In section 81(1) for 'Criminal Appeal Act 1968 (c. 19)' substitute 'Criminal Appeal (Northern Ireland) Act 1980 (c. 47)'.

(6) In section 81(2) –

    (a) for '33' substitute '31', and

    (b) for 'An' substitute 'Subject to the provisions of this Part of this Act, an'.

(7) In section 81(4) –

    (a) for '34(2)' substitute '32(2)', and

    (b) for '33(1B)' substitute '31(1B)'.

(8) In section 82(10) after 'enactment' in each place insert '(including any provision of Northern Ireland legislation)'.

(9) In section 84(1) and (2) for 'preferred' substitute 'presented'.

(10) Section 84(6) has effect –

    (a) as if any reference to a provision of Part 11 were a reference to any corresponding provision contained in an Order in Council to which section 334(1) applies, at any time when such corresponding provision is in force;

    (b) at any other time, with the omission of paragraphs (b) and (c).

(11) After section 84(6) insert –

    '(6A) Article 29 of the Legal Aid, Advice and Assistance (Northern Ireland) Order 1981 (S.I. 1981/228 (N.I. 8)) applies in the case of a person who is to be tried in accordance with subsection (1) as if –

        (a) he had been returned for trial for the offence in question, and

        (b) the reference in paragraph (2)(a) of that Article to a magistrates' court included a reference to the Court of Appeal.'

(12) In section 87 –

    (a) in subsection (3), for 'Part 4 of the 1984 Act' substitute 'Part 5 of the Police and Criminal Evidence (Northern Ireland) Order 1989 (S.I. 1989/1341 (N.I. 12)) ('the 1989 Order')',

    (b) in paragraph (b) of that subsection, for 'section 34(7) of that Act' substitute 'Article 35(8) of that Order',

    (c) in subsection (6) –

(i)   for the words from the beginning to '40(8) of that Act)' substitute 'Article 38 of that Order (including any provision of that Article as applied by Article 41(8) of that Order)',

(ii) for 'subsection' in each place substitute 'paragraph',

(iii) in paragraph (e), for 'subsections (7A), (7B) and (8)' substitute 'paragraph (8)', and

(iv) in paragraph (f), in the inserted paragraph (10A) omit 'above',

(d)   for subsection (7) substitute –

'(7)   Article 41 of that Order has effect as if in paragraphs (8) and (9) of that Article after "(6)" there were inserted "and (10A).".',

(e)   in subsection (8) –

(i)   for 'Section 42 of that Act' substitute 'Article 43 of that Order', and

(ii) for 'subsection (1) of that section' substitute 'paragraph (1) of that Article'.

(13) For section 88(1) substitute –

'(1)   In relation to a person charged in accordance with section 87(4) –

(a)   Article 39 of the 1989 Order (including any provision of that Article as applied by Article 41(10) of that Order) has effect as if, in paragraph (1), for "either on bail or without bail" there were substituted "on bail",

(b)   Article 48 of that Order has effect as if for paragraphs (1) to (11) there were substituted –

"(1)   A person who is released on bail shall be subject to a duty to appear before the Crown Court at such place as the custody officer may appoint and at such time, not later than 24 hours after the person is released, as that officer may appoint.

(2)   The custody officer may require a person who is to be released on bail to enter into a recognisance conditioned upon his subsequent appearance before the Crown Court in accordance with paragraph (1).

(3)   A recognisance under paragraph (2) may be taken before the custody officer.", and

(c)   Article 132A of the Magistrates' Courts (Northern Ireland) Order 1981 (S.I. 1981/1675 (N.I. 26)) does not apply.'

(14) In section 88(2) –

(a)   for paragraph (b) substitute –

'(b)   detained in a place of safety in pursuance of arrangements made under Article 39(6) of the 1989 Order,', and

(b)   for 'section 46 of the 1984 Act' substitute 'Article 47 of the 1989 Order'.

(15) In section 89(6) for 'section 81(5) of the Supreme Court Act 1981 (c. 54)' substitute 'section 51(8) of the Judicature (Northern Ireland) Act 1978 (c. 23)'.

(16) For section 90(4) substitute –

'(4)   The court may at any time, as it sees fit, vary the conditions of bail granted under this section.'

(17) In section 92(1) for the words from the beginning to 'does' substitute 'Sections 30(4) and 36 of the Justice (Northern Ireland) Act 2002 (c. 26) do'.

(18) Until the coming into force of section 36 of that Act of 2002 the reference to that section in subsection (17) is to be read as a reference to Article 4(8) of the Prosecution of Offences (Northern Ireland) Order 1972 (S.I. 1972/538 (N.I. 1)).

(19) In section 93(2) for 'the Criminal Appeal Rules and the Crown Court Rules' substitute 'rules under section 55 of the Judicature (Northern Ireland) Act 1978 and Crown Court Rules'.

(20) In section 93(3) after 'enactment' insert '(including any provision of Northern Ireland legislation)'.

(21) In section 95(1) for the definition of 'police force' substitute –

'"police force" means –

(a) the Police Service of Northern Ireland or the Police Service of Northern Ireland Reserve,

(b) the Ministry of Defence Police,

(c) any body of constables appointed under Article 19 of the Airports (Northern Ireland) Order 1994 (S.I. 1994/426 (N.I. 1)), or

(d) any body of special constables appointed in Northern Ireland under section 79 of the Harbours, Docks and Piers Clauses Act 1847 (c. 27) or section 57 of the Civil Aviation Act 1982 (c. 16),'.

(22) Omit section 95(2).

97 Application of Criminal Appeal Acts to proceedings under Part 10

Subject to the provisions of this Part, the Secretary of State may make an order containing provision, in relation to proceedings before the Court of Appeal under this Part, which corresponds to any provision, in relation to appeals or other proceedings before that court, which is contained in the Criminal Appeal Act 1968 (c. 19) or the Criminal Appeal (Northern Ireland) Act 1980 (c. 47) (subject to any specified modifications).

PART 11   EVIDENCE

CHAPTER 1   EVIDENCE OF BAD CHARACTER

Introductory

98 'Bad character'

References in this Chapter to evidence of a person's 'bad character' are to evidence of, or of a disposition towards, misconduct on his part, other than evidence which –

(a) has to do with the alleged facts of the offence with which the defendant is charged, or

(b) is evidence of misconduct in connection with the investigation or prosecution of that offence.

99 Abolition of common law rules

(1) The common law rules governing the admissibility of evidence of bad character in criminal proceedings are abolished.

(2) Subsection (1) is subject to section 118(1) in so far as it preserves the rule under which in criminal proceedings a person's reputation is admissible for the purposes of proving his bad character.

Persons other than defendants

100 Non-defendant's bad character

(1) In criminal proceedings evidence of the bad character of a person other than the defendant is admissible if and only if –

(a) it is important explanatory evidence,

(b) it has substantial probative value in relation to a matter which –

> (i)   is a matter in issue in the proceedings, and
> (ii) is of substantial importance in the context of the case as a whole, or

(c) all parties to the proceedings agree to the evidence being admissible.

(2) For the purposes of subsection (1)(a) evidence is important explanatory evidence if –

(a) without it, the court or jury would find it impossible or difficult properly to understand other evidence in the case, and

(b) its value for understanding the case as a whole is substantial.

(3) In assessing the probative value of evidence for the purposes of subsection (1)(b) the court must have regard to the following factors (and to any others it considers relevant) –

(a) the nature and number of the events, or other things, to which the evidence relates;

(b) when those events or things are alleged to have happened or existed;

(c) where –

> (i)   the evidence is evidence of a person's misconduct, and
> (ii) it is suggested that the evidence has probative value by reason of similarity between that misconduct and other alleged misconduct,

the nature and extent of the similarities and the dissimilarities between each of the alleged instances of misconduct;

(d) where –

> (i)   the evidence is evidence of a person's misconduct,
> (ii) it is suggested that that person is also responsible for the misconduct charged, and
> (iii) the identity of the person responsible for the misconduct charged is disputed,

the extent to which the evidence shows or tends to show that the same person was responsible each time.

(4) Except where subsection (1)(c) applies, evidence of the bad character of a person other than the defendant must not be given without leave of the court.

Defendants

101 Defendant's bad character

(1) In criminal proceedings evidence of the defendant's bad character is admissible if, but only if –

(a) all parties to the proceedings agree to the evidence being admissible,

(b) the evidence is adduced by the defendant himself or is given in answer to a question asked by him in cross-examination and intended to elicit it,

(c) it is important explanatory evidence,

(d) it is relevant to an important matter in issue between the defendant and the prosecution,

(e) it has substantial probative value in relation to an important matter in issue between the defendant and a co-defendant,

(f) it is evidence to correct a false impression given by the defendant, or

(g) the defendant has made an attack on another person's character.

(2) Sections 102 to 106 contain provision supplementing subsection (1).

(3) The court must not admit evidence under subsection (1)(d) or (g) if, on an application by the defendant to exclude it, it appears to the court that the admission of the evidence would have such an adverse effect on the fairness of the proceedings that the court ought not to admit it.

(4) On an application to exclude evidence under subsection (3) the court must have regard, in particular, to the length of time between the matters to which that evidence relates and the matters which form the subject of the offence charged.

102 'Important explanatory evidence'

For the purposes of section 101(1)(c) evidence is important explanatory evidence if –

   (a) without it, the court or jury would find it impossible or difficult properly to understand other evidence in the case, and
   (b) its value for understanding the case as a whole is substantial.

103 'Matter in issue between the defendant and the prosecution'

(1) For the purposes of section 101(1)(d) the matters in issue between the defendant and the prosecution include –

   (a) the question whether the defendant has a propensity to commit offences of the kind with which he is charged, except where his having such a propensity makes it no more likely that he is guilty of the offence;
   (b) the question whether the defendant has a propensity to be untruthful, except where it is not suggested that the defendant's case is untruthful in any respect.

(2) Where subsection (1)(a) applies, a defendant's propensity to commit offences of the kind with which he is charged may (without prejudice to any other way of doing so) be established by evidence that he has been convicted of –

   (a) an offence of the same description as the one with which he is charged, or
   (b) an offence of the same category as the one with which he is charged.

(3) Subsection (2) does not apply in the case of a particular defendant if the court is satisfied, by reason of the length of time since the conviction or for any other reason, that it would be unjust for it to apply in his case.

(4) For the purposes of subsection (2) –

   (a) two offences are of the same description as each other if the statement of the offence in a written charge or indictment would, in each case, be in the same terms;
   (b) two offences are of the same category as each other if they belong to the same category of offences prescribed for the purposes of this section by an order made by the Secretary of State.

(5) A category prescribed by an order under subsection (4)(b) must consist of offences of the same type.

(6) Only prosecution evidence is admissible under section 101(1)(d).

104 'Matter in issue between the defendant and a co-defendant'

(1) Evidence which is relevant to the question whether the defendant has a propensity to be untruthful is admissible on that basis under section 101(1)(e) only if the nature or conduct of his defence is such as to undermine the co-defendant's defence.

(2) Only evidence –

   (a) which is to be (or has been) adduced by the co-defendant, or
   (b) which a witness is to be invited to give (or has given) in cross-examination by the co-defendant,

is admissible under section 101(1)(e).

105 'Evidence to correct a false impression'

(1) For the purposes of section 101(1)(f) –

   (a) the defendant gives a false impression if he is responsible for the making of an express or implied assertion which is apt to give the court or jury a false or misleading impression about the defendant;

(b)   evidence to correct such an impression is evidence which has probative value in correcting it.

(2) A defendant is treated as being responsible for the making of an assertion if –

(a)   the assertion is made by the defendant in the proceedings (whether or not in evidence given by him),

(b)   the assertion was made by the defendant –

    (i)   on being questioned under caution, before charge, about the offence with which he is charged, or

    (ii)   on being charged with the offence or officially informed that he might be prosecuted for it,

and evidence of the assertion is given in the proceedings,

(c)   the assertion is made by a witness called by the defendant,

(d)   the assertion is made by any witness in cross-examination in response to a question asked by the defendant that is intended to elicit it, or is likely to do so, or

(e)   the assertion was made by any person out of court, and the defendant adduces evidence of it in the proceedings.

(3) A defendant who would otherwise be treated as responsible for the making of an assertion shall not be so treated if, or to the extent that, he withdraws it or disassociates himself from it.

(4) Where it appears to the court that a defendant, by means of his conduct (other than the giving of evidence) in the proceedings, is seeking to give the court or jury an impression about himself that is false or misleading, the court may if it appears just to do so treat the defendant as being responsible for the making of an assertion which is apt to give that impression.

(5) In subsection (4) 'conduct' includes appearance or dress.

(6) Evidence is admissible under section 101(1)(f) only if it goes no further than is necessary to correct the false impression.

(7) Only prosecution evidence is admissible under section 101(1)(f).

106 'Attack on another person's character'

(1) For the purposes of section 101(1)(g) a defendant makes an attack on another person's character if –

(a)   he adduces evidence attacking the other person's character,

(b)   he (or any legal representative appointed under section 38(4) of the Youth Justice and Criminal Evidence Act 1999 (c. 23) to cross-examine a witness in his interests) asks questions in cross-examination that are intended to elicit such evidence, or are likely to do so, or

(c)   evidence is given of an imputation about the other person made by the defendant –

    (i)   on being questioned under caution, before charge, about the offence with which he is charged, or

    (ii)   on being charged with the offence or officially informed that he might be prosecuted for it.

(2) In subsection (1) 'evidence attacking the other person's character' means evidence to the effect that the other person –

(a)   has committed an offence (whether a different offence from the one with which the defendant is charged or the same one), or

(b)   has behaved, or is disposed to behave, in a reprehensible way;

and 'imputation about the other person' means an assertion to that effect.

(3) Only prosecution evidence is admissible under section 101(1)(g).

107 Stopping the case where evidence contaminated

(1) If on a defendant's trial before a judge and jury for an offence –

    (a) evidence of his bad character has been admitted under any of paragraphs (c) to (g) of section 101(1), and

    (b) the court is satisfied at any time after the close of the case for the prosecution that –

        (i) the evidence is contaminated, and

        (ii) the contamination is such that, considering the importance of the evidence to the case against the defendant, his conviction of the offence would be unsafe,

the court must either direct the jury to acquit the defendant of the offence or, if it considers that there ought to be a retrial, discharge the jury.

(2) Where –

    (a) a jury is directed under subsection (1) to acquit a defendant of an offence, and

    (b) the circumstances are such that, apart from this subsection, the defendant could if acquitted of that offence be found guilty of another offence,

the defendant may not be found guilty of that other offence if the court is satisfied as mentioned in subsection (1)(b) in respect of it.

(3) If –

    (a) a jury is required to determine under section 4A(2) of the Criminal Procedure (Insanity) Act 1964 (c. 84) whether a person charged on an indictment with an offence did the act or made the omission charged,

    (b) evidence of the person's bad character has been admitted under any of paragraphs (c) to (g) of section 101(1), and

    (c) the court is satisfied at any time after the close of the case for the prosecution that –

        (i) the evidence is contaminated, and

        (ii) the contamination is such that, considering the importance of the evidence to the case against the person, a finding that he did the act or made the omission would be unsafe,

the court must either direct the jury to acquit the defendant of the offence or, if it considers that there ought to be a rehearing, discharge the jury.

(4) This section does not prejudice any other power a court may have to direct a jury to acquit a person of an offence or to discharge a jury.

(5) For the purposes of this section a person's evidence is contaminated where –

    (a) as a result of an agreement or understanding between the person and one or more others, or

    (b) as a result of the person being aware of anything alleged by one or more others whose evidence may be, or has been, given in the proceedings,

the evidence is false or misleading in any respect, or is different from what it would otherwise have been.

108 Offences committed by defendant when a child

(1) Section 16(2) and (3) of the Children and Young Persons Act 1963 (c. 37) (offences committed by person under 14 disregarded for purposes of evidence relating to previous convictions) shall cease to have effect.

(2) In proceedings for an offence committed or alleged to have been committed by the defendant when aged 21 or over, evidence of his conviction for an offence when under the age of 14 is not admissible unless –

    (a) both of the offences are triable only on indictment, and

(b) the court is satisfied that the interests of justice require the evidence to be admissible.

(3) Subsection (2) applies in addition to section 101.

General

109 Assumption of truth in assessment of relevance or probative value

(1) Subject to subsection (2), a reference in this Chapter to the relevance or probative value of evidence is a reference to its relevance or probative value on the assumption that it is true.

(2) In assessing the relevance or probative value of an item of evidence for any purpose of this Chapter, a court need not assume that the evidence is true if it appears, on the basis of any material before the court (including any evidence it decides to hear on the matter), that no court or jury could reasonably find it to be true.

110 Court's duty to give reasons for rulings

(1) Where the court makes a relevant ruling –

(a) it must state in open court (but in the absence of the jury, if there is one) its reasons for the ruling;

(b) if it is a magistrates' court, it must cause the ruling and the reasons for it to be entered in the register of the court's proceedings.

(2) In this section 'relevant ruling' means –

(a) a ruling on whether an item of evidence is evidence of a person's bad character;

(b) a ruling on whether an item of such evidence is admissible under section 100 or 101 (including a ruling on an application under section 101(3));

(c) a ruling under section 107.

111 Rules of court

(1) Rules of court may make such provision as appears to the appropriate authority to be necessary or expedient for the purposes of this Act; and the appropriate authority is the authority entitled to make the rules.

(2) The rules may, and, where the party in question is the prosecution, must, contain provision requiring a party who –

(a) proposes to adduce evidence of a defendant's bad character, or

(b) proposes to cross-examine a witness with a view to eliciting such evidence,

to serve on the defendant such notice, and such particulars of or relating to the evidence, as may be prescribed.

(3) The rules may provide that the court or the defendant may, in such circumstances as may be prescribed, dispense with a requirement imposed by virtue of subsection (2).

(4) In considering the exercise of its powers with respect to costs, the court may take into account any failure by a party to comply with a requirement imposed by virtue of subsection (2) and not dispensed with by virtue of subsection (3).

(5) The rules may –

(a) limit the application of any provision of the rules to prescribed circumstances;

(b) subject any provision of the rules to prescribed exceptions;

(c) make different provision for different cases or circumstances.

(6) Nothing in this section prejudices the generality of any enactment conferring power to make rules of court; and no particular provision of this section prejudices any general provision of it.

(7) In this section –

'prescribed' means prescribed by rules of court;
'rules of court' means –

(a)   Crown Court Rules;
(b)   Criminal Appeal Rules;
(c)   rules under section 144 of the Magistrates' Courts Act 1980 (c. 43).

112 Interpretation of Chapter 1

(1)   In this Chapter –

'bad character' is to be read in accordance with section 98;
'criminal proceedings' means criminal proceedings in relation to which the strict rules of evidence apply;
'defendant', in relation to criminal proceedings, means a person charged with an offence in those proceedings; and 'co-defendant', in relation to a defendant, means a person charged with an offence in the same proceedings;
'important matter' means a matter of substantial importance in the context of the case as a whole;
'misconduct' means the commission of an offence or other reprehensible behaviour;
'offence' includes a service offence;
'probative value', and 'relevant' (in relation to an item of evidence), are to be read in accordance with section 109;
'prosecution evidence' means evidence which is to be (or has been) adduced by the prosecution, or which a witness is to be invited to give (or has given) in cross-examination by the prosecution;
'service offence' means an offence under the Army Act 1955 (3 & 4 Eliz. 2 c. 18), the Air Force Act 1955 (3 & 4 Eliz. 2 c. 19) or the Naval Discipline Act 1957 (c. 53);
'written charge' has the same meaning as in section 29 and also includes an information.

(2)   Where a defendant is charged with two or more offences in the same criminal proceedings, this Chapter (except section 101(3)) has effect as if each offence were charged in separate proceedings; and references to the offence with which the defendant is charged are to be read accordingly.

(3)   Nothing in this Chapter affects the exclusion of evidence –

(a)   under the rule in section 3 of the Criminal Procedure Act 1865 (c. 18) against a party impeaching the credit of his own witness by general evidence of bad character,

(b)   under section 41 of the Youth Justice and Criminal Evidence Act 1999 (c. 23) (restriction on evidence or questions about complainant's sexual history), or

(c)   on grounds other than the fact that it is evidence of a person's bad character.

113 Armed forces

Schedule 6 (armed forces) has effect.

CHAPTER 2   HEARSAY EVIDENCE

Hearsay: main provisions

114 Admissibility of hearsay evidence

(1)   In criminal proceedings a statement not made in oral evidence in the proceedings is admissible as evidence of any matter stated if, but only if –

(a)   any provision of this Chapter or any other statutory provision makes it admissible,

(b) any rule of law preserved by section 118 makes it admissible,

(c) all parties to the proceedings agree to it being admissible, or

(d) the court is satisfied that it is in the interests of justice for it to be admissible.

(2) In deciding whether a statement not made in oral evidence should be admitted under subsection (1)(d), the court must have regard to the following factors (and to any others it considers relevant) –

(a) how much probative value the statement has (assuming it to be true) in relation to a matter in issue in the proceedings, or how valuable it is for the understanding of other evidence in the case;

(b) what other evidence has been, or can be, given on the matter or evidence mentioned in paragraph (a);

(c) how important the matter or evidence mentioned in paragraph (a) is in the context of the case as a whole;

(d) the circumstances in which the statement was made;

(e) how reliable the maker of the statement appears to be;

(f) how reliable the evidence of the making of the statement appears to be;

(g) whether oral evidence of the matter stated can be given and, if not, why it cannot;

(h) the amount of difficulty involved in challenging the statement;

(i) the extent to which that difficulty would be likely to prejudice the party facing it.

(3) Nothing in this Chapter affects the exclusion of evidence of a statement on grounds other than the fact that it is a statement not made in oral evidence in the proceedings.

115 Statements and matters stated

(1) In this Chapter references to a statement or to a matter stated are to be read as follows.

(2) A statement is any representation of fact or opinion made by a person by whatever means; and it includes a representation made in a sketch, photofit or other pictorial form.

(3) A matter stated is one to which this Chapter applies if (and only if) the purpose, or one of the purposes, of the person making the statement appears to the court to have been –

(a) to cause another person to believe the matter, or

(b) to cause another person to act or a machine to operate on the basis that the matter is as stated.

Principal categories of admissibility

116 Cases where a witness is unavailable

(1) In criminal proceedings a statement not made in oral evidence in the proceedings is admissible as evidence of any matter stated if –

(a) oral evidence given in the proceedings by the person who made the statement would be admissible as evidence of that matter,

(b) the person who made the statement (the relevant person) is identified to the court's satisfaction, and

(c) any of the five conditions mentioned in subsection (2) is satisfied,

(2) The conditions are –

(a) that the relevant person is dead;

(b) that the relevant person is unfit to be a witness because of his bodily or mental condition;

(c) that the relevant person is outside the United Kingdom and it is not reasonably practicable to secure his attendance;

(d) that the relevant person cannot be found although such steps as it is reasonably practicable to take to find him have been taken;

(e) that through fear the relevant person does not give (or does not continue to give) oral evidence in the proceedings, either at all or in connection with the subject matter of the statement, and the court gives leave for the statement to be given in evidence.

(3) For the purposes of subsection (2)(e) 'fear' is to be widely construed and (for example) includes fear of the death or injury of another person or of financial loss.

(4) Leave may be given under subsection (2)(e) only if the court considers that the statement ought to be admitted in the interests of justice, having regard –

(a) to the statement's contents,

(b) to any risk that its admission or exclusion will result in unfairness to any party to the proceedings (and in particular to how difficult it will be to challenge the statement if the relevant person does not give oral evidence),

(c) in appropriate cases, to the fact that a direction under section 19 of the Youth Justice and Criminal Evidence Act 1999 (c. 23) (special measures for the giving of evidence by fearful witnesses etc) could be made in relation to the relevant person, and

(d) to any other relevant circumstances.

(5) A condition set out in any paragraph of subsection (2) which is in fact satisfied is to be treated as not satisfied if it is shown that the circumstances described in that paragraph are caused –

(a) by the person in support of whose case it is sought to give the statement in evidence, or

(b) by a person acting on his behalf,

in order to prevent the relevant person giving oral evidence in the proceedings (whether at all or in connection with the subject matter of the statement).

117 Business and other documents

(1) In criminal proceedings a statement contained in a document is admissible as evidence of any matter stated if –

(a) oral evidence given in the proceedings would be admissible as evidence of that matter,

(b) the requirements of subsection (2) are satisfied, and

(c) the requirements of subsection (5) are satisfied, in a case where subsection (4) requires them to be.

(2) The requirements of this subsection are satisfied if –

(a) the document or the part containing the statement was created or received by a person in the course of a trade, business, profession or other occupation, or as the holder of a paid or unpaid office,

(b) the person who supplied the information contained in the statement (the relevant person) had or may reasonably be supposed to have had personal knowledge of the matters dealt with, and

(c) each person (if any) through whom the information was supplied from the relevant person to the person mentioned in paragraph (a) received the information in the course of a trade, business, profession or other occupation, or as the holder of a paid or unpaid office.

(3) The persons mentioned in paragraphs (a) and (b) of subsection (2) may be the same person.

(4) The additional requirements of subsection (5) must be satisfied if the statement –

(a) was prepared for the purposes of pending or contemplated criminal proceedings, or for a criminal investigation, but

(b) was not obtained pursuant to a request under section 7 of the Crime (International Co-operation) Act 2003 (c. 32) or an order under paragraph 6 of Schedule 13 to the Criminal Justice Act 1988 (c. 33) (which relate to overseas evidence).

(5) The requirements of this subsection are satisfied if –

(a) any of the five conditions mentioned in section 116(2) is satisfied (absence of relevant person etc), or

(b) the relevant person cannot reasonably be expected to have any recollection of the matters dealt with in the statement (having regard to the length of time since he supplied the information and all other circumstances).

(6) A statement is not admissible under this section if the court makes a direction to that effect under subsection (7).

(7) The court may make a direction under this subsection if satisfied that the statement's reliability as evidence for the purpose for which it is tendered is doubtful in view of –

(a) its contents,

(b) the source of the information contained in it,

(c) the way in which or the circumstances in which the information was supplied or received, or

(d) the way in which or the circumstances in which the document concerned was created or received.

118 Preservation of certain common law categories of admissibility

(1) The following rules of law are preserved.

'Public information etc

1   Any rule of law under which in criminal proceedings –

(a) published works dealing with matters of a public nature (such as histories, scientific works, dictionaries and maps) are admissible as evidence of facts of a public nature stated in them,

(b) public documents (such as public registers, and returns made under public authority with respect to matters of public interest) are admissible as evidence of facts stated in them,

(c) records (such as the records of certain courts, treaties, Crown grants, pardons and commissions) are admissible as evidence of facts stated in them, or

(d) evidence relating to a person's age or date or place of birth may be given by a person without personal knowledge of the matter.

Reputation as to character

2   Any rule of law under which in criminal proceedings evidence of a person's reputation is admissible for the purpose of proving his good or bad character.

Note

The rule is preserved only so far as it allows the court to treat such evidence as proving the matter concerned.

Reputation or family tradition

3   Any rule of law under which in criminal proceedings evidence of reputation or family tradition is admissible for the purpose of proving or disproving –

(a) pedigree or the existence of a marriage,

(b) the existence of any public or general right, or

(c) the identity of any person or thing.

Note

The rule is preserved only so far as it allows the court to treat such evidence as proving or disproving the matter concerned.

Res gestae

4   Any rule of law under which in criminal proceedings a statement is admissible as evidence of any matter stated if –

(a)   the statement was made by a person so emotionally overpowered by an event that the possibility of concoction or distortion can be disregarded,

(b)   the statement accompanied an act which can be properly evaluated as evidence only if considered in conjunction with the statement, or

(c)   the statement relates to a physical sensation or a mental state (such as intention or emotion).

Confessions etc

5   Any rule of law relating to the admissibility of confessions or mixed statements in criminal proceedings.

Admissions by agents etc

6   Any rule of law under which in criminal proceedings –

(a)   an admission made by an agent of a defendant is admissible against the defendant as evidence of any matter stated, or

(b)   a statement made by a person to whom a defendant refers a person for information is admissible against the defendant as evidence of any matter stated.

Common enterprise

7   Any rule of law under which in criminal proceedings a statement made by a party to a common enterprise is admissible against another party to the enterprise as evidence of any matter stated.

Expert evidence

8   Any rule of law under which in criminal proceedings an expert witness may draw on the body of expertise relevant to his field.'

(2)   With the exception of the rules preserved by this section, the common law rules governing the admissibility of hearsay evidence in criminal proceedings are abolished.

119 Inconsistent statements

(1)   If in criminal proceedings a person gives oral evidence and –

(a)   he admits making a previous inconsistent statement, or

(b)   a previous inconsistent statement made by him is proved by virtue of section 3, 4 or 5 of the Criminal Procedure Act 1865 (c. 18),

the statement is admissible as evidence of any matter stated of which oral evidence by him would be admissible.

(2)   If in criminal proceedings evidence of an inconsistent statement by any person is given under section 124(2)(c), the statement is admissible as evidence of any matter stated in it of which oral evidence by that person would be admissible.

120 Other previous statements of witnesses

(1)   This section applies where a person (the witness) is called to give evidence in criminal proceedings.

(2)   If a previous statement by the witness is admitted as evidence to rebut a suggestion that his oral evidence has been fabricated, that statement is admissible as evidence of any matter stated of which oral evidence by the witness would be admissible.

(3)   A statement made by the witness in a document –

(a) which is used by him to refresh his memory while giving evidence,

(b) on which he is cross-examined, and

(c) which as a consequence is received in evidence in the proceedings,

is admissible as evidence of any matter stated of which oral evidence by him would be admissible.

(4) A previous statement by the witness is admissible as evidence of any matter stated of which oral evidence by him would be admissible, if –

(a) any of the following three conditions is satisfied, and

(b) while giving evidence the witness indicates that to the best of his belief he made the statement, and that to the best of his belief it states the truth.

(5) The first condition is that the statement identifies or describes a person, object or place.

(6) The second condition is that the statement was made by the witness when the matters stated were fresh in his memory but he does not remember them, and cannot reasonably be expected to remember them, well enough to give oral evidence of them in the proceedings.

(7) The third condition is that –

(a) the witness claims to be a person against whom an offence has been committed,

(b) the offence is one to which the proceedings relate,

(c) the statement consists of a complaint made by the witness (whether to a person in authority or not) about conduct which would, if proved, constitute the offence or part of the offence,

(d) the complaint was made as soon as could reasonably be expected after the alleged conduct,

(e) the complaint was not made as a result of a threat or a promise, and

(f) before the statement is adduced the witness gives oral evidence in connection with its subject matter.

(8) For the purposes of subsection (7) the fact that the complaint was elicited (for example, by a leading question) is irrelevant unless a threat or a promise was involved.

Supplementary

121 Additional requirement for admissibility of multiple hearsay

(1) A hearsay statement is not admissible to prove the fact that an earlier hearsay statement was made unless –

(a) either of the statements is admissible under section 117, 119 or 120,

(b) all parties to the proceedings so agree, or

(c) the court is satisfied that the value of the evidence in question, taking into account how reliable the statements appear to be, is so high that the interests of justice require the later statement to be admissible for that purpose.

(2) In this section 'hearsay statement' means a statement, not made in oral evidence, that is relied on as evidence of a matter stated in it.

122 Documents produced as exhibits

(1) This section applies if on a trial before a judge and jury for an offence –

(a) a statement made in a document is admitted in evidence under section 119 or 120, and

(b) the document or a copy of it is produced as an exhibit.

(2) The exhibit must not accompany the jury when they retire to consider their verdict unless –

(a) the court considers it appropriate, or

(b) all the parties to the proceedings agree that it should accompany the jury.

123 Capability to make statement

(1) Nothing in section 116, 119 or 120 makes a statement admissible as evidence if it was made by a person who did not have the required capability at the time when he made the statement.

(2) Nothing in section 117 makes a statement admissible as evidence if any person who, in order for the requirements of section 117(2) to be satisfied, must at any time have supplied or received the information concerned or created or received the document or part concerned –

(a) did not have the required capability at that time, or

(b) cannot be identified but cannot reasonably be assumed to have had the required capability at that time.

(3) For the purposes of this section a person has the required capability if he is capable of –

(a) understanding questions put to him about the matters stated, and

(b) giving answers to such questions which can be understood.

(4) Where by reason of this section there is an issue as to whether a person had the required capability when he made a statement –

(a) proceedings held for the determination of the issue must take place in the absence of the jury (if there is one);

(b) in determining the issue the court may receive expert evidence and evidence from any person to whom the statement in question was made;

(c) the burden of proof on the issue lies on the party seeking to adduce the statement, and the standard of proof is the balance of probabilities.

124 Credibility

(1) This section applies if in criminal proceedings –

(a) a statement not made in oral evidence in the proceedings is admitted as evidence of a matter stated, and

(b) the maker of the statement does not give oral evidence in connection with the subject matter of the statement.

(2) In such a case –

(a) any evidence which (if he had given such evidence) would have been admissible as relevant to his credibility as a witness is so admissible in the proceedings;

(b) evidence may with the court's leave be given of any matter which (if he had given such evidence) could have been put to him in cross-examination as relevant to his credibility as a witness but of which evidence could not have been adduced by the cross-examining party;

(c) evidence tending to prove that he made (at whatever time) any other statement inconsistent with the statement admitted as evidence is admissible for the purpose of showing that he contradicted himself.

(3) If as a result of evidence admitted under this section an allegation is made against the maker of a statement, the court may permit a party to lead additional evidence of such description as the court may specify for the purposes of denying or answering the allegation.

(4) In the case of a statement in a document which is admitted as evidence under section 117 each person who, in order for the statement to be admissible, must have supplied or received the information concerned or created or received the document or part concerned is to be treated as the maker of the statement for the purposes of subsections (1) to (3) above.

125 Stopping the case where evidence is unconvincing

(1) If on a defendant's trial before a judge and jury for an offence the court is satisfied at any time after the close of the case for the prosecution that –

(a) the case against the defendant is based wholly or partly on a statement not made in oral evidence in the proceedings, and

(b) the evidence provided by the statement is so unconvincing that, considering its importance to the case against the defendant, his conviction of the offence would be unsafe,

the court must either direct the jury to acquit the defendant of the offence or, if it considers that there ought to be a retrial, discharge the jury.

(2) Where –

(a) a jury is directed under subsection (1) to acquit a defendant of an offence, and

(b) the circumstances are such that, apart from this subsection, the defendant could if acquitted of that offence be found guilty of another offence,

the defendant may not be found guilty of that other offence if the court is satisfied as mentioned in subsection (1) in respect of it.

(3) If –

(a) a jury is required to determine under section 4A(2) of the Criminal Procedure (Insanity) Act 1964 (c. 84) whether a person charged on an indictment with an offence did the act or made the omission charged, and

(b) the court is satisfied as mentioned in subsection (1) above at any time after the close of the case for the prosecution that –

(i) the case against the defendant is based wholly or partly on a statement not made in oral evidence in the proceedings, and

(ii) the evidence provided by the statement is so unconvincing that, considering its importance to the case against the person, a finding that he did the act or made the omission would be unsafe,

the court must either direct the jury to acquit the defendant of the offence or, if it considers that there ought to be a rehearing, discharge the jury.

(4) This section does not prejudice any other power a court may have to direct a jury to acquit a person of an offence or to discharge a jury.

126 Court's general discretion to exclude evidence

(1) In criminal proceedings the court may refuse to admit a statement as evidence of a matter stated if –

(a) the statement was made otherwise than in oral evidence in the proceedings, and

(b) the court is satisfied that the case for excluding the statement, taking account of the danger that to admit it would result in undue waste of time, substantially outweighs the case for admitting it, taking account of the value of the evidence.

(2) Nothing in this Chapter prejudices –

(a) any power of a court to exclude evidence under section 78 of the Police and Criminal Evidence Act 1984 (c. 60) (exclusion of unfair evidence), or

(b) any other power of a court to exclude evidence at its discretion (whether by preventing questions from being put or otherwise).

Miscellaneous

127 Expert evidence: preparatory work

(1) This section applies if –

(a) a statement has been prepared for the purposes of criminal proceedings,

(b) the person who prepared the statement had or may reasonably be supposed to have had personal knowledge of the matters stated,

(c) notice is given under the appropriate rules that another person (the expert) will in evidence given in the proceedings orally or under section 9 of the Criminal Justice Act 1967 (c. 80) base an opinion or inference on the statement, and

(d) the notice gives the name of the person who prepared the statement and the nature of the matters stated.

(2) In evidence given in the proceedings the expert may base an opinion or inference on the statement.

(3) If evidence based on the statement is given under subsection (2) the statement is to be treated as evidence of what it states.

(4) This section does not apply if the court, on an application by a party to the proceedings, orders that it is not in the interests of justice that it should apply.

(5) The matters to be considered by the court in deciding whether to make an order under subsection (4) include –

(a) the expense of calling as a witness the person who prepared the statement;

(b) whether relevant evidence could be given by that person which could not be given by the expert;

(c) whether that person can reasonably be expected to remember the matters stated well enough to give oral evidence of them.

(6) Subsections (1) to (5) apply to a statement prepared for the purposes of a criminal investigation as they apply to a statement prepared for the purposes of criminal proceedings, and in such a case references to the proceedings are to criminal proceedings arising from the investigation.

(7) The appropriate rules are rules made –

(a) under section 81 of the Police and Criminal Evidence Act 1984 (advance notice of expert evidence in Crown Court), or

(b) under section 144 of the Magistrates' Courts Act 1980 (c. 43) by virtue of section 20(3) of the Criminal Procedure and Investigations Act 1996 (c. 25) (advance notice of expert evidence in magistrates' courts).

128 Confessions

(1) In the Police and Criminal Evidence Act 1984 (c. 60) the following section is inserted after section 76 –

'76A Confessions may be given in evidence for co-accused

(1) In any proceedings a confession made by an accused person may be given in evidence for another person charged in the same proceedings (a co-accused) in so far as it is relevant to any matter in issue in the proceedings and is not excluded by the court in pursuance of this section.

(2) If, in any proceedings where a co-accused proposes to give in evidence a confession made by an accused person, it is represented to the court that the confession was or may have been obtained –

(a) by oppression of the person who made it; or

(b) in consequence of anything said or done which was likely, in the circumstances existing at the time, to render unreliable any confession which might be made by him in consequence thereof,

the court shall not allow the confession to be given in evidence for the co-accused except in so far as it is proved to the court on the balance of probabilities that the confession (notwithstanding that it may be true) was not so obtained.

(3) Before allowing a confession made by an accused person to be given in evidence for a co-accused in any proceedings, the court may of its own motion require the

fact that the confession was not obtained as mentioned in subsection (2) above to be proved in the proceedings on the balance of probabilities.

(4) The fact that a confession is wholly or partly excluded in pursuance of this section shall not affect the admissibility in evidence –

(a) of any facts discovered as a result of the confession; or

(b) where the confession is relevant as showing that the accused speaks, writes or expresses himself in a particular way, of so much of the confession as is necessary to show that he does so.

(5) Evidence that a fact to which this subsection applies was discovered as a result of a statement made by an accused person shall not be admissible unless evidence of how it was discovered is given by him or on his behalf.

(6) Subsection (5) above applies –

(a) to any fact discovered as a result of a confession which is wholly excluded in pursuance of this section; and

(b) to any fact discovered as a result of a confession which is partly so excluded, if the fact is discovered as a result of the excluded part of the confession.

(7) In this section "oppression" includes torture, inhuman or degrading treatment, and the use or threat of violence (whether or not amounting to torture).'

(2) Subject to subsection (1), nothing in this Chapter makes a confession by a defendant admissible if it would not be admissible under section 76 of the Police and Criminal Evidence Act 1984 (c. 60).

(3) In subsection (2) 'confession' has the meaning given by section 82 of that Act.

129 Representations other than by a person

(1) Where a representation of any fact –

(a) is made otherwise than by a person, but

(b) depends for its accuracy on information supplied (directly or indirectly) by a person,

the representation is not admissible in criminal proceedings as evidence of the fact unless it is proved that the information was accurate.

(2) Subsection (1) does not affect the operation of the presumption that a mechanical device has been properly set or calibrated.

130 Depositions

In Schedule 3 to the Crime and Disorder Act 1998 (c. 37), sub-paragraph (4) of paragraph 5 is omitted (power of the court to overrule an objection to a deposition being read as evidence by virtue of that paragraph).

131 Evidence at retrial

For paragraphs 1 and 1A of Schedule 2 to the Criminal Appeal Act 1968 (c. 19) (oral evidence and use of transcripts etc at retrials under that Act) there is substituted –

'Evidence

1 (1) Evidence given at a retrial must be given orally if it was given orally at the original trial, unless –

(a) all the parties to the retrial agree otherwise;

(b) section 116 of the Criminal Justice Act 2003 applies (admissibility of hearsay evidence where a witness is unavailable); or

(c) the witness is unavailable to give evidence, otherwise than as mentioned in subsection (2) of that section, and section 114(1)(d) of that Act applies (admission of hearsay evidence under residual discretion).

(2)   Paragraph 5 of Schedule 3 to the Crime and Disorder Act 1998 (use of depositions) does not apply at a retrial to a deposition read as evidence at the original trial.'

General

132 Rules of court

(1) Rules of court may make such provision as appears to the appropriate authority to be necessary or expedient for the purposes of this Chapter; and the appropriate authority is the authority entitled to make the rules.

(2) The rules may make provision about the procedure to be followed and other conditions to be fulfilled by a party proposing to tender a statement in evidence under any provision of this Chapter.

(3) The rules may require a party proposing to tender the evidence to serve on each party to the proceedings such notice, and such particulars of or relating to the evidence, as may be prescribed.

(4) The rules may provide that the evidence is to be treated as admissible by agreement of the parties if –

(a) a notice has been served in accordance with provision made under subsection (3), and

(b) no counter-notice in the prescribed form objecting to the admission of the evidence has been served by a party.

(5) If a party proposing to tender evidence fails to comply with a prescribed requirement applicable to it –

(a) the evidence is not admissible except with the court's leave;

(b) where leave is given the court or jury may draw such inferences from the failure as appear proper;

(c) the failure may be taken into account by the court in considering the exercise of its powers with respect to costs.

(6) In considering whether or how to exercise any of its powers under subsection (5) the court shall have regard to whether there is any justification for the failure to comply with the requirement.

(7) A person shall not be convicted of an offence solely on an inference drawn under subsection (5)(b).

(8) Rules under this section may –

(a) limit the application of any provision of the rules to prescribed circumstances;

(b) subject any provision of the rules to prescribed exceptions;

(c) make different provision for different cases or circumstances.

(9) Nothing in this section prejudices the generality of any enactment conferring power to make rules of court; and no particular provision of this section prejudices any general provision of it.

(10) In this section –

'prescribed' means prescribed by rules of court;
'rules of court' means –

(a)   Crown Court Rules;

(b)   Criminal Appeal Rules;

(c)   rules under section 144 of the Magistrates' Courts Act 1980 (c. 43).

133 Proof of statements in documents

Where a statement in a document is admissible as evidence in criminal proceedings, the statement may be proved by producing either –

(a)   the document, or

(b)   (whether or not the document exists) a copy of the document or of the material part of it,

authenticated in whatever way the court may approve.

134 Interpretation of Chapter 2

(1)   In this Chapter –

'copy', in relation to a document, means anything on to which information recorded in the document has been copied, by whatever means and whether directly or indirectly;

'criminal proceedings' means criminal proceedings in relation to which the strict rules of evidence apply;

'defendant', in relation to criminal proceedings, means a person charged with an offence in those proceedings;

'document' means anything in which information of any description is recorded;

'oral evidence' includes evidence which, by reason of any disability, disorder or other impairment, a person called as a witness gives in writing or by signs or by way of any device;

'statutory provision' means any provision contained in, or in an instrument made under, this or any other Act, including any Act passed after this Act.

(2)   Section 115 (statements and matters stated) contains other general interpretative provisions.

(3)   Where a defendant is charged with two or more offences in the same criminal proceedings, this Chapter has effect as if each offence were charged in separate proceedings.

135 Armed forces

Schedule 7 (hearsay evidence: armed forces) has effect.

136 Repeals etc

In the Criminal Justice Act 1988 (c. 33), the following provisions (which are to some extent superseded by provisions of this Chapter) are repealed –

(a)   Part 2 and Schedule 2 (which relate to documentary evidence);

(b)   in Schedule 13, paragraphs 2 to 5 (which relate to documentary evidence in service courts etc).

CHAPTER 3   MISCELLANEOUS AND SUPPLEMENTAL

137 Evidence by video recording

(1)   This section applies where –

(a)   a person is called as a witness in proceedings for an offence triable only on indictment, or for a prescribed offence triable either way,

(b)   the person claims to have witnessed (whether visually or in any other way) –

(i)   events alleged by the prosecution to include conduct constituting the offence or part of the offence, or

(ii)   events closely connected with such events,

(c)   he has previously given an account of the events in question (whether in response to questions asked or otherwise),

(d)   the account was given at a time when those events were fresh in the person's memory (or would have been, assuming the truth of the claim mentioned in paragraph (b)),

    (e) a video recording was made of the account,

    (f) the court has made a direction that the recording should be admitted as evidence in chief of the witness, and the direction has not been rescinded, and

    (g) the recording is played in the proceedings in accordance with the direction.

(2) If, or to the extent that, the witness in his oral evidence in the proceedings asserts the truth of the statements made by him in the recorded account, they shall be treated as if made by him in that evidence.

(3) A direction under subsection (1)(f) –

    (a) may not be made in relation to a recorded account given by the defendant;

    (b) may be made only if it appears to the court that –

        (i) the witness's recollection of the events in question is likely to have been significantly better when he gave the recorded account than it will be when he gives oral evidence in the proceedings, and

        (ii) it is in the interests of justice for the recording to be admitted, having regard in particular to the matters mentioned in subsection (4).

(4) Those matters are –

    (a) the interval between the time of the events in question and the time when the recorded account was made;

    (b) any other factors that might affect the reliability of what the witness said in that account;

    (c) the quality of the recording;

    (d) any views of the witness as to whether his evidence in chief should be given orally or by means of the recording.

(5) For the purposes of subsection (2) it does not matter if the statements in the recorded account were not made on oath.

(6) In this section 'prescribed' means of a description specified in an order made by the Secretary of State.

138 Video evidence: further provisions

(1) Where a video recording is admitted under section 137, the witness may not give evidence in chief otherwise than by means of the recording as to any matter which, in the opinion of the court, has been dealt with adequately in the recorded account.

(2) The reference in subsection (1)(f) of section 137 to the admission of a recording includes a reference to the admission of part of the recording; and references in that section and this one to the video recording or to the witness's recorded account shall, where appropriate, be read accordingly.

(3) In considering whether any part of a recording should be not admitted under section 137, the court must consider –

    (a) whether admitting that part would carry a risk of prejudice to the defendant, and

    (b) if so, whether the interests of justice nevertheless require it to be admitted in view of the desirability of showing the whole, or substantially the whole, of the recorded interview.

(4) A court may not make a direction under section 137(1)(f) in relation to any proceedings unless –

    (a) the Secretary of State has notified the court that arrangements can be made, in the area in which it appears to the court that the proceedings will take place, for implementing directions under that section, and

    (b) the notice has not been withdrawn.

(5) Nothing in section 137 affects the admissibility of any video recording which would be admissible apart from that section.

139 Use of documents to refresh memory

(1) A person giving oral evidence in criminal proceedings about any matter may, at any stage in the course of doing so, refresh his memory of it from a document made or verified by him at an earlier time if –

    (a) he states in his oral evidence that the document records his recollection of the matter at that earlier time, and

    (b) his recollection of the matter is likely to have been significantly better at that time than it is at the time of his oral evidence.

(2) Where –

    (a) a person giving oral evidence in criminal proceedings about any matter has previously given an oral account, of which a sound recording was made, and he states in that evidence that the account represented his recollection of the matter at that time,

    (b) his recollection of the matter is likely to have been significantly better at the time of the previous account than it is at the time of his oral evidence, and

    (c) a transcript has been made of the sound recording,

he may, at any stage in the course of giving his evidence, refresh his memory of the matter from that transcript.

140 Interpretation of Chapter 3

In this Chapter –

    'criminal proceedings' means criminal proceedings in relation to which the strict rules of evidence apply;

    'defendant', in relation to criminal proceedings, means a person charged with an offence in those proceedings;

    'document' means anything in which information of any description is recorded, but not including any recording of sounds or moving images;

    'oral evidence' includes evidence which, by reason of any disability, disorder or other impairment, a person called as a witness gives in writing or by signs or by way of any device;

    'video recording' means any recording, on any medium, from which a moving image may by any means be produced, and includes the accompanying sound-track.

141 Saving

No provision of this Part has effect in relation to criminal proceedings begun before the commencement of that provision.

PART 12   SENTENCING

CHAPTER 1   GENERAL PROVISIONS ABOUT SENTENCING

Matters to be taken into account in sentencing

142 Purposes of sentencing

(1) Any court dealing with an offender in respect of his offence must have regard to the following purposes of sentencing –

    (a) the punishment of offenders,

    (b) the reduction of crime (including its reduction by deterrence),

    (c) the reform and rehabilitation of offenders,

(d) the protection of the public, and
(e) the making of reparation by offenders to persons affected by their offences.

(2) Subsection (1) does not apply –

(a) in relation to an offender who is aged under 18 at the time of conviction,
(b) to an offence the sentence for which is fixed by law,
(c) to an offence the sentence for which falls to be imposed under section 51A(2) of the Firearms Act 1968 (c. 27) (minimum sentence for certain firearms offences), under subsection (2) of section 110 or 111 of the Sentencing Act (required custodial sentences) or under any of sections 225 to 228 of this Act (dangerous offenders), or
(d) in relation to the making under Part 3 of the Mental Health Act 1983 (c. 20) of a hospital order (with or without a restriction order), an interim hospital order, a hospital direction or a limitation direction.

(3) In this Chapter 'sentence', in relation to an offence, includes any order made by a court when dealing with the offender in respect of his offence; and 'sentencing' is to be construed accordingly.

143 Determining the seriousness of an offence

(1) In considering the seriousness of any offence, the court must consider the offender's culpability in committing the offence and any harm which the offence caused, was intended to cause or might foreseeably have caused.

(2) In considering the seriousness of an offence ('the current offence') committed by an offender who has one or more previous convictions, the court must treat each previous conviction as an aggravating factor if (in the case of that conviction) the court considers that it can reasonably be so treated having regard, in particular, to –

(a) the nature of the offence to which the conviction relates and its relevance to the current offence, and
(b) the time that has elapsed since the conviction.

(3) In considering the seriousness of any offence committed while the offender was on bail, the court must treat the fact that it was committed in those circumstances as an aggravating factor.

(4) Any reference in subsection (2) to a previous conviction is to be read as a reference to –

(a) a previous conviction by a court in the United Kingdom, or
(b) a previous finding of guilt in service disciplinary proceedings.

(5) Subsections (2) and (4) do not prevent the court from treating a previous conviction by a court outside the United Kingdom as an aggravating factor in any case where the court considers it appropriate to do so.

144 Reduction in sentences for guilty pleas

(1) In determining what sentence to pass on an offender who has pleaded guilty to an offence in proceedings before that or another court, a court must take into account –

(a) the stage in the proceedings for the offence at which the offender indicated his intention to plead guilty, and
(b) the circumstances in which this indication was given.

(2) In the case of an offence the sentence for which falls to be imposed under subsection (2) of section 110 or 111 of the Sentencing Act, nothing in that subsection prevents the court, after taking into account any matter referred to in subsection (1) of this section, from imposing any sentence which is not less than 80 per cent of that specified in that subsection.

145 Increase in sentences for racial or religious aggravation

(1) This section applies where a court is considering the seriousness of an offence other than one under sections 29 to 32 of the Crime and Disorder Act 1998 (c. 37) (racially or religiously aggravated assaults, criminal damage, public order offences and harassment etc).

(2) If the offence was racially or religiously aggravated, the court –

   (a) must treat that fact as an aggravating factor, and

   (b) must state in open court that the offence was so aggravated.

(3) Section 28 of the Crime and Disorder Act 1998 (meaning of 'racially or religiously aggravated') applies for the purposes of this section as it applies for the purposes of sections 29 to 32 of that Act.

146 Increase in sentences for aggravation related to disability or sexual orientation

(1) This section applies where the court is considering the seriousness of an offence committed in any of the circumstances mentioned in subsection (2).

(2) Those circumstances are –

   (a) that, at the time of committing the offence, or immediately before or after doing so, the offender demonstrated towards the victim of the offence hostility based on –

      (i)   the sexual orientation (or presumed sexual orientation) of the victim, or

      (ii) a disability (or presumed disability) of the victim, or

   (b) that the offence is motivated (wholly or partly) –

      (i)   by hostility towards persons who are of a particular sexual orientation, or

      (ii) by hostility towards persons who have a disability or a particular disability.

(3) The court –

   (a) must treat the fact that the offence was committed in any of those circumstances as an aggravating factor, and

   (b) must state in open court that the offence was committed in such circumstances.

(4) It is immaterial for the purposes of paragraph (a) or (b) of subsection (2) whether or not the offender's hostility is also based, to any extent, on any other factor not mentioned in that paragraph.

(5) In this section 'disability' means any physical or mental impairment.

General restrictions on community sentences

147 Meaning of 'community sentence' etc

(1) In this Part 'community sentence' means a sentence which consists of or includes –

   (a) a community order (as defined by section 177), or

   (b) one or more youth community orders.

(2) In this Chapter 'youth community order' means –

   (a) a curfew order as defined by section 163 of the Sentencing Act,

   (b) an exclusion order under section 40A(1) of that Act,

   (c) an attendance centre order as defined by section 163 of that Act,

   (d) a supervision order under section 63(1) of that Act, or

   (e) an action plan order under section 69(1) of that Act.

148 Restrictions on imposing community sentences

(1) A court must not pass a community sentence on an offender unless it is of the opinion that the offence, or the combination of the offence and one or more offences associated with it, was serious enough to warrant such a sentence.

(2) Where a court passes a community sentence which consists of or includes a community order –

    (a) the particular requirement or requirements forming part of the community order must be such as, in the opinion of the court, is, or taken together are, the most suitable for the offender, and

    (b) the restrictions on liberty imposed by the order must be such as in the opinion of the court are commensurate with the seriousness of the offence, or the combination of the offence and one or more offences associated with it.

(3) Where a court passes a community sentence which consists of or includes one or more youth community orders –

    (a) the particular order or orders forming part of the sentence must be such as, in the opinion of the court, is, or taken together are, the most suitable for the offender, and

    (b) the restrictions on liberty imposed by the order or orders must be such as in the opinion of the court are commensurate with the seriousness of the offence, or the combination of the offence and one or more offences associated with it.

(4) Subsections (1) and (2)(b) have effect subject to section 151(2).

149 Passing of community sentence on offender remanded in custody

(1) In determining the restrictions on liberty to be imposed by a community order or youth community order in respect of an offence, the court may have regard to any period for which the offender has been remanded in custody in connection with the offence or any other offence the charge for which was founded on the same facts or evidence.

(2) In subsection (1) 'remanded in custody' has the meaning given by section 242(2).

150 Community sentence not available where sentence fixed by law etc

The power to make a community order or youth community order is not exercisable in respect of an offence for which the sentence –

    (a) is fixed by law,

    (b) falls to be imposed under section 51A(2) of the Firearms Act 1968 (c. 27) (required custodial sentence for certain firearms offences),

    (c) falls to be imposed under section 110(2) or 111(2) of the Sentencing Act (requirement to impose custodial sentences for certain repeated offences committed by offenders aged 18 or over), or

    (d) falls to be imposed under any of sections 225 to 228 of this Act (requirement to impose custodial sentences for certain offences committed by offenders posing risk to public).

151 Community order for persistent offender previously fined

(1) Subsection (2) applies where –

    (a) a person aged 16 or over is convicted of an offence ('the current offence'),

    (b) on three or more previous occasions he has, on conviction by a court in the United Kingdom of any offence committed by him after attaining the age of 16, had passed on him a sentence consisting only of a fine, and

    (c) despite the effect of section 143(2), the court would not (apart from this section) regard the current offence, or the combination of the current offence and one or more offences associated with it, as being serious enough to warrant a community sentence.

(2) The court may make a community order in respect of the current offence instead of imposing a fine if it considers that, having regard to all the circumstances including

the matters mentioned in subsection (3), it would be in the interests of justice to make such an order.

(3) The matters referred to in subsection (2) are –

(a) the nature of the offences to which the previous convictions mentioned in subsection (1)(b) relate and their relevance to the current offence, and

(b) the time that has elapsed since the offender's conviction of each of those offences.

(4) In subsection (1)(b), the reference to conviction by a court in the United Kingdom includes a reference to the finding of guilt in service disciplinary proceedings; and, in relation to any such finding of guilt, the reference to the sentence passed is a reference to the punishment awarded.

(5) For the purposes of subsection (1)(b), a compensation order does not form part of an offender's sentence.

(6) For the purposes of subsection (1)(b), it is immaterial whether on other previous occasions a court has passed on the offender a sentence not consisting only of a fine.

(7) This section does not limit the extent to which a court may, in accordance with section 143(2), treat any previous convictions of the offender as increasing the seriousness of an offence.

General restrictions on discretionary custodial sentences

152 General restrictions on imposing discretionary custodial sentences

(1) This section applies where a person is convicted of an offence punishable with a custodial sentence other than one –

(a) fixed by law, or

(b) falling to be imposed under section 51A(2) of the Firearms Act 1968 (c. 27), under section 110(2) or 111(2) of the Sentencing Act or under any of sections 225 to 228 of this Act.

(2) The court must not pass a custodial sentence unless it is of the opinion that the offence, or the combination of the offence and one or more offences associated with it, was so serious that neither a fine alone nor a community sentence can be justified for the offence.

(3) Nothing in subsection (2) prevents the court from passing a custodial sentence on the offender if –

(a) he fails to express his willingness to comply with a requirement which is proposed by the court to be included in a community order and which requires an expression of such willingness, or

(b) he fails to comply with an order under section 161(2) (pre-sentence drug testing).

153 Length of discretionary custodial sentences: general provision

(1) This section applies where a court passes a custodial sentence other than one fixed by law or falling to be imposed under section 225 or 226.

(2) Subject to section 51A(2) of the Firearms Act 1968 (c. 27), sections 110(2) and 111(2) of the Sentencing Act and sections 227(2) and 228(2) of this Act, the custodial sentence must be for the shortest term (not exceeding the permitted maximum) that in the opinion of the court is commensurate with the seriousness of the offence, or the combination of the offence and one or more offences associated with it.

General limit on magistrates' court's power to impose imprisonment

154 General limit on magistrates' court's power to impose imprisonment

(1) A magistrates' court does not have power to impose imprisonment for more than 12 months in respect of any one offence.

(2) Unless expressly excluded, subsection (1) applies even if the offence in question is one for which a person would otherwise be liable on summary conviction to imprisonment for more than 12 months.

(3) Subsection (1) is without prejudice to section 133 of the Magistrates' Courts Act 1980 (c. 43) (consecutive terms of imprisonment).

(4) Any power of a magistrates' court to impose a term of imprisonment for non-payment of a fine, or for want of sufficient distress to satisfy a fine, is not limited by virtue of subsection (1).

(5) In subsection (4) 'fine' includes a pecuniary penalty but does not include a pecuniary forfeiture or pecuniary compensation.

(6) In this section 'impose imprisonment' means pass a sentence of imprisonment or fix a term of imprisonment for failure to pay any sum of money, or for want of sufficient distress to satisfy any sum of money, or for failure to do or abstain from doing anything required to be done or left undone.

(7) Section 132 of the Magistrates' Courts Act 1980 contains provisions about the minimum term of imprisonment which may be imposed by a magistrates' court.

155 Consecutive terms of imprisonment

(1) Section 133 of the Magistrates' Courts Act 1980 (consecutive terms of imprisonment) is amended as follows.

(2) In subsection (1), for '6 months' there is substituted '65 weeks'.

(3) Subsection (2) is omitted.

(4) In subsection (3) for 'the preceding subsections' there is substituted 'subsection (1) above'.

Procedural requirements for imposing community sentences and discretionary custodial sentences

156 Pre-sentence reports and other requirements

(1) In forming any such opinion as is mentioned in section 148(1), (2)(b) or (3)(b), section 152(2) or section 153(2), a court must take into account all such information as is available to it about the circumstances of the offence or (as the case may be) of the offence and the offence or offences associated with it, including any aggravating or mitigating factors.

(2) In forming any such opinion as is mentioned in section 148(2)(a) or (3)(a), the court may take into account any information about the offender which is before it.

(3) Subject to subsection (4), a court must obtain and consider a pre-sentence report before –

(a) in the case of a custodial sentence, forming any such opinion as is mentioned in section 152(2), section 153(2), section 225(1)(b), section 226(1)(b), section 227(1)(b) or section 228(1)(b)(i), or

(b) in the case of a community sentence, forming any such opinion as is mentioned in section 148(1), (2)(b) or (3)(b) or any opinion as to the suitability for the offender of the particular requirement or requirements to be imposed by the community order.

(4) Subsection (3) does not apply if, in the circumstances of the case, the court is of the opinion that it is unnecessary to obtain a pre-sentence report.

(5)   In a case where the offender is aged under 18, the court must not form the opinion mentioned in subsection (4) unless –

   (a)   there exists a previous pre-sentence report obtained in respect of the offender, and

   (b)   the court has had regard to the information contained in that report, or, if there is more than one such report, the most recent report.

(6)   No custodial sentence or community sentence is invalidated by the failure of a court to obtain and consider a pre-sentence report before forming an opinion referred to in subsection (3), but any court on an appeal against such a sentence –

   (a)   must, subject to subsection (7), obtain a pre-sentence report if none was obtained by the court below, and

   (b)   must consider any such report obtained by it or by that court.

(7)   Subsection (6)(a) does not apply if the court is of the opinion –

   (a)   that the court below was justified in forming an opinion that it was unnecessary to obtain a pre-sentence report, or

   (b)   that, although the court below was not justified in forming that opinion, in the circumstances of the case at the time it is before the court, it is unnecessary to obtain a pre-sentence report.

(8)   In a case where the offender is aged under 18, the court must not form the opinion mentioned in subsection (7) unless –

   (a)   there exists a previous pre-sentence report obtained in respect of the offender, and

   (b)   the court has had regard to the information contained in that report, or, if there is more than one such report, the most recent report.

157 Additional requirements in case of mentally disordered offender

(1)   Subject to subsection (2), in any case where the offender is or appears to be mentally disordered, the court must obtain and consider a medical report before passing a custodial sentence other than one fixed by law.

(2)   Subsection (1) does not apply if, in the circumstances of the case, the court is of the opinion that it is unnecessary to obtain a medical report.

(3)   Before passing a custodial sentence other than one fixed by law on an offender who is or appears to be mentally disordered, a court must consider –

   (a)   any information before it which relates to his mental condition (whether given in a medical report, a pre-sentence report or otherwise), and

   (b)   the likely effect of such a sentence on that condition and on any treatment which may be available for it.

(4)   No custodial sentence which is passed in a case to which subsection (1) applies is invalidated by the failure of a court to comply with that subsection, but any court on an appeal against such a sentence –

   (a)   must obtain a medical report if none was obtained by the court below, and

   (b)   must consider any such report obtained by it or by that court.

(5)   In this section 'mentally disordered', in relation to any person, means suffering from a mental disorder within the meaning of the Mental Health Act 1983 (c. 20).

(6)   In this section 'medical report' means a report as to an offender's mental condition made or submitted orally or in writing by a registered medical practitioner who is approved for the purposes of section 12 of the Mental Health Act 1983 by the Secretary of State as having special experience in the diagnosis or treatment of mental disorder.

(7)   Nothing in this section is to be taken to limit the generality of section 156.

158 Meaning of 'pre-sentence report'

(1) In this Part 'pre-sentence report' means a report which –

    (a) with a view to assisting the court in determining the most suitable method of dealing with an offender, is made or submitted by an appropriate officer, and

    (b) contains information as to such matters, presented in such manner, as may be prescribed by rules made by the Secretary of State.

(2) In subsection (1) 'an appropriate officer' means –

    (a) where the offender is aged 18 or over, an officer of a local probation board, and

    (b) where the offender is aged under 18, an officer of a local probation board, a social worker of a local authority social services department or a member of a youth offending team.

Disclosure of pre-sentence reports etc

159 Disclosure of pre-sentence reports

(1) This section applies where the court obtains a pre-sentence report, other than a report given orally in open court.

(2) Subject to subsections (3) and (4), the court must give a copy of the report –

    (a) to the offender or his counsel or solicitor,

    (b) if the offender is aged under 18, to any parent or guardian of his who is present in court, and

    (c) to the prosecutor, that is to say, the person having the conduct of the proceedings in respect of the offence.

(3) If the offender is aged under 18 and it appears to the court that the disclosure to the offender or to any parent or guardian of his of any information contained in the report would be likely to create a risk of significant harm to the offender, a complete copy of the report need not be given to the offender or, as the case may be, to that parent or guardian.

(4) If the prosecutor is not of a description prescribed by order made by the Secretary of State, a copy of the report need not be given to the prosecutor if the court considers that it would be inappropriate for him to be given it.

(5) No information obtained by virtue of subsection (2)(c) may be used or disclosed otherwise than for the purpose of –

    (a) determining whether representations as to matters contained in the report need to be made to the court, or

    (b) making such representations to the court.

(6) In relation to an offender aged under 18 for whom a local authority have parental responsibility and who –

    (a) is in their care, or

    (b) is provided with accommodation by them in the exercise of any social services functions,

references in this section to his parent or guardian are to be read as references to that authority.

(7) In this section and section 160 –

       'harm' has the same meaning as in section 31 of the Children Act 1989 (c. 41);

       'local authority' and 'parental responsibility' have the same meanings as in that Act;

       'social services functions', in relation to a local authority, has the meaning given by section 1A of the Local Authority Social Services Act 1970 (c. 42).

160 Other reports of local probation boards and members of youth offending teams

(1) This section applies where –

    (a) a report by an officer of a local probation board or a member of a youth offending team is made to any court (other than a youth court) with a view to assisting the court in determining the most suitable method of dealing with any person in respect of an offence, and

    (b) the report is not a pre-sentence report.

(2) Subject to subsection (3), the court must give a copy of the report –

    (a) to the offender or his counsel or solicitor, and

    (b) if the offender is aged under 18, to any parent or guardian of his who is present in court.

(3) If the offender is aged under 18 and it appears to the court that the disclosure to the offender or to any parent or guardian of his of any information contained in the report would be likely to create a risk of significant harm to the offender, a complete copy of the report need not be given to the offender or, as the case may be, to that parent or guardian.

(4) In relation to an offender aged under 18 for whom a local authority have parental responsibility and who –

    (a) is in their care, or

    (b) is provided with accommodation by them in the exercise of any social services functions,

references in this section to his parent or guardian are to be read as references to that authority.

Pre-sentence drug testing

161 Pre-sentence drug testing

(1) Where a person aged 14 or over is convicted of an offence and the court is considering passing a community sentence or a suspended sentence, it may make an order under subsection (2) for the purpose of ascertaining whether the offender has any specified Class A drug in his body.

(2) The order requires the offender to provide, in accordance with the order, samples of any description specified in the order.

(3) Where the offender has not attained the age of 17, the order must provide for the samples to be provided in the presence of an appropriate adult.

(4) If it is proved to the satisfaction of the court that the offender has, without reasonable excuse, failed to comply with the order it may impose on him a fine of an amount not exceeding level 4.

(5) In subsection (4) 'level 4' means the amount which, in relation to a fine for a summary offence, is level 4 on the standard scale.

(6) The court may not make an order under subsection (2) unless it has been notified by the Secretary of State that the power to make such orders is exercisable by the court and the notice has not been withdrawn.

(7) The Secretary of State may by order amend subsection (1) by substituting for the age for the time being specified there a different age specified in the order.

(8) In this section –

    'appropriate adult', in relation to a person under the age of 17, means –

        (a) his parent or guardian or, if he is in the care of a local authority or voluntary organisation, a person representing that authority or organisation,

        (b) a social worker of a local authority social services department, or

(c)   if no person falling within paragraph (a) or (b) is available, any responsible person aged 18 or over who is not a police officer or a person employed by the police;

'specified Class A drug' has the same meaning as in Part 3 of the Criminal Justice and Court Services Act 2000 (c. 43).

Fines

162 Powers to order statement as to offender's financial circumstances

(1)   Where an individual has been convicted of an offence, the court may, before sentencing him, make a financial circumstances order with respect to him.

(2)   Where a magistrates' court has been notified in accordance with section 12(4) of the Magistrates' Courts Act 1980 (c. 43) that an individual desires to plead guilty without appearing before the court, the court may make a financial circumstances order with respect to him.

(3)   In this section 'a financial circumstances order' means, in relation to any individual, an order requiring him to give to the court, within such period as may be specified in the order, such a statement of his financial circumstances as the court may require.

(4)   An individual who without reasonable excuse fails to comply with a financial circumstances order is liable on summary conviction to a fine not exceeding level 3 on the standard scale.

(5)   If an individual, in furnishing any statement in pursuance of a financial circumstances order –

(a)   makes a statement which he knows to be false in a material particular,

(b)   recklessly furnishes a statement which is false in a material particular, or

(c)   knowingly fails to disclose any material fact,

he is liable on summary conviction to a fine not exceeding level 4 on the standard scale.

(6)   Proceedings in respect of an offence under subsection (5) may, notwithstanding anything in section 127(1) of the Magistrates' Courts Act 1980 (c. 43) (limitation of time), be commenced at any time within two years from the date of the commission of the offence or within six months from its first discovery by the prosecutor, whichever period expires the earlier.

163 General power of Crown Court to fine offender convicted on indictment

Where a person is convicted on indictment of any offence, other than an offence for which the sentence is fixed by law or falls to be imposed under section 110(2) or 111(2) of the Sentencing Act or under any of sections 225 to 228 of this Act, the court, if not precluded from sentencing an offender by its exercise of some other power, may impose a fine instead of or in addition to dealing with him in any other way in which the court has power to deal with him, subject however to any enactment requiring the offender to be dealt with in a particular way.

164 Fixing of fines

(1)   Before fixing the amount of any fine to be imposed on an offender who is an individual, a court must inquire into his financial circumstances.

(2)   The amount of any fine fixed by a court must be such as, in the opinion of the court, reflects the seriousness of the offence.

(3)   In fixing the amount of any fine to be imposed on an offender (whether an individual or other person), a court must take into account the circumstances of the case including, among other things, the financial circumstances of the offender so far as they are known, or appear, to the court.

(4) Subsection (3) applies whether taking into account the financial circumstances of the offender has the effect of increasing or reducing the amount of the fine.

(5) Where –

   (a) an offender has been convicted in his absence in pursuance of section 11 or 12 of the Magistrates' Courts Act 1980 (c. 43) (non-appearance of accused), or

   (b) an offender –

      (i) has failed to furnish a statement of his financial circumstances in response to a request which is an official request for the purposes of section 20A of the Criminal Justice Act 1991 (c.53) (offence of making false statement as to financial circumstances),

      (ii) has failed to comply with an order under section 162(1), or

      (iii) has otherwise failed to co-operate with the court in its inquiry into his financial circumstances,

   and the court considers that it has insufficient information to make a proper determination of the financial circumstances of the offender, it may make such determination as it thinks fit.

165 Remission of fines

(1) This section applies where a court has, in fixing the amount of a fine, determined the offender's financial circumstances under section 164(5).

(2) If, on subsequently inquiring into the offender's financial circumstances, the court is satisfied that had it had the results of that inquiry when sentencing the offender it would –

   (a) have fixed a smaller amount, or

   (b) not have fined him,

   it may remit the whole or part of the fine.

(3) Where under this section the court remits the whole or part of a fine after a term of imprisonment has been fixed under section 139 of the Sentencing Act (powers of Crown Court in relation to fines) or section 82(5) of the Magistrates' Courts Act 1980 (magistrates' powers in relation to default) it must reduce the term by the corresponding proportion.

(4) In calculating any reduction required by subsection (3), any fraction of a day is to be ignored.

Savings for power to mitigate etc

166 Savings for powers to mitigate sentences and deal appropriately with mentally disordered offenders

(1) Nothing in –

   (a) section 148 (imposing community sentences),

   (b) section 152, 153 or 157 (imposing custodial sentences),

   (c) section 156 (pre-sentence reports and other requirements),

   (d) section 164 (fixing of fines),

   prevents a court from mitigating an offender's sentence by taking into account any such matters as, in the opinion of the court, are relevant in mitigation of sentence.

(2) Section 152(2) does not prevent a court, after taking into account such matters, from passing a community sentence even though it is of the opinion that the offence, or the combination of the offence and one or more offences associated with it, was so serious that a community sentence could not normally be justified for the offence.

(3) Nothing in the sections mentioned in subsection (1)(a) to (d) prevents a court –

    (a) from mitigating any penalty included in an offender's sentence by taking into account any other penalty included in that sentence, and

    (b) in the case of an offender who is convicted of one or more other offences, from mitigating his sentence by applying any rule of law as to the totality of sentences.

(4) Subsections (2) and (3) are without prejudice to the generality of subsection (1).

(5) Nothing in the sections mentioned in subsection (1)(a) to (d) is to be taken –

    (a) as requiring a court to pass a custodial sentence, or any particular custodial sentence, on a mentally disordered offender, or

    (b) as restricting any power (whether under the Mental Health Act 1983 (c. 20) or otherwise) which enables a court to deal with such an offender in the manner it considers to be most appropriate in all the circumstances.

(6) In subsection (5) 'mentally disordered', in relation to a person, means suffering from a mental disorder within the meaning of the Mental Health Act 1983.

Sentencing and allocation guidelines

167 The Sentencing Guidelines Council

(1) There shall be a Sentencing Guidelines Council (in this Chapter referred to as the Council) consisting of –

    (a) the Lord Chief Justice, who is to be chairman of the Council,

    (b) seven members (in this section and section 168 referred to as 'judicial members') appointed by the Lord Chancellor after consultation with the Secretary of State and the Lord Chief Justice, and

    (c) four members (in this section and section 168 referred to as 'non- judicial members') appointed by the Secretary of State after consultation with the Lord Chancellor and the Lord Chief Justice.

(2) A person is eligible to be appointed as a judicial member if he is –

    (a) a Lord Justice of Appeal,

    (b) a judge of the High Court,

    (c) a Circuit judge,

    (d) a District Judge (Magistrates' Courts), or

    (e) a lay justice.

(3) The judicial members must include a Circuit judge, a District Judge (Magistrates' Courts) and a lay justice.

(4) A person is eligible for appointment as a non-judicial member if he appears to the Secretary of State to have experience in one or more of the following areas –

    (a) policing,

    (b) criminal prosecution,

    (c) criminal defence, and

    (d) the promotion of the welfare of victims of crime.

(5) The persons eligible for appointment as a non-judicial member by virtue of experience of criminal prosecution include the Director of Public Prosecutions.

(6) The non-judicial members must include at least one person appearing to the Secretary of State to have experience in each area.

(7) The Lord Chief Justice must appoint one of the judicial members or non-judicial members to be deputy chairman of the Council.

(8) In relation to any meeting of the Council from which the Lord Chief Justice is to be absent, he may nominate any person eligible for appointment as a judicial member to act as a member on his behalf at the meeting.

(9) The Secretary of State may appoint a person appearing to him to have experience of sentencing policy and the administration of sentences to attend and speak at any meeting of the Council.

(10) In this section and section 168 'lay justice' means a justice of the peace who is not a District Judge (Magistrates' Courts).

168 Sentencing Guidelines Council: supplementary provisions

(1) In relation to the Council, the Lord Chancellor may by order make provision –

   (a) as to the term of office, resignation and re-appointment of judicial members and non-judicial members,

   (b) enabling the appropriate Minister to remove a judicial member or non-judicial member from office on grounds of incapacity or misbehaviour, and

   (c) as to the proceedings of the Council.

(2) In subsection (1)(b) 'the appropriate Minister' means –

   (a) in relation to a judicial member, the Lord Chancellor, and

   (b) in relation to a non-judicial member, the Secretary of State.

(3) The validity of anything done by the Council is not affected by any vacancy among its members, by any defect in the appointment of a member or by any failure to comply with section 167(3), (6) or (7).

(4) The Lord Chancellor may pay –

   (a) to any judicial member who is appointed by virtue of being a lay justice, such remuneration or expenses as he may determine, and

   (b) to any other judicial member or the Lord Chief Justice, such expenses as he may determine.

(5) The Secretary of State may pay to any non-judicial member such remuneration or expenses as he may determine.

169 The Sentencing Advisory Panel

(1) There shall continue to be a Sentencing Advisory Panel (in this Chapter referred to as 'the Panel') constituted by the Lord Chancellor after consultation with the Secretary of State and the Lord Chief Justice.

(2) The Lord Chancellor must, after consultation with the Secretary of State and the Lord Chief Justice, appoint one of the members of the Panel to be its chairman.

(3) The Lord Chancellor may pay to any member of the Panel such remuneration or expenses as he may determine.

170 Guidelines relating to sentencing and allocation

(1) In this Chapter –

   (a) 'sentencing guidelines' means guidelines relating to the sentencing of offenders, which may be general in nature or limited to a particular category of offence or offender, and

   (b) 'allocation guidelines' means guidelines relating to decisions by a magistrates' court under section 19 of the Magistrates' Courts Act 1980 (c. 43) as to whether an offence is more suitable for summary trial or trial on indictment.

(2) The Secretary of State may at any time propose to the Council –

   (a) that sentencing guidelines be framed or revised by the Council –

      (i)   in respect of offences or offenders of a particular category, or

      (ii) in respect of a particular matter affecting sentencing, or

   (b) that allocation guidelines be framed or revised by the Council.

(3) The Council may from time to time consider whether to frame sentencing guidelines or allocation guidelines and, if it receives –

   (a) a proposal under section 171(2) from the Panel, or

   (b) a proposal under subsection (2) from the Secretary of State,

   must consider whether to do so.

(4) Where sentencing guidelines or allocation guidelines have been issued by the Council as definitive guidelines, the Council must from time to time (and, in particular, if it receives a proposal under section 171(2) from the Panel or under subsection (2) from the Secretary of State) consider whether to revise them.

(5) Where the Council decides to frame or revise sentencing guidelines, the matters to which the Council must have regard include –

(a) the need to promote consistency in sentencing,

(b) the sentences imposed by courts in England and Wales for offences to which the guidelines relate,

(c) the cost of different sentences and their relative effectiveness in preventing re-offending,

(d) the need to promote public confidence in the criminal justice system, and

(e) the views communicated to the Council, in accordance with section 171(3)(b), by the Panel.

(6) Where the Council decides to frame or revise allocation guidelines, the matters to which the Council must have regard include –

(a) the need to promote consistency in decisions under section 19 of the Magistrates' Courts Act 1980 (c. 43), and

(b) the views communicated to the Council, in accordance with section 171(3)(b), by the Panel.

(7) Sentencing guidelines in respect of an offence or category of offences must include criteria for determining the seriousness of the offence or offences, including (where appropriate) criteria for determining the weight to be given to any previous convictions of offenders.

(8) Where the Council has prepared or revised any sentencing guidelines or allocation guidelines, it must –

(a) publish them as draft guidelines, and

(b) consult about the draft guidelines –

(i) the Secretary of State,

(ii) such persons as the Lord Chancellor, after consultation with the Secretary of State, may direct, and

(iii) such other persons as the Council considers appropriate.

(9) The Council may, after making any amendment of the draft guidelines which it considers appropriate, issue the guidelines as definitive guidelines.

171 Functions of Sentencing Advisory Panel in relation to guidelines

(1) Where the Council decides to frame or revise any sentencing guidelines or allocation guidelines, otherwise than in response to a proposal from the Panel under subsection (2), the Council must notify the Panel.

(2) The Panel may at any time propose to the Council –

(a) that sentencing guidelines be framed or revised by the Council –

(i) in respect of offences or offenders of a particular category, or

(ii) in respect of a particular matter affecting sentencing, or

(b) that allocation guidelines be framed or revised by the Council.

(3) Where the Panel receives a notification under subsection (1) or makes a proposal under subsection (2), the Panel must –

(a) obtain and consider the views on the matters in issue of such persons or bodies as may be determined, after consultation with the Secretary of State and the Lord Chancellor, by the Council, and

(b) formulate its own views on those matters and communicate them to the Council.

(4) Paragraph (a) of subsection (3) does not apply where the Council notifies the Panel of the Council's view that the urgency of the case makes it impracticable for the Panel to comply with that paragraph.

172 Duty of court to have regard to sentencing guidelines

(1) Every court must –

    (a) in sentencing an offender, have regard to any guidelines which are relevant to the offender's case, and

    (b) in exercising any other function relating to the sentencing of offenders, have regard to any guidelines which are relevant to the exercise of the function.

(2) In subsection (1) 'guidelines' means sentencing guidelines issued by the Council under section 170(9) as definitive guidelines, as revised by subsequent guidelines so issued.

173 Annual report by Council

(1) The Council must as soon as practicable after the end of each financial year make to the Ministers a report on the exercise of the Council's functions during the year.

(2) If section 167 comes into force after the beginning of a financial year, the first report may relate to a period beginning with the day on which that section comes into force and ending with the end of the next financial year.

(3) The Ministers must lay a copy of the report before each House of Parliament.

(4) The Council must publish the report once the copy has been so laid.

(5) In this section –

    'financial year' means a period of 12 months ending with 31st March;

    'the Ministers' means the Secretary of State and the Lord Chancellor.

Duty of court to explain sentence

174 Duty to give reasons for, and explain effect of, sentence

(1) Subject to subsections (3) and (4), any court passing sentence on an offender –

    (a) must state in open court, in ordinary language and in general terms, its reasons for deciding on the sentence passed, and

    (b) must explain to the offender in ordinary language –

        (i) the effect of the sentence,

        (ii) where the offender is required to comply with any order of the court forming part of the sentence, the effects of non-compliance with the order,

        (iii) any power of the court, on the application of the offender or any other person, to vary or review any order of the court forming part of the sentence, and

        (iv) where the sentence consists of or includes a fine, the effects of failure to pay the fine.

(2) In complying with subsection (1)(a), the court must –

    (a) where guidelines indicate that a sentence of a particular kind, or within a particular range, would normally be appropriate for the offence and the sentence is of a different kind, or is outside that range, state the court's reasons for deciding on a sentence of a different kind or outside that range,

    (b) where the sentence is a custodial sentence and the duty in subsection (2) of section 152 is not excluded by subsection (1)(a) or (b) or (3) of that section, state that it is of the opinion referred to in section 152(2) and why it is of that opinion,

    (c) where the sentence is a community sentence and the case does not fall within section 151(2), state that it is of the opinion that section 148(1) applies and why it is of that opinion,

(d) where as a result of taking into account any matter referred to in section 144(1), the court imposes a punishment on the offender which is less severe than the punishment it would otherwise have imposed, state that fact, and

(e) in any case, mention any aggravating or mitigating factors which the court has regarded as being of particular importance.

(3) Subsection (1)(a) does not apply –

(a) to an offence the sentence for which is fixed by law (provision relating to sentencing for such an offence being made by section 270), or

(b) to an offence the sentence for which falls to be imposed under section 51A(2) of the Firearms Act 1968 (c. 27) or under subsection (2) of section 110 or 111 of the Sentencing Act (required custodial sentences).

(4) The Secretary of State may by order –

(a) prescribe cases in which subsection (1)(a) or (b) does not apply, and

(b) prescribe cases in which the statement referred to in subsection (1)(a) or the explanation referred to in subsection (1)(b) may be made in the absence of the offender, or may be provided in written form.

(5) Where a magistrates' court passes a custodial sentence, it must cause any reason stated by virtue of subsection (2)(b) to be specified in the warrant of commitment and entered on the register.

(6) In this section –

'guidelines' has the same meaning as in section 172;
'the register' has the meaning given by section 163 of the Sentencing Act.

Publication of information by Secretary of State

175 Duty to publish information about sentencing

In section 95 of the Criminal Justice Act 1991 (c. 53) (information for financial and other purposes) in subsection (1) before the 'or' at the end of paragraph (a) there is inserted –

'(aa) enabling such persons to become aware of the relative effectiveness of different sentences –

(i) in preventing re-offending, and

(ii) in promoting public confidence in the criminal justice system;'.

Interpretation of Chapter

176 Interpretation of Chapter 1

In this Chapter –

'allocation guidelines' has the meaning given by section 170(1)(b);
'the Council' means the Sentencing Guidelines Council;
'the Panel' means the Sentencing Advisory Panel;
'sentence' and 'sentencing' are to be read in accordance with section 142(3);
'sentencing guidelines' has the meaning given by section 170(1)(a);
'youth community order' has the meaning given by section 147(2).

CHAPTER 2   COMMUNITY ORDERS: OFFENDERS AGED 16 OR OVER

177 Community orders

(1) Where a person aged 16 or over is convicted of an offence, the court by or before which he is convicted may make an order (in this Part referred to as a 'community order') imposing on him any one or more of the following requirements –

    (a) an unpaid work requirement (as defined by section 199),

    (b) an activity requirement (as defined by section 201),

    (c) a programme requirement (as defined by section 202),

    (d) a prohibited activity requirement (as defined by section 203),

    (e) a curfew requirement (as defined by section 204),

    (f) an exclusion requirement (as defined by section 205),

    (g) a residence requirement (as defined by section 206),

    (h) a mental health treatment requirement (as defined by section 207),

    (i) a drug rehabilitation requirement (as defined by section 209),

    (j) an alcohol treatment requirement (as defined by section 212),

    (k) a supervision requirement (as defined by section 213), and

    (l) in a case where the offender is aged under 25, an attendance centre requirement (as defined by section 214).

(2) Subsection (1) has effect subject to sections 150 and 218 and to the following provisions of Chapter 4 relating to particular requirements –

    (a) section 199(3) (unpaid work requirement),

    (b) section 201(3) and (4) (activity requirement),

    (c) section 202(4) and (5) (programme requirement),

    (d) section 203(2) (prohibited activity requirement),

    (e) section 207(3) (mental health treatment requirement),

    (f) section 209(2) (drug rehabilitation requirement), and

    (g) section 212(2) and (3) (alcohol treatment requirement).

(3) Where the court makes a community order imposing a curfew requirement or an exclusion requirement, the court must also impose an electronic monitoring requirement (as defined by section 215) unless –

    (a) it is prevented from doing so by section 215(2) or 218(4), or

    (b) in the particular circumstances of the case, it considers it inappropriate to do so.

(4) Where the court makes a community order imposing an unpaid work requirement, an activity requirement, a programme requirement, a prohibited activity requirement, a residence requirement, a mental health treatment requirement, a drug rehabilitation requirement, an alcohol treatment requirement, a supervision requirement or an attendance centre requirement, the court may also impose an electronic monitoring requirement unless prevented from doing so by section 215(2) or 218(4).

(5) A community order must specify a date, not more than three years after the date of the order, by which all the requirements in it must have been complied with; and a community order which imposes two or more different requirements falling within subsection (1) may also specify an earlier date or dates in relation to compliance with any one or more of them.

(6) Before making a community order imposing two or more different requirements falling within subsection (1), the court must consider whether, in the circumstances of the case, the requirements are compatible with each other.

178 Power to provide for court review of community orders

(1) The Secretary of State may by order –

    (a)   enable or require a court making a community order to provide for the community order to be reviewed periodically by that or another court,

    (b)   enable a court to amend a community order so as to include or remove a provision for review by a court, and

    (c)   make provision as to the timing and conduct of reviews and as to the powers of the court on a review.

(2)   An order under this section may, in particular, make provision in relation to community orders corresponding to any provision made by sections 191 and 192 in relation to suspended sentence orders.

(3)   An order under this section may repeal or amend any provision of this Part.

179 Breach, revocation or amendment of community order

Schedule 8 (which relates to failures to comply with the requirements of community orders and to the revocation or amendment of such orders) shall have effect.

180 Transfer of community orders to Scotland or Northern Ireland

Schedule 9 (transfer of community orders to Scotland or Northern Ireland) shall have effect.

CHAPTER 3   PRISON SENTENCES OF LESS THAN 12 MONTHS

Prison sentences of less than twelve months

181 Prison sentences of less than 12 months

(1)   Any power of a court to impose a sentence of imprisonment for a term of less than 12 months on an offender may be exercised only in accordance with the following provisions of this section unless the court makes an intermittent custody order (as defined by section 183).

(2)   The term of the sentence –

    (a)   must be expressed in weeks,

    (b)   must be at least 28 weeks,

    (c)   must not be more than 51 weeks in respect of any one offence, and

    (d)   must not exceed the maximum term permitted for the offence.

(3)   The court, when passing sentence, must –

    (a)   specify a period (in this Chapter referred to as 'the custodial period') at the end of which the offender is to be released on a licence, and

    (b)   by order require the licence to be granted subject to conditions requiring the offender's compliance during the remainder of the term (in this Chapter referred to as 'the licence period') or any part of it with one or more requirements falling within section 182(1) and specified in the order.

(4)   In this Part 'custody plus order' means an order under subsection (3)(b).

(5)   The custodial period –

    (a)   must be at least 2 weeks, and

    (b)   in respect of any one offence, must not be more than 13 weeks.

(6)   In determining the term of the sentence and the length of the custodial period, the court must ensure that the licence period is at least 26 weeks in length.

(7)   Where a court imposes two or more terms of imprisonment in accordance with this section to be served consecutively –

    (a)   the aggregate length of the terms of imprisonment must not be more than 65 weeks, and

(b) the aggregate length of the custodial periods must not be more than 26 weeks.

(8) A custody plus order which specifies two or more requirements may, in relation to any requirement, refer to compliance within such part of the licence period as is specified in the order.

(9) Subsection (3)(b) does not apply where the sentence is a suspended sentence.

182 Licence conditions

(1) The requirements falling within this subsection are –

    (a) an unpaid work requirement (as defined by section 199),

    (b) an activity requirement (as defined by section 201),

    (c) a programme requirement (as defined by section 202),

    (d) a prohibited activity requirement (as defined by section 203),

    (e) a curfew requirement (as defined by section 204),

    (f) an exclusion requirement (as defined by section 205),

    (g) a supervision requirement (as defined by section 213), and

    (h) in a case where the offender is aged under 25, an attendance centre requirement (as defined by section 214).

(2) The power under section 181(3)(b) to determine the conditions of the licence has effect subject to section 218 and to the following provisions of Chapter 4 relating to particular requirements –

    (a) section 199(3) (unpaid work requirement),

    (b) section 201(3) and (4) (activity requirement),

    (c) section 202(4) and (5) (programme requirement), and

    (d) section 203(2) (prohibited activity requirement).

(3) Where the court makes a custody plus order requiring a licence to contain a curfew requirement or an exclusion requirement, the court must also require the licence to contain an electronic monitoring requirement (as defined by section 215) unless –

    (a) the court is prevented from doing so by section 215(2) or 218(4), or

    (b) in the particular circumstances of the case, it considers it inappropriate to do so.

(4) Where the court makes a custody plus order requiring a licence to contain an unpaid work requirement, an activity requirement, a programme requirement, a prohibited activity requirement, a supervision requirement or an attendance centre requirement, the court may also require the licence to contain an electronic monitoring requirement unless the court is prevented from doing so by section 215(2) or 218(4).

(5) Before making a custody plus order requiring a licence to contain two or more different requirements falling within subsection (1), the court must consider whether, in the circumstances of the case, the requirements are compatible with each other.

Intermittent custody

183 Intermittent custody

(1) A court may, when passing a sentence of imprisonment for a term complying with subsection (4) –

    (a) specify the number of days that the offender must serve in prison under the sentence before being released on licence for the remainder of the term, and

    (b) by order –

        (i) specify periods during which the offender is to be released temporarily on licence before he has served that number of days in prison, and

        (ii) require any licence to be granted subject to conditions requiring the offender's compliance during the licence periods with one or more requirements falling within section 182(1) and specified in the order.

(2) In this Part 'intermittent custody order' means an order under subsection (1)(b).

(3) In this Chapter –

> 'licence period', in relation to a term of imprisonment to which an intermittent custody order relates, means any period during which the offender is released on licence by virtue of subsection (1)(a) or (b)(i);
>
> 'the number of custodial days', in relation to a term of imprisonment to which an intermittent custody order relates, means the number of days specified under subsection (1)(a).

(4) The term of the sentence –

    (a) must be expressed in weeks,

    (b) must be at least 28 weeks,

    (c) must not be more than 51 weeks in respect of any one offence, and

    (d) must not exceed the maximum term permitted for the offence.

(5) The number of custodial days –

    (a) must be at least 14, and

    (b) in respect of any one offence, must not be more than 90.

(6) A court may not exercise its powers under subsection (1) unless the offender has expressed his willingness to serve the custodial part of the proposed sentence intermittently, during the parts of the sentence that are not to be licence periods.

(7) Where a court exercises its powers under subsection (1) in respect of two or more terms of imprisonment that are to be served consecutively –

    (a) the aggregate length of the terms of imprisonment must not be more than 65 weeks, and

    (b) the aggregate of the numbers of custodial days must not be more than 180.

(8) The Secretary of State may by order require a court, in specifying licence periods under subsection (1)(b)(i), to specify only –

    (a) periods of a prescribed duration,

    (b) periods beginning or ending at prescribed times, or

    (c) periods including, or not including, specified parts of the week.

(9) An intermittent custody order which specifies two or more requirements may, in relation to any requirement, refer to compliance within such licence period or periods, or part of a licence period, as is specified in the order.

184 Restrictions on power to make intermittent custody order

(1) A court may not make an intermittent custody order unless it has been notified by the Secretary of State that arrangements for implementing such orders are available in the area proposed to be specified in the intermittent custody order and the notice has not been withdrawn.

(2) The court may not make an intermittent custody order in respect of any offender unless –

    (a) it has consulted an officer of a local probation board,

    (b) it has received from the Secretary of State notification that suitable prison accommodation is available for the offender during the custodial periods, and

    (c) it appears to the court that the offender will have suitable accommodation available to him during the licence periods.

(3) In this section 'custodial period', in relation to a sentence to which an intermittent custody order relates, means any part of the sentence that is not a licence period.

185 Intermittent custody: licence conditions

(1) Section 183(1)(b) has effect subject to section 218 and to the following provisions of Chapter 4 limiting the power to require the licence to contain particular requirements –

(a) section 199(3) (unpaid work requirement),
(b) section 201(3) and (4) (activity requirement),
(c) section 202(4) and (5) (programme requirement), and
(d) section 203(2) (prohibited activity requirement).

(2) Subsections (3) to (5) of section 182 have effect in relation to an intermittent custody order as they have effect in relation to a custody plus order.

186 Further provisions relating to intermittent custody

(1) Section 21 of the 1952 Act (expenses of conveyance to prison) does not apply in relation to the conveyance to prison at the end of any licence period of an offender to whom an intermittent custody order relates.

(2) The Secretary of State may pay to any offender to whom an intermittent custody order relates the whole or part of any expenses incurred by the offender in travelling to and from prison during licence periods.

(3) In section 49 of the 1952 Act (persons unlawfully at large) after subsection (4) there is inserted –

'(4A) For the purposes of this section a person shall also be deemed to be unlawfully at large if, having been temporarily released in pursuance of an intermittent custody order made under section 183 of the Criminal Justice Act 2003, he remains at large at a time when, by reason of the expiry of the period for which he was temporarily released, he is liable to be detained in pursuance of his sentence.'

(4) In section 23 of the Criminal Justice Act 1961 (c. 39) (prison rules), in subsection (3) for 'The days' there is substituted 'Subject to subsection (3A), the days' and after subsection (3) there is inserted –

'(3A) In relation to a prisoner to whom an intermittent custody order under section 183 of the Criminal Justice Act 2003 relates, the only days to which subsection (3) applies are Christmas Day, Good Friday and any day which under the Banking and Financial Dealings Act 1971 is a bank holiday in England and Wales.'

(5) In section 1 of the Prisoners (Return to Custody) Act 1995 (c. 16) (remaining at large after temporary release) after subsection (1) there is inserted –

'(1A) A person who has been temporarily released in pursuance of an intermittent custody order made under section 183 of the Criminal Justice Act 2003 is guilty of an offence if, without reasonable excuse, he remains unlawfully at large at any time after becoming so at large by virtue of the expiry of the period for which he was temporarily released.'

(6) In this section 'the 1952 Act' means the Prison Act 1952 (c. 52).

Further provision about custody plus orders and intermittent custody orders

187 Revocation or amendment of order

Schedule 10 (which contains provisions relating to the revocation or amendment of custody plus orders and the amendment of intermittent custody orders) shall have effect.

188 Transfer of custody plus orders and intermittent custody orders to Scotland or Northern Ireland

Schedule 11 (transfer of custody plus orders and intermittent custody orders to Scotland or Northern Ireland) shall have effect.

Suspended sentences

189 Suspended sentences of imprisonment

(1) A court which passes a sentence of imprisonment for a term of at least 28 weeks but not more than 51 weeks in accordance with section 181 may –

    (a) order the offender to comply during a period specified for the purposes of this paragraph in the order (in this Chapter referred to as 'the supervision period') with one or more requirements falling within section 190(1) and specified in the order, and

    (b) order that the sentence of imprisonment is not to take effect unless either –

        (i) during the supervision period the offender fails to comply with a requirement imposed under paragraph (a), or

        (ii) during a period specified in the order for the purposes of this sub-paragraph (in this Chapter referred to as 'the operational period') the offender commits in the United Kingdom another offence (whether or not punishable with imprisonment),

    and (in either case) a court having power to do so subsequently orders under paragraph 8 of Schedule 12 that the original sentence is to take effect.

(2) Where two or more sentences imposed on the same occasion are to be served consecutively, the power conferred by subsection (1) is not exercisable in relation to any of them unless the aggregate of the terms of the sentences does not exceed 65 weeks.

(3) The supervision period and the operational period must each be a period of not less than six months and not more than two years beginning with the date of the order.

(4) The supervision period must not end later than the operational period.

(5) A court which passes a suspended sentence on any person for an offence may not impose a community sentence in his case in respect of that offence or any other offence of which he is convicted by or before the court or for which he is dealt with by the court.

(6) Subject to any provision to the contrary contained in the Criminal Justice Act 1967 (c. 80), the Sentencing Act or any other enactment passed or instrument made under any enactment after 31st December 1967, a suspended sentence which has not taken effect under paragraph 8 of Schedule 12 is to be treated as a sentence of imprisonment for the purposes of all enactments and instruments made under enactments.

(7) In this Part –

    (a) 'suspended sentence order' means an order under subsection (1),

    (b) 'suspended sentence' means a sentence to which a suspended sentence order relates, and

    (c) 'community requirement', in relation to a suspended sentence order, means a requirement imposed under subsection (1)(a).

190 Imposition of requirements by suspended sentence order

(1) The requirements falling within this subsection are –

    (a) an unpaid work requirement (as defined by section 199),

    (b) an activity requirement (as defined by section 201),

    (c) a programme requirement (as defined by section 202),

    (d) a prohibited activity requirement (as defined by section 203),

    (e) a curfew requirement (as defined by section 204),

    (f) an exclusion requirement (as defined by section 205),

    (g) a residence requirement (as defined by section 206),

    (h) a mental health treatment requirement (as defined by section 207),

    (i) a drug rehabilitation requirement (as defined by section 209),

    (j) an alcohol treatment requirement (as defined by section 212),

    (k) a supervision requirement (as defined by section 213), and

(l)   in a case where the offender is aged under 25, an attendance centre requirement (as defined by section 214).

(2)   Section 189(1)(a) has effect subject to section 218 and to the following provisions of Chapter 4 relating to particular requirements –

(a)   section 199(3) (unpaid work requirement),
(b)   section 201(3) and (4) (activity requirement),
(c)   section 202(4) and (5) (programme requirement),
(d)   section 203(2) (prohibited activity requirement),
(e)   section 207(3) (mental health treatment requirement),
(f)   section 209(2) (drug rehabilitation requirement), and
(g)   section 212(2) and (3) (alcohol treatment requirement).

(3)   Where the court makes a suspended sentence order imposing a curfew requirement or an exclusion requirement, it must also impose an electronic monitoring requirement (as defined by section 215) unless –

(a)   the court is prevented from doing so by section 215(2) or 218(4), or
(b)   in the particular circumstances of the case, it considers it inappropriate to do so.

(4)   Where the court makes a suspended sentence order imposing an unpaid work requirement, an activity requirement, a programme requirement, a prohibited activity requirement, a residence requirement, a mental health treatment requirement, a drug rehabilitation requirement, an alcohol treatment requirement, a supervision requirement or an attendance centre requirement, the court may also impose an electronic monitoring requirement unless the court is prevented from doing so by section 215(2) or 218(4).

(5)   Before making a suspended sentence order imposing two or more different requirements falling within subsection (1), the court must consider whether, in the circumstances of the case, the requirements are compatible with each other.

191 Power to provide for review of suspended sentence order

(1)   A suspended sentence order may –

(a)   provide for the order to be reviewed periodically at specified intervals,
(b)   provide for each review to be made, subject to section 192(4), at a hearing held for the purpose by the court responsible for the order (a 'review hearing'),
(c)   require the offender to attend each review hearing, and
(d)   provide for the responsible officer to make to the court responsible for the order, before each review, a report on the offender's progress in complying with the community requirements of the order.

(2)   Subsection (1) does not apply in the case of an order imposing a drug rehabilitation requirement (provision for such a requirement to be subject to review being made by section 210).

(3)   In this section references to the court responsible for a suspended sentence order are references –

(a)   where a court is specified in the order in accordance with subsection (4), to that court;
(b)   in any other case, to the court by which the order is made.

(4)   Where the area specified in a suspended sentence order made by a magistrates' court is not the area for which the court acts, the court may, if it thinks fit, include in the order provision specifying for the purpose of subsection (3) a magistrates' court which acts for the area specified in the order.

(5)   Where a suspended sentence order has been made on an appeal brought from the Crown Court or from the criminal division of the Court of Appeal, it is to be taken for the purposes of subsection (3)(b) to have been made by the Crown Court.

192 Periodic reviews of suspended sentence order

(1) At a review hearing (within the meaning of subsection (1) of section 191) the court may, after considering the responsible officer's report referred to in that subsection, amend the community requirements of the suspended sentence order, or any provision of the order which relates to those requirements.

(2) The court –

    (a) may not amend the community requirements of the order so as to impose a requirement of a different kind unless the offender expresses his willingness to comply with that requirement,

    (b) may not amend a mental health treatment requirement, a drug rehabilitation requirement or an alcohol treatment requirement unless the offender expresses his willingness to comply with the requirement as amended,

    (c) may amend the supervision period only if the period as amended complies with section 189(3) and (4),

    (d) may not amend the operational period of the suspended sentence, and

    (e) except with the consent of the offender, may not amend the order while an appeal against the order is pending.

(3) For the purposes of subsection (2)(a) –

    (a) a community requirement falling within any paragraph of section 190(1) is of the same kind as any other community requirement falling within that paragraph, and

    (b) an electronic monitoring requirement is a community requirement of the same kind as any requirement falling within section 190(1) to which it relates.

(4) If before a review hearing is held at any review the court, after considering the responsible officer's report, is of the opinion that the offender's progress in complying with the community requirements of the order is satisfactory, it may order that no review hearing is to be held at that review; and if before a review hearing is held at any review, or at a review hearing, the court, after considering that report, is of that opinion, it may amend the suspended sentence order so as to provide for each subsequent review to be held without a hearing.

(5) If at a review held without a hearing the court, after considering the responsible officer's report, is of the opinion that the offender's progress under the order is no longer satisfactory, the court may require the offender to attend a hearing of the court at a specified time and place.

(6) If at a review hearing the court is of the opinion that the offender has without reasonable excuse failed to comply with any of the community requirements of the order, the court may adjourn the hearing for the purpose of dealing with the case under paragraph 8 of Schedule 12.

(7) At a review hearing the court may amend the suspended sentence order so as to vary the intervals specified under section 191(1).

(8) In this section any reference to the court, in relation to a review without a hearing, is to be read –

    (a) in the case of the Crown Court, as a reference to a judge of the court, and

    (b) in the case of a magistrates' court, as a reference to a justice of the peace acting for the commission area for which the court acts.

193 Breach, revocation or amendment of suspended sentence order, and effect of further conviction

Schedule 12 (which relates to the breach, revocation or amendment of the community requirements of suspended sentence orders, and to the effect of any further conviction) shall have effect.

194 Transfer of suspended sentence orders to Scotland or Northern Ireland

Schedule 13 (transfer of suspended sentence orders to Scotland or Northern Ireland) shall have effect.

Interpretation of Chapter

195 Interpretation of Chapter 3

In this Chapter –

'custodial period', in relation to a term of imprisonment imposed in accordance with section 181, has the meaning given by subsection (3)(a) of that section;

'licence period' –

(a) in relation to a term of imprisonment imposed in accordance with section 181, has the meaning given by subsection (3)(b) of that section, and

(b) in relation to a term of imprisonment to which an intermittent custody order relates, has the meaning given by section 183(3);

'the number of custodial days', in relation to a term of imprisonment to which an intermittent custody order relates, has the meaning given by section 183(3);

'operational period' and 'supervision period', in relation to a suspended sentence, are to be read in accordance with section 189(1);

'sentence of imprisonment' does not include a committal for contempt of court or any kindred offence.

CHAPTER 4   FURTHER PROVISIONS ABOUT ORDERS UNDER CHAPTERS 2 AND 3

Introductory

196 Meaning of 'relevant order'

(1) In this Chapter 'relevant order' means –

(a) a community order,

(b) a custody plus order,

(c) a suspended sentence order, or

(d) an intermittent custody order.

(2) In this Chapter any reference to a requirement being imposed by, or included in, a relevant order is, in relation to a custody plus order or an intermittent custody order, a reference to compliance with the requirement being required by the order to be a condition of a licence.

197 Meaning of 'the responsible officer'

(1) For the purposes of this Part, 'the responsible officer', in relation to an offender to whom a relevant order relates, means –

(a) in a case where the order –

(i) imposes a curfew requirement or an exclusion requirement but no other requirement mentioned in section 177(1) or, as the case requires, section 182(1) or 190(1), and

(ii) imposes an electronic monitoring requirement,

the person who under section 215(3) is responsible for the electronic monitoring required by the order;

(b) in a case where the offender is aged 18 or over and the only requirement imposed by the order is an attendance centre requirement, the officer in charge of the attendance centre in question;

(c) in any other case, the qualifying officer who, as respects the offender, is for the time being responsible for discharging the functions conferred by this Part on the responsible officer.

(2) The following are qualifying officers for the purposes of subsection (1)(c) –

(a) in a case where the offender is aged under 18 at the time when the relevant order is made, an officer of a local probation board appointed for or assigned to the petty sessions area for the time being specified in the order or a member of a youth offending team established by a local authority for the time being specified in the order;

(b) in any other case, an officer of a local probation board appointed for or assigned to the petty sessions area for the time being specified in the order.

(3) The Secretary of State may by order –

(a) amend subsections (1) and (2), and

(b) make any other amendments of this Part that appear to him to be necessary or expedient in consequence of any amendment made by virtue of paragraph (a).

(4) An order under subsection (3) may, in particular, provide for the court to determine which of two or more descriptions of 'responsible officer' is to apply in relation to any relevant order.

198 Duties of responsible officer

(1) Where a relevant order has effect, it is the duty of the responsible officer –

(a) to make any arrangements that are necessary in connection with the requirements imposed by the order,

(b) to promote the offender's compliance with those requirements, and

(c) where appropriate, to take steps to enforce those requirements.

(2) In this section 'responsible officer' does not include a person falling within section 197(1)(a).

Requirements available in case of all offenders

199 Unpaid work requirement

(1) In this Part 'unpaid work requirement', in relation to a relevant order, means a requirement that the offender must perform unpaid work in accordance with section 200.

(2) The number of hours which a person may be required to work under an unpaid work requirement must be specified in the relevant order and must be in the aggregate –

(a) not less than 40, and

(b) not more than 300.

(3) A court may not impose an unpaid work requirement in respect of an offender unless after hearing (if the courts thinks necessary) an appropriate officer, the court is satisfied that the offender is a suitable person to perform work under such a requirement.

(4) In subsection (3) 'an appropriate officer' means –

(a) in the case of an offender aged 18 or over, an officer of a local probation board, and

(b) in the case of an offender aged under 18, an officer of a local probation board, a social worker of a local authority social services department or a member of a youth offending team.

(5) Where the court makes relevant orders in respect of two or more offences of which the offender has been convicted on the same occasion and includes unpaid work

requirements in each of them, the court may direct that the hours of work specified in any of those requirements is to be concurrent with or additional to those specified in any other of those orders, but so that the total number of hours which are not concurrent does not exceed the maximum specified in subsection (2)(b).

200 Obligations of person subject to unpaid work requirement

(1) An offender in respect of whom an unpaid work requirement of a relevant order is in force must perform for the number of hours specified in the order such work at such times as he may be instructed by the responsible officer.

(2) Subject to paragraph 20 of Schedule 8 and paragraph 18 of Schedule 12 (power to extend order), the work required to be performed under an unpaid work requirement of a community order or a suspended sentence order must be performed during a period of twelve months.

(3) Unless revoked, a community order imposing an unpaid work requirement remains in force until the offender has worked under it for the number of hours specified in it.

(4) Where an unpaid work requirement is imposed by a suspended sentence order, the supervision period as defined by section 189(1)(a) continues until the offender has worked under the order for the number of hours specified in the order, but does not continue beyond the end of the operational period as defined by section 189(1)(b)(ii).

201 Activity requirement

(1) In this Part 'activity requirement', in relation to a relevant order, means a requirement that the offender must do either or both of the following –

  (a) present himself to a person or persons specified in the relevant order at a place or places so specified on such number of days as may be so specified;
  (b) participate in activities specified in the order on such number of days as may be so specified.

(2) The specified activities may consist of or include activities whose purpose is that of reparation, such as activities involving contact between offenders and persons affected by their offences.

(3) A court may not include an activity requirement in a relevant order unless –

  (a) it has consulted –

    (i)   in the case of an offender aged 18 or over, an officer of a local probation board,
    (ii) in the case of an offender aged under 18, either an officer of a local probation board or a member of a youth offending team, and

  (b) it is satisfied that it is feasible to secure compliance with the requirement.

(4) A court may not include an activity requirement in a relevant order if compliance with that requirement would involve the co-operation of a person other than the offender and the offender's responsible officer, unless that other person consents to its inclusion.

(5) The aggregate of the number of days specified under subsection (1)(a) and (b) must not exceed 60.

(6) A requirement such as is mentioned in subsection (1)(a) operates to require the offender –

  (a) in accordance with instructions given by his responsible officer, to present himself at a place or places on the number of days specified in the order, and
  (b) while at any place, to comply with instructions given by, or under the authority of, the person in charge of that place.

(7) A place specified under subsection (1)(a) must be –

  (a) a community rehabilitation centre, or

   (b)   a place that has been approved by the local probation board for the area in which the premises are situated as providing facilities suitable for persons subject to activity requirements.

(8) Where the place specified under subsection (1)(a) is a community rehabilitation centre, the reference in subsection (6)(a) to the offender presenting himself at the specified place includes a reference to him presenting himself elsewhere than at the centre for the purpose of participating in activities in accordance with instructions given by, or under the authority of, the person in charge of the centre.

(9) A requirement to participate in activities operates to require the offender –

   (a)   in accordance with instructions given by his responsible officer, to participate in activities on the number of days specified in the order, and

   (b)   while participating, to comply with instructions given by, or under the authority of, the person in charge of the activities.

(10) In this section 'community rehabilitation centre' means premises –

   (a)   at which non-residential facilities are provided for use in connection with the rehabilitation of offenders, and

   (b)   which are for the time being approved by the Secretary of State as providing facilities suitable for persons subject to relevant orders.

202 Programme requirement

(1) In this Part 'programme requirement', in relation to a relevant order, means a requirement that the offender must participate in an accredited programme specified in the order at a place so specified on such number of days as may be so specified.

(2) In this Part 'accredited programme' means a programme that is for the time being accredited by the accreditation body.

(3) In this section –

   (a)   'programme' means a systematic set of activities, and

   (b)   'the accreditation body' means such body as the Secretary of State may designate for the purposes of this section by order.

(4) A court may not include a programme requirement in a relevant order unless –

   (a)   the accredited programme which the court proposes to specify in the order has been recommended to the court as being suitable for the offender –

      (i)   in the case of an offender aged 18 or over, by an officer of a local probation board, or

      (ii)   in the case of an offender aged under 18, either by an officer of a local probation board or by a member of a youth offending team, and

   (b)   the court is satisfied that the programme is (or, where the relevant order is a custody plus order or an intermittent custody order, will be) available at the place proposed to be specified.

(5) A court may not include a programme requirement in a relevant order if compliance with that requirement would involve the co-operation of a person other than the offender and the offender's responsible officer, unless that other person consents to its inclusion.

(6) A requirement to attend an accredited programme operates to require the offender –

   (a)   in accordance with instructions given by the responsible officer, to participate in the accredited programme at the place specified in the order on the number of days specified in the order, and

   (b)   while at that place, to comply with instructions given by, or under the authority of, the person in charge of the programme.

(7) A place specified in an order must be a place that has been approved by the local probation board for the area in which the premises are situated as providing facilities suitable for persons subject to programme requirements.

203 Prohibited activity requirement

(1) In this Part 'prohibited activity requirement', in relation to a relevant order, means a requirement that the offender must refrain from participating in activities specified in the order –

    (a) on a day or days so specified, or

    (b) during a period so specified.

(2) A court may not include a prohibited activity requirement in a relevant order unless it has consulted –

    (a) in the case of an offender aged 18 or over, an officer of a local probation board;

    (b) in the case of an offender aged under 18, either an officer of a local probation board or a member of a youth offending team.

(3) The requirements that may by virtue of this section be included in a relevant order include a requirement that the offender does not possess, use or carry a firearm within the meaning of the Firearms Act 1968 (c. 27).

204 Curfew requirement

(1) In this Part 'curfew requirement', in relation to a relevant order, means a requirement that the offender must remain, for periods specified in the relevant order, at a place so specified.

(2) A relevant order imposing a curfew requirement may specify different places or different periods for different days, but may not specify periods which amount to less than two hours or more than twelve hours in any day.

(3) A community order or suspended sentence order which imposes a curfew requirement may not specify periods which fall outside the period of six months beginning with the day on which it is made.

(4) A custody plus order which imposes a curfew requirement may not specify a period which falls outside the period of six months beginning with the first day of the licence period as defined by section 181(3)(b).

(5) An intermittent custody order which imposes a curfew requirement must not specify a period if to do so would cause the aggregate number of days on which the offender is subject to the requirement for any part of the day to exceed 182.

(6) Before making a relevant order imposing a curfew requirement, the court must obtain and consider information about the place proposed to be specified in the order (including information as to the attitude of persons likely to be affected by the enforced presence there of the offender).

205 Exclusion requirement

(1) In this Part 'exclusion requirement', in relation to a relevant order, means a provision prohibiting the offender from entering a place specified in the order for a period so specified.

(2) Where the relevant order is a community order, the period specified must not be more than two years.

(3) An exclusion requirement –

    (a) may provide for the prohibition to operate only during the periods specified in the order, and

    (b) may specify different places for different periods or days.

(4) In this section 'place' includes an area.

206 Residence requirement

(1) In this Part, 'residence requirement', in relation to a community order or a suspended sentence order, means a requirement that, during a period specified in the relevant order, the offender must reside at a place specified in the order.

(2) If the order so provides, a residence requirement does not prohibit the offender from residing, with the prior approval of the responsible officer, at a place other than that specified in the order.

(3) Before making a community order or suspended sentence order containing a residence requirement, the court must consider the home surroundings of the offender.

(4) A court may not specify a hostel or other institution as the place where an offender must reside, except on the recommendation of an officer of a local probation board.

207 Mental health treatment requirement

(1) In this Part, 'mental health treatment requirement', in relation to a community order or suspended sentence order, means a requirement that the offender must submit, during a period or periods specified in the order, to treatment by or under the direction of a registered medical practitioner or a chartered psychologist (or both, for different periods) with a view to the improvement of the offender's mental condition.

(2) The treatment required must be such one of the following kinds of treatment as may be specified in the relevant order –

    (a) treatment as a resident patient in an independent hospital or care home within the meaning of the Care Standards Act 2000 (c. 14) or a hospital within the meaning of the Mental Health Act 1983 (c. 20), but not in hospital premises where high security psychiatric services within the meaning of that Act are provided;

    (b) treatment as a non-resident patient at such institution or place as may be specified in the order;

    (c) treatment by or under the direction of such registered medical practitioner or chartered psychologist (or both) as may be so specified;

but the nature of the treatment is not to be specified in the order except as mentioned in paragraph (a), (b) or (c).

(3) A court may not by virtue of this section include a mental health treatment requirement in a relevant order unless –

    (a) the court is satisfied, on the evidence of a registered medical practitioner approved for the purposes of section 12 of the Mental Health Act 1983, that the mental condition of the offender –

        (i)   is such as requires and may be susceptible to treatment, but

        (ii) is not such as to warrant the making of a hospital order or guardianship order within the meaning of that Act;

    (b) the court is also satisfied that arrangements have been or can be made for the treatment intended to be specified in the order (including arrangements for the reception of the offender where he is to be required to submit to treatment as a resident patient); and

    (c) the offender has expressed his willingness to comply with such a requirement.

(4) While the offender is under treatment as a resident patient in pursuance of a mental health requirement of a relevant order, his responsible officer shall carry out the supervision of the offender to such extent only as may be necessary for the purpose of the revocation or amendment of the order.

(5) Subsections (2) and (3) of section 54 of the Mental Health Act 1983 (c. 20) have effect with respect to proof for the purposes of subsection (3)(a) of an offender's mental condition as they have effect with respect to proof of an offender's mental condition for the purposes of section 37(2)(a) of that Act.

(6) In this section and section 208, 'chartered psychologist' means a person for the time being listed in the British Psychological Society's Register of Chartered Psychologists.

208 Mental health treatment at place other than that specified in order

(1) Where the medical practitioner or chartered psychologist by whom or under whose direction an offender is being treated for his mental condition in pursuance of a mental health treatment requirement is of the opinion that part of the treatment can be better or more conveniently given in or at an institution or place which –

(a) is not specified in the relevant order, and

(b) is one in or at which the treatment of the offender will be given by or under the direction of a registered medical practitioner or chartered psychologist,

he may, with the consent of the offender, make arrangements for him to be treated accordingly.

(2) Such arrangements as are mentioned in subsection (1) may provide for the offender to receive part of his treatment as a resident patient in an institution or place notwithstanding that the institution or place is not one which could have been specified for that purpose in the relevant order.

(3) Where any such arrangements as are mentioned in subsection (1) are made for the treatment of an offender –

(a) the medical practitioner or chartered psychologist by whom the arrangements are made shall give notice in writing to the offender's responsible officer, specifying the institution or place in or at which the treatment is to be carried out; and

(b) the treatment provided for by the arrangements shall be deemed to be treatment to which he is required to submit in pursuance of the relevant order.

209 Drug rehabilitation requirement

(1) In this Part 'drug rehabilitation requirement', in relation to a community order or suspended sentence order, means a requirement that during a period specified in the order ('the treatment and testing period') the offender –

(a) must submit to treatment by or under the direction of a specified person having the necessary qualifications or experience with a view to the reduction or elimination of the offender's dependency on or propensity to misuse drugs, and

(b) for the purpose of ascertaining whether he has any drug in his body during that period, must provide samples of such description as may be so determined, at such times or in such circumstances as may (subject to the provisions of the order) be determined by the responsible officer or by the person specified as the person by or under whose direction the treatment is to be provided.

(2) A court may not impose a drug rehabilitation requirement unless –

(a) it is satisfied –

(i) that the offender is dependent on, or has a propensity to misuse drugs, and

(ii) that his dependency or propensity is such as requires and may be susceptible to treatment,

(b) it is also satisfied that arrangements have been or can be made for the treatment intended to be specified in the order (including arrangements for the reception of the offender where he is to be required to submit to treatment as a resident),

(c) the requirement has been recommended to the court as being suitable for the offender –

(i) in the case of an offender aged 18 or over, by an officer of a local probation board, or

(ii) in the case of an offender aged under 18, either by an officer of a local probation board or by a member of a youth offending team, and

(d) the offender expresses his willingness to comply with the requirement.

(3) The treatment and testing period must be at least six months.

(4) The required treatment for any particular period must be –

(a) treatment as a resident in such institution or place as may be specified in the order, or

(b) treatment as a non-resident in or at such institution or place, and at such intervals, as may be so specified;

but the nature of the treatment is not to be specified in the order except as mentioned in paragraph (a) or (b) above.

(5) The function of making a determination as to the provision of samples under provision included in the community order or suspended sentence order by virtue of subsection (1)(b) is to be exercised in accordance with guidance given from time to time by the Secretary of State.

(6) A community order or suspended sentence order imposing a drug rehabilitation requirement must provide that the results of tests carried out on any samples provided by the offender in pursuance of the requirement to a person other than the responsible officer are to be communicated to the responsible officer.

(7) In this section 'drug' means a controlled drug as defined by section 2 of the Misuse of Drugs Act 1971 (c. 38).

210 Drug rehabilitation requirement: provision for review by court

(1) A community order or suspended sentence order imposing a drug rehabilitation requirement may (and must if the treatment and testing period is more than 12 months) –

(a) provide for the requirement to be reviewed periodically at intervals of not less than one month,

(b) provide for each review of the requirement to be made, subject to section 211(6), at a hearing held for the purpose by the court responsible for the order (a 'review hearing'),

(c) require the offender to attend each review hearing,

(d) provide for the responsible officer to make to the court responsible for the order, before each review, a report in writing on the offender's progress under the requirement, and

(e) provide for each such report to include the test results communicated to the responsible officer under section 209(6) or otherwise and the views of the treatment provider as to the treatment and testing of the offender.

(2) In this section references to the court responsible for a community order or suspended sentence order imposing a drug rehabilitation requirement are references –

(a) where a court is specified in the order in accordance with subsection (3), to that court;

(b) in any other case, to the court by which the order is made.

(3) Where the area specified in a community order or suspended sentence order which is made by a magistrates' court and imposes a drug rehabilitation requirement is not the area for which the court acts, the court may, if it thinks fit, include in the order provision specifying for the purposes of subsection (2) a magistrates' court which acts for the area specified in the order.

(4) Where a community order or suspended sentence order imposing a drug rehabilitation requirement has been made on an appeal brought from the Crown Court or from the criminal division of the Court of Appeal, for the purposes of subsection (2)(b) it shall be taken to have been made by the Crown Court.

211 Periodic review of drug rehabilitation requirement

(1) At a review hearing (within the meaning given by subsection (1) of section 210) the court may, after considering the responsible officer's report referred to in that subsection, amend the community order or suspended sentence order, so far as it relates to the drug rehabilitation requirement.

(2) The court –

   (a) may not amend the drug rehabilitation requirement unless the offender expresses his willingness to comply with the requirement as amended,

   (b) may not amend any provision of the order so as to reduce the period for which the drug rehabilitation requirement has effect below the minimum specified in section 209(3), and

   (c) except with the consent of the offender, may not amend any requirement or provision of the order while an appeal against the order is pending.

(3) If the offender fails to express his willingness to comply with the drug rehabilitation requirement as proposed to be amended by the court, the court may –

   (a) revoke the community order, or the suspended sentence order and the suspended sentence to which it relates, and

   (b) deal with him, for the offence in respect of which the order was made, in any way in which he could have been dealt with for that offence by the court which made the order if the order had not been made.

(4) In dealing with the offender under subsection (3)(b), the court –

   (a) shall take into account the extent to which the offender has complied with the requirements of the order, and

   (b) may impose a custodial sentence (where the order was made in respect of an offence punishable with such a sentence) notwithstanding anything in section 152(2).

(5) Where the order is a community order made by a magistrates' court in the case of an offender under 18 years of age in respect of an offence triable only on indictment in the case of an adult, any powers exercisable under subsection (3)(b) in respect of the offender after he attains the age of 18 are powers to do either or both of the following –

   (a) to impose a fine not exceeding £5,000 for the offence in respect of which the order was made;

   (b) to deal with the offender for that offence in any way in which the court could deal with him if it had just convicted him of an offence punishable with imprisonment for a term not exceeding twelve months.

(6) If at a review hearing (as defined by section 210(1)(b)) the court, after considering the responsible officer's report, is of the opinion that the offender's progress under the requirement is satisfactory, the court may so amend the order as to provide for each subsequent review to be made by the court without a hearing.

(7) If at a review without a hearing the court, after considering the responsible officer's report, is of the opinion that the offender's progress under the requirement is no longer satisfactory, the court may require the offender to attend a hearing of the court at a specified time and place.

(8) At that hearing the court, after considering that report, may –

   (a) exercise the powers conferred by this section as if the hearing were a review hearing, and

   (b) so amend the order as to provide for each subsequent review to be made at a review hearing.

(9) In this section any reference to the court, in relation to a review without a hearing, is to be read –

   (a) in the case of the Crown Court, as a reference to a judge of the court;

   (b) in the case of a magistrates' court, as a reference to a justice of the peace acting for the commission area for which the court acts.

212 Alcohol treatment requirement

(1) In this Part 'alcohol treatment requirement', in relation to a community order or suspended sentence order, means a requirement that the offender must submit during a period specified in the order to treatment by or under the direction of a specified person having the necessary qualifications or experience with a view to the reduction or elimination of the offender's dependency on alcohol.

(2) A court may not impose an alcohol treatment requirement in respect of an offender unless it is satisfied –

    (a) that he is dependent on alcohol,

    (b) that his dependency is such as requires and may be susceptible to treatment, and

    (c) that arrangements have been or can be made for the treatment intended to be specified in the order (including arrangements for the reception of the offender where he is to be required to submit to treatment as a resident).

(3) A court may not impose an alcohol treatment requirement unless the offender expresses his willingness to comply with its requirements.

(4) The period for which the alcohol treatment requirement has effect must be not less than six months.

(5) The treatment required by an alcohol treatment requirement for any particular period must be –

    (a) treatment as a resident in such institution or place as may be specified in the order,

    (b) treatment as a non-resident in or at such institution or place, and at such intervals, as may be so specified, or

    (c) treatment by or under the direction of such person having the necessary qualification or experience as may be so specified;

but the nature of the treatment shall not be specified in the order except as mentioned in paragraph (a), (b) or (c) above.

213 Supervision requirement

(1) In this Part 'supervision requirement', in relation to a relevant order, means a requirement that, during the relevant period, the offender must attend appointments with the responsible officer or another person determined by the responsible officer, at such time and place as may be determined by the officer.

(2) The purpose for which a supervision requirement may be imposed is that of promoting the offender's rehabilitation.

(3) In subsection (1) 'the relevant period' means –

    (a) in relation to a community order, the period for which the community order remains in force,

    (b) in relation to a custody plus order, the licence period as defined by section 181(3)(b),

    (c) in relation to an intermittent custody order, the licence periods as defined by section 183(3), and

    (d) in relation to a suspended sentence order, the supervision period as defined by section 189(1)(a).

Requirements available only in case of offenders aged under 25

214 Attendance centre requirement

(1) In this Part 'attendance centre requirement', in relation to a relevant order, means a requirement that the offender must attend at an attendance centre specified in the relevant order for such number of hours as may be so specified.

(2) The aggregate number of hours for which the offender may be required to attend at an attendance centre must not be less than 12 or more than 36.

(3) The court may not impose an attendance centre requirement unless the court is satisfied that the attendance centre to be specified in it is reasonably accessible to the offender concerned, having regard to the means of access available to him and any other circumstances.

(4) The first time at which the offender is required to attend at the attendance centre is a time notified to the offender by the responsible officer.

(5) The subsequent hours are to be fixed by the officer in charge of the centre, having regard to the offender's circumstances.

(6) An offender may not be required under this section to attend at an attendance centre on more than one occasion on any day, or for more than three hours on any occasion.

Electronic monitoring

215 Electronic monitoring requirement

(1) In this Part 'electronic monitoring requirement', in relation to a relevant order, means a requirement for securing the electronic monitoring of the offender's compliance with other requirements imposed by the order during a period specified in the order, or determined by the responsible officer in accordance with the relevant order.

(2) Where –

    (a) it is proposed to include in a relevant order a requirement for securing electronic monitoring in accordance with this section, but

    (b) there is a person (other than the offender) without whose co-operation it will not be practicable to secure the monitoring,

the requirement may not be included in the order without that person's consent.

(3) A relevant order which includes an electronic monitoring requirement must include provision for making a person responsible for the monitoring; and a person who is made so responsible must be of a description specified in an order made by the Secretary of State.

(4) Where an electronic monitoring requirement is required to take effect during a period determined by the responsible officer in accordance with the relevant order, the responsible officer must, before the beginning of that period, notify –

    (a) the offender,

    (b) the person responsible for the monitoring, and

    (c) any person falling within subsection (2)(b),

of the time when the period is to begin.

Provisions applying to relevant orders generally

216 Petty sessions area to be specified in relevant order

(1) A community order or suspended sentence order must specify the petty sessions area in which the offender resides or will reside.

(2) A custody plus order or an intermittent custody order must specify the petty sessions area in which the offender will reside –

    (a) in the case of a custody plus order, during the licence period as defined by section 181(3)(b), or

    (b) in the case of an intermittent custody order, during the licence periods as defined by section 183(3).

217 Requirement to avoid conflict with religious beliefs, etc

(1) The court must ensure, as far as practicable, that any requirement imposed by a relevant order is such as to avoid –

    (a) any conflict with the offender's religious beliefs or with the requirements of any other relevant order to which he may be subject; and

    (b) any interference with the times, if any, at which he normally works or attends school or any other educational establishment.

(2) The responsible officer in relation to an offender to whom a relevant order relates must ensure, as far as practicable, that any instruction given or requirement imposed by him in pursuance of the order is such as to avoid the conflict or interference mentioned in subsection (1).

(3) The Secretary of State may by order provide that subsection (1) or (2) is to have effect with such additional restrictions as may be specified in the order.

218 Availability of arrangements in local area

(1) A court may not include an unpaid work requirement in a relevant order unless the court is satisfied that provision for the offender to work under such a requirement can be made under the arrangements for persons to perform work under such a requirement which exist in the petty sessions area in which he resides or will reside.

(2) A court may not include an activity requirement in a relevant order unless the court is satisfied that provision for the offender to participate in the activities proposed to be specified in the order can be made under the arrangements for persons to participate in such activities which exist in the petty sessions area in which he resides or will reside.

(3) A court may not include an attendance centre requirement in a relevant order in respect of an offender unless the court has been notified by the Secretary of State that an attendance centre is available for persons of his description.

(4) A court may not include an electronic monitoring requirement in a relevant order in respect of an offender unless the court –

    (a) has been notified by the Secretary of State that electronic monitoring arrangements are available in the relevant areas mentioned in subsections (5) to (7), and

    (b) is satisfied that the necessary provision can be made under those arrangements.

(5) In the case of a relevant order containing a curfew requirement or an exclusion requirement, the relevant area for the purposes of subsection (4) is the area in which the place proposed to be specified in the order is situated.

(6) In the case of a relevant order containing an attendance centre requirement, the relevant area for the purposes of subsection (4) is the area in which the attendance centre proposed to be specified in the order is situated.

(7) In the case of any other relevant order, the relevant area for the purposes of subsection (4) is the petty sessions area proposed to be specified in the order.

(8) In subsection (5) 'place', in relation to an exclusion requirement, has the same meaning as in section 205.

219 Provision of copies of relevant orders

(1) The court by which any relevant order is made must forthwith provide copies of the order –

    (a) to the offender,

    (b) if the offender is aged 18 or over, to an officer of a local probation board assigned to the court,

    (c) if the offender is aged 16 or 17, to an officer of a local probation board assigned to the court or to a member of a youth offending team assigned to the court, and

    (d) where the order specifies a petty sessions area for which the court making the order does not act, to the local probation board acting for that area.

(2) Where a relevant order imposes any requirement specified in the first column of Schedule 14, the court by which the order is made must also forthwith provide the person specified in relation to that requirement in the second column of that Schedule with a copy of so much of the order as relates to that requirement.

(3) Where a relevant order specifies a petty sessions area for which the court making the order does not act, the court making the order must provide to the magistrates' court acting for that area –

(a) a copy of the order, and

(b) such documents and information relating to the case as it considers likely to be of assistance to a court acting for that area in the exercise of its functions in relation to the order.

220 Duty of offender to keep in touch with responsible officer

(1) An offender in respect of whom a community order or a suspended sentence order is in force –

(a) must keep in touch with the responsible officer in accordance with such instructions as he may from time to time be given by that officer, and

(b) must notify him of any change of address.

(2) The obligation imposed by subsection (1) is enforceable as if it were a requirement imposed by the order.

Powers of Secretary of State

221 Provision of attendance centres

(1) The Secretary of State may continue to provide attendance centres.

(2) In this Part 'attendance centre' means a place at which offenders aged under 25 may be required to attend and be given under supervision appropriate occupation or instruction in pursuance of –

(a) attendance centre requirements of relevant orders, or

(b) attendance centre orders under section 60 of the Sentencing Act.

(3) For the purpose of providing attendance centres, the Secretary of State may make arrangements with any local authority or police authority for the use of premises of that authority.

222 Rules

(1) The Secretary of State may make rules for regulating –

(a) the supervision of persons who are subject to relevant orders,

(b) without prejudice to the generality of paragraph (a), the functions of responsible officers in relation to offenders subject to relevant orders,

(c) the arrangements to be made by local probation boards for persons subject to unpaid work requirements to perform work and the performance of such work,

(d) the provision and carrying on of attendance centres and community rehabilitation centres,

(e) the attendance of persons subject to activity requirements or attendance centre requirements at the places at which they are required to attend, including hours of attendance, reckoning days of attendance and the keeping of attendance records,

(f) electronic monitoring in pursuance of an electronic monitoring requirement, and

(g) without prejudice to the generality of paragraph (f), the functions of persons made responsible for securing electronic monitoring in pursuance of such a requirement.

(2) Rules under subsection (1)(c) may, in particular, make provision –

    (a) limiting the number of hours of work to be done by a person on any one day,

    (b) as to the reckoning of hours worked and the keeping of work records, and

    (c) for the payment of travelling and other expenses in connection with the performance of work.

223 Power to amend limits

(1) The Secretary of State may by order amend –

    (a) subsection (2) of section 199 (unpaid work requirement), or

    (b) subsection (2) of section 204 (curfew requirement),

by substituting, for the maximum number of hours for the time being specified in that subsection, such other number of hours as may be specified in the order.

(2) The Secretary of State may by order amend any of the provisions mentioned in subsection (3) by substituting, for any period for the time being specified in the provision, such other period as may be specified in the order.

(3) Those provisions are –

    (a) section 204(3) (curfew requirement);

    (b) section 205(2) (exclusion requirement);

    (c) section 209(3) (drug rehabilitation requirement);

    (d) section 212(4) (alcohol treatment requirement).

CHAPTER 5   DANGEROUS OFFENDERS

224 Meaning of 'specified offence' etc.

(1) An offence is a 'specified offence' for the purposes of this Chapter if it is a specified violent offence or a specified sexual offence.

(2) An offence is a 'serious offence' for the purposes of this Chapter if and only if –

    (a) it is a specified offence, and

    (b) it is, apart from section 225, punishable in the case of a person aged 18 or over by –

        (i) imprisonment for life, or

        (ii) imprisonment for a determinate period of ten years or more.

(3) In this Chapter –

    'relevant offence' has the meaning given by section 229(4);

    'serious harm' means death or serious personal injury, whether physical or psychological;

    'specified violent offence' means an offence specified in Part 1 of Schedule 15;

    'specified sexual offence' means an offence specified in Part 2 of that Schedule.

225 Life sentence or imprisonment for public protection for serious offences

(1) This section applies where –

    (a) a person aged 18 or over is convicted of a serious offence committed after the commencement of this section, and

    (b) the court is of the opinion that there is a significant risk to members of the public of serious harm occasioned by the commission by him of further specified offences.

(2) If –

    (a) the offence is one in respect of which the offender would apart from this section be liable to imprisonment for life, and

(b) the court considers that the seriousness of the offence, or of the offence and one or more offences associated with it, is such as to justify the imposition of a sentence of imprisonment for life,

the court must impose a sentence of imprisonment for life.

(3) In a case not falling within subsection (2), the court must impose a sentence of imprisonment for public protection.

(4) A sentence of imprisonment for public protection is a sentence of imprisonment for an indeterminate period, subject to the provisions of Chapter 2 of Part 2 of the Crime (Sentences) Act 1997 (c. 43) as to the release of prisoners and duration of licences.

(5) An offence the sentence for which is imposed under this section is not to be regarded as an offence the sentence for which is fixed by law.

226 Detention for life or detention for public protection for serious offences committed by those under 18

(1) This section applies where –

(a) a person aged under 18 is convicted of a serious offence committed after the commencement of this section, and

(b) the court is of the opinion that there is a significant risk to members of the public of serious harm occasioned by the commission by him of further specified offences.

(2) If –

(a) the offence is one in respect of which the offender would apart from this section be liable to a sentence of detention for life under section 91 of the Sentencing Act, and

(b) the court considers that the seriousness of the offence, or of the offence and one or more offences associated with it, is such as to justify the imposition of a sentence of detention for life,

the court must impose a sentence of detention for life under that section.

(3) If, in a case not falling within subsection (2), the court considers that an extended sentence under section 228 would not be adequate for the purpose of protecting the public from serious harm occasioned by the commission by the offender of further specified offences, the court must impose a sentence of detention for public protection.

(4) A sentence of detention for public protection is a sentence of detention for an indeterminate period, subject to the provisions of Chapter 2 of Part 2 of the Crime (Sentences) Act 1997 (c. 43) as to the release of prisoners and duration of licences.

(5) An offence the sentence for which is imposed under this section is not to be regarded as an offence the sentence for which is fixed by law.

227 Extended sentence for certain violent or sexual offences: persons 18 or over

(1) This section applies where –

(a) a person aged 18 or over is convicted of a specified offence, other than a serious offence, committed after the commencement of this section, and

(b) the court considers that there is a significant risk to members of the public of serious harm occasioned by the commission by the offender of further specified offences.

(2) The court must impose on the offender an extended sentence of imprisonment, that is to say, a sentence of imprisonment the term of which is equal to the aggregate of –

(a) the appropriate custodial term, and

(b) a further period ('the extension period') for which the offender is to be subject to a licence and which is of such length as the court considers necessary for the purpose of protecting members of the public from serious harm occasioned by the commission by him of further specified offences.

(3) In subsection (2) 'the appropriate custodial term' means a term of imprisonment (not exceeding the maximum term permitted for the offence) which –

(a) is the term that would (apart from this section) be imposed in compliance with section 153(2), or

(b) where the term that would be so imposed is a term of less than 12 months, is a term of 12 months.

(4) The extension period must not exceed –

(a) five years in the case of a specified violent offence, and

(b) eight years in the case of a specified sexual offence.

(5) The term of an extended sentence of imprisonment passed under this section in respect of an offence must not exceed the maximum term permitted for the offence.

228 Extended sentence for certain violent or sexual offences: persons under 18

(1) This section applies where –

(a) a person aged under 18 is convicted of a specified offence committed after the commencement of this section, and

(b) the court considers –

(i) that there is a significant risk to members of the public of serious harm occasioned by the commission by the offender of further specified offences, and

(ii) where the specified offence is a serious offence, that the case is not one in which the court is required by section 226(2) to impose a sentence of detention for life under section 91 of the Sentencing Act or by section 226(3) to impose a sentence of detention for public protection.

(2) The court must impose on the offender an extended sentence of detention, that is to say, a sentence of detention the term of which is equal to the aggregate of –

(a) the appropriate custodial term, and

(b) a further period ('the extension period') for which the offender is to be subject to a licence and which is of such length as the court considers necessary for the purpose of protecting members of the public from serious harm occasioned by the commission by him of further specified offences.

(3) In subsection (2) 'the appropriate custodial term' means such term as the court considers appropriate, which –

(a) must be at least 12 months, and

(b) must not exceed the maximum term of imprisonment permitted for the offence.

(4) The extension period must not exceed –

(a) five years in the case of a specified violent offence, and

(b) eight years in the case of a specified sexual offence.

(5) The term of an extended sentence of detention passed under this section in respect of an offence must not exceed the maximum term of imprisonment permitted for the offence.

(6) Any reference in this section to the maximum term of imprisonment permitted for an offence is a reference to the maximum term of imprisonment that is, apart from section 225, permitted for the offence in the case of a person aged 18 or over.

229 The assessment of dangerousness

(1) This section applies where –

(a) a person has been convicted of a specified offence, and

(b) it falls to a court to assess under any of sections 225 to 228 whether there is a significant risk to members of the public of serious harm occasioned by the commission by him of further such offences.

(2) If at the time when that offence was committed the offender had not been convicted in any part of the United Kingdom of any relevant offence or was aged under 18, the court in making the assessment referred to in subsection (1)(b) –

(a) must take into account all such information as is available to it about the nature and circumstances of the offence,

(b) may take into account any information which is before it about any pattern of behaviour of which the offence forms part, and

(c) may take into account any information about the offender which is before it.

(3) If at the time when that offence was committed the offender was aged 18 or over and had been convicted in any part of the United Kingdom of one or more relevant offences, the court must assume that there is such a risk as is mentioned in subsection (1)(b) unless, after taking into account –

(a) all such information as is available to it about the nature and circumstances of each of the offences,

(b) where appropriate, any information which is before it about any pattern of behaviour of which any of the offences forms part, and

(c) any information about the offender which is before it,

the court considers that it would be unreasonable to conclude that there is such a risk.

(4) In this Chapter 'relevant offence' means –

(a) a specified offence,

(b) an offence specified in Schedule 16 (offences under the law of Scotland), or

(c) an offence specified in Schedule 17 (offences under the law of Northern Ireland).

230 Imprisonment or detention for public protection: release on licence

Schedule 18 (release of prisoners serving sentences of imprisonment or detention for public protection) shall have effect.

231 Appeals where previous convictions set aside

(1) This section applies where –

(a) a sentence has been imposed on any person under section 225 or 227, and

(b) any previous conviction of his without which the court would not have been required to make the assumption mentioned in section 229(3) has been subsequently set aside on appeal.

(2) Notwithstanding anything in section 18 of the Criminal Appeal Act 1968 (c. 19), notice of appeal against the sentence may be given at any time within 28 days from the date on which the previous conviction was set aside.

232 Certificates of convictions for purposes of section 229

Where –

(a) on any date after the commencement of this section a person is convicted in England and Wales of a relevant offence, and

(b) the court by or before which he is so convicted states in open court that he has been convicted of such an offence on that date, and

(c) that court subsequently certifies that fact,

that certificate shall be evidence, for the purposes of section 229, that he was convicted of such an offence on that date.

233 Offences under service law

Where –

    (a) a person has at any time been convicted of an offence under section 70 of the Army Act 1955 (3 & 4 Eliz. 2 c. 18), section 70 of the Air Force Act 1955 (3 & 4 Eliz. 2 c. 19) or section 42 of the Naval Discipline Act 1957 (c. 53), and

    (b) the corresponding civil offence (within the meaning of that Act) was a relevant offence,

section 229 shall have effect as if he had at that time been convicted in England and Wales of the corresponding civil offence.

234 Determination of day when offence committed

Where an offence is found to have been committed over a period of two or more days, or at some time during a period of two or more days, it shall be taken for the purposes of section 229 to have been committed on the last of those days.

235 Detention under sections 226 and 228

A person sentenced to be detained under section 226 or 228 is liable to be detained in such place, and under such conditions, as may be determined by the Secretary of State or by such other person as may be authorised by him for the purpose.

236 Conversion of sentences of detention into sentences of imprisonment

For section 99 of the Sentencing Act (conversion of sentence of detention and custody into sentence of imprisonment) there is substituted –

'Conversion of sentence of detention to sentence of imprisonment

99 Conversion of sentence of detention to sentence of imprisonment

    (1) Subject to the following provisions of this section, where an offender has been sentenced by a relevant sentence of detention to a term of detention and either –

        (a) he has attained the age of 21, or

        (b) he has attained the age of 18 and has been reported to the Secretary of State by the board of visitors of the institution in which he is detained as exercising a bad influence on the other inmates of the institution or as behaving in a disruptive manner to the detriment of those inmates,

    the Secretary of State may direct that he shall be treated as if he had been sentenced to imprisonment for the same term.

    (2) Where the Secretary of State gives a direction under subsection (1) above in relation to an offender, the portion of the term of detention imposed under the relevant sentence of detention which he has already served shall be deemed to have been a portion of a term of imprisonment.

    (3) Where the Secretary of State gives a direction under subsection (1) above in relation to an offender serving a sentence of detention for public protection under section 226 of the Criminal Justice Act 2003 the offender shall be treated as if he had been sentenced under section 225 of that Act; and where the Secretary of State gives such a direction in relation to an offender serving an extended sentence of detention under section 228 of that Act the offender shall be treated as if he had been sentenced under section 227 of that Act.

    (4) Rules under section 47 of the Prison Act 1952 may provide that any award for an offence against discipline made in respect of an offender serving a relevant sentence of detention shall continue to have effect after a direction under subsection (1) has been given in relation to him.

    (5) In this section "relevant sentence of detention" means –

(a) a sentence of detention under section 90 or 91 above,

(b) a sentence of detention for public protection under section 226 of the Criminal Justice Act 2003, or

(c) an extended sentence of detention under section 228 of that Act.'

CHAPTER 6   RELEASE ON LICENCE

Preliminary

237 Meaning of 'fixed-term prisoner'

(1) In this Chapter 'fixed-term prisoner' means –

(a) a person serving a sentence of imprisonment for a determinate term, or

(b) a person serving a determinate sentence of detention under section 91 of the Sentencing Act or under section 228 of this Act.

(2) In this Chapter, unless the context otherwise requires, 'prisoner' includes a person serving a sentence falling within subsection (1)(b); and 'prison' includes any place where a person serving such a sentence is liable to be detained.

Power of court to recommend licence conditions

238 Power of court to recommend licence conditions for certain prisoners

(1) A court which sentences an offender to a term of imprisonment of twelve months or more in respect of any offence may, when passing sentence, recommend to the Secretary of State particular conditions which in its view should be included in any licence granted to the offender under this Chapter on his release from prison.

(2) In exercising his powers under section 250(4)(b) in respect of an offender, the Secretary of State must have regard to any recommendation under subsection (1).

(3) A recommendation under subsection (1) is not to be treated for any purpose as part of the sentence passed on the offender.

(4) This section does not apply in relation to a sentence of detention under section 91 of the Sentencing Act or section 228 of this Act.

239 The Parole Board

(1) The Parole Board is to continue to be, by that name, a body corporate and as such is –

(a) to be constituted in accordance with this Chapter, and

(b) to have the functions conferred on it by this Chapter in respect of fixed-term prisoners and by Chapter 2 of Part 2 of the Crime (Sentences) Act 1997 (c. 43) (in this Chapter referred to as 'the 1997 Act') in respect of life prisoners within the meaning of that Chapter.

(2) It is the duty of the Board to advise the Secretary of State with respect to any matter referred to it by him which is to do with the early release or recall of prisoners.

(3) The Board must, in dealing with cases as respects which it makes recommendations under this Chapter or under Chapter 2 of Part 2 of the 1997 Act, consider –

(a) any documents given to it by the Secretary of State, and

(b) any other oral or written information obtained by it;

and if in any particular case the Board thinks it necessary to interview the person to whom the case relates before reaching a decision, the Board may authorise one of its members to interview him and must consider the report of the interview made by that member.

(4) The Board must deal with cases as respects which it gives directions under this Chapter or under Chapter 2 of Part 2 of the 1997 Act on consideration of all such evidence as may be adduced before it.

(5) Without prejudice to subsections (3) and (4), the Secretary of State may make rules with respect to the proceedings of the Board, including proceedings authorising cases to be dealt with by a prescribed number of its members or requiring cases to be dealt with at prescribed times.

(6) The Secretary of State may also give to the Board directions as to the matters to be taken into account by it in discharging any functions under this Chapter or under Chapter 2 of Part 2 of the 1997 Act; and in giving any such directions the Secretary of State must have regard to –

   (a) the need to protect the public from serious harm from offenders, and
   (b) the desirability of preventing the commission by them of further offences and of securing their rehabilitation.

(7) Schedule 19 shall have effect with respect to the Board.

Effect of remand in custody

240 Crediting of periods of remand in custody: terms of imprisonment and detention

(1) This section applies where –

   (a) a court sentences an offender to imprisonment for a term in respect of an offence committed after the commencement of this section, and
   (b) the offender has been remanded in custody (within the meaning given by section 242) in connection with the offence or a related offence, that is to say, any other offence the charge for which was founded on the same facts or evidence.

(2) It is immaterial for that purpose whether the offender –

   (a) has also been remanded in custody in connection with other offences; or
   (b) has also been detained in connection with other matters.

(3) Subject to subsection (4), the court must direct that the number of days for which the offender was remanded in custody in connection with the offence or a related offence is to count as time served by him as part of the sentence.

(4) Subsection (3) does not apply if and to the extent that –

   (a) rules made by the Secretary of State so provide in the case of –

      (i) a remand in custody which is wholly or partly concurrent with a sentence of imprisonment, or
      (ii) sentences of imprisonment for consecutive terms or for terms which are wholly or partly concurrent, or

   (b) it is in the opinion of the court just in all the circumstances not to give a direction under that subsection.

(5) Where the court gives a direction under subsection (3), it shall state in open court –

   (a) the number of days for which the offender was remanded in custody, and
   (b) the number of days in relation to which the direction is given.

(6) Where the court does not give a direction under subsection (3), or gives such a direction in relation to a number of days less than that for which the offender was remanded in custody, it shall state in open court –

   (a) that its decision is in accordance with rules made under paragraph (a) of subsection (4), or
   (b) that it is of the opinion mentioned in paragraph (b) of that subsection and what the circumstances are.

(7) For the purposes of this section a suspended sentence –

(a) is to be treated as a sentence of imprisonment when it takes effect under paragraph 8(2)(a) or (b) of Schedule 12, and

(b) is to be treated as being imposed by the order under which it takes effect.

(8) For the purposes of the reference in subsection (3) to the term of imprisonment to which a person has been sentenced (that is to say, the reference to his 'sentence'), consecutive terms and terms which are wholly or partly concurrent are to be treated as a single term if –

(a) the sentences were passed on the same occasion, or

(b) where they were passed on different occasions, the person has not been released under this Chapter at any time during the period beginning with the first and ending with the last of those occasions.

(9) Where an offence is found to have been committed over a period of two or more days, or at some time during a period of two or more days, it shall be taken for the purposes of subsection (1) to have been committed on the last of those days.

(10) This section applies to a determinate sentence of detention under section 91 of the Sentencing Act or section 228 of this Act as it applies to an equivalent sentence of imprisonment.

241 Effect of direction under section 240 on release on licence

(1) In determining for the purposes of this Chapter or Chapter 3 (prison sentences of less than twelve months) whether a person to whom a direction under section 240 relates –

(a) has served, or would (but for his release) have served, a particular proportion of his sentence, or

(b) has served a particular period,

the number of days specified in the direction are to be treated as having been served by him as part of that sentence or period.

(2) In determining for the purposes of section 183 (intermittent custody) whether any part of a sentence to which an intermittent custody order relates is a licence period, the number of custodial days, as defined by subsection (3) of that section, is to be taken to be reduced by the number of days specified in a direction under section 240.

242 Interpretation of sections 240 and 241

(1) For the purposes of sections 240 and 241, the definition of 'sentence of imprisonment' in section 305 applies as if for the words from the beginning of the definition to the end of paragraph (a) there were substituted –

'"sentence of imprisonment" does not include a committal –

(a) in default of payment of any sum of money, other than one adjudged to be paid on a conviction,';

and references in those sections to sentencing an offender to imprisonment, and to an offender's sentence, are to be read accordingly.

(2) References in sections 240 and 241 to an offender's being remanded in custody are references to his being –

(a) remanded in or committed to custody by order of a court,

(b) remanded or committed to local authority accommodation under section 23 of the Children and Young Persons Act 1969 (c. 54) and kept in secure accommodation or detained in a secure training centre pursuant to arrangements under subsection (7A) of that section, or

(c) remanded, admitted or removed to hospital under section 35, 36, 38 or 48 of the Mental Health Act 1983 (c. 20).

(3) In subsection (2), 'secure accommodation' has the same meaning as in section 23 of the Children and Young Persons Act 1969.

243 Persons extradited to the United Kingdom

(1) A fixed-term prisoner is an extradited prisoner for the purposes of this section if –

    (a) he was tried for the offence in respect of which his sentence was imposed –

        (i) after having been extradited to the United Kingdom, and

        (ii) without having first been restored or had an opportunity of leaving the United Kingdom, and

    (b) he was for any period kept in custody while awaiting his extradition to the United Kingdom as mentioned in paragraph (a).

(2) In the case of an extradited prisoner, section 240 has effect as if the days for which he was kept in custody while awaiting extradition were days for which he was remanded in custody in connection with the offence, or any other offence the charge for which was founded on the same facts or evidence.

(3) In this section –

    'extradited to the United Kingdom' means returned to the United Kingdom –

        (a) in pursuance of extradition arrangements,

        (b) under any law of a designated Commonwealth country corresponding to the Extradition Act 1989 (c. 33),

        (c) under that Act as extended to a British overseas territory or under any corresponding law of a British overseas territory,

        (d) in pursuance of a warrant of arrest endorsed in the Republic of Ireland under the law of that country corresponding to the Backing of Warrants (Republic of Ireland) Act 1965 (c. 45), or

        (e) in pursuance of arrangements with a foreign state in respect of which an Order in Council under section 2 of the Extradition Act 1870 (c. 52) is in force;

    'extradition arrangements' has the meaning given by section 3 of the Extradition Act 1989;

    'designated Commonwealth country' has the meaning given by section 5(1) of that Act.

Release on licence

244 Duty to release prisoners

(1) As soon as a fixed-term prisoner, other than a prisoner to whom section 247 applies, has served the requisite custodial period, it is the duty of the Secretary of State to release him on licence under this section.

(2) Subsection (1) is subject to section 245.

(3) In this section 'the requisite custodial period' means –

    (a) in relation to a person serving a sentence of imprisonment for a term of twelve months or more or any determinate sentence of detention under section 91 of the Sentencing Act, one-half of his sentence,

    (b) in relation to a person serving a sentence of imprisonment for a term of less than twelve months (other than one to which an intermittent custody order relates), the custodial period within the meaning of section 181,

    (c) in relation to a person serving a sentence of imprisonment to which an intermittent custody order relates, any part of the term which is not a licence period as defined by section 183(3), and

    (d) in relation to a person serving two or more concurrent or consecutive sentences, the period determined under sections 263(2) and 264(2).

245 Restrictions on operation of section 244(1) in relation to intermittent custody prisoners

(1) Where an intermittent custody prisoner returns to custody after being unlawfully at large within the meaning of section 49 of the Prison Act 1952 (c. 52) at any time during the currency of his sentence, section 244(1) does not apply until –

    (a) the relevant time (as defined in subsection (2)), or

    (b) if earlier, the date on which he has served in prison the number of custodial days required by the intermittent custody order.

(2) In subsection (1)(a) 'the relevant time' means –

    (a) in a case where, within the period of 72 hours beginning with the return to custody of the intermittent custody prisoner, the Secretary of State or the responsible officer has applied to the court for the amendment of the intermittent custody order under paragraph 6(1)(b) of Schedule 10, the date on which the application is withdrawn or determined, and

    (b) in any other case, the end of that 72-hour period.

(3) Section 244(1) does not apply in relation to an intermittent custody prisoner at any time after he has been recalled under section 254, unless after his recall the Board has directed his further release on licence.

246 Power to release prisoners on licence before required to do so

(1) Subject to subsections (2) to (4), the Secretary of State may –

    (a) release on licence under this section a fixed-term prisoner, other than an intermittent custody prisoner, at any time during the period of 135 days ending with the day on which the prisoner will have served the requisite custodial period, and

    (b) release on licence under this section an intermittent custody prisoner when 135 or less of the required custodial days remain to be served.

(2) Subsection (1)(a) does not apply in relation to a prisoner unless –

    (a) the length of the requisite custodial period is at least 6 weeks,

    (b) he has served –

        (i) at least 4 weeks of his sentence, and

        (ii) at least one-half of the requisite custodial period.

(3) Subsection (1)(b) does not apply in relation to a prisoner unless –

    (a) the number of required custodial days is at least 42, and

    (b) the prisoner has served –

        (i) at least 28 of those days, and

        (ii) at least one-half of the total number of those days.

(4) Subsection (1) does not apply where –

    (a) the sentence is imposed under section 227 or 228,

    (b) the sentence is for an offence under section 1 of the Prisoners (Return to Custody) Act 1995 (c. 16),

    (c) the prisoner is subject to a hospital order, hospital direction or transfer direction under section 37, 45A or 47 of the Mental Health Act 1983 (c. 20),

    (d) the sentence was imposed by virtue of paragraph 9(1)(b) or (c) or 10(1)(b) or (c) of Schedule 8 in a case where the prisoner has failed to comply with a curfew requirement of a community order,

    (e) the prisoner is subject to the notification requirements of Part 2 of the Sexual Offences Act 2003 (c. 42),

    (f) the prisoner is liable to removal from the United Kingdom,

    (g) the prisoner has been released on licence under this section during the currency of the sentence, and has been recalled to prison under section 255(1)(a),

(h)   the prisoner has been released on licence under section 248 during the currency of the sentence, and has been recalled to prison under section 254, or

(i)   in the case of a prisoner to whom a direction under section 240 relates, the interval between the date on which the sentence was passed and the date on which the prisoner will have served the requisite custodial period is less than 14 days or, where the sentence is one of intermittent custody, the number of the required custodial days remaining to be served is less than 14.

(5)   The Secretary of State may by order –

(a)   amend the number of days for the time being specified in subsection (1)(a) or (b), (3) or (4)(i),

(b)   amend the number of weeks for the time being specified in subsection (2)(a) or (b)(i), and

(c)   amend the fraction for the time being specified in subsection (2)(b)(ii) or (3)(b)(ii).

(6)   In this section –

'the required custodial days', in relation to an intermittent custody prisoner, means –

(a)   the number of custodial days specified under section 183, or

(b)   in the case of two or more sentences of intermittent custody, the aggregate of the numbers so specified;

'the requisite custodial period' in relation to a person serving any sentence other than a sentence of intermittent custody, has the meaning given by paragraph (a), (b) or (d) of section 244(3);

'sentence of intermittent custody' means a sentence to which an intermittent custody order relates.

247 Release on licence of prisoner serving extended sentence under section 227 or 228

(1)   This section applies to a prisoner who is serving an extended sentence imposed under section 227 or 228.

(2)   As soon as –

(a)   a prisoner to whom this section applies has served one-half of the appropriate custodial term, and

(b)   the Parole Board has directed his release under this section,

it is the duty of the Secretary of State to release him on licence.

(3)   The Parole Board may not give a direction under subsection (2) unless the Board is satisfied that it is no longer necessary for the protection of the public that the prisoner should be confined.

(4)   As soon as a prisoner to whom this section applies has served the appropriate custodial term, it is the duty of the Secretary of State to release him on licence unless the prisoner has previously been recalled under section 254.

(5)   Where a prisoner to whom this section applies is released on a licence, the Secretary of State may not by virtue of section 250(4)(b) include, or subsequently insert, a condition in the licence, or vary or cancel a condition in the licence, except after consultation with the Board.

(6)   For the purposes of subsection (5), the Secretary of State is to be treated as having consulted the Board about a proposal to include, insert, vary or cancel a condition in any case if he has consulted the Board about the implementation of proposals of that description generally or in that class of case.

(7)   In this section 'the appropriate custodial term' means the period determined by the court as the appropriate custodial term under section 227 or 228.

248 Power to release prisoners on compassionate grounds

(1) The Secretary of State may at any time release a fixed-term prisoner on licence if he is satisfied that exceptional circumstances exist which justify the prisoner's release on compassionate grounds.

(2) Before releasing under this section a prisoner to whom section 247 applies, the Secretary of State must consult the Board, unless the circumstances are such as to render such consultation impracticable.

249 Duration of licence

(1) Subject to subsections (2) and (3), where a fixed-term prisoner is released on licence, the licence shall, subject to any revocation under section 254 or 255, remain in force for the remainder of his sentence.

(2) Where an intermittent custody prisoner is released on licence under section 244, the licence shall, subject to any revocation under section 254, remain in force –

(a) until the time when he is required to return to prison at the beginning of the next custodial period of the sentence, or

(b) where it is granted at the end of the last custodial period, for the remainder of his sentence.

(3) Subsection (1) has effect subject to sections 263(2) (concurrent terms) and 264(3) and (4) (consecutive terms).

(4) In subsection (2) 'custodial period', in relation to a sentence to which an intermittent custody order relates, means any period which is not a licence period as defined by section 183(3).

250 Licence conditions

(1) In this section –

(a) 'the standard conditions' means such conditions as may be prescribed for the purposes of this section as standard conditions, and

(b) 'prescribed' means prescribed by the Secretary of State by order.

(2) Subject to subsection (6) and section 251, any licence under this Chapter in respect of a prisoner serving one or more sentences of imprisonment of less than twelve months and no sentence of twelve months or more –

(a) must include –

(i) the conditions required by the relevant court order, and

(ii) so far as not inconsistent with them, the standard conditions, and

(b) may also include –

(i) any condition which is authorised by section 62 of the Criminal Justice and Court Services Act 2000 (c. 43) (electronic monitoring) or section 64 of that Act (drug testing requirements) and which is compatible with the conditions required by the relevant court order, and

(ii) such other conditions of a kind prescribed for the purposes of this paragraph as the Secretary of State may for the time being consider to be necessary for the protection of the public and specify in the licence.

(3) For the purposes of subsection (2)(a)(i), any reference in the relevant court order to the licence period specified in the order is, in relation to a prohibited activity requirement, exclusion requirement, residence requirement or supervision requirement, to be taken to include a reference to any other period during which the prisoner is released on licence under section 246 or 248.

(4) Any licence under this Chapter in respect of a prisoner serving a sentence of imprisonment for a term of 12 months or more (including such a sentence imposed under section 227) or any sentence of detention under section 91 of the Sentencing Act or section 228 of this Act –

(a) must include the standard conditions, and

(b) may include –

- (i) any condition authorised by section 62 or 64 of the Criminal Justice and Court Services Act 2000, and
- (ii) such other conditions of a kind prescribed by the Secretary of State for the purposes of this paragraph as the Secretary of State may for the time being specify in the licence.

(5) A licence under section 246 must also include a curfew condition complying with section 253.

(6) Where –

- (a) a licence under section 246 is granted to a prisoner serving one or more sentences of imprisonment of less than 12 months and no sentence of 12 months or more, and
- (b) the relevant court order requires the licence to be granted subject to a condition requiring his compliance with a curfew requirement (as defined by section 204),

that condition is not to be included in the licence at any time while a curfew condition required by section 253 is in force.

(7) The preceding provisions of this section have effect subject to section 263(3) (concurrent terms) and section 264(3) and (4) (consecutive terms).

(8) In exercising his powers to prescribe standard conditions or the other conditions referred to in subsection (4)(b)(ii), the Secretary of State must have regard to the following purposes of the supervision of offenders while on licence under this Chapter –

- (a) the protection of the public,
- (b) the prevention of re-offending, and
- (c) securing the successful re-integration of the prisoner into the community.

251 Licence conditions on re-release of prisoner serving sentence of less than 12 months

(1) In relation to any licence under this Chapter which is granted to a prisoner serving one or more sentences of imprisonment of less than twelve months and no sentence of twelve months or more on his release in pursuance of a decision of the Board under section 254 or 256, subsections (2) and (3) apply instead of section 250(2).

(2) The licence –

- (a) must include the standard conditions, and
- (b) may include –
    - (i) any condition authorised by section 62 or 64 of the Criminal Justice and Court Services Act 2000 (c. 43), and
    - (ii) such other conditions of a kind prescribed by the Secretary of State for the purposes of section 250(4)(b)(ii) as the Secretary of State may for the time being specify in the licence.

(3) In exercising his powers under subsection (2)(b)(ii), the Secretary of State must have regard to the terms of the relevant court order.

(4) In this section 'the standard conditions' has the same meaning as in section 250.

252 Duty to comply with licence conditions

A person subject to a licence under this Chapter must comply with such conditions as may for the time being be specified in the licence.

253 Curfew condition to be included in licence under section 246

(1) For the purposes of this Chapter, a curfew condition is a condition which –

(a) requires the released person to remain, for periods for the time being specified in the condition, at a place for the time being so specified (which may be premises approved by the Secretary of State under section 9 of the Criminal Justice and Court Services Act 2000 (c. 43)), and

(b) includes requirements for securing the electronic monitoring of his whereabouts during the periods for the time being so specified.

(2) The curfew condition may specify different places or different periods for different days, but may not specify periods which amount to less than 9 hours in any one day (excluding for this purpose the first and last days of the period for which the condition is in force).

(3) The curfew condition is to remain in force until the date when the released person would (but for his release) fall to be released on licence under section 244.

(4) Subsection (3) does not apply in relation to a released person to whom an intermittent custody order relates; and in relation to such a person the curfew condition is to remain in force until the number of days during which it has been in force is equal to the number of the required custodial days, as defined in section 246(6), that remained to be served at the time when he was released under section 246.

(5) The curfew condition must include provision for making a person responsible for monitoring the released person's whereabouts during the periods for the time being specified in the condition; and a person who is made so responsible shall be of a description specified in an order made by the Secretary of State.

(6) Nothing in this section is to be taken to require the Secretary of State to ensure that arrangements are made for the electronic monitoring of released persons' whereabouts in any particular part of England and Wales.

Recall after release

254 Recall of prisoners while on licence

(1) The Secretary of State may, in the case of any prisoner who has been released on licence under this Chapter, revoke his licence and recall him to prison.

(2) A person recalled to prison under subsection (1) –

(a) may make representations in writing with respect to his recall, and

(b) on his return to prison, must be informed of the reasons for his recall and of his right to make representations.

(3) The Secretary of State must refer to the Board the case of a person recalled under subsection (1).

(4) Where on a reference under subsection (3) relating to any person the Board recommends his immediate release on licence under this Chapter, the Secretary of State must give effect to the recommendation.

(5) In the case of an intermittent custody prisoner who has not yet served in prison the number of custodial days specified in the intermittent custody order, any recommendation by the Board as to immediate release on licence is to be a recommendation as to his release on licence until the end of one of the licence periods specified by virtue of section 183(1)(b) in the intermittent custody order.

(6) On the revocation of the licence of any person under this section, he shall be liable to be detained in pursuance of his sentence and, if at large, is to be treated as being unlawfully at large.

(7) Nothing in subsections (2) to (6) applies in relation to a person recalled under section 255.

255 Recall of prisoners released early under section 246

(1) If it appears to the Secretary of State, as regards a person released on licence under section 246 –

(a) that he has failed to comply with any condition included in his licence, or
(b) that his whereabouts can no longer be electronically monitored at the place for the time being specified in the curfew condition included in his licence,

the Secretary of State may, if the curfew condition is still in force, revoke the licence and recall the person to prison under this section.

(2) A person whose licence under section 246 is revoked under this section –

(a) may make representations in writing with respect to the revocation, and
(b) on his return to prison, must be informed of the reasons for the revocation and of his right to make representations.

(3) The Secretary of State, after considering any representations under subsection (2)(b) or any other matters, may cancel a revocation under this section.

(4) Where the revocation of a person's licence is cancelled under subsection (3), the person is to be treated for the purposes of section 246 as if he had not been recalled to prison under this section.

(5) On the revocation of a person's licence under section 246, he is liable to be detained in pursuance of his sentence and, if at large, is to be treated as being unlawfully at large.

256 Further release after recall

(1) Where on a reference under section 254(3) in relation to any person, the Board does not recommend his immediate release on licence under this Chapter, the Board must either –

(a) fix a date for the person's release on licence, or
(b) fix a date as the date for the next review of the person's case by the Board.

(2) Any date fixed under subsection (1)(a) or (b) must not be later than the first anniversary of the date on which the decision is taken.

(3) The Board need not fix a date under subsection (1)(a) or (b) if the prisoner will fall to be released unconditionally at any time within the next 12 months.

(4) Where the Board has fixed a date under subsection (1)(a), it is the duty of the Secretary of State to release him on licence on that date.

(5) On a review required by subsection (1)(b) in relation to any person, the Board may –

(a) recommend his immediate release on licence, or
(b) fix a date under subsection (1)(a) or (b).

Additional days

257 Additional days for disciplinary offences

(1) Prison rules, that is to say, rules made under section 47 of the Prison Act 1952 (c. 52), may include provision for the award of additional days –

(a) to fixed-term prisoners, or
(b) conditionally on their subsequently becoming such prisoners, to persons on remand,

who (in either case) are guilty of disciplinary offences.

(2) Where additional days are awarded to a fixed-term prisoner, or to a person on remand who subsequently becomes such a prisoner, and are not remitted in accordance with prison rules –

(a) any period which he must serve before becoming entitled to or eligible for release under this Chapter,
(b) any period which he must serve before he can be removed from prison under section 260, and

(c) any period for which a licence granted to him under this Chapter remains in force,

is extended by the aggregate of those additional days.

Fine defaulters and contemnors

258 Early release of fine defaulters and contemnors

(1) This section applies in relation to a person committed to prison –

  (a) in default of payment of a sum adjudged to be paid by a conviction, or
  (b) for contempt of court or any kindred offence.

(2) As soon as a person to whom this section applies has served one-half of the term for which he was committed, it is the duty of the Secretary of State to release him unconditionally.

(3) Where a person to whom this section applies is also serving one or more sentences of imprisonment, nothing in this section requires the Secretary of State to release him until he is also required to release him in respect of that sentence or each of those sentences.

(4) The Secretary of State may at any time release unconditionally a person to whom this section applies if he is satisfied that exceptional circumstances exist which justify the person's release on compassionate grounds.

Persons liable to removal from the United Kingdom

259 Persons liable to removal from the United Kingdom

For the purposes of this Chapter a person is liable to removal from the United Kingdom if –

  (a) he is liable to deportation under section 3(5) of the Immigration Act 1971 (c. 77) and has been notified of a decision to make a deportation order against him,
  (b) he is liable to deportation under section 3(6) of that Act,
  (c) he has been notified of a decision to refuse him leave to enter the United Kingdom,
  (d) he is an illegal entrant within the meaning of section 33(1) of that Act, or
  (e) he is liable to removal under section 10 of the Immigration and Asylum Act 1999 (c. 33).

260 Early removal of prisoners liable to removal from United Kingdom

(1) Subject to subsections (2) and (3), where a fixed-term prisoner is liable to removal from the United Kingdom, the Secretary of State may remove him from prison under this section at any time during the period of 135 days ending with the day on which the prisoner will have served the requisite custodial period.

(2) Subsection (1) does not apply in relation to a prisoner unless –

  (a) the length of the requisite custodial period is at least 6 weeks, and
  (b) he has served –

    (i) at least 4 weeks of his sentence, and
    (ii) at least one-half of the requisite custodial period.

(3) Subsection (1) does not apply where –

  (a) the sentence is imposed under section 227 or 228,
  (b) the sentence is for an offence under section 1 of the Prisoners (Return to Custody) Act 1995 (c. 16),

- (c) the prisoner is subject to a hospital order, hospital direction or transfer direction under section 37, 45A or 47 of the Mental Health Act 1983 (c. 20),
- (d) the prisoner is subject to the notification requirements of Part 2 of the Sexual Offences Act 2003 (c. 42), or
- (e) in the case of a prisoner to whom a direction under section 240 relates, the interval between the date on which the sentence was passed and the date on which the prisoner will have served the requisite custodial period is less than 14 days.

(4) A prisoner removed from prison under this section –

- (a) is so removed only for the purpose of enabling the Secretary of State to remove him from the United Kingdom under powers conferred by –
  - (i) Schedule 2 or 3 to the Immigration Act 1971, or
  - (ii) section 10 of the Immigration and Asylum Act 1999 (c. 33), and
- (b) so long as remaining in the United Kingdom, remains liable to be detained in pursuance of his sentence until he has served the requisite custodial period.

(5) So long as a prisoner removed from prison under this section remains in the United Kingdom but has not been returned to prison, any duty or power of the Secretary of State under section 244 or 248 is exercisable in relation to him as if he were in prison.

(6) The Secretary of State may by order –

- (a) amend the number of days for the time being specified in subsection (1) or (3)(e),
- (b) amend the number of weeks for the time being specified in subsection (2)(a) or (b)(i), and
- (c) amend the fraction for the time being specified in subsection (2)(b)(ii).

(7) In this section 'the requisite custodial period' has the meaning given by paragraph (a), (b) or (d) of section 244(3).

261 Re-entry into United Kingdom of offender removed from prison early

(1) This section applies in relation to a person who, after being removed from prison under section 260, has been removed from the United Kingdom before he has served the requisite custodial period.

(2) If a person to whom this section applies enters the United Kingdom at any time before his sentence expiry date, he is liable to be detained in pursuance of his sentence from the time of his entry into the United Kingdom until whichever is the earlier of the following –

- (a) the end of a period ('the further custodial period') beginning with that time and equal in length to the outstanding custodial period, and
- (b) his sentence expiry date.

(3) A person who is liable to be detained by virtue of subsection (2) is, if at large, to be taken for the purposes of section 49 of the Prison Act 1952 (c. 52) (persons unlawfully at large) to be unlawfully at large.

(4) Subsection (2) does not prevent the further removal from the United Kingdom of a person falling within that subsection.

(5) Where, in the case of a person returned to prison by virtue of subsection (2), the further custodial period ends before the sentence expiry date, section 244 has effect in relation to him as if the reference to the requisite custodial period were a reference to the further custodial period.

(6) In this section –

'further custodial period' has the meaning given by subsection (2)(a);
'outstanding custodial period', in relation to a person to whom this section applies, means the period beginning with the date of his removal from the United Kingdom and ending with the date on which he would, but for his removal, have served the requisite custodial period;

'requisite custodial period' has the meaning given by paragraph (a), (b) or (d) of section 244(3);

'sentence expiry date', in relation to a person to whom this section applies, means the date on which, but for his removal from the United Kingdom, he would have ceased to be subject to a licence.

262 Prisoners liable to removal from United Kingdom: modifications of Criminal Justice Act 1991

Part 2 of the Criminal Justice Act 1991 (c. 53) (early release of prisoners) shall (until the coming into force of its repeal by this Act) have effect subject to the modifications set out in Schedule 20 (which relate to persons liable to removal from the United Kingdom).

Consecutive or concurrent terms

263 Concurrent terms

(1) This section applies where –

    (a) a person ('the offender') has been sentenced by any court to two or more terms of imprisonment which are wholly or partly concurrent, and

    (b) the sentences were passed on the same occasion or, where they were passed on different occasions, the person has not been released under this Chapter at any time during the period beginning with the first and ending with the last of those occasions.

(2) Where this section applies –

    (a) nothing in this Chapter requires the Secretary of State to release the offender in respect of any of the terms unless and until he is required to release him in respect of each of the others,

    (b) section 244 does not authorise the Secretary of State to release him on licence under that section in respect of any of the terms unless and until that section authorises the Secretary of State to do so in respect of each of the others,

    (c) on and after his release under this Chapter the offender is to be on licence for so long, and subject to such conditions, as is required by this Chapter in respect of any of the sentences.

(3) Where the sentences include one or more sentences of twelve months or more and one or more sentences of less than twelve months, the terms of the licence may be determined by the Secretary of State in accordance with section 250(4)(b), without regard to the requirements of any custody plus order or intermittent custody order.

(4) In this section 'term of imprisonment' includes a determinate sentence of detention under section 91 of the Sentencing Act or under section 228 of this Act.

264 Consecutive terms

(1) This section applies where –

    (a) a person ('the offender') has been sentenced to two or more terms of imprisonment which are to be served consecutively on each other, and

    (b) the sentences were passed on the same occasion or, where they were passed on different occasions, the person has not been released under this Chapter at any time during the period beginning with the first and ending with the last of those occasions.

(2) Nothing in this Chapter requires the Secretary of State to release the offender on licence until he has served a period equal in length to the aggregate of the length of the custodial periods in relation to each of the terms of imprisonment.

(3) Where any of the terms of imprisonment is a term of twelve months or more, the offender is, on and after his release under this Chapter, to be on licence –

(a) until he would, but for his release, have served a term equal in length to the aggregate length of the terms of imprisonment, and

(b) subject to such conditions as are required by this Chapter in respect of each of those terms of imprisonment.

(4) Where each of the terms of imprisonment is a term of less than twelve months, the offender is, on and after his release under this Chapter, to be on licence until the relevant time, and subject to such conditions as are required by this Chapter in respect of any of the terms of imprisonment, and none of the terms is to be regarded for any purpose as continuing after the relevant time.

(5) In subsection (4) 'the relevant time' means the time when the offender would, but for his release, have served a term equal in length to the aggregate of –

(a) all the custodial periods in relation to the terms of imprisonment, and

(b) the longest of the licence periods in relation to those terms.

(6) In this section –

(a) 'custodial period' –

(i) in relation to an extended sentence imposed under section 227 or 228, means the appropriate custodial term determined under that section,

(ii) in relation to a term of twelve months or more, means one-half of the term, and

(iii) in relation to a term of less than twelve months complying with section 181, means the custodial period as defined by subsection (3)(a) of that section;

(b) 'licence period', in relation to a term of less than twelve months complying with section 181, has the meaning given by subsection (3)(b) of that section.

(7) This section applies to a determinate sentence of detention under section 91 of the Sentencing Act or under section 228 of this Act as it applies to a term of imprisonment of 12 months or more.

Restriction on consecutive sentences for released prisoners

265 Restriction on consecutive sentences for released prisoners

(1) A court sentencing a person to a term of imprisonment may not order or direct that the term is to commence on the expiry of any other sentence of imprisonment from which he has been released early under this Chapter.

(2) In this section 'sentence of imprisonment' includes a sentence of detention under section 91 of the Sentencing Act or section 228 of this Act, and 'term of imprisonment' is to be read accordingly.

Drug testing requirements

266 Release on licence etc: drug testing requirements

(1) Section 64 of the Criminal Justice and Court Services Act 2000 (c. 43) (release on licence etc: drug testing requirements) is amended as follows.

(2) In subsection (1) for paragraph (a) there is substituted –

'(a) the Secretary of State releases from prison a person aged 14 or over on whom a sentence of imprisonment has been imposed,

(aa) a responsible officer is of the opinion –

(i) that the offender has a propensity to misuse specified Class A drugs, and

    (ii)   that the misuse by the offender of any specified Class A drug caused or contributed to any offence of which he has been convicted, or is likely to cause or contribute to the commission of further offences, and'.

(3) After subsection (4) there is inserted –

'(4A) A person under the age of 17 years may not be required by virtue of this section to provide a sample otherwise than in the presence of an appropriate adult.'

(4) In subsection (5), after paragraph (e) there is inserted 'and

    (f)   a sentence of detention under section 226 or 228 of the Criminal Justice Act 2003,'.

(5) After subsection (5) there is inserted –

'(6) In this section –

"appropriate adult", in relation to a person aged under 17, means –

    (a)   his parent or guardian or, if he is in the care of a local authority or voluntary organisation, a person representing that authority or organisation,

    (b)   a social worker of a local authority social services department, or

    (c)   if no person falling within paragraph (a) or (b) is available, any responsible person aged 18 or over who is not a police officer or a person employed by the police;

"responsible officer" means –

    (a)   in relation to an offender aged under 18, an officer of a local probation board or a member of a youth offending team;

    (b)   in relation to an offender aged 18 or over, an officer of a local probation board.'

Supplemental

267 Alteration by order of relevant proportion of sentence

The Secretary of State may by order provide that any reference in section 244(3)(a), section 247(2) or section 264(6)(a)(ii) to a particular proportion of a prisoner's sentence is to be read as a reference to such other proportion of a prisoner's sentence as may be specified in the order.

268 Interpretation of Chapter 6

In this Chapter –

    'the 1997 Act' means the Crime (Sentences) Act 1997 (c. 43);

    'the Board' means the Parole Board;

    'fixed-term prisoner' has the meaning given by section 237(1);

    'intermittent custody prisoner' means a prisoner serving a sentence of imprisonment to which an intermittent custody order relates;

    'prison' and 'prisoner' are to be read in accordance with section 237(2);

    'release', in relation to a prisoner serving a sentence of imprisonment to which an intermittent custody order relates, includes temporary release;

    'relevant court order', in relation to a person serving a sentence of imprisonment to which a custody plus order or intermittent custody order relates, means that order.

CHAPTER 7   EFFECT OF LIFE SENTENCE

269 Determination of minimum term in relation to mandatory life sentence

(1) This section applies where after the commencement of this section a court passes a life sentence in circumstances where the sentence is fixed by law.

(2) The court must, unless it makes an order under subsection (4), order that the provisions of section 28(5) to (8) of the Crime (Sentences) Act 1997 (referred to in this Chapter as 'the early release provisions') are to apply to the offender as soon as he has served the part of his sentence which is specified in the order.

(3) The part of his sentence is to be such as the court considers appropriate taking into account –

    (a) the seriousness of the offence, or of the combination of the offence and any one or more offences associated with it, and

    (b) the effect of any direction which it would have given under section 240 (crediting periods of remand in custody) if it had sentenced him to a term of imprisonment.

(4) If the offender was 21 or over when he committed the offence and the court is of the opinion that, because of the seriousness of the offence, or of the combination of the offence and one or more offences associated with it, no order should be made under subsection (2), the court must order that the early release provisions are not to apply to the offender.

(5) In considering under subsection (3) or (4) the seriousness of an offence (or of the combination of an offence and one or more offences associated with it), the court must have regard to –

    (a) the general principles set out in Schedule 21, and

    (b) any guidelines relating to offences in general which are relevant to the case and are not incompatible with the provisions of Schedule 21.

(6) The Secretary of State may by order amend Schedule 21.

(7) Before making an order under subsection (6), the Secretary of State shall consult the Sentencing Guidelines Council.

270 Duty to give reasons

(1) Any court making an order under subsection (2) or (4) of section 269 must state in open court, in ordinary language, its reasons for deciding on the order made.

(2) In stating its reasons the court must, in particular –

    (a) state which of the starting points in Schedule 21 it has chosen and its reasons for doing so, and

    (b) state its reasons for any departure from that starting point.

271 Appeals

(1) In section 9 of the Criminal Appeal Act 1968 (c. 19) (appeal against sentence following conviction on indictment), after subsection (1) there is inserted –

    '(1A) In subsection (1) of this section, the reference to a sentence fixed by law does not include a reference to an order made under subsection (2) or (4) of section 269 of the Criminal Justice Act 2003 in relation to a life sentence (as defined in section 277 of that Act) that is fixed by law.'.

(2) In section 8 of the Courts-Martial (Appeals) Act 1968 (c. 20) (right of appeal from court-martial to Courts-Martial Appeal Court) after subsection (1) there is inserted –

    '(1ZA) In subsection (1) above, the reference to a sentence fixed by law does not include a reference to an order made under subsection (2) or (4) of section 269 of the Criminal Justice Act 2003 in relation to a life sentence (as defined in section 277 of that Act) that is fixed by law.'.

272 Review of minimum term on a reference by Attorney General

(1) In section 36 of the Criminal Justice Act 1988 (c. 33) (reviews of sentencing) after subsection (3) there is inserted –

'(3A) Where a reference under this section relates to an order under subsection (2) of section 269 of the Criminal Justice Act 2003 (determination of minimum term in relation to mandatory life sentence), the Court of Appeal shall not, in deciding what order under that section is appropriate for the case, make any allowance for the fact that the person to whom it relates is being sentenced for a second time.'.

(2) Each of the following sections (which relate to the review by the Courts-Martial Appeal Court of sentences passed by courts-martial) –

  (a) section 113C of the Army Act 1955 (3 & 4 Eliz. 2 c. 18),
  (b) section 113C of the Air Force Act 1955 (3 & 4 Eliz. 2 c. 19), and
  (c) section 71AC of the Naval Discipline Act 1957 (c. 53),

  is amended as follows.

(3) After subsection (3) there is inserted –

'(3A) Where a reference under this section relates to an order under subsection (2) of section 269 of the Criminal Justice Act 2003 (determination of minimum term in relation to mandatory life sentence), the Courts-Martial Appeal Court shall not, in deciding what order under that section is appropriate for the case, make any allowance for the fact that the person to whom it relates is being sentenced for a second time.'.

273 Life prisoners transferred to England and Wales

(1) The Secretary of State must refer the case of any transferred life prisoner to the High Court for the making of one or more relevant orders.

(2) In subsection (1) 'transferred life prisoner' means a person –

  (a) on whom a court in a country or territory outside the British Islands has imposed one or more sentences of imprisonment or detention for an indeterminate period, and
  (b) who has been transferred to England and Wales after the commencement of this section in pursuance of –

    (i) an order made by the Secretary of State under section 2 of the Colonial Prisoners Removal Act 1884 (c. 31), or
    (ii) a warrant issued by the Secretary of State under the Repatriation of Prisoners Act 1984 (c. 47),

  there to serve his sentence or sentences or the remainder of his sentence or sentences.

(3) In subsection (1) 'a relevant order' means –

  (a) in the case of an offence which appears to the court to be an offence for which, if it had been committed in England and Wales, the sentence would have been fixed by law, an order under subsection (2) or (4) of section 269, and
  (b) in any other case, an order under subsection (2) or (4) of section 82A of the Sentencing Act.

(4) In section 34(1) of the Crime (Sentences) Act 1997 (c. 43) (meaning of 'life prisoner' in Chapter 2 of Part 2 of that Act) at the end there is inserted 'and includes a transferred life prisoner as defined by section 273 of the Criminal Justice Act 2003'.

274 Further provisions about references relating to transferred life prisoners

(1) A reference to the High Court under section 273 is to be determined by a single judge of that court without an oral hearing.

(2) In relation to a reference under that section, any reference to 'the court' in subsections (2) to (5) of section 269, in Schedule 21 or in section 82A(2) to (4) of the Sentencing Act is to be read as a reference to the High Court.

(3) A person in respect of whom a reference has been made under section 273 may with the leave of the Court of Appeal appeal to the Court of Appeal against the decision of the High Court on the reference.

(4) Section 1(1) of the Administration of Justice Act 1960 (c. 65) (appeal to House of Lords from decision of High Court in a criminal cause or matter) and section 18(1)(a) of the Supreme Court Act 1981 (c. 54) (exclusion of appeal from High Court to Court of Appeal in a criminal cause or matter) do not apply in relation to a decision to which subsection (3) applies.

(5) The jurisdiction conferred on the Court of Appeal by subsection (3) is to be exercised by the criminal division of that court.

(6) Section 33(3) of the Criminal Appeal Act 1968 (c. 19) (limitation on appeal from criminal division of Court of Appeal) does not prevent an appeal to the House of Lords under this section.

(7) In relation to appeals to the Court of Appeal or the House of Lords under this section, the Secretary of State may make an order containing provision corresponding to any provision in the Criminal Appeal Act 1968 (subject to any specified modifications).

275 Duty to release certain life prisoners

(1) Section 28 of the Crime (Sentences) Act 1997 (c. 43) (duty to release certain life prisoners) is amended as follows.

(2) For subsection (1A) there is substituted –

'(1A) This section applies to a life prisoner in respect of whom a minimum term order has been made; and any reference in this section to the relevant part of such a prisoner's sentence is a reference to the part of the sentence specified in the order.'

(3) In subsection (1B)(a) –

(a) for the words from the beginning to 'applies' there is substituted 'this section does not apply to him', and

(b) for the words from 'such an order' to 'appropriate stage' there is substituted 'a minimum term order has been made in respect of each of those sentences'.

(4) After subsection (8) there is inserted –

'(8A) In this section 'minimum term order' means an order under –

(a) subsection (2) of section 82A of the Powers of Criminal Courts (Sentencing) Act 2000 (determination of minimum term in respect of life sentence that is not fixed by law), or

(b) subsection (2) of section 269 of the Criminal Justice Act 2003 (determination of minimum term in respect of mandatory life sentence).'.

276 Mandatory life sentences: transitional cases

Schedule 22 (which relates to the effect in transitional cases of mandatory life sentences) shall have effect.

277 Interpretation of Chapter 7

In this Chapter –

'court' includes a court-martial;
'guidelines' has the same meaning as in section 172(1);
'life sentence' means –

(a) a sentence of imprisonment for life,

(b) a sentence of detention during Her Majesty's pleasure, or

(c)   a sentence of custody for life passed before the commencement of section 61(1) of the Criminal Justice and Court Services Act 2000 (c. 43) (which abolishes that sentence).

CHAPTER 8   OTHER PROVISIONS ABOUT SENTENCING

Deferment of sentence

278 Deferment of sentence

Schedule 23 (deferment of sentence) shall have effect.

Power to include drug treatment and testing requirement in certain orders in respect of young offenders

279 Drug treatment and testing requirement in action plan order or supervision order

Schedule 24 (which enables a requirement as to drug treatment and testing to be included in an action plan order or a supervision order) shall have effect.

Alteration of penalties for offences

280 Alteration of penalties for specified summary offences

(1)   The summary offences listed in Schedule 25 are no longer punishable with imprisonment.

(2)   Schedule 26 (which contains amendments increasing the maximum term of imprisonment for certain summary offences from 4 months or less to 51 weeks) shall have effect.

(3)   This section does not affect the penalty for any offence committed before the commencement of this section.

281 Alteration of penalties for other summary offences

(1)   Subsection (2) applies to any summary offence which –

(a)   is an offence under a relevant enactment,

(b)   is punishable with a maximum term of imprisonment of five months or less, and

(c)   is not listed in Schedule 25 or Schedule 26.

(2)   The Secretary of State may by order amend any relevant enactment so as to –

(a)   provide that any summary offence to which this subsection applies is no longer punishable with imprisonment, or

(b)   increase to 51 weeks the maximum term of imprisonment to which a person is liable on conviction of the offence.

(3)   An order under subsection (2) may make such supplementary, incidental or consequential provision as the Secretary of State considers necessary or expedient, including provision amending any relevant enactment.

(4)   Subsection (5) applies to any summary offence which –

(a)   is an offence under a relevant enactment, and

(b)   is punishable with a maximum term of imprisonment of six months.

(5)   The maximum term of imprisonment to which a person is liable on conviction of an offence to which this subsection applies is, by virtue of this subsection, 51 weeks (and the relevant enactment in question is to be read as if it had been amended accordingly).

(6) Neither of the following –

    (a) an order under subsection (2), or

    (b) subsection (5),

affects the penalty for any offence committed before the commencement of that order or subsection (as the case may be).

(7) In this section and section 282 'relevant enactment' means any enactment contained in –

    (a) an Act passed before or in the same Session as this Act, or

    (b) any subordinate legislation made before the passing of this Act.

(8) In subsection (7) 'subordinate legislation' has the same meaning as in the Interpretation Act 1978 (c. 30).

282 Increase in maximum term that may be imposed on summary conviction of offence triable either way

(1) In section 32 of the Magistrates' Courts Act 1980 (c. 43) (penalties on summary conviction for offences triable either way) in subsection (1) (offences listed in Schedule 1 to that Act) for 'not exceeding 6 months' there is substituted 'not exceeding 12 months'.

(2) Subsection (3) applies to any offence triable either way which –

    (a) is an offence under a relevant enactment,

    (b) is punishable with imprisonment on summary conviction, and

    (c) is not listed in Schedule 1 to the Magistrates' Courts Act 1980.

(3) The maximum term of imprisonment to which a person is liable on summary conviction of an offence to which this subsection applies is by virtue of this subsection 12 months (and the relevant enactment in question is to be read as if it had been amended accordingly).

(4) Nothing in this section affects the penalty for any offence committed before the commencement of this section.

283 Enabling powers: power to alter maximum penalties

(1) The Secretary of State may by order, in accordance with subsection (2) or (3), amend any relevant enactment which confers a power (however framed or worded) by subordinate legislation to make a person –

    (a) as regards a summary offence, liable on conviction to a term of imprisonment;

    (b) as regards an offence triable either way, liable on summary conviction to a term of imprisonment.

(2) An order made by virtue of paragraph (a) of subsection (1) may amend the relevant enactment in question so as to –

    (a) restrict the power so that a person may no longer be made liable on conviction of a summary offence to a term of imprisonment, or

    (b) increase to 51 weeks the maximum term of imprisonment to which a person may be made liable on conviction of a summary offence under the power.

(3) An order made by virtue of paragraph (b) of that subsection may amend the relevant enactment in question so as to increase the maximum term of imprisonment to which a person may be made liable on summary conviction of an offence under the power to 12 months.

(4) Schedule 27 (which amends the maximum penalties which may be imposed by virtue of certain enabling powers) shall have effect.

(5) The power conferred by subsection (1) shall not apply to the enactments amended under Schedule 27.

(6) An order under subsection (1) may make such supplementary, incidental or consequential provision as the Secretary of State considers necessary or expedient, including provision amending any relevant enactment.

(7) None of the following –

    (a) an order under subsection (1), or

    (b) Schedule 27,

affects the penalty for any offence committed before the commencement of that order or Schedule (as the case may be).

(8) In subsection (1) 'subordinate legislation' has the same meaning as in the Interpretation Act 1978 (c. 30).

(9) In this section 'relevant enactment' means any enactment contained in an Act passed before or in the same Session as this Act.

284 Increase in penalties for drug-related offences

(1) Schedule 28 (increase in penalties for certain drug-related offences) shall have effect.

(2) That Schedule does not affect the penalty for any offence committed before the commencement of that Schedule.

285 Increase in penalties for certain driving-related offences

(1) In section 12A of the Theft Act 1968 (c. 60) (aggravated vehicle-taking), in subsection (4), for 'five years' there is substituted 'fourteen years'.

(2) Part 1 of Schedule 2 to the Road Traffic Offenders Act 1988 (c. 53) (prosecution and punishment of offences) is amended in accordance with subsections (3) and (4).

(3) In the entry relating to section 1 of the Road Traffic Act 1988 (c. 52) (causing death by dangerous driving), in column 4, for '10 years' there is substituted '14 years'.

(4) In the entry relating to section 3A of that Act (causing death by careless driving when under influence of drink or drugs), in column 4, for '10 years' there is substituted '14 years'.

(5) Part I of Schedule 1 to the Road Traffic Offenders (Northern Ireland) Order 1996 (S.I. 1996/1320 (N.I. 10)) (prosecution and punishment of offences) is amended in accordance with subsections (6) and (7).

(6) In the entry relating to Article 9 of the Road Traffic (Northern Ireland) Order 1995 (S.I. 1995/2994 (N.I. 18)) (causing death or grievous bodily injury by dangerous driving), in column 4, for '10 years' there is substituted '14 years'.

(7) In the entry relating to Article 14 of that Order (causing death or grievous bodily injury by careless driving when under the influence of drink or drugs), in column 4, for '10 years' there is substituted '14 years'.

(8) This section does not affect the penalty for any offence committed before the commencement of this section.

286 Increase in penalties for offences under section 174 of Road Traffic Act 1988

(1) In Part 1 of Schedule 2 to the Road Traffic Offenders Act 1988 (c. 53) (prosecution and punishment of offences), in the entry relating to section 174 of the Road Traffic Act 1988 (c. 52) (false statements and withholding material information), for columns (3) and (4) there is substituted –

'(a) Summarily	(a) 6 months or the statutory maximum or both
(b) On indictment	(b) 2 years or a fine or both.'

(2) Section 282(3) (increase in maximum term that may be imposed on summary conviction of offence triable either way) has effect in relation to the entry amended by

subsection (1) as it has effect in relation to any other enactment contained in an Act passed before this Act.

(3) This section does not apply in relation to any offence committed before the commencement of this section.

Firearms offences

287 Minimum sentence for certain firearms offences

After section 51 of the Firearms Act 1968 (c. 27) there is inserted the following section –

'51A Minimum sentence for certain offences under s. 5

(1) This section applies where –

   (a)   an individual is convicted of –

      (i)   an offence under section 5(1)(a), (ab), (aba), (ac), (ad), (ae), (af) or (c) of this Act, or

      (ii)   an offence under section 5(1A)(a) of this Act, and

   (b)   the offence was committed after the commencement of this section and at a time when he was aged 16 or over.

(2) The court shall impose an appropriate custodial sentence (or order for detention) for a term of at least the required minimum term (with or without a fine) unless the court is of the opinion that there are exceptional circumstances relating to the offence or to the offender which justify its not doing so.

(3) Where an offence is found to have been committed over a period of two or more days, or at some time during a period of two or more days, it shall be taken for the purposes of this section to have been committed on the last of those days.

(4) In this section "appropriate custodial sentence (or order for detention)" means –

   (a)   in relation to England and Wales –

      (i)   in the case of an offender who is aged 18 or over when convicted, a sentence of imprisonment, and

      (ii)   in the case of an offender who is aged under 18 at that time, a sentence of detention under section 91 of the Powers of Criminal Courts (Sentencing) Act 2000;

   (b)   in relation to Scotland –

      (i)   in the case of an offender who is aged 21 or over when convicted, a sentence of imprisonment,

      (ii)   in the case of an offender who is aged under 21 at that time (not being an offender mentioned in sub-paragraph (iii)), a sentence of detention under section 207 of the Criminal Procedure (Scotland) Act 1995, and

      (iii)   in the case of an offender who is aged under 18 at that time and is subject to a supervision requirement, an order for detention under section 44, or sentence of detention under section 208, of that Act.

(5) In this section "the required minimum term" means –

   (a)   in relation to England and Wales –

      (i)   in the case of an offender who was aged 18 or over when he committed the offence, five years, and

      (ii)   in the case of an offender who was under 18 at that time, three years, and

    (b)   in relation to Scotland –

        (i)   in the case of an offender who was aged 21 or over when he committed the offence, five years, and

        (ii) in the case of an offender who was aged under 21 at that time, three years.'

288 Certain firearms offences to be triable only on indictment

In Part 1 of Schedule 6 to the Firearms Act 1968 (c. 27) (prosecution and punishment of offences) for the entries relating to offences under section 5(1) (possessing or distributing prohibited weapons or ammunition) and section 5(1A) (possessing or distributing other prohibited weapons) there is substituted –

'Section 5(1)(a), (ab), (aba), (ac), (ad), (ae), (af) or (c)	Possessing or distributing prohibited weapons or ammunition.	On indictment	10 years or a fine, or both.
Section 5(1)(b)	Possessing or distributing prohibited weapon designed for discharge of noxious liquid etc.	(a) Summary	6 months or a fine of the statutory maximum, or both.
		(b) On indictment	10 years or a fine or both.
Section 5(1A)(a)	Possessing or distributing firearm disguised as other object.	On indictment	10 years or a fine, or both.
Section 5(1A)(b), (c), (d), (e), (f) or (g)	Possessing or distributing other prohibited weapons.	(a) Summary	6 months or a fine of the statutory maximum, or both.
		(b) On indictment	10 years or a fine, or both.'

289 Power to sentence young offender to detention in respect of certain firearms offences: England and Wales

(1) Section 91 of the Sentencing Act (offenders under 18 convicted of certain serious offences: power to detain for specified period) is amended as follows.

(2) After subsection (1) there is inserted –

    '(1A) Subsection (3) below also applies where –

        (a)   a person aged under 18 is convicted on indictment of an offence –

            (i)   under subsection (1)(a), (ab), (aba), (ac), (ad), (ae), (af) or (c) of section 5 of the Firearms Act 1968 (prohibited weapons), or

            (ii) under subsection (1A)(a) of that section,

        (b)   the offence was committed after the commencement of section 51A of that Act and at a time when he was aged 16 or over, and

(c)   the court is of the opinion mentioned in section 51A(2) of that Act (exceptional circumstances which justify its not imposing required custodial sentence).'

(3) After subsection (4) there is inserted –

'(5) Where subsection (2) of section 51A of the Firearms Act 1968 requires the imposition of a sentence of detention under this section for a term of at least the required minimum term (within the meaning of that section), the court shall sentence the offender to be detained for such period, of at least that term but not exceeding the maximum term of imprisonment with which the offence is punishable in the case of a person aged 18 or over, as may be specified in the sentence.'.

290 Power to sentence young offender to detention in respect of certain firearms offences: Scotland

(1) The Criminal Procedure (Scotland) Act 1995 (c. 46) is amended as follows.

(2) In section 49(3) (children's hearing for purpose of obtaining advice as to treatment of child), at the end there is added 'except that where the circumstances are such as are mentioned in paragraphs (a) and (b) of section 51A(1) of the Firearms Act 1968 it shall itself dispose of the case'.

(3) In section 208 (detention of children convicted on indictment), the existing provisions become subsection (1); and after that subsection there is added –

'(2) Subsection (1) does not apply where the circumstances are such as are mentioned in paragraphs (a) and (b) of section 51A(1) of the Firearms Act 1968.'.

291 Power by order to exclude application of minimum sentence to those under 18

(1) The Secretary of State may by order –

(a)   amend section 51A(1)(b) of the Firearms Act 1968 (c. 27) by substituting for the word '16' the word '18',

(b)   repeal section 91(1A)(c) and (5) of the Sentencing Act,

(c)   amend subsection (3) of section 49 of the Criminal Procedure (Scotland) Act 1995 by repealing the exception to that subsection,

(d)   repeal section 208(2) of that Act, and

(e)   make such other provision as he considers necessary or expedient in consequence of, or in connection with, the provision made by virtue of paragraphs (a) to (d).

(2) The provision that may be made by virtue of subsection (1)(e) includes, in particular, provision amending or repealing any provision of an Act (whenever passed), including any provision of this Act.

292 Sentencing for firearms offences in Northern Ireland

Schedule 29 (which contains amendments of the Firearms (Northern Ireland) Order 1981 (S.I. 1981/155 (N.I. 2)) relating to sentencing) shall have effect.

293 Increase in penalty for offences relating to importation or exportation of certain firearms

(1) The Customs and Excise Management Act 1979 (c. 2) is amended as follows.

(2) In section 50 (penalty for improper importation of goods), for subsection (5A) there is substituted –

'(5A) In the case of –

(a)   an offence under subsection (2) or (3) above committed in Great Britain in connection with a prohibition or restriction on the importation of any weapon or ammunition that is of a kind mentioned in section 5(1)(a), (ab), (aba), (ac), (ad), (ae), (af) or (c) or (1A)(a) of the Firearms Act 1968,

(b) any such offence committed in Northern Ireland in connection with a prohibition or restriction on the importation of any weapon or ammunition that is of a kind mentioned in Article 6(1)(a), (ab), (ac), (ad), (ae) or (c) or (1A)(a) of the Firearms (Northern Ireland) Order 1981, or

(c) any such offence committed in connection with the prohibition contained in section 20 of the Forgery and Counterfeiting Act 1981,

subsection (4)(b) above shall have effect as if for the words "7 years" there were substituted the words "10 years".'

(3) In section 68 (offences in relation to exportation of prohibited or restricted goods) for subsection (4A) there is substituted –

'(4A) In the case of –

(a) an offence under subsection (2) or (3) above committed in Great Britain in connection with a prohibition or restriction on the exportation of any weapon or ammunition that is of a kind mentioned in section 5(1)(a), (ab), (aba), (ac), (ad), (ae), (af) or (c) or (1A)(a) of the Firearms Act 1968,

(b) any such offence committed in Northern Ireland in connection with a prohibition or restriction on the exportation of any weapon or ammunition that is of a kind mentioned in Article 6(1)(a), (ab), (ac), (ad), (ae) or (c) or (1A)(a) of the Firearms (Northern Ireland) Order 1981, or

(c) any such offence committed in connection with the prohibition contained in section 21 of the Forgery and Counterfeiting Act 1981,

subsection (3)(b) above shall have effect as if for the words "7 years" there were substituted the words "10 years".'

(4) In section 170 (penalty for fraudulent evasion of duty, etc), for subsection (4A) there is substituted –

'(4A) In the case of –

(a) an offence under subsection (2) or (3) above committed in Great Britain in connection with a prohibition or restriction on the importation or exportation of any weapon or ammunition that is of a kind mentioned in section 5(1)(a), (ab), (aba), (ac), (ad), (ae), (af) or (c) or (1A)(a) of the Firearms Act 1968,

(b) any such offence committed in Northern Ireland in connection with a prohibition or restriction on the importation or exportation of any weapon or ammunition that is of a kind mentioned in Article 6(1)(a), (ab), (ac), (ad), (ae) or (c) or (1A)(a) of the Firearms (Northern Ireland) Order 1981, or

(c) any such offence committed in connection with the prohibitions contained in sections 20 and 21 of the Forgery and Counterfeiting Act 1981,

subsection (3)(b) above shall have effect as if for the words "7 years" there were substituted the words "10 years".'

(5) This section does not affect the penalty for any offence committed before the commencement of this section.

Offenders transferred to mental hospital

294 Duration of directions under Mental Health Act 1983 in relation to offenders

(1) Section 50 of the Mental Health Act 1983 (c. 20) (further provisions as to prisoners under sentence) is amended as follows.

(2) In subsection (1), for 'the expiration of that person's sentence' there is substituted 'his release date'.

(3) For subsections (2) and (3) there is substituted –

'(2) A restriction direction in the case of a person serving a sentence of imprisonment shall cease to have effect, if it has not previously done so, on his release date.

(3) In this section, references to a person's release date are to the day (if any) on which he would be entitled to be released (whether unconditionally or on licence) from any prison or other institution in which he might have been detained if the transfer direction had not been given; and in determining that day there shall be disregarded –

    (a) any powers that would be exercisable by the Parole Board if he were detained in such a prison or other institution, and

    (b) any practice of the Secretary of State in relation to the early release under discretionary powers of persons detained in such a prison or other institution.'.

295 Access to Parole Board for certain patients serving prison sentences

In section 74 of the Mental Health Act 1983 (restricted patients subject to restriction directions) after subsection (5) there is inserted –

'(5A) Where the tribunal have made a recommendation under subsection (1)(b) above in the case of a patient who is subject to a restriction direction or a limitation direction –

    (a) the fact that the restriction direction or limitation direction remains in force does not prevent the making of any application or reference to the Parole Board by or in respect of him or the exercise by him of any power to require the Secretary of State to refer his case to the Parole Board, and

    (b) if the Parole Board make a direction or recommendation by virtue of which the patient would become entitled to be released (whether unconditionally or on licence) from any prison or other institution in which he might have been detained if he had not been removed to hospital, the restriction direction or limitation direction shall cease to have effect at the time when he would become entitled to be so released.'

296 Duration of directions under Mental Health (Northern Ireland) Order 1986 in relation to offenders

(1) Article 56 of the Mental Health (Northern Ireland) Order 1986 (S.I. 1986/595 (N.I. 4)) (further provisions as to prisoners under sentence) is amended as follows.

(2) In paragraph (1), for 'the expiration of that person's sentence' there is substituted 'his release date'.

(3) For paragraphs (2) and (3) there is substituted –

'(2) A restriction direction in the case of a person serving a sentence of imprisonment shall cease to have effect, if it has not previously done so, on his release date.

(3) In this Article, references to a person's release date are to the day (if any) on which he would be entitled to be released (whether unconditionally or on licence) from any prison or juvenile justice centre in which he might have been detained if the transfer direction had not been given; and in determining that day any powers that would be exercisable by the Sentence Review Commissioners or the Life Sentence Review Commissioners if he were detained in such a prison or juvenile justice centre shall be disregarded.'

297 Access to Sentence Review Commissioners and Life Sentence Review Commissioners for certain Northern Ireland patients

In Article 79 of the Mental Health (Northern Ireland) Order 1986 (restricted patients subject to restriction directions) after paragraph (5) there is inserted –

'(5A) Where the tribunal have made a recommendation under paragraph (1)(b) in the case of a patient who is subject to a restriction direction –

(a)   the fact that the restriction direction remains in force does not prevent –

   (i)   the making of any application or reference to the Life Sentence Review Commissioners by or in respect of him or the exercise by him of any power to require the Secretary of State to refer his case to those Commissioners, or

   (ii)   the making of any application by him to the Sentence Review Commissioners, and

(b)   if –

   (i)   the Life Sentence Review Commissioners give a direction by virtue of which the patient would become entitled to be released (whether unconditionally or on licence) from any prison or juvenile justice centre in which he might have been detained if the transfer direction had not been given, or

   (ii)   the Sentence Review Commissioners grant a declaration by virtue of which he would become so entitled,

the restriction direction shall cease to have effect at the time at which he would become so entitled.'.

Term of detention and training order

298 Term of detention and training order

(1)   Section 101 of the Sentencing Act (which relates to detention and training orders) is amended as follows.

(2)   In subsection (1), for 'subsection (2)' there is substituted 'subsections (2) and (2A)'.

(3)   After subsection (2) there is inserted –

'(2A)   Where –

   (a)   the offence is a summary offence,

   (b)   the maximum term of imprisonment that a court could (in the case of an offender aged 18 or over) impose for the offence is 51 weeks,

the term of a detention and training order may not exceed 6 months.'

Disqualification from working with children

299 Disqualification from working with children

Schedule 30 (which contains amendments of Part 2 of the Criminal Justice and Court Services Act 2000 (c. 43) relating to disqualification orders under that Part) shall have effect.

Fine defaulters

300 Power to impose unpaid work requirement or curfew requirement on fine defaulter

(1)   Subsection (2) applies in any case where, in respect of a person aged 16 or over, a magistrates' court –

   (a)   has power under Part 3 of the Magistrates' Courts Act 1980 (c. 43) to issue a warrant of commitment for default in paying a sum adjudged to be paid by a conviction (other than a sum ordered to be paid under section 6 of the Proceeds of Crime Act 2002 (c. 29)), or

(b) would, but for section 89 of the Sentencing Act (restrictions on custodial sentences for persons under 18), have power to issue such a warrant for such default.

(2) The magistrates' court may, instead of issuing a warrant of commitment or, as the case may be, proceeding under section 81 of the Magistrates' Courts Act 1980 (enforcement of fines imposed on young offender), order the person in default to comply with –

    (a) an unpaid work requirement (as defined by section 199), or
    (b) a curfew requirement (as defined by section 204).

(3) In this Part 'default order' means an order under subsection (2).

(4) Subsections (3) and (4) of section 177 (which relate to electronic monitoring) have effect in relation to a default order as they have effect in relation to a community order.

(5) Where a magistrates' court has power to make a default order, it may, if it thinks it expedient to do so, postpone the making of the order until such time and on such conditions (if any) as it thinks just.

(6) Schedule 8 (breach, revocation or amendment of community order), Schedule 9 (transfer of community orders to Scotland or Northern Ireland) and Chapter 4 (further provisions about orders under Chapters 2 and 3) have effect in relation to default orders as they have effect in relation to community orders, but subject to the modifications contained in Schedule 31.

(7) Where a default order has been made for default in paying any sum –

    (a) on payment of the whole sum to any person authorised to receive it, the order shall cease to have effect, and
    (b) on payment of a part of the sum to any such person, the total number of hours or days to which the order relates is to be taken to be reduced by a proportion corresponding to that which the part paid bears to the whole sum.

(8) In calculating any reduction required by subsection (7)(b), any fraction of a day or hour is to be disregarded.

301 Fine defaulters: driving disqualification

(1) Subsection (2) applies in any case where a magistrates' court –

    (a) has power under Part 3 of the Magistrates' Courts Act 1980 (c. 43) to issue a warrant of commitment for default in paying a sum adjudged to be paid by a conviction (other than a sum ordered to be paid under section 6 of the Proceeds of Crime Act 2002 (c. 29)), or
    (b) would, but for section 89 of the Sentencing Act (restrictions on custodial sentences for persons under 18), have power to issue such a warrant for such default.

(2) The magistrates' court may, instead of issuing a warrant of commitment or, as the case may be, proceeding under section 81 of the Magistrates' Courts Act 1980 (enforcement of fines imposed on young offenders), order the person in default to be disqualified, for such period not exceeding twelve months as it thinks fit, for holding or obtaining a driving licence.

(3) Where an order has been made under subsection (2) for default in paying any sum –

    (a) on payment of the whole sum to any person authorised to receive it, the order shall cease to have effect, and
    (b) on payment of part of the sum to any such person, the total number of weeks or months to which the order relates is to be taken to be reduced by a proportion corresponding to that which the part paid bears to the whole sum.

(4) In calculating any reduction required by subsection (3)(b) any fraction of a week or month is to be disregarded.

(5) The Secretary of State may by order amend subsection (2) by substituting, for the period there specified, such other period as may be specified in the order.

(6) A court which makes an order under this section disqualifying a person for holding or obtaining a driving licence shall require him to produce –

(a) any such licence held by him together with its counterpart; or

(b) in the case where he holds a Community licence (within the meaning of Part 3 of the Road Traffic Act 1988 (c. 52)), his Community licence and its counterpart (if any).

(7) In this section –

'driving licence' means a licence to drive a motor vehicle granted under Part 3 of the Road Traffic Act 1988;

'counterpart' –

(a) in relation to a driving licence, has the meaning given in relation to such a licence by section 108(1) of that Act; and

(b) in relation to a Community licence, has the meaning given by section 99B of that Act.

CHAPTER 9   SUPPLEMENTARY

302 Execution of process between England and Wales and Scotland

Section 4 of the Summary Jurisdiction (Process) Act 1881 (c. 24) (execution of process of English and Welsh courts in Scotland) applies to any process issued by a magistrates' court under –

paragraph 7(2) or (4), 13(6) or 25(1) of Schedule 8,
paragraph 12 of Schedule 9,
paragraph 8(1) of Schedule 10, or
paragraph 6(2) or (4), 12(1) or 20(1) of Schedule 12,

as it applies to process issued under the Magistrates' Courts Act 1980 by a magistrates' court.

303 Sentencing: repeals

The following enactments (which are superseded by the provisions of this Part) shall cease to have effect –

(a) Part 2 of the Criminal Justice Act 1991 (c. 53) (early release of prisoners),

(b) in the Crime (Sentences) Act 1997 (c. 43) –

(i) section 29 (power of Secretary of State to release life prisoners to whom section 28 of that Act does not apply),

(ii) section 33 (transferred prisoners), and

(iii) sections 35 and 40 (fine defaulters),

(c) sections 80 and 81 of the Crime and Disorder Act 1998 (c. 37) (sentencing guidelines), and

(d) in the Sentencing Act –

(i) Chapter 3 of Part 4 (community orders available only where offender 16 or over),

(ii) section 85 (sexual or violent offences: extension of custodial term for licence purposes),

(iii) sections 87 and 88 (remand in custody),

(iv) section 109 (life sentence for second serious offence), and

(v) Chapter 5 of Part 5 (suspended sentences).

304 Amendments relating to sentencing

Schedule 32 (which contains amendments related to the provisions of this Part) shall have effect.

305 Interpretation of Part 12

(1) In this Part, except where the contrary intention appears –

'accredited programme' has the meaning given by section 202(2);

'activity requirement', in relation to a community order, custody plus order, intermittent custody order or suspended sentence order, has the meaning given by section 201;

'alcohol treatment requirement', in relation to a community order or suspended sentence order, has the meaning given by section 212;

'the appropriate officer of the court' means, in relation to a magistrates' court, the clerk of the court;

'associated', in relation to offences, is to be read in accordance with section 161(1) of the Sentencing Act;

'attendance centre' has the meaning given by section 221(2);

'attendance centre requirement', in relation to a community order, custody plus order, intermittent custody order or suspended sentence order, has the meaning given by section 214;

'community order' has the meaning given by section 177(1);

'community requirement', in relation to a suspended sentence order, has the meaning given by section 189(7);

'community sentence' has the meaning given by section 147(1);

'court' (without more), except in Chapter 7, does not include a service court;

'curfew requirement', in relation to a community order, custody plus order, intermittent custody order or suspended sentence order, has the meaning given by section 204;

'custodial sentence' has the meaning given by section 76 of the Sentencing Act;

'custody plus order' has the meaning given by section 181(4);

'default order' has the meaning given by section 300(3);

'drug rehabilitation requirement', in relation to a community order or suspended sentence order, has the meaning given by section 209;

'electronic monitoring requirement', in relation to a community order, custody plus order, intermittent custody order or suspended sentence order, has the meaning given by section 215;

'exclusion requirement', in relation to a community order, custody plus order, intermittent custody order or suspended sentence order, has the meaning given by section 205;

'guardian' has the same meaning as in the Children and Young Persons Act 1933 (c. 12);

'intermittent custody order' has the meaning given by section 183(2);

'licence' means a licence under Chapter 6;

'local probation board' means a local probation board established under section 4 of the Criminal Justice and Court Services Act 2000 (c. 43);

'mental health treatment requirement', in relation to a community order or suspended sentence order, has the meaning given by section 207;

'pre-sentence report' has the meaning given by section 158(1);

'programme requirement', in relation to a community order, custody plus order, intermittent custody order or suspended sentence order, has the meaning given by section 202;

'prohibited activity requirement', in relation to a community order, custody plus order, intermittent custody order or suspended sentence order, has the meaning given by section 203;

'residence requirement', in relation to a community order or suspended sentence order, has the meaning given by section 206;

'responsible officer', in relation to an offender to whom a community order, a custody plus order, an intermittent custody order or a suspended sentence order relates, has the meaning given by section 197;

'sentence of imprisonment' does not include a committal –

(a)   in default of payment of any sum of money,

(b)   for want of sufficient distress to satisfy any sum of money, or

(c)   for failure to do or abstain from doing anything required to be done or left undone,

and references to sentencing an offender to imprisonment are to be read accordingly;

'the Sentencing Act' means the Powers of Criminal Courts (Sentencing) Act 2000 (c. 6);

'service court' means –

(a)   a court-martial constituted under the Army Act 1955 (3 & 4 Eliz. 2 c. 18), the Air Force Act 1955 (3 & 4 Eliz. 2 c. 19) or the Naval Discipline Act 1957 (c. 53);

(b)   a summary appeal court constituted under section 83ZA of the Army Act 1955, section 83ZA of the Air Force Act 1955 or section 52FF of the Naval Discipline Act 1957;

(c)   the Courts-Martial Appeal Court; or

(d)   a Standing Civilian Court;

'service disciplinary proceedings' means –

(a)   any proceedings under the Army Act 1955, the Air Force Act 1955 or the Naval Discipline Act 1957 (whether before a court-martial or any other court or person authorised under any of those Acts to award a punishment in respect of any offence), and

(b)   any proceedings before a Standing Civilian Court;

'supervision requirement', in relation to a community order, custody plus order, intermittent custody order or suspended sentence order, has the meaning given by section 213;

'suspended sentence' and 'suspended sentence order' have the meaning given by section 189(7);

'unpaid work requirement', in relation to a community order, custody plus order, intermittent custody order or suspended sentence order, has the meaning given by section 199;

'youth offending team' means a team established under section 39 of the Crime and Disorder Act 1998 (c. 37).

(2)   For the purposes of any provision of this Part which requires the determination of the age of a person by the court or the Secretary of State, his age is to be taken to be that which it appears to the court or (as the case may be) the Secretary of State to be after considering any available evidence.

(3)   Any reference in this Part to an offence punishable with imprisonment is to be read without regard to any prohibition or restriction imposed by or under any Act on the imprisonment of young offenders.

(4)   For the purposes of this Part –

(a)   a sentence falls to be imposed under subsection (2) of section 51A of the Firearms Act 1968 (c. 27) if it is required by that subsection and the court is not of the opinion there mentioned,

(b)   a sentence falls to be imposed under section 110(2) or 111(2) of the Sentencing Act if it is required by that provision and the court is not of the opinion there mentioned,

(c) a sentence falls to be imposed under section 225 or 227 if, because the court is of the opinion mentioned in subsection (1)(b) of that section, the court is obliged to pass a sentence complying with that section,

(d) a sentence falls to be imposed under section 226 if, because the court is of the opinion mentioned in subsection (1)(b) of that section and considers that the case falls within subsection (2) or (3) of that section, the court is obliged to pass a sentence complying with that section, and

(e) a sentence falls to be imposed under section 228 if, because the court is of the opinion mentioned in subsection (1)(b)(i) and (ii) of that section, the court is obliged to pass a sentence complying with that section.

PART 13   MISCELLANEOUS

Detention of suspected terrorists

306 Limit on period of detention without charge of suspected terrorists

(1) Schedule 8 to the Terrorism Act 2000 (c. 11) (detention) is amended as follows.

(2) At the beginning of paragraph 29(3) (duration of warrants of further detention) there is inserted 'Subject to paragraph 36(3A),'.

(3) In sub-paragraph (3) of paragraph 36 (extension of warrants) –

(a) at the beginning there is inserted 'Subject to sub-paragraph (3A),', and

(b) for the words from 'beginning' onwards there is substituted 'beginning with the relevant time'.

(4) After that sub-paragraph there is inserted –

'(3A) Where the period specified in a warrant of further detention –

(a)   ends at the end of the period of seven days beginning with the relevant time, or

(b)   by virtue of a previous extension (or further extension) under this sub-paragraph, ends after the end of that period,

the specified period may, on an application under this paragraph, be extended or further extended to a period ending not later than the end of the period of fourteen days beginning with the relevant time.

(3B) In this paragraph "the relevant time", in relation to a person, means –

(a)   the time of his arrest under section 41, or

(b)   if he was being detained under Schedule 7 when he was arrested under section 41, the time when his examination under that Schedule began.'

Enforcement of legislation on endangered species

307 Enforcement of regulations implementing Community legislation on endangered species

(1) In this section –

'the 1972 Act' means the European Communities Act 1972 (c. 68);
'relevant Community instrument' means –

(a)   Council Regulation 338/97/EC on the protection of species of wild fauna and flora by regulating the trade therein, and

(b)   Commission Regulation 1808/01/EC on the implementation of the Council Regulation mentioned in paragraph (a).

(2) Regulations made under section 2(2) of the 1972 Act for the purpose of implementing any relevant Community instrument may, notwithstanding paragraph 1(1)(d) of

Schedule 2 to the 1972 Act, create offences punishable on conviction on indictment with imprisonment for a term not exceeding five years.

(3) In relation to Scotland and Northern Ireland, regulations made under section 2(2) of the 1972 Act for the purpose of implementing any relevant Community instrument may, notwithstanding paragraph 1(1)(d) of Schedule 2 to the 1972 Act, create offences punishable on summary conviction with imprisonment for a term not exceeding six months.

(4) In Scotland, a constable may arrest without a warrant a person –

   (a) who has committed or attempted to commit an offence under regulations made under section 2(2) of the 1972 Act for the purpose of implementing any relevant Community instrument, or

   (b) whom he has reasonable grounds for suspecting to have committed or to have attempted to commit such an offence.

(5) Until the coming into force of paragraph 3 of Schedule 27 (which amends paragraph 1 of Schedule 2 to the 1972 Act), subsection (3) has effect –

   (a) with the omission of the words 'in relation to Scotland and Northern Ireland', and

   (b) as if, in relation to England and Wales, the definition of 'relevant Community instrument' also included Council Directive 92/43/EEC on the conservation of natural habitats and wild fauna and flora as amended by the Act of Accession to the European Union of Austria, Finland and Sweden and by Council Directive 97/62/EC.

(6) Any reference in this section to a Community instrument is to be read –

   (a) as a reference to that instrument as amended from time to time, and

   (b) where any provision of that instrument has been repealed, as including a reference to any instrument that re-enacts the repealed provision (with or without amendment).

Miscellaneous provisions about criminal proceedings

308 Non-appearance of defendant: plea of guilty

In section 12 of the Magistrates' Courts Act 1980 (c. 43) (non-appearance of accused: plea of guilty) subsection (1)(a)(i) (which excludes offences punishable with imprisonment for term exceeding 3 months) is omitted.

309 Preparatory hearings for serious offences not involving fraud

In section 29 of the Criminal Procedure and Investigations Act 1996 (c. 25) (power to order preparatory hearings) in subsection (1) (preparatory hearing may be held in complex or lengthy trial) after 'complexity' there is inserted 'a case of such seriousness'.

310 Preparatory hearings to deal with severance and joinder of charges

(1) In section 7(1) of the Criminal Justice Act 1987 (c. 38) (which sets out the purposes of preparatory hearings in fraud cases) after paragraph (d) there is inserted 'or

   (e) considering questions as to the severance or joinder of charges.'

(2) In section 9(3) of that Act (determinations as to the admissibility of evidence etc) after paragraph (c) there is inserted 'and

   (d) any question as to the severance or joinder of charges.'

(3) In section 9(11) of that Act (appeals against orders or rulings under section 9(3)(b) or (c)) for 'or (c)' there is substituted '(c) or (d)'.

(4) In section 29(2) of the Criminal Procedure and Investigations Act 1996 (purposes of preparatory hearings in non-fraud cases) after paragraph (d) there is inserted –

'(e)   considering questions as to the severance or joinder of charges,'.

(5) In section 31(3) of that Act (rulings as to the admissibility of evidence etc) after paragraph (b) there is inserted –

'(c)   any question as to the severance or joinder of charges.'

311 Reporting restrictions for preparatory hearings

(1) The Criminal Justice Act 1987 is amended as follows.

(2) In paragraphs (a) and (b) of section 11(1) (restrictions on reporting) for 'Great Britain' there is substituted 'the United Kingdom'.

(3) In section 11A (offences in connection with reporting) after subsection (3) there is inserted –

'(3A) Proceedings for an offence under this section shall not be instituted in Northern Ireland otherwise than by or with the consent of the Attorney General for Northern Ireland.'

(4) In section 17(3) (extent) after 'sections 2 and 3;' there is inserted 'sections 11 and 11A;'.

(5) The Criminal Procedure and Investigations Act 1996 (c. 25) is amended as follows.

(6) In paragraphs (a) and (b) of section 37(1) (restrictions on reporting) for 'Great Britain' there is substituted 'the United Kingdom'.

(7) In section 38 (offences in connection with reporting) after subsection (3) there is inserted –

'(3A) Proceedings for an offence under this section shall not be instituted in Northern Ireland otherwise than by or with the consent of the Attorney General for Northern Ireland.'

(8) In paragraphs (a) and (b) of section 41(1) (restrictions on reporting) for 'Great Britain' there is substituted 'the United Kingdom'.

(9) In section 79(3) (extent) after 'Parts III' there is inserted '(other than sections 37 and 38)'.

(10) In Schedule 4 (modifications for Northern Ireland) paragraph 16 is omitted.

312 Awards of costs

(1) The Prosecution of Offences Act 1985 (c. 23) is amended as follows.

(2) In section 16(4A) (defence costs on an appeal under section 9(11) of Criminal Justice Act 1987 (c. 38) may be met out of central funds) after '1987' there is inserted 'or section 35(1) of the Criminal Procedure and Investigations Act 1996'.

(3) In section 18(2) (award of costs against accused in case of dismissal of appeal under section 9(11) of the Criminal Justice Act 1987 etc) after paragraph (c) there is inserted 'or

(d)   an appeal or application for leave to appeal under section 35(1) of the Criminal Procedure and Investigations Act 1996.'

313 Extension of investigations by Criminal Cases Review Commission in England and Wales

(1) Section 23A of the Criminal Appeal Act 1968 (c. 19) (power to order investigations by Criminal Cases Review Commission) is amended as follows.

(2) In subsection (1) after 'conviction' there is inserted 'or an application for leave to appeal against conviction,'.

(3) In paragraph (a) of that subsection –

(a)   at the beginning there is inserted 'in the case of an appeal,', and

(b)   for 'case', in both places where it occurs, there is substituted 'appeal'.

(4) After paragraph (a) of that subsection there is inserted –

'(aa) in the case of an application for leave to appeal, the matter is relevant to the determination of the application and ought, if possible, to be resolved before the application is determined;'.

(5) After that subsection there is inserted –

'(1A) A direction under subsection (1) above may not be given by a single judge, notwithstanding that, in the case of an application for leave to appeal, the application may be determined by a single judge as provided for by section 31 of this Act.'

(6) After subsection (4) there is inserted –

'(5) In this section "respondent" includes a person who will be a respondent if leave to appeal is granted.'

314 Extension of investigations by Criminal Cases Review Commission in Northern Ireland

(1) Section 25A of the Criminal Appeal (Northern Ireland) Act 1980 (c. 47) (power to order investigations by Criminal Cases Review Commission) is amended as follows.

(2) In subsection (1) after 'conviction' there is inserted 'or an application for leave to appeal against conviction,'.

(3) In paragraph (a) of that subsection –

(a) at the beginning there is inserted 'in the case of an appeal,', and
(b) for 'case', in both places where it occurs, there is substituted 'appeal'.

(4) After paragraph (a) of that subsection there is inserted –

'(aa) in the case of an application for leave to appeal, the matter is relevant to the determination of the application and ought, if possible, to be resolved before the application is determined;'.

(5) After that subsection there is inserted –

'(1A) A direction under subsection (1) above may not be given by a single judge, notwithstanding that, in the case of an application for leave to appeal, the application may be determined by a single judge as provided for by section 45 below.'

(6) After subsection (4) there is inserted –

'(5) In this section "respondent" includes a person who will be a respondent if leave to appeal is granted.'

315 Appeals following reference by Criminal Cases Review Commission

(1) Section 14 of the Criminal Appeal Act 1995 (c. 35) (further provision about references by Criminal Cases Review Commission) is amended as follows.

(2) After subsection (4) there is inserted –

'(4A) Subject to subsection (4B), where a reference under section 9 or 10 is treated as an appeal against any conviction, verdict, finding or sentence, the appeal may not be on any ground which is not related to any reason given by the Commission for making the reference.

(4B) The Court of Appeal may give leave for an appeal mentioned in subsection (4A) to be on a ground relating to the conviction, verdict, finding or sentence which is not related to any reason given by the Commission for making the reference.'

(3) In subsection (5) for 'any of sections 9 to' there is substituted 'section 11 or'.

316 Power to substitute conviction of alternative offence on appeal in England and Wales

(1) The Criminal Appeal Act 1968 (c. 19) is amended as follows.
(2) In section 3 (power to substitute conviction of alternative offence) in subsection (1) after 'an offence' there is inserted 'to which he did not plead guilty'.
(3) After section 3 there is inserted –

'**3A Power to substitute conviction of alternative offence after guilty plea**

(1) This section applies on an appeal against conviction where –

(a) an appellant has been convicted of an offence to which he pleaded guilty,
(b) if he had not so pleaded, he could on the indictment have pleaded, or been found, guilty of some other offence, and
(c) it appears to the Court of Appeal that the plea of guilty indicates an admission by the appellant of facts which prove him guilty of the other offence.

(2) The Court of Appeal may, instead of allowing or dismissing the appeal, substitute for the appellant's plea of guilty a plea of guilty of the other offence and pass such sentence in substitution for the sentence passed at the trial as may be authorised by law for the other offence, not being a sentence of greater severity.'

317 Power to substitute conviction of alternative offence on appeal in Northern Ireland

(1) The Criminal Appeal (Northern Ireland) Act 1980 (c. 47) is amended as follows.
(2) In section 3 (power to substitute conviction of alternative offence) in subsection (1) after 'an offence' there is inserted 'to which he did not plead guilty'.
(3) After section 3 there is inserted –

'**3A Power to substitute conviction of alternative offence after guilty plea**

(1) This section applies where –

(a) an appellant has been convicted of an offence to which he pleaded guilty,
(b) if he had not so pleaded, he could on the indictment have pleaded, or been found, guilty of some other offence, and
(c) it appears to the Court of Appeal that the plea of guilty indicates an admission by the appellant of facts which prove him guilty of that other offence.

(2) The Court may, instead of allowing or dismissing the appeal, substitute for the appellant's plea of guilty a plea of guilty of that other offence and pass such sentence in substitution for the sentence passed at the trial as may be warranted in law by the plea so substituted.'

318 Substitution of conviction on different charge on appeal from court-martial

(1) The Courts-Martial (Appeals) Act 1968 (c. 20) is amended as follows.
(2) In section 14 (substitution of conviction on different charge) in subsection (1) after 'an offence' there is inserted 'to which he did not plead guilty'.
(3) After section 14 there is inserted –

'**14A Substitution of conviction on different charge after guilty plea**

(1) This section applies where –

(a) an appellant has been convicted of an offence to which he pleaded guilty,
(b) if he had not so pleaded, he could lawfully have pleaded, or been found, guilty of some other offence, and
(c) it appears to the Appeal Court on an appeal against conviction that the plea of guilty indicates an admission by the appellant of facts which prove him guilty of that other offence.

(2)   The Appeal Court may, instead of allowing or dismissing the appeal, substitute for the appellant's plea of guilty a plea of guilty of the other offence, and may pass on the appellant, in substitution for the sentence passed on him by the court-martial, such sentence as they think proper, being a sentence warranted by the relevant Service Act for that other offence, but not a sentence of greater severity.'

319 Appeals against sentences in England and Wales

(1)   The Criminal Appeal Act 1968 (c. 19) is amended as follows.

(2)   In section 10 (appeal against sentence in certain cases) for subsection (3) there is substituted –

'(3)   An offender dealt with for an offence before the Crown Court in a proceeding to which subsection (2) of this section applies may appeal to the Court of Appeal against any sentence passed on him for the offence by the Crown Court.'

(3)   In section 11 (supplementary provisions as to appeal against sentence) after subsection (6) there is inserted –

'(7)   For the purposes of this section, any two or more sentences are to be treated as passed in the same proceeding if –

(a)   they are passed on the same day; or

(b)   they are passed on different days but the court in passing any one of them states that it is treating that one together with the other or others as substantially one sentence.'

Outraging public decency

320 Offence of outraging public decency triable either way

(1)   After paragraph 1 of Schedule 1 to the Magistrates' Courts Act 1980 (c. 43) (offences triable either way by virtue of section 17) there is inserted –

'1A   An offence at common law of outraging public decency.'

(2)   This section does not apply in relation to any offence committed before the commencement of this section.

Jury service

321 Jury service

Schedule 33 (jury service) shall have effect.

Individual support orders

322 Individual support orders

After section 1A of the Crime and Disorder Act 1998 (c. 37) there is inserted –

'1AA Individual support orders

(1)   Where a court makes an anti-social behaviour order in respect of a defendant who is a child or young person when that order is made, it must consider whether the individual support conditions are fulfilled.

(2)   If it is satisfied that those conditions are fulfilled, the court must make an order under this section ("an individual support order") which –

(a)   requires the defendant to comply, for a period not exceeding six months, with such requirements as are specified in the order; and

(b)   requires the defendant to comply with any directions given by the responsible officer with a view to the implementation of the requirements under paragraph (a) above.

(3) The individual support conditions are –

(a)   that an individual support order would be desirable in the interests of preventing any repetition of the kind of behaviour which led to the making of the anti-social behaviour order;

(b)   that the defendant is not already subject to an individual support order; and

(c)   that the court has been notified by the Secretary of State that arrangements for implementing individual support orders are available in the area in which it appears to it that the defendant resides or will reside and the notice has not been withdrawn.

(4) If the court is not satisfied that the individual support conditions are fulfilled, it shall state in open court that it is not so satisfied and why it is not.

(5) The requirements that may be specified under subsection (2)(a) above are those that the court considers desirable in the interests of preventing any repetition of the kind of behaviour which led to the making of the anti-social behaviour order.

(6) Requirements included in an individual support order, or directions given under such an order by a responsible officer, may require the defendant to do all or any of the following things –

(a)   to participate in activities specified in the requirements or directions at a time or times so specified;

(b)   to present himself to a person or persons so specified at a place or places and at a time or times so specified;

(c)   to comply with any arrangements for his education so specified.

(7) But requirements included in, or directions given under, such an order may not require the defendant to attend (whether at the same place or at different places) on more than two days in any week; and "week" here means a period of seven days beginning with a Sunday.

(8) Requirements included in, and directions given under, an individual support order shall, as far as practicable, be such as to avoid –

(a)   any conflict with the defendant's religious beliefs; and

(b)   any interference with the times, if any, at which he normally works or attends school or any other educational establishment.

(9) Before making an individual support order, the court shall obtain from a social worker of a local authority social services department or a member of a youth offending team any information which it considers necessary in order –

(a)   to determine whether the individual support conditions are fulfilled, or

(b)   to determine what requirements should be imposed by an individual support order if made,

and shall consider that information.

(10) In this section and section 1AB below "responsible officer", in relation to an individual support order, means one of the following who is specified in the order, namely –

(a)   a social worker of a local authority social services department;

(b)   a person nominated by a person appointed as chief education officer under section 532 of the Education Act 1996 (c. 56);

(c)   a member of a youth offending team.

1AB Individual support orders: explanation, breach, amendment etc

(1) Before making an individual support order, the court shall explain to the defendant in ordinary language –

(a) the effect of the order and of the requirements proposed to be included in it;

(b) the consequences which may follow (under subsection (3) below) if he fails to comply with any of those requirements; and

(c) that the court has power (under subsection (6) below) to review the order on the application either of the defendant or of the responsible officer.

(2) The power of the Secretary of State under section 174(4) of the Criminal Justice Act 2003 includes power by order to –

(a) prescribe cases in which subsection (1) above does not apply; and

(b) prescribe cases in which the explanation referred to in that subsection may be made in the absence of the defendant, or may be provided in written form.

(3) If the person in respect of whom an individual support order is made fails without reasonable excuse to comply with any requirement included in the order, he is guilty of an offence and liable on summary conviction to a fine not exceeding –

(a) if he is aged 14 or over at the date of his conviction, £1,000;

(b) if he is aged under 14 then, £250.

(4) No referral order under section 16(2) or (3) of the Powers of Criminal Courts (Sentencing) Act 2000 (referral of young offenders to youth offender panels) may be made in respect of an offence under subsection (3) above.

(5) If the anti-social behaviour order as a result of which an individual support order was made ceases to have effect, the individual support order (if it has not previously ceased to have effect) ceases to have effect when the anti-social behaviour order does.

(6) On an application made by complaint by –

(a) the person subject to an individual support order, or

(b) the responsible officer,

the court which made the individual support order may vary or discharge it by a further order.

(7) If the anti-social behaviour order as a result of which an individual support order was made is varied, the court varying the anti-social behaviour order may by a further order vary or discharge the individual support order.'

323 Individual support orders: consequential amendments

(1) The Crime and Disorder Act 1998 (c. 37) is amended as mentioned in subsections (2) to (5).

(2) In section 4 of that Act (appeals against orders) –

(a) in subsection (1) after 'an anti-social behaviour order' there is inserted ', an individual support order', and

(b) in subsection (3) after '1(8)' there is inserted ', 1AB(6)'.

(3) In section 18(1) of that Act (interpretation of Chapter 1) –

(a) after the definition of 'curfew notice' there is inserted –

'"individual support order" has the meaning given by section 1AA(2) above;', and

(b) in the definition of 'responsible officer', before paragraph (a) there is inserted –

'(za) in relation to an individual support order, has the meaning given by section 1AA(10) above;'.

(4) In section 18(4) of that Act (cases where social worker or member of a youth offending team to give supervision or directions) –

   (a) after 'directions under' there is inserted 'an individual support order or', and
   (b) for 'the child or, as the case may be, the parent' there is substituted 'the child, defendant or parent, as the case may be,'.

(5) In section 38 of that Act (local provision of youth justice services), in subsection (4)(f) after 'in relation to' there is inserted 'individual support orders,'.

(6) In section 143(2) (provisions in which sums may be altered) of the Magistrates' Courts Act 1980 (c. 43), after paragraph (d) there is inserted –

   '(da) section 1AB(3) of the Crime and Disorder Act 1998 (failure to comply with individual support order);'.

Parenting orders and referral orders

324 Parenting orders and referral orders

Schedule 34 (parenting orders and referral orders) shall have effect.

Assessing etc. risks posed by sexual or violent offenders

325 Arrangements for assessing etc risks posed by certain offenders

(1) In this section –

   'relevant sexual or violent offender' has the meaning given by section 327;
   'responsible authority', in relation to any area, means the chief officer of police, the local probation board for that area and the Minister of the Crown exercising functions in relation to prisons, acting jointly.

(2) The responsible authority for each area must establish arrangements for the purpose of assessing and managing the risks posed in that area by –

   (a) relevant sexual and violent offenders, and
   (b) other persons who, by reason of offences committed by them (wherever committed), are considered by the responsible authority to be persons who may cause serious harm to the public.

(3) In establishing those arrangements, the responsible authority must act in co-operation with the persons specified in subsection (6); and it is the duty of those persons to co-operate in the establishment by the responsible authority of those arrangements, to the extent that such co-operation is compatible with the exercise by those persons of their functions under any other enactment.

(4) Co-operation under subsection (3) may include the exchange of information.

(5) The responsible authority for each area ('the relevant area') and the persons specified in subsection (6) must together draw up a memorandum setting out the ways in which they are to co-operate.

(6) The persons referred to in subsections (3) and (5) are –

   (a) every youth offending team established for an area any part of which falls within the relevant area,
   (b) the Ministers of the Crown exercising functions in relation to social security, child support, war pensions, employment and training,
   (c) every local education authority any part of whose area falls within the relevant area,
   (d) every local housing authority or social services authority any part of whose area falls within the relevant area,

(e) every registered social landlord which provides or manages residential accom-
     modation in the relevant area in which persons falling within subsection (2)(a)
     or (b) reside or may reside,
(f) every Health Authority or Strategic Health Authority any part of whose area falls
     within the relevant area,
(g) every Primary Care Trust or Local Health Board any part of whose area falls
     within the relevant area,
(h) every NHS trust any part of whose area falls within the relevant area, and
(i) every person who is designated by the Secretary of State by order for the
     purposes of this paragraph as a provider of electronic monitoring services.

(7) The Secretary of State may by order amend subsection (6) by adding or removing any
     person or description of person.
(8) The Secretary of State may issue guidance to responsible authorities on the discharge
     of the functions conferred by this section and section 326.
(9) In this section –

     'local education authority' has the same meaning as in the Education Act 1996
          (c. 56);
     'local housing authority' has the same meaning as in the Housing Act 1985
          (c. 68);
     'Minister of the Crown' has the same meaning as in the Ministers of the Crown
          Act 1975 (c. 26);
     'NHS trust' has the same meaning as in the National Health Service Act 1977
          (c. 49);
     'prison' has the same meaning as in the Prison Act 1952 (c. 52);
     'registered social landlord' has the same meaning as in Part 1 of the Housing Act
          1996 (c. 52);
     'social services authority' means a local authority for the purposes of the Local
          Authority Social Services Act 1970 (c. 42).

326 Review of arrangements

(1) The responsible authority for each area must keep the arrangements established by it
     under section 325 under review with a view to monitoring their effectiveness and
     making any changes to them that appear necessary or expedient.
(2) The responsible authority for any area must exercise their functions under subsection
     (1) in consultation with persons appointed by the Secretary of State as lay advisers in
     relation to that authority.
(3) The Secretary of State must appoint two lay advisers under subsection (2) in relation
     to each responsible authority.
(4) The responsible authority must pay to or in respect of the persons so appointed such
     allowances as the Secretary of State may determine.
(5) As soon as practicable after the end of each period of 12 months beginning with 1st
     April, the responsible authority for each area must –

     (a) prepare a report on the discharge by it during that period of the functions
          conferred by section 325 and this section, and
     (b) publish the report in that area.

(6) The report must include –

     (a) details of the arrangements established by the responsible authority, and
     (b) information of such descriptions as the Secretary of State has notified to the
          responsible authority that he wishes to be included in the report.

327 Section 325: interpretation

(1) For the purposes of section 325, a person is a relevant sexual or violent offender if he
     falls within one or more of subsections (2) to (5).

(2)   A person falls within this subsection if he is subject to the notification requirements of Part 2 of the Sexual Offences Act 2003 (c. 42).

(3)   A person falls within this subsection if –

    (a)   he is convicted by a court in England or Wales of murder or an offence specified in Schedule 15, and

    (b)   one of the following sentences is imposed on him in respect of the conviction –

        (i)   a sentence of imprisonment for a term of 12 months or more,

        (ii)   a sentence of detention in a young offender institution for a term of 12 months or more,

        (iii) a sentence of detention during Her Majesty's pleasure,

        (iv)   a sentence of detention for public protection under section 226,

        (v)   a sentence of detention for a period of 12 months or more under section 91 of the Sentencing Act (offenders under 18 convicted of certain serious offences),

        (vi)   a sentence of detention under section 228,

        (vii) a detention and training order for a term of 12 months or more, or

        (viii) a hospital or guardianship order within the meaning of the Mental Health Act 1983 (c. 20).

(4)   A person falls within this subsection if –

    (a)   he is found not guilty by a court in England and Wales of murder or an offence specified in Schedule 15 by reason of insanity or to be under a disability and to have done the act charged against him in respect of such an offence, and

    (b)   one of the following orders is made in respect of the act charged against him as the offence –

        (i)   an order that he be admitted to hospital, or

        (ii)   a guardianship order within the meaning of the Mental Health Act 1983.

(5)   A person falls within this subsection if –

    (a)   the first condition set out in section 28(2) or 29(2) of the Criminal Justice and Court Services Act 2000 (c. 43) or the second condition set out in section 28(3) or 29(3) of that Act is satisfied in his case, or

    (b)   an order under section 29A of that Act has been made in respect of him.

(6)   In this section 'court' does not include a service court, as defined by section 305(1).

Criminal record certificates

328 Criminal record certificates: amendments of Part 5 of Police Act 1997

Schedule 35 (which contains amendments of Part 5 of the Police Act 1997 (c. 50)) shall have effect.

Civil proceedings brought by offenders

329 Civil proceedings for trespass to the person brought by offender

(1)   This section applies where –

    (a)   a person ('the claimant') claims that another person ('the defendant') did an act amounting to trespass to the claimant's person, and

    (b)   the claimant has been convicted in the United Kingdom of an imprisonable offence committed on the same occasion as that on which the act is alleged to have been done.

(2)   Civil proceedings relating to the claim may be brought only with the permission of the court.

(3) The court may give permission for the proceedings to be brought only if there is evidence that either –

    (a) the condition in subsection (5) is not met, or

    (b) in all the circumstances, the defendant's act was grossly disproportionate.

(4) If the court gives permission and the proceedings are brought, it is a defence for the defendant to prove both –

    (a) that the condition in subsection (5) is met, and

    (b) that, in all the circumstances, his act was not grossly disproportionate.

(5) The condition referred to in subsection (3)(a) and (4)(a) is that the defendant did the act only because –

    (a) he believed that the claimant –

        (i)   was about to commit an offence,

        (ii) was in the course of committing an offence, or

        (iii) had committed an offence immediately beforehand; and

    (b) he believed that the act was necessary to –

        (i)   defend himself or another person,

        (ii) protect or recover property,

        (iii) prevent the commission or continuation of an offence, or

        (iv) apprehend, or secure the conviction, of the claimant after he had committed an offence;

or was necessary to assist in achieving any of those things.

(6) Subsection (4) is without prejudice to any other defence.

(7) Where –

    (a) in service disciplinary proceedings, as defined by section 305(1), a person has been found guilty of an offence under section 70 of the Army Act 1955 (3 & 4 Eliz. 2 c. 18), section 70 of the Air Force Act 1955 (3 & 4 Eliz. 2 c. 19) or section 42 of the Naval Discipline Act 1957 (c. 53), and

    (b) the corresponding civil offence (within the meaning of that Act) was an imprisonable offence,

he is to be treated for the purposes of this section as having been convicted in the United Kingdom of the corresponding civil offence.

(8) In this section –

    (a) the reference to trespass to the person is a reference to –

        (i)   assault,

        (ii) battery, or

        (iii) false imprisonment;

    (b) references to a defendant's belief are to his honest belief, whether or not the belief was also reasonable;

    (c) 'court' means the High Court or a county court; and

    (d) 'imprisonable offence' means an offence which, in the case of a person aged 18 or over, is punishable by imprisonment.

PART 14   GENERAL

330 Orders and rules

(1) This section applies to –

    (a) any power conferred by this Act on the Secretary of State to make an order or rules;

    (b) the power conferred by section 168 on the Lord Chancellor to make an order.

(2) The power is exercisable by statutory instrument.

(3) The power –

    (a) may be exercised so as to make different provision for different purposes or different areas, and

    (b) may be exercised either for all the purposes to which the power extends, or for those purposes subject to specified exceptions, or only for specified purposes.

(4) The power includes power to make –

    (a) any supplementary, incidental or consequential provision, and

    (b) any transitory, transitional or saving provision,

which the Minister making the instrument considers necessary or expedient.

(5) A statutory instrument containing –

    (a) an order under any of the following provisions –

        section 25(5),
        section 103,
        section 161(7),
        section 178,
        section 197(3),
        section 223,
        section 246(5),
        section 260,
        section 267,
        section 269(6),
        section 281(2),
        section 283(1),
        section 291,
        section 301(5),
        section 325(7), and
        paragraph 5 of Schedule 31,

    (b) an order under section 336(3) bringing section 43 into force,

    (c) an order making any provision by virtue of section 333(2)(b) which adds to, replaces or omits any part of the text of an Act, or

    (d) rules under section 240(4)(a),

may only be made if a draft of the statutory instrument has been laid before, and approved by a resolution of, each House of Parliament.

(6) Any other statutory instrument made in the exercise of a power to which this section applies is subject to annulment in pursuance of a resolution of either House of Parliament.

(7) Subsection (6) does not apply to a statutory instrument containing only an order made under one or more of the following provisions –

        section 202(3)(b),
        section 215(3),
        section 253(5),
        section 325(6)(i), and
        section 336.

331 Further minor and consequential amendments

Schedule 36 (further minor and consequential amendments) shall have effect.

332 Repeals

Schedule 37 (repeals) shall have effect.

333 Supplementary and consequential provision, etc.

(1) The Secretary of State may by order make –

   (a) any supplementary, incidental or consequential provision, and

   (b) any transitory, transitional or saving provision,

   which he considers necessary or expedient for the purposes of, in consequence of, or for giving full effect to any provision of this Act.

(2) An order under subsection (1) may, in particular –

   (a) provide for any provision of this Act which comes into force before another such provision has come into force to have effect, until that other provision has come into force, with such modifications as are specified in the order, and

   (b) amend or repeal –

      (i) any Act passed before, or in the same Session as, this Act, and

      (ii) subordinate legislation made before the passing of this Act.

(3) Nothing in this section limits the power by virtue of section 330(4)(b) to include transitional or saving provision in an order under section 336.

(4) The amendments that may be made under subsection (2)(b) are in addition to those made by or under any other provision of this Act.

(5) In this section 'subordinate legislation' has the same meaning as in the Interpretation Act 1978 (c. 30).

(6) Schedule 38 (which contains transitory and transitional provisions and savings) shall have effect.

334 Provision for Northern Ireland

(1) An Order in Council under section 85 of the Northern Ireland Act 1998 (c. 47) (provision dealing with certain reserved matters) which contains a statement that it is made only for purposes corresponding to those of any provisions of this Act specified in subsection (2) –

   (a) shall not be subject to subsections (3) to (9) of that section (affirmative resolution of both Houses of Parliament), but

   (b) shall be subject to annulment in pursuance of a resolution of either House of Parliament.

(2) The provisions are –

   (a) in Part 1, sections 1, 3(3), 4, 7 to 10 and 12 and paragraphs 1, 2, 5 to 10 and 20 of Schedule 1, and

   (b) Parts 8, 9 and 11.

(3) In relation to any time when section 1 of the Northern Ireland Act 2000 (c. 1) is in force (suspension of devolved government in Northern Ireland) –

   (a) the reference in subsection (1) above to section 85 of the Northern Ireland Act 1998 shall be read as a reference to paragraph 1 of the Schedule to the Northern Ireland Act 2000 (legislation by Order in Council during suspension), and

   (b) the reference in subsection (1)(a) above to subsections (3) to (9) of that section shall be read as a reference to paragraph 2 of that Schedule.

(4) The reference in section 41(2) of the Justice (Northern Ireland) Act 2002 (c. 26) (transfer of certain functions to Director of Public Prosecutions for Northern Ireland) to any function of the Attorney General for Northern Ireland of consenting to the institution of criminal proceedings includes any such function which is conferred by an amendment made by this Act.

(5) Any reference to any provision of the Criminal Appeal (Northern Ireland) Act 1980 (c. 47) in the Access to Justice (Northern Ireland) Order 2003 (S.I. 2003/435 (N.I. 10)) is to be read as a reference to that provision as amended by this Act.

335 Expenses

There shall be paid out of money provided by Parliament –

    (a) any expenditure incurred by a Minister of the Crown by virtue of this Act, and

    (b) any increase attributable to this Act in the sums payable out of money so provided under any other enactment.

336 Commencement

(1) The following provisions of this Act come into force on the passing of this Act –

        section 168(1) and (2),
        section 183(8),
        section 307(1) to (3), (5) and (6),
        section 330,
        section 333(1) to (5),
        sections 334 and 335,
        this section and sections 337, 338 and 339, and
        the repeal in Part 9 of Schedule 37 of section 81(2) and (3) of the Countryside and Rights of Way Act 2000 (c. 37) (and section 332 so far as relating to that repeal), and
        paragraphs 1 and 6 of Schedule 38 (and section 333(6) so far as relating to those paragraphs).

(2) The following provisions of this Act come into force at the end of the period of four weeks beginning with the day on which this Act is passed –

        Chapter 7 of Part 12 (and Schedules 21 and 22);
        section 303(b)(i) and (ii);
        paragraphs 42, 43(3), 66, 83(1) to (3), 84 and 109(2), (3)(b), (4) and (5) of Schedule 32 (and section 304 so far as relating to those provisions);
        Part 8 of Schedule 37 (and section 332 so far as relating to that Part of that Schedule).

(3) The remaining provisions of this Act come into force in accordance with provision made by the Secretary of State by order.

(4) Different provision may be made for different purposes and different areas.

337 Extent

(1) Subject to the following provisions of this section and to section 338, this Act extends to England and Wales only.

(2) The following provisions extend also to Scotland and Northern Ireland –

        sections 71 and 72;
        sections 82 and 83;
        section 180 and Schedule 9;
        section 188 and Schedule 11;
        section 194 and Schedule 13;
        section 293;
        section 306
        section 307;
        section 311;
        this Part, except sections 331, 332 and 334(5);
        paragraphs 19, 70 and 71 of Schedule 3;
        paragraph 12(3) of Schedule 12;
        paragraphs 3, 6, 7 and 8 of Schedule 27;
        paragraphs 6 to 8 of Schedule 31.

(3) The following provisions extend also to Scotland –

> section 50(14);
> section 286;
> sections 287, 288, and 291;
> section 302;
> paragraph 2 of Schedule 23;
> paragraphs 1, 2 and 5 of Schedule 27;
> paragraph 7 of Schedule 38.

(4) Section 290 extends to Scotland only.

(5) The following provisions extend also to Northern Ireland –

> Part 5;
> Part 7;
> sections 75 to 81;
> sections 84 to 93;
> sections 95 to 97;
> section 315;
> Schedule 5.

(6) The following provisions extend to Northern Ireland only –

> section 292 and Schedule 29;
> sections 296 and 297;
> section 314;
> section 317;
> section 334(5).

(7) The amendment or repeal of any enactment by any provision of –

- (a) Part 1,
- (b) section 285,
- (c) Part 2 of Schedule 3 (except as mentioned in subsection (8)),
- (d) Schedule 27,
- (e) Schedule 28,
- (f) Part 1 of Schedule 32,
- (g) Parts 1 to 4 and 6 of Schedule 36, and
- (h) Parts 1 to 4, 6 to 8, 10 and 12 of Schedule 37 (except as mentioned in subsection (9)),

extends to the part or parts of the United Kingdom to which the enactment extends.

(8) Paragraphs 29, 30, 31, 39, 41, 50, 53 and 63 of Schedule 3 do not extend to Northern Ireland.

(9) The repeals in Part 4 of Schedule 37 relating to –

- (a) the Bankers' Books Evidence Act 1879 (c. 11),
- (b) the Explosive Substances Act 1883 (c. 3),
- (c) the Backing of Warrants (Republic of Ireland) Act 1965 (c. 45),
- (d) the Customs and Excise Management Act 1979 (c. 2), and
- (e) the Contempt of Court Act 1981 (c. 49),

do not extend to Northern Ireland.

(10) The provisions mentioned in subsection (11), so far as relating to proceedings before a particular service court, have the same extent as the Act under which the court is constituted.

(11) Those provisions are –

> section 113 and Schedule 6;
> section 135 and Schedule 7.

(12) Nothing in subsection (1) affects –

(a) the extent of Chapter 7 of Part 12 so far as relating to sentences passed by a court-martial, or

(b) the extent of section 299 and Schedule 30 so far as relating to the making of orders by, or orders made by, courts-martial or the Courts-Martial Appeal Court.

(13) Any provision of this Act which –

(a) relates to any enactment contained in –

(i)   the Army Act 1955 (3 & 4 Eliz. 2 c. 18),

(ii)   the Air Force Act 1955 (3 & 4 Eliz. 2 c. 19),

(iii)   the Naval Discipline Act 1957 (c. 53),

(iv)   the Courts-Martial (Appeals) Act 1968 (c. 20),

(v)   the Armed Forces Act 1976 (c. 52),

(vi)   section 113 of the Police and Criminal Evidence Act 1984 (c. 60),

(vii)   the Reserve Forces Act 1996 (c. 14), or

(viii)   the Armed Forces Act 2001 (c. 19), and

(b) is not itself contained in Schedule 25 or Part 9 of Schedule 37,

has the same extent as the enactment to which it relates.

338 Channel Islands and Isle of Man

(1) Subject to subsections (2) and (3), Her Majesty may by Order in Council extend any provision of this Act, with such modifications as appear to Her Majesty in Council to be appropriate, to any of the Channel Islands or the Isle of Man.

(2) Subsection (1) does not authorise the extension to any place of a provision of this Act so far as the provision amends an enactment that does not itself extend there and is not itself capable of being extended there in the exercise of a power conferred on Her Majesty in Council.

(3) Subsection (1) does not apply in relation to any provision that extends to the Channel Islands or the Isle of Man by virtue of any of subsections (10) to (13) of section 337.

(4) Subsection (4) of section 330 applies to the power to make an Order in Council under subsection (1) as it applies to any power of the Secretary of State to make an order under this Act, but as if references in that subsection to the Minister making the instrument were references to Her Majesty in Council.

339 Short title

This Act may be cited as the Criminal Justice Act 2003.

SCHEDULES

SCHEDULE 1   AMENDMENTS RELATED TO PART 1   Section 12

The 1984 Act

1   The 1984 Act is amended as follows.

2   In section 18 (entry and search after arrest), for subsection (5) there is substituted –

'(5)   A constable may conduct a search under subsection (1) –

(a)   before the person is taken to a police station or released on bail under section 30A, and

(b)   without obtaining an authorisation under subsection (4),

if the condition in subsection (5A) is satisfied.

(5A)The condition is that the presence of the person at a place (other than a police station) is necessary for the effective investigation of the offence.'

3   In section 21 (access and copying), at the end there is inserted –

'(9)   The references to a constable in subsections (1), (2), (3)(a) and (5) include a person authorised under section 16(2) to accompany a constable executing a warrant.'

4   In section 22 (retention), at the end there is inserted –

'(7)   The reference in subsection (1) to anything seized by a constable includes anything seized by a person authorised under section 16(2) to accompany a constable executing a warrant.'

5   In section 34 (limitation on police detention), for subsection (7) there is substituted –

'(7)   For the purposes of this Part a person who –

(a)   attends a police station to answer to bail granted under section 30A,

(b)   returns to a police station to answer to bail granted under this Part, or

(c)   is arrested under section 30D or 46A,

is to be treated as arrested for an offence and that offence is the offence in connection with which he was granted bail.'

6   In section 35(1) (designated police stations), for 'section 30(3) and (5) above' there is substituted 'sections 30(3) and (5), 30A(5) and 30D(2)'.

7   In section 36 (custody officers at police stations), after subsection (7) there is inserted –

'(7A)   Subject to subsection (7B), subsection (7) applies where a person attends a police station which is not a designated station to answer to bail granted under section 30A as it applies where a person is taken to such a station.

(7B)   Where subsection (7) applies because of subsection (7A), the reference in subsection (7)(b) to the officer who took him to the station is to be read as a reference to the officer who granted him bail.'

8   In section 41(2) (calculation of periods of time), after paragraph (c) there is inserted –

'(ca)   in the case of a person who attends a police station to answer to bail granted under section 30A, the time when he arrives at the police station;'.

9   In section 45A(2)(a) (functions which may be performed by video-conferencing), after 'taken to' there is inserted ', or answering to bail at,'.

10   In section 47 (bail after arrest) –

(a)   in subsection (6), after 'granted bail' there is inserted 'under this Part', and

(b)   in subsection (7), after 'released on bail' there is inserted 'under this Part'.

Criminal Justice Act 1987 (c. 38)

11   In section 2 of the Criminal Justice Act 1987 (director's investigation powers), after subsection (6) there is inserted –

'(6A)   Where an appropriate person accompanies a constable, he may exercise the powers conferred by subsection (5) but only in the company, and under the supervision, of the constable.'

12   In subsection (7) of that section (meaning of appropriate person), for 'subsection (6) above' there is substituted 'this section'.

13   In subsection (8D) of that section (references to evidence obtained by Director), after 'by a constable' there is inserted 'or by an appropriate person'.

Criminal Justice and Police Act 2001 (c. 16)

14   In section 56 of the Criminal Justice and Police Act 2001 (property seized by constables etc.), after subsection (4) there is inserted –

'(4A)   Subsection (1)(a) includes property seized on any premises –

(a)   by a person authorised under section 16(2) of the 1984 Act to accompany a constable executing a warrant, or

(b)   by a person accompanying a constable under section 2(6) of the Criminal Justice Act 1987 in the execution of a warrant under section 2(4) of that Act.'

Armed Forces Act 2001 (c. 19)

15   In section 2(9) of the Armed Forces Act 2001 (offences for purpose of definition of prohibited article), at the end of paragraph (d) there is inserted '; and

(e)   offences under section 1 of the Criminal Damage Act 1971 (destroying or damaging property).'

Police Reform Act 2002 (c. 30)

16   Schedule 4 to the Police Reform Act 2002 (powers exercisable by police civilians) is amended as follows.

17   In paragraph 17 (access to excluded and special procedure material) after paragraph (b) there is inserted –

'(bb)   section 15 of that Act (safeguards) shall have effect in relation to the issue of any warrant under paragraph 12 of that Schedule to that person as it has effect in relation to the issue of a warrant under that paragraph to a constable;

(bc)   section 16 of that Act (execution of warrants) shall have effect in relation to any warrant to enter and search premises that is issued under paragraph 12 of that Schedule (whether to that person or to any other person) in respect of premises in the relevant police area as if references in that section to a constable included references to that person;'.

18   In paragraph 20 (access and copying in case of things seized by constables) after 'by a constable' there is inserted 'or by a person authorised to accompany him under section 16(2) of that Act'.

19   After paragraph 24 (extended powers of seizure) there is inserted –

24A 'Persons accompanying investigating officers

(1) This paragraph applies where a person ("an authorised person") is authorised by virtue of section 16(2) of the 1984 Act to accompany an investigating officer designated for the purposes of paragraph 16 (or 17) in the execution of a warrant.

(2) The reference in paragraph 16(h) (or 17(e)) to the seizure of anything by a designated person in exercise of a particular power includes a reference to the seizure of anything by the authorised person in exercise of that power by virtue of section 16(2A) of the 1984 Act.

(3) In relation to any such seizure, paragraph 16(h) (or 17(e)) is to be read as if it provided for the references to a constable and to an officer in section 21(1) and (2) of the 1984 Act to include references to the authorised person.

(4) The reference in paragraph 16(i) (or 17(f)) to anything seized by a designated person in exercise of a particular power includes a reference to anything seized by the authorised person in exercise of that power by virtue of section 16(2A) of the 1984 Act.

(5) In relation to anything so seized, paragraph 16(i)(ii) (or 17(f)(ii)) is to be read as if it provided for –

(a) the references to the supervision of a constable in subsections (3) and (4) of section 21 of the 1984 Act to include references to the supervision of a person designated for the purposes of paragraph 16 (or paragraph 17), and

(b) the reference to a constable in subsection (5) of that section to include a reference to such a person or an authorised person accompanying him.

(6) Where an authorised person accompanies an investigating officer who is also designated for the purposes of paragraph 24, the references in sub-paragraphs (a) and (b) of that paragraph to the designated person include references to the authorised person.'

20   In paragraph 34 (powers of escort officer to take arrested person to prison), in sub-paragraph (1)(a), for 'subsection (1) of section 30' there is substituted 'subsection (1A) of section 30'.

SCHEDULE 2   CHARGING OR RELEASE OF PERSONS IN POLICE DETENTION   Section 28

1   The Police and Criminal Evidence Act 1984 (c. 60) is amended as follows.

2   (1) Section 37 (duties of custody officers before charge) is amended as follows.

(2) In subsection (7) for paragraphs (a) and (b) there is substituted –

'(a) shall be released without charge and on bail for the purpose of enabling the Director of Public Prosecutions to make a decision under section 37B below,

(b) shall be released without charge and on bail but not for that purpose,

(c) shall be released without charge and without bail, or

(d) shall be charged.'

(3) After that subsection there is inserted –

'(7A) The decision as to how a person is to be dealt with under subsection (7) above shall be that of the custody officer.

(7B) Where a person is released under subsection (7)(a) above, it shall be the duty of the custody officer to inform him that he is being released to enable the Director of Public Prosecutions to make a decision under section 37B below.'

(4) In subsection (8)(a) after '(7)(b)' there is inserted 'or (c)'.

3   After that section there is inserted –

'37A Guidance

(1) The Director of Public Prosecutions may issue guidance –

(a) for the purpose of enabling custody officers to decide how persons should be dealt with under section 37(7) above or 37C(2) below, and

(b) as to the information to be sent to the Director of Public Prosecutions under section 37B(1) below.

(2) The Director of Public Prosecutions may from time to time revise guidance issued under this section.

(3) Custody officers are to have regard to guidance under this section in deciding how persons should be dealt with under section 37(7) above or 37C(2) below.

(4) A report under section 9 of the Prosecution of Offences Act 1985 (report by DPP to Attorney General) must set out the provisions of any guidance issued, and any revisions to guidance made, in the year to which the report relates.

(5) The Director of Public Prosecutions must publish in such manner as he thinks fit –

(a) any guidance issued under this section, and

(b) any revisions made to such guidance.

(6) Guidance under this section may make different provision for different cases, circumstances or areas.

37B Consultation with the Director of Public Prosecutions

(1) Where a person is released on bail under section 37(7)(a) above, an officer involved in the investigation of the offence shall, as soon as is practicable, send to the Director of Public Prosecutions such information as may be specified in guidance under section 37A above.

(2) The Director of Public Prosecutions shall decide whether there is sufficient evidence to charge the person with an offence.

(3) If he decides that there is sufficient evidence to charge the person with an offence, he shall decide –

(a) whether or not the person should be charged and, if so, the offence with which he should be charged, and

(b) whether or not the person should be given a caution and, if so, the offence in respect of which he should be given a caution.

(4) The Director of Public Prosecutions shall give written notice of his decision to an officer involved in the investigation of the offence.

(5) If his decision is –

(a) that there is not sufficient evidence to charge the person with an offence, or

(b) that there is sufficient evidence to charge the person with an offence but that the person should not be charged with an offence or given a caution in respect of an offence,

a custody officer shall give the person notice in writing that he is not to be prosecuted.

(6) If the decision of the Director of Public Prosecutions is that the person should be charged with an offence, or given a caution in respect of an offence, the person shall be charged or cautioned accordingly.

(7) But if his decision is that the person should be given a caution in respect of the offence and it proves not to be possible to give the person such a caution, he shall instead be charged with the offence.

(8) For the purposes of this section, a person is to be charged with an offence either –

(a) when he is in police detention after returning to a police station to answer bail or is otherwise in police detention at a police station, or

(b) in accordance with section 29 of the Criminal Justice Act 2003.

(9) In this section "caution" includes –

(a) a conditional caution within the meaning of Part 3 of the Criminal Justice Act 2003, and

(b) a warning or reprimand under section 65 of the Crime and Disorder Act 1998.

37C Breach of bail following release under section 37(7)(a)

(1) This section applies where –

(a) a person released on bail under section 37(7)(a) above or subsection (2)(b) below is arrested under section 46A below in respect of that bail, and

(b) at the time of his detention following that arrest at the police station mentioned in section 46A(2) below, notice under section 37B(4) above has not been given.

(2) The person arrested –

(a) shall be charged, or

(b) shall be released without charge, either on bail or without bail.

(3) The decision as to how a person is to be dealt with under subsection (2) above shall be that of a custody officer.

(4) A person released on bail under subsection (2)(b) above shall be released on bail subject to the same conditions (if any) which applied immediately before his arrest.

37D Release under section 37(7)(a): further provision

(1) Where a person is released on bail under section 37(7)(a) or section 37C(2)(b) above, a custody officer may subsequently appoint a different time, or an additional time, at which the person is to attend at the police station to answer bail.

(2) The custody officer shall give the person notice in writing of the exercise of the power under subsection (1).

(3) The exercise of the power under subsection (1) shall not affect the conditions (if any) to which bail is subject.

(4) Where a person released on bail under section 37(7)(a) or 37C(2)(b) above returns to a police station to answer bail or is otherwise in police detention at a police station, he may be kept in police detention to enable him to be dealt with in accordance with section 37B or 37C above or to enable the power under subsection (1) above to be exercised.

(5) If the person is not in a fit state to enable him to be so dealt with or to enable that power to be exercised, he may be kept in police detention until he is.

(6) Where a person is kept in police detention by virtue of subsection (4) or (5) above, section 37(1) to (3) and (7) above (and section 40(8) below so far as it relates to section 37(1) to (3)) shall not apply to the offence in connection with which he was released on bail under section 37(7)(a) or 37C(2)(b) above.'

4   In section 40 (review of police detention) in subsection (9) after '37(9)' there is inserted 'or 37D(5)'.

5   In section 46A (power of arrest for failure to answer police bail) after subsection (1) insert –

    '(1A) A person who has been released on bail under section 37(7)(a) or 37C(2)(b) above may be arrested without warrant by a constable if the constable has reasonable grounds for suspecting that the person has broken any of the conditions of bail.'

6   (1) Section 47 (bail after arrest) is amended as follows.

    (2) In subsection (1) (release on bail under Part 4 shall be release on bail granted in accordance with certain provisions of the Bail Act 1976) for 'Subject to subsection (2) below' there is substituted 'Subject to the following provisions of this section'.

    (3) In subsection (1A) (bail conditions may be imposed when a person is released under section 38(1)) after 'section', in the first place where it occurs, there is inserted '37(7)(a) above or section'.

    (4) After that subsection there is inserted –

    '(1B) No application may be made under section 5B of the Bail Act 1976 if a person is released on bail under section 37(7)(a) or 37C(2)(b) above.

    (1C) Subsections (1D) to (1F) below apply where a person released on bail under section 37(7)(a) or 37C(2)(b) above is on bail subject to conditions.

    (1D) The person shall not be entitled to make an application under section 43B of the Magistrates' Courts Act 1980.

    (1E) A magistrates' court may, on an application by or on behalf of the person, vary the conditions of bail; and in this subsection 'vary' has the same meaning as in the Bail Act 1976.

    (1F) Where a magistrates' court varies the conditions of bail under subsection (1E) above, that bail shall not lapse but shall continue subject to the conditions as so varied.'

SCHEDULE 3   ALLOCATION OF CASES TRIABLE EITHER WAY, AND SENDING CASES TO THE CROWN COURT ETC

Section 41

PART 1

PRINCIPAL AMENDMENTS

Magistrates' Courts Act 1980 (c. 43)

1   The Magistrates' Courts Act 1980 is amended as follows.

2   (1) Section 17A (initial indication as to plea) is amended as follows.

    (2) For paragraph (b) of subsection (4) there is substituted –

    '(b)   he may (unless section 17D(2) below were to apply) be committed to the Crown Court under section 3 or (if applicable) 3A of the Powers of Criminal Courts (Sentencing) Act 2000 if the court is of such opinion as is mentioned in subsection (2) of the applicable section.'

    (3) After subsection (9) there is inserted –

    '(10) If in respect of the offence the court receives a notice under section 51B or 51C of the Crime and Disorder Act 1998 (which relate to serious or complex fraud cases and to certain cases involving children respectively), the preceding provisions of this section and the provisions of section 17B below shall not apply, and the court shall proceed in relation to the offence in accordance with section 51 or, as the case may be, section 51A of that Act.'

3   After section 17C there is inserted –

'17D Maximum penalty under section 17A(6) or 17B(2)(c) for certain offences

    (1)   If –

        (a) the offence is a scheduled offence (as defined in section 22(1) below);

        (b) the court proceeds in relation to the offence in accordance with section 17A(6) or 17B(2)(c) above; and

        (c) the court convicts the accused of the offence,

the court shall consider whether, having regard to any representations made by him or by the prosecutor, the value involved (as defined in section 22(10) below) appears to the court to exceed the relevant sum (as specified for the purposes of section 22 below).

    (2)   If it appears to the court clear that the value involved does not exceed the relevant sum, or it appears to the court for any reason not clear whether the value involved does or does not exceed the relevant sum –

        (a) subject to subsection (4) below, the court shall not have power to impose on the accused in respect of the offence a sentence in excess of the limits mentioned in section 33(1)(a) below; and

        (b) sections 3 and 4 of the Powers of Criminal Courts (Sentencing) Act 2000 shall not apply as regards that offence.

    (3)   Subsections (9) to (12) of section 22 below shall apply for the purposes of this section as they apply for the purposes of that section (reading the reference to subsection (1) in section 22(9) as a reference to subsection (1) of this section).

    (4)   Subsection (2)(a) above does not apply to an offence under section 12A of the Theft Act 1968 (aggravated vehicle-taking).

17E Functions under sections 17A to 17D capable of exercise by single justice

    (1)   The functions of a magistrates' court under sections 17A to 17D above may be discharged by a single justice.

    (2)   Subsection (1) above shall not be taken as authorising –

        (a) the summary trial of an information (otherwise than in accordance with section 17A(6) or 17B(2)(c) above); or

        (b) the imposition of a sentence,

by a magistrates' court composed of fewer than two justices.'

4   In section 18 (initial procedure on information against adult for offence triable either way), for subsection (5) there is substituted –

    '(5)   The functions of a magistrates' court under sections 19 to 23 below may be discharged by a single justice, but this subsection shall not be taken as authorising –

        (a) the summary trial of an information (otherwise than in accordance with section 20(7) below); or

        (b) the imposition of a sentence,

by a magistrates' court composed of fewer than two justices.'

5   For section 19 (court to begin by considering which mode of trial appears more suitable) there is substituted –

'19 Decision as to allocation

(1)   The court shall decide whether the offence appears to it more suitable for summary trial or for trial on indictment.

(2)   Before making a decision under this section, the court –

(a) shall give the prosecution an opportunity to inform the court of the accused's previous convictions (if any); and

(b) shall give the prosecution and the accused an opportunity to make representations as to whether summary trial or trial on indictment would be more suitable.

(3)   In making a decision under this section, the court shall consider –

(a) whether the sentence which a magistrates' court would have power to impose for the offence would be adequate; and

(b) any representations made by the prosecution or the accused under subsection (2)(b) above,

and shall have regard to any allocation guidelines (or revised allocation guidelines) issued as definitive guidelines under section 170 of the Criminal Justice Act 2003.

(4)   Where –

(a) the accused is charged with two or more offences; and

(b) it appears to the court that the charges for the offences could be joined in the same indictment or that the offences arise out of the same or connected circumstances,

subsection (3)(a) above shall have effect as if references to the sentence which a magistrates' court would have power to impose for the offence were a reference to the maximum aggregate sentence which a magistrates' court would have power to impose for all of the offences taken together.

(5)   In this section any reference to a previous conviction is a reference to –

(a) a previous conviction by a court in the United Kingdom; or

(b) a previous finding of guilt in –

(i) any proceedings under the Army Act 1955, the Air Force Act 1955 or the Naval Discipline Act 1957 (whether before a court-martial or any other court or person authorised under any of those Acts to award a punishment in respect of any offence); or

(ii) any proceedings before a Standing Civilian Court.

(6)   If, in respect of the offence, the court receives a notice under section 51B or 51C of the Crime and Disorder Act 1998 (which relate to serious or complex fraud cases and to certain cases involving children respectively), the preceding provisions of this section and sections 20, 20A and 21 below shall not apply, and the court shall proceed in relation to the offence in accordance with section 51(1) of that Act.'

6   For section 20 (procedure where summary trial appears more suitable) there is substituted –

'20 Procedure where summary trial appears more suitable

(1)   If the court decides under section 19 above that the offence appears to it more suitable for summary trial, the following provisions of this section shall apply (unless they are excluded by section 23 below).

(2)   The court shall explain to the accused in ordinary language –

(a) that it appears to the court more suitable for him to be tried summarily for the offence;

(b) that he can either consent to be so tried or, if he wishes, be tried on indictment; and

(c) in the case of a specified offence (within the meaning of section 224 of the Criminal Justice Act 2003), that if he is tried summarily and is convicted by the court, he may be committed for sentence to the Crown Court under section 3A of the Powers of Criminal Courts (Sentencing) Act 2000 if the committing court is of such opinion as is mentioned in subsection (2) of that section.

(3) The accused may then request an indication ("an indication of sentence") of whether a custodial sentence or non-custodial sentence would be more likely to be imposed if he were to be tried summarily for the offence and to plead guilty.

(4) If the accused requests an indication of sentence, the court may, but need not, give such an indication.

(5) If the accused requests and the court gives an indication of sentence, the court shall ask the accused whether he wishes, on the basis of the indication, to reconsider the indication of plea which was given, or is taken to have been given, under section 17A or 17B above.

(6) If the accused indicates that he wishes to reconsider the indication under section 17A or 17B above, the court shall ask the accused whether (if the offence were to proceed to trial) he would plead guilty or not guilty.

(7) If the accused indicates that he would plead guilty the court shall proceed as if –

(a) the proceedings constituted from that time the summary trial of the information; and

(b) section 9(1) above were complied with and he pleaded guilty under it.

(8) Subsection (9) below applies where –

(a) the court does not give an indication of sentence (whether because the accused does not request one or because the court does not agree to give one);

(b) the accused either –

(i) does not indicate, in accordance with subsection (5) above, that he wishes; or

(ii) indicates, in accordance with subsection (5) above, that he does not wish,

to reconsider the indication of plea under section 17A or 17B above; or

(c) the accused does not indicate, in accordance with subsection (6) above, that he would plead guilty.

(9) The court shall ask the accused whether he consents to be tried summarily or wishes to be tried on indictment and –

(a) if he consents to be tried summarily, shall proceed to the summary trial of the information; and

(b) if he does not so consent, shall proceed in relation to the offence in accordance with section 51(1) of the Crime and Disorder Act 1998.

20A Procedure where summary trial appears more suitable: supplementary

(1) Where the case is dealt with in accordance with section 20(7) above, no court (whether a magistrates' court or not) may impose a custodial sentence for the offence unless such a sentence was indicated in the indication of sentence referred to in section 20 above.

(2) Subsection (1) above is subject to sections 3A(4), 4(8) and 5(3) of the Powers of Criminal Courts (Sentencing) Act 2000.

(3) Except as provided in subsection (1) above –

(a) an indication of sentence shall not be binding on any court (whether a magistrates' court or not); and

(b) no sentence may be challenged or be the subject of appeal in any court on the ground that it is not consistent with an indication of sentence.

(4) Subject to section 20(7) above, the following shall not for any purpose be taken to constitute the taking of a plea –

(a) asking the accused under section 20 above whether (if the offence were to proceed to trial) he would plead guilty or not guilty; or

(b) an indication by the accused under that section of how he would plead.

(5) Where the court gives an indication of sentence under section 20 above, it shall cause each such indication to be entered in the register.

(6) In this section and in section 20 above, references to a custodial sentence are to a custodial sentence within the meaning of section 76 of the Powers of Criminal Courts (Sentencing) Act 2000, and references to a non-custodial sentence shall be construed accordingly.'

7   For section 21 (procedure where trial on indictment appears more suitable) there is substituted –

'21 Procedure where trial on indictment appears more suitable

If the court decides under section 19 above that the offence appears to it more suitable for trial on indictment, the court shall tell the accused that the court has decided that it is more suitable for him to be tried on indictment, and shall proceed in relation to the offence in accordance with section 51(1) of the Crime and Disorder Act 1998.'

8   (1) Section 23 (power of court, with consent of legally represented accused, to proceed in his absence) is amended as follows.

(2) In subsection (4) –

(a) for the words preceding paragraph (a) there is substituted 'If the court decides under section 19 above that the offence appears to it more suitable for trial on indictment then – ', and

(b) in paragraph (b), for the words from 'to inquire' to the end there is substituted 'in relation to the offence in accordance with section 51(1) of the Crime and Disorder Act 1998.'.

(3) For subsection (5) there is substituted –

'(5) If the court decides under section 19 above that the offence appears to it more suitable for trial on indictment, section 21 above shall not apply and the court shall proceed in relation to the offence in accordance with section 51(1) of the Crime and Disorder Act 1998.'

9   (1) Section 24 (summary trial of information against child or young persons for indictable offence), as amended by section 42 of this Act, is amended as follows.

(2) For subsection (1) there is substituted –

'(1) Where a person under the age of 18 years appears or is brought before a magistrates' court on an information charging him with an indictable offence he shall, subject to sections 51 and 51A of the Crime and Disorder Act 1998 and to sections 24A and 24B below, be tried summarily.'

(3) Subsections (1A) and (2) are omitted.

10   After section 24 there is inserted –

'24A Child or young person to indicate intention as to plea in certain cases

(1) This section applies where –

(a) a person under the age of 18 years appears or is brought before a magistrates' court on an information charging him with an offence other than one falling within section 51A(12) of the Crime and Disorder Act 1998 ("the 1998 Act"); and

(b) but for the application of the following provisions of this section, the court would be required at that stage, by virtue of section 51(7) or (8) or 51A(3)(b), (4) or (5) of the 1998 Act to determine, in relation to the offence, whether to send the person to the Crown Court for trial (or to determine any matter, the effect of which would be to determine whether he is sent to the Crown Court for trial).

(2) Where this section applies, the court shall, before proceeding to make any such determination as is referred to in subsection (1)(b) above (the "relevant determination"), follow the procedure set out in this section.

(3) Everything that the court is required to do under the following provisions of this section must be done with the accused person in court.

(4) The court shall cause the charge to be written down, if this has not already been done, and to be read to the accused.

(5) The court shall then explain to the accused in ordinary language that he may indicate whether (if the offence were to proceed to trial) he would plead guilty or not guilty, and that if he indicates that he would plead guilty –

(a) the court must proceed as mentioned in subsection (7) below; and

(b) (in cases where the offence is one mentioned in section 91(1) of the Powers of Criminal Courts (Sentencing) Act 2000) he may be sent to the Crown Court for sentencing under section 3B or (if applicable) 3C of that Act if the court is of such opinion as is mentioned in subsection (2) of the applicable section.

(6) The court shall then ask the accused whether (if the offence were to proceed to trial) he would plead guilty or not guilty.

(7) If the accused indicates that he would plead guilty, the court shall proceed as if –

(a) the proceedings constituted from the beginning the summary trial of the information; and

(b) section 9(1) above was complied with and he pleaded guilty under it,

and, accordingly, the court shall not (and shall not be required to) proceed to make the relevant determination or to proceed further under section 51 or (as the case may be) section 51A of the 1998 Act in relation to the offence.

(8) If the accused indicates that he would plead not guilty, the court shall proceed to make the relevant determination and this section shall cease to apply.

(9) If the accused in fact fails to indicate how he would plead, for the purposes of this section he shall be taken to indicate that he would plead not guilty.

(10) Subject to subsection (7) above, the following shall not for any purpose be taken to constitute the taking of a plea –

(a) asking the accused under this section whether (if the offence were to proceed to trial) he would plead guilty or not guilty;

(b) an indication by the accused under this section of how he would plead.

24B Intention as to plea by child or young person: absence of accused

(1) This section shall have effect where –

(a) a person under the age of 18 years appears or is brought before a magistrates' court on an information charging him with an offence other than one falling within section 51A(12) of the Crime and Disorder Act 1998;

(b) but for the application of the following provisions of this section, the court would be required at that stage to make one of the determinations referred to in paragraph (b) of section 24A(1) above ("the relevant determination");

(c) the accused is represented by a legal representative;

(d) the court considers that by reason of the accused's disorderly conduct before the court it is not practicable for proceedings under section 24A above to be conducted in his presence; and

(e) the court considers that it should proceed in the absence of the accused.

(2) In such a case –

(a) the court shall cause the charge to be written down, if this has not already been done, and to be read to the representative;

(b) the court shall ask the representative whether (if the offence were to proceed to trial) the accused would plead guilty or not guilty;

(c) if the representative indicates that the accused would plead guilty the court shall proceed as if the proceedings constituted from the beginning the summary trial of the information, and as if section 9(1) above was complied with and the accused pleaded guilty under it;

(d) if the representative indicates that the accused would plead not guilty the court shall proceed to make the relevant determination and this section shall cease to apply.

(3) If the representative in fact fails to indicate how the accused would plead, for the purposes of this section he shall be taken to indicate that the accused would plead not guilty.

(4) Subject to subsection (2)(c) above, the following shall not for any purpose be taken to constitute the taking of a plea –

(a) asking the representative under this section whether (if the offence were to proceed to trial) the accused would plead guilty or not guilty;

(b) an indication by the representative under this section of how the accused would plead.

24C Intention as to plea by child or young person: adjournment

(1) A magistrates' court proceeding under section 24A or 24B above may adjourn the proceedings at any time, and on doing so on any occasion when the accused is present may remand the accused.

(2) Where the court remands the accused, the time fixed for the resumption of proceedings shall be that at which he is required to appear or be brought before the court in pursuance of the remand or would be required to be brought before the court but for section 128(3A) below.

24D Functions under sections 24A to 24C capable of exercise by single justice

(1) The functions of a magistrates' court under sections 24A to 24C above may be discharged by a single justice.

(2) Subsection (1) above shall not be taken as authorising –

(a) the summary trial of an information (other than a summary trial by virtue of section 24A(7) or 24B(2)(c) above); or

(b) the imposition of a sentence,

by a magistrates' court composed of fewer than two justices.'

11 (1) Section 25 (power to change from summary trial to committal proceedings and vice versa), as amended by section 42 of this Act, is amended as follows.

(2) In subsection (1), for '(2) to (4)' there is substituted '(2) to (2D)'.

(3) For subsection (2) there is substituted –

'(2) Where the court is required under section 20(9) above to proceed to the summary trial of the information, the prosecution may apply to the court for the offence to be tried on indictment instead.

(2A) An application under subsection (2) above –

    (a) must be made before the summary trial begins; and

    (b) must be dealt with by the court before any other application or issue in relation to the summary trial is dealt with.

(2B) The court may grant an application under subsection (2) above but only if it is satisfied that the sentence which a magistrates' court would have power to impose for the offence would be inadequate.

(2C) Where –

    (a) the accused is charged on the same occasion with two or more offences; and

    (b) it appears to the court that they constitute or form part of a series of two or more offences of the same or a similar character,

subsection (2B) above shall have effect as if references to the sentence which a magistrates' court would have power to impose for the offence were a reference to the maximum aggregate sentence which a magistrates' court would have power to impose for all of the offences taken together.

(2D) Where the court grants an application under subsection (2) above, it shall proceed in relation to the offence in accordance with section 51(1) of the Crime and Disorder Act 1998.'

(4) Subsections (3) to (8) are omitted.

12   For subsections (1) and (2) of section 26 (power to issue summons to accused in certain circumstances) there is substituted –

'(1) Where, in the circumstances mentioned in section 23(1)(a) above, the court is not satisfied that there is good reason for proceeding in the absence of the accused, the justice or any of the justices of which the court is composed may issue a summons directed to the accused requiring his presence before the court.

(2) In a case within subsection (1) above, if the accused is not present at the time and place appointed for the proceedings under section 19 or section 22(1) above, the court may issue a warrant for his arrest.'

13   In section 33 (maximum penalties on summary conviction in pursuance of section 22), in subsection (1), paragraph (b) and the word 'and' immediately preceding it are omitted.

14   Section 42 (restriction on justices sitting after dealing with bail) shall cease to have effect.

Crime and Disorder Act 1998 (c. 37)

15   The Crime and Disorder Act 1998 is amended as follows.

16   In section 50 (early administrative hearings), in subsection (1) (court may consist of single justice unless accused falls to be dealt with under section 51), the words 'unless the accused falls to be dealt with under section 51 below' are omitted.

17   After section 50 there is inserted –

'50A Order of consideration for either-way offences

(1) Where an adult appears or is brought before a magistrates' court charged with an either-way offence (the "relevant offence"), the court shall proceed in the manner described in this section.

(2) If notice is given in respect of the relevant offence under section 51B or 51C below, the court shall deal with the offence as provided in section 51 below.

(3)   Otherwise –

(a)   if the adult (or another adult with whom the adult is charged jointly with the relevant offence) is or has been sent to the Crown Court for trial for an offence under section 51(2)(a) or 51(2)(c) below –

(i)   the court shall first consider the relevant offence under subsection (3), (4), (5) or, as the case may be, (6) of section 51 below and, where applicable, deal with it under that subsection;

(ii)   if the adult is not sent to the Crown Court for trial for the relevant offence by virtue of sub-paragraph (i) above, the court shall then proceed to deal with the relevant offence in accordance with sections 17A to 23 of the 1980 Act;

(b)   in all other cases –

(i)   the court shall first consider the relevant offence under sections 17A to 20 (excluding subsections (8) and (9) of section 20) of the 1980 Act;

(ii)   if, by virtue of sub-paragraph (i) above, the court would be required to proceed in relation to the offence as mentioned in section 17A(6), 17B(2)(c) or 20(7) of that Act (indication of guilty plea), it shall proceed as so required (and, accordingly, shall not consider the offence under section 51 or 51A below);

(iii)   if sub-paragraph (ii) above does not apply –

(a)   the court shall consider the relevant offence under sections 51 and 51A below and, where applicable, deal with it under the relevant section;

(b)   if the adult is not sent to the Crown Court for trial for the relevant offence by virtue of paragraph (a) of this sub-paragraph, the court shall then proceed to deal with the relevant offence as contemplated by section 20(9) or, as the case may be, section 21 of the 1980 Act.

(4)   Subsection (3) above is subject to any requirement to proceed as mentioned in subsections (2) or (6)(a) of section 22 of the 1980 Act (certain offences where value involved is small).

(5)   Nothing in this section shall prevent the court from committing the adult to the Crown Court for sentence pursuant to any enactment, if he is convicted of the relevant offence.'

18   For section 51 (no committal proceedings for indictable-only offences) there is substituted –

'51 Sending cases to the Crown Court: adults

(1)   Where an adult appears or is brought before a magistrates' court ("the court") charged with an offence and any of the conditions mentioned in subsection (2) below is satisfied, the court shall send him forthwith to the Crown Court for trial for the offence.

(2)   Those conditions are –

(a)   that the offence is an offence triable only on indictment other than one in respect of which notice has been given under section 51B or 51C below;

(b)   that the offence is an either-way offence and the court is required under section 20(9)(b), 21, 23(4)(b) or (5) or 25(2D) of the Magistrates' Courts Act 1980 to proceed in relation to the offence in accordance with subsection (1) above;

(c)   that notice is given to the court under section 51B or 51C below in respect of the offence.

(3) Where the court sends an adult for trial under subsection (1) above, it shall at the same time send him to the Crown Court for trial for any either-way or summary offence with which he is charged and which –

    (a) (if it is an either-way offence) appears to the court to be related to the offence mentioned in subsection (1) above; or

    (b) (if it is a summary offence) appears to the court to be related to the offence mentioned in subsection (1) above or to the either-way offence, and which fulfils the requisite condition (as defined in subsection (11) below).

(4) Where an adult who has been sent for trial under subsection (1) above subsequently appears or is brought before a magistrates' court charged with an either-way or summary offence which –

    (a) appears to the court to be related to the offence mentioned in subsection (1) above; and

    (b) (in the case of a summary offence) fulfils the requisite condition, the court may send him forthwith to the Crown Court for trial for the either-way or summary offence.

(5) Where –

    (a) the court sends an adult ("A") for trial under subsection (1) or (3) above;

    (b) another adult appears or is brought before the court on the same or a subsequent occasion charged jointly with A with an either-way offence; and

    (c) that offence appears to the court to be related to an offence for which A was sent for trial under subsection (1) or (3) above,

the court shall where it is the same occasion, and may where it is a subsequent occasion, send the other adult forthwith to the Crown Court for trial for the either-way offence.

(6) Where the court sends an adult for trial under subsection (5) above, it shall at the same time send him to the Crown Court for trial for any either-way or summary offence with which he is charged and which –

    (a) (if it is an either-way offence) appears to the court to be related to the offence for which he is sent for trial; and

    (b) (if it is a summary offence) appears to the court to be related to the offence for which he is sent for trial or to the either-way offence, and which fulfils the requisite condition.

(7) Where –

    (a) the court sends an adult ("A") for trial under subsection (1), (3) or (5) above; and

    (b) a child or young person appears or is brought before the court on the same or a subsequent occasion charged jointly with A with an indictable offence for which A is sent for trial under subsection (1), (3) or (5) above, or an indictable offence which appears to the court to be related to that offence,

the court shall, if it considers it necessary in the interests of justice to do so, send the child or young person forthwith to the Crown Court for trial for the indictable offence.

(8) Where the court sends a child or young person for trial under subsection (7) above, it may at the same time send him to the Crown Court for trial for any indictable or summary offence with which he is charged and which –

    (a) (if it is an indictable offence) appears to the court to be related to the offence for which he is sent for trial; and

     (b) (if it is a summary offence) appears to the court to be related to the offence for which he is sent for trial or to the indictable offence, and which fulfils the requisite condition.

(9) Subsections (7) and (8) above are subject to sections 24A and 24B of the Magistrates' Courts Act 1980 (which provide for certain cases involving children and young persons to be tried summarily).

(10) The trial of the information charging any summary offence for which a person is sent for trial under this section shall be treated as if the court had adjourned it under section 10 of the 1980 Act and had not fixed the time and place for its resumption.

(11) A summary offence fulfils the requisite condition if it is punishable with imprisonment or involves obligatory or discretionary disqualification from driving.

(12) In the case of an adult charged with an offence –

     (a) if the offence satisfies paragraph (c) of subsection (2) above, the offence shall be dealt with under subsection (1) above and not under any other provision of this section or section 51A below;

     (b) subject to paragraph (a) above, if the offence is one in respect of which the court is required to, or would decide to, send the adult to the Crown Court under –

          (i) subsection (5) above; or
          (ii) subsection (6) of section 51A below,

the offence shall be dealt with under that subsection and not under any other provision of this section or section 51A below.

(13) The functions of a magistrates' court under this section, and its related functions under section 51D below, may be discharged by a single justice.

51A Sending cases to the Crown Court: children and young persons

(1) This section is subject to sections 24A and 24B of the Magistrates' Courts Act 1980 (which provide for certain offences involving children or young persons to be tried summarily).

(2) Where a child or young person appears or is brought before a magistrates' court ("the court") charged with an offence and any of the conditions mentioned in subsection (3) below is satisfied, the court shall send him forthwith to the Crown Court for trial for the offence.

(3) Those conditions are –

     (a) that the offence falls within subsection (12) below;

     (b) that the offence is such as is mentioned in subsection (1) of section 91 of the Powers of Criminal Courts (Sentencing) Act 2000 (other than one mentioned in paragraph (d) below in relation to which it appears to the court as mentioned there) and the court considers that if he is found guilty of the offence it ought to be possible to sentence him in pursuance of subsection (3) of that section;

     (c) that notice is given to the court under section 51B or 51C below in respect of the offence;

     (d) that the offence is a specified offence (within the meaning of section 224 of the Criminal Justice Act 2003) and it appears to the court that if he is found guilty of the offence the criteria for the imposition of a sentence under section 226(3) or 228(2) of that Act would be met.

(4) Where the court sends a child or young person for trial under subsection (2) above, it may at the same time send him to the Crown Court for trial for any indictable or summary offence with which he is charged and which –

    (a) (if it is an indictable offence) appears to the court to be related to the offence mentioned in subsection (2) above; or

    (b) (if it is a summary offence) appears to the court to be related to the offence mentioned in subsection (2) above or to the indictable offence, and which fulfils the requisite condition (as defined in subsection (9) below).

(5) Where a child or young person who has been sent for trial under subsection (2) above subsequently appears or is brought before a magistrates' court charged with an indictable or summary offence which –

    (a) appears to the court to be related to the offence mentioned in subsection (2) above; and

    (b) (in the case of a summary offence) fulfils the requisite condition,

the court may send him forthwith to the Crown Court for trial for the indictable or summary offence.

(6) Where –

    (a) the court sends a child or young person ("C") for trial under subsection (2) or (4) above; and

    (b) an adult appears or is brought before the court on the same or a subsequent occasion charged jointly with C with an either-way offence for which C is sent for trial under subsection (2) or (4) above, or an either-way offence which appears to the court to be related to that offence,

the court shall where it is the same occasion, and may where it is a subsequent occasion, send the adult forthwith to the Crown Court for trial for the either-way offence.

(7) Where the court sends an adult for trial under subsection (6) above, it shall at the same time send him to the Crown Court for trial for any either-way or summary offence with which he is charged and which –

    (a) (if it is an either-way offence) appears to the court to be related to the offence for which he was sent for trial; and

    (b) (if it is a summary offence) appears to the court to be related to the offence for which he was sent for trial or to the either- way offence, and which fulfils the requisite condition.

(8) The trial of the information charging any summary offence for which a person is sent for trial under this section shall be treated as if the court had adjourned it under section 10 of the 1980 Act and had not fixed the time and place for its resumption.

(9) A summary offence fulfils the requisite condition if it is punishable with imprisonment or involves obligatory or discretionary disqualification from driving.

(10) In the case of a child or young person charged with an offence –

    (a) if the offence satisfies any of the conditions in subsection (3) above, the offence shall be dealt with under subsection (2) above and not under any other provision of this section or section 51 above;

    (b) subject to paragraph (a) above, if the offence is one in respect of which the requirements of subsection (7) of section 51 above for sending the child or young person to the Crown Court are satisfied, the offence shall be dealt with under that subsection and not under any other provision of this section or section 51 above.

(11) The functions of a magistrates' court under this section, and its related functions under section 51D below, may be discharged by a single justice.

(12) An offence falls within this subsection if –

    (a) it is an offence of homicide; or

(b) each of the requirements of section 51A(1) of the Firearms Act 1968 would be satisfied with respect to –

    (i) the offence; and

    (ii) the person charged with it,

if he were convicted of the offence.

51B Notices in serious or complex fraud cases

(1) A notice may be given by a designated authority under this section in respect of an indictable offence if the authority is of the opinion that the evidence of the offence charged –

    (a) is sufficient for the person charged to be put on trial for the offence; and

    (b) reveals a case of fraud of such seriousness or complexity that it is appropriate that the management of the case should without delay be taken over by the Crown Court.

(2) That opinion must be certified by the designated authority in the notice.

(3) The notice must also specify the proposed place of trial, and in selecting that place the designated authority must have regard to the same matters as are specified in paragraphs (a) to (c) of section 51D(4) below.

(4) A notice under this section must be given to the magistrates' court at which the person charged appears or before which he is brought.

(5) Such a notice must be given to the magistrates' court before any summary trial begins.

(6) The effect of such a notice is that the functions of the magistrates' court cease in relation to the case, except –

    (a) for the purposes of section 51D below;

    (b) as provided by paragraph 2 of Schedule 3 to the Access to Justice Act 1999; and

    (c) as provided by section 52 below.

(7) The functions of a designated authority under this section may be exercised by an officer of the authority acting on behalf of the authority.

(8) A decision to give a notice under this section shall not be subject to appeal or liable to be questioned in any court (whether a magistrates' court or not).

(9) In this section "designated authority" means –

    (a) the Director of Public Prosecutions;

    (b) the Director of the Serious Fraud Office;

    (c) the Commissioners of the Inland Revenue;

    (d) the Commissioners of Customs and Excise; or

    (e) the Secretary of State.

51C Notices in certain cases involving children

(1) A notice may be given by the Director of Public Prosecutions under this section in respect of an offence falling within subsection (3) below if he is of the opinion –

    (a) that the evidence of the offence would be sufficient for the person charged to be put on trial for the offence;

    (b) that a child would be called as a witness at the trial; and

    (c) that, for the purpose of avoiding any prejudice to the welfare of the child, the case should be taken over and proceeded with without delay by the Crown Court.

(2) That opinion must be certified by the Director of Public Prosecutions in the notice.

(3) This subsection applies to an offence –

(a) which involves an assault on, or injury or a threat of injury to, a person;

(b) under section 1 of the Children and Young Persons Act 1933 (cruelty to persons under 16);

(c) under the Sexual Offences Act 1956, the Protection of Children Act 1978 or the Sexual Offences Act 2003;

(d) of kidnapping or false imprisonment, or an offence under section 1 or 2 of the Child Abduction Act 1984;

(e) which consists of attempting or conspiring to commit, or of aiding, abetting, counselling, procuring or inciting the commission of, an offence falling within paragraph (a), (b), (c) or (d) above.

(4) Subsections (4), (5) and (6) of section 51B above apply for the purposes of this section as they apply for the purposes of that.

(5) The functions of the Director of Public Prosecutions under this section may be exercised by an officer acting on behalf of the Director.

(6) A decision to give a notice under this section shall not be subject to appeal or liable to be questioned in any court (whether a magistrates' court or not).

(7) In this section "child" means –

(a) a person who is under the age of 17; or

(b) any person of whom a video recording (as defined in section 63(1) of the Youth Justice and Criminal Evidence Act 1999) was made when he was under the age of 17 with a view to its admission as his evidence in chief in the trial referred to in subsection (1) above.

51D Notice of offence and place of trial

(1) The court shall specify in a notice –

(a) the offence or offences for which a person is sent for trial under section 51 or 51A above; and

(b) the place at which he is to be tried (which, if a notice has been given under section 51B above, must be the place specified in that notice).

(2) A copy of the notice shall be served on the accused and given to the Crown Court sitting at that place.

(3) In a case where a person is sent for trial under section 51 or 51A above for more than one offence, the court shall specify in that notice, for each offence –

(a) the subsection under which the person is so sent; and

(b) if applicable, the offence to which that offence appears to the court to be related.

(4) Where the court selects the place of trial for the purposes of subsection (1) above, it shall have regard to –

(a) the convenience of the defence, the prosecution and the witnesses;

(b) the desirability of expediting the trial; and

(c) any direction given by or on behalf of the Lord Chief Justice with the concurrence of the Lord Chancellor under section 75(1) of the Supreme Court Act 1981.

51E Interpretation of sections 50A to 51D

For the purposes of sections 50A to 51D above –

(a) "adult" means a person aged 18 or over, and references to an adult include a corporation;

(b) "either-way offence" means an offence triable either way;

(c) an either-way offence is related to an indictable offence if the charge for the either-way offence could be joined in the same indictment as the charge for the indictable offence;

(d) a summary offence is related to an indictable offence if it arises out of circumstances which are the same as or connected with those giving rise to the indictable offence.'

19 (1) After section 52 there is inserted –

'52A Restrictions on reporting

(1) Except as provided by this section, it shall not be lawful –

(a) to publish in the United Kingdom a written report of any allocation or sending proceedings in England and Wales; or

(b) to include in a relevant programme for reception in the United Kingdom a report of any such proceedings,

if (in either case) the report contains any matter other than that permitted by this section.

(2) Subject to subsections (3) and (4) below, a magistrates' court may, with reference to any allocation or sending proceedings, order that subsection (1) above shall not apply to reports of those proceedings.

(3) Where there is only one accused and he objects to the making of an order under subsection (2) above, the court shall make the order if, and only if, it is satisfied, after hearing the representations of the accused, that it is in the interests of justice to do so.

(4) Where in the case of two or more accused one of them objects to the making of an order under subsection (2) above, the court shall make the order if, and only if, it is satisfied, after hearing the representations of the accused, that it is in the interests of justice to do so.

(5) An order under subsection (2) above shall not apply to reports of proceedings under subsection (3) or (4) above, but any decision of the court to make or not to make such an order may be contained in reports published or included in a relevant programme before the time authorised by subsection (6) below.

(6) It shall not be unlawful under this section to publish or include in a relevant programme a report of allocation or sending proceedings containing any matter other than that permitted by subsection (7) below –

(a) where, in relation to the accused (or all of them, if there are more than one), the magistrates' court is required to proceed as mentioned in section 20(7) of the 1980 Act, after the court is so required;

(b) where, in relation to the accused (or any of them, if there are more than one), the court proceeds other than as mentioned there, after conclusion of his trial or, as the case may be, the trial of the last to be tried.

(7) The following matters may be contained in a report of allocation or sending proceedings published or included in a relevant programme without an order under subsection (2) above before the time authorised by subsection (6) above –

(a) the identity of the court and the name of the justice or justices;

(b) the name, age, home address and occupation of the accused;

(c) in the case of an accused charged with an offence in respect of which notice has been given to the court under section 51B above, any relevant business information;

(d) the offence or offences, or a summary of them, with which the accused is or are charged;

(e) the names of counsel and solicitors engaged in the proceedings;

(f) where the proceedings are adjourned, the date and place to which they are adjourned;

(g) the arrangements as to bail;

(h) whether a right to representation funded by the Legal Services Commission as part of the Criminal Defence Service was granted to the accused or any of the accused.

(8) The addresses that may be published or included in a relevant programme under subsection (7) above are addresses –

(a) at any relevant time; and

(b) at the time of their publication or inclusion in a relevant programme.

(9) The following is relevant business information for the purposes of subsection (7) above –

(a) any address used by the accused for carrying on a business on his own account;

(b) the name of any business which he was carrying on on his own account at any relevant time;

(c) the name of any firm in which he was a partner at any relevant time or by which he was engaged at any such time;

(d) the address of any such firm;

(e) the name of any company of which he was a director at any relevant time or by which he was otherwise engaged at any such time;

(f) the address of the registered or principal office of any such company;

(g) any working address of the accused in his capacity as a person engaged by any such company;

and here "engaged" means engaged under a contract of service or a contract for services.

(10) Subsection (1) above shall be in addition to, and not in derogation from, the provisions of any other enactment with respect to the publication of reports of court proceedings.

(11) In this section –

"allocation or sending proceedings" means, in relation to an information charging an indictable offence –

(a) any proceedings in the magistrates' court at which matters are considered under any of the following provisions –

(i) sections 19 to 23 of the 1980 Act;

(ii) section 51, 51A or 52 above;

(b) any proceedings in the magistrates' court before the court proceeds to consider any matter mentioned in paragraph (a) above; and

(c) any proceedings in the magistrates' court at which an application under section 25(2) of the 1980 Act is considered;

"publish", in relation to a report, means publish the report, either by itself or as part of a newspaper or periodical, for distribution to the public;

"relevant programme" means a programme included in a programme service (within the meaning of the Broadcasting Act 1990);

"relevant time" means a time when events giving rise to the charges to which the proceedings relate occurred.

52B Offences in connection with reporting

(1) If a report is published or included in a relevant programme in contravention of section 52A above, each of the following persons is guilty of an offence –

(a) in the case of a publication of a written report as part of a newspaper or periodical, any proprietor, editor or publisher of the newspaper or periodical;

(b) in the case of a publication of a written report otherwise than as part of a newspaper or periodical, the person who publishes it;

(c) in the case of the inclusion of a report in a relevant programme, any body corporate which is engaged in providing the service in which the programme is included and any person having functions in relation to the programme corresponding to those of the editor of a newspaper.

(2) A person guilty of an offence under this section is liable on summary conviction to a fine not exceeding level 5 on the standard scale.

(3) Proceedings for an offence under this section shall not, in England and Wales, be instituted otherwise than by or with the consent of the Attorney General.

(4) Proceedings for an offence under this section shall not, in Northern Ireland, be instituted otherwise than by or with the consent of the Attorney General for Northern Ireland.

(5) Subsection (11) of section 52A above applies for the purposes of this section as it applies for the purposes of that section.'.

(2) In section 121 (short title, commencement and extent) –

    (a) in subsection (6), after paragraph (b) there is inserted –

       '(bb) sections 52A and 52B;', and

    (b) in subsection (8), after '(5) above,' there is inserted 'sections 52A and 52B above,'.

20 (1) Schedule 3 (procedure where persons are sent for trial under section 51 of the Crime and Disorder Act 1998) is amended as follows.

(2) In paragraph 1(1) –

    (a) after '51' there is inserted 'or 51A', and

    (b) in paragraph (b), for 'subsection (7) of that section' there is substituted 'section 51D(1) of this Act'.

(3) In paragraph 2 –

    (a) in sub-paragraph (1) –

       (i) after '51' there is inserted 'or 51A', and

       (ii) for 'subsection (7) of that section' there is substituted 'section 51D(1) of this Act', and

    (b) sub-paragraphs (4) and (5) are omitted.

(4) In paragraph 4, in sub-paragraph (1)(a), after '51' there is inserted 'or 51A'.

(5) In paragraph 5, in sub-paragraph (2), after '51' there is inserted 'or 51A'.

(6) Paragraph 6 is amended as follows –

    (a) in sub-paragraph (1), after '51' there is inserted 'or 51A',

    (b) in sub-paragraph (2), for the words from the second 'offence' to the end there is substituted 'indictable offence for which he was sent for trial or, as the case may be, any of the indictable offences for which he was so sent', and

    (c) in sub-paragraph (9), for 'indictable-only' there is substituted 'indictable'.

(7) In paragraph 7 –

    (a) in sub-paragraph (1)(a), after '51' there is inserted 'or 51A',

    (b) in sub-paragraph (1)(b), for 'offence that is triable only on indictment' there is substituted 'main offence',

    (c) in sub-paragraph (3), after 'each' there is inserted 'remaining',

(d) in sub-paragraph (7), for 'consider' there is substituted 'decide', and

(e) after sub-paragraph (8) there is inserted –

'(9) In this paragraph, a "main offence" is –

(a) an offence for which the person has been sent to the Crown Court for trial under section 51(1) of this Act; or

(b) an offence –

(i) for which the person has been sent to the Crown Court for trial under subsection (5) of section 51 or subsection (6) of section 51A of this Act ("the applicable subsection"); and

(ii) in respect of which the conditions for sending him to the Crown Court for trial under the applicable subsection (as set out in paragraphs (a) to (c) of section 51(5) or paragraphs (a) and (b) of section 51A(6)) continue to be satisfied.'

(8) In paragraph 8 –

(a) in sub-paragraph (1)(a), after '51' there is inserted 'or 51A',

(b) in sub-paragraph (1)(b), for 'offence that is triable only on indictment' there is substituted 'main offence (within the meaning of paragraph 7 above)',

(c) in sub-paragraph (2)(a), after 'each' there is inserted 'remaining', and

(d) in sub-paragraph (2)(d), for 'consider' there is substituted 'decide'.

(9) In paragraph 9 –

(a) in sub-paragraph (1), for 'consider' there is substituted 'decide', and

(b) for sub-paragraphs (2) and (3), there is substituted –

'(2) Before deciding the question, the court –

(a) shall give the prosecution an opportunity to inform the court of the accused's previous convictions (if any); and

(b) shall give the prosecution and the accused an opportunity to make representations as to whether summary trial or trial on indictment would be more suitable.

(3) In deciding the question, the court shall consider –

(a) whether the sentence which a magistrates' court would have power to impose for the offence would be adequate; and

(b) any representations made by the prosecution or the accused under sub-paragraph (2)(b) above,

and shall have regard to any allocation guidelines (or revised allocation guidelines) issued as definitive guidelines under section 170 of the Criminal Justice Act 2003.

(4) Where –

(a) the accused is charged on the same occasion with two or more offences; and

(b) it appears to the court that they constitute or form part of a series of two or more offences of the same or a similar character;

sub-paragraph (3)(a) above shall have effect as if references to the sentence which a magistrates' court would have power to impose for the offence were a reference to the maximum aggregate sentence which a magistrates' court would have power to impose for all of the offences taken together.

(5) In this paragraph any reference to a previous conviction is a reference to –

(a) a previous conviction by a court in the United Kingdom, or

(b) a previous finding of guilt in –

    (i) any proceedings under the Army Act 1955, the Air Force Act 1955 or the Naval Discipline Act 1957 (whether before a court-martial or any other court or person authorised under any of those Acts to award a punishment in respect of any offence), or

    (ii) any proceedings before a Standing Civilian Court.'

(10) In paragraph 10 –

  (a) for sub-paragraph (2), there is substituted –

'(2) The court shall explain to the accused in ordinary language –

    (a) that it appears to the court more suitable for him to be tried summarily for the offence;

    (b) that he can either consent to be so tried or, if he wishes, be tried on indictment; and

    (c) in the case of a specified offence (within the meaning of section 224 of the Criminal Justice Act 2003), that if he is tried summarily and is convicted by the court, he may be committed for sentence to the Crown Court under section 3A of the Powers of Criminal Courts (Sentencing) Act 2000 if the committing court is of such opinion as is mentioned in subsection (2) of that section.', and

  (b) in sub-paragraph (3), for 'by a jury' there is substituted 'on indictment'.

(11) In paragraph 11, in sub-paragraph (a), for 'by a jury' there is substituted 'on indictment'.

(12) Paragraph 12 shall cease to have effect.

(13) In paragraph 13 –

  (a) in sub-paragraph (1)(a), after '51' there is inserted 'or 51A',

  (b) in sub-paragraph (1)(b), for 'offence that is triable only on indictment' there is substituted 'main offence',

  (c) in sub-paragraph (2), the words from 'unless' to the end are omitted, and

  (d) for sub-paragraph (3) there is substituted –

'(3) In this paragraph, a "main offence" is –

    (a) an offence for which the child or young person has been sent to the Crown Court for trial under section 51A(2) of this Act; or

    (b) an offence –

      (i) for which the child or young person has been sent to the Crown Court for trial under subsection (7) of section 51 of this Act; and

      (ii) in respect of which the conditions for sending him to the Crown Court for trial under that subsection (as set out in paragraphs (a) and (b) of that subsection) continue to be satisfied.'

(14) In paragraph 15, in each of sub-paragraphs (3) and (4), for 'considered' there is substituted 'decided'.

Powers of Criminal Courts (Sentencing) Act 2000 (c. 6)

21   The Powers of Criminal Courts (Sentencing) Act 2000 is amended as follows.

22   For section 3 (committal for sentence on summary trial of offence triable either way) there is substituted –

'3 Committal for sentence on indication of guilty plea to serious offence triable either way

   (1) Subject to subsection (4) below, this section applies where –

      (a) a person aged 18 or over appears or is brought before a magistrates' court ("the court") on an information charging him with an offence triable either way ("the offence");

      (b) he or his representative indicates under section 17A or (as the case may be) 17B of the Magistrates' Courts Act 1980 (initial procedure: accused to indicate intention as to plea), but not section 20(7) of that Act, that he would plead guilty if the offence were to proceed to trial; and

      (c) proceeding as if section 9(1) of that Act were complied with and he pleaded guilty under it, the court convicts him of the offence.

   (2) If the court is of the opinion that –

      (a) the offence; or

      (b) the combination of the offence and one or more offences associated with it,

      was so serious that the Crown Court should, in the court's opinion, have the power to deal with the offender in any way it could deal with him if he had been convicted on indictment, the court may commit him in custody or on bail to the Crown Court for sentence in accordance with section 5(1) below.

   (3) Where the court commits a person under subsection (2) above, section 6 below (which enables a magistrates' court, where it commits a person under this section in respect of an offence, also to commit him to the Crown Court to be dealt with in respect of certain other offences) shall apply accordingly.

   (4) This section does not apply in relation to an offence as regards which this section is excluded by section 17D of the Magistrates' Courts Act 1980 (certain offences where value involved is small).

   (5) The preceding provisions of this section shall apply in relation to a corporation as if –

      (a) the corporation were an individual aged 18 or over; and

      (b) in subsection (2) above, the words "in custody or on bail" were omitted.'

23 After section 3 there is inserted –

'3A Committal for sentence of dangerous adult offenders

   (1) This section applies where on the summary trial of a specified offence triable either way a person aged 18 or over is convicted of the offence.

   (2) If, in relation to the offence, it appears to the court that the criteria for the imposition of a sentence under section 225(3) or 227(2) of the Criminal Justice Act 2003 would be met, the court must commit the offender in custody or on bail to the Crown Court for sentence in accordance with section 5(1) below.

   (3) Where the court commits a person under subsection (2) above, section 6 below (which enables a magistrates' court, where it commits a person under this section in respect of an offence, also to commit him to the Crown Court to be dealt with in respect of certain other offences) shall apply accordingly.

   (4) In reaching any decision under or taking any step contemplated by this section –

      (a) the court shall not be bound by any indication of sentence given in respect of the offence under section 20 of the Magistrates' Courts Act 1980 (procedure where summary trial appears more suitable); and

(b) nothing the court does under this section may be challenged or be the subject of any appeal in any court on the ground that it is not consistent with an indication of sentence.

(5) Nothing in this section shall prevent the court from committing a specified offence to the Crown Court for sentence under section 3 above if the provisions of that section are satisfied.

(6) In this section, references to a specified offence are to a specified offence within the meaning of section 224 of the Criminal Justice Act 2003.

3B Committal for sentence on indication of guilty plea by child or young person

(1) This section applies where –

(a) a person aged under 18 appears or is brought before a magistrates' court ("the court") on an information charging him with an offence mentioned in subsection (1) of section 91 below ("the offence");

(b) he or his representative indicates under section 24A or (as the case may be) 24B of the Magistrates' Courts Act 1980 (child or young person to indicate intention as to plea in certain cases) that he would plead guilty if the offence were to proceed to trial; and

(c) proceeding as if section 9(1) of that Act were complied with and he pleaded guilty under it, the court convicts him of the offence.

(2) If the court is of the opinion that –

(a) the offence; or

(b) the combination of the offence and one or more offences associated with it,

was such that the Crown Court should, in the court's opinion, have power to deal with the offender as if the provisions of section 91(3) below applied, the court may commit him in custody or on bail to the Crown Court for sentence in accordance with section 5A(1) below.

(3) Where the court commits a person under subsection (2) above, section 6 below (which enables a magistrates' court, where it commits a person under this section in respect of an offence, also to commit him to the Crown Court to be dealt with in respect of certain other offences) shall apply accordingly.

3C Committal for sentence of dangerous young offenders

(1) This section applies where on the summary trial of a specified offence a person aged under 18 is convicted of the offence.

(2) If, in relation to the offence, it appears to the court that the criteria for the imposition of a sentence under section 226(3) or 228(2) of the Criminal Justice Act 2003 would be met, the court must commit the offender in custody or on bail to the Crown Court for sentence in accordance with section 5A(1) below.

(3) Where the court commits a person under subsection (2) above, section 6 below (which enables a magistrates' court, where it commits a person under this section in respect of an offence, also to commit him to the Crown Court to be dealt with in respect of certain other offences) shall apply accordingly.

(4) Nothing in this section shall prevent the court from committing a specified offence to the Crown Court for sentence under section 3B above if the provisions of that section are satisfied.

(5)   In this section, references to a specified offence are to a specified offence within the meaning of section 224 of the Criminal Justice Act 2003.'

24 (1) Section 4 (committal for sentence on indication of guilty plea to offence triable either way) is amended as follows.

    (2) For subsection (1)(b), there is substituted –

        '(b) he or (where applicable) his representative indicates under section 17A, 17B or 20(7) of the Magistrates' Courts Act 1980 that he would plead guilty if the offence were to proceed to trial; and'.

    (3) In subsection (1)(c), for 'the Magistrates' Courts Act 1980' there is substituted 'that Act'.

    (4) After subsection (1) there is inserted –

    '(1A) But this section does not apply to an offence as regards which this section is excluded by section 17D of that Act (certain offences where value involved is small).'

    (5) For subsection (3), there is substituted –

    '(3) If the power conferred by subsection (2) above is not exercisable but the court is still to determine to, or to determine whether to, send the offender to the Crown Court for trial under section 51 or 51A of the Crime and Disorder Act 1998 for one or more related offences –

        (a) it shall adjourn the proceedings relating to the offence until after it has made those determinations; and

        (b) if it sends the offender to the Crown Court for trial for one or more related offences, it may then exercise that power.'

    (6) In subsection (4)(b), after 'section 3(2)' there is inserted 'or, as the case may be, section 3A(2)'.

    (7) After subsection (7) there is inserted –

    '(8) In reaching any decision under or taking any step contemplated by this section –

        (a) the court shall not be bound by any indication of sentence given in respect of the offence under section 20 of the Magistrates' Courts Act 1980 (procedure where summary trial appears more suitable); and

        (b) nothing the court does under this section may be challenged or be the subject of any appeal in any court on the ground that it is not consistent with an indication of sentence.'

25 After section 4 there is inserted –

'4A Committal for sentence on indication of guilty plea by child or young person with related offences

    (1) This section applies where –

        (a) a person aged under 18 appears or brought before a magistrates' court ("the court") on an information charging him with an offence mentioned in subsection (1) of section 91 below ("the offence");

        (b) he or his representative indicates under section 24A or (as the case may be) 24B of the Magistrates' Courts Act 1980 (child or young person to indicate intention as to plea in certain cases) that he would plead guilty if the offence were to proceed to trial; and

        (c) proceeding as if section 9(1) of that Act were complied with and he pleaded guilty under it, the court convicts him of the offence.

    (2) If the court has sent the offender to the Crown Court for trial for one or more related offences, that is to say one or more offences which, in its opinion, are related to the offence, it may commit him in custody or on bail to

the Crown Court to be dealt with in respect of the offence in accordance with section 5A(1) below.

(3)   If the power conferred by subsection (2) above is not exercisable but the court is still to determine to, or to determine whether to, send the offender to the Crown Court for trial under section 51 or 51A of the Crime and Disorder Act 1998 for one or more related offences –

(a) it shall adjourn the proceedings relating to the offence until after it has made those determinations; and

(b) if it sends the offender to the Crown Court for trial for one or more related offences, it may then exercise that power.

(4)   Where the court –

(a) under subsection (2) above commits the offender to the Crown Court to be dealt with in respect of the offence; and

(b) does not state that, in its opinion, it also has power so to commit him under section 3B(2) or, as the case may be, section 3C(2) above,

section 5A(1) below shall not apply unless he is convicted before the Crown Court of one or more of the related offences.

(5)   Where section 5A(1) below does not apply, the Crown Court may deal with the offender in respect of the offence in any way in which the magistrates' court could deal with him if it had just convicted him of the offence.

(6)   Where the court commits a person under subsection (2) above, section 6 below (which enables a magistrates' court, where it commits a person under this section in respect of an offence, also to commit him to the Crown Court to be dealt with in respect of certain other offences) shall apply accordingly.

(7)   Section 4(7) above applies for the purposes of this section as it applies for the purposes of that section.'

26   For section 5 (power of Crown Court on committal for sentence under sections 3 and 4) there is substituted –

'5 Power of Crown Court on committal for sentence under sections 3, 3A and 4

(1)   Where an offender is committed by a magistrates' court for sentence under section 3, 3A or 4 above, the Crown Court shall inquire into the circumstances of the case and may deal with the offender in any way in which it could deal with him if he had just been convicted of the offence on indictment before the court.

(2)   In relation to committals under section 4 above, subsection (1) above has effect subject to section 4(4) and (5) above.

(3)   Section 20A(1) of the Magistrates' Courts Act 1980 (which relates to the effect of an indication of sentence under section 20 of that Act) shall not apply in respect of any specified offence (within the meaning of section 224 of the Criminal Justice Act 2003) –

(a) in respect of which the offender is committed under section 3A(2) above; or

(b) in respect of which –

(i) the offender is committed under section 4(2) above; and

(ii) the court states under section 4(4) above that, in its opinion, it also has power to commit the offender under section 3A(2) above.'

27   After section 5 there is inserted –

'5A Power of Crown Court on committal for sentence under sections 3B, 3C and 4A

(1)   Where an offender is committed by a magistrates' court for sentence under section 3B, 3C or 4A above, the Crown Court shall inquire into the circumstances of the case and may deal with the offender in any way in which it could deal with him if he had just been convicted of the offence on indictment before the court.

(2)   In relation to committals under section 4A above, subsection (1) above has effect subject to section 4A(4) and (5) above.'

28   In section 6 (committal for sentence in certain cases where offender committed in respect of another offence), in subsection (4)(b), for '3 and 4' there is substituted '3 to 4A'.

PART 2

MINOR AND CONSEQUENTIAL AMENDMENTS

Territorial Waters Jurisdiction Act 1878 (c. 73)

29   In section 4 of the Territorial Waters Jurisdiction Act 1878 (provisions as to procedure), in the paragraph beginning 'Proceedings before a justice of the peace', for the words from the beginning to 'his trial' there is substituted –

'Any stage of proceedings –

(a)   before the summary trial of the offence; or

(b)   before the offender has been sent for trial for the offence,'.

Bankers' Books Evidence Act 1879 (c. 11)

30   (1)   The Bankers' Books Evidence Act 1879 is amended as follows.

(2)   In section 4 (proof that book is a banker's book), the paragraph beginning 'Where the proceedings' is omitted.

(3)   In section 5 (verification of copy), the paragraph beginning 'Where the proceedings' is omitted.

Explosive Substances Act 1883 (c. 3)

31   In section 6 of Explosive Substances Act 1883 (inquiry by Attorney-General, and apprehension of absconding witnesses), subsection (3) is omitted.

Criminal Justice Act 1925 (c. 86)

32   In section 49 of the Criminal Justice Act 1925 (interpretation, etc), subsection (2) is omitted.

Children and Young Persons Act 1933 (c. 12)

33   In section 42 of the Children and Young Persons Act 1933 (extension of power to take deposition of child or young person), in subsection (2)(a), for 'committed' in both places there is substituted 'sent'.

Administration of Justice (Miscellaneous Provisions) Act 1933 (c. 36)

34   (1)   Section 2 of the Administration of Justice (Miscellaneous Provisions) Act 1933 (procedure for indictment of offenders) is amended as follows.

    (2)   In subsection (2) –

        (a)   in paragraph (a), for 'committed' there is substituted 'sent',

        (b)   paragraphs (aa) to (ac) are omitted,

        (c)   for paragraph (i) there is substituted –

            '(i) where the person charged has been sent for trial, the bill of indictment against him may include, either in substitution for or in addition to any count charging an offence specified in the notice under section 57D(1) of the Crime and Disorder Act 1998, any counts founded on material which, in pursuance of regulations made under paragraph 1 of Schedule 3 to that Act, was served on the person charged, being counts which may lawfully be joined in the same indictment;',

        (d)   paragraphs (iA) and (iB) are omitted,

        (e)   in paragraph (ii), for 'the committal' there is substituted 'such notice', and

        (f)   the words from 'and in paragraph (iA)' to the end are omitted.

    (3)   In subsection (3)(b), for 'committed' there is substituted 'sent'.

Criminal Justice Act 1948 (c. 58)

35   (1)   The Criminal Justice Act 1948 is amended as follows.

    (2)   In section 27 (remand and committal of persons aged 17 to 20), in subsection (1), for 'commits him for trial or' there is substituted 'sends him to the Crown Court for trial or commits him there for'.

    (3)   In section 41 (evidence by certificate), subsection (5A) is omitted.

    (4)   In section 80 (interpretation), the definition of 'Court of summary jurisdiction' is omitted.

Prison Act 1952 (c. 52)

36   Until their repeal by (respectively) section 59 of, and paragraph 10(a)(ii) of Schedule 7 to, the Criminal Justice and Court Services Act 2000, paragraph (a) of subsection (1), and paragraphs (b) and (c) of subsection (2), of section 43 of the Prison Act 1952 (remand centres, detention centres and youth custody centres) are to have effect as if references to being committed for trial were references to being sent for trial.

Army Act 1955 (3 & 4 Eliz. 2 c. 18)

37   In section 187 of the Army Act 1955 (proceedings before a civil court where persons suspected of illegal absence), at the end of subsection (4) there is inserted –

    'The references in this subsection to provisions of the Magistrates' Courts Act 1980 and to corresponding enactments are to be taken to refer to those provisions and enactments as if no amendment to them had been made by the Criminal Justice Act 2003.'

Air Force Act 1955 (3 & 4 Eliz. 2 c. 19)

38   In section 187 of the Air Force Act 1955 (proceedings before a civil court where persons suspected of illegal absence), at the end of subsection (4) there is inserted –

'The references in this subsection to provisions of the Magistrates' Courts Act 1980 and to corresponding enactments are to be taken to refer to those provisions and enactments as if no amendment to them had been made by the Criminal Justice Act 2003.'

Geneva Conventions Act 1957 (c. 52)

39   In section 5 of the Geneva Conventions Act 1957 (reduction of sentence and custody of protected persons) –

(a)   in subsection (1), for 'committal' there is substituted 'having been sent',

(b)   in subsection (2), for 'committal', where it first appears, there is substituted 'having been sent'.

Naval Discipline Act 1957 (c. 53)

40   In section 109 of the Naval Discipline Act 1957 (proceedings before summary courts), at the end of subsection (4) there is inserted –

'The references in this subsection to provisions are to be taken to refer to those provisions as if no amendment to them had been made by the Criminal Justice Act 2003.'

Backing of Warrants (Republic of Ireland) Act 1965 (c. 45)

41   In paragraph 4 of the Schedule to the Backing of Warrants (Republic of Ireland) Act 1965 (supplementary procedures as to proceedings under section 2) –

(a)   the words 'and section 2 of the Poor Prisoners Defence Act 1930 (legal aid before examining justices)' are omitted, and

(b)   for 'it had determined not to commit for trial' there is substituted 'the offence were to be dealt with summarily and the court had dismissed the information'.

Criminal Procedure (Attendance of Witnesses) Act 1965 (c. 69)

42   In section 2 of the Criminal Procedure (Attendance of Witnesses) Act 1965 (issue of witness summons on application to Crown Court) –

(a)   for subsection (4) there is substituted –

'(4) Where a person has been sent for trial for any offence to which the proceedings concerned relate, an application must be made as soon as is reasonably practicable after service on that person, in pursuance of regulations made under paragraph 1 of Schedule 3 to the Crime and Disorder Act 1998, of the documents relevant to that offence.', and

(b)   subsection (5) is omitted.

Criminal Justice Act 1967 (c. 80)

43   (1) The Criminal Justice Act 1967 is amended as follows.

 (2) In section 9 (proof by written statement), in subsection (1), the words ', other than committal proceedings,' are omitted.

 (3) In section 36 (interpretation), in subsection (1), the definition of 'committal proceedings' is omitted.

Criminal Appeal Act 1968 (c. 19)

44   (1) The Criminal Appeal Act 1968 is amended as follows.

 (2) In section 1 (right of appeal), in subsection (3), for 'committed him' there is substituted 'sent him to the Crown Court'.

 (3) In section 9 (appeal against sentence following conviction on indictment), in subsection (2), the words from 'section 41' to 'either way offence' are omitted.

Firearms Act 1968 (c. 27)

45   In Schedule 6 to the Firearms Act 1968 (prosecution and punishment of offences), in Part 2, paragraph 3 is omitted.

Theft Act 1968 (c. 60)

46   In section 27 of the Theft Act 1968 (evidence and procedure on charge of theft or handling stolen goods), subsection (4A) is omitted.

Criminal Justice Act 1972 (c. 71)

47   In section 46 of the Criminal Justice Act 1972 (admissibility of written statements outside England and Wales), subsections (1A) to (1C) are omitted.

Bail Act 1976 (c. 63)

48   (1) The Bail Act 1976 is amended as follows.

 (2) In section 3 (general provisions) –

 (a)   in subsection (8) –

 (i) for 'committed' there is substituted 'sent', and
 (ii) after 'for trial or' there is inserted 'committed him on bail to the Crown Court', and

 (b)   subsections (8A) and (8B), and the subsection (10) inserted by paragraph 12(b) of Schedule 9 to the Criminal Justice and Public Order Act 1994 (c. 33), are omitted.

 (3) In section 5 (supplementary provisions about decisions on bail) –

 (a)   in subsection (6)(a), for 'committing' there is substituted 'sending', and
 (b)   in subsection (6A)(a) –

 (i) after 'under' there is inserted 'section 52(5) of the Crime and Disorder Act 1998,',
 (ii) sub-paragraph (i) is omitted,
 (iii) after sub-paragraph (ii) there is inserted –

 '(iia) section 17C (intention as to plea: adjournment);', and

(iv) at the end of sub-paragraph (iii) there is inserted 'or

(iv) section 24C (intention as to plea by child or young person: adjournment),'.

(4) In section 6 (offence of absconding by person released on bail), in subsection (6)(b), for 'commits' there is substituted 'sends'.

(5) In section 9 (offence of agreeing to indemnify sureties in criminal proceedings), in subsection (3)(b), for 'commits' there is substituted 'sends'.

Interpretation Act 1978 (c. 30)

49   In Schedule 1 to the Interpretation Act 1978 (words and expressions defined) –

(a)   in the definition of 'Committed for trial', paragraph (a) is omitted,

(b)   after the entry for 'Secretary of State' there is inserted –

'"Sent for trial" means, in relation to England and Wales, sent by a magistrates' court to the Crown Court for trial pursuant to section 51 or 51A of the Crime and Disorder Act 1998.'

Customs and Excise Management Act 1979 (c. 2)

50   In section 147 of the Customs and Excise Management Act 1979 (proceedings for offences), subsection (2) is omitted.

Magistrates' Courts Act 1980 (c. 43)

51   (1)   The Magistrates' Courts Act 1980 is amended as follows.

(2)   In section 2, as substituted by the Courts Act 2003 (trial of summary offences), in subsection (2), for 'as examining justices over' there is substituted 'under sections 51 and 51A of the Crime and Disorder Act 1998 in respect of'.

(3)   Sections 4 to 8 (which relate to committal proceedings) shall cease to have effect and the cross-heading preceding section 4 is omitted.

(4)   In section 8B, as inserted by the Courts Act 2003 (effect of rulings at pre-trial hearing), in subsection (6), the words 'commits or' are omitted.

(5)   In section 29 (power of magistrates' court to remit a person under 17 for trial to a juvenile court in certain circumstances), in subsection (2)(b)(i), for the words from 'proceeds' to the end there is substituted 'sends him to the Crown Court for trial under section 51 or 51A of the Crime and Disorder Act 1998; and'.

(6)   The following sections shall cease to have effect –

(a)   section 97A (summons or warrant as to committal proceedings),

(b)   section 103 (evidence of persons under 14 in committal proceedings for assault, sexual offences etc), and

(c)   section 106 (false written statements tendered in evidence).

(7)   In section 128 (remand in custody or on bail) –

(a)   in subsection (1)(b), the words 'inquiring into or' are omitted,

(b)   in subsection (1A)(a) –

(i)   '5,' is omitted, and

(ii)   for 'or 18(4)' there is substituted ', 18(4) or 24C',

(c)   in subsection (3A) –

(i)   '5,' is omitted, and

(ii)   for 'or 18(4)' there is substituted ', 18(4) or 24C',

(d)   in subsection (3C)(a) –

  (i) '5,' is omitted, and
  (ii) for 'or 18(4)' there is substituted ', 18(4) or 24C', and

(e)   in subsection (3E)(a) –

  (i) '5,' is omitted, and
  (ii) for 'or 18(4)' there is substituted ', 18(4) or 24C'.

(8) In section 129 (further remand), in subsection (4) –

  (a)   for 'commits a person' there is substituted 'sends a person to the Crown Court', and
  (b)   for 'committed' there is substituted 'sent'.

(9) In section 130 (transfer of remand hearings), in subsection (1) –

  (a)   '5,' is omitted, and
  (b)   for 'or 18(4)' there is substituted ', 18(4) or 24C'.

(10) In section 145 (rules: supplementary provisions), in subsection (1), paragraph (f) is omitted.

(11) In section 150 (interpretation of other terms), in subsection (1), the definition of 'committal proceedings' is omitted.

(12) In section 155 (short title, extent and commencement), in subsection (2)(a), the words '8 (except subsection (9))' are omitted.

(13) In Schedule 3 (corporations) –

  (a)   in paragraph 2, sub-paragraph (a) is omitted,
  (b)   in paragraph 6, for 'inquiry into, and trial of,' there is substituted 'trial of'.

(14) In Schedule 5 (transfer of remand hearings) –

  (a)   paragraph 2 is omitted, and
  (b)   in paragraph 5, for '5, 10 or 18(4)' there is substituted '10, 17C, 18(4) or 24C'.

Criminal Attempts Act 1981 (c. 47)

52   In section 2 of the Criminal Attempts Act 1981 (application of procedures and other provisions to offences under section 1), in subsection (2)(g), the words 'or committed for trial' are omitted.

53   In section 4 of the Contempt of Court Act 1981 (contemporary reports of proceedings), in subsection (3), for paragraph (b) there is substituted –

  '(b)   in the case of a report of allocation or sending proceedings of which publication is permitted by virtue only of subsection (6) of section 52A of the Crime and Disorder Act 1998 ("the 1998 Act"), if published as soon as practicable after publication is so permitted;

  (c)   in the case of a report of an application of which publication is permitted by virtue only of sub-paragraph (5) or (7) of paragraph 3 of Schedule 3 to the 1998 Act, if published as soon as practicable after publication is so permitted.'

Supreme Court Act 1981 (c. 54)

54   (1)   The Supreme Court Act 1981 is amended as follows.

  (2)   In section 76 (committal for trial: alteration of place of trial) –

  (a)   in subsection (1), for the words from 'varying' (where it first appears) to 'to Crown Court)' there is substituted 'substituting some other place for the place specified in a notice under section 51D(1) of the Crime and Disorder Act 1998 (a "section 51D notice")',

(b) in subsection (3), for the words 'fixed by the magistrates' court, as specified in a notice under a relevant transfer provision' there is substituted 'specified in a section 51D notice',

(c) subsection (5) is omitted, and

(d) in the heading, for '**Committal**' there is substituted '**Sending**'.

(3) In section 77 (committal for trial: date of trial) –

(a) in subsection (1), for 'committal for trial or the giving of a notice of transfer under a relevant transfer provision' there is substituted 'being sent for trial',

(b) in subsection (2), for 'committed by a magistrates' court or in respect of whom a notice of transfer under a relevant transfer provision has been given' there is substituted 'sent for trial',

(c) in subsection (3), for 'of committal for trial or of a notice of transfer' there is substituted 'when the defendant is sent for trial',

(d) subsection (4) is omitted, and

(e) in the heading, for '**Committal**' there is substituted '**Sending**'.

(4) In section 80 (process to compel appearance), in subsection (2), for 'committed' there is substituted 'sent'.

(5) In section 81 –

(a) in subsection (1) –

(i) in paragraph (a) –

(a) the words 'who has been committed in custody for appearance before the Crown Court or in relation to whose case a notice of transfer has been given under a relevant transfer provision or' are omitted, and

(b) after '51' there is inserted 'or 51A',

(ii) in paragraph (g), sub-paragraph (i) is omitted, and

(b) subsection (7) is omitted.

Mental Health Act 1983 (c. 20)

55 (1) The Mental Health Act 1983 is amended as follows.

(2) In section 43 (power of magistrates' court to commit for restriction order), for subsection (4) there is substituted –

'(4) The powers of a magistrates' court under section 3 or 3B of the Powers of Criminal Courts (Sentencing) Act 2000 (which enable such a court to commit an offender to the Crown Court where the court is of the opinion, or it appears to the court, as mentioned in the section in question) shall also be exercisable by a magistrates' court where it is of that opinion (or it so appears to it) unless a hospital order is made in the offender's case with a restriction order.'

(3) In section 52 (further provisions as to persons remanded by magistrates' courts) –

(a) in subsection (2), for 'committed' there is substituted 'sent',

(b) in subsection (5), for 'committed' there is substituted 'sent',

(c) in subsection (6), for 'committed' there is substituted 'sent', and

(d) in subsection (7), for the words from 'inquire' to '1980' there is substituted 'send him to the Crown Court for trial under section 51 or 51A of the Crime and Disorder Act 1998', and in paragraph (b) of that subsection, the words 'where the court proceeds under subsection (1) of that section' are omitted.

Police and Criminal Evidence Act 1984 (c. 60)

56 (1) The Police and Criminal Evidence Act 1984 is amended as follows.

    (2) In section 62 (intimate samples), in subsection (10) –

        (a) sub-paragraph (i) of paragraph (a) is omitted, and

        (b) in paragraph (aa), for sub-paragraphs (i) and (ii) there is substituted 'paragraph 2 of Schedule 3 to the Crime and Disorder Act 1998 (applications for dismissal); and'.

    (3) In section 71 (microfilm copies), the paragraph beginning 'Where the proceedings' is omitted.

    (4) In section 76 (confessions), subsection (9) is omitted.

    (5) In section 78 (exclusion of unfair evidence), subsection (3) is omitted.

Prosecution of Offences Act 1985 (c. 23)

57 (1) The Prosecution of Offences Act 1985 is amended as follows.

    (2) In section 7A (powers of non-legal staff), for subsection (6) there is substituted –

        '(6) This section applies to an offence if it is triable only on indictment or is an offence for which the accused has been sent for trial.'

    (3) In section 16 (defence costs) –

        (a) in subsection (1), paragraph (b) is omitted, and

        (b) in subsection (2) –

            (i) in paragraph (a), for 'committed' there is substituted 'sent', and

            (ii) paragraph (aa) is omitted, and

        (c) subsection (12) is omitted.

    (4) In section 21 (interpretation), in subsection (6)(b), for 'committed' there is substituted 'sent'.

    (5) In section 22 (power of Secretary of State to set time limits in relation to preliminary stages of criminal proceedings), in subsection (11) –

        (a) in paragraph (a) of the definition of 'appropriate court', for 'committed for trial, sent for trial under section 51 of the Crime and Disorder Act 1998' there is substituted 'sent for trial',

        (b) for the definition of 'custody of the Crown Court' there is substituted –

        '"custody of the Crown Court" includes custody to which a person is committed in pursuance of –

            (a) section 43A of the Magistrates' Courts Act 1980 (magistrates' court dealing with a person brought before it following his arrest in pursuance of a warrant issued by the Crown Court); or

            (b) section 52 of the Crime and Disorder Act 1998 (provisions supplementing section 51);'.

    (6) In section 23 (discontinuance of proceedings in magistrates' court), in subsection (2), for paragraphs (a) to (c) there is substituted –

        '(a) any stage of the proceedings after the court has begun to hear evidence for the prosecution at a summary trial of the offence; or

        (b) any stage of the proceedings after the accused has been sent for trial for the offence.'

    (7) In section 23A (discontinuance of proceedings after accused has been sent for trial) –

        (a) in paragraph (b) of subsection (1), the words from 'under' to '1998' are omitted, and

        (b) in subsection (2), for '51(7)' there is substituted '51D(1)'.

Criminal Justice Act 1987 (c. 38)

58   (1)   The Criminal Justice Act 1987 is amended as follows.
     (2)   Sections 4 to 6 (which relate to the transfer of cases to the Crown Court) shall cease to have effect.
     (3)   In section 11 (restrictions on reporting) –
         (a)   in subsection (2), paragraph (a) is omitted,
         (b)   subsection (3) is omitted,
         (c)   in subsection (7), '(3),' is omitted,
         (d)   in subsection (8), '(3),' is omitted,
         (e)   subsections (9) and (10) are omitted,
         (f)   in subsection (11), paragraphs (a) and (d) are omitted.

Coroners Act 1988 (c. 13)

59   (1)   The Coroners Act 1988 is amended as follows.
     (2)   In section 16 (adjournment of inquest in event of criminal proceedings) –
         (a)   in subsection (1)(b), for 'charged before examining justices with' there is substituted 'sent for trial for', and
         (b)   for subsection (8) there is substituted –
             '(8) In this section, the "relevant criminal proceedings" means the proceedings –
                 (a)   before a magistrates' court to determine whether the person charged is to be sent to the Crown Court for trial; or
                 (b)   before any court to which that person is sent for trial.'
     (3)   In section 17 (provisions supplementary to section 16) –
         (a)   in subsection (2), for 'committed' there is substituted 'sent', and
         (b)   in subsection (3)(b), for 'committed' there is substituted 'sent'.

Criminal Justice Act 1988 (c. 33)

60   (1)   The Criminal Justice Act 1988 is amended as follows.
     (2)   In section 23 (first-hand hearsay), subsection (5) is omitted.
     (3)   In section 24 (business etc documents), subsection (5) is omitted.
     (4)   In section 26 (statements in certain documents), the paragraph beginning 'This section shall not apply' is omitted.
     (5)   In section 27 (proof of statements contained in documents), the paragraph beginning 'This section shall not apply' is omitted.
     (6)   In section 30 (expert reports), subsection (4A) is omitted.
     (7)   In section 40 (power to join in indictment count for common assault etc), in subsection (1) –
         (a)   the words 'were disclosed to a magistrates' court inquiring into the offence as examining justices or' are omitted,
         (b)   after '51' there is inserted 'or 51A'.
     (8)   Section 41 (power of Crown Court to deal with summary offence where person committed for either way offence) shall cease to have effect.

Road Traffic Offenders Act 1988 (c. 53)

61   (1)   The Road Traffic Offenders Act 1988 is amended as follows.
    (2)   In section 11 (evidence by certificate as to driver, user or owner), subsection (3A) is omitted.
    (3)   In section 13 (admissibility of records as evidence), subsection (7) is omitted.
    (4)   In section 16 (documentary evidence as to specimens), subsection (6A) is omitted.
    (5)   In section 20 (speeding offences etc), subsection (8A) is omitted.

Criminal Justice Act 1991 (c. 53)

62   (1)   The Criminal Justice Act 1991 is amended as follows.
    (2)   Section 53 (notices of transfer in certain cases involving children) shall cease to have effect.
    (3)   Schedule 6 (notices of transfer: procedures in lieu of committal) shall cease to have effect.

Sexual Offences (Amendment) Act 1992 (c. 34)

63   In section 6 of the Sexual Offences (Amendment) Act 1992 (interpretation), in subsection (3)(c), for 'commits him' there is substituted 'sends him to the Crown Court'.

Criminal Justice and Public Order Act 1994 (c. 33)

64   (1)   The Criminal Justice and Public Order Act 1994 is amended as follows.
    (2)   In section 34 (effect of accused's failure to mention facts when questioned or charged), in subsection (2) –
        (a)   paragraph (a) is omitted, and
        (b)   in paragraph (b), for sub-paragraphs (i) and (ii), there is substituted 'paragraph 2 of Schedule 3 to the Crime and Disorder Act 1998'.
    (3)   In section 36 (effect of accused's failure or refusal to account for objects, substances or marks), in subsection (2) –
        (a)   paragraph (a) is omitted, and
        (b)   in paragraph (b), for sub-paragraphs (i) and (ii), there is substituted 'paragraph 2 of Schedule 3 to the Crime and Disorder Act 1998'.
    (4)   In section 37 (effect of accused's failure or refusal to account for presence at a particular place), in subsection (2) –
        (a)   paragraph (a) is omitted, and
        (b)   in paragraph (b), for sub-paragraphs (i) and (ii), there is substituted 'paragraph 2 of Schedule 3 to the Crime and Disorder Act 1998'.

Reserve Forces Act 1996 (c. 14)

65   In Schedule 2 to the Reserve Forces Act 1996 (deserters and absentees without leave), in paragraph 3, after sub-paragraph (2) there is inserted –
    '(2A)   The reference in sub-paragraph (2) to provisions of the Magistrates' Courts Act 1980 is to be taken to refer to those provisions as if no amendment to them had been made by the Criminal Justice Act 2003.'

Criminal Procedure and Investigations Act 1996 (c. 25)

66 (1) The Criminal Procedure and Investigations Act 1996 is amended as follows.

(2) In section 1 (application of this Part), in subsection (2) –

(a) paragraphs (a) to (c) are omitted, and

(b) in paragraph (cc), the words from 'under' to the end are omitted.

(3) In section 5 (compulsory disclosure by accused) –

(a) in subsection (1), for '(2) to' there is substituted '(3A) and',

(b) subsections (2) and (3) are omitted, and

(c) in subsection (3A), in paragraph (b), for 'subsection (7) of section 51' there is substituted 'subsection (1) of section 51D'.

(4) In section 13 (time limits: transitional), in subsection (1), paragraphs (a) to (c) of the modified section 3(8) are omitted.

(5) In section 21 (common law rules as to disclosure), in subsection (3), for paragraphs (b) and (c) there is substituted –

'(b) the accused is sent for trial (where this Part applies by virtue of section 1(2)(cc)),'.

(6) In section 28 (introduction to Part 3), in subsection (1) –

(a) for paragraph (a) there is substituted –

'(a) on or after the appointed day the accused is sent for trial for the offence concerned,', and

(b) paragraph (b) is omitted.

(7) In section 39 (meaning of pre-trial hearing), in subsection (1), for paragraph (a) there is substituted –

'(a) after the accused has been sent for trial for the offence, and'.

(8) Section 68 (use of written statements and depositions at trial) and Schedule 2 (statements and depositions) shall cease to have effect.

Sexual Offences (Protected Material) Act 1997 (c. 39)

67   In section 9 of the Sexual Offences (Protected Material) Act 1997 (modification and amendment of certain enactments), subsection (1) is omitted.

Crime and Disorder Act 1998 (c. 37)

68   The Crime and Disorder Act 1998 is amended as follows.

69   In section 52 (provisions supplementing section 51) –

(a) in subsection (1), after '51' there is inserted 'or 51A',

(b) in subsection (3), after '51' there is inserted 'or 51A',

(c) in subsection (5), after '51' there is inserted 'or 51A',

(d) in subsection (6), after '51' there is inserted 'or 51A', and

(e) in the heading, after '**51**' there is inserted '**and 51A**'.

70   In section 121 (short title, commencement and extent), in subsection (8), before 'paragraphs 7(1)' there is inserted 'paragraph 3 of Schedule 3 to this Act, section 52(6) above so far as relating to that paragraph,'.

71   In paragraph 3 of Schedule 3 (reporting restrictions) –

(a) in each of paragraphs (a) and (b) of sub-paragraph (1), for 'Great Britain' there is substituted 'the United Kingdom',

(b)   in sub-paragraph (8), after paragraph (b) there is inserted –

'(bb) where the application made by the accused under paragraph 2(1) above relates to a charge for an offence in respect of which notice has been given to the court under section 51B of this Act, any relevant business information;',

(c)   after sub-paragraph (9) there is inserted –

'(9A) The following is relevant business information for the purposes of sub-paragraph (8) above –

(a)   any address used by the accused for carrying on a business on his own account;

(b)   the name of any business which he was carrying on on his own account at any relevant time;

(c)   the name of any firm in which he was a partner at any relevant time or by which he was engaged at any such time;

(d)   the address of any such firm;

(e)   the name of any company of which he was a director at any relevant time or by which he was otherwise engaged at any such time;

(f)   the address of the registered or principal office of any such company;

(g)   any working address of the accused in his capacity as a person engaged by any such company;

and here "engaged" means engaged under a contract of service or a contract for services.', and

(d)   after sub-paragraph (11) there is inserted –

'(11A) Proceedings for an offence under this paragraph shall not, in Northern Ireland, be instituted otherwise than by or with the consent of the Attorney General for Northern Ireland.'

72   In paragraph 4 of Schedule 3 (power of justice to take depositions etc), in sub-paragraph (12), for the definition of 'the relevant date' there is substituted –

'"the relevant date" means the expiry of the period referred to in paragraph 1(1) above.'

Youth Justice and Criminal Evidence Act 1999 (c. 23)

73   (1)   The Youth Justice and Criminal Evidence Act 1999 is amended as follows.

(2)   In section 27 (video recorded evidence in chief), subsection (10) is omitted.

(3)   In section 42 (interpretation and application of section 41), in subsection (3) –

(a)   paragraphs (a) and (b) are omitted, and

(b)   in paragraph (c), after '51' there is inserted 'or 51A'.

Powers of Criminal Courts (Sentencing) Act 2000 (c. 6)

74   (1)   The Powers of Criminal Courts (Sentencing) Act 2000 is amended as follows.

(2)   In section 8 (power and duty to remit young offenders to youth courts for sentence), in subsection (2), for paragraph (a) there is substituted –

'(a)   if the offender was sent to the Crown Court for trial under section 51 or 51A of the Crime and Disorder Act 1998, to a youth court acting for the place where he was sent to the Crown Court for trial;'.

(3)   In section 89 (restriction on imposing imprisonment), in subsection (2) –

(a)   in paragraph (b), the words 'trial or' are omitted, and

(b)   in paragraph (c), after '51' there is inserted 'or 51A'.

(4) In section 140 (enforcement of fines etc), in subsection (1)(b) –

    (a)   the words 'was committed to the Crown Court to be tried or dealt with or by which he' are omitted, and

    (b)   after '51' there is inserted 'or 51A'.

(5) In section 148 (restitution orders), in subsection (6), for paragraph (b) there is substituted –

    '(b)   such documents as were served on the offender in pursuance of regulations made under paragraph 1 of Schedule 3 to the Crime and Disorder Act 1998.'

(6) In Schedule 11, paragraph 9 is omitted.

Proceeds of Crime Act 2002 (c. 29)

75 (1) The Proceeds of Crime Act 2002 is amended as follows.

    (2) In section 6 (making of confiscation order), in subsection (2)(b), for 'section 3, 4 or 6' there is substituted 'section 3, 3A, 3B, 3C, 4, 4A or 6'.

    (3) In section 27 (defendant absconds after being convicted or committed), in subsection (2)(b), for 'section 3, 4 or 6' there is substituted 'section 3, 3A, 3B, 3C, 4, 4A or 6'.

    (4) In section 70 (committal by magistrates' court), in subsection (5), after 'way)' there is inserted 'or under section 3B(2) of that Act (committal of child or young person)'.

SCHEDULE 4 QUALIFYING OFFENCES FOR PURPOSES OF SECTION 62

Section 62

PART 1

LIST OF OFFENCES

OFFENCES AGAINST THE PERSON

Murder

1 Murder.

Attempted murder

2 An offence under section 1 of the Criminal Attempts Act 1981 (c. 47) of attempting to commit murder.

Soliciting murder

3 An offence under section 4 of the Offences against the Person Act 1861 (c. 100).

Manslaughter

4 Manslaughter.

Wounding or causing grievous bodily harm with intent

5   An offence under section 18 of the Offences against the Person Act 1861 (c. 100).

Kidnapping

6   Kidnapping.

SEXUAL OFFENCES

Rape

7   An offence under section 1 of the Sexual Offences Act 1956 (c. 69) or section 1 of the Sexual Offences Act 2003 (c. 42).

Attempted rape

8   An offence under section 1 of the Criminal Attempts Act 1981 (c. 47) of attempting to commit an offence under section 1 of the Sexual Offences Act 1956 or section 1 of the Sexual Offences Act 2003.

Intercourse with a girl under thirteen

9   An offence under section 5 of the Sexual Offences Act 1956.

Incest by a man with a girl under thirteen

10   An offence under section 10 of the Sexual Offences Act 1956 alleged to have been committed with a girl under thirteen.

Assault by penetration

11   An offence under section 2 of the Sexual Offences Act 2003.

Causing a person to engage in sexual activity without consent

12   An offence under section 4 of the Sexual Offences Act 2003 where it is alleged that the activity caused involved penetration within subsection (4)(a) to (d) of that section.

Rape of a child under thirteen

13   An offence under section 5 of the Sexual Offences Act 2003.

Attempted rape of a child under thirteen

14   An offence under section 1 of the Criminal Attempts Act 1981 of attempting to commit an offence under section 5 of the Sexual Offences Act 2003.

Assault of a child under thirteen by penetration

15   An offence under section 6 of the Sexual Offences Act 2003.

Causing a child under thirteen to engage in sexual activity

16   An offence under section 8 of the Sexual Offences Act 2003 (c. 42) where it is alleged that an activity involving penetration within subsection (2)(a) to (d) of that section was caused.

Sexual activity with a person with a mental disorder impeding choice

17   An offence under section 30 of the Sexual Offences Act 2003 where it is alleged that the touching involved penetration within subsection (3)(a) to (d) of that section.

Causing or inciting a person with a mental disorder impeding choice to engage in sexual activity

18   An offence under section 31 of the Sexual Offences Act 2003 where it is alleged that an activity involving penetration within subsection (3)(a) to (d) of that section was caused.

DRUGS OFFENCES

Unlawful importation of a Class A drug

19   An offence under section 50(2) of the Customs and Excise Management Act 1979 (c. 2) alleged to have been committed in respect of a Class A drug (as defined by section 2 of the Misuse of Drugs Act 1971 (c. 38)).

Unlawful exportation of Class A drug

20   An offence under section 68(2) of the Customs and Excise Management Act 1979 alleged to have been committed in respect of a Class A drug (as defined by section 2 of the Misuse of Drugs Act 1971).

Fraudulent evasion in respect of Class A drug

21   An offence under section 170(1) or (2) of the Customs and Excise Management Act 1979 alleged to have been committed in respect of a Class A drug (as defined by section 2 of the Misuse of Drugs Act 1971).

Producing or being concerned in production of Class A drug

22   An offence under section 4(2) of the Misuse of Drugs Act 1971 alleged to have been committed in relation to a Class A drug (as defined by section 2 of that Act).

Supplying or offering to supply Class A drug

23 An offence under section 4(3) of the Misuse of Drugs Act 1971 alleged to have been committed in relation to a Class A drug (as defined by section 2 of that Act).

THEFT OFFENCES

Robbery

24 An offence under section 8(1) of the Theft Act 1968 (c. 60) where it is alleged that, at some time during the commission of the offence, the defendant had in his possession a firearm or imitation firearm (as defined by section 57 of the Firearms Act 1968 (c. 27)).

CRIMINAL DAMAGE OFFENCES

Arson endangering life

25 An offence under section 1(2) of the Criminal Damage Act 1971 (c.48) alleged to have been committed by destroying or damaging property by fire.

Causing explosion likely to endanger life or property

26 An offence under section 2 of the Explosive Substances Act 1883 (c. 3).

Intent or conspiracy to cause explosion likely to endanger life or property

27 An offence under section 3(1)(a) of the Explosive Substances Act 1883.

WAR CRIMES AND TERRORISM

Genocide, crimes against humanity and war crimes

28 An offence under section 51 or 52 of the International Criminal Court Act 2001 (c. 17).

Grave breaches of the Geneva Conventions

29 An offence under section 1 of the Geneva Conventions Act 1957 (c. 52).

Directing terrorist organisation

30 An offence under section 56 of the Terrorism Act 2000 (c. 11).

Hostage-taking

31 An offence under section 1 of the Taking of Hostages Act 1982 (c. 28).

HIJACKING AND OTHER OFFENCES RELATING TO AVIATION, MARITIME AND RAIL SECURITY

Hijacking of aircraft

32   An offence under section 1 of the Aviation Security Act 1982 (c. 36).

Destroying, damaging or endangering the safety of an aircraft

33   An offence under section 2 of the Aviation Security Act 1982.

Hijacking of ships

34   An offence under section 9 of the Aviation and Maritime Security Act 1990 (c. 31).

Seizing or exercising control of fixed platforms

35   An offence under section 10 of the Aviation and Maritime Security Act 1990.

Destroying ships or fixed platforms or endangering their safety

36   An offence under section 11 of the Aviation and Maritime Security Act 1990.

Hijacking of Channel Tunnel trains

37   An offence under article 4 of the Channel Tunnel (Security) Order 1994 (S.I.1994/570).

Seizing or exercising control of the Channel Tunnel system

38   An offence under article 5 of the Channel Tunnel (Security) Order 1994 (S.I.1994/570).

CONSPIRACY

Conspiracy

39   An offence under section 1 of the Criminal Law Act 1977 (c. 45) of conspiracy to commit an offence listed in this Part of this Schedule.

PART 2

SUPPLEMENTARY

40   A reference in Part 1 of this Schedule to an offence includes a reference to an offence of aiding, abetting, counselling or procuring the commission of the offence.

41   A reference in Part 1 of this Schedule to an enactment includes a reference to the enactment as enacted and as amended from time to time.

SCHEDULE 5   QUALIFYING OFFENCES FOR PURPOSES OF PART 10

Section 75

PART 1

LIST OF OFFENCES FOR ENGLAND AND WALES

OFFENCES AGAINST THE PERSON

Murder

1   Murder.

Attempted murder

2   An offence under section 1 of the Criminal Attempts Act 1981 (c. 47) of attempting to commit murder.

Soliciting murder

3   An offence under section 4 of the Offences against the Person Act 1861 (c. 100).

Manslaughter

4   Manslaughter.

Kidnapping

5   Kidnapping.

SEXUAL OFFENCES

Rape

6   An offence under section 1 of the Sexual Offences Act 1956 (c. 69) or section 1 of the Sexual Offences Act 2003 (c. 42).

Attempted rape

7   An offence under section 1 of the Criminal Attempts Act 1981 of attempting to commit an offence under section 1 of the Sexual Offences Act 1956 or section 1 of the Sexual Offences Act 2003.

Intercourse with a girl under thirteen

8   An offence under section 5 of the Sexual Offences Act 1956.

Incest by a man with a girl under thirteen

9   An offence under section 10 of the Sexual Offences Act 1956 alleged to have been committed with a girl under thirteen.

Assault by penetration

10   An offence under section 2 of the Sexual Offences Act 2003 (c. 42).

Causing a person to engage in sexual activity without consent

11   An offence under section 4 of the Sexual Offences Act 2003 where it is alleged that the activity caused involved penetration within subsection (4)(a) to (d) of that section.

Rape of a child under thirteen

12   An offence under section 5 of the Sexual Offences Act 2003.

Attempted rape of a child under thirteen

13   An offence under section 1 of the Criminal Attempts Act 1981 (c. 47) of attempting to commit an offence under section 5 of the Sexual Offences Act 2003.

Assault of a child under thirteen by penetration

14   An offence under section 6 of the Sexual Offences Act 2003.

Causing a child under thirteen to engage in sexual activity

15   An offence under section 8 of the Sexual Offences Act 2003 where it is alleged that an activity involving penetration within subsection (2)(a) to (d) of that section was caused.

Sexual activity with a person with a mental disorder impeding choice

16   An offence under section 30 of the Sexual Offences Act 2003 where it is alleged that the touching involved penetration within subsection (3)(a) to (d) of that section.

Causing a person with a mental disorder impeding choice to engage in sexual activity

17   An offence under section 31 of the Sexual Offences Act 2003 where it is alleged that an activity involving penetration within subsection (3)(a) to (d) of that section was caused.

DRUGS OFFENCES

Unlawful importation of Class A drug

18   An offence under section 50(2) of the Customs and Excise Management Act 1979 (c. 2) alleged to have been committed in respect of a Class A drug (as defined by section 2 of the Misuse of Drugs Act 1971 (c. 38)).

Unlawful exportation of Class A drug

19   An offence under section 68(2) of the Customs and Excise Management Act 1979 alleged to have been committed in respect of a Class A drug (as defined by section 2 of the Misuse of Drugs Act 1971).

Fraudulent evasion in respect of Class A drug

20   An offence under section 170(1) or (2) of the Customs and Excise Management Act 1979 (c. 2) alleged to have been committed in respect of a Class A drug (as defined by section 2 of the Misuse of Drugs Act 1971 (c. 38)).

Producing or being concerned in production of Class A drug

21   An offence under section 4(2) of the Misuse of Drugs Act 1971 alleged to have been committed in relation to a Class A drug (as defined by section 2 of that Act).

CRIMINAL DAMAGE OFFENCES

Arson endangering life

22   An offence under section 1(2) of the Criminal Damage Act 1971 (c.48) alleged to have been committed by destroying or damaging property by fire.

Causing explosion likely to endanger life or property

23   An offence under section 2 of the Explosive Substances Act 1883 (c. 3).

Intent or conspiracy to cause explosion likely to endanger life or property

24   An offence under section 3(1)(a) of the Explosive Substances Act 1883.

WAR CRIMES AND TERRORISM

Genocide, crimes against humanity and war crimes

25   An offence under section 51 or 52 of the International Criminal Court Act 2001 (c. 17).

Grave breaches of the Geneva Conventions

26 An offence under section 1 of the Geneva Conventions Act 1957 (c. 52).

Directing terrorist organisation

27 An offence under section 56 of the Terrorism Act 2000 (c. 11).

Hostage-taking

28 An offence under section 1 of the Taking of Hostages Act 1982 (c. 28).

CONSPIRACY

Conspiracy

29 An offence under section 1 of the Criminal Law Act 1977 (c. 45) of conspiracy to commit an offence listed in this Part of this Schedule.

PART 2

LIST OF OFFENCES FOR NORTHERN IRELAND

OFFENCES AGAINST THE PERSON

Murder

30 Murder.

Attempted murder

31 An offence under Article 3 of the Criminal Attempts and Conspiracy (Northern Ireland) Order 1983 of attempting to commit murder.

Soliciting murder

32 An offence under section 4 of the Offences against the Person Act 1861 (c. 100).

Manslaughter

33 Manslaughter.

Kidnapping

34 Kidnapping.

SEXUAL OFFENCES

Rape

35   Rape.

Attempted rape

36   An offence under section 2 of the Attempted Rape, etc., Act (Northern Ireland) 1960.

Intercourse with a girl under fourteen

37   An offence under section 4 of the Criminal Law Amendment Act 1885 (c. 69) of unlawfully and carnally knowing a girl under fourteen.

Incest by a man with a girl under fourteen

38   An offence under section 1(1) of the Punishment of Incest Act 1908 (c. 45) alleged to have been committed with a girl under fourteen.

DRUGS OFFENCES

Unlawful importation of Class A drug

39   An offence under section 50(2) of the Customs and Excise Management Act 1979 (c. 2) alleged to have been committed in respect of a Class A drug (as defined by section 2 of the Misuse of Drugs Act 1971 (c. 38)).

Unlawful exportation of Class A drug

40   An offence under section 68(2) of the Customs and Excise Management Act 1979 alleged to have been committed in respect of a Class A drug (as defined by section 2 of the Misuse of Drugs Act 1971).

Fraudulent evasion in respect of Class A drug

41   An offence under section 170(1) or (2) of the Customs and Excise Management Act 1979 alleged to have been committed in respect of a Class A drug (as defined by section 2 of the Misuse of Drugs Act 1971).

Producing or being concerned in production of Class A drug

42   An offence under section 4(2) of the Misuse of Drugs Act 1971 alleged to have been committed in respect of a Class A drug (as defined by section 2 of that Act).

CRIMINAL DAMAGE OFFENCES

Arson endangering life

43   An offence under Article 3(2) of the Criminal Damage (Northern Ireland) Order 1977 alleged to have been committed by destroying or damaging property by fire.

Causing explosion likely to endanger life or property

44   An offence under section 2 of the Explosive Substances Act 1883 (c. 3).

Intent or conspiracy to cause explosion likely to endanger life or property

45   An offence under section 3(1)(a) of the Explosive Substances Act 1883.

WAR CRIMES AND TERRORISM

Genocide, crimes against humanity and war crimes

46   An offence under section 51 or 52 of the International Criminal Court Act 2001 (c. 17).

Grave breaches of the Geneva Conventions

47   An offence under section 1 of the Geneva Conventions Act 1957 (c. 52).

Directing terrorist organisation

48   An offence under section 56 of the Terrorism Act 2000 (c. 11).

Hostage-taking

49   An offence under section 1 of the Taking of Hostages Act 1982 (c. 28).

CONSPIRACY

Conspiracy

50   An offence under Article 9 of the Criminal Attempts and Conspiracy (Northern Ireland) Order 1983 of conspiracy to commit an offence listed in this Part of this Schedule.

PART 3

SUPPLEMENTARY

51   A reference in this Schedule to an offence includes a reference to an offence of aiding, abetting, counselling or procuring the commission of the offence.
52   A reference in this Schedule to an enactment includes a reference to the enactment as enacted and as amended from time to time.

SCHEDULE 6   EVIDENCE OF BAD CHARACTER: ARMED FORCES   Section 113

1   Sections 98 to 106, 109, 110 and 112, in so far as they are not applied in relation to proceedings before service courts by provision contained in or made under any other Act, have effect in relation to such proceedings (whether in the United Kingdom or elsewhere) as they have effect in relation to criminal proceedings.
2   Section 103, as it applies in relation to proceedings before service courts, has effect with the substitution in subsection (4)(a) of 'charge sheet' for 'written charge or indictment'.
3   (1)   Section 107 has effect in relation to proceedings before courts-martial (whether in the United Kingdom or elsewhere) with the following modifications.
     (2)   In subsection (1) –
          (a)   for 'judge and jury' substitute 'court-martial';
          (b)   for 'the court is satisfied' substitute 'the judge advocate is satisfied';
          (c)   for the words after paragraph (b) substitute 'the judge advocate must either direct the court to acquit the defendant of the offence or, if he considers that there ought to be a retrial, dissolve the court.'
     (3)   In subsection (2) –
          (a)   for 'jury' substitute 'court';
          (b)   for 'the court is satisfied' substitute 'the judge advocate is satisfied'.
     (4)   In subsection (3) –
          (a)   for paragraph (a) substitute –
               '(a) a court is required to determine under section 115B(2) of the Army Act 1955, section 115B(2) of the Air Force Act 1955 or section 62B(2) of the Naval Discipline Act 1957 whether a person charged with an offence did the act or made the omission charged,';
          (b)   for 'the court is satisfied' substitute 'the judge advocate is satisfied';
          (c)   for the words after paragraph (c) substitute 'the judge advocate must either direct the court to acquit the defendant of the offence or, if he considers that there ought to be a rehearing, dissolve the court.'
     (5)   For subsection (4) substitute –
               '(4)   This section does not prejudice any other power a judge advocate may have to direct a court to acquit a person of an offence or to dissolve a court.'
4   Section 110, as it applies in relation to proceedings before service courts, has effect with the substitution of the following for subsection (1) –
     '(1) Where the court makes a relevant ruling –
          (a)   it must state in open court (but, in the case of a ruling by a judge advocate in proceedings before a court-martial, in the absence of the other members of the court) its reasons for the ruling;

(b) if it is a Standing Civilian Court, it must cause the ruling and the reasons for it to be entered in the note of the court's proceedings.'

5 Section 111 has effect as if, in subsection (7), the definition of 'rules of court' included rules regulating the practice and procedure of service courts.

6 (1) In this Schedule, and in section 107 as applied by this Schedule, 'court-martial' means a court-martial constituted under the Army Act 1955 (3 & 4 Eliz. 2 c. 18), the Air Force Act 1955 (3 & 4 Eliz. 2 c. 19) or the Naval Discipline Act 1957 (c. 53).

(2) In this Schedule 'service court' means –

(a) a court-martial;

(b) a summary appeal court constituted under section 83ZA of the Army Act 1955, section 83ZA of the Air Force Act 1955 or section 52FF of the Naval Discipline Act 1957;

(c) the Courts-Martial Appeal Court;

(d) a Standing Civilian Court.

SCHEDULE 7 HEARSAY EVIDENCE: ARMED FORCES   Section 135

Application to proceedings before service courts

1 Sections 114 to 121, 123, 124, 126, 127 to 129 and 133 and 134, in so far as they are not applied in relation to proceedings before service courts by provision contained in or made under any other Act, have effect in relation to such proceedings (whether in the United Kingdom or elsewhere) as they have effect in relation to criminal proceedings.

2 (1) In their application to such proceedings those sections have effect with the following modifications.

(2) In section 116(2)(c) for 'United Kingdom' substitute 'country where the court is sitting'.

(3) In section 117 insert after subsection (7) –

'(8) In subsection (4) "criminal proceedings" includes summary proceedings under section 76B of the Army Act 1955, section 76B of the Air Force Act 1955 or section 52D of the Naval Discipline Act 1957; and the definition of "criminal proceedings" in section 134(1) has effect accordingly.'

(4) In section 123(4) for paragraph (a) substitute –

'(a) in the case of proceedings before a court-martial, proceedings held for the determination of the issue must take place before the judge advocate in the absence of the other members of the court;'.

(5) In section 127, for subsection (7) substitute –

'(7) The appropriate rules are those regulating the practice and procedure of service courts.'

(6) In section 132(10), at the end of the definition of 'rules of court' insert –

'(d) rules regulating the practice and procedure of service courts.'

(7) In section 134 insert after subsection (1) –

'(1A) In this Part "criminal investigation" includes any investigation which may lead –

(a) to proceedings before a court-martial or Standing Civilian Court, or

(b) to summary proceedings under section 76B of the Army Act 1955, section 76B of the Air Force Act 1955 or section 52D of the Naval Discipline Act 1957.'

3   (1) Section 122 has effect in relation to proceedings before courts-martial (whether in the United Kingdom or elsewhere) with the following modifications.

(2) In subsection (1) for 'judge and jury' substitute 'court-martial'.

(3) In subsection (2) –

(a) for 'jury when they retire to consider their' substitute 'court when it retires to consider its';

(b) for 'the court' in paragraph (a) substitute 'the judge advocate';

(c) for 'the jury' in paragraph (b) substitute 'the court'.

4   (1) Section 125 has effect in relation to proceedings before courts-martial (whether in the United Kingdom or elsewhere) with the following modifications.

(2) In subsection (1) –

(a) for 'judge and jury' substitute 'court-martial';

(b) for 'the court is satisfied' substitute 'the judge advocate is satisfied';

(c) for the words after paragraph (b) substitute 'the judge advocate must either direct the court to acquit the defendant of the offence or, if he considers that there ought to be a retrial, dissolve the court.'

(3) In subsection (2) –

(a) for 'jury' substitute 'court';

(b) for 'the court is satisfied' substitute 'the judge advocate is satisfied'.

(4) In subsection (3) –

(a) for paragraph (a) substitute –

'(a) a court is required to determine under section 115B(2) of the Army Act 1955, section 115B(2) of the Air Force Act 1955 or section 62B(2) of the Naval Discipline Act 1957 whether a person charged with an offence did the act or made the omission charged,';

(b) for 'the court is satisfied' substitute 'the judge advocate is satisfied';

(c) for the words after paragraph (b) substitute 'the judge advocate must either direct the court to acquit the defendant of the offence or, if he considers that there ought to be a rehearing, dissolve the court.'

(5) For subsection (4) substitute –

'(4) This section does not prejudice any other power a judge advocate may have to direct a court to acquit a person of an offence or to dissolve a court.'

Amendments

5   For paragraph 1 of Schedule 1 to the Courts-Martial (Appeals) Act 1968 (c. 20) (use at retrial under Naval Discipline Act 1957 of record of evidence given at original trial) substitute –

'1   Evidence given at the retrial of any person under section 1 of this Act shall be given orally if it was given orally at the original trial, unless –

(a) all the parties to the retrial agree otherwise;

(b) section 116 of the Criminal Justice Act 2003 applies (admissibility of hearsay evidence where a witness is unavailable); or

(c) the witness is unavailable to give evidence, otherwise than as mentioned in subsection (2) of that section, and section 114(1)(d) of that Act applies (admission of hearsay evidence under residual discretion).'

6   For paragraph 3 of that Schedule (use at retrial under Army Act 1955 of record of evidence given at original trial) substitute –

'3   Evidence given at the retrial of any person under section 19 of this Act shall be given orally if it was given orally at the original trial, unless –

   (a)   all the parties to the retrial agree otherwise;

   (b)   section 116 of the Criminal Justice Act 2003 applies (admissibility of hearsay evidence where a witness is unavailable); or

   (c)   the witness is unavailable to give evidence, otherwise than as mentioned in subsection (2) of that section, and section 114(1)(d) of that Act applies (admission of hearsay evidence under residual discretion).'

7   For paragraph 5 of that Schedule (use at retrial under Air Force Act 1955 of record of evidence given at original trial) substitute –

'5   Evidence given at the retrial of any person under section 19 of this Act shall be given orally if it was given orally at the original trial, unless –

   (a)   all the parties to the retrial agree otherwise;

   (b)   section 116 of the Criminal Justice Act 2003 applies (admissibility of hearsay evidence where a witness is unavailable); or

   (c)   the witness is unavailable to give evidence, otherwise than as mentioned in subsection (2) of that section, and section 114(1)(d) of that Act applies (admission of hearsay evidence under residual discretion).'

Interpretation

8   In this Schedule, and in any provision of this Part as applied by this Schedule –

   'court-martial' means a court-martial constituted under the Army Act 1955 (3 & 4 Eliz. 2 c. 18), the Air Force Act 1955 (3 & 4 Eliz. 2 c. 19) or the Naval Discipline Act 1957 (c. 53);

   'service court' means –

      (a) a court-martial;

      (b) a summary appeal court constituted under section 83ZA of the Army Act 1955, section 83ZA of the Air Force Act 1955 or section 52FF of the Naval Discipline Act 1957;

      (c) the Courts-Martial Appeal Court;

      (d) a Standing Civilian Court.

SCHEDULE 8   BREACH, REVOCATION OR AMENDMENT OF COMMUNITY ORDER   Section 179

PART 1

PRELIMINARY

Interpretation

1   In this Schedule –

   'the offender', in relation to a community order, means the person in respect of whom the order is made;

   'the petty sessions area concerned', in relation to a community order, means the petty sessions area for the time being specified in the order;

   'the responsible officer' has the meaning given by section 197.

2   In this Schedule –

   (a) references to a drug rehabilitation requirement of a community order being
        subject to review are references to that requirement being subject to review in
        accordance with section 210(1)(b);

   (b) references to the court responsible for a community order imposing a drug
        rehabilitation requirement which is subject to review are to be construed in
        accordance with section 210(2).

3   For the purposes of this Schedule –

   (a) a requirement falling within any paragraph of section 177(1) is of the same kind
        as any other requirement falling within that paragraph, and

   (b) an electronic monitoring requirement is a requirement of the same kind as any
        requirement falling within section 177(1) to which it relates.

Orders made on appeal

4   Where a community order has been made on appeal, it is to be taken for the purposes
     of this Schedule to have been made by the Crown Court.

PART 2

BREACH OF REQUIREMENT OF ORDER

Duty to give warning

5   (1) If the responsible officer is of the opinion that the offender has failed without
          reasonable excuse to comply with any of the requirements of a community order,
          the officer must give him a warning under this paragraph unless –

        (a) the offender has within the previous twelve months been given a warning
             under this paragraph in relation to a failure to comply with any of the
             requirements of the order, or

        (b) the officer causes an information to be laid before a justice of the peace in
             respect of the failure.

     (2) A warning under this paragraph must –

        (a) describe the circumstances of the failure,

        (b) state that the failure is unacceptable, and

        (c) inform the offender that, if within the next twelve months he again fails to
             comply with any requirement of the order, he will be liable to be brought
             before a court.

     (3) The responsible officer must, as soon as practicable after the warning has been
          given, record that fact.

     (4) In relation to any community order which was made by the Crown Court and
          does not include a direction that any failure to comply with the requirements
          of the order is to be dealt with by a magistrates' court, the reference in sub-
          paragraph (1)(b) to a justice of the peace is to be read as a reference to the
          Crown Court.

Breach of order after warning

6   (1)   If –
   (a)   the responsible officer has given a warning under paragraph 5 to the offender in respect of a community order, and
   (b)   at any time within the twelve months beginning with the date on which the warning was given, the responsible officer is of the opinion that the offender has since that date failed without reasonable excuse to comply with any of the requirements of the order,

the officer must cause an information to be laid before a justice of the peace in respect of the failure in question.

   (2)   In relation to any community order which was made by the Crown Court and does not include a direction that any failure to comply with the requirements of the order is to be dealt with by a magistrates' court, the reference in sub-paragraph (1) to a justice of the peace is to be read as a reference to the Crown Court.

Issue of summons or warrant by justice of the peace

7   (1)   This paragraph applies to –
   (a)   a community order made by a magistrates' court, or
   (b)   any community order which was made by the Crown Court and includes a direction that any failure to comply with the requirements of the order is to be dealt with by a magistrates' court.

   (2)   If at any time while a community order to which this paragraph applies is in force it appears on information to a justice of the peace acting for the petty sessions area concerned that the offender has failed to comply with any of the requirements of the order, the justice may –
   (a)   issue a summons requiring the offender to appear at the place and time specified in it, or
   (b)   if the information is in writing and on oath, issue a warrant for his arrest.

   (3)   Any summons or warrant issued under this paragraph must direct the offender to appear or be brought –
   (a)   in the case of a community order imposing a drug rehabilitation requirement which is subject to review, before the magistrates' court responsible for the order, or
   (b)   in any other case, before a magistrates' court acting for the petty sessions area concerned.

   (4)   Where a summons issued under sub-paragraph (2)(a) requires the offender to appear before a magistrates' court and the offender does not appear in answer to the summons, the magistrates' court may issue a warrant for the arrest of the offender.

Issue of summons or warrant by Crown Court

8   (1)   This paragraph applies to a community order made by the Crown Court which does not include a direction that any failure to comply with the requirements of the order is to be dealt with by a magistrates' court.

   (2)   If at any time while a community order to which this paragraph applies is in force it appears on information to the Crown Court that the offender has failed to comply with any of the requirements of the order, the Crown Court may –
   (a)   issue a summons requiring the offender to appear at the place and time specified in it, or

(b)   if the information is in writing and on oath, issue a warrant for his arrest.

(3)   Any summons or warrant issued under this paragraph must direct the offender to appear or be brought before the Crown Court.

(4)   Where a summons issued under sub-paragraph (2)(a) requires the offender to appear before the Crown Court and the offender does not appear in answer to the summons, the Crown Court may issue a warrant for the arrest of the offender.

Powers of magistrates' court

9   (1)   If it is proved to the satisfaction of a magistrates' court before which an offender appears or is brought under paragraph 7 that he has failed without reasonable excuse to comply with any of the requirements of the community order, the court must deal with him in respect of the failure in any one of the following ways –

(a)   by amending the terms of the community order so as to impose more onerous requirements which the court could include if it were then making the order;

(b)   where the community order was made by a magistrates' court, by dealing with him, for the offence in respect of which the order was made, in any way in which the court could deal with him if he had just been convicted by it of the offence;

(c)   where –

(i)   the community order was made by a magistrates' court,

(ii)   the offence in respect of which the order was made was not an offence punishable by imprisonment,

(iii)   the offender is aged 18 or over, and

(iv)   the offender has wilfully and persistently failed to comply with the requirements of the order,

by dealing with him, in respect of that offence, by imposing a sentence of imprisonment for a term not exceeding 51 weeks.

(2)   In dealing with an offender under sub-paragraph (1), a magistrates' court must take into account the extent to which the offender has complied with the requirements of the community order.

(3)   In dealing with an offender under sub-paragraph (1)(a), the court may extend the duration of particular requirements (subject to any limit imposed by Chapter 4 of Part 12 of this Act) but may not extend the period specified under section 177(5).

(4)   In dealing with an offender under sub-paragraph (1)(b), the court may, in the case of an offender who has wilfully and persistently failed to comply with the requirements of the community order, impose a custodial sentence (where the order was made in respect of an offence punishable with such a sentence) notwithstanding anything in section 152(2).

(5)   Where a magistrates' court deals with an offender under sub-paragraph (1)(b) or (c), it must revoke the community order if it is still in force.

(6)   Where a community order was made by the Crown Court and a magistrates' court would (apart from this sub-paragraph) be required to deal with the offender under sub-paragraph (1)(a), (b) or (c), it may instead commit him to custody or release him on bail until he can be brought or appear before the Crown Court.

(7)   A magistrates' court which deals with an offender's case under sub-paragraph (6) must send to the Crown Court –

(a) a certificate signed by a justice of the peace certifying that the offender has failed to comply with the requirements of the community order in the respect specified in the certificate, and

(b) such other particulars of the case as may be desirable;

and a certificate purporting to be so signed is admissible as evidence of the failure before the Crown Court.

(8) A person sentenced under sub-paragraph (1)(b) or (c) for an offence may appeal to the Crown Court against the sentence.

Powers of Crown Court

10 (1) Where under paragraph 8 or by virtue of paragraph 9(6) an offender appears or is brought before the Crown Court and it is proved to the satisfaction of that court that he has failed without reasonable excuse to comply with any of the requirements of the community order, the Crown Court must deal with him in respect of the failure in any one of the following ways –

(a) by amending the terms of the community order so as to impose more onerous requirements which the Crown Court could impose if it were then making the order;

(b) by dealing with him, for the offence in respect of which the order was made, in any way in which he could have been dealt with for that offence by the court which made the order if the order had not been made;

(c) where –

(i) the offence in respect of which the order was made was not an offence punishable by imprisonment,

(ii) the offender is aged 18 or over,

(iii) the offender has wilfully and persistently failed to comply with the requirements of the order,

by dealing with him, in respect of that offence, by imposing a sentence of imprisonment for a term not exceeding 51 weeks.

(2) In dealing with an offender under sub-paragraph (1), the Crown Court must take into account the extent to which the offender has complied with the requirements of the community order.

(3) In dealing with an offender under sub-paragraph (1)(a), the court may extend the duration of particular requirements (subject to any limit imposed by Chapter 4 of Part 12 of this Act) but may not extend the period specified under section 177(5).

(4) In dealing with an offender under sub-paragraph (1)(b), the Crown Court may, in the case of an offender who has wilfully and persistently failed to comply with the requirements of the community order, impose a custodial sentence (where the order was made in respect of an offence punishable with such a sentence) notwithstanding anything in section 152(2).

(5) Where the Crown Court deals with an offender under sub-paragraph (1)(b) or (c), it must revoke the community order if it is still in force.

(6) In proceedings before the Crown Court under this paragraph any question whether the offender has failed to comply with the requirements of the community order is to be determined by the court and not by the verdict of a jury.

Restriction of powers in paragraphs 9 and 10 where treatment required

11 (1) An offender who is required by any of the following requirements of a community order –

    (a) a mental health treatment requirement,

    (b) a drug rehabilitation requirement, or

    (c) an alcohol treatment requirement,

to submit to treatment for his mental condition, or his dependency on or propensity to misuse drugs or alcohol, is not to be treated for the purposes of paragraph 9 or 10 as having failed to comply with that requirement on the ground only that he had refused to undergo any surgical, electrical or other treatment if, in the opinion of the court, his refusal was reasonable having regard to all the circumstances.

    (2) A court may not under paragraph 9(1)(a) or 10(1)(a) amend a mental health treatment requirement, a drug rehabilitation requirement or an alcohol treatment requirement unless the offender expresses his willingness to comply with the requirement as amended.

Supplementary

12 Where a community order was made by a magistrates' court in the case of an offender under 18 years of age in respect of an offence triable only on indictment in the case of an adult, any powers exercisable under paragraph 9(1)(b) in respect of the offender after he attains the age of 18 are powers to do either or both of the following –

    (a) to impose a fine not exceeding £5,000 for the offence in respect of which the order was made;

    (b) to deal with the offender for that offence in any way in which a magistrates' court could deal with him if it had just convicted him of an offence punishable with imprisonment for a term not exceeding 51 weeks.

PART 3

REVOCATION OF ORDER

Revocation of order with or without re-sentencing: powers of magistrates' court

13 (1) This paragraph applies where a community order, other than an order made by the Crown Court and falling within paragraph 14(1)(a), is in force and on the application of the offender or the responsible officer it appears to the appropriate magistrates' court that, having regard to circumstances which have arisen since the order was made, it would be in the interests of justice –

    (a) for the order to be revoked, or

    (b) for the offender to be dealt with in some other way for the offence in respect of which the order was made.

    (2) The appropriate magistrates' court may –

    (a) revoke the order, or

    (b) both –

      (i) revoke the order, and

      (ii) deal with the offender, for the offence in respect of which the order was made, in any way in which it could deal with him if he had just been convicted by the court of the offence.

(3) The circumstances in which a community order may be revoked under sub-paragraph (2) include the offender's making good progress or his responding satisfactorily to supervision or treatment (as the case requires).

(4) In dealing with an offender under sub-paragraph (2)(b), a magistrates' court must take into account the extent to which the offender has complied with the requirements of the community order.

(5) A person sentenced under sub-paragraph (2)(b) for an offence may appeal to the Crown Court against the sentence.

(6) Where a magistrates' court proposes to exercise its powers under this paragraph otherwise than on the application of the offender, it must summon him to appear before the court and, if he does not appear in answer to the summons, may issue a warrant for his arrest.

(7) In this paragraph 'the appropriate magistrates' court' means –

    (a) in the case of an order imposing a drug rehabilitation requirement which is subject to review, the magistrates' court responsible for the order, and

    (b) in the case of any other community order, a magistrates' court acting for the petty sessions area concerned.

Revocation of order with or without re-sentencing: powers of Crown Court

14 (1) This paragraph applies where –

    (a) there is in force a community order made by the Crown Court which does not include a direction that any failure to comply with the requirements of the order is to be dealt with by a magistrates' court, and

    (b) the offender or the responsible officer applies to the Crown Court for the order to be revoked or for the offender to be dealt with in some other way for the offence in respect of which the order was made.

(2) If it appears to the Crown Court to be in the interests of justice to do so, having regard to circumstances which have arisen since the order was made, the Crown Court may –

    (a) revoke the order, or

    (b) both –

      (i) revoke the order, and

      (ii) deal with the offender, for the offence in respect of which the order was made, in any way in which he could have been dealt with for that offence by the court which made the order if the order had not been made.

(3) The circumstances in which a community order may be revoked under sub-paragraph (2) include the offender's making good progress or his responding satisfactorily to supervision or treatment (as the case requires).

(4) In dealing with an offender under sub-paragraph (2)(b), the Crown Court must take into account the extent to which the offender has complied with the requirements of the order.

(5) Where the Crown Court proposes to exercise its powers under this paragraph otherwise than on the application of the offender, it must summon him to appear before the court and, if he does not appear in answer to the summons, may issue a warrant for his arrest.

Supplementary

15   Paragraph 12 applies for the purposes of paragraphs 13 and 14 as it applies for the purposes of paragraph 9 above, but as if for the words 'paragraph 9(1)(b)' there were substituted 'paragraph 13(2)(b)(ii) or 14(2)(b)(ii)'.

PART 4

AMENDMENT OF ORDER

Amendment by reason of change of residence

16   (1)   This paragraph applies where, at any time while a community order is in force in respect of an offender, the appropriate court is satisfied that the offender proposes to change, or has changed, his residence from the petty sessions area concerned to another petty sessions area.

(2)   Subject to sub-paragraphs (3) and (4), the appropriate court may, and on the application of the responsible officer must, amend the community order by substituting the other petty sessions area for the area specified in the order.

(3)   The court may not under this paragraph amend a community order which contains requirements which, in the opinion of the court, cannot be complied with unless the offender continues to reside in the petty sessions area concerned unless, in accordance with paragraph 17, it either –

(a)   cancels those requirements, or

(b)   substitutes for those requirements other requirements which can be complied with if the offender ceases to reside in that area.

(4)   The court may not amend under this paragraph a community order imposing a programme requirement unless it appears to the court that the accredited programme specified in the requirement is available in the other petty sessions area.

(5)   In this paragraph 'the appropriate court' means –

(a)   in relation to any community order imposing a drug rehabilitation requirement which is subject to review, the court responsible for the order,

(b)   in relation to any community order which was made by the Crown Court and does not include any direction that any failure to comply with the requirements of the order is to be dealt with by a magistrates' court, the Crown Court, and

(c)   in relation to any other community order, a magistrates' court acting for the petty sessions area concerned.

Amendment of requirements of community order

17   (1)   The appropriate court may, on the application of the offender or the responsible officer, by order amend a community order –

(a)   by cancelling any of the requirements of the order, or

(b)   by replacing any of those requirements with a requirement of the same kind, which the court could include if it were then making the order.

(2)   The court may not under this paragraph amend a mental health treatment requirement, a drug rehabilitation requirement or an alcohol treatment requirement unless the offender expresses his willingness to comply with the requirement as amended.

(3) If the offender fails to express his willingness to comply with a mental health treatment requirement, drug rehabilitation requirement or alcohol treatment requirement as proposed to be amended by the court under this paragraph, the court may –

    (a)   revoke the community order, and

    (b)   deal with him, for the offence in respect of which the order was made, in any way in which he could have been dealt with for that offence by the court which made the order if the order had not been made.

(4) In dealing with the offender under sub-paragraph (3)(b), the court –

    (a)   must take into account the extent to which the offender has complied with the requirements of the order, and

    (b)   may impose a custodial sentence (where the order was made in respect of an offence punishable with such a sentence) notwithstanding anything in section 152(2).

(5) Paragraph 12 applies for the purposes of this paragraph as it applies for the purposes of paragraph 9, but as if for the words 'paragraph 9(1)(b)' there were substituted 'paragraph 17(3)(b)'.

(6) In this paragraph 'the appropriate court' has the same meaning as in paragraph 16.

Amendment of treatment requirements of community order on report of practitioner

18   (1) Where the medical practitioner or other person by whom or under whose direction an offender is, in pursuance of any requirement to which this sub-paragraph applies, being treated for his mental condition or his dependency on or propensity to misuse drugs or alcohol –

    (a)   is of the opinion mentioned in sub-paragraph (3), or

    (b)   is for any reason unwilling to continue to treat or direct the treatment of the offender,

he must make a report in writing to that effect to the responsible officer and that officer must apply under paragraph 17 to the appropriate court for the variation or cancellation of the requirement.

(2) The requirements to which sub-paragraph (1) applies are –

    (a)   a mental health treatment requirement,

    (b)   a drug rehabilitation requirement, and

    (c)   an alcohol treatment requirement.

(3) The opinion referred to in sub-paragraph (1) is –

    (a)   that the treatment of the offender should be continued beyond the period specified in that behalf in the order,

    (b)   that the offender needs different treatment,

    (c)   that the offender is not susceptible to treatment, or

    (d)   that the offender does not require further treatment.

(4) In this paragraph 'the appropriate court' has the same meaning as in paragraph 16.

Amendment in relation to review of drug rehabilitation requirement

19   Where the responsible officer is of the opinion that a community order imposing a drug rehabilitation requirement which is subject to review should be so amended as to provide for each subsequent periodic review (required by section 211) to be made

without a hearing instead of at a review hearing, or vice versa, he must apply under paragraph 17 to the court responsible for the order for the variation of the order.

Extension of unpaid work requirement

20 (1) Where –

    (a) a community order imposing an unpaid work requirement is in force in respect of any offender, and

    (b) on the application of the offender or the responsible officer, it appears to the appropriate court that it would be in the interests of justice to do so having regard to circumstances which have arisen since the order was made,

the court may, in relation to the order, extend the period of 12 months specified in section 200(2).

    (2) In this paragraph 'the appropriate court' has the same meaning as in paragraph 16.

PART 5

POWERS OF COURT IN RELATION TO ORDER FOLLOWING SUBSEQUENT CONVICTION

Powers of magistrates' court following subsequent conviction

21 (1) This paragraph applies where –

    (a) an offender in respect of whom a community order made by a magistrates' court is in force is convicted of an offence by a magistrates' court, and

    (b) it appears to the court that it would be in the interests of justice to exercise its powers under this paragraph, having regard to circumstances which have arisen since the community order was made.

    (2) The magistrates' court may –

    (a) revoke the order, or

    (b) both –

        (i) revoke the order, and

        (ii) deal with the offender, for the offence in respect of which the order was made, in any way in which he could have been dealt with for that offence by the court which made the order if the order had not been made.

    (3) In dealing with an offender under sub-paragraph (2)(b), a magistrates' court must take into account the extent to which the offender has complied with the requirements of the community order.

    (4) A person sentenced under sub-paragraph (2)(b) for an offence may appeal to the Crown Court against the sentence.

22 (1) Where an offender in respect of whom a community order made by the Crown Court is in force is convicted of an offence by a magistrates' court, the magistrates' court may commit the offender in custody or release him on bail until he can be brought before the Crown Court.

    (2) Where the magistrates' court deals with an offender's case under sub-paragraph (1), it must send to the Crown Court such particulars of the case as may be desirable.

Powers of Crown Court following subsequent conviction

23 (1) This paragraph applies where –

(a) an offender in respect of whom a community order is in force –

(i) is convicted of an offence by the Crown Court, or

(ii) is brought or appears before the Crown Court by virtue of paragraph 22 or having been committed by the magistrates' court to the Crown Court for sentence, and

(b) it appears to the Crown Court that it would be in the interests of justice to exercise its powers under this paragraph, having regard to circumstances which have arisen since the community order was made.

(2) The Crown Court may –

(a) revoke the order, or

(b) both –

(i) revoke the order, and

(ii) deal with the offender, for the offence in respect of which the order was made, in any way in which he could have been dealt with for that offence by the court which made the order if the order had not been made.

(3) In dealing with an offender under sub-paragraph (2)(b), the Crown Court must take into account the extent to which the offender has complied with the requirements of the community order.

PART 6

SUPPLEMENTARY

24 (1) No order may be made under paragraph 16, and no application may be made under paragraph 13, 17 or 20, while an appeal against the community order is pending.

(2) Sub-paragraph (1) does not apply to an application under paragraph 17 which –

(a) relates to a mental health treatment requirement, a drug rehabilitation requirement or an alcohol treatment requirement, and

(b) is made by the responsible officer with the consent of the offender.

25 (1) Subject to sub-paragraph (2), where a court proposes to exercise its powers under Part 4 or 5 of this Schedule, otherwise than on the application of the offender, the court –

(a) must summon him to appear before the court, and

(b) if he does not appear in answer to the summons, may issue a warrant for his arrest.

(2) This paragraph does not apply to an order cancelling a requirement of a community order or reducing the period of any requirement, or substituting a new petty sessions area or a new place for the one specified in the order.

26 Paragraphs 9(1)(a), 10(1)(a) and 17(1)(b) have effect subject to the provisions mentioned in subsection (2) of section 177, and to subsections (3) and (6) of that section.

27 (1) On the making under this Schedule of an order revoking or amending a community order, the proper officer of the court must –

(a) provide copies of the revoking or amending order to the offender and the responsible officer,

(b)   in the case of an amending order which substitutes a new petty sessions area, provide a copy of the amending order to –

(i)   the local probation board acting for that area, and
(ii)   the magistrates' court acting for that area, and

(c)   in the case of an amending order which imposes or amends a requirement specified in the first column of Schedule 14, provide a copy of so much of the amending order as relates to that requirement to the person specified in relation to that requirement in the second column of that Schedule.

(2)   Where under sub-paragraph (1)(b) the proper officer of the court provides a copy of an amending order to a magistrates' court acting for a different area, the officer must also provide to that court such documents and information relating to the case as it considers likely to be of assistance to a court acting for that area in the exercise of its functions in relation to the order.

(3)   In this paragraph 'proper officer' means –

(a)   in relation to a magistrates' court, the justices' chief executive for the court; and

(b)   in relation to the Crown Court, the appropriate officer.

SCHEDULE 9   TRANSFER OF COMMUNITY ORDERS TO SCOTLAND OR NORTHERN IRELAND

Section 180

PART 1

SCOTLAND

1   (1)   Where the court considering the making of a community order is satisfied that the offender resides in Scotland, or will reside there when the order comes into force, the court may not make a community order in respect of the offender unless it appears to the court –

(a)   in the case of an order imposing a requirement mentioned in sub-paragraph (2), that arrangements exist for persons to comply with such a requirement in the locality in Scotland in which the offender resides, or will be residing when the order comes into force, and that provision can be made for him to comply with the requirement under those arrangements, and

(b)   in any case, that suitable arrangements for his supervision can be made by the council constituted under section 2 of the Local Government etc. (Scotland) Act 1994 (c. 39) in whose area he resides, or will be residing when the order comes into force.

(2)   The requirements referred to in sub-paragraph (1)(a) are –

(a)   an unpaid work requirement,
(b)   an activity requirement,
(c)   a programme requirement,
(d)   a mental health treatment requirement,
(e)   a drug rehabilitation requirement,
(f)   an alcohol treatment requirement, and
(g)   an electronic monitoring requirement.

(3) Where –

    (a) the appropriate court for the purposes of paragraph 16 of Schedule 8 (amendment by reason of change of residence) is satisfied that an offender in respect of whom a community order is in force proposes to reside or is residing in Scotland, and

    (b) it appears to the court that the conditions in sub-paragraph (1)(a) and (b) are satisfied,

the power of the court to amend the order under Part 4 of Schedule 8 includes power to amend it by requiring it to be complied with in Scotland and the offender to be supervised in accordance with the arrangements referred to in sub-paragraph (1)(b).

(4) For the purposes of sub-paragraph (3), any reference in sub-paragraph (1)(a) and (b) to the time when the order comes into force is to be treated as a reference to the time when the amendment comes into force.

(5) The court may not by virtue of sub-paragraph (1) or (3) require an attendance centre requirement to be complied with in Scotland.

(6) A community order made or amended in accordance with this paragraph must –

    (a) specify the locality in Scotland in which the offender resides or will be residing when the order or amendment comes into force;

    (b) specify as the corresponding order for the purposes of this Schedule an order that may be made by a court in Scotland;

    (c) specify as the appropriate court for the purposes of subsection (4) of section 228 of the Criminal Procedure (Scotland) Act 1995 (c. 46) a court of summary jurisdiction (which, in the case of an offender convicted on indictment, must be the sheriff court) having jurisdiction in the locality specified under paragraph (a);

and section 216 (petty sessions area to be specified) does not apply in relation to an order so made or amended.

2 (1) Where a court is considering the making or amendment of a community order by virtue of paragraph 1, Chapter 4 of Part 12 of this Act has effect subject to the following modifications.

(2) Any reference to the responsible officer has effect as a reference to the officer of a council constituted under section 2 of the Local Government etc. (Scotland) Act 1994 (c. 39) responsible for the offender's supervision or, as the case may be, discharging in relation to him the functions in respect of community service orders assigned by sections 239 to 245 of the Criminal Procedure (Scotland) Act 1995.

(3) The following provisions are omitted –

    (a) subsection (7) of section 201 (activity requirement),

    (b) subsection (7) of section 202 (programme requirement),

    (c) subsection (4) of section 206 (residence requirement), and

    (d) subsection (4) of section 218 (availability of arrangements in local area).

(4) In section 207 (mental health treatment requirement), for subsection (2)(a) there is substituted –

    '(a) treatment as a resident patient in a hospital within the meaning of the Mental Health (Care and Treatment) (Scotland) Act 2003, not being a State hospital within the meaning of that Act;'.

(5) In section 215 (electronic monitoring requirement), in subsection (3), the words from 'and' onwards are omitted.

PART 2

NORTHERN IRELAND

3   (1)   Where the court considering the making of a community order is satisfied that the offender resides in Northern Ireland, or will reside there when the order comes into force, the court may not make a community order in respect of the offender unless it appears to the court –

    (a)   in the case of an order imposing a requirement mentioned in sub-paragraph (2), that arrangements exist for persons to comply with such a requirement in the petty sessions district in Northern Ireland in which the offender resides, or will be residing when the order comes into force, and that provision can be made for him to comply with the requirement under those arrangements, and

    (b)   in any case, that suitable arrangements for his supervision can be made by the Probation Board for Northern Ireland.

  (2)   The requirements referred to in sub-paragraph (1) are –

    (a)   an unpaid work requirement,
    (b)   an activity requirement,
    (c)   a programme requirement,
    (d)   a mental health treatment requirement,
    (e)   a drug rehabilitation requirement,
    (f)   an alcohol treatment requirement,
    (g)   an attendance centre requirement, and
    (h)   an electronic monitoring requirement.

  (3)   Where –

    (a)   the appropriate court for the purposes of paragraph 16 of Schedule 8 (amendment by reason of change of residence) is satisfied that the offender to whom a community order relates proposes to reside or is residing in Northern Ireland, and

    (b)   it appears to the court that the conditions in sub-paragraphs (1)(a) and (b) are satisfied,

the power of the court to amend the order under Part 4 of Schedule 8 includes power to amend it by requiring it to be complied with in Northern Ireland and the offender to be supervised in accordance with the arrangements referred to in sub-paragraph (1)(b).

  (4)   For the purposes of sub-paragraph (3), any reference in sub-paragraph (1)(a) and (b) to the time when the order comes into force is to be treated as a reference to the time when the amendment comes into force.

  (5)   A community order made or amended in accordance with this paragraph must specify the petty sessions district in Northern Ireland in which the offender resides or will be residing when the order or amendment comes into force; and section 216 (petty sessions area to be specified) does not apply in relation to an order so made or amended.

  (6)   A community order made or amended in accordance with this paragraph must also specify as the corresponding order for the purposes of this Schedule an order that may be made by a court in Northern Ireland.

4   (1)   Where a court is considering the making or amendment of a community order by virtue of paragraph 3, Chapter 4 of Part 12 of this Act has effect subject to the following modifications.

  (2)   Any reference to the responsible officer has effect as a reference to the probation officer responsible for the offender's supervision or, as the case may be, discharging

in relation to the offender the functions conferred by Part 2 of the Criminal Justice (Northern Ireland) Order 1996 (S.I. 1996/3160 (N.I. 24)).

(3) The following provisions are omitted –

    (a)   subsection (7) of section 201 (activity requirement),

    (b)   subsection (7) of section 202 (programme requirement),

    (c)   subsection (4) of section 206 (residence requirement), and

    (d)   subsection (4) of section 218 (availability of arrangements in local area).

(4) In section 207 (mental health treatment requirement), for subsection (2)(a) there is substituted –

    '(a) treatment (whether as an in-patient or an out-patient) at such hospital as may be specified in the order, being a hospital within the meaning of the Health and Personal Social Services (Northern Ireland) Order 1972, approved by the Department of Health, Social Services and Public Safety for the purposes of paragraph 4(3) of Schedule 1 to the Criminal Justice (Northern Ireland) Order 1996 (S.I. 1996/3160 (N.I. 24));'.

(5) In section 214 (attendance centre requirement), any reference to an attendance centre has effect as a reference to a day centre, as defined by paragraph 3(6) of Schedule 1 to the Criminal Justice (Northern Ireland) Order 1996 (S.I. 1996/3160 (N.I. 24)).

(6) In section 215 (electronic monitoring requirement), in subsection (3), the words from 'and' onwards are omitted.

PART 3

GENERAL PROVISIONS

5   In this Part of this Schedule –

    'corresponding order' means the order specified under paragraph 1(6)(b) or 3(6);

    'home court' means –

    (a)   if the offender resides in Scotland, or will be residing there at the relevant time, the sheriff court having jurisdiction in the locality in which he resides or proposes to reside, and

    (b)   if he resides in Northern Ireland, or will be residing there at the relevant time, the court of summary jurisdiction acting for the petty sessions district in which he resides or proposes to reside;

    'the local authority officer concerned', in relation to an offender, means the officer of a council constituted under section 2 of the Local Government etc. (Scotland) Act 1994 (c. 39) responsible for his supervision or, as the case may be, discharging in relation to him the functions in respect of community service orders assigned by sections 239 to 245 of the Criminal Procedure (Scotland) Act 1995 (c. 46);

    'the probation officer concerned', in relation to an offender, means the probation officer responsible for his supervision or, as the case may be, discharging in relation to him the functions conferred by Part 2 of the Criminal Justice (Northern Ireland) Order 1996;

    'the relevant time' means the time when the order or the amendment to it comes into force.

6   Where a community order is made or amended in accordance with paragraph 1 or 3, the court which makes or amends the order must provide the home court with a copy of the order as made or amended, together with such other documents and informa-

tion relating to the case as it considers likely to be of assistance to that court; and paragraphs (b) to (d) of subsection (1) of section 219 (provision of copies of relevant orders) do not apply.

7   In section 220 (duty of offender to keep in touch with responsible officer) the reference to the responsible officer is to be read in accordance with paragraph 2(2) or 4(2).

8   Where a community order is made or amended in accordance with paragraph 1 or 3, then, subject to the following provisions of this Part of this Schedule –

    (a)   the order is to be treated as if it were a corresponding order made in the part of the United Kingdom in which the offender resides, or will be residing at the relevant time, and

    (b)   the legislation relating to such orders which has effect in that part of the United Kingdom applies accordingly.

9   Before making or amending a community order in those circumstances the court must explain to the offender in ordinary language –

    (a)   the requirements of the legislation relating to corresponding orders which has effect in the part of the United Kingdom in which he resides or will be residing at the relevant time,

    (b)   the powers of the home court under that legislation, as modified by this Part of this Schedule, and

    (c)   its own powers under this Part of this Schedule.

10   The home court may exercise in relation to the community order any power which it could exercise in relation to the corresponding order made by a court in the part of the United Kingdom in which the home court exercises jurisdiction, by virtue of the legislation relating to such orders which has effect in that part, except the following –

    (a)   any power to discharge or revoke the order (other than a power to revoke the order where the offender has been convicted of a further offence and the court has imposed a custodial sentence),

    (b)   any power to deal with the offender for the offence in respect of which the order was made,

    (c)   in the case of a community order imposing an unpaid work requirement, any power to vary the order by substituting for the number of hours of work specified in it any greater number than the court which made the order could have specified, and

    (d)   in the case of a community order imposing a curfew requirement, any power to vary the order by substituting for the period specified in it any longer period than the court which made the order could have specified.

11   If at any time while legislation relating to corresponding orders which has effect in Scotland or Northern Ireland applies by virtue of paragraph 7 to a community order made in England and Wales –

    (a)   it appears to the home court –

        (i)   if that court is in Scotland, on information from the local authority officer concerned, or

        (ii)   if that court is in Northern Ireland, upon a complaint being made to a justice of the peace acting for the petty sessions district for the time being specified in the order,

        that the offender has failed to comply with any of the requirements of the order, or

(b) it appears to the home court –

(i) if that court is in Scotland, on the application of the offender or of the local authority officer concerned, or

(ii) if it is in Northern Ireland, on the application of the offender or of the probation officer concerned,

that it would be in the interests of justice for a power conferred by paragraph 13 or 14 of Schedule 8 to be exercised,

the home court may require the offender to appear before the court which made the order or the court which last amended the order in England and Wales.

12 Where an offender is required by virtue of paragraph 11 to appear before a court in England and Wales that court –

(a) may issue a warrant for his arrest, and

(b) may exercise any power which it could exercise in respect of the community order if the offender resided in England and Wales,

and any enactment relating to the exercise of such powers has effect accordingly, and with any reference to the responsible officer being read as a reference to the local authority officer or probation officer concerned.

13 Paragraph 12(b) does not enable the court to amend the community order unless –

(a) where the offender resides in Scotland, it appears to the court that the conditions in paragraph 1(1)(a) and (b) are satisfied in relation to any requirement to be imposed, or

(b) where the offender resides in Northern Ireland, it appears to the court that the conditions in paragraph 3(1)(a) and (b) are satisfied in relation to any requirement to be imposed.

14 The preceding paragraphs of this Schedule have effect in relation to the amendment of a community order by virtue of paragraph 12(b) as they have effect in relation to the amendment of such an order by virtue of paragraph 1(3) or 3(3).

15 Where an offender is required by virtue of paragraph (a) of paragraph 11 to appear before a court in England and Wales –

(a) the home court must send to that court a certificate certifying that the offender has failed to comply with such of the requirements of the order as may be specified in the certificate, together with such other particulars of the case as may be desirable, and

(b) a certificate purporting to be signed by the clerk of the home court is admissible as evidence of the failure before the court which made the order.

SCHEDULE 10   REVOCATION OR AMENDMENT OF CUSTODY PLUS ORDERS AND AMENDMENT OF INTERMITTENT CUSTODY ORDERS

Section 187

Interpretation

1 (1) In this Schedule –

'the appropriate court' means –

(a) where the custody plus order or intermittent custody order was made by the Crown Court, the Crown Court, and

(b) in any other case, a magistrates' court acting for the petty sessions area concerned;

'the offender', in relation to a custody plus order or intermittent custody order, means the person in respect of whom the order is made;

'the petty sessions area concerned', in relation to a custody plus order or intermittent custody order, means the petty sessions area for the time being specified in the order;

'the responsible officer' has the meaning given by section 197.

(2) In this Schedule any reference to a requirement being imposed by, or included in, a custody plus order or intermittent custody order is to be read as a reference to compliance with the requirement being required by the order to be a condition of a licence.

Orders made on appeal

2   Where a custody plus order or intermittent custody order has been made on appeal, it is to be taken for the purposes of this Schedule to have been made by the Crown Court.

Revocation of custody plus order or removal from intermittent custody order of requirements as to licence conditions

3   (1) Where at any time while a custody plus order or intermittent custody order is in force, it appears to the appropriate court on the application of the offender or the responsible officer that, having regard to circumstances which have arisen since the order was made, it would be in the interests of justice to do so, the court may –

(a) in the case of a custody plus order, revoke the order, and

(b) in the case of an intermittent custody order, amend the order so that it contains only provision specifying periods for the purposes of section 183(1)(b)(i).

(2) The revocation under this paragraph of a custody plus order does not affect the sentence of imprisonment to which the order relates, except in relation to the conditions of the licence.

Amendment by reason of change of residence

4   (1) This paragraph applies where, at any time during the term of imprisonment to which a custody plus order or intermittent custody order relates, the appropriate court is satisfied that the offender proposes to change, or has changed, his residence during the licence period from the petty sessions area concerned to another petty sessions area.

(2) Subject to sub-paragraphs (3) and (4), the appropriate court may, and on the application of the Secretary of State or the responsible officer must, amend the custody plus order or intermittent custody order by substituting the other petty sessions area for the area specified in the order.

(3) The court may not amend under this paragraph a custody plus order or intermittent custody order which contains requirements which, in the opinion of the court, cannot be complied with unless the offender resides in the petty sessions area concerned unless, in accordance with paragraph 5, it either –

    (a)   cancels those requirements, or

    (b)   substitutes for those requirements other requirements which can be complied with if the offender does not reside in that area.

(4)   The court may not amend under this paragraph any custody plus order or intermittent custody order imposing a programme requirement unless it appears to the court that the accredited programme specified in the requirement is available in the other petty sessions area.

Amendment of requirements of custody plus order or intermittent custody order

5   (1)   At any time during the term of imprisonment to which a custody plus order or intermittent custody order relates, the appropriate court may, on the application of the offender, the Secretary of State or the responsible officer, by order amend any requirement of the custody plus order or intermittent custody order –

    (a)   by cancelling the requirement, or

    (b)   by replacing it with a requirement of the same kind imposing different obligations, which the court could include if it were then making the order.

(2)   For the purposes of sub-paragraph (1) –

    (a)   a requirement falling within any paragraph of section 182(1) is of the same kind as any other requirement falling within that paragraph, and

    (b)   an electronic monitoring requirement is a requirement of the same kind as any requirement falling within section 182(1) to which it relates.

(3)   Sub-paragraph (1)(b) has effect subject to the provisions mentioned in subsection (2) of section 182, and to subsections (3) and (5) of that section.

Alteration of pattern of temporary release

6   (1)   At any time during the term of imprisonment to which an intermittent custody order relates, the appropriate court may, on the application of the offender, the Secretary of State or the responsible officer, amend the order –

    (a)   so as to specify different periods for the purposes of section 183(1)(b)(i), or

    (b)   so as to provide that he is to remain in prison until the number of days served by him in prison is equal to the number of custodial days.

(2)   The appropriate court may not by virtue of sub-paragraph (1) amend an intermittent custody order unless it has received from the Secretary of State notification that suitable prison accommodation is available for the offender during the periods which, under the order as amended, will be custodial periods.

(3)   In this paragraph 'custodial period' has the same meaning as in section 184(3).

Supplementary

7   No application may be made under paragraph 3(1), 5(1) or 6(1) while an appeal against the sentence of which the custody plus or intermittent custody order forms part is pending.

8   (1)   Subject to sub-paragraph (2), where a court proposes to exercise its powers under paragraph 5 or 6, otherwise than on the application of the offender, the court –

(a) must summon him to appear before the court, and

(b) if he does not appear in answer to the summons, may issue a warrant for his arrest.

(2) This paragraph does not apply to an order cancelling any requirement of a custody plus or intermittent custody order.

9   (1) On the making under this Schedule of an order revoking or amending a custody plus order or amending an intermittent custody order, the proper officer of the court must –

(a) provide copies of the revoking or amending order to the offender and the responsible officer,

(b) in the case of an amending order which substitutes a new petty sessions area, provide a copy of the amending order to –

(i) the local probation board acting for that area, and

(ii) the magistrates' court acting for that area,

(c) in the case of an order which cancels or amends a requirement specified in the first column of Schedule 14, provide a copy of so much of the amending order as relates to that requirement to the person specified in relation to that requirement in the second column of that Schedule.

(2) Where under sub-paragraph (1)(b) the proper officer of the court provides a copy of an amending order to a magistrates' court acting for a different area, the officer must also provide to that court such documents and information relating to the case as it considers likely to be of assistance to a court acting for that area in the exercise of its functions in relation to the order.

SCHEDULE 11   TRANSFER OF CUSTODY PLUS ORDERS AND INTERMITTENT CUSTODY ORDERS TO SCOTLAND OR NORTHERN IRELAND

Section 188

PART 1

INTRODUCTORY

1   In this Schedule –

(a) 'the 1997 Act' means the Crime (Sentences) Act 1997 (c. 43), and

(b) any reference to a requirement being imposed by, or included in a custody plus order or intermittent custody order is a reference to compliance with the requirement being required by the order to be a condition of a licence.

PART 2

SCOTLAND

2   (1) Where the court making a custody plus order is satisfied that the offender resides in Scotland, or will reside there during the licence period, the court may, subject to sub-paragraph (2), impose requirements that are to be complied with in Scotland and require the offender's compliance with the order to be supervised

in accordance with arrangements made by the local authority in Scotland in whose area he resides or will reside.

(2) The court may not make an order by virtue of this paragraph unless it appears to the court –

(a) in the case of an order imposing a requirement mentioned in sub-paragraph (3), that arrangements exist for persons to comply with such a requirement in the locality in Scotland in which the offender resides, or will be residing during the licence period, and that provision can be made for him to comply with the requirement under those arrangements, and

(b) in any case, that suitable arrangements for supervising his compliance with the order can be made by the local authority in whose area he resides, or will be residing during the licence period.

(3) The requirements referred to in sub-paragraph (2)(a) are –

(a) an unpaid work requirement,

(b) an activity requirement,

(c) a programme requirement, and

(d) an electronic monitoring requirement.

(4) If an order has been made in accordance with this paragraph in relation to an offender but –

(a) the Secretary of State decides not to make an order under paragraph 1 or 4 of Schedule 1 to the 1997 Act in relation to him, and

(b) the offender has not applied under paragraph 22 of this Schedule for the amendment of the custody plus order or intermittent custody order,

the Secretary of State must apply to the court under paragraph 22 of this Schedule for the amendment of the order.

3   Where –

(a) the appropriate court for the purposes of paragraph 4 of Schedule 10 (amendment by reason of change of residence) is satisfied that the offender in respect of whom a custody plus order or intermittent custody order is in force is residing in Scotland, or proposes to reside there during the licence period,

(b) the Secretary of State has made, or has indicated his willingness to make, an order under paragraph 1 or 4 of Schedule 1 to the 1997 Act in relation to the offender, and

(c) it appears to the court that the conditions in paragraph 2(2)(a) and (b) are satisfied,

the power of the court to amend the order under Schedule 10 includes power to amend it by requiring the requirements included in the order to be complied with in Scotland and the offender's compliance with them to be supervised in accordance with the arrangements referred to in paragraph 2(2)(b).

4   A court may not by virtue of paragraph 2 or 3 require an attendance centre requirement to be complied with in Scotland.

5   A custody plus order made in accordance with paragraph 2 or a custody plus order or intermittent order amended in accordance with paragraph 3 must –

(a) specify the local authority area in which the offender resides or will reside during the licence period, and

(b) require the local authority for that area to appoint or assign an officer who will be responsible for discharging in relation to him the functions conferred on responsible officers by Part 12 of this Act;

and section 216 (petty sessions area to be specified) does not apply in relation to an order so made or amended.

6   (1) Where a court makes a custody plus order in accordance with paragraph 2 or
          amends a custody plus order or intermittent custody order in accordance with
          paragraph 3, the court must provide the relevant documents to –

     (a)   the local authority for the area specified in the order, and
     (b)   the sheriff court having jurisdiction in the locality in which the offender
           resides or proposes to reside;

     and paragraphs (b) to (d) of subsection (1) of section 219 (which relate to the
     provision of copies) do not apply in relation to an order so made or amended.

     (2) In this paragraph, 'the relevant documents' means –

     (a)   a copy of the order as made or amended, and
     (b)   such other documents and information relating to the case as the court
           making or amending the order considers likely to be of assistance.

7   (1) In relation to the making of a custody plus order by virtue of paragraph 2, in
          relation to the amendment of a custody plus order or intermittent custody
          order by virtue of paragraph 3, and (except for the purposes of paragraph 22)
          in relation to an order so made or amended, Chapter 4 of Part 12 of this Act
          has effect subject to the following modifications.

     (2) Any reference to the responsible officer has effect as a reference to the officer
          appointed or assigned under paragraph 5(b).

     (3) The following provisions are omitted –

     (a)   subsection (7) of section 201 (activity requirement);
     (b)   subsection (7) of section 202 (programme requirement);
     (c)   subsection (4) of section 218 (availability of arrangements in local area).

     (4) In section 215 (electronic monitoring requirement), in subsection (3), the words
          from 'and' onwards are omitted.

8   In this Part of this Schedule 'local authority' means a council constituted under sec-
     tion 2 of the Local Government etc. (Scotland) Act 1994 (c. 39); and any reference to
     the area of such an authority is a reference to the local government area within the
     meaning of that Act.

PART 3

NORTHERN IRELAND

9   (1) Where the court making a custody plus order is satisfied that the offender resides
          in Northern Ireland, or will reside there during the licence period, the court may,
          subject to sub-paragraph (2), impose requirements that are to be complied with
          in Northern Ireland and require the offender's compliance with the order to be
          supervised in accordance with arrangements made by the Probation Board for
          Northern Ireland.

     (2) The court may not make an order by virtue of this paragraph unless it appears to
          the court –

     (a)   in the case of an order imposing a requirement mentioned in sub-paragraph
           (3), that arrangements exist for persons to comply with such a requirement in
           the petty sessions district in Northern Ireland in which the offender resides,
           or will be residing during the licence period, and that provision can be made
           for him to comply with the requirement under those arrangements, and
     (b)   in any case, that suitable arrangements for supervising his compliance with
           the order can be made by the Probation Board for Northern Ireland.

(3) The requirements referred to in sub-paragraph (1)(a) are –
  (a) an unpaid work requirement,
  (b) an activity requirement,
  (c) a programme requirement,
  (d) an attendance centre requirement, and
  (e) an electronic monitoring requirement.

(4) If an order has been made in accordance with this paragraph in relation to an offender but –
  (a) the Secretary of State decides not to make an order under paragraph 1 or 4 of Schedule 1 to the 1997 Act in relation to him, and
  (b) the offender has not applied under paragraph 22 of this Schedule for the amendment of the custody plus order or intermittent custody order,

the Secretary of State must apply to the court under paragraph 22 for the amendment of the order.

10 Where –
  (a) the appropriate court for the purposes of paragraph 4 of Schedule 10 (amendment by reason of change of residence) is satisfied that the offender in respect of whom a custody plus order or intermittent custody order is in force is residing in Northern Ireland, or proposes to reside there during the licence period,
  (b) the Secretary of State has made, or has indicated his willingness to make, an order under paragraph 1 or 4 of Schedule 1 to the 1997 Act in relation to the offender, and
  (c) it appears to the court that the conditions in paragraph 9(2)(a) and (b) are satisfied,

the power of the court to amend the order under Schedule 10 includes power to amend it by requiring the requirements included in the order to be complied with in Northern Ireland and the offender's compliance with them to be supervised in accordance with the arrangements referred to in paragraph 9(2)(b).

11 A custody plus order made in accordance with paragraph 9 or a custody plus order or intermittent custody order amended in accordance with paragraph 10 must –
  (a) specify the petty sessions district in Northern Ireland in which the offender resides or will reside during the licence period, and
  (b) require the Probation Board for Northern Ireland to appoint or assign a probation officer who will be responsible for discharging in relation to him the functions conferred on responsible officers by Part 11 of this Act;

and section 216 (petty sessions area to be specified) does not apply in relation to an order so made or amended.

12 (1) Where a court makes a custody plus order in accordance with paragraph 9 or amends a custody plus order or intermittent custody order in accordance with paragraph 10, the court must provide the relevant documents to –
  (a) the Probation Board for Northern Ireland, and
  (b) the court of summary jurisdiction acting for the petty sessions district in which the offender resides or proposes to reside;

and paragraphs (b) to (d) of subsection (1) of section 219 (which relate to the provision of copies) do not apply in relation to an order so made or amended.

(2) In this paragraph, 'the relevant documents' means –

> (a)   a copy of the order as made or amended, and
>
> (b)   such other documents and information relating to the case as the court making or amending the order considers likely to be of assistance.

13   (1)   In relation to the making of a custody plus order by virtue of paragraph 9, in relation to the amendment of a custody plus order or intermittent custody order by virtue of paragraph 10, and (except for the purposes of paragraph 22) in relation to an order so made or amended, Chapter 4 of Part 12 of this Act has effect subject to the following modifications.

(2)   Any reference to the responsible officer has effect as a reference to the probation officer appointed or assigned under paragraph 11(b).

(3)   The following provisions are omitted –

> (a)   subsection (7) of section 201 (activity requirement);
>
> (b)   subsection (7) of section 202 (programme requirement);
>
> (c)   subsection (4) of section 218 (availability of arrangements in local area).

(4)   In section 214 (attendance centre requirement), any reference to an attendance centre has effect as a reference to a day centre, as defined by paragraph 3(6) of Schedule 1 to the Criminal Justice (Northern Ireland) Order 1996 (S.I. 1996/3160 (N.I. 24)).

(5)   In section 215 (electronic monitoring requirement), in subsection (3), the words from 'and' onwards are omitted.

PART 4

GENERAL PROVISIONS

14   This Part of this Schedule applies at any time while a custody plus order made in accordance with paragraph 2 or 9 or amended in accordance with paragraph 3 or 10, or an intermittent custody order amended in accordance with paragraph 3 or 10, is in force in respect of an offender.

15   In this Part of this Schedule –

'home court' means –

> (a)   if the offender resides in Scotland, or will be residing there during the licence period, the sheriff court having jurisdiction in the locality in which the offender resides or proposes to reside, and
>
> (b)   if he resides in Northern Ireland, or will be residing there during the licence period, the court of summary jurisdiction acting for the petty sessions district in which he resides or proposes to reside;

'local authority' and 'local authority area' are to be read in accordance with paragraph 8;

'original court' means the court in England and Wales which made or last amended the custody plus order or intermittent custody order;

'the relevant officer' means –

> (a)   where the order specifies a local authority area in Scotland, the local authority officer appointed or assigned under paragraph 5(b), and
>
> (b)   where the order specifies a local authority district in Northern Ireland, the probation officer appointed or assigned under paragraph 11(b).

16   (1)   Where this Part of this Schedule applies, Schedule 10 has effect subject to the following modifications.

(2)   Any reference to the responsible officer has effect as a reference to the relevant officer.

(3) Any reference to the appropriate court has effect as a reference to the original court.

(4) Where the order specifies a local authority area in Scotland –

    (a) any reference to the petty sessions area concerned has effect as a reference to that local authority area, and

    (b) any other reference to a petty sessions area has effect as a reference to a local authority area.

(5) Where the order specifies a petty sessions district in Northern Ireland –

    (a) any reference to the petty sessions area concerned has effect as a reference to that petty sessions district, and

    (b) any other reference to a petty sessions area has effect as a reference to a petty sessions district.

(6) Paragraph 9 is omitted.

17 (1) The home court may exercise any power under paragraph 4 or 5 of Schedule 10 (amendment of custody plus order or intermittent custody order) as if it were the original court.

(2) Subject to sub-paragraph (3), where the home court proposes to exercise the power conferred by paragraph 5 of Schedule 10, otherwise than on the application of the offender, the court –

    (a) if it is in Scotland –

        (i) must issue a citation requiring the offender to appear before it, and

        (ii) if he does not appear in answer to the citation, may issue a warrant for the offender's arrest;

    (b) if it is in Northern Ireland –

        (i) must issue a summons requiring the offender to appear before it, and

        (ii) if he does not appear in answer to the summons, may issue a warrant for the offender's arrest;

and paragraph 8 of Schedule 10 does not apply to the home court.

(3) Sub-paragraph (2) does not apply to any order cancelling any requirement of a custody plus order or intermittent custody order.

(4) Where the home court is considering amending a custody plus or intermittent custody order, any reference in Chapter 4 of Part 12 of this Act to a local probation board has effect as a reference to a local authority in Scotland or, as the case may be, the Probation Board for Northern Ireland.

18 Where by virtue of paragraph 17 any application is made to the home court under paragraph 4 or 5 of Schedule 10, the home court may (instead of dealing with the application) require the offender to appear before the original court.

19 No court may amend or further amend a custody plus order or an intermittent custody order unless it appears to the court that the conditions in paragraph 2(2)(a) and (b) or, as the case may be, the conditions in paragraph 9(2)(a) and (b) are satisfied in relation to any requirement to be imposed; but this paragraph does not apply to any amendment made by virtue of paragraph 22(1).

20 The preceding paragraphs of this Schedule have effect in relation to any amendment of a custody plus or intermittent custody order by any court as they have effect in relation to the amendment of such an order by virtue of paragraph 3 or 10.

21 On the making of an order amending a custody plus order or intermittent custody order –

    (a) the court must provide copies of the amending order to the offender and the relevant officer, and

    (b)   in the case of an amending order which substitutes a new local authority area or petty sessions district, paragraphs 5 and 6, or as the case may be paragraphs 11 and 12, have effect in relation to the order as they have effect in relation to an order made or amended in accordance with paragraph 2 or 3 or, as the case may be, 9 or 10.

22 (1) Where –

    (a)   a custody plus order has been made in accordance with paragraph 2 or 9, or a custody plus or intermittent custody order has been amended in accordance with paragraph 3 or 10, but (in any of those cases) the Secretary of State has not made an order under paragraph 1 or 4 of Schedule 1 to the 1997 Act in relation to the offender, or

    (b)   the Secretary of State has made, or indicated his willingness to make, an order under paragraph 7(1) of Schedule 1 to the 1997 Act transferring the offender or his supervision back to England and Wales,

the court may, on the application of the offender or the Secretary of State, amend the custody plus order or intermittent custody order by requiring it to be complied with in England and Wales.

(2) In sub-paragraph (1) 'the court', in a case falling within paragraph (a) of that sub-paragraph, means the original court.

(3) In a case where paragraph 2(4) or 9(4) requires the Secretary of State to apply under this paragraph, the court must make an amending order under this paragraph.

(4) Where under this paragraph the court amends a custody plus order or intermittent custody order which contains requirements which, in the opinion of the court, cannot be complied with in the petty sessions area in which the offender is residing or proposes to reside, the court must, in accordance with paragraph 5 of Schedule 10, either –

    (a)   cancel those requirements, or

    (b)   substitute for those requirements other requirements which can be complied with if the offender resides in that area.

(5) Where the court amends under this paragraph any custody plus order or intermittent custody order imposing a programme requirement, the court must ensure that the requirement as amended specifies a programme which is available in the petty sessions area in England and Wales in which the offender is residing or proposes to reside.

(6) The custody plus order or intermittent custody order as amended under this paragraph must specify the petty sessions area in which the offender resides or proposes to reside in the licence period.

(7) On the making under this paragraph of an order amending a custody plus order or intermittent custody order, the court must –

    (a)   provide copies of the amending order to the offender, the relevant officer and the local probation board acting for the new petty sessions area, and

    (b)   provide the magistrates' court acting for that area with a copy of the amending order and such other documents and information relating to the case as the home court considers likely to be of assistance to the court acting for that area in the exercise of its functions in relation to the order.

(8) Where an order has been amended under this paragraph, the preceding paragraphs of this Schedule shall cease to apply to the order as amended.

PART 5

SUPPLEMENTARY

23   Subsections (1) and (3) of section 245C of the Criminal Procedure (Scotland) Act
1995 (c. 46) (provision of remote monitoring) have effect as if they included a reference to the electronic monitoring of the requirements of a custody plus order made
in accordance with paragraph 2 or a custody plus order or intermittent custody order
made in accordance with paragraph 3.

24   (1)   Section 4 of the Summary Jurisdiction (Process) Act 1881 (c. 24) (which provides, among other things, for service in England and Wales of Scottish citations
or warrants) applies to any citation or warrant issued under paragraph 17(2)(a)
as it applies to a citation or warrant granted under section 134 of the Criminal
Procedure (Scotland) Act 1995.

   (2)   A summons issued by a court in Northern Ireland under paragraph 17(2)(b) may,
in such circumstances as may be prescribed by rules of court, be served in
England and Wales or Scotland.

SCHEDULE 12   BREACH OR AMENDMENT OF SUSPENDED SENTENCE ORDER, AND EFFECT OF FURTHER CONVICTION   Section 193

PART 1

PRELIMINARY

Interpretation

1   In this Schedule –

   'the offender', in relation to a suspended sentence order, means the person in
respect of whom the order is made;
   'the petty sessions area concerned', in relation to a suspended sentence order,
means the petty sessions area for the time being specified in the order;
   'the responsible officer' has the meaning given by section 197.

2   In this Schedule –

   (a)   any reference to a suspended sentence order being subject to review is a reference to such an order being subject to review in accordance with section
191(1)(b) or to a drug rehabilitation requirement of such an order being
subject to review in accordance with section 210(1)(b);

   (b)   any reference to the court responsible for a suspended sentence order
which is subject to review is to be construed in accordance with section
191(3) or, as the case may be, 210(2).

Orders made on appeal

3   Where a suspended sentence order is made on appeal it is to be taken for the purposes
of this Schedule to have been made by the Crown Court.

PART 2

BREACH OF COMMUNITY REQUIREMENT OR CONVICTION OF FURTHER OFFENCE

Duty to give warning in relation to community requirement

4   (1) If the responsible officer is of the opinion that the offender has failed without reasonable excuse to comply with any of the community requirements of a suspended sentence order, the officer must give him a warning under this paragraph unless –

   (a)   the offender has within the previous 12 months been given a warning under this paragraph in relation to a failure to comply with any of the community requirements of the order, or
   (b)   the officer causes an information to be laid before a justice of the peace in respect of the failure.

   (2) A warning under this paragraph must –

   (a)   describe the circumstances of the failure,
   (b)   state that the failure is unacceptable, and
   (c)   inform the offender that if within the next twelve months he again fails to comply with any requirement of the order, he will be liable to be brought before a court.

   (3) The responsible officer must, as soon as practicable after the warning has been given, record that fact.

   (4) In relation to any suspended sentence order which is made by the Crown Court and does not include a direction that any failure to comply with the community requirements of the order is to be dealt with by a magistrates' court, the reference in sub-paragraph (1)(b) to a justice of the peace is to be read as a reference to the Crown Court.

Breach of order after warning

5   (1) If –

   (a)   the responsible officer has given a warning under paragraph 4 to the offender in respect of a suspended sentence order, and
   (b)   at any time within the twelve months beginning with the date on which the warning was given, the responsible officer is of the opinion that the offender has since that date failed without reasonable excuse to comply with any of the community requirements of the order,

   the officer must cause an information to be laid before a justice of the peace in respect of the failure in question.

   (2) In relation to any suspended sentence order which is made by the Crown Court and does not include a direction that any failure to comply with the community requirements of the order is to be dealt with by a magistrates' court, the reference in sub-paragraph (1) to a justice of the peace is to be read as a reference to the Crown Court.

Issue of summons or warrant by justice of the peace

6   (1)   This paragraph applies to –

   (a)   a suspended sentence order made by a magistrates' court, or

   (b)   any suspended sentence order which was made by the Crown Court and includes a direction that any failure to comply with the community requirements of the order is to be dealt with by a magistrates' court.

   (2)   If at any time while a suspended sentence order to which this paragraph applies is in force it appears on information to a justice of the peace acting for the petty sessions area concerned that the offender has failed to comply with any of the community requirements of the order, the justice may –

   (a)   issue a summons requiring the offender to appear at the place and time specified in it, or

   (b)   if the information is in writing and on oath, issue a warrant for his arrest.

   (3)   Any summons or warrant issued under this paragraph must direct the offender to appear or be brought –

   (a)   in the case of a suspended sentence order which is subject to review, before the court responsible for the order,

   (b)   in any other case, before a magistrates' court acting for the petty sessions area concerned.

   (4)   Where a summons issued under sub-paragraph (2)(a) requires the offender to appear before a magistrates' court and the offender does not appear in answer to the summons, the magistrates' court may issue a warrant for the arrest of the offender.

Issue of summons or warrant by Crown Court

7   (1)   This paragraph applies to a suspended sentence order made by the Crown Court which does not include a direction that any failure to comply with the community requirements of the order is to be dealt with by a magistrates' court.

   (2)   If at any time while a suspended sentence order to which this paragraph applies is in force it appears on information to the Crown Court that the offender has failed to comply with any of the community requirements of the order, the Crown Court may –

   (a)   issue a summons requiring the offender to appear at the place and time specified in it, or

   (b)   if the information is in writing and on oath, issue a warrant for his arrest.

   (3)   Any summons or warrant issued under this paragraph must direct the offender to appear or be brought before the Crown Court.

   (4)   Where a summons issued under sub-paragraph (1)(a) requires the offender to appear before the Crown Court and the offender does not appear in answer to the summons, the Crown Court may issue a warrant for the arrest of the offender.

Powers of court on breach of community requirement or conviction of further offence

8   (1)   This paragraph applies where –

   (a)   it is proved to the satisfaction of a court before which an offender appears or is brought under paragraph 6 or 7 or by virtue of section 192(6) that he has failed without reasonable excuse to comply with any of the community requirements of the suspended sentence order, or

    (b)   an offender is convicted of an offence committed during the operational period of a suspended sentence (other than one which has already taken effect) and either –

        (i) he is so convicted by or before a court having power under paragraph 11 to deal with him in respect of the suspended sentence, or

        (ii) he subsequently appears or is brought before such a court.

(2)   The court must consider his case and deal with him in one of the following ways –

    (a)   the court may order that the suspended sentence is to take effect with its original term and custodial period unaltered,

    (b)   the court may order that the sentence is to take effect with either or both of the following modifications –

        (i) the substitution for the original term of a lesser term complying with section 181(2), and

        (ii) the substitution for the original custodial period of a lesser custodial period complying with section 181(5) and (6),

    (c)   the court may amend the order by doing any one or more of the following –

        (i) imposing more onerous community requirements which the court could include if it were then making the order,

        (ii) subject to subsections (3) and (4) of section 189, extending the supervision period, or

        (iii) subject to subsection (3) of that section, extending the operational period.

(3)   The court must make an order under sub-paragraph (2)(a) or (b) unless it is of the opinion that it would be unjust to do so in view of all the circumstances, including the matters mentioned in sub-paragraph (4); and where it is of that opinion the court must state its reasons.

(4)   The matters referred to in sub-paragraph (3) are –

    (a)   the extent to which the offender has complied with the community requirements of the suspended sentence order, and

    (b)   in a case falling within sub-paragraph (1)(b), the facts of the subsequent offence.

(5)   Where a court deals with an offender under sub-paragraph (2) in respect of a suspended sentence, the appropriate officer of the court must notify the appropriate officer of the court which passed the sentence of the method adopted.

(6)   Where a suspended sentence order was made by the Crown Court and a magistrates' court would (apart from this sub-paragraph) be required to deal with the offender under sub-paragraph (2)(a), (b) or (c) it may instead commit him to custody or release him on bail until he can be brought or appear before the Crown Court.

(7)   A magistrates' court which deals with an offender's case under sub-paragraph (6) must send to the Crown Court –

    (a)   a certificate signed by a justice of the peace certifying that the offender has failed to comply with the community requirements of the suspended sentence order in the respect specified in the certificate, and

    (b)   such other particulars of the case as may be desirable;

and a certificate purporting to be so signed is admissible as evidence of the failure before the Crown Court.

(8)   In proceedings before the Crown Court under this paragraph any question whether the offender has failed to comply with the community requirements of the suspended sentence order and any question whether the offender has been convicted of an offence committed during the operational period of the suspended sentence is to be determined by the court and not by the verdict of a jury.

Further provisions as to order that suspended sentence is to take effect

9   (1) When making an order under paragraph 8(2)(a) or (b) that a sentence is to take effect (with or without any variation of the original term and custodial period), the court –

    (a) must also make a custody plus order, and

    (b) may order that the sentence is to take effect immediately or that the term of that sentence is to commence on the expiry of another term of imprisonment passed on the offender by that or another court.

   (2) The power to make an order under sub-paragraph (1)(b) has effect subject to section 265 (restriction on consecutive sentences for released prisoners).

   (3) For the purpose of any enactment conferring rights of appeal in criminal cases, any order made by the court under paragraph 8(2)(a) or (b) is to be treated as a sentence passed on the offender by that court for the offence for which the suspended sentence was passed.

Restriction of powers in paragraph 8 where treatment required

10   (1) An offender who is required by any of the following community requirements of a suspended sentence order –

    (a) a mental health treatment requirement,

    (b) a drug rehabilitation requirement, or

    (c) an alcohol treatment requirement,

to submit to treatment for his mental condition, or his dependency on or propensity to misuse drugs or alcohol, is not to be treated for the purposes of paragraph 8(1)(a) as having failed to comply with that requirement on the ground only that he had refused to undergo any surgical, electrical or other treatment if, in the opinion of the court, his refusal was reasonable having regard to all the circumstances.

   (2) A court may not under paragraph 8(2)(c)(i) amend a mental health treatment requirement, a drug rehabilitation requirement or an alcohol treatment requirement unless the offender expresses his willingness to comply with the requirement as amended.

Court by which suspended sentence may be dealt with under paragraph 8(1)(b)

11   (1) An offender may be dealt with under paragraph 8(1)(b) in respect of a suspended sentence by the Crown Court or, where the sentence was passed by a magistrates' court, by any magistrates' court before which he appears or is brought.

   (2) Where an offender is convicted by a magistrates' court of any offence and the court is satisfied that the offence was committed during the operational period of a suspended sentence passed by the Crown Court –

    (a) the court may, if it thinks fit, commit him in custody or on bail to the Crown Court, and

    (b) if it does not, must give written notice of the conviction to the appropriate officer of the Crown Court.

Procedure where court convicting of further offence does not deal with suspended sentence

12   (1)   If it appears to the Crown Court, where that court has jurisdiction in accordance with sub-paragraph (2), or to a justice of the peace having jurisdiction in accordance with that sub-paragraph –

    (a)   that an offender has been convicted in the United Kingdom of an offence committed during the operational period of a suspended sentence, and

    (b)   that he has not been dealt with in respect of the suspended sentence, that court or justice may, subject to the following provisions of this paragraph, issue a summons requiring the offender to appear at the place and time specified in it, or a warrant for his arrest.

    (2)   Jurisdiction for the purposes of sub-paragraph (1) may be exercised –

        (a)   if the suspended sentence was passed by the Crown Court, by that court;

        (b)   if it was passed by a magistrates' court, by a justice acting for the petty sessions area for which that court acted.

    (3)   Where –

        (a)   an offender is convicted in Scotland or Northern Ireland of an offence, and

        (b)   the court is informed that the offence was committed during the operational period of a suspended sentence passed in England or Wales,

the court must give written notice of the conviction to the appropriate officer of the court by which the suspended sentence was passed.

    (4)   Unless he is acting in consequence of a notice under sub-paragraph (3), a justice of the peace may not issue a summons under this paragraph except on information and may not issue a warrant under this paragraph except on information in writing and on oath.

    (5)   A summons or warrant issued under this paragraph must direct the offender to appear or be brought before the court by which the suspended sentence was passed.

PART 3

AMENDMENT OF SUSPENDED SENTENCE ORDER

Cancellation of community requirements of suspended sentence order

13   (1)   Where at any time while a suspended sentence order is in force, it appears to the appropriate court on the application of the offender or the responsible officer that, having regard to the circumstances which have arisen since the order was made, it would be in the interests of justice to do so, the court may cancel the community requirements of the suspended sentence order.

    (2)   The circumstances in which the appropriate court may exercise its power under sub-paragraph (1) include the offender's making good progress or his responding satisfactorily to supervision.

    (3)   In this paragraph 'the appropriate court' means –

        (a)   in the case of a suspended sentence order which is subject to review, the court responsible for the order,

        (b)   in the case of a suspended sentence order which was made by the Crown Court and does not include any direction that any failure to comply with the community requirements of the order is to be dealt with by a magistrates' court, the Crown Court, and

(c)   in any other case, a magistrates' court acting for the petty sessions area concerned.

Amendment by reason of change of residence

14   (1)   This paragraph applies where, at any time while a suspended sentence order is in force, the appropriate court is satisfied that the offender proposes to change, or has changed, his residence from the petty sessions area concerned to another petty sessions area.

  (2)   Subject to sub-paragraphs (3) and (4), the appropriate court may, and on the application of the responsible officer must, amend the suspended sentence order by substituting the other petty sessions area for the area specified in the order.

  (3)   The court may not amend under this paragraph a suspended sentence order which contains requirements which, in the opinion of the court, cannot be complied with unless the offender resides in the petty sessions area concerned unless, in accordance with paragraph 15 it either –

    (a)   cancels those requirements, or
    (b)   substitutes for those requirements other requirements which can be complied with if the offender does not reside in that area.

  (4)   The court may not amend under this paragraph any suspended sentence order imposing a programme requirement unless it appears to the court that the accredited programme specified in the requirement is available in the other petty sessions area.

  (5)   In this paragraph 'the appropriate court' has the same meaning as in paragraph 13.

Amendment of community requirements of suspended sentence order

15   (1)   At any time during the supervision period, the appropriate court may, on the application of the offender or the responsible officer, by order amend any community requirement of a suspended sentence order –

    (a)   by cancelling the requirement, or
    (b)   by replacing it with a requirement of the same kind, which the court could include if it were then making the order.

  (2)   For the purposes of sub-paragraph (1) –

    (a)   a requirement falling within any paragraph of section 190(1) is of the same kind as any other requirement falling within that paragraph, and
    (b)   an electronic monitoring requirement is a requirement of the same kind as any requirement falling within section 190(1) to which it relates.

  (3)   The court may not under this paragraph amend a mental health treatment requirement, a drug rehabilitation requirement or an alcohol treatment requirement unless the offender expresses his willingness to comply with the requirement as amended.

  (4)   If the offender fails to express his willingness to comply with a mental health treatment requirement, drug rehabilitation requirement or alcohol treatment requirement as proposed to be amended by the court under this paragraph, the court may –

    (a)   revoke the suspended sentence order and the suspended sentence to which it relates, and
    (b)   deal with him, for the offence in respect of which the suspended sentence was imposed, in any way in which it could deal with him if he had just been convicted by or before the court of the offence.

(5) In dealing with the offender under sub-paragraph (4)(b), the court must take into account the extent to which the offender has complied with the requirements of the order.

(6) In this paragraph 'the appropriate court' has the same meaning as in paragraph 13.

Amendment of treatment requirements on report of practitioner

16 (1) Where the medical practitioner or other person by whom or under whose direction an offender is, in pursuance of any requirement to which this sub-paragraph applies, being treated for his mental condition or his dependency on or propensity to misuse drugs or alcohol –

(a) is of the opinion mentioned in sub-paragraph (3), or

(b) is for any reason unwilling to continue to treat or direct the treatment of the offender,

he must make a report in writing to that effect to the responsible officer and that officer must apply under paragraph 15 to the appropriate court for the variation or cancellation of the requirement.

(2) The requirements to which sub-paragraph (1) applies are –

(a) a mental health treatment requirement,

(b) a drug rehabilitation requirement, and

(c) an alcohol treatment requirement.

(3) The opinion referred to in sub-paragraph (1) is –

(a) that the treatment of the offender should be continued beyond the period specified in that behalf in the order,

(b) that the offender needs different treatment,

(c) that the offender is not susceptible to treatment, or

(d) that the offender does not require further treatment.

(4) In this paragraph 'the appropriate court' has the same meaning as in paragraph 13.

Amendment in relation to review of drug rehabilitation requirement

17 Where the responsible officer is of the opinion that a suspended sentence order imposing a drug rehabilitation requirement which is subject to review should be so amended as to provide for each periodic review (required by section 211) to be made without a hearing instead of at a review hearing, or vice versa, he must apply under paragraph 15 to the court responsible for the order for the variation of the order.

Extension of unpaid work requirement

18 (1) Where –

(a) a suspended sentence order imposing an unpaid work requirement is in force in respect of the offender, and

(b) on the application of the offender or the responsible officer, it appears to the appropriate court that it would be in the interests of justice to do so having regard to circumstances which have arisen since the order was made,

the court may, in relation to the order, extend the period of twelve months specified in section 200(2).

(2) In this paragraph 'the appropriate court' has the same meaning as in paragraph 13.

Supplementary

19 (1) No application may be made under paragraph 13, 15 or 18, and no order may be made under paragraph 14, while an appeal against the suspended sentence is pending.

     (2) Sub-paragraph (1) does not apply to an application under paragraph 15 which –

        (a) relates to a mental health treatment requirement, a drug rehabilitation requirement or an alcohol treatment requirement, and

        (b) is made by the responsible officer with the consent of the offender.

20 (1) Subject to sub-paragraph (2), where a court proposes to exercise its powers under paragraph 15, otherwise than on the application of the offender, the court –

        (a) must summon him to appear before the court, and

        (b) if he does not appear in answer to the summons, may issue a warrant for his arrest.

     (2) This paragraph does not apply to an order cancelling any community requirement of a suspended sentence order.

21 Paragraphs 8(2)(c) and 15(1)(b) have effect subject to the provisions mentioned in subsection (2) of section 190, and to subsections (3) and (5) of that section.

22 (1) On the making under this Schedule of an order amending a suspended sentence order, the proper officer of the court must –

        (a) provide copies of the amending order to the offender and the responsible officer,

        (b) in the case of an amending order which substitutes a new petty sessions area, provide a copy of the amending order to –

           (i) the local probation board acting for that area, and

           (ii) the magistrates' court acting for that area, and

        (c) in the case of an amending order which imposes or amends a requirement specified in the first column of Schedule 14, provide a copy of so much of the amending order as relates to that requirement to the person specified in relation to that requirement in the second column of that Schedule.

     (2) Where under sub-paragraph (1)(b) the proper officer of the court provides a copy of an amending order to a magistrates' court acting for a different area, the officer must also provide to that court such documents and information relating to the case as it considers likely to be of assistance to a court acting for that area in the exercise of its functions in relation to the order.

     (3) In this paragraph 'proper officer' means –

        (a) in relation to a magistrates' court, the justices' chief executive for the court; and

        (b) in relation to the Crown Court, the appropriate officer.

SCHEDULE 13   TRANSFER OF SUSPENDED SENTENCE ORDERS TO SCOTLAND OR NORTHERN IRELAND

Section 194

PART 1

SCOTLAND

1   (1) Where the court considering the making of a suspended sentence order is satisfied that the offender resides in Scotland, or will reside there when the order comes into force, the court may not make a suspended sentence order in respect of the offender unless it appears to the court –

   (a) in the case of an order imposing a requirement mentioned in sub-paragraph (2), that arrangements exist for persons to comply with such a requirement in the locality in Scotland in which the offender resides, or will be residing when the order comes into force, and that provision can be made for him to comply with the requirement under those arrangements, and

   (b) in any case, that suitable arrangements for his supervision can be made by the local authority in whose area he resides, or will be residing when the order comes into force.

   (2) The requirements referred to in sub-paragraph (1)(a) are –

   (a) an unpaid work requirement,
   (b) an activity requirement,
   (c) a programme requirement,
   (d) a mental health treatment requirement,
   (e) a drug rehabilitation requirement,
   (f) an alcohol treatment requirement, and
   (g) an electronic monitoring requirement.

   (3) Where –

   (a) the appropriate court for the purposes of paragraph 14 of Schedule 12 (amendment by reason of change of residence) is satisfied that an offender in respect of whom a suspended sentence order is in force proposes to reside or is residing in Scotland, and

   (b) it appears to the court that the conditions in sub-paragraph (1)(a) and (b) are satisfied,

   the power of the court to amend the order under Part 3 of Schedule 12 includes power to amend it by requiring it to be complied with in Scotland and the offender to be supervised in accordance with the arrangements referred to in sub-paragraph (1)(b).

   (4) For the purposes of sub-paragraph (3), any reference in sub-paragraph (1)(a) and (b) to the time when the order comes into force is to be treated as a reference to the time when the amendment comes into force.

   (5) The court may not by virtue of sub-paragraph (1) or (3) require an attendance centre requirement to be complied with in Scotland.

   (6) The court may not provide for an order made in accordance with this paragraph to be subject to review under section 191 or 210; and where an order which is subject to review under either of those sections is amended in accordance with this paragraph, the order shall cease to be so subject.

2   A suspended sentence order made or amended in accordance with paragraph 1 must –

    (a)   specify the local authority area in which the offender resides or will be residing when the order or amendment comes into force, and

    (b)   require the local authority for that area to appoint or assign an officer who will be responsible for discharging in relation to him the functions conferred on responsible officers by Part 12 of this Act;

and section 216 (petty sessions area to be specified) does not apply in relation to an order so made or amended.

3   (1) Where a court makes or amends a suspended sentence order in accordance with paragraph 1, the court must provide the relevant documents to –

    (a)   the local authority for the area specified in the order, and

    (b)   the sheriff court having jurisdiction in the locality in which the offender resides or proposes to reside;

and paragraphs (b) to (d) of subsection (1) of section 219 (provision of copies of relevant orders) do not apply in relation to an order so made or amended.

   (2) In this paragraph, 'the relevant documents' means –

    (a)   a copy of the order as made or amended, and

    (b)   such other documents and information relating to the case as the court making or amending the order considers likely to be of assistance.

4   (1) In relation to the making or amendment of a suspended sentence order in accordance with paragraph 1, and (except for the purposes of paragraph 20) in relation to an order so made or amended, Chapter 4 of Part 12 of this Act has effect subject to the following modifications.

   (2) Any reference to the responsible officer has effect as a reference to the officer appointed or assigned under paragraph 2(b).

   (3) The following provisions are omitted –

    (a)   subsection (7) of section 201 (activity requirement),

    (b)   subsection (7) of section 202 (programme requirement),

    (c)   subsection (4) of section 206 (residence requirement),

    (d)   subsection (4) of section 218 (availability of arrangements in local area).

   (4) In section 207 (mental health treatment requirement), for subsection (2)(a) there is substituted –

   '(a)   treatment as a resident patient in a hospital within the meaning of the Mental Health (Care and Treatment) (Scotland) Act 2003, not being a state hospital within the meaning of that Act;'.

   (5) In section 215 (electronic monitoring requirement), in subsection (3), the words from 'and' onwards are omitted.

5   In this Part of this Schedule 'local authority' means a council constituted under section 2 of the Local Government etc. (Scotland) Act 1994 (c. 39); and any reference to the area of such an authority is a reference to the local government area within the meaning of that Act.

PART 2

NORTHERN IRELAND

6   (1) Where the court considering the making of a suspended sentence order is satisfied that the offender resides in Northern Ireland, or will reside there when the order comes into force, the court may not make a suspended sentence order in respect of the offender unless it appears to the court –

(a)   in the case of an order imposing a requirement mentioned in sub-paragraph (2), that arrangements exist for persons to comply with such a requirement in the petty sessions district in Northern Ireland in which the offender resides, or will be residing when the order comes into force, and that provision can be made for him to comply with the requirement under those arrangements, and

(b)   in any case, that suitable arrangements for his supervision can be made by the Probation Board for Northern Ireland.

(2)   The requirements referred to in sub-paragraph (1)(a) are –

(a)   an unpaid work requirement,

(b)   an activity requirement,

(c)   a programme requirement,

(d)   a mental health treatment requirement,

(e)   a drug rehabilitation requirement,

(f)   an alcohol treatment requirement,

(g)   an attendance centre requirement, and

(h)   an electronic monitoring requirement.

(3)   Where –

(a)   the appropriate court for the purposes of paragraph 14 of Schedule 12 (amendment by reason of change of residence) is satisfied that an offender in respect of whom a suspended sentence order is in force proposes to reside or is residing in Northern Ireland, and

(b)   it appears to the court that the conditions in sub-paragraphs (1)(a) and (b) are satisfied,

the power of the court to amend the order under Part 3 of Schedule 12 includes power to amend it by requiring it to be complied with in Northern Ireland and the offender to be supervised in accordance with the arrangements referred to in sub-paragraph (1)(b).

(4)   For the purposes of sub-paragraph (3), any reference in sub-paragraph (1)(a) and (b) to the time when the order comes into force is to be treated as a reference to the time when the amendment comes into force.

(5)   The court may not provide for an order made in accordance with this paragraph to be subject to review under section 191 or 210; and where an order which is subject to review under either of those sections is amended in accordance with this paragraph, the order shall cease to be so subject.

7   A suspended sentence order made or amended in accordance with paragraph 6 must –

(a)   specify the petty sessions district in Northern Ireland in which the offender resides or will be residing when the order or amendment comes into force, and

(b)   require the Probation Board for Northern Ireland to appoint or assign a probation officer who will be responsible for discharging in relation to him the functions conferred on responsible officers by Part 12 of this Act;

and section 216 (petty sessions area to be specified) does not apply in relation to an order so made or amended.

8   (1)   Where a court makes or amends a suspended sentence order in accordance with paragraph 6, the court must provide the relevant documents to –

(a)   the Probation Board for Northern Ireland, and

(b)   the court of summary jurisdiction acting for the petty sessions district in which the offender resides or proposes to reside;

and paragraphs (b) to (d) of subsection (1) of section 219 (provision of copies of relevant orders) do not apply in relation to an order so made or amended.

(2) In this paragraph, 'the relevant documents' means –

    (a) a copy of the order as made or amended, and

    (b) such other documents and information relating to the case as the court making or amending the order considers likely to be of assistance.

9 (1) In relation to the making or amendment of a suspended sentence order in accordance with paragraph 6, and (except for the purposes of paragraph 20) in relation to an order so made or amended, Chapter 4 of Part 12 of this Act has effect subject to the following modifications.

(2) Any reference to the responsible officer has effect as a reference to the probation officer appointed or assigned under paragraph 7(b).

(3) The following provisions are omitted –

    (a) subsection (7) of section 201 (activity requirement),

    (b) subsection (7) of section 202 (programme requirement),

    (c) subsection (4) of section 206 (residence requirement),

    (d) subsection (4) of section 218 (availability of arrangements in local area).

(4) In section 207 (mental health treatment requirement), for subsection (2)(a) there is substituted –

    '(a) treatment (whether as an in-patient or an out-patient) at such hospital as may be specified in the order, being a hospital within the meaning of the Health and Personal Social Services (Northern Ireland) Order 1972, approved by the Department of Health, Social Services and Public Safety for the purposes of paragraph 4(3) of Schedule 1 to the Criminal Justice (Northern Ireland) Order 1996 (S.I. 1996/3160 (N.I. 24));'.

(5) In section 214 (attendance centre requirement), any reference to an attendance centre has effect as a reference to a day centre, as defined by paragraph 3(6) of Schedule 1 to the Criminal Justice (Northern Ireland) Order 1996 (S.I. 1996/3160 (N.I. 24)).

(6) In section 215 (electronic monitoring requirement), in subsection (3), the words from 'and' onwards are omitted.

PART 3

GENERAL PROVISIONS: BREACH OR AMENDMENT

10 This Part of this Schedule applies at any time while a suspended sentence order made or amended in accordance with paragraph 1 or 6 is in force in respect of an offender.

11 In this Part of this Schedule –

'home court' means –

    (a) if the offender resides in Scotland, or will be residing there at the relevant time, the sheriff court having jurisdiction in the locality in which the offender resides or proposes to reside, and

    (b) if he resides in Northern Ireland, or will be residing there at the relevant time, the court of summary jurisdiction acting for the petty sessions district in which he resides or proposes to reside;

'local authority' and 'local authority area' are to be read in accordance with paragraph 5;

'original court' means the court in England and Wales which made or last amended the order;

'the relevant officer' means –

(a) where the order specifies a local authority area in Scotland, the local authority officer appointed or assigned under paragraph 2(b), and

(b) where the court specifies a petty sessions district in Northern Ireland, the probation officer appointed or assigned under paragraph 7(b);

'the relevant time' means the time when the order or the amendment to it comes into force.

12 (1) Where this Part of this Schedule applies, Schedule 12 has effect subject to the following modifications.

(2) Any reference to the responsible officer has effect as a reference to the relevant officer.

(3) Any reference to a magistrates' court acting for the petty sessions area concerned has effect as a reference to a magistrates' court acting for the same petty sessions area as the original court; and any reference to a justice of the peace acting for the petty sessions area concerned has effect as a reference to a justice of the peace acting for the same petty sessions area as that court.

(4) Any reference to the appropriate court has effect as a reference to the original court.

(5) In paragraphs 4 and 5, any reference to causing an information to be laid before a justice of the peace has effect –

(a) if the home court is in Scotland, as a reference to providing information to the home court with a view to it issuing a citation, and

(b) if the home court is in Northern Ireland, as a reference to making a complaint to a justice of the peace in Northern Ireland.

(6) In paragraph 14 –

(a) if the home court is in Scotland –

(i) any reference to the petty sessions area concerned has effect as a reference to the local authority area specified in the order, and

(ii) any other reference to a petty sessions area has effect as a reference to a local authority area, and

(b) if the home court is in Northern Ireland –

(i) any reference to the petty sessions area concerned has effect as a reference to the petty sessions district specified in the order, and

(ii) any other reference to a petty sessions area has effect as a reference to a petty sessions district.

(7) Paragraph 22 is omitted.

(8) No court in England and Wales may –

(a) exercise any power in relation to any failure by the offender to comply with any community requirement of the order unless the offender has been required in accordance with paragraph 14(1)(b) or (2)(a) of this Schedule to appear before that court;

(b) exercise any power under Part 3 of Schedule 12 unless the offender has been required in accordance with paragraph 15(2) or 16 of this Schedule to appear before that court.

13 (1) Sub-paragraph (2) applies where it appears to the home court –

(a) if that court is in Scotland, on information from the relevant officer, or

(b) if that court is in Northern Ireland, upon a complaint being made by the relevant officer,

that the offender has failed without reasonable excuse to comply with any of the community requirements of the suspended sentence order.

   (2) The home court may –

      (a) if it is in Scotland –

         (i) issue a citation requiring the offender to appear before it at the time specified in the citation, or

         (ii) issue a warrant for the offender's arrest;

      (b) if it is in Northern Ireland –

         (i) issue a summons requiring the offender to appear before it at the time specified in the summons, or

         (ii) issue a warrant for the offender's arrest.

14 (1) The court before which an offender appears or is brought by virtue of paragraph 13 must –

      (a) determine whether the offender has failed without reasonable excuse to comply with any of the community requirements of the suspended sentence order, or

      (b) require the offender to appear before the original court.

   (2) If the home court determines that the offender has failed without reasonable excuse to comply with any of the community requirements of the order –

      (a) the home court must require the offender to appear before the original court, and

      (b) when the offender appears before the original court, paragraph 8 of Schedule 12 applies as if it had already been proved to the satisfaction of the original court that the offender failed without reasonable excuse to comply with such of the community requirements of the order as may have been determined.

   (3) An offender who is required by any of the following community requirements of a suspended sentence order –

      (a) a mental health treatment requirement,

      (b) a drug rehabilitation requirement, or

      (c) an alcohol treatment requirement,

   to submit to treatment for his mental condition, or his dependency on or propensity to misuse drugs or alcohol, is not to be treated for the purposes of sub-paragraph (2) as having failed to comply with that requirement on the ground only that he had refused to undergo any surgical, electrical or other treatment if, in the opinion of the court, his refusal was reasonable having regard to all the circumstances.

   (4) The evidence of one witness shall, for the purposes of sub-paragraph (2), be sufficient.

   (5) Where the home court is in Scotland and the order contains an electronic monitoring requirement, section 245H of the Criminal Procedure (Scotland) Act 1995 (c. 46) (documentary evidence) applies to proceedings under this paragraph as it applies to proceedings under section 245F of that Act (breach of restriction of liberty order).

   (6) Where an offender is required by virtue of sub-paragraph (2) to appear before the original court –

      (a) the home court must send to the original court a certificate certifying that the offender has failed without reasonable excuse to comply with the requirements of the order in the respect specified, and

      (b) such a certificate signed by the clerk of the home court is admissible before the original court as conclusive evidence of the matters specified in it.

15 (1) The home court may exercise any power under Part 3 of Schedule 12 (amendment of suspended sentence order) as if it were the original court, except that the

home court may not exercise the power conferred by paragraph 15(4) of that Schedule.

(2) Where paragraph 15(4) of Schedule 12 applies the home court must require the offender to appear before the original court.

(3) Subject to sub-paragraph (4), where the home court proposes to exercise the power conferred by paragraph 15(1) of Schedule 12, otherwise than on the application of the offender, the court –

   (a)   if it is in Scotland –

      (i) must issue a citation requiring the offender to appear before it, and
      (ii) if he does not appear in answer to the citation, may issue a warrant for the offender's arrest;

   (b)   if it is in Northern Ireland –

      (i) must issue a summons requiring the offender to appear before it, and
      (ii) if he does not appear in answer to the summons, may issue a warrant for the offender's arrest;

   and paragraph 20 of Schedule 12 does not apply to the home court.

(4) Sub-paragraph (3) does not apply to an order cancelling any community requirement of a suspended sentence order.

(5) Where the home court is considering amending a suspended sentence order, any reference in Chapter 4 of Part 12 of this Act to a local probation board has effect as a reference to a local authority in Scotland or, as the case may be, the Probation Board for Northern Ireland.

16   Where by virtue of paragraph 15 any application is made to the home court under Part 3 of Schedule 12, the home court may (instead of dealing with the application) require the offender to appear before the original court.

17   No court may amend or further amend a suspended sentence order unless it appears to the court that the conditions in paragraph 1(1)(a) and (b) or, as the case may be, paragraph 6(1)(a) and (b) are satisfied in relation to any requirement to be imposed; but this paragraph does not apply to any amendment by virtue of paragraph 20(2).

18   The preceding paragraphs of this Schedule have effect in relation to any amendment of a suspended order by any court as they have effect in relation to the amendment of such an order by virtue of paragraph 1(3) or 6(3).

19   On the making of an order amending a suspended sentence order –

   (a)   the court must provide copies of the amending order to the offender and the relevant officer, and

   (b)   in the case of an amending order which substitutes a new local authority area or petty sessions district, paragraphs 2 and 3 or, as the case may be, 7 and 8 have effect in relation to the order as they have effect in relation to an order made or amended in accordance with paragraph 1 or 6.

20   (1)   This paragraph applies where the home court is satisfied that the offender is residing or proposes to reside in England and Wales.

   (2)   Subject to sub-paragraphs (3) and (4), the home court may, and on the application of the relevant officer must, amend the suspended sentence order by requiring it to be complied with in England and Wales.

   (3)   The court may not amend under this paragraph a suspended sentence order which contains requirements which, in the opinion of the court, cannot be complied with in the petty sessions area in which the offender is residing or proposes to reside unless, in accordance with paragraph 15 of Schedule 12 it either –

   (a)   cancels those requirements, or

   (b)   substitutes for those requirements other requirements which can be complied with if the offender resides in that area.

(4) The court may not amend under this paragraph any suspended sentence order imposing a programme requirement unless it appears to the court that the accredited programme specified in the requirement is available in the petty sessions area in England and Wales in which the offender is residing or proposes to reside.

(5) The suspended sentence order as amended must specify the petty sessions area in which the offender resides or proposes to reside.

(6) On the making under this paragraph of an order amending a suspended sentence order, the home court must –

    (a) provide copies of the amending order to the offender, the relevant officer and the local probation board acting for the new petty sessions area, and

    (b) provide the magistrates' court acting for that area with a copy of the amending order and such other documents and information relating to the case as the home court considers likely to be of assistance to a court acting for that area in the exercise of its functions in relation to the order.

(7) Where an order has been amended under this paragraph, the preceding paragraphs of this Schedule shall cease to apply to the order as amended.

PART 4

SUPPLEMENTARY

21 Subsections (1) and (3) of section 245C of the Criminal Procedure (Scotland) Act 1995 (c. 46) (provision of remote monitoring) have effect as if they included a reference to the electronic monitoring of the community requirements of a suspended sentence order made or amended in accordance with paragraph 1 of this Schedule.

22 (1) Section 4 of the Summary Jurisdiction (Process) Act 1881 (c. 24) (which provides, among other things, for service in England and Wales of Scottish citations or warrants) applies to any citation or warrant issued under paragraph 13(2)(a) or 15(3)(a) as it applies to a citation or warrant granted under section 134 of the Criminal Procedure (Scotland) Act 1995.

    (2) A summons issued by a court in Northern Ireland under paragraph 13(2)(b) or 15(3)(b) may, in such circumstances as may be prescribed by rules of court, be served in England and Wales or Scotland.

SCHEDULE 14   PERSONS TO WHOM COPIES OF REQUIREMENTS TO BE PROVIDED IN PARTICULAR CASES

Section 219

Requirement	Person to whom copy of requirement is to be given
An activity requirement.	The person specified under section 201(1)(a).
An exclusion requirement imposed for the purpose (or partly for the purpose) of protecting a person from being approached by the offender.	The person intended to be protected.
A residence requirement relating to residence in an institution.	The person in charge of the institution.
A mental health treatment requirement.	The person specified under section 207(2)(c) or the person in charge of the institution or place specified under section 207(2)(a) or (b).
A drug rehabilitation requirement.	The person in charge of the institution or place specified under section 209(4)(a) or (b).
An alcohol treatment requirement.	The person specified under section 212(5)(c) or the person in charge of the institution or place specified under section 212(5)(a) or (b).
An attendance centre requirement.	The officer in charge of the attendance centre specified in the requirement.
An electronic monitoring requirement.	Any person who by virtue of section 215(3) will be responsible for the electronic monitoring. Any person by virtue of whose consent the requirement is included in the order.

SCHEDULE 15   SPECIFIED OFFENCES FOR PURPOSES OF CHAPTER 5 OF PART 12

Section 224

PART 1

SPECIFIED VIOLENT OFFENCES

1   Manslaughter.
2   Kidnapping.
3   False imprisonment.
4   An offence under section 4 of the Offences against the Person Act 1861 (c. 100) (soliciting murder).
5   An offence under section 16 of that Act (threats to kill).
6   An offence under section 18 of that Act (wounding with intent to cause grievous bodily harm).
7   An offence under section 20 of that Act (malicious wounding).
8   An offence under section 21 of that Act (attempting to choke, suffocate or strangle in order to commit or assist in committing an indictable offence).

9   An offence under section 22 of that Act (using chloroform etc. to commit or assist in the committing of any indictable offence).

10 An offence under section 23 of that Act (maliciously administering poison etc. so as to endanger life or inflict grievous bodily harm).

11 An offence under section 27 of that Act (abandoning children).

12 An offence under section 28 of that Act (causing bodily injury by explosives).

13 An offence under section 29 of that Act (using explosives etc. with intent to do grievous bodily harm).

14 An offence under section 30 of that Act (placing explosives with intent to do bodily injury).

15 An offence under section 31 of that Act (setting spring guns etc. with intent to do grievous bodily harm).

16 An offence under section 32 of that Act (endangering the safety of railway passengers).

17 An offence under section 35 of that Act (injuring persons by furious driving).

18 An offence under section 37 of that Act (assaulting officer preserving wreck).

19 An offence under section 38 of that Act (assault with intent to resist arrest).

20 An offence under section 47 of that Act (assault occasioning actual bodily harm).

21 An offence under section 2 of the Explosive Substances Act 1883 (c. 3) (causing explosion likely to endanger life or property).

22 An offence under section 3 of that Act (attempt to cause explosion, or making or keeping explosive with intent to endanger life or property).

23 An offence under section 1 of the Infant Life (Preservation) Act 1929 (c. 34) (child destruction).

24 An offence under section 1 of the Children and Young Persons Act 1933 (c. 12) (cruelty to children).

25 An offence under section 1 of the Infanticide Act 1938 (c. 36) (infanticide).

26 An offence under section 16 of the Firearms Act 1968 (c. 27) (possession of firearm with intent to endanger life).

27 An offence under section 16A of that Act (possession of firearm with intent to cause fear of violence).

28 An offence under section 17(1) of that Act (use of firearm to resist arrest).

29 An offence under section 17(2) of that Act (possession of firearm at time of committing or being arrested for offence specified in Schedule 1 to that Act).

30 An offence under section 18 of that Act (carrying a firearm with criminal intent).

31 An offence under section 8 of the Theft Act 1968 (c. 60) (robbery or assault with intent to rob).

32 An offence under section 9 of that Act of burglary with intent to –

    (a) inflict grievous bodily harm on a person, or
    (b) do unlawful damage to a building or anything in it.

33 An offence under section 10 of that Act (aggravated burglary).

34 An offence under section 12A of that Act (aggravated vehicle-taking) involving an accident which caused the death of any person.

35 An offence of arson under section 1 of the Criminal Damage Act 1971 (c. 48).

36 An offence under section 1(2) of that Act (destroying or damaging property) other than an offence of arson.

37 An offence under section 1 of the Taking of Hostages Act 1982 (c.28) (hostage-taking).

38 An offence under section 1 of the Aviation Security Act 1982 (c. 36) (hijacking).

39 An offence under section 2 of that Act (destroying, damaging or endangering safety of aircraft).

40 An offence under section 3 of that Act (other acts endangering or likely to endanger safety of aircraft).

41 An offence under section 4 of that Act (offences in relation to certain dangerous articles).

42   An offence under section 127 of the Mental Health Act 1983 (c. 20) (ill-treatment of patients).

43   An offence under section 1 of the Prohibition of Female Circumcision Act 1985 (c. 38) (prohibition of female circumcision).

44   An offence under section 1 of the Public Order Act 1986 (c. 64) (riot).

45   An offence under section 2 of that Act (violent disorder).

46   An offence under section 3 of that Act (affray).

47   An offence under section 134 of the Criminal Justice Act 1988 (c.33) (torture).

48   An offence under section 1 of the Road Traffic Act 1988 (c. 52) (causing death by dangerous driving).

49   An offence under section 3A of that Act (causing death by careless driving when under influence of drink or drugs).

50   An offence under section 1 of the Aviation and Maritime Security Act 1990 (c. 31) (endangering safety at aerodromes).

51   An offence under section 9 of that Act (hijacking of ships).

52   An offence under section 10 of that Act (seizing or exercising control of fixed platforms).

53   An offence under section 11 of that Act (destroying fixed platforms or endangering their safety).

54   An offence under section 12 of that Act (other acts endangering or likely to endanger safe navigation).

55   An offence under section 13 of that Act (offences involving threats).

56   An offence under Part II of the Channel Tunnel (Security) Order 1994 (S.I. 1994/570) (offences relating to Channel Tunnel trains and the tunnel system).

57   An offence under section 4 of the Protection from Harassment Act 1997 (c. 40) (putting people in fear of violence).

58   An offence under section 29 of the Crime and Disorder Act 1998 (c. 37) (racially or religiously aggravated assaults).

59   An offence falling within section 31(1)(a) or (b) of that Act (racially or religiously aggravated offences under section 4 or 4A of the Public Order Act 1986 (c. 64)).

60   An offence under section 51 or 52 of the International Criminal Court Act 2001 (c. 17) (genocide, crimes against humanity, war crimes and related offences), other than one involving murder.

61   An offence under section 1 of the Female Genital Mutilation Act 2003 (c. 31) (female genital mutilation).

62   An offence under section 2 of that Act (assisting a girl to mutilate her own genitalia).

63   An offence under section 3 of that Act (assisting a non-UK person to mutilate overseas a girl's genitalia).

64   An offence of –

   (a)   aiding, abetting, counselling, procuring or inciting the commission of an offence specified in this Part of this Schedule,
   (b)   conspiring to commit an offence so specified, or
   (c)   attempting to commit an offence so specified.

65   An attempt to commit murder or a conspiracy to commit murder.

PART 2

SPECIFIED SEXUAL OFFENCES

66 An offence under section 1 of the Sexual Offences Act 1956 (c. 69) (rape).
67 An offence under section 2 of that Act (procurement of woman by threats).
68 An offence under section 3 of that Act (procurement of woman by false pretences).
69 An offence under section 4 of that Act (administering drugs to obtain or facilitate intercourse).
70 An offence under section 5 of that Act (intercourse with girl under thirteen).
71 An offence under section 6 of that Act (intercourse with girl under 16).
72 An offence under section 7 of that Act (intercourse with a defective).
73 An offence under section 9 of that Act (procurement of a defective).
74 An offence under section 10 of that Act (incest by a man).
75 An offence under section 11 of that Act (incest by a woman).
76 An offence under section 14 of that Act (indecent assault on a woman).
77 An offence under section 15 of that Act (indecent assault on a man).
78 An offence under section 16 of that Act (assault with intent to commit buggery).
79 An offence under section 17 of that Act (abduction of woman by force or for the sake of her property).
80 An offence under section 19 of that Act (abduction of unmarried girl under eighteen from parent or guardian).
81 An offence under section 20 of that Act (abduction of unmarried girl under sixteen from parent or guardian).
82 An offence under section 21 of that Act (abduction of defective from parent or guardian).
83 An offence under section 22 of that Act (causing prositution of women).
84 An offence under section 23 of that Act (procuration of girl under twenty-one).
85 An offence under section 24 of that Act (detention of woman in brothel).
86 An offence under section 25 of that Act (permitting girl under thirteen to use premises for intercourse).
87 An offence under section 26 of that Act (permitting girl under sixteen to use premises for intercourse).
88 An offence under section 27 of that Act (permitting defective to use premises for intercourse).
89 An offence under section 28 of that Act (causing or encouraging the prostitution of, intercourse with or indecent assault on girl under sixteen).
90 An offence under section 29 of that Act (causing or encouraging prostitution of defective).
91 An offence under section 32 of that Act (soliciting by men).
92 An offence under section 33 of that Act (keeping a brothel).
93 An offence under section 128 of the Mental Health Act 1959 (c. 72) (sexual intercourse with patients).
94 An offence under section 1 of the Indecency with Children Act 1960 (c. 33) (indecent conduct towards young child).
95 An offence under section 4 of the Sexual Offences Act 1967 (c. 60) (procuring others to commit homosexual acts).
96 An offence under section 5 of that Act (living on earnings of male prostitution).
97 An offence under section 9 of the Theft Act 1968 (c. 60) of burglary with intent to commit rape.
98 An offence under section 54 of the Criminal Law Act 1977 (c. 45) (inciting girl under sixteen to have incestuous sexual intercourse).

99 An offence under section 1 of the Protection of Children Act 1978 (c. 37) (indecent photographs of children).

100 An offence under section 170 of the Customs and Excise Management Act 1979 (c. 2) (penalty for fraudulent evasion of duty etc.) in relation to goods prohibited to be imported under section 42 of the Customs Consolidation Act 1876 (c. 36) (indecent or obscene articles).

101 An offence under section 160 of the Criminal Justice Act 1988 (c. 33) (possession of indecent photograph of a child).

102 An offence under section 1 of the Sexual Offences Act 2003 (c. 42) (rape).

103 An offence under section 2 of that Act (assault by penetration).

104 An offence under section 3 of that Act (sexual assault).

105 An offence under section 4 of that Act (causing a person to engage in sexual activity without consent).

106 An offence under section 5 of that Act (rape of a child under 13).

107 An offence under section 6 of that Act (assault of a child under 13 by penetration).

108 An offence under section 7 of that Act (sexual assault of a child under 13).

109 An offence under section 8 of that Act (causing or inciting a child under 13 to engage in sexual activity).

110 An offence under section 9 of that Act (sexual activity with a child).

111 An offence under section 10 of that Act (causing or inciting a child to engage in sexual activity).

112 An offence under section 11 of that Act (engaging in sexual activity in the presence of a child).

113 An offence under section 12 of that Act (causing a child to watch a sexual act).

114 An offence under section 13 of that Act (child sex offences committed by children or young persons).

115 An offence under section 14 of that Act (arranging or facilitating commission of a child sex offence).

116 An offence under section 15 of that Act (meeting a child following sexual grooming etc.).

117 An offence under section 16 of that Act (abuse of position of trust: sexual activity with a child).

118 An offence under section 17 of that Act (abuse of position of trust: causing or inciting a child to engage in sexual activity).

119 An offence under section 18 of that Act (abuse of position of trust: sexual activity in the presence of a child).

120 An offence under section 19 of that Act (abuse of position of trust: causing a child to watch a sexual act).

121 An offence under section 25 of that Act (sexual activity with a child family member).

122 An offence under section 26 of that Act (inciting a child family member to engage in sexual activity).

123 An offence under section 30 of that Act (sexual activity with a person with a mental disorder impeding choice).

124 An offence under section 31 of that Act (causing or inciting a person with a mental disorder impeding choice to engage in sexual activity).

125 An offence under section 32 of that Act (engaging in sexual activity in the presence of a person with a mental disorder impeding choice).

126 An offence under section 33 of that Act (causing a person with a mental disorder impeding choice to watch a sexual act).

127 An offence under section 34 of that Act (inducement, threat or deception to procure sexual activity with a person with a mental disorder).

128 An offence under section 35 of that Act (causing a person with a mental disorder to engage in or agree to engage in sexual activity by inducement, threat or deception).

129 An offence under section 36 of that Act (engaging in sexual activity in the presence, procured by inducement, threat or deception, of a person with a mental disorder).

130 An offence under section 37 of that Act (causing a person with a mental disorder to watch a sexual act by inducement, threat or deception).

131 An offence under section 38 of that Act (care workers: sexual activity with a person with a mental disorder).

132 An offence under section 39 of that Act (care workers: causing or inciting sexual activity).

133 An offence under section 40 of that Act (care workers: sexual activity in the presence of a person with a mental disorder).

134 An offence under section 41 of that Act (care workers: causing a person with a mental disorder to watch a sexual act).

135 An offence under section 47 of that Act (paying for sexual services of a child).

136 An offence under section 48 of that Act (causing or inciting child prostitution or pornography).

137 An offence under section 49 of that Act (controlling a child prostitute or a child involved in pornography).

138 An offence under section 50 of that Act (arranging or facilitating child prostitution or pornography).

139 An offence under section 52 of that Act (causing or inciting prostitution for gain).

140 An offence under section 53 of that Act (controlling prostitution for gain).

141 An offence under section 57 of that Act (trafficking into the UK for sexual exploitation).

142 An offence under section 58 of that Act (trafficking within the UK for sexual exploitation).

143 An offence under section 59 of that Act (trafficking out of the UK for sexual exploitation).

144 An offence under section 61 of that Act (administering a substance with intent).

145 An offence under section 62 of that Act (committing an offence with intent to commit a sexual offence).

146 An offence under section 63 of that Act (trespass with intent to commit a sexual offence).

147 An offence under section 64 of that Act (sex with an adult relative: penetration).

148 An offence under section 65 of that Act (sex with an adult relative: consenting to penetration).

149 An offence under section 66 of that Act (exposure).

150 An offence under section 67 of that Act (voyeurism).

151 An offence under section 69 of that Act (intercourse with an animal).

152 An offence under section 70 of that Act (sexual penetration of a corpse).

153 An offence of –

(a) aiding, abetting, counselling, procuring or inciting the commission of an offence specified in this Part of this Schedule,

(b) conspiring to commit an offence so specified, or

(c) attempting to commit an offence so specified.

SCHEDULE 16   SCOTTISH OFFENCES SPECIFIED FOR THE PURPOSES OF SECTION 229(4)   Section 229

1 Rape.
2 Clandestine injury to women.
3 Abduction of woman or girl with intent to rape or ravish.
4 Assault with intent to rape or ravish.
5 Indecent assault.
6 Lewd, indecent or libidinous behaviour or practices.
7 Shameless indecency.
8 Sodomy.
9 An offence under section 170 of the Customs and Excise Management Act 1979 (c. 2) in relation to goods prohibited to be imported under section 42 of the Customs Consolidation Act 1876 (c. 36), but only where the prohibited goods include indecent photographs of persons.
10 An offence under section 52 of the Civic Government (Scotland) Act 1982 (c. 45) (taking and distribution of indecent images of children).
11 An offence under section 52A of that Act (possession of indecent images of children).
12 An offence under section 1 of the Criminal Law (Consolidation) (Scotland) Act 1995 (c. 39) (incest).
13 An offence under section 2 of that Act (intercourse with a stepchild).
14 An offence under section 3 of that Act (intercourse with child under 16 by person in position of trust).
15 An offence under section 5 of that Act (unlawful intercourse with girl under 16).
16 An offence under section 6 of that Act (indecent behaviour towards girl between 12 and 16).
17 An offence under section 8 of that Act (detention of woman in brothel or other premises).
18 An offence under section 10 of that Act (person having parental responsibilities causing or encouraging sexual activity in relation to a girl under 16).
19 An offence under subsection (5) of section 13 of that Act (homosexual offences).
20 An offence under section 3 of the Sexual Offences (Amendment) Act 2000 (c. 44) (abuse of position of trust).
21 An offence of –

   (a) attempting, conspiring or inciting another to commit any offence specified in the preceding paragraphs, or
   (b) aiding, abetting, counselling or procuring the commission of any offence specified in paragraphs 9 to 20.

22 Any offence (other than an offence specified in any of the preceding paragraphs) inferring personal violence.

SCHEDULE 17 NORTHERN IRELAND OFFENCES SPECIFIED FOR THE PURPOSES OF SECTION 229(4)

Section 229

PART 1

VIOLENT OFFENCES

1 Manslaughter.
2 Kidnapping.
3 Riot.
4 Affray.
5 False imprisonment.
6 An offence under section 4 of the Offences against the Person Act 1861 (c. 100) (soliciting murder).
7 An offence under section 16 of that Act (threats to kill).
8 An offence under section 18 of that Act (wounding with intent to cause grievous bodily harm).
9 An offence under section 20 of that Act (malicious wounding).
10 An offence under section 21 of that Act (attempting to choke, suffocate or strangle in order to commit or assist in committing an indictable offence).
11 An offence under section 22 of that Act (using chloroform etc. to commit or assist in the committing of any indictable offence).
12 An offence under section 23 of that Act (maliciously administering poison etc. so as to endanger life or inflict grievous bodily harm).
13 An offence under section 27 of that Act (abandoning children).
14 An offence under section 28 of that Act (causing bodily injury by explosives).
15 An offence under section 29 of that Act (using explosives etc. with intent to do grievous bodily harm).
16 An offence under section 30 of that Act (placing explosives with intent to do bodily injury).
17 An offence under section 31 of that Act (setting spring guns etc. with intent to do grievous bodily harm).
18 An offence under section 32 of that Act (endangering the safety of railway passengers).
19 An offence under section 35 of that Act (injuring persons by furious driving).
20 An offence under section 37 of that Act (assaulting officer preserving wreck).
21 An offence under section 47 of that Act of assault occasioning actual bodily harm.
22 An offence under section 2 of the Explosive Substances Act 1883 (c. 3) (causing explosion likely to endanger life or property).
23 An offence under section 3 of that Act (attempt to cause explosion, or making or keeping explosive with intent to endanger life of property).
24 An offence under section 25 of the Criminal Justice (Northern Ireland) Act 1945 (c. 15) (child destruction).
25 An offence under section 1 of the Infanticide Act (Northern Ireland) 1939 (c. 5) (infanticide).
26 An offence under section 7(1)(b) of the Criminal Justice (Miscellaneous Provisions) Act (Northern Ireland) 1968 (c. 28) (assault with intent to resist arrest).
27 An offence under section 20 of the Children and Young Persons Act (Northern Ireland) 1968 (c. 34) (cruelty to children).
28 An offence under section 8 of the Theft Act (Northern Ireland) 1969 (c. 16) (robbery or assault with intent to rob).

29   An offence under section 9 of that Act of burglary with intent to –

(a)   inflict grievous bodily harm on a person, or

(b)   do unlawful damage to a building or anything in it.

30   An offence under section 10 of that Act (aggravated burglary).

31   An offence of arson under Article 3 of the Criminal Damage (Northern Ireland) Order 1977 (S.I. 1977/426 (N.I. 4)).

32   An offence under Article 3(2) of that Order (destroying or damaging property) other than an offence of arson.

33   An offence under Article 17 of the Firearms (Northern Ireland) Order 1981 (S.I. 1981/155 (N.I. 2)) (possession of firearm with intent to endanger life).

34   An offence under Article 17A of that Order (possession of firearm with intent to cause fear of violence).

35   An offence under Article 18(1) of that Order (use of firearm to resist arrest).

36   An offence under Article 18(2) of that Order (possession of firearm at time of committing or being arrested for an offence specified in Schedule 1 to that Order).

37   An offence under Article 19 of that Order (carrying a firearm with criminal intent).

38   An offence under section 1 of the Taking of Hostages Act 1982 (c. 28) (hostage-taking).

39   An offence under section 1 of the Aviation Security Act 1982 (c. 36) (hijacking).

40   An offence under section 2 of that Act (destroying, damaging or endangering safety of aircraft).

41   An offence under section 3 of that Act (other acts endangering or likely to endanger safety of aircraft).

42   An offence under section 4 of that Act (offences in relation to certain dangerous articles).

43   An offence under section 1 of the Prohibition of Female Circumcision Act 1985 (c. 38) (prohibition of female circumcision).

44   An offence under Article 121 of the Mental Health (Northern Ireland) Order 1986 (S.I. 1986/595 (N.I. 4) (ill-treatment of patients).

45   An offence under section 134 of the Criminal Justice Act 1988 (c. 33) (torture).

46   An offence under section 1 of the Aviation and Maritime Security Act 1990 (c. 31) (endangering safety at aerodromes).

47   An offence under section 9 of that Act (hijacking of ships).

48   An offence under section 10 of that Act (seizing or exercising control of fixed platforms).

49   An offence under section 11 of that Act (destroying fixed platforms or endangering their safety).

50   An offence under section 12 of that Act (other acts endangering or likely to endanger safe navigation).

51   An offence under section 13 of that Act (offences involving threats).

52   An offence under Part II of the Channel Tunnel (Security) Order 1994 (S.I. 1994/570) (offences relating to Channel Tunnel trains and the tunnel system).

53   An offence under Article 9 of the Road Traffic (Northern Ireland) Order 1995 (S.I. 1995/2994 (N.I. 18)) (causing death or grievous bodily injury by dangerous driving).

54   An offence under Article 14 of that Order (causing death or grievous bodily injury by careless driving when under the influence of drink or drugs).

55   An offence under Article 6 of the Protection from Harassment (Northern Ireland) Order 1997 (S.I. 1997/1180 (N.I. 9)) (putting people in fear of violence).

56   An offence under section 66 of the Police (Northern Ireland) Act 1998 (c. 32) (assaulting or obstructing a constable etc.).

57   An offence under section 51 or 52 of the International Criminal Court Act 2001 (c. 17) (genocide, crimes against humanity, war crimes and related offences), other than one involving murder.

58 An offence under section 1 of the Female Genital Mutilation Act 2003 (c. 31) (female genital mutilation).

59 An offence under section 2 of that Act (assisting a girl to mutilate her own genitalia).

60 An offence under section 3 of that Act (assisting a non-UK person to mutilate overseas a girl's genitalia).

61 An offence of –

(a) aiding, abetting, counselling, procuring or inciting the commission of an offence specified in this Part of this Schedule,

(b) conspiring to commit an offence so specified, or

(c) attempting to commit an offence so specified.

62 An attempt to commit murder or a conspiracy to commit murder.

PART 2

SEXUAL OFFENCES

63 Rape.

64 Indecent assault upon a female.

65 An offence under section 52 of the Offences against the Person Act 1861 (c. 100) (indecent assault upon a female).

66 An offence under section 53 of that Act (abduction of woman etc.).

67 An offence under section 54 of that Act (abduction of woman by force).

68 An offence under section 55 of that Act (abduction of unmarried girl under 16 from parent or guardian).

69 An offence under section 2 of the Criminal Law Amendment Act 1885 (c. 69) (procuration).

70 An offence under section 3 of that Act (procurement of woman or girl by threats etc. or administering drugs).

71 An offence under section 4 of that Act (intercourse or attempted intercourse with girl under 14).

72 An offence under section 5 of that Act (intercourse or attempted intercourse with girl under 17).

73 An offence under section 6 of that Act (permitting girl under 17 to use premises for intercourse).

74 An offence under section 7 of that Act (abduction of girl under 18 from parent or guardian).

75 An offence under section 8 of that Act (unlawful detention of woman or girl in brothel etc.).

76 An offence under section 1 of the Vagrancy Act 1898 (c. 39) (living on earnings of prostitution or soliciting or importuning in a public place).

77 An offence under section 1 of the Punishment of Incest Act 1908 (c. 45) (incest by a man).

78 An offence under section 2 of that Act (incest by a woman).

79 An offence under section 21 of the Children and Young Persons Act (Northern Ireland) 1968 (c. 34) (causing or encouraging seduction or prostitution of girl under 17).

80 An offence under section 22 of that Act (indecent conduct towards child).

81 An offence under section 9 of the Theft Act (Northern Ireland) 1969 (c. 16) of burglary with intent to commit rape.

82 An offence under Article 3 of the Protection of Children (Northern Ireland) Order 1978 (S.I. 1978/1047 (N.I. 17)) (indecent photographs of children).

83 An offence under section 170 of the Customs and Excise Management Act 1979 (c. 2) (penalty for fraudulent evasion of duty etc.) in relation to goods prohibited to be imported under section 42 of the Customs Consolidation Act 1876 (c. 36) (indecent or obscene articles).

84 An offence under Article 9 of the Criminal Justice (Northern Ireland) Order 1980 (S.I. 1980/704 (N.I. 6)) (inciting girl under 16 to have incestuous sexual intercourse).

85 An offence under Article 7 of the Homosexual Offences (Northern Ireland) Order 1982 (S.I. 1982/1536 (N.I. 19)) (procuring others to commit homosexual acts).

86 An offence under Article 8 of that Order (living on earnings of male prostitution).

87 An offence under Article 122 of the Mental Health (Northern Ireland) Order 1986 (S.I. 1986/595 (N.I. 4)) (protection of women suffering from severe mental handicap).

88 An offence under Article 123 of that Order (protection of patients).

89 An offence under Article 15 of the Criminal Justice (Evidence, etc.) (Northern Ireland) Order 1988 (S.I. 1988/1847 (N.I. 17) (possession of indecent photograph of a child).

90 An offence under section 15 of the Sexual Offences Act 2003 (c. 42) (meeting a child following sexual grooming etc.).

91 An offence under section 16 of that Act (abuse of position of trust: sexual activity with a child).

92 An offence under section 17 of that Act (abuse of position of trust: causing or inciting a child to engage in sexual activity).

93 An offence under section 18 of that Act (abuse of position of trust: sexual activity in the presence of a child).

94 An offence under section 19 of that Act (abuse of position of trust: causing a child to watch a sexual act).

95 An offence under section 47 of that Act (paying for sexual services of a child).

96 An offence under section 48 of that Act (causing or inciting child prostitution or pornography).

97 An offence under section 49 of that Act (controlling a child prostitute or a child involved in pornography).

98 An offence under section 50 of that Act (arranging or facilitating child prostitution or pornography).

99 An offence under section 52 of that Act (causing or inciting prostitution for gain).

100 An offence under section 53 of that Act (controlling prostitution for gain).

101 An offence under section 57 of that Act (trafficking into the UK for sexual exploitation).

102 An offence under section 58 of that Act (trafficking within the UK for sexual exploitation).

103 An offence under section 59 of that Act (trafficking out of the UK for sexual exploitation).

104 An offence under section 66 of that Act (exposure).

105 An offence under section 67 of that Act (voyeurism).

106 An offence under section 69 of that Act (intercourse with an animal).

107 An offence under section 70 of that Act (sexual penetration of a corpse).

108 An offence under Article 20 of the Criminal Justice (Northern Ireland) Order 2003 (S.I. 2003/1247 (N.I. 13)) (assault with intent to commit buggery).

109 An offence under Article 21 of that Order (indecent assault on a male).

110 An offence of –

   (a) aiding, abetting, counselling, procuring or inciting the commission of an offence specified in this Part of this Schedule,

   (b) conspiring to commit an offence so specified, or

   (c) attempting to commit an offence so specified.

SCHEDULE 18   RELEASE OF PRISONERS SERVING SENTENCES OF IMPRISONMENT OR DETENTION FOR PUBLIC PROTECTION

Section 230

Release on licence

1   (1)   Section 31 of the Crime (Sentences) Act 1997 (c. 43) (duration and conditions of licences for life prisoners), is amended as follows.

    (2)   In subsection (1) (licence to remain in force until death), after 'life prisoner' there is inserted ', other than a prisoner to whom section 31A below applies,'.

    (3)   After that subsection there is inserted –

    '(1A) Where a prisoner to whom section 31A below applies is released on licence, the licence shall remain in force until his death unless –

      (a)   it is previously revoked under section 32(1) or (2) below; or

      (b)   it ceases to have effect in accordance with an order made by the Secretary of State under section 31A below.'

2   After that section there is inserted –

'31A Imprisonment or detention for public protection: termination of licences

    (1)   This section applies to a prisoner who –

      (a)   is serving one or more preventive sentences, and

      (b)   is not serving any other life sentence.

    (2)   Where –

      (a)   the prisoner has been released on licence under this Chapter; and

      (b)   the qualifying period has expired,

    the Secretary of State shall, if directed to do so by the Parole Board, order that the licence is to cease to have effect.

    (3)   Where –

      (a)   the prisoner has been released on licence under this Chapter;

      (b)   the qualifying period has expired; and

      (c)   if he has made a previous application under this subsection, a period of at least twelve months has expired since the disposal of that application,

    the prisoner may make an application to the Parole Board under this subsection.

    (4)   Where an application is made under subsection (3) above, the Parole Board –

      (a)   shall, if it is satisfied that it is no longer necessary for the protection of the public that the licence should remain in force, direct the Secretary of State to make an order that the licence is to cease to have effect;

      (b)   shall otherwise dismiss the application.

    (5)   In this section –

    "preventive sentence" means a sentence of imprisonment for public protection under section 225 of the Criminal Justice Act 2003 or a sentence of detention for public protection under section 226 of that Act;

    "the qualifying period", in relation to a prisoner who has been released on licence, means the period of ten years beginning with the date of his release.'

3   In section 34(2) of that Act (meaning of 'life sentence'), after paragraph (c) there is inserted –

'(d)   a sentence of imprisonment for public protection under section 225 of the Criminal Justice Act 2003, and

(e)   a sentence of detention for public protection under section 226 of that Act.'

Determination of tariffs

4   In section 82A of the Sentencing Act (determination of tariffs), after subsection (4) there is inserted –

'(4A)   No order under subsection (4) above may be made where the life sentence is –

(a)   a sentence of imprisonment for public protection under section 225 of the Criminal Justice Act 2003, or

(b)   a sentence of detention for public protection under section 226 of that Act.'

SCHEDULE 19   THE PAROLE BOARD: SUPPLEMENTARY PROVISIONS   Section 239(7)

Status and Capacity

1   (1)   The Board is not to be regarded as the servant or agent of the Crown or as enjoying any status, immunity or privilege of the Crown; and the Board's property is not to be regarded as property of, or held on behalf of, the Crown.

(2)   It is within the capacity of the Board as a statutory corporation to do such things and enter into such transactions as are incidental to or conducive to the discharge of –

(a)   its functions under Chapter 6 of Part 12 in respect of fixed-term prisoners, and

(b)   its functions under Chapter 2 of Part 2 of the Crime (Sentences) Act 1997 (c. 43) in relation to life prisoners within the meaning of that Chapter.

Membership

2   (1)   The Board is to consist of a chairman and not less than four other members appointed by the Secretary of State.

(2)   The Board must include among its members –

(a)   a person who holds or has held judicial office;

(b)   a registered medical practitioner who is a psychiatrist;

(c)   a person appearing to the Secretary of State to have knowledge and experience of the supervision or after-care of discharged prisoners; and

(d)   a person appearing to the Secretary of State to have made a study of the causes of delinquency or the treatment of offenders.

(3)   A member of the Board –

(a)   holds and vacates office in accordance with the terms of his appointment;

(b)   may resign his office by notice in writing addressed to the Secretary of State;

and a person who ceases to hold office as a member of the Board is eligible for re-appointment.

Payments to members

3   (1) The Board may pay to each member such remuneration and allowances as the Secretary of State may determine.

(2) The Board may pay or make provision for paying to or in respect of any member such sums by way of pension, allowances or gratuities as the Secretary of State may determine.

(3) If a person ceases to be a member otherwise than on the expiry of his term of office and it appears to the Secretary of State that there are special circumstances that make it right that he should receive compensation, the Secretary of State may direct the Board to make to that person a payment of such amount as the Secretary of State may determine.

(4) A determination or direction of the Secretary of State under this paragraph requires the approval of the Treasury.

Proceedings

4   (1) Subject to the provisions of section 239(5), the arrangements relating to meetings of the Board are to be such as the Board may determine.

(2) The arrangements may provide for the discharge, under the general direction of the Board, of any of the Board's functions by a committee or by one or more of the members or employees of the Board.

(3) The validity of the proceedings of the Board are not to be affected by any vacancy among the members or by any defect in the appointment of a member.

Staff

5   (1) The Board may appoint such number of employees as it may determine.

(2) The remuneration and other conditions of service of the persons appointed under this paragraph are to be determined by the Board.

(3) Any determination under sub-paragraph (1) or (2) requires the approval of the Secretary of State given with the consent of the Treasury.

(4) The Employers' Liability (Compulsory Insurance) Act 1969 (c. 57) shall not require insurance to be effected by the Board.

6   (1) Employment with the Board shall continue to be included among the kinds of employment to which a scheme under section 1 of the Superannuation Act 1972 (c. 11) can apply, and accordingly in Schedule 1 to that Act (in which those kinds of employment are listed) at the end of the list of Other Bodies there shall continue to be inserted –

'Parole Board.'.

(2) The Board shall pay to the Treasury, at such times as the Treasury may direct, such sums as the Treasury may determine in respect of the increase attributable to this paragraph in the sums payable under the Superannuation Act 1972 out of money provided by Parliament.

Financial provisions

7   (1) The Secretary of State shall pay to the Board –

(a) any expenses incurred or to be incurred by the Board by virtue of paragraph 3 or 5; and

(b) with the consent of the Treasury, such sums as he thinks fit for enabling the Board to meet other expenses.

(2) Any sums required by the Secretary of State for making payments under sub-paragraph (1) are to be paid out of money provided by Parliament.

Authentication of Board's seal

8 The application of the seal of the Board is to be authenticated by the signature of the Chairman or some other person authorised for the purpose.

Presumption of authenticity of documents issued by Board

9 Any document purporting to be an instrument issued by the Board and to be duly executed under the seal of the Board or to be signed on behalf of the Board shall be received in evidence and shall be deemed to be such an instrument unless the contrary is shown.

Accounts and audit

10 (1) It is the duty of the Board –

    (a) to keep proper accounts and proper records in relation to the accounts;

    (b) to prepare in respect of each financial year a statement of accounts in such form as the Secretary of State may direct with the approval of the Treasury; and

    (c) to send copies of each such statement to the Secretary of State and the Comptroller and Auditor General not later than 31st August next following the end of the financial year to which the statement relates.

(2) The Comptroller and Auditor General shall examine, certify and report on each statement of accounts sent to him by the Board and shall lay a copy of every such statement and of his report before each House of Parliament.

(3) In this paragraph and paragraph 11 'financial year' means a period of 12 months ending with 31st March.

Reports

11 The Board must as soon as practicable after the end of each financial year make to the Secretary of State a report on the performance of its functions during the year; and the Secretary of State must lay a copy of the report before each House of Parliament.

SCHEDULE 20   PRISONERS LIABLE TO REMOVAL FROM UNITED KINGDOM: MODIFICATIONS OF CRIMINAL JUSTICE ACT 1991   Section 262

1 In this Schedule 'the 1991 Act' means the Criminal Justice Act 1991 (c. 53).

2 In section 42 of the 1991 Act (additional days for disciplinary offences), in subsection (2) before the word 'and' at the end of paragraph (a) there is inserted –

'(aa) any period which he must serve before he can be removed under section 46A below;'.

3 (1) In section 46 of the 1991 Act (persons liable to removal from the United Kingdom) in subsection (3) after paragraph (d) there is inserted 'or

(e)   he is liable to removal under section 10 of the Immigration and Asylum Act 1999'.

(2)   Sub-paragraph (1) does not apply to any prisoner whose sentence relates to an offence committed before the commencement of this Schedule.

4   After section 46 of the 1991 Act there is inserted –

'46A   Early removal of persons liable to removal from United Kingdom

(1)   Subject to subsection (2) below, where a short-term or long-term prisoner is liable to removal from the United Kingdom, the Secretary of State may under this section remove him from prison at any time after he has served the requisite period.

(2)   Subsection (1) above does not apply where –

(a)   the sentence is an extended sentence within the meaning of section 85 of the Powers of Criminal Courts (Sentencing) Act 2000,

(b)   the sentence is for an offence under section 1 of the Prisoners (Return to Custody) Act 1995,

(c)   the prisoner is subject to a hospital order, hospital direction or transfer direction under section 37, 45A or 47 of the Mental Health Act 1983,

(d)   the prisoner is subject to the notification requirements of Part 2 of the Sexual Offences Act 2003, or

(e)   the interval between –

(i)   the date on which the prisoner will have served the requisite period for the term of the sentence, and

(ii)   the date on which he will have served one-half of the sentence,

is less than 14 days.

(3)   A prisoner removed from prison under this section –

(a)   is so removed only for the purpose of enabling the Secretary of State to remove him from the United Kingdom under powers conferred by –

(i)   Schedule 2 or 3 to the Immigration Act 1971, or

(ii)   section 10 of the Immigration and Asylum Act 1999, and

(b)   so long as remaining in the United Kingdom, remains liable to be detained in pursuance of his sentence until he falls to be released under section 33 or 35 above.

(4)   So long as a prisoner removed from prison under this section remains in the United Kingdom but has not been returned to prison, any duty or power of the Secretary of State under section 33, 35 or 36 is exercisable in relation to him as if he were in prison.

(5)   In this section "the requisite period" means –

(a)   for a term of three months or more but less than four months, a period of 30 days;

(b)   for a term of four months or more but less than 18 months, a period equal to one-quarter of the term;

(c)   for a term of 18 months or more, a period that is 135 days less than one-half of the term.

(6)   The Secretary of State may by order made by statutory instrument –

(a)   amend the definition of "the requisite period" in subsection (5) above,

(b)   make such transitional provision as appears to him necessary or expedient in connection with the amendment.

(7)   No order shall be made under subsection (6) above unless a draft of the order has been laid before and approved by a resolution of each House of Parliament.

(8)   In relation to any time before the commencement of sections 80 and 81 of the Sexual Offences Act 2003, the reference in subsection (2)(d) above to Part 2 of that Act is to be read as a reference to Part 1 of the Sex Offenders Act 1997.

46B Re-entry into United Kingdom of offender removed early from prison

(1)   This section applies in relation to a person who, after being removed from prison under section 46A above, has been removed from the United Kingdom before he has served one-half of his sentence.

(2)   If a person to whom this section applies enters the United Kingdom at any time before his sentence expiry date, he is liable to be detained in pursuance of his sentence from the time of his entry into the United Kingdom until whichever is the earlier of the following –

(a)   the end of a period ("the further custodial period") beginning with that time and equal in length to the outstanding custodial period, and

(b)   his sentence expiry date.

(3)   A person who is liable to be detained by virtue of subsection (2) above is, if at large, to be taken for the purposes of section 49 of the Prison Act 1952 (persons unlawfully at large) to be unlawfully at large.

(4)   Subsection (2) above does not prevent the further removal from the United Kingdom of a person falling within that subsection.

(5)   Where, in the case of a person returned to prison by virtue of subsection (2) above, the further custodial period ends before the sentence expiry date, subsections (1) and (2) of section 33 above apply in relation to him as if any reference to one-half or two-thirds of the prisoner's sentence were a reference to the further custodial period.

(6)   If a person returned to prison by virtue of subsection (2) above falls by virtue of subsection (5) above to be released on licence under section 33(1) or (2) above after the date on which (but for his removal from the United Kingdom) he would have served three-quarters of his sentence, section 37(1) above has effect in relation to him as if for the reference to three-quarters of his sentence there were substituted a reference to the whole of his sentence.

(7)   If a person who is released on licence under section 33(1) or (2) above at the end of the further custodial period is recalled to prison under section 39(1) or (2) above, section 33A(3) above shall not apply, but it shall be the duty of the Secretary of State –

(a)   if the person is recalled before the date on which (but for his removal from the United Kingdom) he would have served three-quarters of his sentence, to release him on licence on that date, and

(b)   if he is recalled after that date, to release him on the sentence expiry date.

(8)   A licence granted by virtue of subsection (7)(a) above shall remain in force until the sentence expiry date.

(9)   In this section –

"further custodial period" has the meaning given by subsection (2)(a) above;

"outstanding custodial period", in relation to a person to whom this section applies, means the period beginning with the date on which he was removed from the United Kingdom and ending with the date on which (but for his removal) he would have served one-half of his sentence;

"sentence expiry date", in relation to a person to whom this section applies, means the date on which (but for his removal from the United Kingdom) he would have served the whole of this sentence.'

SCHEDULE 21   DETERMINATION OF MINIMUM TERM IN RELATION TO MANDATORY LIFE SENTENCE

Section 269(5)

Interpretation

1   In this Schedule –

'child' means a person under 18 years;

'mandatory life sentence' means a life sentence passed in circumstances where the sentence is fixed by law;

'minimum term', in relation to a mandatory life sentence, means the part of the sentence to be specified in an order under section 269(2);

'whole life order' means an order under subsection (4) of section 269.

2   Section 28 of the Crime and Disorder Act 1998 (c. 37) (meaning of 'racially or religiously aggravated') applies for the purposes of this Schedule as it applies for the purposes of sections 29 to 32 of that Act.

3   For the purposes of this Schedule an offence is aggravated by sexual orientation if it is committed in circumstances falling within subsection (2)(a)(i) or (b)(i) of section 146.

Starting points

4   (1)   If –

    (a)   the court considers that the seriousness of the offence (or the combination of the offence and one or more offences associated with it) is exceptionally high, and

    (b)   the offender was aged 21 or over when he committed the offence,

the appropriate starting point is a whole life order.

    (2)   Cases that would normally fall within sub-paragraph (1)(a) include –

    (a)   the murder of two or more persons, where each murder involves any of the following –

        (i)   a substantial degree of premeditation or planning,

        (ii)   the abduction of the victim, or

        (iii)   sexual or sadistic conduct,

    (b)   the murder of a child if involving the abduction of the child or sexual or sadistic motivation,

    (c)   a murder done for the purpose of advancing a political, religious or ideological cause, or

    (d)   a murder by an offender previously convicted of murder.

5   (1)   If –

    (a)   the case does not fall within paragraph 4(1) but the court considers that the seriousness of the offence (or the combination of the offence and one or more offences associated with it) is particularly high, and

    (b)   the offender was aged 18 or over when he committed the offence,

the appropriate starting point, in determining the minimum term, is 30 years.

    (2)   Cases that (if not falling within paragraph 4(1)) would normally fall within sub-paragraph (1)(a) include –

    (a)   the murder of a police officer or prison officer in the course of his duty,

    (b)   a murder involving the use of a firearm or explosive,

(c)   a murder done for gain (such as a murder done in the course or further-
ance of robbery or burglary, done for payment or done in the expectation
of gain as a result of the death),

(d)   a murder intended to obstruct or interfere with the course of justice,

(e)   a murder involving sexual or sadistic conduct,

(f)   the murder of two or more persons,

(g)   a murder that is racially or religiously aggravated or aggravated by sexual
orientation, or

(h)   a murder falling within paragraph 4(2) committed by an offender who was
aged under 21 when he committed the offence.

6   If the offender was aged 18 or over when he committed the offence and the case does
not fall within paragraph 4(1) or 5(1), the appropriate starting point, in determining
the minimum term, is 15 years.

7   If the offender was aged under 18 when he committed the offence, the appropriate
starting point, in determining the minimum term, is 12 years.

Aggravating and mitigating factors

8   Having chosen a starting point, the court should take into account any aggravating or
mitigating factors, to the extent that it has not allowed for them in its choice of starting
point.

9   Detailed consideration of aggravating or mitigating factors may result in a minimum
term of any length (whatever the starting point), or in the making of a whole life
order.

10   Aggravating factors (additional to those mentioned in paragraph 4(2) and 5(2)) that
may be relevant to the offence of murder include –

(a)   a significant degree of planning or premeditation,

(b)   the fact that the victim was particularly vulnerable because of age or disability,

(c)   mental or physical suffering inflicted on the victim before death,

(d)   the abuse of a position of trust,

(e)   the use of duress or threats against another person to facilitate the commission
of the offence,

(f)   the fact that the victim was providing a public service or performing a public
duty, and

(g)   concealment, destruction or dismemberment of the body.

11   Mitigating factors that may be relevant to the offence of murder include –

(a)   an intention to cause serious bodily harm rather than to kill,

(b)   lack of premeditation,

(c)   the fact that the offender suffered from any mental disorder or mental disability
which (although not falling within section 2(1) of the Homicide Act 1957 (c. 11)),
lowered his degree of culpability,

(d)   the fact that the offender was provoked (for example, by prolonged stress) in a
way not amounting to a defence of provocation,

(e)   the fact that the offender acted to any extent in self-defence,

(f)   a belief by the offender that the murder was an act of mercy, and

(g)   the age of the offender.

12   Nothing in this Schedule restricts the application of –

(a)   section 143(2) (previous convictions),

(b)   section 143(3) (bail), or

(c)   section 144 (guilty plea).

SCHEDULE 22 MANDATORY LIFE SENTENCES: TRANSITIONAL CASES

Section 276

Interpretation

1 In this Schedule –

'the commencement date' means the day on which section 269 comes into force;

'the early release provisions' means the provisions of section 28(5) to (8) of the Crime (Sentences) Act 1997 (c. 43);

'existing prisoner' means a person serving one or more mandatory life sentences passed before the commencement date (whether or not he is also serving any other sentence);

'life sentence' means a sentence of imprisonment for life or custody for life passed in England and Wales or by a court-martial outside England and Wales;

'mandatory life sentence' means a life sentence passed in circumstances where the sentence was fixed by law.

Existing prisoners notified by Secretary of State

2 Paragraph 3 applies in relation to any existing prisoner who, in respect of any mandatory life sentence, has before the commencement date been notified in writing by the Secretary of State (otherwise than in a notice that is expressed to be provisional) either –

(a) of a minimum period which in the view of the Secretary of State should be served before the prisoner's release on licence, or

(b) that the Secretary of State does not intend that the prisoner should ever be released on licence.

3 (1) On the application of the existing prisoner, the High Court must, in relation to the mandatory life sentence, either –

(a) order that the early release provisions are to apply to him as soon as he has served the part of the sentence which is specified in the order, which in a case falling within paragraph 2(a) must not be greater than the notified minimum term, or

(b) in a case falling within paragraph 2(b), order that the early release provisions are not to apply to the offender.

(2) In a case falling within paragraph 2(a), no application may be made under this paragraph after the end of the notified minimum term.

(3) Where no application under this paragraph is made in a case falling within paragraph 2(a), the early release provisions apply to the prisoner in respect of the sentence as soon as he has served the notified minimum term (or, if he has served that term before the commencement date but has not been released, from the commencement date).

(4) In this paragraph 'the notified minimum term' means the minimum period notified as mentioned in paragraph 2(a), or where the prisoner has been so notified on more than one occasion, the period most recently so notified.

4 (1) In dealing with an application under paragraph 3, the High Court must have regard to –

(a) the seriousness of the offence, or of the combination of the offence and one or more offences associated with it,

(b) where the court is satisfied that, if the prisoner had been sentenced to a term of imprisonment, the length of his sentence would have been treated by section 67 of the Criminal Justice Act 1967 (c. 80) as being reduced by a particular period, the effect which that section would have had if he had been sentenced to a term of imprisonment, and

(c)   the length of the notified minimum term or, where a notification falling within paragraph 2(b) has been given to the prisoner, to the fact that such a notification has been given.

(2)   In considering under sub-paragraph (1) the seriousness of the offence, or of the combination of the offence and one or more offences associated with it, the High Court must have regard to –

(a)   the general principles set out in Schedule 21, and

(b)   any recommendation made to the Secretary of State by the trial judge or the Lord Chief Justice as to the minimum term to be served by the offender before release on licence.

(3)   In this paragraph 'the notified minimum term' has the same meaning as in paragraph 3.

Existing prisoners not notified by Secretary of State

5   Paragraph 6 applies in relation to any existing prisoner who, in respect of any mandatory life sentence, has not before the commencement date been notified as mentioned in paragraph 2(a) or (b) by the Secretary of State.

6   The Secretary of State must refer the prisoner's case to the High Court for the making by the High Court of an order under subsection (2) or (4) of section 269 in relation to the mandatory life sentence.

7   In considering under subsection (3) or (4) of section 269 the seriousness of an offence (or the combination of an offence and one or more offences associated with it) in a case referred to the High Court under paragraph 6, the High Court must have regard not only to the matters mentioned in subsection (5) of that section but also to any recommendation made to the Secretary of State by the trial judge or the Lord Chief Justice as to the minimum term to be served by the offender before release on licence.

8   In dealing with a reference under paragraph 6, the High Court –

(a)   may not make an order under subsection (2) of section 269 specifying a part of the sentence which in the opinion of the court is greater than that which, under the practice followed by the Secretary of State before December 2002, the Secretary of State would have been likely to notify as mentioned in paragraph 2(a), and

(b)   may not make an order under subsection (4) of section 269 unless the court is of the opinion that, under the practice followed by the Secretary of State before December 2002, the Secretary of State would have been likely to give the prisoner a notification falling within paragraph 2(b).

Sentences passed on or after commencement date in respect of offences committed before that date

9   Paragraph 10 applies where –

(a)   on or after the commencement date a court passes a life sentence in circumstances where the sentence is fixed by law, and

(b)   the offence to which the sentence relates was committed before the commencement date.

10   The court –

(a)   may not make an order under subsection (2) of section 269 specifying a part of the sentence which in the opinion of the court is greater than that which, under the practice followed by the Secretary of State before December 2002, the Secretary of State would have been likely to notify as mentioned in paragraph 2(a), and

(b) may not make an order under subsection (4) of section 269 unless the court is of the opinion that, under the practice followed by the Secretary of State before December 2002, the Secretary of State would have been likely to give the prisoner a notification falling within paragraph 2(b).

Proceedings in High Court

11 (1) An application under paragraph 3 or a reference under paragraph 6 is to be determined by a single judge of the High Court without an oral hearing.

(2) In relation to such an application or reference, any reference to 'the court' in section 269(2) to (5) and Schedule 21 is to be read as a reference to the High Court.

Giving of reasons

12 (1) Where the High Court makes an order under paragraph 3(1)(a) or (b), it must state in open court, in ordinary language, its reasons for deciding on the order made.

(2) Where the order is an order under paragraph 3(1)(a) specifying a part of the sentence shorter than the notified minimum term the High Court must, in particular, state its reasons for departing from the notified minimum term.

13 Where the High Court makes an order under subsection (2) or (4) of section 269 on a reference under paragraph 6, subsection (2) of section 270 does not apply.

Right of appeal

14 (1) A person who has made an application under paragraph 3 or in respect of whom a reference has been made under paragraph 6 may with the leave of the Court of Appeal appeal to the Court of Appeal against the decision of the High Court on the application or reference.

(2) Section 1(1) of the Administration of Justice Act 1960 (c. 65) (appeal to House of Lords from decision of High Court in a criminal cause or matter) and section 18(1)(a) of the Supreme Court Act 1981 (c. 54) (exclusion of appeal from High Court to Court of Appeal in a criminal cause or matter) do not apply in relation to a decision to which sub-paragraph (1) applies.

(3) The jurisdiction conferred on the Court of Appeal by this paragraph is to be exercised by the criminal division of that court.

(4) Section 33(3) of the Criminal Appeal Act 1968 (c. 19) (limitation on appeal from criminal division of Court of Appeal) does not prevent an appeal to the House of Lords under this paragraph.

(5) In relation to appeals to the Court of Appeal or the House of Lords under this paragraph, the Secretary of State may make an order containing provision corresponding to any provision in the Criminal Appeal Act 1968 (subject to any specified modifications).

Review of minimum term on reference by Attorney General

15   Section 36 of the Criminal Justice Act 1988 (c. 33) applies in relation to an order made by the High Court under paragraph 3(1)(a) as it applies in relation to an order made by the Crown Court under section 269(2).

Modification of early release provisions

16   (1)   In relation to an existing prisoner, section 28 of the Crime (Sentences) Act 1997 (c. 43) has effect subject to the following modifications.

(2)   Any reference to a life prisoner in respect of whom a minimum term order has been made includes a reference to –

(a)   an existing prisoner in respect of whom an order under paragraph 3(1)(a) has been made, and

(b)   an existing prisoner serving a sentence in respect of which paragraph 3(3) applies.

(3)   Any reference to the relevant part of the sentence is to be read –

(a)   in relation to a sentence in respect of which an order under paragraph 3(1)(a) has been made, as a reference to the part specified in the order, and

(b)   in relation to a sentence in respect of which paragraph 3(3) applies, as a reference to the notified minimum term as defined by paragraph 3(4).

(4)   In subsection (1B) (life prisoner serving two or more sentences), paragraph (a) is to be read as if it referred to each of the sentences being one –

(a)   in respect of which a minimum term order or an order under paragraph 3(1)(a) has been made, or

(b)   in respect of which paragraph 3(3) applies.

17   In section 34(1) of the Crime (Sentences) Act 1997 (c. 43) (interpretation of Chapter 2 of that Act), in the definition of 'life prisoner', the reference to a transferred prisoner as defined by section 273 of this Act includes a reference to an existing prisoner who immediately before the commencement date is a transferred life prisoner for the purposes of section 33 of that Act.

Transferred life prisoners

18   In relation to an existing prisoner who immediately before the commencement date is a transferred life prisoner for the purposes of section 33 of the Crime (Sentences) Act 1997, this Schedule is to be read as if –

(a)   any certificate under subsection (2) of that section were a notification falling within paragraph 2(a) of this Schedule, and

(b)   references to any recommendation of the trial judge or the Lord Chief Justice were omitted.

SCHEDULE 23   DEFERMENT OF SENTENCE   Section 278

1   For sections 1 and 2 of the Sentencing Act (deferment of sentence) there is substituted –

'Deferment of sentence

1   **Deferment of sentence**

(1)   The Crown Court or a magistrates' court may defer passing sentence on an offender for the purpose of enabling the court, or any other court to which it falls to deal with him, to have regard in dealing with him to –

    (a)   his conduct after conviction (including, where appropriate, the making by him of reparation for his offence); or

    (b)   any change in his circumstances;

but this is subject to subsections (3) and (4) below.

(2)   Without prejudice to the generality of subsection (1) above, the matters to which the court to which it falls to deal with the offender may have regard by virtue of paragraph (a) of that subsection include the extent to which the offender has complied with any requirements imposed under subsection (3)(b) below.

(3)   The power conferred by subsection (1) above shall be exercisable only if –

    (a)   the offender consents;

    (b)   the offender undertakes to comply with any requirements as to his conduct during the period of the deferment that the court considers it appropriate to impose; and

    (c)   the court is satisfied, having regard to the nature of the offence and the character and circumstances of the offender, that it would be in the interests of justice to exercise the power.

(4)   Any deferment under this section shall be until such date as may be specified by the court, not being more than six months after the date on which the deferment is announced by the court; and, subject to section 1D(3) below, where the passing of sentence has been deferred under this section it shall not be further so deferred.

(5)   Where a court has under this section deferred passing sentence on an offender, it shall forthwith give a copy of the order deferring the passing of sentence and setting out any requirements imposed under subsection (3)(b) above –

    (a)   to the offender,

    (b)   where an officer of a local probation board has been appointed to act as a supervisor in relation to him, to that board, and

    (c)   where a person has been appointed under section 1A(2)(b) below to act as a supervisor in relation to him, to that person.

(6)   Notwithstanding any enactment, a court which under this section defers passing sentence on an offender shall not on the same occasion remand him.

(7)   Where –

    (a)   a court which under this section has deferred passing sentence on an offender proposes to deal with him on the date originally specified by the court, or

    (b)   the offender does not appear on the day so specified, the court may issue a summons requiring him to appear before the court at a time and place specified in the summons, or may issue a warrant to arrest him and bring him before the court at a time and place specified in the warrant.

(8) Nothing in this section or sections 1A to 1D below shall affect –

(a) the power of the Crown Court to bind over an offender to come up for judgment when called upon; or

(b) the power of any court to defer passing sentence for any purpose for which it may lawfully do so apart from this section.

1A   Further provision about undertakings ·

(1) Without prejudice to the generality of paragraph (b) of section 1(3) above, the requirements that may be imposed by virtue of that paragraph include requirements as to the residence of the offender during the whole or any part of the period of deferment.

(2) Where an offender has undertaken to comply with any requirements imposed under section 1(3)(b) above the court may appoint –

(a) an officer of a local probation board, or

(b) any other person whom the court thinks appropriate,

to act as a supervisor in relation to him.

(3) A person shall not be appointed under subsection (2)(b) above without his consent.

(4) It shall be the duty of a supervisor appointed under subsection (2) above –

(a) to monitor the offender's compliance with the requirements; and

(b) to provide the court to which it falls to deal with the offender in respect of the offence in question with such information as the court may require relating to the offender's compliance with the requirements.

1B   Breach of undertakings

(1) A court which under section 1 above has deferred passing sentence on an offender may deal with him before the end of the period of deferment if –

(a) he appears or is brought before the court under subsection (3) below; and

(b) the court is satisfied that he has failed to comply with one or more requirements imposed under section 1(3)(b) above in connection with the deferment.

(2) Subsection (3) below applies where –

(a) a court has under section 1 above deferred passing sentence on an offender;

(b) the offender undertook to comply with one or more requirements imposed under section 1(3)(b) above in connection with the deferment; and

(c) a person appointed under section 1A(2) above to act as a supervisor in relation to the offender has reported to the court that the offender has failed to comply with one or more of those requirements.

(3) Where this subsection applies, the court may issue –

(a) a summons requiring the offender to appear before the court at a time and place specified in the summons; or

(b) a warrant to arrest him and bring him before the court at a time and place specified in the warrant.

1C **Conviction of offence during period of deferment**

(1) A court which under section 1 above has deferred passing sentence on an offender may deal with him before the end of the period of deferment if during that period he is convicted in Great Britain of any offence.

(2) Subsection (3) below applies where a court has under section 1 above deferred passing sentence on an offender in respect of one or more offences and during the period of deferment the offender is convicted in England and Wales of any offence ('the later offence').

(3) Where this subsection applies, then (without prejudice to subsection (1) above and whether or not the offender is sentenced for the later offence during the period of deferment), the court which passes sentence on him for the later offence may also, if this has not already been done, deal with him for the offence or offences for which passing of sentence has been deferred, except that –

(a) the power conferred by this subsection shall not be exercised by a magistrates' court if the court which deferred passing sentence was the Crown Court; and

(b) the Crown Court, in exercising that power in a case in which the court which deferred passing sentence was a magistrates' court, shall not pass any sentence which could not have been passed by a magistrates' court in exercising that power.

(4) Where a court which under section 1 above has deferred passing sentence on an offender proposes to deal with him by virtue of subsection (1) above before the end of the period of deferment, the court may issue –

(a) a summons requiring him to appear before the court at a time and place specified in the summons; or

(b) a warrant to arrest him and bring him before the court at a time and place specified in the warrant.

1D **Deferment of sentence: supplementary**

(1) In deferring the passing of sentence under section 1 above a magistrates' court shall be regarded as exercising the power of adjourning the trial conferred by section 10(1) of the Magistrates' Courts Act 1980, and accordingly sections 11(1) and 13(1) to (3A) and (5) of that Act (non-appearance of the accused) apply (without prejudice to section 1(7) above) if the offender does not appear on the date specified under section 1(4) above.

(2) Where the passing of sentence on an offender has been deferred by a court ("the original court") under section 1 above, the power of that court under that section to deal with the offender at the end of the period of deferment and any power of that court under section 1B(1) or 1C(1) above, or of any court under section 1C(3) above, to deal with the offender –

(a) is power to deal with him, in respect of the offence for which passing of sentence has been deferred, in any way in which the original court could have dealt with him if it had not deferred passing sentence; and

(b) without prejudice to the generality of paragraph (a) above, in the case of a magistrates' court, includes the power conferred by section 3 below to commit him to the Crown Court for sentence.

(3) Where –

(a) the passing of sentence on an offender in respect of one or more offences has been deferred under section 1 above, and

(b) a magistrates' court deals with him in respect of the offence or any of the offences by committing him to the Crown Court under section 3 below, the power of the Crown Court to deal with him includes the same power to defer passing sentence on him as if he had just been convicted of the offence or offences on indictment before the court.

(4) Subsection (5) below applies where –

   (a)   the passing of sentence on an offender in respect of one or more offences has been deferred under section 1 above;

   (b)   it falls to a magistrates' court to determine a relevant matter; and

   (c)   a justice of the peace is satisfied –

      (i)   that a person appointed under section 1A(2)(b) above to act as a supervisor in relation to the offender is likely to be able to give evidence that may assist the court in determining that matter; and

      (ii)   that that person will not voluntarily attend as a witness.

(5) The justice may issue a summons directed to that person requiring him to attend before the court at the time and place appointed in the summons to give evidence.

(6) For the purposes of subsection (4) above a court determines a relevant matter if it –

   (a)   deals with the offender in respect of the offence, or any of the offences, for which the passing of sentence has been deferred; or

   (b)   determines, for the purposes of section 1B(1)(b) above, whether the offender has failed to comply with any requirements imposed under section 1(3)(b) above.'

2   In section 159 of the Sentencing Act (execution of process between England and Wales and Scotland), for 'section 2(4),' there is substituted 'section 1(7), 1B(3), 1C(4),'.

SCHEDULE 24   DRUG TREATMENT AND TESTING REQUIREMENT IN ACTION PLAN ORDER OR SUPERVISION ORDER   Section 279

1   (1)   Section 70 of the Sentencing Act (requirements which may be included in action plan orders and directions) is amended as follows.

   (2)   After subsection (4) there is inserted –

    '(4A) Subsection (4B) below applies where a court proposing to make an action plan order is satisfied –

      (a) that the offender is dependent on, or has a propensity to misuse, drugs, and

      (b) that his dependency or propensity is such as requires and may be susceptible to treatment.

    (4B) Where this subsection applies, requirements included in an action plan order may require the offender for a period specified in the order ("the treatment period") to submit to treatment by or under the direction of a specified person having the necessary qualifications and experience ("the treatment provider") with a view to the reduction or elimination of the offender's dependency on or propensity to misuse drugs.

    (4C) The required treatment shall be –

      (a) treatment as a resident in such institution or place as may be specified in the order, or

      (b) treatment as a non-resident at such institution or place, and at such intervals, as may be so specified;

but the nature of the treatment shall not be specified in the order except as mentioned in paragraph (a) or (b) above.

(4D) A requirement shall not be included in an action plan order by virtue of subsection (4B) above –

(a) in any case, unless –

    (i) the court is satisfied that arrangements have been or can be made for the treatment intended to be specified in the order (including arrangements for the reception of the offender where he is to be required to submit to treatment as a resident), and

    (ii) the requirement has been recommended to the court as suitable for the offender by an officer of a local probation board or by a member of a youth offending team; and

(b) in the case of an order made or to be made in respect of a person aged 14 or over, unless he consents to its inclusion.

(4E) Subject to subsection (4F), an action plan order which includes a requirement by virtue of subsection (4B) above may, if the offender is aged 14 or over, also include a requirement ("a testing requirement") that, for the purpose of ascertaining whether he has any drug in his body during the treatment period, the offender shall during that period, at such times or in such circumstances as may (subject to the provisions of the order) be determined by the responsible officer or the treatment provider, provide samples of such description as may be so determined.

(4F) A testing requirement shall not be included in an action plan order by virtue of subsection (4E) above unless –

(a) the offender is aged 14 or over and consents to its inclusion, and

(b) the court has been notified by the Secretary of State that arrangements for implementing such requirements are in force in the area proposed to be specified in the order

(4G) A testing requirement shall specify for each month the minimum number of occasions on which samples are to be provided.

(4H) An action plan order including a testing requirement shall provide for the results of tests carried out on any samples provided by the offender in pursuance of the requirement to a person other than the responsible officer to be communicated to the responsible officer.'

2   (1) Schedule 6 to the Sentencing Act (requirements which may be included in supervision orders) is amended as follows.

(2) In paragraph 1, after '6' there is inserted ', 6A'.

(3) After paragraph 6 there is inserted –

'Requirements as to drug treatment and testing

6A (1) This paragraph applies where a court proposing to make a supervision order is satisfied –

(a)   that the offender is dependent on, or has a propensity to misuse, drugs, and

(b)   that his dependency or propensity is such as requires and may be susceptible to treatment.

(2) Where this paragraph applies, the court may include in the supervision order a requirement that the offender shall, for a period specified in the order ("the treatment period"), submit to treatment by or under the direction of a specified person having the necessary qualifications and experience

("the treatment provider") with a view to the reduction or elimination of the offender's dependency on or propensity to misuse drugs.

(3) The required treatment shall be –

(a) treatment as a resident in such institution or place as may be specified in the order, or

(b) treatment as a non-resident at such institution or place, and at such intervals, as may be so specified;

but the nature of the treatment shall not be specified in the order except as mentioned in paragraph (a) or (b) above.

(4) A requirement shall not be included in a supervision order by virtue of sub-paragraph (2) above –

(a) in any case, unless –

(i) the court is satisfied that arrangements have been or can be made for the treatment intended to be specified in the order (including arrangements for the reception of the offender where he is to be required to submit to treatment as a resident), and

(ii) the requirement has been recommended to the court as suitable for the offender by an officer of a local probation board or by a member of a youth offending team; and

(b) in the case of an order made or to be made in respect of a person aged 14 or over, unless he consents to its inclusion.

(5) Subject to sub-paragraph (6), a supervision order which includes a treatment requirement may also include a requirement ("a testing requirement") that, for the purpose of ascertaining whether he has any drug in his body during the treatment period, the offender shall during that period, at such times or in such circumstances as may (subject to the provisions of the order) be determined by the supervisor or the treatment provider, provide samples of such description as may be so determined.

(6) A testing requirement shall not be included in a supervision order by virtue of sub-paragraph (5) above unless –

(a) the offender is aged 14 or over and consents to its inclusion, and

(b) the court has been notified by the Secretary of State that arrangements for implementing such requirements are in force in the area proposed to be specified in the order.

(7) A testing requirement shall specify for each month the minimum number of occasions on which samples are to be provided.

(8) A supervision order including a testing requirement shall provide for the results of tests carried out on any samples provided by the offender in pursuance of the requirement to a person other than the supervisor to be communicated to the supervisor.'

3   In Schedule 7 to the Sentencing Act (breach, revocation and amendment of supervision orders), in paragraph 2(1), before 'or 7' there is inserted ', 6A'.

SCHEDULE 25   SUMMARY OFFENCES NO LONGER PUNISHABLE WITH IMPRISONMENT   Section 280(1)

Vagrancy Act 1824 (c. 83)

1   The offence under section 3 of the Vagrancy Act 1824 (idle and disorderly persons) of causing or procuring or encouraging any child or children to wander abroad, or

place himself or herself in any public place, street, highway, court, or passage, to beg or gather alms.

2 The following offences under section 4 of that Act (rogues and vagabonds) –

(a) the offence of going about as a gatherer or collector of alms, or endeavouring to procure charitable contributions of any nature or kind, under any false or fraudulent pretence,

(b) the offence of being found in or upon any dwelling house, warehouse, coach-house, stable, or outhouse, or in any inclosed yard, garden, or area, for any unlawful purpose, and

(c) the offence of being apprehended as an idle and disorderly person, and violently resisting any constable, or other peace officer so apprehending him or her, and being subsequently convicted of the offence for which he or she shall have been so apprehended.

Railway Regulation Act 1842 (c. 55)

3 An offence under section 17 of the Railway Regulation Act 1842 (punishment of railway employees guilty of misconduct).

London Hackney Carriages Act 1843 (c. 86)

4 An offence under section 28 of the London Hackney Carriages Act 1843 (punishment for furious driving etc.).

Town Police Clauses Act 1847 (c. 89)

5 An offence under section 26 of the Town Police Clauses Act 1847 (unlawful release of impounded stray cattle).

6 An offence under section 28 of that Act (offences relating to obstructions and nuisances).

7 An offence under section 29 of that Act (drunken persons, etc. guilty of violent or indecent behaviour).

8 An offence under section 36 of that Act (keeping places for bear-baiting, cock-fighting etc.).

Ecclesiastical Courts Jurisdiction Act 1860 (c. 32)

9 An offence under section 2 of the Ecclesiastical Courts Jurisdiction Act 1860 (making a disturbance in churches, chapels, churchyards, etc.).

Town Gardens Protection Act 1863 (c. 13)

10 An offence under section 5 of the Town Gardens Protection Act 1863 (injuring gardens).

Public Stores Act 1875 (c. 25)

11 An offence under section 8 of the Public Stores Act 1875 (sweeping, etc., near dock-yards, artillery ranges, etc.).

North Sea Fisheries Act 1893 (c. 17)

12   An offence under section 2 of the North Sea Fisheries Act 1893 (penalty for supplying, exchanging, or otherwise selling spirits).

13   An offence under section 3 of that Act (penalty for purchasing spirits by exchange or otherwise).

Seamen's and Soldiers' False Characters Act 1906 (c. 5)

14   An offence under section 1 of the Seamen's and Soldiers' False Characters Act 1906 (forgery of service or discharge certificate and personation).

Aliens Restriction (Amendment) Act 1919 (c. 92)

15   An offence under section 3(2) of the Aliens Restriction (Amendment) Act 1919 (promoting industrial unrest).

Children and Young Persons Act 1933 (c. 12)

16   An offence under section 4 of the Children and Young Persons Act 1933 (causing or allowing persons under sixteen to be used for begging).

Protection of Animals Act 1934 (c. 21)

17   An offence under section 2 of the Protection of Animals Act 1934 (offences relating to the prohibition of certain public contests, performances, and exhibitions with animals).

Public Health Act 1936 (c. 49)

18   An offence under section 287 of the Public Health Act 1936 (power to enter premises).

Essential Commodities Reserves Act 1938 (c. 51)

19   An offence under section 4(2) of the Essential Commodities Reserves Act 1938 (enforcement).

London Building Acts (Amendment) Act 1939 (c. xcvii)

20   An offence under section 142 of the London Building Acts (Amendment) Act 1939 (power of Council and others to enter buildings etc).

Cancer Act 1939 (c. 13)

21   An offence under section 4 of the Cancer Act 139 (prohibition of of certain advertisements).

Civil Defence Act 1939 (c. 31)

22   An offence under section 77 of the Civil Defence Act 1939 (penalty for false statements).

Hill Farming Act 1946 (c. 73)

23   An offence under section 19(2) or (3) of the Hill Farming Act 1946 (offences in relation to the control of rams).

Polish Resettlement Act 1947 (c. 19)

24   An offence under paragraph 7 of the Schedule to the Polish Resettlement Act 1947 (false representation or making a false statement).

Agriculture Act 1947 (c. 48)

25   An offence under section 14(7) of the Agriculture Act 1947, as remaining in force for the purposes of section 95 of that Act, (directions to secure good estate management and good husbandry).
26   An offence under section 95 of that Act (failure to comply with a direction to secure production).

Civil Defence Act 1948 (c. 5)

27   An offence under section 4 of the Civil Defence Act 1948 (powers as to land).

Agricultural Wages Act 1948 (c. 47)

28   An offence under section 12 of the Agricultural Wages Act 1948 (hindering investigation of complaints etc.).

Wireless Telegraphy Act 1949 (c. 54)

29   An offence under section 11(7) of the Wireless Telegraphy Act 1949 (enforcement of regulations as to use of apparatus), other than one within section 14(1A)(c) of that Act.

Prevention of Damage by Pests Act 1949 (c. 55)

30   An offence under section 22(5) of the Prevention of Damage by Pests Act 1949 (wrongful disclosure of information).

Coast Protection Act 1949 (c. 74)

31   An offence under section 25(9) of the Coast Protection Act 1949 (powers of entry and inspection).

Pet Animals Act 1951 (c. 35)

32   An offence under the Pet Animals Act 1951 (offences relating to licensing of pet shops and the sale of pets), other than one under section 4 of that Act.

Cockfighting Act 1952 (c. 59)

33   An offence under section 1 of the Cockfighting Act 1952 (possession of appliances for use in fighting of domestic fowl).

Agricultural Land (Removal of Surface Soil) Act 1953 (c. 10)

34   An offence under the Agricultural Land (Removal of Surface Soil) Act 1953 (removal of surface soil without planning permission).

Accommodation Agencies Act 1953 (c. 23)

35   An offence under section 1 of the Accommodation Agencies Act 1953 (illegal commissions and advertisements).

Army Act 1955 (3 & 4 Eliz. 2 c. 18)

36   An offence under section 19 of the Army Act 1955 (false answers in attestation paper).
37   An offence under section 161 of that Act (refusal to receive persons billeted, etc.).
38   An offence under section 171 of that Act (offences relating to the enforcement of provisions as to requisitioning).
39   An offence under section 191 of that Act (pretending to be a deserter).
40   An offence under section 193 of that Act (obstructing members of regular forces in execution of duty).
41   An offence under section 196 of the Act (illegal dealings in documents relating to pay, pensions, mobilisation etc.).
42   An offence under section 197 of that Act (unauthorised use of and dealing in decorations etc.).

Air Force Act 1955 (3 & 4 Eliz. 2 c. 19)

43   An offence under section 19 of the Air Force Act 1955 (false answers in attestation paper).
44   An offence under section 161 of that Act (refusal to receive persons billeted, etc.).
45   An offence under section 171 of that Act (offences relating to the enforcement of provisions as to requisitioning).
46   An offence under section 191 of that Act (pretending to be a deserter).
47   An offence under section 193 of that Act (obstructing members of regular air force in execution of duty).
48   An offence under section 196 of that Act (illegal dealings in documents relating to pay, pensions, mobilisation etc.).
49   An offence under section 197 of that Act (unauthorised use of and dealing in decorations etc.).

Naval Discipline Act 1957 (c. 53)

50   An offence under section 96 of the Naval Discipline Act 1957 (false pretence of desertion or absence without leave).

51   An offence under sectiion 99 of that Act (illegal dealings in official documents).

Agricultural Marketing Act 1958 (c. 47)

52   An offence under section 45 of the Agricultural Marketing Act 1958 (failure to comply with demand for information or knowingly making any false statement in reply thereto).

Rivers (Prevention of Pollution) Act 1961 (c. 50)

53   An offence under section 12(1) of the Rivers (Prevention of Pollution) Act 1961 (restriction of disclosure of information).

Betting, Gaming and Lotteries Act 1963 (c. 2)

54   An offence under section 8 of the Betting, Gaming and Lotteries Act 1963 (betting in streets and public places).

Children and Young Persons Act 1963 (c. 37)

55   An offence under section 40 of the Children and Young Persons Act 1963 (offences relating to persons under 16 taking part in public performances etc.).

Animal Boarding Establishments Act 1963 (c. 43)

56   An offence under the Animal Boarding Establishments Act 1963 (offences in connection with the licensing and inspection of boarding establishments for animals), other than an offence under section 2 of that Act.

Agriculture and Horticulture Act 1964 (c. 28)

57   An offence under Part 3 of the Agriculture and Horticulture Act 1964 (offences relating to the grading and transport of fresh horticultural produce), other than an offence under section 15(1) of that Act.

Emergency Laws (Re-enactments and Repeals) Act 1964 (c. 60)

58   An offence under paragraph 1(3) or 2(4) of Schedule 1 to the Emergency Laws (Re-enactments and Repeals) Act 1964 (offences relating to the production of documents).

Riding Establishments Act 1964 (c. 70)

59   An offence under the Riding Establishments Act 1964 (offences relating to the keeping of riding establishments), other than an offence under section 2(4) of that Act.

Industrial and Provident Societies Act 1965 (c. 12)

60   An offence under section 16 of the Industrial and Provident Societies Act 1965 (cancellation of registration of society).
61   An offence under section 48 of that Act (production of documents and provision of information for certain purposes).

Cereals Marketing Act 1965 (c. 14)

62   An offence under section 17(1) of the Cereals Marketing Act 1965 (failure to comply with a requirement of a scheme).

Gas Act 1965 (c. 36)

63   An offence under paragraph 9 of Schedule 6 to the Gas Act 1965 (wrongful disclosure of information).

Armed Forces Act 1966 (c. 45)

64   An offence under section 8 of the Armed Forces Act 1966 (false statements on entry into Royal Navy).

Agriculture Act 1967 (c. 22)

65   An offence under section 6(9) of the Agriculture Act 1967 (compulsory use of systems of classification of carcases).
66   An offence under section 14(2) of that Act (levy schemes: requirements in relation to registration, returns and records).
67   An offence under section 69 of that Act (false statements to obtain grants etc).

Sea Fisheries (Shellfish) Act 1967 (c. 83)

68   An offence under section 14(2) of the Sea Fisheries (Shellfish) Act 1967 (offences relating to the deposit and importation of shellfish).

Theatres Act 1968 (c. 54)

69   An offence under section 13(1) or (2) of the Theatres Act 1968 (offences relating to licensing of premises for public performances of plays).

Theft Act 1968 (c. 60)

70   An offence under paragraph 2(1) of Schedule 1 to the Theft Act 1968 (taking or destroying fish).

Agriculture Act 1970 (c. 40)

71   An offence under section 106(8) of the Agriculture Act 1970 (eradication of brucellosis: obstructing or impeding an officer in the exercise of powers to obtain information).

Breeding of Dogs Act 1973 (c. 60)

72   An offence under the Breeding of Dogs Act 1973 (offences connected with the licensing of breeding establishments for dogs), other than under section 2 of that Act.

Slaughterhouses Act 1974 (c. 3)

73   An offence under section 4(5) of the Slaughterhouses Act 1974 (knacker's yard licences and applications for such licences).

National Health Service Act 1977 (c. 49)

74   An offence under paragraph 8(3) or 9(4) of Schedule 11 to the National Health Service Act 1977 (offences relating to the production of documents etc.).

Magistrates' Courts Act 1980 (c. 43)

75   An offence under section 84(3) of the Magistrates' Courts Act 1980 (making of false statement as to means).

Animal Health Act 1981 (c. 22)

76   An offence under paragraph 6 of Schedule 1 to the Animal Health Act 1981 (offences relating to the manufacture of veterinary therapeutic substances).

Fisheries Act 1981 (c. 29)

77   An offence under section 5(4) of the Fisheries Act 1981 (alteration of records or furnishing false information).

Civil Aviation Act 1982 (c. 16)

78   An offence under section 82 of the Civil Aviation Act 1982 (using an aircraft for advertising, etc.).

Mental Health Act 1983 (c. 20)

79   An offence under section 103 of the Mental Health Act 1983 (wrongful disclosure of a report made by a Visitor).
80   An offence under section 129 of that Act (obstruction).

Building Act 1984 (c. 55)

81   An offence under section 96(3) of the Building Act 1984 (wrongful disclosure of information).

Surrogacy Arrangements Act 1985 (c. 49)

82   An offence under section 2 of the Surrogacy Arrangements Act 1985 (negotiating surrogacy arrangements on a commercial basis, etc.).

Animals (Scientific Procedures) Act 1986 (c. 14)

83   An offence under section 22(3), 23 or 25(3) of the Animals (Scientific Procedures) Act 1986 (false statements and offences in relation to powers of entry).

Motor Cycle Noise Act 1987 (c. 34)

84   An offence under paragraph 1 of Schedule 1 to the Motor Cycle Noise Act 1987 (supply of exhaust systems etc. not complying with prescribed requirements).

Human Organ Transplants Act 1989 (c. 31)

85   An offence under section 2 of the Human Organ Transplants Act 1989 (restrictions on organ transplants).

Town and Country Planning Act 1990 (c. 8)

86   An offence under paragraph 14(4) of Schedule 15 to the Town and Country Planning Act 1990 (wrongful disclosure of information).

Environmental Protection Act 1990 (c. 43)

87   An offence under section 118(1)(g), (h) or (i) of the Environmental Protection Act 1990 (offences relating to inspection of genetically modified organisms).

Criminal Justice Act 1991 (c. 53)

88   An offence under section 20A of the Criminal Justice Act 1991 (false statements as to financial circumstances).

Deer Act 1991 (c. 54)

89   An offence under section 10(3) of the Deer Act 1991 (offences relating to sale and purchase etc. of venison).

Water Industry Act 1991 (c. 56)

90   An offence under section 206(2) of the Water Industry Act 1991 (wrongful disclosure of information).
91   An offence that falls within paragraph 5(5) of Schedule 6 to that Act (wrongful disclosure of information).

Social Security Administration Act 1992 (c. 5)

92   An offence under section 105 of the Social Security Administration Act 1992 (failure of person to maintain himself or another).
93   An offence under section 182 of that Act (illegal possession of documents).

Local Government Finance Act 1992 (c. 14)

94 An offence under section 27(5) of the Local Government Finance Act 1992 (false statements in relation to properties).

Trade Union and Labour Relations (Consolidation) Act 1992 (c. 52)

95 An offence under section 240 of the Trade Union and Labour Relations (Consolidation) Act 1992 (breach of contract involving injury to persons or property).

Merchant Shipping Act 1995 (c. 21)

96 An offence under section 57 of the Merchant Shipping Act 1995 (offences relating to merchant navy uniforms).

Reserve Forces Act 1996 (c. 14)

97 An offence under section 75(5) of the Reserve Forces Act 1996 (making false statements).
98 An offence under section 82(1) of that Act (offences in connection with regulations under sections 78 and 79 of that Act).
99 An offence under section 87(1) of that Act (offences in connection with claims for payment).
100 An offence under section 99 of that Act (false pretence of illegal absence).
101 An offence under paragraph 5(1) of Schedule 1 to that Act (false answers in attestation papers).

Housing Act 1996 (c. 52)

102 An offence under paragraph 23 or 24 of Schedule 1 to the Housing Act 1996 (contravening order not to part with money etc. held on behalf of a social landlord).

Broadcasting Act 1996 (c. 55)

103 An offence under section 144 of the Broadcasting Act 1996 (providing false information in connection with licences).

Breeding and Sale of Dogs (Welfare) Act 1999 (c. 11)

104 An offence under section 8 or 9(6) of the Breeding and Sale of Dogs (Welfare) Act 1999 (offences relating to the sale of dogs and connected matters).

Transport Act 2000 (c. 38)

105 An offence under section 82(2) of the Transport Act 2000 (wrongful disclosure of information).

SCHEDULE 26   INCREASE IN MAXIMUM TERM FOR CERTAIN SUMMARY OFFENCES

Section 280(2)

Railway Regulation Act 1840 (c. 97)

1   In section 16 of the Railway Regulation Act 1840 (obstructing officers or trespassing upon railway), for 'one month', there is substituted '51 weeks'.

Licensing Act 1872 (c. 94)

2   In section 12 of the Licensing Act 1872 (penalty for being found drunk), for 'one month' there is substituted '51 weeks'.

Regulation of Railways Act 1889 (c. 57)

3   In section 5 of the Regulation of Railways Act 1889 (avoiding payment of fares, etc.), in subsection (3), for 'three months' there is substituted '51 weeks'.

Witnesses (Public Inquiries) Protection Act 1892 (c. 64)

4   In section 2 of the Witnesses (Public Inquiries) Protection Act 1892 (persons obstructing or intimidating witnesses), for 'three months' there is substituted '51 weeks'.

Licensing Act 1902 (c. 28)

5   In section 2 of the Licensing Act 1902 (penalty for being drunk while in charge of a child), in subsection (1), for 'one month' there is substituted '51 weeks'.

Emergency Powers Act 1920 (c. 55)

6   In section 2 of the Emergency Powers Act 1920 (emergency regulations), in subsection (3), for 'three months' there is substituted '51 weeks'.

Judicial Proceedings (Regulation of Reports) Act 1926 (c. 61)

7   In section 1 of the Judicial Proceedings (Regulation of Reports) Act 1926 (restriction on publication of reports of judicial proceedings), in subsection (2), for 'four months' there is substituted '51 weeks'.

Public Order Act 1936 (1 Edw. 8 & 1 Geo. 6 c. 6)

8   In section 7 of the Public Order Act 1936 (enforcement), in subsection (2), for 'three months' there is substituted '51 weeks'.

Cinematograph Films (Animals) Act 1937 (c. 59)

9   In section 1 of the Cinematograph Films (Animals) Act 1937 (prohibition of films involving cruelty to animals), in subsection (3), for 'three months' there is substituted '51 weeks'.

House to House Collections Act 1939 (c. 44)

10   In section 8 of the House to House Collections Act 1939, in subsection (2), for 'three months' there is substituted '51 weeks'.

Fire Services Act 1947 (c. 41)

11   In section 31 of the Fire Services Act 1947 (false alarms of fire), in subsection (1), for 'three months' there is substituted '51 weeks'.

National Assistance Act 1948 (c. 29)

12   (1)   The National Assistance Act 1948 is amended as follows.
     (2)   In section 51 (failure to maintain), in subsection (3)(a) and (b), for 'three months' there is substituted '51 weeks'.
     (3)   In section 52 (false statements), in subsection (1), for 'three months' there is substituted '51 weeks'.

Docking and Nicking of Horses Act 1949 (c. 70)

13   (1)   The Docking and Nicking of Horses Act 1949 is amended as follows.
     (2)   In section 1 (prohibition of docking and nicking except in certain cases), in subsection (3), for 'three months' there is substituted '51 weeks'.
     (3)   In section 2 (restriction on landing docked horses) –

         (a)   in subsection (3), and
         (b)   in subsection (4),

     for '3 months' there is substituted '51 weeks'.

Protection of Animals (Amendment) Act 1954 (c. 40)

14   In section 2 of the Protection of Animals (Amendment) Act 1954 (breach of disqualification order), for 'three months' there is substituted '51 weeks'.

Children and Young Persons (Harmful Publications) Act 1955 (c. 28)

15   In section 2 of the Children and Young Persons (Harmful Publications) Act 1955 (penalty for publishing certain works etc.), in subsection (1), for 'four months' there is substituted '51 weeks'.

Agriculture Act 1957 (c. 57)

16   In section 7 of the Agriculture Act 1957 (penalties) –

     (a)   in subsection (1), for 'three months' there is substituted '51 weeks', and
     (b)   in subsection (2), for 'one month' there is substituted '51 weeks'.

Animals (Cruel Poisons) Act 1962 (c. 26)

17   In section 1 of the Animals (Cruel Poisons) Act 1962 (offences and penalties under regulations), in paragraph (b), for 'three months' there is substituted '51 weeks'.

Plant Varieties and Seeds Act 1964 (c. 14)

18   In section 27 of the Plant Varieties and Seeds Act 1964 (tampering with samples), in subsection (1), for 'three months' there is substituted '51 weeks'.

Agriculture Act 1967 (c. 22)

19   (1) The Agriculture Act 1967 is amended as follows.
      (2) In section 6 (penalties), in subsection (4), for 'three months' there is substituted '51 weeks'.
      (3) In section 21 (inquiry by Meat and Livestock Commission), in subsection (11), for 'three months' there is substituted '51 weeks'.

Firearms Act 1968 (c. 27)

20   (1) Part 1 of Schedule 6 to the Firearms Act 1968 (prosecution and punishment of offences) is amended as follows.
      (2) In the entry relating to section 3(6) of that Act (business and other transactions with firearms and ammunition), in the fourth column, for '3 months' there is substituted '51 weeks'.
      (3) In the entry relating to section 6(3) of that Act (power to prohibit movement of arms and ammunition), in the fourth column, for '3 months' there is substituted '51 weeks'.
      (4) In the entry relating to section 20(2) of that Act (trespassing with firearm), in the fourth column, for '3 months' there is substituted '51 weeks'.
      (5) In the entry relating to section 22(1A) of that Act (acquisition and possession of firearms by minors), in the fourth column, for '3 months' there is substituted '51 weeks'.
      (6) In the entry relating to section 25 of that Act (supplying firearm to person drunk or insane), in the fourth column, for '3 months' there is substituted '51 weeks'.
      (7) In the entry relating to section 32C(6) of that Act (variation endorsement etc. of European documents), in the fourth column, for '3 months' there is substituted '51 weeks'.
      (8) In the entry relating to section 42A of that Act (information as to transactions under visitors' permits), in the fourth column, for '3 months' there is substituted '51 weeks'.
      (9) In the entry relating to section 47(2) of that Act (powers of constables to stop and search), in the fourth column, for '3 months' there is substituted '51 weeks'.
      (10) In the entry relating to section 49(3) of that Act (police powers in relation to arms traffic), in the fourth column, for '3 months' there is substituted '51 weeks'.

Agriculture (Miscellaneous Provisions) Act 1968 (c. 34)

21   In section 7 of the Agriculture (Miscellaneous Provisions) Act 1968 (punishment of offences under Part 1), in subsection (1), for 'three months' there is substituted '51 weeks'.

Agriculture Act 1970 (c. 40)

22   (1) The Agriculture Act 1970 is amended as follows.

(2) In section 68 (duty to give statutory statement), in subsection (4), for 'three months' there is substituted '51 weeks'.

(3) In section 69 (marking of material prepared for sale), in subsection (4), for 'three months' there is substituted '51 weeks'.

(4) In section 70 (use of names or expressions with prescribed meanings), in subsection (2), for 'three months' there is substituted '51 weeks'.

(5) In section 71 (particulars to be given of attributes if claimed to be present), in subsection (2), for 'three months' there is substituted '51 weeks'.

(6) In section 73 (deleterious ingredients in feeding stuff), in subsection (4), for 'three months' there is substituted '51 weeks'.

(7) In section 73A (unwholesome feeding stuff), in subsection (4), for 'three months' there is substituted '51 weeks'.

(8) In section 74A (regulations controlling the contents of feeding stuff), in subsection (3), for 'three months' there is substituted '51 weeks'.

(9) In section 79 (supplementary provision relating to samples and analysis), in subsection (10), for 'three months' there is substituted '51 weeks'.

(10) In section 83 (exercise of powers by inspectors), in subsection (3), for 'three months' there is substituted '51 weeks'.

(11) In section 106 (eradication of brucellosis), in subsection (7), for 'three months' there is substituted '51 weeks'.

Slaughterhouses Act 1974 (c. 3)

23   (1) The Slaughterhouses Act 1974 is amended as follows.

(2) In section 20 (wrongful disclosure of information), in subsection (4), for 'three months' there is substituted '51 weeks'.

(3) In section 21 (obstruction), in subsection (1), for 'one month' there is substituted '51 weeks'.

(4) In section 23 (prosecution and punishment of offences), in subsection (2)(a), for 'three months' there is substituted '51 weeks'.

Criminal Law Act 1977 (c. 45)

24   In section 8 of the Criminal Law Act 1977 (trespassing with a weapon of offence), in subsection (3), for 'three months' there is substituted '51 weeks'.

Refuse Disposal (Amenity) Act 1978 (c. 3)

25   In section 2 of the Refuse Disposal (Amenity) Act 1978 (penalty for unauthorised dumping), in subsection (1), for 'three months' there is substituted '51 weeks'.

Customs and Excise Management Act 1979 (c. 2)

26   (1) The Customs and Excise Management Act 1979 is amended as follows.

(2) In section 21 (control of movement of aircraft), in subsection (6), for '3 months' there is substituted '51 weeks'.

(3) In section 33 (power to inspect aircraft etc.), in subsection (4), for '3 months' there is substituted '51 weeks'.

(4) In section 34 (power to prevent flight of aircraft) –

(a)   in subsection (2), and
(b)   in subsection (3),

for '3 months' there is substituted '51 weeks'.

Licensed Premises (Exclusion of Certain Persons) Act 1980 (c. 32)

27   In section 2 of the Licensed Premises (Exclusion of Certain Persons) Act 1980 (penalty for non-compliance with an exclusion order), in subsection (1), for 'one month' there is substituted '51 weeks'.

Criminal Attempts Act 1981 (c. 47)

28   In section 9 of the Criminal Attempts Act 1981 (interference with vehicles), in subsection (3), for 'three months' there is substituted '51 weeks'.

British Nationality Act 1981 (c. 61)

29   In section 46 of the British Nationality Act 1981 (offences and proceedings), in subsection (1) for 'three months' there is substituted '51 weeks'.

Civil Aviation Act 1982 (c. 16)

30   (1)   The Civil Aviation Act 1982 is amended as follows.
     (2)   In section 44 (offences relating to the power to obtain rights over land), in subsection (10), for 'three months' there is substituted '51 weeks'.
     (3)   In section 75 (investigation of accidents), in subsection (5), for 'three months' there is substituted '51 weeks'.

Anatomy Act 1984 (c. 14)

31   In section 11 of the Anatomy Act 1984 (offences), in subsection (6), for '3 months' there is substituted '51 weeks'.

Public Health (Control of Disease) Act 1984 (c. 22)

32   (1)   The Public Health (Control of Disease) Act 1984 is amended as follows.
     (2)   In section 29 (letting of house after recent case of notifiable disease), in subsection (1), for 'one month' there is substituted '51 weeks'.
     (3)   In section 30 (duty on ceasing to occupy house after recent case of notifiable disease), in subsection (1), for 'one month' there is substituted '51 weeks'.
     (4)   In section 62 (powers of entry), in subsection (3), for '3 months' there is substituted '51 weeks'.

County Courts Act 1984 (c. 28)

33   (1)   The County Courts Act 1984 is amended as follows.
     (2)   In section 14 (penalty for assaulting officers), in subsection (1)(a), for '3 months' there is substituted '51 weeks'.
     (3)   In section 92 (penalty for rescuing goods seized), in subsection (1)(a), for 'one month' there is substituted '51 weeks.'

Animal Health and Welfare Act 1984 (c. 40)

34   In section 10 of the Animal Health and Welfare Act 1984 (artificial breeding of livestock), in subsection (6), for 'three months' there is substituted '51 weeks'.

Police and Criminal Evidence Act 1984 (c. 60)

35   In section 63C of the Police and Criminal Evidence Act 1984 (testing for presence of drugs), in subsection (1), for 'three months' there is substituted '51 weeks'.

Sporting Events (Control of Alcohol etc.) Act 1985 (c. 57)

36   In section 8 of the Sporting Events (Control of Alcohol etc.) Act 1985 (penalties for offences), in paragraph (b), for 'three months' there is substituted '51 weeks'.

Public Order Act 1986 (c. 64)

37   (1)   The Public Order Act 1986 is amended as follows.
     (2)   In section 12 (imposing conditions on public processions) –

    (a)   in subsection (8), and
    (b)   in subsection (10),

for '3 months' there is substituted '51 weeks'.
     (3)   In section 13 (prohibiting public processions) –

    (a)   in subsection (11), and
    (b)   in subsection (13),

for '3 months' there is substituted '51 weeks'.
     (4)   In section 14 (imposing conditions on public assemblies) –

    (a)   in subsection (8), and
    (b)   in subsection (10),

for '3 months' there is substituted '51 weeks'.
     (5)   In section 14B (offences in connection with trespassory assemblies and arrest therefor) –

    (a)   in subsection (5), and
    (b)   in subsection (7),

for '3 months' there is substituted '51 weeks'.

Road Traffic Offenders Act 1988 (c. 53)

38   (1)   Part 1 of Schedule 2 to the Road Traffic Offenders Act 1988 (prosecution and punishment of offenders) is amended as follows.
     (2)   In the entry relating to section 4(2) of the Road Traffic Act 1988 (driving, or being in charge, when under the influence of drink or drugs), in column 4, for '3 months' there is substituted '51 weeks'.
     (3)   In the entry relating to section 5(1)(b) of that Act (driving or being in charge of a motor vehicle with alcohol concentration above prescribed limit), in column 4, for '3 months' there is substituted '51 weeks'.
     (4)   In the entry relating to section 7 of that Act (provision of specimens for analysis), in column 4, for '3 months' there is substituted '51 weeks'.
     (5)   In the entry relating to section 7A of that Act (failing to allow specimen to be subjected to analysis), in column 4, for '3 months' there is substituted '51 weeks'.

Official Secrets Act 1989 (c. 6)

39   In section 10 of the Official Secrets Act 1989 (penalties), in subsection (2), for 'three months' there is substituted '51 weeks'.

Human Organ Transplants Act 1989 (c. 31)

40   In section 1 of the Human Organ Transplants Act 1989 (prohibition of commercial dealings in human organs), in subsection (5), for 'three months' there is substituted '51 weeks'.

Football Spectators Act 1989 (c. 37)

41   In section 2 of the Football Spectators Act 1989 (unauthorised attendance at designated football matches), in subsection (3), for 'one month' there is substituted '51 weeks'.

Food Safety Act 1990 (c. 16)

42   In section 35 of the Food Safety Act 1990 (punishment of offences), in subsection (1), for 'three months' there is substituted '51 weeks'.

Deer Act 1991 (c. 54)

43   In section 9 of the Deer Act 1991 (penalties for offences relating to deer), in subsection (1), for 'three months' there is substituted '51 weeks'.

Social Security Administration Act 1992 (c. 5)

44   In section 112 of the Social Security Administration Act 1992 (false representations for obtaining benefit etc.), in subsection (2), for '3 months' there is substituted '51 weeks'.

Criminal Justice and Public Order Act 1994 (c. 33)

45   (1) The Criminal Justice and Public Order Act 1994 is amended as follows.
       (2) In section 60 (failing to stop), in subsection (8), for 'one month' there is substituted '51 weeks'.
       (3) In section 60AA (powers to require removal of disguises), in subsection (7), for 'one month' there is substituted '51 weeks'.
       (4) In section 61 (power to remove trespasser on land), in subsection (4), for 'three months' there is substituted '51 weeks'.
       (5) In section 62B (failure to comply with direction under section 62A: offences), in subsection (3), for '3 months' there is substituted '51 weeks'.
       (6) In section 63 (powers to remove persons attending or preparing for a rave), in subsections (6) and (7B), for 'three months' there is substituted '51 weeks'.
       (7) In section 68 (offence of aggravated trespass), in subsection (3), for 'three months' there is substituted '51 weeks'.
       (8) In section 69 (powers to remove persons committing or participating in aggravated trespass), in subsection (3), for 'three months' there is substituted '51 weeks'.

London Local Authorities Act 1995 (c. x)

46   In section 24 of the London Local Authorities Act 1995 (enforcement), in subsection (1), for 'three months' there is substituted '51 weeks'.

Police Act 1996 (c. 16)

47   In section 89 of the Police Act 1996 (assaults on constables etc.), in subsection (2), for 'one month' there is substituted '51 weeks'.

Treasure Act 1996 (c. 24)

48   In section 8 of the Treasure Act 1996 (duty of finder of treasure to notify coroner), in subsection (3)(a), for 'three months' there is substituted '51 weeks'.

Education Act 1996 (c. 56)

49   (1) The Education Act 1996 is amended as follows.
     (2) In section 444 (failure to secure regular attendance at school), in subsection (8A)(b), for 'three months' there is substituted '51 weeks'.
     (3) In section 559 (prohibition or restriction on employment of children), in subsection (4)(b), for 'one month' there is substituted '51 weeks'.

Government of Wales Act 1998 (c. 38)

50   In section 75 of the Government of Wales Act 1998 (witnesses and documents: supplementary), in subsection (3)(b), for 'three months' there is substituted '51 weeks'.

Access to Justice Act 1999 (c. 22)

51   In section 21 of the Access to Justice Act 1999 (misrepresentation etc), in subsection (2)(b), for 'three months' there is substituted '51 weeks'.

Greater London Authority Act 1999 (c. 29)

52   In section 64 of the Greater London Authority Act 1999 (failure to attend proceedings etc), in subsection (2)(b), for 'three months' there is substituted '51 weeks'.

Immigration and Asylum Act 1999 (c. 33)

53   (1) The Immigration and Asylum Act 1999 is amended as follows.
     (2) In section 105 (false representation), in subsection (2), for 'three months' there is substituted '51 weeks'.
     (3) In section 108 (failure of sponsor to maintain), in subsection (2), for '3 months' there is substituted '51 weeks'.

Financial Services and Markets Act 2000 (c. 8)

54   (1)   The Financial Services and Markets Act 2000 is amended as follows.
     (2)   In section 177 (offences), in subsection (6), for 'three months' there is sub-
           stituted '51 weeks'.
     (3)   In section 352 (offences), in subsection (5), for 'three months' there is sub-
           stituted '51 weeks'.

Terrorism Act 2000 (c. 11)

55   (1)   The Terrorism Act 2000 is amended as follows.
     (2)   In section 36 (police powers), in subsection (4)(a), for 'three months' there is
           substituted '51 weeks'.
     (3)   In section 51 (offences in relation to parking), in subsection (6)(a), for 'three
           months' there is substituted '51 weeks'.
     (4)   In Schedule 5 (terrorist investigations: information) –

           (a)   in paragraph 3(8)(a), and
           (b)   in paragraph 15(5)(a),

           for 'three months' there is substituted '51 weeks'.
     (5)   In Schedule 7 (ports and border controls), in paragraph 18(2)(a), for 'three
           months' there is substituted '51 weeks'.

Criminal Justice and Police Act 2001 (c. 16)

56   (1)   The Criminal Justice and Police Act 2001 is amended as follows.
     (2)   In section 25 (enforcement of closure orders) –

           (a)   in subsection (3)(a), for 'one month' there is substituted '51 weeks', and
           (b)   in subsections (4) and (5), for 'three months' there is substituted '51
                 weeks'.
     (3)   In section 42 (prevention of intimidation), in subsection (7), for 'three months'
           there is substituted '51 weeks'.

Police Reform Act 2002 (c. 30)

57   In section 46 of the Police Reform Act 2002 (offences against designated and accred-
     ited persons etc.), in subsection (2), for 'one month' there is substituted '51 weeks'.

Nationality, Immigration and Asylum Act 2002 (c. 41)

58   In section 137 of the Nationality, Immigration and Asylum Act 2002 (offences relat-
     ing to the disclosure of information), in subsection (2)(a), for 'three months' there is
     substituted '51 weeks'.

Anti-social Behaviour Act 2003 (c. 38)

59   In section 40 of the Anti-social Behaviour Act 2003 (closure of noisy premises), in
     subsection (5)(a), for 'three months' there is substituted '51 weeks'.

SCHEDULE 27   ENABLING POWERS: ALTERATION
OF MAXIMUM PENALTIES ETC.   Section 283

Plant Health Act 1967 (c. 8)

1   (1) Section 3 of the Plant Health Act 1967 (control of spread of pests in Great
          Britain) is amended as follows.
     (2) In subsection (4A), for 'three months' there is substituted 'the prescribed term'.
     (3) After that subsection there is inserted –

          '(4B) In subsection (4A) above, "the prescribed term" means –

                 (a) in relation to England and Wales, 51 weeks;
                 (b) in relation to Scotland, three months.'

Agriculture Act 1967 (c. 22)

2   (1) Section 9 of the Agriculture Act 1967 (powers to meet future developments in
          livestock and livestock products industries) is amended as follows.
     (2) In subsection (10), for 'three months' there is substituted 'the prescribed term'.
     (3) After that subsection there is inserted –

          '(10A) In subsection (10), "the prescribed term" means –

                  (a) in relation to England and Wales, 51 weeks;
                  (b) in relation to Scotland, three months.'

European Communities Act 1972 (c. 68)

3   (1) Paragraph 1 of Schedule 2 to the European Communities Act 1972 (provisions
          as to powers conferred by section 2(2)) is amended as follows.
     (2) In sub-paragraph (1)(d), for 'three months' there is substituted 'the prescribed
          term'.
     (3) After sub-paragraph (2) there is inserted –

          '(3) In sub-paragraph (1)(d), "the prescribed term" means –

                (a) in relation to England and Wales, where the offence is a summary
                     offence, 51 weeks;
                (b) in relation to England and Wales, where the offence is triable either
                     way, twelve months;
                (c) in relation to Scotland and Northern Ireland, three months.'

Slaughterhouses Act 1974 (c. 3)

4   In section 38(5) of the Slaughterhouses Act 1974 (maximum penalties to be pre-
     scribed by regulations), the words 'or imprisonment for a term of three months or
     both' are omitted.

Anatomy Act 1984 (c. 14)

5   (1) Section 11 of the Anatomy Act 1984 (offences) is amended as follows.
     (2) In subsection (7), for '3 months' there is substituted 'the prescribed term'.
     (3) After that subsection there is inserted –

'(7A) In subsection (7), "the prescribed term" means –

(a) in relation to England and Wales, 51 weeks;
(b) in relation to Scotland, 3 months.'

Environmental Protection Act 1990 (c. 43)

6   (1) Section 141 of the Environmental Protection Act 1990 (power to prohibit or restrict the importation or exportation of waste) is amended as follows.

(2) In paragraph (g) of subsection (5), for 'six months' there is substituted 'the prescribed term'.

(3) After that subsection there is inserted –

'(5A) In subsection (5)(g), "the prescribed term" means –

(a) in relation to England and Wales, where the offence is a summary offence, 51 weeks;
(b) in relation to England and Wales, where the offence is triable either way, twelve months;
(c) in relation to Scotland and Northern Ireland, six months.'

Scotland Act 1998 (c. 46)

7   (1) Section 113 of the Scotland Act 1998 (subordinate legislation: scope of powers) is amended as follows.

(2) In paragraph (a) of subsection (10), for 'three months' there is substituted 'the prescribed term'.

(3) After that subsection there is inserted –

'(10A) In subsection (10)(a), "the prescribed term" means –

(a) in relation to England and Wales, where the offence is a summary offence, 51 weeks;
(b) in relation to England and Wales, where the offence is triable either way, twelve months;
(c) in relation to Scotland and Northern Ireland, three months.'

Regulatory Reform Act 2001 (c. 6)

8   (1) Section 3 of the Regulatory Reform Act 2001 (limitations on order-making power) is amended as follows.

(2) In paragraph (b) of subsection (3), for 'six months' there is substituted 'the prescribed term'.

(3) After that subsection there is inserted –

'(3A) In subsection (3)(b), "the prescribed term" means –

(a) in relation to England and Wales, where the offence is a summary offence, 51 weeks;
(b) in relation to England and Wales, where the offence is triable either way, twelve months;
(c) in relation to Scotland and Northern Ireland, six months.'

SCHEDULE 28   INCREASE IN PENALTIES FOR
DRUG-RELATED OFFENCES
Section 284

Misuse of Drugs Act 1971 (c. 38)

1 (1) Schedule 4 to the Misuse of Drugs Act 1971 (prosecution and punishment of offences) is amended as follows.

   (2) In column 6 of that Schedule (punishments for offences under that Act committed in relation to Class C drugs), in each of the following entries, for '5 years' there is substituted '14 years'.

   (3) Those entries are the entries relating to the punishment, on conviction on indictment, of offences under the following provisions of that Act –

   (a) section 4(2) (production, or being concerned in the production, of a controlled drug),

   (b) section 4(3) (supplying or offering to supply a controlled drug or being concerned in the doing of either activity by another),

   (c) section 5(3) (having possession of a controlled drug with intent to supply it to another),

   (d) section 8 (being the occupier, or concerned in the management, of premises and permitting or suffering certain activities to take place there),

   (e) section 12(6) (contravention of direction prohibiting practitioner etc from possessing, supplying etc controlled drugs), and

   (f) section 13(3) (contravention of direction prohibiting practitioner etc from prescribing, supplying etc controlled drugs).

Customs and Excise Management Act 1979 (c. 2)

2 In Schedule 1 to the Customs and Excise Management Act 1979 (controlled drugs: variation of punishments for certain offences under that Act), in paragraph 2(c) (punishment on conviction on indictment of offences under that Act committed in relation to Class C drugs), for '5 years' there is substituted '14 years'.

Criminal Justice (International Co-operation) Act 1990 (c. 5)

3 In section 19 of the Criminal Justice (International Co-operation) Act 1990 (ships used for illicit traffic), in subsection (4)(c)(ii) (punishment on conviction on indictment of offences under that section committed in relation to Class C drugs), for 'five years' there is substituted 'fourteen years'.

SCHEDULE 29   SENTENCING FOR FIREARMS OFFENCES
IN NORTHERN IRELAND
Section 292

1 The Firearms (Northern Ireland) Order 1981 (S.I. 1981/155 (N.I. 2)) is amended as follows.

2 In Article 2(2) (interpretation) after the definition of 'firearms dealer' there is inserted –

'"handgun" means any firearm which either has a barrel less than 30 centimetres in length or is less than 60 centimetres in length overall, other than an air weapon, a muzzle-loading gun or a firearm designed as signalling apparatus;'.

3 In Article 3(1) (requirement of firearm certificate) for sub-paragraph (a) there is substituted –

'(aa) has in his possession, or purchases or acquires, a handgun without holding a firearm certificate in force at the time, or otherwise than as authorised by such a certificate;

(ab) has in his possession, or purchases or acquires, any firearm, other than a handgun, without holding a firearm certificate in force at the time, or otherwise than as authorised by such a certificate; or'.

4   After Article 52 of that Order there is inserted –

'52A Minimum sentence for certain offences

(1)   This Article applies where –

(a)   an individual is convicted of –

(i) an offence under Article 3(1)(aa),

(ii) an offence under Article 6(1)(a), (ab), (ac), (ad), (ae) or (c), or

(iii) an offence under Article 6(1A)(a), and

(b)   the offence was committed after the commencement of this Article and at a time when he was aged 16 or over.

(2)   The court shall –

(a)   in the case of an offence under Article 3(1)(aa) committed by a person who was aged 21 or over when he committed the offence, impose a sentence of imprisonment for a term of five years (with or without a fine), and

(b)   in any other case, impose an appropriate custodial sentence for a term of at least the required minimum term (with or without a fine)

unless (in any of those cases) the court is of the opinion that there are exceptional circumstances relating to the offence or to the offender which justify its not doing so.

(3)   Where an offence is found to have been committed over a period of two or more days, or at some time during a period of two or more days, it shall be taken for the purposes of this Article to have been committed on the last of those days.

(4)   In this Article –

"appropriate custodial sentence" means –

(a)   in the case of an offender who is aged 21 or over when convicted, a sentence of imprisonment, and

(b)   in the case of an offender who is aged under 21 at that time, a sentence of detention under section 5(1) of the Treatment of Offenders Act (Northern Ireland) 1968;

"the required minimum term" means –

(a)   in the case of an offender who was aged 21 or over when he committed the offence, five years, and

(b)   in the case of an offender who was aged under 21 at that time, three years.'

5   After Article 52A there is inserted –

'52B Power by order to exclude application of minimum sentence to those under 18

(1)   The Secretary of State may by order –

(a)   amend Article 52A(1)(b) by substituting for the word "16" the word "18", and

(b)   make such other provision as he considers necessary or expedient in consequence of, or in connection with, the provision made by virtue of sub-paragraph (a).

(2) The provision that may be made by virtue of paragraph (1)(b) includes, in particular, provision amending or repealing any statutory provision within the meaning of section 1(f) of the Interpretation Act (Northern Ireland) 1954 (whenever passed or made).

(3) An order under paragraph (1) shall be subject to annulment in pursuance of a resolution of either House of Parliament in like manner as a statutory instrument and section 5 of the Statutory Instruments Act 1946 shall apply accordingly.'

6 (1) Schedule 2 (table of punishments) is amended as follows.

(2) For the entry relating to offences under Article 3(1) (purchase, acquisition or possession of firearm or ammunition without firearm certificate) there is substituted –

'Article 3(1)(aa)	Purchase, acquisition or possession of handgun without firearm certificate	Indictment	10 years or a fine, or both
Article 3(1)(ab)	Purchase, acquisition or possession without firearm certificate of firearm other than handgun	(a) Summary	1 year or a fine of the statutory maximum, or both
		(b) Indictment	5 years or a fine, or both
Article 3(1)(b)	Purchase, acquisition or possession of ammunition without firearm certificate	(a) Summary	1 year or a fine of the statutory maximum, or both
		(b) Indictment	5 years or a fine, or both'.

(3) For the entries relating to offences under Article 6(1) (manufacture, dealing in or possession of prohibited weapons) and Article 6(1A) (possession of or dealing in other prohibited weapons) there is substituted –

'Article 6(1)(a), (ab), (ac), (ad), (ae) and (c)	Manufacture, dealing in or possession of prohibited weapons.	Indictment	10 years or a fine, or both

Article 6(1)(b)	Manufacture, dealing in or possession of prohibited weapon designed for discharge of noxious liquid etc.	(a) Summary	1 year or a fine of the statutory maximum, or both
		(b) Indictment	10 years or a fine, or both
Article 6 (1A)(a)	Possession of or dealing in firearm disguised as other object	Indictment	10 years or a fine, or both
Article 6(1A)(b), (c), (d), (e), (f) or (g)	Possession of or dealing in other prohibited weapons	(a) Summary	6 months or a fine of the statutory maximum, or both
		(b) Indictment	10 years or a fine, or both'.

SCHEDULE 30   DISQUALIFICATION FROM WORKING WITH CHILDREN

Section 299

1   The Criminal Justice Court Services Act 2000 (c. 43) is amended as follows.
2   After section 29 there is inserted –

'29A Disqualification at discretion of court: adults and juveniles

(1)   This section applies where –

   (a)   an individual is convicted of an offence against a child (whether or not committed when he was aged 18 or over),
   (b)   the individual is sentenced by a senior court, and
   (c)   no qualifying sentence is imposed in respect of the conviction.

(2)   If the court is satisfied, having regard to all the circumstances, that it is likely that the individual will commit a further offence against a child, it may order the individual to be disqualified from working with children.

(3)   If the court makes an order under this section, it must state its reasons for doing so and cause those reasons to be included in the record of the proceedings.

29B Subsequent application for order under section 28 or 29

(1)   Where –

   (a)   section 28 applies but the court has neither made an order under that section nor complied with subsection (6) of that section, or
   (b)   section 29 applies but the court has not made an order under that section, and it appears to the prosecutor that the court has not considered the making of an order under that section,

the prosecutor may at any time apply to that court for an order under section 28 or 29.

(2) Subject to subsection (3), on an application under subsection (1) –

    (a) in a case falling within subsection (1)(a), the court –

        (i) must make an order under section 28 unless it is satisfied as mentioned in subsection (5) of that section, and

        (ii) if it does not make an order under that section, must comply with subsection (6) of that section,

    (b) in a case falling within subsection (1)(b), the court –

        (i) must make an order under section 29 if it is satisfied as mentioned in subsection (4) of that section, and

        (ii) if it does so, must comply with subsection (5) of that section.

(3) Subsection (2) does not enable or require an order under section 28 or 29 to be made where the court is satisfied that it had considered the making of an order under that section at the time when it imposed the qualifying sentence or made the relevant order.'

3 (1) Section 30 (supplemental provisions) is amended as follows.

  (2) In the heading for 'and 29' there is substituted 'to 29B'.

  (3) In subsection (1) –

    (a) for 'and 29' there is substituted 'to 29B', and

    (b) in the definition of 'qualifying sentence', after paragraph (d) there is inserted –

    '(dd) a sentence of detention under section 198 or 200 of the Criminal Justice Act 2003,'.

  (4) In subsection (5) –

    (a) in paragraph (a), for 'or 29' there is substituted ', 29 or 29A',

    (b) after paragraph (b) there is inserted –

    '(c) in relation to an individual to whom section 29A applies and on whom a sentence has been passed, references to his sentence are to that sentence.'

4 In section 31 (appeals), in subsection (1), after paragraph (b) there is inserted –

'(c) where an order is made under section 29A, as if the order were a sentence passed on him for the offence of which he has been convicted.'

5 (1) Section 33 (conditions for application under section 32) is amended as follows.

  (2) In subsection (6), after paragraph (d) there is inserted –

    '(e) in relation to an individual not falling within any of paragraphs (a) to (d), the day on which the disqualification order is made.'.

  (3) For subsection (8) there is substituted –

    '(8) In subsection (7) "detention" means detention (or detention and training) –

      (a) under any sentence or order falling within paragraphs (b) to (f) of the definition of "qualifying sentence" in section 30(1), or

      (b) under any sentence or order which would fall within those paragraphs if it were for a term or period of 12 months or more.'.

SCHEDULE 31   DEFAULT ORDERS: MODIFICATION OF PROVISIONS RELATING TO COMMUNITY ORDERS

Section 300

General

1   Any reference to the offender is, in relation to a default order, to be read as a reference to the person in default.

Unpaid work requirement

2   (1) In its application to a default order, section 199 (unpaid work requirement) is modified as follows.

(2) In subsection (2), for paragraphs (a) and (b) there is substituted –

'(a) not less than 20 hours, and

(b) in the case of an amount in default which is specified in the first column of the following Table, not more than the number of hours set out opposite that amount in the second column.

TABLE

Amount	Number of Hours
An amount not exceeding £200	40 hours
An amount exceeding £200 but not exceeding £500	60 hours
An amount exceeding £500	100 hours'

(3) Subsection (5) is omitted.

Curfew requirement

3   (1) In its application to a default order, section 204 (curfew requirement) is modified as follows.

(2) After subsection (2) there is inserted –

'(2A) In the case of an amount in default which is specified in the first column of the following Table, the number of days on which the person in default is subject to the curfew requirement must not exceed the number of days set out opposite that amount in the second column.

TABLE

Amount	Number of days
An amount not exceeding £200	20 days
An amount exceeding £200 but not exceeding £500	30 days
An amount exceeding £500 but not exceeding £1,000	60 days
An amount exceeding £1,000 but not exceeding £2,500	90 days
An amount exceeding £2,500	180 days'

Enforcement, revocation and amendment of default order

4 (1) In its application to a default order, Schedule 8 (breach, revocation or amendment of community orders) is modified as follows.

(2) Any reference to the offence in respect of which the community order was made is to be taken to be a reference to the default in respect of which the default order was made.

(3) Any power of the court to revoke the community order and deal with the offender for the offence is to be taken to be a power to revoke the default order and deal with him in any way in which the court which made the default order could deal with him for his default in paying the sum in question.

(4) In paragraph 4 the reference to the Crown Court is to be taken as a reference to a magistrates' court.

(5) The following provisions are omitted –

(a) paragraph 9(1)(c), (5) and (8),
(b) paragraph 12,
(c) paragraph 13(5),
(d) paragraph 15,
(e) paragraph 17(5),
(f) paragraph 21(4), and
(g) paragraph 23(2)(b).

Power to alter amount of money or number of hours or days

5 The Secretary of State may by order amend paragraph 2 or 3 by substituting for any reference to an amount of money or a number of hours or days there specified a reference to such other amount or number as may be specified in the order.

Transfer of default orders to Scotland or Northern Ireland)

6 In its application to a default order, Schedule 9 (transfer of community orders to Scotland or Northern Ireland) is modified as follows.

7 After paragraph 8 there is inserted –

"8A Nothing in paragraph 8 affects the application of section 300(7) to a default order made or amended in accordance with paragraph 1 or 3."

8   In paragraph 10, after paragraph (b) there is inserted –

"(bb) any power to impose a fine on the offender"

SCHEDULE 32   AMENDMENTS RELATING TO SENTENCING

Section 304

PART 1

GENERAL

Piracy Act 1837 (c. 88)

1   Section 3 of the Piracy Act 1837 (punishment for offence under certain repealed Acts relating to piracy) shall cease to have effect.

Children and Young Persons Act 1933 (c. 12)

2   (1) Section 49 of the Children and Young Persons Act 1933 (restrictions on reports of proceedings in which young persons are concerned) is amended as follows.

(2) In subsection (4A)(d), for 'section 62(3) of the Powers of Criminal Courts (Sentencing) Act 2000' there is substituted 'section 222(1)(d) or (e) of the Criminal Justice Act 2003'.

(3) In subsection (11) –

(a) in the definition of 'sexual offence', for 'has the same meaning as in the Powers of Criminal Courts (Sentencing) Act 2000' there is substituted 'means an offence listed in Part 2 of Schedule 15 to the Criminal Justice Act 2003', and

(b) in the definition of 'violent offence', for 'has the same meaning as in the Powers of Criminal Courts (Sentencing) Act 2000' there is substituted 'means an offence listed in Part 1 of Schedule 15 to the Criminal Justice Act 2003'.

Prison Act 1952 (c. 52)

3   In section 53 of the Prison Act 1952 (interpretation), for 'section 62 of the Powers of Criminal Courts (Sentencing) Act 2000' there is substituted 'section 221 of the Criminal Justice Act 2003'.

Criminal Justice Act 1967 (c. 80)

4   The Criminal Justice Act 1967 is amended as follows.

5   In section 32 (amendments of Costs in Criminal Cases Act 1952), in subsection (3)(a), for 'make an order under paragraph 5 of Schedule 2 to the Powers of Criminal Courts (Sentencing) Act 2000 (probation orders requiring treatment for mental condition) or' there is substituted 'include in a community order (within the meaning of Part 12 of the Criminal Justice Act 2003) a mental health requirement under section 207 of that Act or make an order under'.

6   In section 104 (general provisions as to interpretation) –

(a)   in subsection (1), the definition of 'suspended sentence' is omitted, and

(b)   subsection (2) is omitted.

Criminal Appeal Act 1968 (c. 19)

7   The Criminal Appeal Act 1968 is amended as follows.

8   (1)   Section 10 (appeal against sentence in cases dealt with by Crown Court otherwise than on conviction on indictment) is amended as follows.

(2)   In subsection (2) –

(a)   in paragraph (b), for 'or a community order within the meaning of the Powers of Criminal Courts (Sentencing) Act 2000' there is substituted 'a youth community order within the meaning of the Powers of Criminal Courts (Sentencing) Act 2000 or a community order within the meaning of Part 12 of the Criminal Justice Act 2003', and

(b)   paragraph (c) and the word 'or' immediately preceding it are omitted.

9   In section 11 (supplementary provisions as to appeal against sentence), subsection (4) is omitted.

10   In Schedule 2 (procedural and other provisions applicable on order for retrial), in paragraph 2(4), for the words from the beginning to 'apply' there is substituted 'Section 240 of the Criminal Justice Act 2003 (crediting of periods of remand in custody: terms of imprisonment and detention) shall apply'.

Firearms Act 1968 (c. 27)

11   The Firearms Act 1968 is amended as follows.

12   (1)   Section 21 (possession of firearms by persons previously convicted of crime) is amended as follows.

(2)   In subsection (2A), after paragraph (c) there is inserted –

'(d)   in the case of a person who has been subject to a sentence of imprisonment to which an intermittent custody order under section 183(1)(b) of the Criminal Justice Act 2003 relates, the date of his final release.'

(3)   After subsection (2A) there is inserted –

'(2B)   A person who is serving a sentence of imprisonment to which an intermittent custody order under section 183 of the Criminal Justice Act 2003 relates shall not during any licence period specified for the purposes of subsection (1)(b)(i) of that section have a firearm or ammunition in his possession.'

(4)   In subsection (3)(b), for 'probation order' there is substituted 'community order'.

(5)   After subsection (3) there is inserted –

'(3ZA)   In subsection (3)(b) above, 'community order' means –

(a)   a community order within the meaning of Part 12 of the Criminal Justice Act 2003 made in England and Wales, or

(b)   a probation order made in Scotland.'

(6)   In subsection (6), after '(2)' there is inserted, '(2B)'.

13   (1)   Section 52 (forfeiture and disposal of firearms; cancellation of certificate by convicting court) is amended as follows.

(2)   In subsection (1)(c), for 'probation order' there is substituted 'community order'.

(3)   After subsection (1) there is inserted –

'(1A) In subsection (1)(c) "community order" means –

> (a) a community order within the meaning of Part 12 of the Criminal Justice Act 2003 made in England and Wales, or
>
> (b) a probation order made in Scotland.'

Social Work (Scotland) Act 1968 (c. 49)

14   In section 94 of the Social Work (Scotland) Act 1968 (interpretation), in the definition of 'probation order' in subsection (1), for 'community rehabilitation order' there is substituted 'community order within the meaning of Part 12 of the Criminal Justice Act 2003'.

Children and Young Persons Act 1969 (c. 54)

15   In section 23 of the Children and Young Persons Act 1969 (remands and committals to local authority accommodation), for the definition of 'sexual offence' and 'violent offence' in subsection (12) there is substituted –

'"sexual offence" means an offence specified in Part 2 of Schedule 15 to the Criminal Justice Act 2003;

"violent offence" means murder or an offence specified in Part 1 of Schedule 15 to the Criminal Justice Act 2003;'.

Immigraton Act 1971 (c. 77)

16   In section 7 of the Immigration Act 1971 (exemption from deportation for certain existing residents), in subsection (4), for 'section 67 of the Criminal Justice Act 1967' there is substituted 'section 240 of the Criminal Justice Act 2003'.

Thames Barrier and Flood Prevention Act 1972 (c. xiv)

17   In section 56 of the Thames Barrier and Flood Prevention Act 1972 (orders for carrying out certain defence works), in subsection (3)(a)(ii), for 'six months' there is substituted '12 months'.

Rehabilitation of Offenders Act 1974 (c. 53)

18   (1) Section 5 of the Rehabilitation of Offenders Act 1974 (rehabilitation periods for particular offences) is amended as follows.

(2) In subsection (1) –

> (a) at the end of paragraph (e), there is inserted 'and', and
>
> (b) after that paragraph, there is inserted the following paragraph –
>
> > '(f) a sentence of imprisonment for public protection under section 225 of the Criminal Justice Act 2003, a sentence of detention for public protection under section 226 of that Act or an extended sentence under section 227 or 228 of that Act'.

(3) In subsection (4A), after the words 'probation order' there is inserted 'or a community order under section 177 of the Criminal Justice Act 2003'.

Armed Forces Act 1976 (c. 52)

19 (1) Section 8 of the Armed Forces Act 1976 (powers of Standing Civilian Courts in relation to civilians) is amended as follows.

(2) In subsection (1)(a), for 'six months' there is substituted '12 months'.

(3) In subsection (2), for '12 months' there is substituted '65 weeks'.

Bail Act 1976 (c. 63)

20 The Bail Act 1976 is amended as follows.

21 (1) Section 2 (other definitions) is amended as follows.

(2) In subsection (1)(d) –

(a) the words 'placing the offender on probation or' are omitted, and

(b) for 'him' there is substituted 'the offender'.

(3) In subsection (2), in the definition of 'probation hostel', for the words from 'by' onwards there is substituted 'by a community order under section 177 of the Criminal Justice Act 2003'.

22 In section 4 (general right to bail of accused persons and others), in subsection (3), for the words from 'to be dealt with' onwards there is substituted 'or the Crown Court to be dealt with under –

(a) Part 2 of Schedule 3 to the Powers of Criminal Courts (Sentencing) Act 2000 (breach of certain youth community orders), or

(b) Part 2 of Schedule 8 to the Criminal Justice Act 2003 (breach of requirement of community order).'

23 In Part 3 of Schedule 1 (interpretation), in the definition of 'default' in paragraph 4, for the words from 'Part II' onwards there is substituted 'Part 2 of Schedule 8 to the Criminal Justice Act 2003 (breach of requirement of order)'.

Criminal Law Act 1977 (c. 45)

24 In section 3 of the Criminal Law Act 1977 (penalties for conspiracy), in subsection (1), for 'section 127 of the Powers of Criminal Courts (Sentencing) Act 2000' there is substituted 'section 163 of the Criminal Justice Act 2003'.

Magistrates' Courts Act 1980 (c. 43)

25 The Magistrates' Courts Act 1980 is amended as follows.

26 In section 11 (non appearance of accused), in subsection (3), for 'section 119 of the Powers of Criminal Courts (Sentencing) Act 2000' there is substituted 'paragraph 8(2)(a) or (b) of Schedule 12 to the Criminal Justice Act 2003'.

27 In section 33 (maximum penalties on summary conviction in pursuance of section 22), in subsection (1)(a), for '3 months' there is substituted '51 weeks'.

28 In section 85 (power to remit fine), in subsection (2A), for 'section 35(2)(a) or (b) of the Crime (Sentences) Act 1997' there is substituted 'section 300(2) of the Criminal Justice Act 2003'.

29 In section 131 (remand of accused already in custody), after subsection (2) there is inserted –

'(2A) Where the accused person is serving a sentence of imprisonment to which an intermittent custody order under section 183 of the Criminal Justice Act 2003 relates, the reference in subsection (2) to the expected date of his release is to be read as a reference to the expected date of his next release on licence.'.

30   In section 133 (consecutive terms of imprisonment), in subsection (1), for 'Subject to section 84 of the Powers of Criminal Courts (Sentencing) Act 2000,' there is substituted 'Subject to section 265 of the Criminal Justice Act 2003,'.

Law Reform (Miscellaneous Provisions) (Scotland) Act 1980 (c. 55)

31   In Schedule 1 to the Law Reform (Miscellaneous Provisions) (Scotland) Act 1980 (ineligibility for and disqualification and excusal from jury service), in Part 2, in paragraph (bb), for sub-paragraph (v) there is substituted –

'(v) a community order within the meaning of section 177 of the Criminal Justice Act 2003;

(va) a youth community order as defined by section 33 of the Powers of Criminal Courts (Sentencing) Act 2000;'.

Public Passenger Vehicles Act 1981 (c. 14)

32   (1) In Schedule 3 to the Public Passenger Vehicles Act 1981 (supplementary provisions as to qualifications for PSV operators licence), paragraph 1 is amended as follows.

(2) In sub-paragraph (4)(a), for 'a community service order for more than 60 hours' there is substituted 'a community order requiring the offender to perform unpaid work for more than 60 hours'.

(3) In sub-paragraph (6), for the words from 'a community' onwards there is substituted '"a community order" means an order under section 177 of the Criminal Justice Act 2003, a community punishment order made before the commencement of that section or a community service order under the Community Service by Offenders (Scotland) Act 1978'.

Criminal Attempts Act 1981 (c. 47)

33   In section 4 of the Criminal Attempts Act 1981 (trials and penalties), in subsection (5)(b), for sub-paragraph (ii) there is substituted –

'(ii) in section 154(1) and (2) (general limit on magistrates' court's powers to impose imprisonment) of the Criminal Justice Act 2003.'.

Criminal Justice Act 1982 (c. 48)

34   The Criminal Justice Act 1982 is amended as follows.

35   In section 32 (early release of prisoners), in subsection (1)(a), after 'life' there is inserted ', imprisonment for public protection under section 225 of the Criminal Justice Act 2003 or an extended sentence under section 227 of that Act'.

36   (1) Part 3 of Schedule 13 (reciprocal arrangements (Northern Ireland): persons residing in England and Wales or Scotland) is amended as follows.

(2) In paragraph 7 –

(a) in sub-paragraph (2)(b), for 'such orders' there is substituted 'an unpaid work requirement of a community order (within the meaning of Part 12 of the Criminal Justice Act 2003)', and

(b) in sub-paragraph (3)(b), for the words from 'community service orders' onwards there is substituted 'community orders within the meaning of Part 12 of the Criminal Justice Act 2003 conferred on responsible officers by that Part of that Act.'.

(3) For paragraph 9(3) there is substituted –

'(3) Subject to the following provisions of this paragraph –

(a) a community service order made or amended in the circumstances specified in paragraph 7 above shall be treated as if it were a community order made in England and Wales under section 177 of the Criminal Justice Act 2003 and the provisions of Part 12 of that Act (so far as relating to such orders) shall apply accordingly; and

(b) a community service order made or amended in the circumstances specified in paragraph 8 above shall be treated as if it were a community service order made in Scotland and the legislation relating to community service orders in Scotland shall apply accordingly.'

(4) In paragraph 9(4)(a), after 'community service orders' there is inserted 'or, as the case may be, community orders (within the meaning of Part 12 of the Criminal Justice Act 2003)'.

(5) In paragraph 9(5), after 'a community service order' there is inserted 'or, as the case may be, a community order (within the meaning of Part 12 of the Criminal Justice Act 2003)'.

(6) In paragraph 9(6) –

(a) after 'community service orders', where first occurring, there is inserted 'or, as the case may be, community orders (within the meaning of Part 12 of the Criminal Justice Act 2003)', and

(b) in paragraph (b)(i), for 'the Powers of Criminal Courts (Sentencing) Act 2000' there is substituted 'Part 12 of the Criminal Justice Act 2003'.

Mental Health Act 1983 (c. 20)

37 The Mental Health Act 1983 is amended as follows.

38 In section 37 (powers of courts to order hospital admission or guardianship) –

(a) in subsection (1), the words 'or falls to be imposed under section 109(2) of the Powers of Criminal Courts (Sentencing) Act 2000' are omitted,

(b) for subsections (1A) and (1B) there is substituted –

'(1A) In the case of an offence the sentence for which would otherwise fall to be imposed –

(a) under section 51A(2) of the Firearms Act 1968,

(b) under section 110(2) or 111(2) of the Powers of Criminal Courts (Sentencing) Act 2000, or

(c) under any of sections 225 to 228 of the Criminal Justice Act 2003,

nothing in those provisions shall prevent a court from making an order under subsection (1) above for the admission of the offender to a hospital.

(1B) References in subsection (1A) above to a sentence falling to be imposed under any of the provisions mentioned in that subsection are to be read in accordance with section 305(4) of the Criminal Justice Act 2003.'

(c) in subsection (8), for 'probation order' there is substituted 'community order (within the meaning of Part 12 of the Criminal Justice Act 2003)'.

39 In section 45A (powers of higher courts to direct hospital admission), in subsection (1)(b), the words from 'except' to '1997' are omitted.

Repatriation of Prisoners Act 1984 (c. 47)

40 The Repatriation of Prisoners Act 1984 is amended as follows.

41 In section 2 (transfer out of the United Kingdom), in subsection (4)(b), for sub-paragraph (i) there is substituted –

'(i)   released on licence under section 28(5) of the Crime (Sentences) Act 1997 or
under section 244 or 246 of the Criminal Justice Act 2003; or'.

42   In section 3 (transfer into the United Kingdom), subsection (9) is omitted.

43   (1)   The Schedule (operation of certain enactments in relation to the prisoner) is
amended as follows in relation to prisoners repatriated to England and Wales.

(2)   In paragraph 2, for sub-paragraphs (1A) and (2) there is substituted –

'(2)   If the warrant specifies a period to be taken into account for the purposes
of this paragraph, the amount of time the prisoner has served shall, so far
only as the question whether he has served a particular part of a life
sentence is concerned, be deemed to be increased by that period.

(3)   Where the prisoner's sentence is for a term of less than twelve months,
Chapter 6 of Part 12 of the Criminal Justice Act 2003 shall apply as if the
sentence were for a term of twelve months or more.

(4)   In this paragraph –

"the enactments relating to release on licence" means section 28(5) and (7)
of the Crime (Sentences) Act 1997 and Chapter 6 of Part 12 of the
Criminal Justice Act 2003;

"sentence", means the provision included in the warrant which is equivalent
to sentence.'.

(3)   Paragraph 3 is omitted.

Police and Criminal Evidence Act 1984 (c. 60)

44   In section 38 of the Police and Criminal Evidence Act 1984 (duties of custody officer
after charge), for the definitions of 'sexual offence' and 'violent offence' in subsection
(6A) there is substituted –

'"sexual offence" means an offence specified in Part 2 of Schedule 15 to the Criminal
Justice Act 2003;

"violent offence" means murder or an offence specified in Part 1 of that Schedule;'.

Criminal Justice Act 2003 (c. 44)

45   The Criminal Justice Act 1988 is amended as follows.

46   In section 36 (reviews of sentencing), in subsection (2), for the words from 'erred in
law' onwards there is substituted –

'(a)   erred in law as to his powers of sentencing; or

(b)   failed to impose a sentence required by –

(i)   section 51A(2) of the Firearms Act 1968;

(ii)   section 110(2) or 111(2) of the Powers of Criminal Courts (Sentencing)
Act 2000; or

(iii)   any of sections 225 to 228 of the Criminal Justice Act 2003.'

47   In section 50 (suspended and partly suspended sentences on certain civilians in
courts-martial and Standing Civilian Courts), in subsection (3)(b)(i), for 'Powers of
Criminal Courts (Sentencing) Act 2000' there is substituted 'Criminal Justice Act
2003'.

Firearms (Amendment) Act 1988 (c. 45)

48   The Firearms (Amendment) Act 1988 is amended as follows.

49   In section 1 (prohibited weapons and ammunition), in subsection (4A) after paragraph
(b) there is inserted –

'(bb) may amend subsection (1A)(a) of section 91 of the Powers of Criminal Courts (Sentencing) Act 2000 (offenders under 18 convicted of certain serious offences: power to detain for specified period) so as to include a reference to any provision added by the order to section 5(1) of the principal Act,

(bc) may amend section 50(5A)(a), 68(4A)(a) or 170(4A)(a) of the Customs and Excise Management Act 1979 (offences relating to improper importation or exportation) so as to include a reference to anything added by the order to section 5(1) of the principal Act,'.

50 In section 27(4) (which relates to Northern Ireland), after 'Except for' there is inserted 'section 1, so far as enabling provision to be made amending the Customs and Excise Management Act 1979, and'.

Road Traffic Act 1988 (c. 52)

51 In section 164 of the Road Traffic Act 1988 (power of constables to require production of driving licence and in certain cases statement of date of birth), in subsection (5), for 'section 40 of the Crime (Sentences) Act 1997' there is substituted 'section 301 of the Criminal Justice Act 2003'.

Road Traffic Offenders Act 1988 (c. 53)

52 The Road Traffic Offenders Act 1988 is amended as follows.
53 In section 27 (production of licence), in subsection (3), for 'section 40 of the Crime (Sentences) Act 1997' there is substituted 'section 301 of the Criminal Justice Act 2003'.
54 In section 46 (combination of disqualification and endorsement with probation orders and orders for discharge), in subsection (1), paragraph (a) and the word 'or' following it shall cease to have effect.

Football Spectators Act 1989 (c. 37)

55 The Football Spectators Act 1989 is amended as follows.
56 In section 7 (disqualification for membership of scheme), subsection (9) is omitted.
57 In section 14E (banning orders: general), after subsection (6) there is inserted –

'(7) A person serving a sentence of imprisonment to which an intermittent custody order under section 183 of the Criminal Justice Act 2003 relates is to be treated for the purposes of this section as having been detained in legal custody until his final release; and accordingly any reference in this section to release is, in relation to a person serving such a sentence, a reference to his final release.'

58 In section 18 (information), after subsection (4) there is inserted –

'(5) In relation to a person serving a sentence of imprisonment to which an intermittent custody order under section 183 of the Criminal Justice Act 2003 relates, any reference in this section to his detention or to his release shall be construed in accordance with section 14E(7).'

Children Act 1989 (c. 41)

59 The Children Act 1989 is amended as follows.
60 (1) Section 68 (persons disqualified from being foster parents) is amended as follows.
(2) In subsection (2)(d), the words 'a probation order has been made in respect of him or he has been' are omitted.

(3)   After subsection (2) there is inserted –

'(2A)   A conviction in respect of which a probation order was made before 1st October 1992 (which would not otherwise be treated as a conviction) is to be treated as a conviction for the purposes of subsection (2)(d).'

61   (1)   In Schedule 9A (child minding and day care for young children), paragraph 4 is amended as follows.

(2)   In sub-paragraph (2)(g), the words 'placed on probation or' are omitted.

(3)   At the end there is inserted –

'(7)   A conviction in respect of which a probation order was made before 1st October 1992 (which would not otherwise be treated as a conviction) is to be treated as a conviction for the purposes of this paragraph.'.

Criminal Justice Act 1991 (c. 53)

62   The Criminal Justice Act 1991 is amended as follows.

63   Section 65 (supervision of young offenders after release) is omitted.

64   (1)   Schedule 3 (reciprocal enforcement of certain orders) is amended as follows.

(2)   In paragraph 10(3)(d), for the words from 'paragraph 3 of Schedule 2' onwards there is substituted 'section 201 of the Criminal Justice Act 2003'.

(3)   In paragraph 11(2) –

(a)   in paragraph (a) –

(i)   for 'probation order' there is substituted 'community order', and

(ii)   after 'England and Wales' there is inserted 'under section 177 of the Criminal Justice Act 2003', and

(b)   for paragraph (b) there is substituted –

'(b)   the provisions of Part 12 of that Act (so far as relating to such orders) shall apply accordingly.'.

(4)   In paragraph 11(3), for paragraphs (a) and (b) there is substituted –

'(a)   the requirements of Part 12 of the Criminal Justice Act 2003 relating to community orders (within the meaning of that Part);

(b)   the powers of the home court under Schedule 8 to that Act, as modified by this paragraph; and'.

(5)   In paragraph 11(4), for the words from 'probation order made by a court' onwards there is substituted 'community order made by a court in England and Wales under section 177 of the Criminal Justice Act 2003, except a power conferred by paragraph 9(1)(b) or (c) or 13(2) of Schedule 8 to that Act'.

(6)   In paragraph 11(5), for 'the Powers of Criminal Courts (Sentencing) Act 2000' there is substituted 'Part 12 of the Criminal Justice Act 2003'.

Aggravated Vehicle-Taking Act 1992 (c. 11)

65   In section 1 of the Aggravated Vehicle-Taking Act 1992 (new offence of aggravated vehicle taking), in subsection (2)(a), for 'section 127 of the Powers of Criminal Courts (Sentencing) Act 2000' there is substituted 'section 163 of the Criminal Justice Act 2003'.

Prisoners and Criminal Proceedings (Scotland) Act 1993 (c. 9)

66   In section 10 of the Prisoners and Criminal Proceedings (Scotland) Act 1993 (life prisoners transferred to Scotland) –

(a) in subsection (1) –

    (i) in paragraph (a), sub-paragraph (i), and the succeeding 'or', are omitted, and

    (ii) after paragraph (a)(ii) there is inserted 'or

        (iii) subsections (5) to (8) of section 28 (early release of life prisoners to whom that section applies) of the Crime (Sentences) Act 1997 (c. 43) (in this section, the "1997 Act") apply by virtue of an order made under section 28(2)(b) of that Act (while that provision was in force) or an order made under section 269(2) of, or paragraph 3(1)(a) of Schedule 22 to, the Criminal Justice Act 2003;', and

    (iii) for '28(2)(b) or 82A(2) or paragraph' there is substituted '82A(2), 28(2)(b) or 269(2) or paragraph 3(1)(a) or';

(b) after subsection (1) there is inserted –

    '(1AA) This Part of this Act, except section 2(9), applies also to a transferred life prisoner –

        (a) who is transferred from England and Wales on or after the date on which section 269 of the Criminal Justice Act 2003 comes into force,

        (b) in relation to whom paragraph 3 of Schedule 22 to that Act applies by virtue of paragraph 2(a) of that Schedule, but

        (c) in respect of whom, under the paragraph so applying, no order has been made,

    as if the prisoner were a life prisoner within the meaning of section 2 of this Act and the punishment part of his sentence within the meaning of that section were the notified minimum term defined by paragraph 3(4) of that Schedule.'; and

(c) in subsection (5)(b) –

    (i) for 'the Crime (Sentences) Act 1997' there is substituted 'the 1997 Act', and

    (ii) after the words 'Powers of Criminal Courts (Sentencing) Act 2000 (c. 6)' there is inserted 'section 269(2) of, or paragraph 3(1)(a) of Schedule 22 to, the Criminal Justice Act 2003,'.

Criminal Justice and Public Order Act 1994 (c. 33)

67 In section 25 of the Criminal Justice and Public Order Act 1994 (no bail for defendants charged with or convicted of homicide or rape after previous conviction of such offences), in paragraph (c) of the definition of 'conviction' in subsection (5) –

(a) the words 'placing the offender on probation or' are omitted, and

(b) for 'him' there is substituted 'the offender'.

Goods Vehicles (Licensing of Operators) Act 1995 (c. 23)

68 (1) In Schedule 3 to the Goods Vehicles (Licensing of Operators) Act 1995 (qualifications for standard licence), paragraph 3 is amended as follows.

    (2) In sub-paragraph (2)(a), for 'exceeding three months' there is substituted 'of 12 months or more or, before the commencement of section 181 of the Criminal Justice Act 2003, a term exceeding three months'.

    (3) In sub-paragraph (2)(c), for 'community service order' there is substituted 'community order'.

    (4) For sub-paragraph (3)(b), there is substituted –

        '(b) "community order" means a community order under section 177 of the Criminal Justice Act 2003, a community punishment order made under section 46 of the Powers of Criminal Courts (Sentencing) Act 2000 or a community service order under the Community Service by Offenders (Scotland) Act 1978.'.

Criminal Procedure (Scotland) Act 1995 (c. 46)

69   The Criminal Procedure (Scotland) Act 1995 is amended as follows.

70   (1)   Section 234 (probation orders: persons residing in England and Wales) is amended as follows.

(2)   In subsection (1), the words after paragraph (b) are omitted.

(3)   For subsection (2) there is substituted –

'(2)   Subsection (1) above applies to any probation order made under section 228 unless the order includes requirements which are more onerous than those which a court in England and Wales could impose on an offender under section 177 of the Criminal Justice Act 2003.'

(4)   In subsection (3), the words from 'or to vary' to 'one hundred' are omitted.

(5)   In subsection (4) –

(a)   in paragraph (a) –

(i)   for 'paragraph 5(3) of Schedule 2 to the 2000 Act' there is substituted 'section 207(2) of the Criminal Justice Act 2003',

(ii)   for 'or, as the case may be, community rehabilitation orders' there is substituted 'or, as the case may be, community orders under Part 12 of that Act', and

(iii)   for 'paragraph 5 of the said Schedule 2' there is substituted 'section 207 of the Criminal Justice Act 2003', and

(b)   in paragraph (b), for 'sub-paragraphs (5) to (7) of the said paragraph 5' there is substituted 'sections 207(4) and 208(1) and (2) of the Criminal Justice Act 2003'.

(6)   After subsection (4) there is inserted –

'(4A) A probation order made or amended under this section must specify as the corresponding requirements for the purposes of this section requirements which could be included in a community order made under section 177 of the Criminal Justice Act 2003.'

(7)   In subsection (5), for 'Schedule 3' onwards there is substituted 'Schedule 8 to the Criminal Justice Act 2003 shall apply as if it were a community order made by a magistrates' court under section 177 of that Act and imposing the requirements specified under subsection (4A) above'.

(8)   For subsection (6) there is substituted –

'(6)   In its application to a probation order made or amended under this section, Schedule 8 to the Criminal Justice Act 2003 has effect subject to the following modifications –

(a)   any reference to the responsible officer has effect as a reference to the person appointed or assigned under subsection (1)(a) above,

(b)   in paragraph 9 –

(i)   paragraphs (b) and (c) of sub-paragraph (1) are omitted,

(ii)   in sub-paragraph (6), the first reference to the Crown Court has effect as a reference to a court in Scotland, and

(iii)   any other reference in sub-paragraphs (6) or (7) to the Crown Court has effect as a reference to the court in Scotland, and

(c)   Parts 3 and 5 are omitted.'

(9) In subsection (10) –

    (a) for the words from 'paragraph 6' to 'community rehabilitation orders' there is substituted 'paragraph 8 of Schedule 9 (which relates to community orders', and

    (b) for 'an order made under section 41' there is substituted 'a community order made under Part 12'.

71 In section 242 (community service orders: persons residing in England and Wales) –

    (a) in subsection (1) –

        (i) in paragraph (a)(ii), for 'a community punishment order' there is substituted 'an unpaid work requirement imposed by a community order (within the meaning of Part 12 of the Criminal Justice Act 2003)', and

        (ii) in paragraph (a)(iii), for 'community punishment orders made under section 46 of the Powers of Criminal Courts (Sentencing) Act 2000' there is substituted 'unpaid work requirements imposed by community orders made under section 177 of the Criminal Justice Act 2003',

    (b) in subsection (2)(b), for 'community punishment orders made under section 46 of the Powers of Criminal Courts (Sentencing) Act 2000' there is substituted 'unpaid work requirements imposed by community orders made under section 177 of the Criminal Justice Act 2003', and

    (c) in subsection (3)(b), for 'in respect of community punishment orders conferred on responsible officers by the Powers of Criminal Courts (Sentencing) Act 2000' there is substituted 'conferred on responsible officers by Part 12 of the Criminal Justice Act 2003 in respect of unpaid work requirements imposed by community orders (within the meaning of that Part)'.

72 In section 244 (community service orders: provisions relating to persons living in England and Wales or Northern Ireland) –

    (a) in subsection (3)(a) –

        (i) for 'community punishment order' there is substituted 'community order (within the meaning of Part 12 of the Criminal Justice Act 2003)', and

        (ii) for 'community punishment orders' there is substituted 'such community orders',

    (b) in subsection (4)(a), for 'community punishment orders' there is substituted 'community orders (within the meaning of Part 12 of the Criminal Justice Act 2003)',

    (c) in subsection (5), for 'community punishment order' there is substituted 'a community order (within the meaning of Part 12 of the Criminal Justice Act 2003)', and

    (d) in subsection (6) –

        (i) for 'community punishment orders', where first occurring, there is substituted 'community orders (within the meaning of Part 12 of the Criminal Justice Act 2003)', and

        (ii) in paragraph (b)(ii), for 'the Powers of Criminal Courts (Sentencing) Act 2000' there is substituted 'Part 12 of the Criminal Justice Act 2003'.

Education Act 1996 (c. 56)

73 In section 562 of the Education Act 1996 (Act not to apply to persons detained under order of a court), for 'probation order' there is substituted 'community order under section 177 of the Criminal Justice Act 2003'.

Criminal Justice (Northern Ireland) Order 1996 (S.I. 1996/3160 (N.I. 24))

74   The Criminal Justice (Northern Ireland) Order 1996 is amended as follows.

75   In Article 2 (interpretation) after paragraph (8) there is inserted –

'(9) For the purposes of this Order, a sentence falls to be imposed under paragraph (2) of Article 52A of the Firearms (Northern Ireland) Order 1981 if it is required by that paragraph and the court is not of the opinion there mentioned.'

76   In Article 4 (absolute and conditional discharge), in paragraph (1), for '(not being an offence for which the sentence is fixed by law)' there is substituted '(not being an offence for which the sentence is fixed by law or falls to be imposed under Article 52A(2) of the Firearms (Northern Ireland) Order 1981)'.

77   In Article 10 (probation orders), in paragraph (1) for '(not being an offence for which the sentence is fixed by law)' there is substituted '(not being an offence for which the sentence is fixed by law or falls to be imposed under Article 52A(2) of the Firearms (Northern Ireland) Order 1981)'.

78   (1)   Article 13 (community service orders) is amended as follows.

(2)   In paragraph (1) for '(not being an offence for which the sentence is fixed by law)' there is substituted '(not being an offence for which the sentence is fixed by law or falls to be imposed under Article 52A(2) of the Firearms (Northern Ireland) Order 1981)'.

(3)   In paragraph (4)(b) as it has effect pursuant to paragraph 7(1) of Schedule 13 to the Criminal Justice Act 1982 (reciprocal arrangements), for 'such orders' there is substituted 'an unpaid work requirement of a community order (within the meaning of Part 12 of the Criminal Justice Act 2003)'.

79   In Article 15 (orders combining probation and community service), in paragraph (1) for '(not being an offence for which the sentence is fixed by law)' there is substituted '(not being an offence for which the sentence is fixed by law or falls to be imposed under Article 52A(2) of the Firearms (Northern Ireland) Order 1981)'.

80   In Article 19 (restrictions on imposing custodial sentences), at the end of paragraph (1) there is inserted 'or falling to be imposed under Article 52A(2) of the Firearms (Northern Ireland) Order 1981'.

81   (1)   In Article 20 (length of custodial sentences), at the end of paragraph (1) there is inserted 'or falling to be imposed under Article 52A(2) of the Firearms (Northern Ireland) Order 1981'.

(2)   In Article 24 (custody probation orders), in paragraph (1) for 'other than one fixed by law' there is substituted ', other than an offence for which the sentence is fixed by law or falls to be imposed under Article 52A(2) of the Firearms (Northern Ireland) Order 1981,'.

Crime (Sentences) Act 1997 (c. 43)

82   The Crime (Sentences) Act 1997 is amended as follows.

83   (1)   Section 31 (duration and conditions of licences) is amended as follows.

(2)   In subsection (3), for the words from 'except' onwards there is substituted 'except in accordance with recommendations of the Parole Board'.

(3)   Subsection (4) is omitted.

(4)   In subsection (6), for 'section 46(3) of the 1991 Act' there is substituted 'section 259 of the Criminal Justice Act 2003'.

84   In section 32 (recall of life prisoners while on licence) for subsection (5) there is substituted –

'(5) Where on a reference under subsection (4) above the Parole Board directs the immediate release on licence under this section of the life prisoner, the Secretary of State shall give effect to the direction.'

85　(1)　Schedule 1 (transfers of prisoners within the British Islands) is amended as follows.

(2)　In paragraph 6, after sub-paragraph (3) there is inserted –

'(4)　In this Part of this Schedule –

"the 2003 Act" means the Criminal Justice Act 2003;
"custody plus order" has the meaning given by section 181(4) of that Act;
"intermittent custody order" has the meaning given by section 183(2) of that Act.'

(3)　In paragraph 8 (restricted transfers from England and Wales to Scotland) –

(a)　for sub-paragraph (2)(a) there is substituted –

'(a)　sections 241, 244, 247 to 252 and 254 to 264 of the 2003 Act (fixed-term prisoners) or, as the case may require, sections 102 to 104 of the Powers of Criminal Courts (Sentencing) Act 2000 (detention and training orders) or sections 28 to 34 of this Act (life sentences) shall apply to him in place of the corresponding provisions of the law of Scotland;

(aa)　sections 62 and 64 of the Criminal Justice and Court Services Act 2000 (which relate to licence conditions) shall apply to him in place of the corresponding provisions of the law of Scotland;

(ab)　where a custody plus order or intermittent custody order has effect in relation to him, the provisions of Chapters 3 and 4 of Part 12 of the 2003 Act relating to such orders shall also apply to him (subject to Schedule 11 to that Act); and',

(b)　for sub-paragraph (4)(a) there is substituted –

'(a)　sections 241, 249 to 252 and 254 to 264 of the 2003 Act (fixed-term prisoners) or, as the case may require, sections 103 and 104 of the Powers of Criminal Courts (Sentencing) Act 2000 (detention and training orders) or sections 31 to 34 of this Act (life sentences) shall apply to him in place of the corresponding provisions of the law of Scotland;

(aa)　sections 62 and 64 of the Criminal Justice and Court Services Act 2000 (which relate to licence conditions) shall apply to him in place of the corresponding provisions of the law of Scotland;

(ab)　where a custody plus order or intermittent custody order has effect in relation to him, the provisions of Chapters 3 and 4 of Part 12 of the 2003 Act relating to such orders shall also apply to him (subject to Schedule 11 to that Act); and', and

(c)　for sub-paragraphs (5) to (7) there is substituted –

'(5)　Section 31(2A) of this Act (conditions as to supervision after release), as applied by sub-paragraph (2) or (4) above, shall have effect as if for paragraphs (a) to (c) there were substituted the words "a relevant officer of such local authority as may be specified in the licence".

(6)　Any provision of sections 102 to 104 of the Powers of Criminal Courts (Sentencing) Act 2000 which is applied by sub-paragraph (2) or (4) above shall have effect (as so applied) as if –

(a)　any reference to secure accommodation were a reference to secure accommodation within the meaning of Part 2 of the Children (Scotland) Act 1995 or a young offenders institution provided under section 19(1)(b) of the Prisons (Scotland) Act 1989,

(b)　except in section 103(2), any reference to the Secretary of State were a reference to the Scottish Ministers,

>> (c) any reference to an officer of a local probation board were a reference to a relevant officer as defined by section 27(1) of the Prisoners and Criminal Proceedings (Scotland) Act 1993,
>> (d) any reference to a youth court were a reference to a sheriff court,
>> (e) in section 103, any reference to a petty sessions area were a reference to a local government area within the meaning of the Local Government etc. (Scotland) Act 1994,
>> (f) in section 103(3), for paragraphs (b) and (c) there were substituted a reference to an officer of a local authority constituted under that Act for the local government area in which the offender resides for the time being,
>> (g) section 103(5) were omitted,
>> (h) in section 104, for subsection (1) there were substituted –

>>> "(1) Where a detention and training order is in force in respect of an offender and it appears on information to a sheriff court having jurisdiction in the locality in which the offender resides that the offender has failed to comply with requirements under section 103(6)(b), the court may –

>>>> (a) issue a citation requiring the offender to appear before it at the time specified in the citation, or
>>>> (b) issue a warrant for the offender's arrest.",

>> (i) section 104(2) were omitted, and
>> (j) in section 104(6), the reference to the Crown Court were a reference to the High Court of Justiciary.'

> (4) In paragraph 9 (restricted transfers from England and Wales to Northern Ireland) –

>> (a) for sub-paragraph (2)(a) there is substituted –

>>> '(a) sections 241, 244, 247 to 252 and 254 to 264 of the 2003 Act (fixed-term prisoners) or, as the case may require, sections 102 to 104 of the Powers of Criminal Courts (Sentencing) Act 2000 (detention and training orders) or sections 28 to 34 of this Act (life sentences) shall apply to him in place of the corresponding provisions of the law of Northern Ireland;
>>> (aa) sections 62 and 64 of the Criminal Justice and Court Services Act 2000 (which relate to licence conditions) shall apply to him in place of the corresponding provisions of the law of Northern Ireland;
>>> (ab) where a custody plus order or intermittent custody order has effect in relation to him, the provisions of Chapters 3 and 4 of Part 12 of the 2003 Act relating to such orders shall apply to him (subject to Schedule 11 to that Act); and',

>> (b) for sub-paragraph (4)(a) there is substituted –

>>> '(a) sections 241, 249 to 252 and 254 to 264 of the 2003 Act (fixed-term prisoners) or, as the case may require, sections 103 and 104 of the Powers of Criminal Courts (Sentencing) Act 2000 (detention and training orders) or sections 31 to 34 of this Act (life sentences) shall apply to him in place of the corresponding provisions of the law of Northern Ireland;
>>> (aa) sections 62 and 64 of the Criminal Justice and Court Services Act 2000 (which relate to licence conditions) shall apply to him in place of the corresponding provisions of the law of Northern Ireland;
>>> (ab) where a custody plus order or intermittent custody order has effect in relation to him, the provisions of Chapters 3 and 4 of Part 12 of the 2003 Act relating to such orders shall apply to him (subject to Schedule 11 to that Act); and',

(c)   for sub-paragraphs (5) to (7) there is substituted –

'(5)   Section 31(2A) of this Act (conditions as to supervision after release), as applied by sub-paragraph (2) or (4) above, shall have effect as if for paragraphs (a) to (c) there were substituted the words "a probation appointed for or assigned to the petty sessions district within which the prisoner for the time being resides".'

(5)   In paragraph 15 (unrestricted transfers: general provisions), sub-paragraph (5) is omitted.

86   In Schedule 2 (repatriation of prisoners to the British Islands) paragraphs 2 and 3 are omitted.

Crime and Disorder Act 1998 (c. 37)

87   The Crime and Disorder Act 1998 is amended as follows.
88   In section 18 (interpretation etc. of Chapter 1) –

(a)   after the definition of 'responsible officer' in subsection (1) there is inserted –

' "serious harm" shall be construed in accordance with section 224 of the Criminal Justice Act 2003;'; and

(b)   subsection (2) is omitted.

89   (1)   Section 38 (local provision of youth justice services) is amended as follows.
(2)   In subsection (4)(g), for 'probation order, a community service order or a combination order' there is substituted 'community order under section 177 of the Criminal Justice Act 2003'.
(3)   In subsection (4)(i), after '1997 Act")' there is inserted 'or by virtue of conditions imposed under section 250 of the Criminal Justice Act 2003'.

Powers of Criminal Courts (Sentencing) Act 2000 (c. 6)

90   The Powers of Criminal Courts (Sentencing) Act 2000 is amended as follows.
91   (1)   Section 6 (committal for sentence in certain cases where offender committed in respect of another offence) is amended as follows.
(2)   In subsection (3)(b), for 'section 120(1) below' there is substituted 'paragraph 11(1) of Schedule 12 to the Criminal Justice Act 2003'.
(3)   For subsection (4)(e), there is substituted –

'(e)   paragraph 11(2) of Schedule 12 to the Criminal Justice Act 2003 (committal to Crown Court where offender convicted during operational period of suspended sentence).'.

92   In section 7 (power of Crown Court on committal for sentence under section 6), in subsection (2), for 'section 119 below' there is substituted 'paragraphs 8 and 9 of Schedule 12 to the Criminal Justice Act 2003'.
93   In section 12 (absolute and conditional discharge) –

(a)   in subsection (1) for '109(2), 110(2) or 111(2) below' there is substituted 'section 110(2) or 111(2) below, section 51A(2) of the Firearms Act 1968 or section 225, 226, 227 or 228 of the Criminal Justice Act 2003', and
(b)   subsection (4) (duty to explain effect of order for conditional discharge) is omitted.

94   In the heading to Part 4, and the heading to Chapter 1 of that Part, for 'COMMUNITY ORDERS' there is substituted 'YOUTH COMMUNITY ORDERS'.
95   For section 33 there is substituted –

'33 Meaning of "youth community order" and "community sentence"

(1) In this Act "youth community order" means any of the following orders –

    (a)   a curfew order;
    (b)   an exclusion order;
    (c)   an attendance centre order;
    (d)   a supervision order;
    (e)   an action plan order.

(2) In this Act "community sentence" means a sentence which consists of or includes –

    (a)   a community order under section 177 of the Criminal Justice Act 2003, or
    (b)   one or more youth community orders.'

96 (1) Section 36B (electronic monitoring of requirements in community orders) is amended as follows.

(2) In the heading for '**community orders**' there is substituted '**youth community orders**', and

(3) In subsection (1) –

    (a)   for 'to (4)' there is substituted 'and (3)', and
    (b)   for 'community order' there is substituted 'youth community order'.

(4) In subsection (2) and (6)(a), for 'community order' there is substituted 'youth community order'.

97 (1) Section 37 (curfew orders) is amended as follows.

(2) In subsection (1) –

    (a)   after the word 'person' there is inserted 'aged under 16', and
    (b)   for 'sections 34 to 36 above' there is substituted 'sections 148, 150 and 156 of the Criminal Justice Act 2003'.

(3) In subsection (5), for 'community order' there is substituted 'youth community order'.

(4) Subsection (10) is omitted.

98 In section 39 (breach, revocation and amendment of curfew orders), for 'community orders' there is substituted 'youth community orders'.

99 In section 40 (curfew orders: supplementary), in subsection (3), for 'paragraphs 2A(4) and (5) and 19(3)' there is substituted 'paragraph 16(2)'.

100 (1) Section 40A (exclusion orders) is amended as follows.

(2) In subsection (1) –

    (a)   after 'person' there is inserted 'aged under 16',
    (b)   for 'sections 34 to 36 above' there is substituted 'sections 148, 150 and 156 of the Criminal Justice Act 2003', and
    (c)   for 'two years' there is substituted 'three months'.

(3) In subsection (5), for 'community order' there is substituted 'youth community order'.

(4) Subsection (10) is omitted.

101 In section 40B (breach, revocation and amendment of exclusion orders), for 'community orders' there is substituted 'youth community orders'.

102 (1) Section 60 (attendance centre orders) is amended as follows.

(2) In subsection (1) –

    (a)   in paragraph (a), for 'sections 34 to 36 above' there is substituted 'sections 148, 150 and 156 of the Criminal Justice Act 2003' and for '21' there is substituted '16', and
    (b)   in paragraph (b), for '21' there is substituted '16', and
    (c)   paragraph (c) and the word 'or' immediately preceding it are omitted.

(3) In subsection (4), for paragraphs (a) and (b) there is substituted 'shall not exceed 24'.

(4) In subsection (7), for 'community order' there is substituted 'youth community order'.

103 In section 63 (supervision orders), in subsection (1), for 'sections 34 to 36 above' there is substituted 'sections 148, 150 and 156 of the Criminal Justice Act 2003'.

104 (1) Section 69 (action plan orders) is amended as follows.

(2) In subsection (1), for 'sections 34 to 36 above' there is substituted 'sections 148, 150 and 156 of the Criminal Justice Act 2003', and

(3) In subsection (5)(b), for 'a community rehabilitation order, a community punishment order, a community punishment and rehabilitation order,' there is substituted 'a community order under section 177 of the Criminal Justice Act 2003'.

(4) Subsection (11) is omitted.

105 In section 70 (requirements which may be included in action plan orders and directions), in subsection (5)(a), after the word 'other' there is inserted 'youth community order or any'.

106 (1) Section 73 (reparation orders) is amended as follows.

(2) In subsection (4)(b), for 'a community punishment order, a community punishment and rehabilitation order,' there is substituted 'a community order under section 177 of the Criminal Justice Act 2003'.

(3) Subsection (7) is omitted.

107 In section 74 (requirements and provisions of reparation order, and obligations of person subject to it), in subsection (3)(a), after 'community order' there is inserted 'or any youth community order'.

108 In section 76 (meaning of custodial sentence), in subsection (1) after paragraph (b) there is inserted –

'(bb) a sentence of detention for public protection under section 226 of the Criminal Justice Act 2003;

(bc) a sentence of detention under section 228 of that Act;'.

109 (1) Section 82A (determination of tariffs) is amended as follows.

(2) In subsection (1), for the words from 'where' onwards there is substituted 'where the sentence is not fixed by law'.

(3) In subsection (3) –

(a) in paragraph (b), for 'section 87' there is substituted 'section 240 of the Criminal Justice Act 2003', and

(b) in paragraph (c), for 'sections 33(2) and 35(1) of the Criminal Justice Act 1991' there is substituted 'section 244(1) of the Criminal Justice Act 2003'.

(4) In subsection (4) –

(a) after 'If' there is inserted 'the offender was aged 21 or over when he committed the offence and', and

(b) the words 'subject to subsection (5) below' are omitted.

(5) Subsections (5) and (6) are omitted.

110 (1) Section 91 (offenders under 18 convicted of certain serious offences) is amended as follows.

(2) In subsection (3), for 'none of the other methods in which the case may legally be dealt with' there is substituted 'neither a community sentence nor a detention and training order'.

(3) In subsection (4), for 'section 79 and 80 above' there is substituted 'section 152 and 153 of the Criminal Justice Act 2003'.

111 (1) Section 100 (detention and training orders) is amended as follows.

(2) In subsection (1) –

    (a) for the words from the beginning to 'subsection (2)' there is substituted 'Subject to sections 90 and 91 above, sections 226 and 228 of the Criminal Justice Act 2003, and subsection (2)', and

    (b) for paragraph (b) there is substituted –

        '(b) the court is of the opinion that subsection (2) of section 152 of the Criminal Justice Act 2003 applies or the case falls within subsection (3) of that section,'.

(3) Subsection (4) is omitted.

112 In section 106 (interaction of detention and training orders with sentences of detention in a young offender institution), subsections (2) and (3) are omitted.

113 After section 106 there is inserted –

'106A   Interaction with sentences of detention

(1) In this section –

"the 2003 Act" means the Criminal Justice Act 2003;
"sentence of detention" means –

    (a) a sentence of detention under section 91 above, or

    (b) a sentence of detention under section 228 of the 2003 Act (extended sentence for certain violent or sexual offences: persons under 18).

(2) Where a court passes a sentence of detention in the case of an offender who is subject to a detention and training order, the sentence shall take effect as follows –

    (a) if the offender has at any time been released by virtue of subsection (2), (3), (4) or (5) of section 102 above, at the beginning of the day on which the sentence is passed, and

    (b) if not, either as mentioned in paragraph (a) above or, if the court so orders, at the time when the offender would otherwise be released by virtue of subsection (2), (3), (4) or (5) of section 102.

(3) Where a court makes a detention and training order in the case of an offender who is subject to a sentence of detention, the order shall take effect as follows –

    (a) if the offender has at any time been released under Chapter 6 of Part 12 of the 2003 Act (release on licence of fixed-term prisoners), at the beginning of the day on which the order is made, and

    (b) if not, either as mentioned in paragraph (a) above or, if the court so orders, at the time when the offender would otherwise be released under that Chapter.

(4) Where an order under section 102(5) above is made in the case of a person in respect of whom a sentence of detention is to take effect as mentioned in subsection (2)(b) above, the order is to be expressed as an order that the period of detention attributable to the detention and training order is to end at the time determined under section 102(5)(a) or (b) above.

(5) In determining for the purposes of subsection (3)(b) the time when an offender would otherwise be released under Chapter 6 of Part 12 of the 2003 Act, section 246 of that Act (power of Secretary of State to release prisoners on licence before he is required to do so) is to be disregarded.

(6) Where by virtue of subsection (3)(b) above a detention and training order made in the case of a person who is subject to a sentence of detention under section 228 of the 2003 Act is to take effect at the time when he would otherwise be released under Chapter 6 of Part 12 of that Act, any direction by

the Parole Board under subsection (2)(b) of section 247 of that Act in respect of him is to be expressed as a direction that the Board would, but for the detention and training order, have directed his release under that section.

(7) Subject to subsection (9) below, where at any time an offender is subject concurrently –

(a) to a detention and training order, and

(b) to a sentence of detention,

he shall be treated for the purposes of the provisions specified in subsection (8) below as if he were subject only to the sentence of detention.

(8) Those provisions are –

(a) sections 102 to 105 above,

(b) section 92 above and section 235 of the 2003 Act (place of detention, etc.), and

(c) Chapter 6 of Part 12 of the 2003 Act.

(9) Nothing in subsection (7) above shall require the offender to be released in respect of either the order or the sentence unless and until he is required to be released in respect of each of them.'

114 In section 110 (required custodial sentence for third class A drug trafficking offence), subsection (3) is omitted.

115 In section 111 (minimum of three years for third domestic burglary) subsection (3) is omitted.

116 Sections 116 and 117 (return to prison etc. where offence committed during original sentence) shall cease to have effect.

117 In section 130 (compensation orders against convicted persons), in subsection (2), for '109(2), 110(2) or 111(2) above,' there is substituted '110(2) or 111(2) above, section 51A(2) of the Firearms Act 1968 or section 225, 226, 227 or 228 of the Criminal Justice Act 2003,'.

118 In section 136 (power to order statement as to financial circumstances of parent or guardian) in subsection (2), for 'section 126 above' there is substituted 'section 162 of the Criminal Justice Act 2003'.

119 (1) Section 138 (fixing of fine or compensation to be paid by parent or guardian) is amended as follows.

(2) In subsection (1)(a), for 'section 128 above' there is substituted 'section 164 of the Criminal Justice Act 2003'.

(3) In subsection (2), for 'sections 128(1) (duty to inquire into financial circumstances) and' there is substituted 'section 164(1) of the Criminal Justice Act 2003 and section'.

(4) In subsection (4) –

(a) for 'section 129 above' there is substituted 'section 165 of the Criminal Justice Act 2003',

(b) for 'section 129(1)' there is substituted 'section 165(1)', and

(c) for 'section 129(2)' there is substituted 'section 165(2)'.

120 In section 146 (driving disqualification for any offence), in subsection (2), for '109(2), 110(2) or 111(2) above' there is substituted '110(2) or 111(2) above, section 51A(2) of the Firearms Act 1968 or section 225, 226, 227 or 228 of the Criminal Justice Act 2003'.

121 In section 154 (commencement of Crown Court sentence), in subsection (2), for 'section 84 above' there is substituted 'section 265 of the Criminal Justice Act 2003'.

122 In section 159 (execution of process between England and Wales and Scotland), for '10(7) or 24(1)' there is substituted '10(6) or 18(1)'.

123 (1) Section 163 (interpretation) is amended as follows.

(2)   In the definition of 'attendance centre' for 'section 62(2) above' there is substituted 'section 221(2) of the Criminal Justice Act 2003'.

(3)   In the definition of 'attendance centre order' for the words from 'by virtue of' to 'Schedule 3' there is substituted 'by virtue of paragraph 4(2)(b) or 5(2)(b) of Schedule 3'.

(4)   In the definition of 'community order', for 'section 33(1) above' there is substituted 'section 177(1) of the Criminal Justice Act 2003'.

(5)   For the definition of 'curfew order' there is substituted –

'curfew order' means an order under section 37(1) above (and, except where the contrary intention is shown by paragraph 7 of Schedule 3 or paragraph 3 of Schedule 7 or 8, includes orders made under section 37(1) by virtue of paragraph 4(2)(a) or 5(2)(a) of Schedule 3 or paragraph 2(2)(a) of Schedule 7 or 8).'.

(6)   In the definition of 'operational period', for 'section 118(3) above' there is substituted 'section 189(1)(b)(ii) of the Criminal Justice Act 2003'.

(7)   In the definition of 'suspended sentence', for 'section 118(3) above' there is substituted 'section 189(7) of the Criminal Justice Act 2003'.

(8)   At the end there is inserted –

'"youth community order" has the meaning given by section 33(1) above.'.

124   In section 164 (further interpretative provision) for subsection (3) there is substituted –

'(3) References in this Act to a sentence falling to be imposed –

(a)   under section 110(2) or 111(2) above,

(b)   under section 51A(2) of the Firearms Act 1968, or

(c)   under any of sections 225 to 228 of the Criminal Justice Act 2003,

are to be read in accordance with section 305(4) of the Criminal Justice Act 2003.'

125   For Schedule 3 (breach revocation and amendment of certain community orders) there is substituted –

'SCHEDULE 3   BREACH, REVOCATION AND AMENDMENT OF CURFEW ORDERS AND EXCLUSION ORDERS

PART 1

PRELIMINARY

Definitions

1   In this Schedule –

"the petty sessions area concerned" means –

(a)   in relation to a curfew order, the petty sessions area in which the place for the time being specified in the order is situated; and

(b)   in relation to an exclusion order, the petty sessions area for the time being specified in the order;

"relevant order" means a curfew order or an exclusion order.

Orders made on appeal

2   Where a relevant order has been made on appeal, for the purposes of this
     Schedule it shall be deemed –

   (a) if it was made on an appeal brought from a magistrates' court, to have been
           made by a magistrates' court;

   (b) if it was made on an appeal brought from the Crown Court or from the
           criminal division of the Court of Appeal, to have been made by the Crown
           Court.

PART 2

BREACH OF REQUIREMENT OF ORDER

Issue of summons or warrant

3   (1) If at any time while a relevant order is in force in respect of an offender it
           appears on information to a justice of the peace acting for the petty sessions
           area concerned that the offender has failed to comply with any of the
           requirements of the order, the justice may –

     (a) issue a summons requiring the offender to appear at the place and time
               specified in it; or

     (b) if the information is in writing and on oath, issue a warrant for his
               arrest.

   (2) Any summons or warrant issued under this paragraph shall direct the
           offender to appear or be brought –

     (a) in the case of any relevant order which was made by the Crown Court
               and included a direction that any failure to comply with any of the
               requirements of the order be dealt with by the Crown Court, before
               the Crown Court; and

     (b) in the case of a relevant order which is not an order to which para-
               graph (a) above applies, before a magistrates' court acting for the petty
               sessions area concerned.

   (3) Where a summons issued under sub-paragraph (1)(a) above requires an
           offender to appear before the Crown Court and the offender does not appear
           in answer to the summons, the Crown Court may issue a further summons
           requiring the offender to appear at the place and time specified in it.

   (4) Where a summons issued under sub-paragraph (1)(a) above or a further
           summons issued under sub-paragraph (3) above requires an offender to
           appear before the Crown Court and the offender does not appear in answer
           to the summons, the Crown Court may issue a warrant for the arrest of the
           offender.

Powers of magistrates' court

4   (1) This paragraph applies if it is proved to the satisfaction of a magistrates'
           court before which an offender appears or is brought under paragraph 3
           above that he has failed without reasonable excuse to comply with any of
           the requirements of the relevant order.

   (2) The magistrates' court may deal with the offender in respect of the failure in
           one of the following ways (and must deal with him in one of those ways if the
           relevant order is in force) –

(a)   by making a curfew order in respect of him (subject to paragraph 7 below);

(b)   by making an attendance centre order in respect of him (subject to paragraph 8 below); or

(c)   where the relevant order was made by a magistrates' court, by dealing with him, for the offence in respect of which the order was made, in any way in which he could have been dealt with for that offence by the court which made the order if the order had not been made.

(3)   In dealing with an offender under sub-paragraph (2)(c) above, a magistrates' court –

(a)   shall take into account the extent to which the offender has complied with the requirements of the relevant order; and

(b)   in the case of an offender who has wilfully and persistently failed to comply with those requirements, may impose a custodial sentence (where the relevant order was made in respect of an offence punishable with such a sentence) notwithstanding anything in section 152(2) of the Criminal Justice Act 2003.

(4)   Where a magistrates' court deals with an offender under sub-paragraph (2)(c) above, it shall revoke the relevant order if it is still in force.

(5)   Where a relevant order was made by the Crown Court and a magistrates' court has power to deal with the offender under sub-paragraph (2)(a) or (b) above, it may instead commit him to custody or release him on bail until he can be brought or appear before the Crown Court.

(6)   A magistrates' court which deals with an offender's case under sub-paragraph (5) above shall send to the Crown Court –

(a)   a certificate signed by a justice of the peace certifying that the offender has failed to comply with the requirements of the relevant order in the respect specified in the certificate; and

(b)   such other particulars of the case as may be desirable;

and a certificate purporting to be so signed shall be admissible as evidence of the failure before the Crown Court.

(7)   A person sentenced under sub-paragraph (2)(c) above for an offence may appeal to the Crown Court against the sentence.

Powers of Crown Court

5   (1)   This paragraph applies where under paragraph 3 or by virtue of paragraph 4(5) above an offender is brought or appears before the Crown Court and it is proved to the satisfaction of that court that he has failed without reasonable excuse to comply with any of the requirements of the relevant order.

(2)   The Crown Court may deal with the offender in respect of the failure in one of the following ways (and must deal with him in one of those ways if the relevant order is in force) –

(a)   by making a curfew order in respect of him (subject to paragraph 7 below);

(b)   by making an attendance centre order in respect of him (subject to paragraph 8 below); or

(c)   by dealing with him, for the offence in respect of which the order was made, in any way in which he could have been dealt with for that offence by the court which made the order if the order had not been made.

(3) In dealing with an offender under sub-paragraph (2)(c) above, the Crown
Court –

    (a) shall take into account the extent to which the offender has complied
with the requirements of the relevant order; and

    (b) in the case of an offender who has wilfully and persistently failed to
comply with those requirements, may impose a custodial sentence
(where the relevant order was made in respect of an offence punishable with such a sentence) notwithstanding anything in section
152(2) of the Criminal Justice Act 2003.

(4) Where the Crown Court deals with an offender under sub-paragraph (2)(c)
above, it shall revoke the relevant order if it is still in force.

(5) In proceedings before the Crown Court under this paragraph any question
whether the offender has failed to comply with the requirements of the relevant order shall be determined by the court and not by the verdict of a jury.

Exclusions from paragraphs 4 and 5

6 Without prejudice to paragraphs 10 and 11 below, an offender who is convicted
of a further offence while a relevant order is in force in respect of him shall not
on that account be liable to be dealt with under paragraph 4 or 5 in respect of a
failure to comply with any requirement of the order.

Curfew orders imposed for breach of relevant order

7 (1) Section 37 of this Act (curfew orders) shall apply for the purposes of paragraphs 4(2)(a) and 5(2)(a) above as if for the words from the beginning to
"make" there were substituted "Where a court has power to deal with an
offender under Part 2 of Schedule 3 to this Act for failure to comply with any
of the requirements of a relevant order, the court may make in respect of the
offender".

(2) The following provisions of this Act, namely –

    (a) section 37(3) to (12), and

    (b) so far as applicable, sections 36B and 40 and this Schedule so far as
relating to curfew orders;

have effect in relation to a curfew order made by virtue of paragraphs
4(2)(a) and 5(2)(a) as they have effect in relation to any other curfew order,
subject to sub-paragraph (3) below.

(3) This Schedule shall have effect in relation to such a curfew order as if –

    (a) the power conferred on the court by each of paragraphs 4(2)(c),
5(2)(c) and 10(3)(b) to deal with the offender for the offence in
respect of which the order was made were a power to deal with the
offender, for his failure to comply with the relevant order, in any way
in which the appropriate court could deal with him for that failure if
it had just been proved to the satisfaction of the court;

    (b) the reference in paragraph 10(1)(b) to the offence in respect of which
the order was made were a reference to the failure to comply in respect
of which the curfew order was made; and

    (c) the power conferred on the Crown Court by paragraph 11(2)(b) to
deal with the offender for the offence in respect of which the order was
made were a power to deal with the offender, for his failure to comply
with the relevant order, in any way in which the appropriate court (if
the relevant order was made by the magistrates' court) or the Crown

Court (if that order was made by the Crown Court) could deal with him for that failure if it had just been proved to its satisfaction.

(4) For the purposes of the provisions mentioned in paragraphs (a) and (c) of sub-paragraph (3) above, as applied by that sub-paragraph, if the relevant order is no longer in force the appropriate court's powers shall be determined on the assumption that it is still in force.

(5) Sections 148 and 156 of the Criminal Justice Act 2003 (restrictions and procedural requirements for community sentences) do not apply in relation to a curfew order made by virtue of paragraph 4(2)(a) or 5(2)(a) above.

Attendance centre orders imposed for breach of relevant order

8 (1) Section 60(1) of this Act (attendance centre orders) shall apply for the purposes of paragraphs 4(2)(b) and 5(2)(b) above as if for the words from the beginning to "the court may," there were substituted "Where a court has power to deal with an offender under Part 2 of Schedule 3 to this Act for failure to comply with any of the requirements of a relevant order, the court may,".

(2) The following provisions of this Act, namely –

(a) subsections (3) to (11) of section 60, and
(b) so far as applicable, section 36B and Schedule 5,

have effect in relation to an attendance centre order made by virtue of paragraph 4(2)(b) or 5(2)(b) above as they have effect in relation to any other attendance centre order, but as if there were omitted from each of paragraphs 2(1)(b), 3(1) and 4(3) of Schedule 5 the words ", for the offence in respect of which the order was made," and "for that offence".

(3) Sections 148 and 156 of the Criminal Justice Act 2003 (restrictions and procedural requirements for community sentences) do not apply in relation to an attendance centre order made by virtue of paragraph 4(2)(b) or 5(2)(b) above.

Supplementary

9 Any exercise by a court of its powers under paragraph 4(2)(a) or (b) or 5(2)(a) or (b) above shall be without prejudice to the continuance of the relevant order.

PART 3

REVOCATION OF ORDER

Revocation of order with or without re-sentencing: powers of magistrates' court

10 (1) This paragraph applies where a relevant order made by a magistrates' court is in force in respect of any offender and on the application of the offender or the responsible officer it appears to the appropriate magistrates' court that, having regard to circumstances which have arisen since the order was made, it would be in the interests of justice –

(a) for the order to be revoked; or
(b) for the offender to be dealt with in some other way for the offence in respect of which the order was made.

(2) In this paragraph "the appropriate magistrates' court" means a magistrates' court acting for the petty sessions area concerned.

(3) The appropriate magistrates' court may –

(a) revoke the order; or

(b) both –

(i) revoke the order; and

(ii) deal with the offender for the offence in respect of which the order was made, in any way in which he could have been dealt with for that offence by the court which made the order if the order had not been made.

(4) In dealing with an offender under sub-paragraph (3)(b) above, a magistrates' court shall take into account the extent to which the offender has complied with the requirements of the relevant order.

(5) A person sentenced under sub-paragraph (3)(b) above for an offence may appeal to the Crown Court against the sentence.

(6) Where a magistrates' court proposes to exercise its powers under this paragraph otherwise than on the application of the offender, it shall summon him to appear before the court and, if he does not appear in answer to the summons, may issue a warrant for his arrest.

(7) No application may be made by the offender under sub-paragraph (1) above while an appeal against the relevant order is pending.

Revocation of order with or without re-sentencing: powers of Crown Court on conviction etc.

11 (1) This paragraph applies where –

(a) a relevant order made by the Crown Court is in force in respect of an offender and the offender or the responsible officer applies to the Crown Court for the order to be revoked or for the offender to be dealt with in some other way for the offence in respect of which the order was made; or

(b) an offender in respect of whom a relevant order is in force is convicted of an offence before the Crown Court or, having been committed by a magistrates' court to the Crown Court for sentence, is brought or appears before the Crown Court.

(2) If it appears to the Crown Court to be in the interests of justice to do so, having regard to circumstances which have arisen since the order was made, the Crown Court may –

(a) revoke the order; or

(b) both –

(i) revoke the order; and

(ii) deal with the offender for the offence in respect of which the order was made, in any way in which he could have been dealt with for that offence by the court which made the order if the order had not been made.

(3) In dealing with an offender under sub-paragraph (2)(b) above, the Crown Court shall take into account the extent to which the offender has complied with the requirements of the relevant order.

Revocation following custodial sentence by magistrates' court unconnected with order

12   (1)   This paragraph applies where –

(a)   an offender in respect of whom a relevant order is in force is convicted of an offence by a magistrates' court unconnected with the order;

(b)   the court imposes a custodial sentence on the offender; and

(c)   it appears to the court, on the application of the offender or the responsible officer, that it would be in the interests of justice to exercise its powers under this paragraph having regard to circumstances which have arisen since the order was made.

(2)   In sub-paragraph (1) above "a magistrates' court unconnected with the order" means a magistrates' court not acting for the petty sessions area concerned.

(3)   The court may –

(a)   if the order was made by a magistrates' court, revoke it;

(b)   if the order was made by the Crown Court, commit the offender in custody or release him on bail until he can be brought or appear before the Crown Court.

(4)   Where the court deals with an offender's case under sub-paragraph (3)(b) above, it shall send to the Crown Court such particulars of the case as may be desirable.

13   Where by virtue of paragraph 12(3)(b) above an offender is brought or appears before the Crown Court and it appears to the Crown Court to be in the interests of justice to do so, having regard to circumstances which have arisen since the relevant order was made, the Crown Court may revoke the order.

Supplementary

14   (1)   On the making under this Part of this Schedule of an order revoking a relevant order, the proper officer of the court shall forthwith give copies of the revoking order to the responsible officer.

(2)   In sub-paragraph (1) above "proper officer" means –

(a)   in relation to a magistrates' court, the justices' chief executive for the court; and

(b)   in relation to the Crown Court, the appropriate officer.

(3)   A responsible officer to whom in accordance with sub-paragraph (1) above copies of a revoking order are given shall give a copy to the offender and to the person in charge of any institution in which the offender was required by the order to reside.

PART 4

AMENDMENT OF ORDER

Amendment by reason of change of residence

15   (1)   This paragraph applies where, at any time while a relevant order is in force in respect of an offender, a magistrates' court acting for the petty sessions area concerned is satisfied that the offender proposes to change, or has

changed, his residence from that petty sessions area to another petty sessions area.

(2) Subject to sub-paragraph (3) below, the court may, and on the application of the responsible officer shall, amend the relevant order by substituting the other petty sessions area for the area specified in the order or, in the case of a curfew order, a place in that other area for the place so specified.

(3) The court shall not amend under this paragraph a curfew order which contains requirements which, in the opinion of the court, cannot be complied with unless the offender continues to reside in the petty sessions area concerned unless, in accordance with paragraph 16 below, it either –

(a) cancels those requirements; or

(b) substitutes for those requirements other requirements which can be complied with if the offender ceases to reside in that area.

Amendment of requirements of order

16 (1) Without prejudice to the provisions of paragraph 15 above but subject to the following provisions of this paragraph, a magistrates' court acting for the petty sessions area concerned may, on the application of an eligible person, by order amend a relevant order –

(a) by cancelling any of the requirements of the order; or

(b) by inserting in the order (either in addition to or in substitution for any of its requirements) any requirement which the court could include if it were then making the order.

(2) A magistrates' court shall not under sub-paragraph (1) above amend a curfew order by extending the curfew periods beyond the end of six months from the date of the original order.

(3) A magistrates' court shall not under sub-paragraph (1) above amend an exclusion order by extending the period for which the offender is prohibited from entering the place in question beyond the end of three months from the date of the original order.

(4) For the purposes of this paragraph the eligible persons are –

(a) the offender;

(b) the responsible officer; and

(c) in relation to an exclusion order, any affected person.

But an application under sub-paragraph (1) by a person such as is mentioned in paragraph (c) above must be for the cancellation of a requirement which was included in the order by virtue of his consent or for the purpose (or partly for the purpose) of protecting him from being approached by the offender, or for the insertion of a requirement which will, if inserted, be such a requirement.

Supplementary

17 No order may be made under paragraph 15 above, and no application may be made under paragraph 16 above, while an appeal against the relevant order is pending.

18 (1) Subject to sub-paragraph (2) below, where a court proposes to exercise its powers under this Part of this Schedule, otherwise than on the application of the offender, the court –

(a) shall summon him to appear before the court; and

(b)   if he does not appear in answer to the summons, may issue a warrant for his arrest.

(2)   This paragraph shall not apply to an order cancelling a requirement of a relevant order or reducing the period of any requirement, or to an order under paragraph 15 above substituting a new petty sessions area or a new place for the one specified in a relevant order.

19   (1)   On the making under this Part of this Schedule of an order amending a relevant order, the justices' chief executive for the court shall forthwith –

(a)   if the order amends the relevant order otherwise than by substituting, by virtue of paragraph 15 above, a new petty session area or a new place for the one specified in the relevant order, give copies of the amending order to the responsible officer;

(b)   if the order amends the relevant order in the manner excepted by paragraph (a) above, send to the chief executive to the justices for the new petty sessions area or, as the case may be, for the petty sessions area in which the new place is situated –

(i)   copies of the amending order; and

(ii)   such documents and information relating to the case as he considers likely to be of assistance to a court acting for that area in the exercise of its functions in relation to the order;

and in a case falling within paragraph (b) above the chief executive of the justices for that area shall give copies of the amending order to the responsible officer.

(2)   A responsible officer to whom in accordance with sub-paragraph (1) above copies of an order are given shall give a copy to the offender and to the person in charge of any institution in which the offender is or was required by the order to reside.'

126   In Schedule 5 (breach, revocation and amendment of attendance centre orders) –

(a)   in paragraph 1(1)(b), for 'section 62(3) of this Act' there is substituted 'section 222(1)(d) or (e) of the Criminal Justice Act 2003',

(b)   in paragraph 2(5)(b), for 'section 79(2) of this Act' there is substituted 'section 152(2) of the Criminal Justice Act 2003', and

(c)   in paragraph 3(3)(b), for 'section 79(2) of this Act' there is substituted 'section 152(2) of the Criminal Justice Act 2003'.

127   In Schedule 6 (requirements which may be included in supervision orders) –

(a)   in paragraph 2(7)(a), after the word 'other' there is inserted 'youth community order or any', and

(b)   in paragraph 3(6)(a), for 'community order' there is substituted 'youth community order'.

128   In Schedule 7 (breach, revocation and amendment of supervision orders) –

(a)   in paragraph 3 –

(i)   in sub-paragraph (2), for 'sub-paragraphs (4) and (5)' there is substituted 'sub-paragraph (5)',

(ii)   in sub-paragraph (3), for 'Sections 35 and 36 of this Act' there is substituted 'Sections 148 and 156 of the Criminal Justice Act 2003',

(iii)   sub-paragraph (4) is omitted, and

(iv)   in sub-paragraph (5)(a), for the words from the beginning to 'and' there is substituted 'the power conferred on the court by each of paragraphs 4(2)(c) and', and

(b)   in paragraph 4(3), for 'Sections 35 and 36 of this Act' there is substituted 'Sections 148 and 156 of the Criminal Justice Act 2003'.

129 In Schedule 8 (breach, revocation and amendment of action plan orders and reparation orders) –

   (a) in paragraph 3 –

      (i) in sub-paragraph (2), for 'sub-paragraphs (4) and (5)' there is substituted 'sub-paragraph (5)',

      (ii) in sub-paragraph (3), for 'Sections 35 and 36 of this Act' there is substituted 'Sections 148 and 156 of the Criminal Justice Act 2003',

     (iii) sub-paragraph (4) is omitted, and

     (iv) in sub-paragraph (5)(a), for the words from the beginning to 'and' there is substituted 'The power conferred on the court by each of paragraphs 4(2)(c) and', and

   (b) in paragraph 4(3), for 'Sections 35 and 36 of this Act' there is substituted 'Sections 148 and 156 of the Criminal Justice Act 2003'.

Child Support, Pensions and Social Security Act 2000 (c. 19)

130 The Child Support, Pensions and Social Security Act 2000 is amended as follows.

131 (1) Section 62 (loss of benefit for breach of community order) is amended as follows.

   (2) In subsection (8), for the definition of 'relevant community order' there is substituted –

   '"relevant community order" means –

      (a) a community order made under section 177 of the Criminal Justice Act 2003; or

      (b) any order falling in England or Wales to be treated as such an order.'

   (3) In subsection (11)(c)(ii), for 'to (e)' there is substituted 'and (b)'.

132 In section 64 (information provision), in subsection (6)(a), after 'community orders' there is inserted '(as defined by section 177 of the Criminal Justice Act 2003)'.

Criminal Justice and Court Services Act 2000 (c. 43)

133 The Criminal Justice and Court Services Act 2000 is amended as follows.

134 In section 1 (purposes of Chapter 1 of Part 1 of the Act), in subsection (2) –

   (a) in paragraph (a), after 'community orders' there is inserted '(as defined by section 177 of the Criminal Justice Act 2003)', and

   (b) after paragraph (c) there is inserted –

   '(d) giving effect to suspended sentence orders (as defined by section 189 of the Criminal Justice Act 2003).'

135 In section 42 (interpretation of Part 2), in subsection (2)(a), for 'section 119 of the Powers of Criminal Court (Sentencing) Act 2000' there is substituted 'paragraph 8(2)(a) or (b) of Schedule 11 of the Criminal Justice Act 2003'.

136 (1) Section 62 (release on licence etc: conditions as to monitoring) is amended as follows.

   (2) For subsection (3) there is substituted –

   '(3) In relation to a prisoner released under section 246 of the Criminal Justice Act 2003 (power to release prisoners on licence before required to do so), the monitoring referred to in subsection (2)(a) does not include the monitoring of his compliance with conditions imposed under section 253 of that Act (curfew condition).'

   (3) In subsection (5) after paragraph (e) there is inserted ', and

(f)   a sentence of detention under section 226 or 228 of the Criminal Justice Act 2003'.

137 In section 69 (duties of local probation boards in connection with victims of certain offences), in subsection (8), for paragraph (a) there is substituted –

'(a) murder or an offence specified in Schedule 15 to the Criminal Justice Act 2003,'.

138 In section 70 (general interpretation), in subsection (5), for the words 'any community order' there is substituted 'a curfew order, an exclusion order, a community rehabilitation order, a community punishment order, a community punishment and rehabilitation order, a drug treatment and testing order, a drug abstinence order, an attendance centre order, a supervision order or an action plan order'.

International Criminal Court Act 2001 (c. 17)

139 (1) Schedule 7 to the International Criminal Court Act 2001 (domestic provisions not applicable to ICC prisoners), is amended as follows.

(2) In paragraph 2(1), for paragraph (d) there is substituted –

'(d) section 240 of the Criminal Justice Act 2003 (crediting of periods of remand in custody).'

(3) In paragraph 3(1), for 'Part 2 of the Criminal Justice Act 1991' there is substituted 'sections 244 to 264 of the Criminal Justice Act 2003'.

Armed Forces Act 2001 (c. 19)

140 In section 30 of the Armed Forces Act 2001 (conditional release from custody), in subsection (6)(a) for 'six months' there is substituted 'the term specified in subsection (1)(a) of section 8 of the Armed Forces Act 1976 (powers of courts in relation to civilians)'.

Proceeds of Crime Act 2002 (c. 29)

141 In section 38 of the Proceeds of Crime Act 2002 (provisions about imprisonment or detention), in subsection (4)(a), for 'section 118(1) of the Sentencing Act' there is substituted 'section 189(1) of the Criminal Justice Act 2003'.

Sexual Offences Act 2003 (c. 42)

142 The Sexual Offences Act 2003 is amended as follows.

143 In section 131 (application of Part 2 to young offenders), after paragraph (j) there is inserted –

'(k) a sentence of detention for public protection under section 226 of the Criminal Justice Act 2003,

(l) an extended sentence under section 228 of that Act,'.

144 In section 133 (general interpretation), at the end of paragraph (a) of the definition of 'community order' there is inserted '(as that Act had effect before the passing of the Criminal Justice Act 2003)'.

PART 2

OFFENCES: ABOLITION OF IMPRISONMENT AND CONVERSION TO SUMMARY OFFENCE

Vagrancy Act 1824 (c. 83)

145 In section 3 of the Vagrancy Act 1824 (idle and disorderly persons), for the words from 'subject to' to the end there is substituted 'it shall be lawful for any justice of the peace to impose on such person (being thereof convicted before him by his own view, or by the confession of such person, or by the evidence on oath of one or more credible witnesses) a fine not exceeding level 3 on the standard scale'.

146 (1) Section 4 of that Act (rogues and vagabonds) is amended as follows.

(2) In that section, for the words from 'shall be' to the end there is substituted 'commits an offence under this section'.

(3) At the end of that section (which becomes subsection (1)) there is inserted –

'(2) It shall be lawful for any justice of the peace to impose on any person who commits an offence under this section (being thereof convicted before him by the confession of such person, or by the evidence on oath of one or more credible witnesses) –

(a) in the case of a person convicted of the offence of wandering abroad and lodging in any barn or outhouse, or in any deserted or unoccupied building, or in the open air, or under a tent, or in any cart or waggon, and not giving a good account of himself, a fine not exceeding level 1 on the standard scale, and

(b) in the case of a person convicted of any other offence under this section, a fine not exceeding level 3 on the standard scale.'

London Hackney Carriages Act 1843 (c. 86)

147 In section 28 of the London Hackney Carriages Act 1843, after 'for every such offence', there is inserted 'of which he is convicted before the justice'.

Town Police Clauses Act 1847 (c. 89)

148 In section 26 of the Town Police Clauses Act 1847, for the words from 'committed by them' to the end, there is substituted 'liable to a fine not exceeding level 3 on the standard scale'.

149 In section 28 of that Act, after 'for each offence', there is inserted 'of which he is convicted before the justice'.

150 In section 29 of that Act, after 'for every such offence', there is inserted 'of which he is convicted before the justice'.

151 In section 36 of that Act, after 'liable', there is inserted 'on conviction before the justices'.

Seamen's and Soldiers' False Characters Act 1906 (c. 5)

152 In section 1 of the Seamen's and Soldiers' False Characters Act 1906, for 'imprisonment for a term not exceeding three months' there is substituted 'a fine not exceeding level 2 on the standard scale'.

Aliens Restriction (Amendment) Act 1919 (c. 92)

153 In section 3(2) of the Aliens Restriction (Amendment) Act 1919, for 'imprisonment for a term not exceeding three months' there is substituted 'a fine not exceeding level 3 on the standard scale'.

Polish Resettlement Act 1947 (c. 19)

154 In the Schedule to the Polish Resettlement Act 1947, in paragraph 7, for 'imprisonment for a term not exceeding three months' there is substituted 'a fine not exceeding level 1 on the standard scale'.

Army Act 1955 (3 & 4 Eliz. 2 c. 18)

155 In section 61 of the Army Act 1955, for the words from 'the like' to 'section nineteen of this Act' there is substituted 'dismissal from Her Majesty's service with or without disgrace, to detention for a term not exceeding three months,'.

Air Force Act 1955 (3 & 4 Eliz. 2 c. 19)

156 In section 61 of the Air Force Act 1955, for the words from 'the like' to 'section nineteen of this Act' there is substituted 'dismissal from Her Majesty's service with or without disgrace, to detention for a term not exceeding three months,'.

Naval Discipline Act 1957 (c. 53)

157 In section 34A of the Naval Discipline Act 1957, for the words 'imprisonment for a term not exceeding three months' there is substituted 'dismissal from Her Majesty's service with or without disgrace, detention for a term not exceeding three months,'.

Slaughterhouses Act 1974 (c. 3)

158 In section 4 of the Slaughterhouses Act 1974, after subsection (5) there is inserted –

'(5A) A person guilty of an offence under subsection (5) above shall be liable to a fine not exceeding level 3 on the standard scale.'

Water Industry Act 1991 (c. 56)

159 In Schedule 6 to the Water Industry Act 1991, in paragraph 5(4), for paragraphs (a) and (b) there is substituted ', on summary conviction, to a fine not exceeding level 5 on the standard scale'.

Water Resources Act 1991 (c. 57)

160 In section 205(6) of the Water Resources Act 1991, for paragraphs (a) and (b) there is substituted 'on summary conviction to a fine not exceeding level 5 on the standard scale'.

Transport Act 2000 (c. 38)

161 In section 82(4) of the Transport Act 2000, after 'subsection (1)' there is inserted 'or (2)'.

Reserve Forces Act 1996 (c. 14)

162 In paragraph 5(3) of Schedule 1 to the Reserve Forces Act 1996, for the words 'imprisonment for a term not exceeding three months' there is substituted 'dismissal from Her Majesty's service with or without disgrace, to detention for a term not exceeding 3 months,'.

SCHEDULE 33   JURY SERVICE   Section 321

1 The Juries Act 1974 (c. 23) is amended as follows.
2 For section 1 (qualification for jury service) there is substituted –

'1 Qualification for jury service

(1) Subject to the provisions of this Act, every person shall be qualified to serve as a juror in the Crown Court, the High Court and county courts and be liable accordingly to attend for jury service when summoned under this Act if –

   (a) he is for the time being registered as a parliamentary or local government elector and is not less than eighteen nor more than seventy years of age;
   (b) he has been ordinarily resident in the United Kingdom, the Channel Islands or the Isle of Man for any period of at least five years since attaining the age of thirteen;
   (c) he is not a mentally disordered person; and
   (d) he is not disqualified for jury service.

(2) In subsection (1) above "mentally disordered person" means any person listed in Part 1 of Schedule 1 to this Act.

(3) The persons who are disqualified for jury service are those listed in Part 2 of that Schedule.'

3 Section 9(1) (certain persons entitled to be excused from jury service) shall cease to have effect.
4 In section 9(2) (discretionary excusal) after 'may' there is inserted ', subject to section 9A(1A) of this Act,'.
5 After section 9(2) (discretionary excusal) there is inserted –

'(2A) Without prejudice to subsection (2) above, the appropriate officer shall excuse a full-time serving member of Her Majesty's naval, military or air forces from attending in pursuance of a summons if –

   (a) that member's commanding officer certifies to the appropriate officer that it would be prejudicial to the efficiency of the service if that member were to be required to be absent from duty, and
   (b) subsection (2A) or (2B) of section 9A of this Act applies.

(2B) Subsection (2A) above does not affect the application of subsection (2) above to a full-time serving member of Her Majesty's naval, military or air forces in a case where he is not entitled to be excused under subsection (2A).'

6 In section 9(3) (discretionary excusal) after 'above' there is inserted 'or any failure by the appropriate officer to excuse him as required by subsection (2A) above'.
·7 In section 9A(1) (discretionary deferral) after 'may' there is inserted ', subject to subsection (2) below,'.

8   After section 9A(1) (discretionary deferral) there is inserted –

'(1A)   Without prejudice to subsection (1) above and subject to subsection (2) below, the appropriate officer –

(a)   shall defer the attendance of a full-time serving member of Her Majesty's naval, military or air forces in pursuance of a summons if subsection (1B) below applies, and

(b)   for this purpose, shall vary the dates upon which that member is summoned to attend and the summons shall have effect accordingly.

(1B)   This subsection applies if that member's commanding officer certifies to the appropriate officer that it would be prejudicial to the efficiency of the service if that member were to be required to be absent from duty.

(1C)   Nothing in subsection (1A) or (1B) above shall affect the application of subsection (1) above to a full-time serving member of Her Majesty's naval, military or air forces in a case where subsection (1B) does not apply.'

9   For section 9A(2) (discretionary deferral) there is substituted –

'(2)   The attendance of a person in pursuance of a summons shall not be deferred under subsection (1) or (1A) above if subsection (2A) or (2B) below applies.'

10   After section 9A(2) (discretionary deferral) there is inserted –

'(2A)   This subsection applies where a deferral of the attendance of the person in pursuance of the summons has previously been made or refused under subsection (1) above or has previously been made under subsection (1A) above.

(2B)   This subsection applies where –

(a)   the person is a full-time serving member of Her Majesty's naval, military or air forces, and

(b)   in addition to certifying to the appropriate officer that it would be prejudicial to the efficiency of the service if that member were to be required to be absent from duty, that member's commanding officer certifies that this position is likely to remain for any period specified for the purpose of this subsection in guidance issued under section 9AA of this Act.'

11   In section 9A(3) (discretionary deferral) after 'above' there is inserted 'or any failure by the appropriate officer to defer his attendance as required by subsection (1A) above'.

12   After section 9A (discretionary deferral) there is inserted –

'9AA   Requirement to issue guidance

(1)   The Lord Chancellor shall issue guidance as to the manner in which the functions of the appropriate officer under sections 9 and 9A of this Act are to be exercised.

(2)   The Lord Chancellor shall –

(a)   lay before each House of Parliament the guidance, and any revised guidance, issued under this section, and

(b)   arrange for the guidance, or revised guidance, to be published in a manner which he considers appropriate.'

13   In section 19 (payment for jury service), after subsection (1) there is inserted –

'(1A)   The reference in subsection (1) above to payments by way of allowance for subsistence includes a reference to vouchers and other benefits which may be used to pay for subsistence, whether or not their use is subject to any limitations.'

14   In section 20 (offences), for subsection (5)(d) there is substituted –

'(d)   knowing that he is disqualified under Part 2 of Schedule 1 to this Act, serves on a jury;'

15   For Schedule 1 (ineligibility and disqualification for and excusal from jury service) there is substituted –

'SCHEDULE 1

MENTALLY DISORDERED PERSONS AND PERSONS DISQUALIFIED FOR JURY SERVICE

PART 1

MENTALLY DISORDERED PERSONS

1   A person who suffers or has suffered from mental illness, psychopathic disorder, mental handicap or severe mental handicap and on account of that condition either –

(a)   is resident in a hospital or similar institution; or
(b)   regularly attends for treatment by a medical practitioner.

2   A person for the time being under guardianship under section 7 of the Mental Health Act 1983.

3   A person who, under Part 7 of that Act, has been determined by a judge to be incapable, by reason of mental disorder, of managing and administering his property and affairs.

4   (1)   In this Part of this Schedule –

(a)   "mental handicap" means a state of arrested or incomplete development of mind (not amounting to severe mental handicap) which includes significant impairment of intelligence and social functioning;
(b)   "severe mental handicap" means a state of arrested or incomplete development of mind which includes severe impairment of intelligence and social functioning;
(c)   other expressions are to be construed in accordance with the Mental Health Act 1983.

(2)   For the purposes of this Part a person is to be treated as being under guardianship under section 7 of the Mental Health Act 1983 at any time while he is subject to guardianship pursuant to an order under section 116A(2)(b) of the Army Act 1955, section 116A(2)(b) of the Air Force Act 1955 or section 63A(2)(b) of the Naval Discipline Act 1957.

PART 2

PERSONS DISQUALIFIED

5   A person who is on bail in criminal proceedings (within the meaning of the Bail Act 1976).

6   A person who has at any time been sentenced in the United Kingdom, the Channel Islands or the Isle of Man –

(a)   to imprisonment for life, detention for life or custody for life,
(b)   to detention during her Majesty's pleasure or during the pleasure of the Secretary of State,
(c)   to imprisonment for public protection or detention for public protection,
(d)   to an extended sentence under section 227 or 228 of the Criminal Justice Act 2003 or section 210A of the Criminal Procedure (Scotland) Act 1995, or

(e) to a term of imprisonment of five years or more or a term of detention of five years or more.

7   A person who at any time in the last ten years has –

(a) in the United Kingdom, the Channel Islands or the Isle of Man –

(i) served any part of a sentence of imprisonment or a sentence of detention, or

(ii) had passed on him a suspended sentence of imprisonment or had made in respect of him a suspended order for detention,

(b) in England and Wales, had made in respect of him a community order under section 177 of the Criminal Justice Act 2003, a community rehabilitation order, a community punishment order, a community punishment and rehabilitation order, a drug treatment and testing order or a drug abstinence order, or

(c) had made in respect of him any corresponding order under the law of Scotland, Northern Ireland, the Isle of Man or any of the Channel Islands.

8   For the purposes of this Part of this Schedule –

(a) a sentence passed by a court-martial is to be treated as having been passed in the United Kingdom, and

(b) a person is sentenced to a term of detention if, but only if –

(i) a court passes on him, or makes in respect of him on conviction, any sentence or order which requires him to be detained in custody for any period, and

(ii) the sentence or order is available only in respect of offenders below a certain age,

and any reference to serving a sentence of detention is to be construed accordingly.'

SCHEDULE 34   PARENTING ORDERS AND REFERRAL ORDERS

Section 324

Crime and Disorder Act 1998 (c. 37)

1   In section 8 of the Crime and Disorder Act 1998 (parenting orders), in subsection (2) the words from 'and to section 19(5)' to '2000' shall cease to have effect.

2   (1) Section 9 of that Act (parenting orders: supplemental) is amended as follows.

(2) For subsection (1A) there is substituted –

'(1A) The requirements of subsection (1) do not apply where the court makes a referral order in respect of the offence.'

(3) After subsection (2) there is inserted –

'(2A) In a case where a court proposes to make both a referral order in respect of a child or young person convicted of an offence and a parenting order, before making the parenting order the court shall obtain and consider a report by an appropriate officer –

(a) indicating the requirements proposed by that officer to be included in the parenting order;

(b) indicating the reasons why he considers those requirements would be desirable in the interests of preventing the commission of any further offence by the child or young person; and

(c) if the child or young person is aged under 16, containing the information required by subsection (2) above.

(2B) In subsection (2A) above "an appropriate officer" means –

    (a) an officer of a local probation board;

    (b) a social worker of a local authority social services department; or

    (c) a member of a youth offending team.'

(4) After subsection (7) there is inserted –

'(7A) In this section "referral order" means an order under section 16(2) or (3) of the Powers of Criminal Courts (Sentencing) Act 2000 (referral of offender to youth offender panel).'

Powers of Criminal Courts (Sentencing) Act 2000 (c. 6)

3   In section 19(5) of the Powers of Criminal Courts (Sentencing) Act 2000 (orders that cannot be made with referral orders) –

(a) at the end of paragraph (a) there is inserted 'or', and

(b) paragraph (c) (parenting orders) and the word 'or' immediately preceding it shall cease to have effect.

4   In section 22 of that Act (referral orders: attendance at panel meetings), after subsection (2) there is inserted –

'(2A) If –

    (a) a parent or guardian of the offender fails to comply with an order under section 20 above (requirement to attend the meetings of the panel), and

    (b) the offender is aged under 18 at the time of the failure,

the panel may refer that parent or guardian to a youth court acting for the petty sessions area in which it appears to the panel that the offender resides or will reside.'

5   (1) Section 28 of that Act (which introduces Schedule 1) is amended as follows.

    (2) In the sidenote, for 'Offender referred back to court or' there is substituted 'Offender or parent referred back to court: offender'.

    (3) After paragraph (a) there is inserted –

'(aa) in Part 1A makes provision for what is to happen when a youth offender panel refers a parent or guardian to the court under section 22(2A) above, and'.

6   In Schedule 1 to that Act (youth offender panels: further court proceedings), after Part 1 there is inserted –

'PART 1A

REFERRAL OF PARENT OR GUARDIAN FOR BREACH OF SECTION 20 ORDER

Introductory

9A   (1) This Part of this Schedule applies where, under section 22(2A) of this Act, a youth offender panel refers an offender's parent or guardian to a youth court.

    (2) In this Part of this Schedule –

        (a) "the offender" means the offender whose parent or guardian is referred under section 22(2A);

(b)   "the parent" means the parent or guardian so referred; and

(c)   "the youth court" means a youth court as mentioned in section 22(2A).

Mode of referral to court

9B   The panel shall make the referral by sending a report to the youth court explaining why the parent is being referred to it.

Bringing the parent before the court

9C   (1)   Where the youth court receives such a report it shall cause the parent to appear before it.

(2)   For the purpose of securing the attendance of the parent before the court, a justice acting for the petty sessions area for which the court acts may –

(a)   issue a summons requiring the parent to appear at the place and time specified in it; or

(b)   if the report is substantiated on oath, issue a warrant for the parent's arrest.

(3)   Any summons or warrant issued under sub-paragraph (2) above shall direct the parent to appear or be brought before the youth court.

Power of court to make parenting order: application of supplemental provisions

9D   (1)   Where the parent appears or is brought before the youth court under paragraph 9C above, the court may make a parenting order in respect of the parent if –

(a)   it is proved to the satisfaction of the court that the parent has failed without reasonable excuse to comply with the order under section 20 of this Act; and

(b)   the court is satisfied that the parenting order would be desirable in the interests of preventing the commission of any further offence by the offender.

(2)   A parenting order is an order which requires the parent –

(a)   to comply, for a period not exceeding twelve months, with such requirements as are specified in the order, and

(b)   subject to sub-paragraph (4) below, to attend, for a concurrent period not exceeding three months, such counselling or guidance programme as may be specified in directions given by the responsible officer.

(3)   The requirements that may be specified under sub-paragraph (2)(a) above are those which the court considers desirable in the interests of preventing the commission of any further offence by the offender.

(4)   A parenting order under this paragraph may, but need not, include a requirement mentioned in subsection (2)(b) above in any case where a parenting order under this paragraph or any other enactment has been made in respect of the parent on a previous occasion.

(5)   A counselling or guidance programme which a parent is required to attend by virtue of subsection (2)(b) above may be or include a residential course but only if the court is satisfied –

(a) that the attendance of the parent at a residential course is likely to be more effective than his attendance at a non-residential course in preventing the commission of any further offence by the offender, and

(b) that any interference with family life which is likely to result from the attendance of the parent at a residential course is proportionate in all the circumstances.

(6) Before making a parenting order under this paragraph where the offender is aged under 16, the court shall obtain and consider information about his family circumstances and the likely effect of the order on those circumstances.

(7) Sections 8(3) and (8), 9(3) to (7) and 18(3) and (4) of the Crime and Disorder Act 1998 apply in relation to a parenting order made under this paragraph as they apply in relation to any other parenting order.

Appeal

9E (1) An appeal shall lie to the Crown Court against the making of a parenting order under paragraph 9D above.

(2) Subsections (2) and (3) of section 10 of the Crime and Disorder Act 1998 (appeals against parenting orders) apply in relation to an appeal under this paragraph as they apply in relation to an appeal under subsection (1)(b) of that section.

Effect on section 20 order

9F (1) The making of a parenting order under paragraph 9D above is without prejudice to the continuance of the order under section 20 of this Act.

(2) Section 63(1) to (4) of the Magistrates' Courts Act 1980 (power of magistrates' court to deal with person for breach of order, etc) apply (as well as section 22(2A) of this Act and this Part of this Schedule) in relation to an order under section 20 of this Act.'

SCHEDULE 35 CRIMINAL RECORD CERTIFICATES: AMENDMENTS OF PART 5 OF POLICE ACT 1997 Section 328

1 The Police Act 1997 (c. 50) is amended as follows.

2 In section 112 (criminal conviction certificates), in subsection (1)(a), after 'prescribed' there is inserted 'manner and'.

3 (1) Section 113 (criminal record certificates) is amended as follows.

(2) In subsection (1) –

(a) at the beginning there is inserted 'Subject to subsection (4A)',

(b) in paragraph (a), after 'prescribed' there is inserted 'manner and', and

(c) in paragraph (b), after 'pays' there is inserted 'in the prescribed manner'.

(3) After subsection (4) there is inserted –

'(4A) The Secretary of State may treat an application' under this section as an application under section 115 if –

(a) in his opinion the certificate is required for a purpose prescribed under subsection (2) of that section,

(b) the registered person provides him with the statement required by subsection (2) of that section, and

(c) the applicant consents and pays to the Secretary of State the amount (if any) by which the fee payable in relation to an application under section 115 exceeds the fee paid in relation to the application under this section.'.

4   (1) Section 115 (enhanced criminal record certificates) is amended as follows.

(2) In subsection (1) –

(a)   at the beginning there is inserted 'Subject to subsection (9A),',

(b)   in paragraph (a), after 'prescribed' there is inserted 'manner and', and

(c)   in paragraph (b), after 'pays' there is inserted 'in the prescribed manner'.

(3) In subsection (2), for paragraphs (a) to (c) there is substituted 'for such purposes as may be prescribed under this subsection'.

(4) Subsections (3) to (5) and subsections (6C) to (6E) are omitted.

(5) After subsection (9) there is inserted –

'(9A) The Secretary of State may treat an application under this section as an application under section 113 if in his opinion the certificate is not required for a purpose prescribed under subsection (2).

(9B) Where by virtue of subsection (9A) the Secretary of State treats an application under this section as an application under section 113, he must refund to the applicant the amount (if any) by which the fee paid in relation to the application under this section exceeds the fee payable in relation to an application under section 113.'

5   In section 116 (enhanced criminal record certificates: judicial appointments and Crown employment), in subsection (2)(b), for the words from 'to which' onwards there is substituted 'of such description as may be prescribed'.

6   (1) Section 120 (registered persons) is amended as follows.

(2) For subsection (2) there is substituted –

'(2)   Subject to regulations under section 120ZA and 120AA and to section 120A the Secretary of State shall include in the register any person who –

(a) applies to him in writing to be registered,

(b) satisfies the conditions in subsections (4) to (6), and

(c) has not in the period of two years ending with the date of the application been removed from the register under section 120A or 120AA.'

(3) Subsection (3) is omitted.

7   After section 120 there is inserted –

'120ZA Regulations about registration

(1)   The Secretary of State may by regulations make further provision about registration.

(2)   Regulations under this section may in particular make provision for –

(a)   the payment of fees,

(b)   the information to be included in the register,

(c)   the registration of any person to be subject to conditions,

(d)   the nomination by –

(i) a body corporate or unincorporate, or

(ii) a person appointed to an office by virtue of any enactment,

of the individuals authorised to act for it or, as the case may be, him in relation to the countersigning of applications under this Part, and

(e)   the refusal by the Secretary of State, on such grounds as may be specified in or determined under the regulations, to accept or to continue to accept the nomination of a person as so authorised.

(3) The provision which may be made by virtue of subsection (2)(c) includes provision –

    (a) for the registration or continued registration of any person to be subject to prescribed conditions or, if the regulations so provide, such conditions as the Secretary of State thinks fit, and

    (b) for the Secretary of State to vary or revoke those conditions.

(4) The conditions imposed by virtue of subsection (2)(c) may in particular include conditions –

    (a) requiring a registered person, before he countersigns an application at an individual's request, to verify the identity of that individual in the prescribed manner,

    (b) requiring an application under section 113 or 115 to be transmitted by electronic means to the Secretary of State by the registered person who countersigns it, and

    (c) requiring a registered person to comply with any code of practice for the time being in force under section 122.'

8 At the end of the sidenote to section 120A (refusal and cancellation of registration) there is inserted 'on grounds related to disclosure'.

9 After section 120A there is inserted –

'120AA Refusal, cancellation or suspension of registration on other grounds

(1) Regulations may make provision enabling the Secretary of State in prescribed cases to refuse to register a person who, in the opinion of the Secretary of State, is likely to countersign fewer applications under this Part in any period of twelve months than a prescribed minimum number.

(2) Subsection (3) applies where a registered person –

    (a) is, in the opinion of the Secretary of State, no longer likely to wish to countersign applications under this Part,

    (b) has, in any period of twelve months during which he was registered, countersigned fewer applications under this Part than the minimum number specified in respect of him by regulations under subsection (1), or

    (c) has failed to comply with any condition of his registration.

(3) Subject to section 120AB, the Secretary of State may –

    (a) suspend that person's registration for such period not exceeding 6 months as the Secretary of State thinks fit, or

    (b) remove that person from the register.

120AB Procedure for cancellation or suspension under section 120AA

(1) Before cancelling or suspending a person's registration by virtue of section 120AA, the Secretary of State must send him written notice of his intention to do so.

(2) Every such notice must –

    (a) give the Secretary of State's reasons for proposing to cancel or suspend the registration, and

    (b) inform the person concerned of his right under subsection (3) to make representations.

(3) A person who receives such a notice may, within 21 days of service, make representations in writing to the Secretary of State as to why the registration should not be cancelled or suspended.

(4) After considering such representations, the Secretary of State must give the registered person written notice –

    (a) that at the end of a further period of six weeks beginning with the date of service, the person's registration will be cancelled or suspended, or

(b)   that he does not propose to take any further action.

(5)   If no representations are received within the period mentioned in subsection (3) the Secretary of State may cancel or suspend the person's registration at the end of the period mentioned in that subsection.

(6)   Subsection (1) does not prevent the Secretary of State from imposing on the registered person a lesser sanction than that specified in the notice under that subsection.

(7)   Any notice under this section that is required to be given in writing may be given by being transmitted electronically.

(8)   This section does not apply where –

(a)   the Secretary of State is satisfied, in the case of a registered person other than a body, that the person has died or is incapable, by reason of physical or mental impairment, of countersigning applications under this Part, or

(b)   the registered person has requested to be removed from the register.

(9)   The Secretary of State may by regulations amend subsection (4)(a) by substituting for the period there specified, such other period as may be specified in the regulations.'

10   After section 122 there is inserted –

'122A Delegation of functions of Secretary of State

(1)   The Secretary of State may, to such extent and subject to such conditions as he thinks fit, delegate any relevant function of his under this Part to such person as he may determine.

(2)   A function is relevant for the purposes of subsection (1) if it does not consist of a power –

(a)   to make regulations, or

(b)   to publish or revise a code of practice or to lay any such code before Parliament.

(3)   A delegation under subsection (1) may be varied or revoked at any time.'

11   After section 124 (offences: disclosure) there is inserted –

'124A Further offences: disclosure of information obtained in connection with delegated function

(1)   Any person who is engaged in the discharge of functions conferred by this Part on the Secretary of State commits an offence if he discloses information which has been obtained by him in connection with those functions and which relates to a particular person unless he discloses the information, in the course of his duties, –

(a)   to another person engaged in the discharge of those functions,

(b)   to the chief officer of a police force in connection with a request under this Part to provide information to the Secretary of State, or

(c)   to an applicant or registered person who is entitled under this Part to the information disclosed to him.

(2)   Where information is disclosed to a person and the disclosure –

(a)   is an offence under subsection (1), or

(b)   would be an offence under subsection (1) but for subsection (3)(a), (d) or (e),

the person to whom the information is disclosed commits an offence if he discloses it to any other person.

(3)   Subsection (1) does not apply to a disclosure of information which is made –

    (a)   with the written consent of the person to whom the information relates,

    (b)   to a government department,

    (c)   to a person appointed to an office by virtue of any enactment,

    (d)   in accordance with an obligation to provide information under or by virtue of any enactment, or

    (e)   for some other purpose specified in regulations made by the Secretary of State.

(4)   A person who is guilty of an offence under this section shall be liable on summary conviction to imprisonment for a term not exceeding 51 weeks or to a fine not exceeding level 3 on the standard scale, or to both.

(5)   In relation to an offence committed before the commencement of section 281(5) of the Criminal Justice Act 2003, the reference in subsection (4) to 51 weeks is to be read as a reference to 6 months.'

12   In section 125 (regulations) –

(a)   subsection (3) is omitted, and

(b)   in subsection (4), the words 'to which subsection (3) does not apply' are omitted.

SCHEDULE 36   FURTHER MINOR AND CONSEQUENTIAL AMENDMENTS   Section 331

PART 1

BAIL

Bail Act 1976 (c. 63)

1   The Bail Act 1976 is amended as follows.

2   (1)   Section 5(6A)(a) (supplementary provisions about decisions on bail) is amended as follows.

    (2)   After 'examination)' there is inserted ', section 52(5) of the Crime and Disorder Act 1998 (adjournment of proceedings under section 51 etc)'.

    (3)   After sub-paragraph (ii) there is inserted –

    '(iia) section 17C (intention as to plea: adjournment), or'.

    (4)   After sub-paragraph (iii) there is inserted 'or

    (iiia) section 24C (intention as to plea by child or young person: adjournment),'.

3   In Part 3 of Schedule 1 (interpretation) for paragraph 2 there is substituted –

'2   References in this Schedule to previous grants of bail include –

    (a)   bail granted before the coming into force of this Act;

    (b)   as respects the reference in paragraph 2A of Part 1 of this Schedule (as substituted by section 14(1) of the Criminal Justice Act 2003), bail granted before the coming into force of that paragraph;

    (c)   as respects the references in paragraph 6 of Part 1 of this Schedule (as substituted by section 15(1) of the Criminal Justice Act 2003), bail granted before the coming into force of that paragraph;

    (d)   as respects the references in paragraph 9AA of Part 1 of this Schedule, bail granted before the coming into force of that paragraph;

    (e)   as respects the references in paragraph 9AB of Part 1 of this Schedule, bail granted before the coming into force of that paragraph;

(f)   as respects the reference in paragraph 5 of Part 2 of this Schedule (as substituted by section 13(4) of the Criminal Justice Act 2003), bail granted before the coming into force of that paragraph.'

Supreme Court Act 1981 (c. 54)

4   (1)   Section 81 of the Supreme Court Act 1981 (bail) is amended as follows.

(2)   In subsection (1)(g) after 'examination)' there is inserted ', section 52(5) of the Crime and Disorder Act 1998 (adjournment of proceedings under section 51 etc)'.

(3)   In subsection (1)(g) the word 'or' at the end of sub-paragraph (ii) is omitted and after that sub-paragraph there is inserted –

'(iia)   section 17C (intention as to plea: adjournment);'.

(4)   In subsection (1)(g) after sub-paragraph (iii) there is inserted 'or

(iiia)   section 24C (intention as to plea by child or young person: adjournment);'.

Police and Criminal Evidence Act 1984 (c. 60)

5   In section 38(2A) of the Police and Criminal Evidence Act 1984 (bail granted by custody officer after charge) –

(a)   for '2' there is substituted '2(1)', and

(b)   after '1976' there is inserted '(disregarding paragraph 2(2) of that Part)'.

PART 2

CHARGING ETC

Criminal Law Act 1977 (c. 45)

6   In section 39 of the Criminal Law Act 1977 (service of summons and citation throughout United Kingdom) for subsection (1) there is substituted –

'(1)   The following documents, namely –

(a)   a summons requiring a person charged with an offence to appear before a court in England or Wales,

(b)   a written charge (within the meaning of section 29 of the Criminal Justice Act 2003) charging a person with an offence,

(c)   a requisition (within the meaning of that section) requiring a person charged with an offence to appear before a court in England or Wales, and

(d)   any other document which, by virtue of any enactment, may or must be served on a person with, or at the same time as, a document mentioned in paragraph (a), (b) or (c) above,

may, in such manner as may be prescribed by rules of court, be served on him in Scotland or Northern Ireland.'

Magistrates' Courts Act 1980 (c. 43)

7   The Magistrates' Courts Act 1980 is amended as follows.

8   (1)   Section 1 (issue of summons to accused or warrant for his arrest) is amended as follows.

(2) In subsection (3) after 'section' there is inserted 'upon an information being laid'.

(3) In subsection (4) after 'summons' there is inserted ', or a written charge and requisition,'.

(4) In subsection (6) after 'has' there is inserted ', or a written charge and requisition have,'.

(5) After subsection (6) there is inserted –

'(6A) Where the offence charged is an indictable offence and a written charge and requisition have previously been issued, a warrant may be issued under this section by a justice of the peace upon a copy of the written charge (rather than an information) being laid before the justice by a public prosecutor.'

(6) After subsection (7) there is inserted –

'(7A) For the purposes of subsection (6A) above, a copy of a written charge may be laid before, and a warrant under this section may be issued by, a single justice of the peace.'

9   In section 150(1) (interpretation of other terms) after the definition of 'prescribed' there is inserted –

'public prosecutor', 'requisition' and 'written charge' have the same meaning as in section 29 of the Criminal Justice Act 2003;'.

Prosecution of Offences Act 1985 (c. 23)

10   (1) Section 15 of the Prosecution of Offences Act 1985 (interpretation) is amended as follows.

(2) In subsection (1) after the definition of 'public authority' there is inserted –

'"public prosecutor", "requisition" and "written charge" have the same meaning as in section 29 of the Criminal Justice Act 2003;'.

(3) In subsection (2), after paragraph (b) there is inserted –

'(ba) where a public prosecutor issues a written charge and requisition for the offence, when the written charge and requisition are issued;'.

Criminal Justice and Public Order Act 1994 (c. 33)

11   (1) Section 51 of the Criminal Justice and Public Order Act 1994 (intimidation, etc, of witnesses, jurors and others) is amended as follows.

(2) In subsection (9), for the word 'and' at the end of the definition of 'potential' there is substituted –

'"public prosecutor", "requisition" and "written charge" have the same meaning as in section 29 of the Criminal Justice Act 2003;'.

(3) In subsection (10)(a), after sub-paragraph (i) there is inserted –

'(ia) when a public prosecutor issues a written charge and requisition in respect of the offence;'.

Drug Trafficking Act 1994 (c. 37)

12   (1) Section 60 of the Drug Trafficking Act 1994 (prosecution by order of Commissioners of Customs and Excise) is amended as follows.

(2) In subsection (6) for the word 'and' at the end of the definition of 'officer' there is substituted –

'"public prosecutor", "requisition" and "written charge" have the same meaning as in section 29 of the Criminal Justice Act 2003;'.

(3) In subsection (6A), after paragraph (a) there is inserted –

'(aa) when a public prosecutor issues a written charge and requisition in respect of the offence;'.

Merchant Shipping Act 1995 (c. 21)

13 (1) Section 145 of the Merchant Shipping Act 1995 (interpretation of section 144) is amended as follows.

(2) In subsection (2)(a), after sub-paragraph (i) there is inserted –

'(ia) when a public prosecutor issues a written charge and requisition in respect of the offence;'.

(3) After subsection (2) there is inserted –

'(2A) In subsection (2) above "public prosecutor", "requisition" and "written charge" have the same meaning as in section 29 of the Criminal Justice Act 2003.'

Terrorism Act 2000 (c. 11)

14 (1) Paragraph 11 of Schedule 4 to the Terrorism Act 2000 (proceedings for an offence: timing) is amended as follows.

(2) In sub-paragraph (1), after paragraph (a) there is inserted –

'(aa) when a public prosecutor issues a written charge and requisition in respect of the offence;'.

(3) After sub-paragraph (2) there is inserted –

'(2A) In sub-paragraph (1) "public prosecutor", "requisition" and "written charge" have the same meaning as in section 29 of the Criminal Justice Act 2003.'

Proceeds of Crime Act 2002 (c. 29)

15 (1) Section 85 of the Proceeds of Crime Act 2002 (proceedings) is amended as follows.

(2) In subsection (1), after paragraph (a) there is inserted –

'(aa) when a public prosecutor issues a written charge and requisition in respect of the offence;'.

(3) After subsection (8) there is inserted –

'(9) In this section "public prosecutor", "requisition" and "written charge" have the same meaning as in section 29 of the Criminal Justice Act 2003.'

Crime (International Co-operation) Act 2003 (c. 32)

16 After section 4 of the Crime (International Co-operation) Act 2003 there is inserted –

'**4A General requirements for service of written charge or requisition**

(1)   This section applies to the following documents issued for the purposes of criminal proceedings in England and Wales by a prosecutor –

    (a)   a written charge (within the meaning of section 29 of the Criminal Justice Act 2003),

    (b)   a requisition (within the meaning of that section).

(2)   The written charge or requisition may be issued in spite of the fact that the person on whom it is to be served is outside the United Kingdom.

(3)   Where the written charge or requisition is to be served outside the United Kingdom and the prosecutor believes that the person on whom it is to be served does not understand English, the written charge or requisition must be accompanied by a translation of it in an appropriate language.

(4)   A written charge or requisition served outside the United Kingdom must be accompanied by a notice giving any information required to be given by rules of court.

(5)   If a requisition is served outside the United Kingdom, no obligation under the law of England and Wales to comply with the requisition is imposed by virtue of the service.

(6)   Accordingly, failure to comply with the requisition is not a ground for issuing a warrant to secure the attendance of the person in question.

(7)   But the requisition may subsequently be served on the person in question in the United Kingdom (with the usual consequences for non-compliance).

4B Service of written charge or requisition otherwise than by post

(1)   A written charge or requisition to which section 4A applies may, instead of being served by post, be served on a person outside the United Kingdom in accordance with arrangements made by the Secretary of State.

(2)   But where the person is in a participating country, the written charge or requisition may be served in accordance with those arrangements only if one of the following conditions is met.

(3)   The conditions are –

    (a)   that the correct address of the person is unknown,

    (b)   that it has not been possible to serve the written charge or requisition by post,

    (c)   that there are good reasons for thinking that service by post will not be effective or is inappropriate.'

PART 3

DISCLOSURE

Prosecution of Offences Act 1985 (c. 23)

17   In section 22B of the Prosecution of Offences Act 1985 (re-institution of proceedings stayed under section 22(4) or 22A(5)), in subsection (5)(a) for 'section 3, 4, 7 or 9' there is substituted 'section 3, 4 or 7A'.

Criminal Justice Act 1987 (c. 38)

18   In section 9 of the Criminal Justice Act 1987 (preparatory hearings in serious fraud cases etc.), paragraphs (i) and (iii) of subsection (5) are omitted.

Criminal Justice (Serious Fraud) (Northern Ireland) Order 1988 (S.I. 1988/1846 (N.I. 16))

19   In Article 8 of the Criminal Justice (Serious Fraud) (Northern Ireland) Order 1988 (preparatory hearings in serious fraud cases etc.), sub-paragraphs (i) and (iii) of paragraph (5) are omitted.

Criminal Procedure and Investigations Act 1996 (c. 25)

20   The Criminal Procedure and Investigations Act 1996 is amended as follows.

21   In section 3 (primary disclosure by prosecutor), for the heading there is substituted 'Initial duty of prosecutor to disclose'.

22   In section 4 (primary disclosure: further provisions), in the heading for 'Primary disclosure' there is substituted 'Initial duty to disclose'.

23   In section 5 (compulsory disclosure by accused), subsections (6) to (9) are omitted.

24   In section 6 (voluntary disclosure by accused), subsection (3) is omitted.

25   Section 7 (secondary disclosure by prosecutor) shall cease to have effect.

26   Section 9 (continuing duty of prosecutor to disclose) shall cease to have effect.

27   In section 10 (prosecutor's failure to observe time limits), in subsection (1), for paragraph (b) there is substituted –

'(b)   purports to act under section 7A(5) after the end of the period which, by virtue of section 12, is the relevant period for section 7A.'

28   In section 12 (time limits) –

(a)   in subsection (1), for 'and 7' there is substituted ', 6B, 6C and 7A(5)';

(b)   in subsection (5), for '7' there is substituted '7A(5)'.

29   In section 13 (time limits: transitional), for subsection (2) there is substituted –

'(2)   As regards a case in relation to which no regulations under section 12 have come into force for the purposes of section 7A, section 7A(5) shall have effect as if –

(a)   in paragraph (a) for the words from "during the period" to the end, and

(b)   in paragraph (b) for "during that period",

there were substituted "as soon as is reasonably practicable after the accused gives the statement in question".'

30   In section 14 (public interest: review for summary trials), in subsection (2)(a), for '7(5), 8(5) or 9(8)' there is substituted '7A(8) or 8(5)'.

31   In section 15 (public interest: review in other cases), in subsection (2)(a), for '7(5), 8(5) or 9(8)' there is substituted '7A(8) or 8(5)'.

32   In section 16 (applications: opportunity to be heard), in paragraph (a) and in the words after paragraph (c), for '7(5), 8(5), 9(8)' there is substituted '7A(8), 8(5)'.

33   In section 17 (confidentiality of disclosed information), in subsection (1)(a), for '7, 9' there is substituted '7A'.

34   In section 19 (rules of court) in subsection (2)(b) and (d), for '7(5), 8(2) or (5), 9(8)' there is substituted '5(5B), 6B(6), 6E(5), 7A(8), 8(2) or (5)'.

35   In section 20 (other statutory rules as to disclosure) –

(a)   subsection (2) is omitted, and

(b)   in subsection (5)(a), for 'sections 3 to 9' there is substituted 'sections 3 to 8'.

36   In section 31 (preparatory hearings in complex cases etc.), paragraphs (a) and (c) of subsection (6) are omitted.

37   (1)   Section 77 (orders and regulations) is amended as follows.

(2)   In subsection (5) –

(a)   after 'No' there is inserted 'regulations or', and

(b)   after 'section' there is inserted '6A or'.

(3) In subsection (6)(b) after 'regulations' there is inserted '(other than regulations under section 6A)'.

38 In Schedule 4 (modifications for Northern Ireland), in paragraph 7, for '3(6), 7(5), 8(5) or 9(8)' there is substituted '3(6), 7A(8) or 8(5)'.

Sexual Offences (Protected Material) Act 1997 (c. 39)

39 In section 9(4) of the Sexual Offences (Protected Material) Act 1997 (which, when in force, will add a subsection (6) to section 1 of the Criminal Procedure and Investigations Act 1996), for 'section 3, 7 or 9' there is substituted 'section 3 or 7A'.

PART 4

TRIALS ON INDICTMENT WITHOUT A JURY

Indictments Act 1915 (c. 90)

40 (1) Section 5 of the Indictments Act 1915 (orders for amendment of indictment, separate trial and postponement of trial) is amended as follows.

(2) In subsection (5)(a) for 'are to' there is substituted '(if there is one)'.

(3) In subsection (5)(b) after 'discharged' there is inserted 'under paragraph (a)'.

Criminal Law Act 1967 (c. 58)

41 In section 6(4) of the Criminal Law Act 1967 (trial of offences) after 'jury' there is inserted 'or otherwise act'.

Criminal Justice Act 1967 (c. 80)

42 In section 17 of the Criminal Justice Act 1967 (entry of verdict of not guilty by order of a judge) –

(a) for 'the defendant being given in charge to a jury' there is substituted 'any further steps being taken in the proceedings', and

(b) after 'verdict of a jury' there is inserted 'or a court'.

Criminal Law Act (Northern Ireland) 1967 (c. 18)

43 In section 6(3) of the Criminal Law Act (Northern Ireland) 1967 (trial of offences) after 'jury' there is inserted 'or otherwise act'.

Criminal Appeal Act 1968 (c. 19)

44 In section 7(2)(c) of the Criminal Appeal Act 1968 (power to order retrial) –

(a) for 'the jury were discharged from giving a verdict' there is substituted 'no verdict was given', and

(b) for 'convicting him' there is substituted 'his being convicted'.

Judicature (Northern Ireland) Act 1978 (c. 23)

45 (1) Section 48 of the Judicature (Northern Ireland) Act 1978 (committal for trial on indictment) is amended as follows.

(2) In subsection (6A) for 'the jury are sworn' there is substituted 'the time when the jury are sworn'.

(3) After subsection (6A) there is inserted –

'(6B) The reference in subsection (6A) to the time when the jury are sworn includes the time when the jury would be sworn but for –

(a) the making of an order under Part 7 of the Criminal Justice Act 2003, or

(b) the application of section 75 of the Terrorism Act 2000.'

Criminal Appeal (Northern Ireland) Act 1980 (c. 47)

46 In section 6(3)(c) of the Criminal Appeal (Northern Ireland) Act 1980 (power to order retrial) for 'the jury were discharged from giving a verdict' there is substituted 'no verdict was given'.

Supreme Court Act 1981 (c. 54)

47 (1) Section 76 of the Supreme Court Act 1981 (committal for trial: alteration of place of trial) is amended as follows.

(2) In subsection (2A) for 'the jury are sworn' there is substituted 'the time when the jury are sworn'

(3) After subsection (2A) there is inserted –

'(2B) The reference in subsection (2A) to the time when the jury are sworn includes the time when the jury would be sworn but for the making of an order under Part 7 of the Criminal Justice Act 2003.'

Police and Criminal Evidence Act 1984 (c. 60)

48 (1) Section 77 of the Police and Criminal Evidence Act 1984 (confessions of mentally handicapped persons) is amended as follows.

(2) In subsection (1) after 'indictment' there is inserted 'with a jury'.

(3) In subsection (2) after 'indictment' there is inserted 'with a jury'.

(4) After subsection (2) there is inserted –

'(2A) In any case where at the trial on indictment without a jury of a person for an offence it appears to the court that a warning under subsection (1) above would be required if the trial were with a jury, the court shall treat the case as one in which there is a special need for caution before convicting the accused on his confession.'

Prosecution of Offences Act 1985 (c. 23)

49 The Prosecution of Offences Act 1985 is amended as follows.

50 In section 7A(6)(a) (powers of non-legal staff) for 'by a jury' there is substituted 'on indictment'.

51 (1) Section 22 (power of Secretary of State to set time limits in relation to preliminary stages of criminal proceedings) is amended as follows.

(2) In subsection (11A) –

(a)   for 'when a jury is sworn' there is substituted 'at the time when a jury is sworn',

(b)   for 'a jury is sworn' there is substituted 'the time when a jury is sworn'.

(3)   After that subsection there is inserted –

'(11AA) The references in subsection (11A) above to the time when a jury is sworn include the time when that jury would be sworn but for the making of an order under Part 7 of the Criminal Justice Act 2003.'

Criminal Justice Act 1987 (c. 38)

52   The Criminal Justice Act 1987 is amended as follows.

53   (1)   Section 7 (power to order preparatory hearing) is amended as follows.
(2)   In subsection (1) for 'the jury are sworn' there is substituted 'the time when the jury are sworn'.
(3)   After subsection (2) there is inserted –

'(2A) The reference in subsection (1) above to the time when the jury are sworn includes the time when the jury would be sworn but for the making of an order under Part 7 of the Criminal Justice Act 2003.'

54   (1)   Section 9 (the preparatory hearing) is amended as follows.
(2)   In subsection (4)(b) for 'the jury' there is substituted 'a jury'.
(3)   In subsection (13) for 'no jury shall be sworn' there is substituted 'the preparatory hearing shall not be concluded'.

55   (1)   Section 10 (later stages of trial) is amended as follows.
(2)   In subsection (2) after 'jury' there is inserted 'or, in the case of a trial without a jury, the judge'.
(3)   In subsection (3) for 'deciding whether to give leave' there is substituted 'doing anything under subsection (2) above or in deciding whether to do anything under it'.
(4)   In subsection (4) for 'Except as provided by this section' there is substituted 'Except as provided by this section, in the case of a trial with a jury'.

Criminal Justice (Serious Fraud) (Northern Ireland) Order 1988 (S.I. 1988/1846 (N.I. 16))

56   The Criminal Justice (Serious Fraud) (Northern Ireland) Order 1988 is amended as follows.

57   (1)   Article 6 (power to order preparatory hearing) is amended as follows.
(2)   In paragraph (1) for 'the jury are sworn' there is substituted 'the time when the jury are sworn'.
(3)   After paragraph (2) there is inserted –

'(2A) The reference in paragraph (1) to the time when the jury are sworn includes the time when the jury would be sworn but for –

(a)   the making of an order under Part 7 of the Criminal Justice Act 2003, or

(b)   the application of section 75 of the Terrorism Act 2000.'

58   (1)   Article 8 (the preparatory hearing) is amended as follows.
(2)   In paragraph (4)(b) for 'the jury' there is substituted 'a jury'.
(3)   In paragraph (12) for 'no jury shall be sworn' there is substituted 'the preparatory hearing shall not be concluded'.

59   (1)   Article 9 (later stages of trial) (as originally enacted) is amended as follows.

(2) In paragraph (1) after 'jury' there is inserted 'or, in the case of a trial without a jury, the judge'.

(3) In paragraph (2) for 'deciding whether to give leave' there is substituted 'doing anything under paragraph (1) or in deciding whether to do anything under it'.

(4) In paragraph (3) for 'Except as provided by this Article' there is substituted 'Except as provided by this Article, in the case of a trial with a jury'.

60 (1) Article 9 (later stages of trial) (as substituted by paragraph 6 of Schedule 3 to the Criminal Procedure and Investigations Act 1996 (c. 25)) is amended as follows.

(2) In paragraph (2) after 'jury' there is inserted 'or, in the case of a trial without a jury, the judge'.

(3) In paragraph (3) for 'deciding whether to give leave' there is substituted 'doing anything under paragraph (2) or in deciding whether to do anything under it'.

(4) In paragraph (4) for 'Except as provided by this Article' there is substituted 'Except as provided by this Article, in the case of a trial with a jury'.

Police and Criminal Evidence (Northern Ireland) Order 1989 (S.I. 1989/1341 (N.I. 12))

61 (1) Article 75 of the Police and Criminal Evidence (Northern I reland) Order 1989 (confessions of mentally handicapped persons) is amended as follows.

(2) In paragraph (1) after 'indictment' there is inserted 'with a jury'.

(3) In paragraph (2) after 'indictment' there is inserted 'with a jury'.

(4) After paragraph (2) there is inserted –

'(2A) In any case where at the trial on indictment without a jury of a person for an offence it appears to the court that a warning under paragraph (1) would be required if the trial were with a jury, the court shall treat the case as one in which there is a special need for caution before convicting the accused on his confession.'

Criminal Justice and Public Order Act 1994 (c. 33)

62 The Criminal Justice and Public Order Act 1994 is amended as follows.

63 In section 35(2) (effect of accused's silence at trial) after 'indictment' there is inserted 'with a jury'.

64 In section 51(10)(b) (intimidation of witnesses, jurors and others) after 'finding' there is inserted 'otherwise than in circumstances where the proceedings are continued without a jury'.

Criminal Procedure and Investigations Act 1996 (c. 25)

65 The Criminal Procedure and Investigations Act 1996 is amended as follows.

66 (1) Section 29 (power to order preparatory hearing) is amended as follows.

(2) In subsection (1)(a) for 'the jury are sworn' there is substituted 'the time when the jury are sworn'.

(3) After subsection (4) there is inserted –

'(5) The reference in subsection (1)(a) to the time when the jury are sworn includes the time when the jury would be sworn but for the making of an order under Part 7 of the Criminal Justice Act 2003.'

67 In section 31(4)(b) (the preparatory hearing) for 'the jury' there is substituted 'a jury'.

68 (1) Section 34 (later stages of trial) is amended as follows.

(2) In subsection (2) after 'jury' there is inserted 'or, in the case of a trial without a jury, the judge'.

(3) In subsection (3) for 'deciding whether to give leave' there is substituted 'doing anything under subsection (2) or in deciding whether to do anything under it'.

(4) In subsection (4) for 'Except as provided by this section' there is substituted 'Except as provided by this section, in the case of a trial with a jury'.

69 In section 35(2) (appeals to Court of Appeal) for 'no jury shall be sworn' there is substituted 'the preparatory hearing shall not be concluded'.

70 In section 36(2) (appeals to House of Lords) for 'no jury shall be sworn' there is substituted 'the preparatory hearing shall not be concluded'.

71 (1) Section 39 (meaning of pre-trial hearing) is amended as follows.

(2) In subsection (3) –

    (a) for 'when a jury is sworn' there is substituted 'at the time when a jury is sworn',

    (b) for 'a jury is sworn' there is substituted 'the time when a jury is sworn'.

(3) After that subsection there is inserted –

    '(4) The references in subsection (3) to the time when a jury is sworn include the time when that jury would be sworn but for the making of an order under Part 7 of the Criminal Justice Act 2003.'

72 (1) Schedule 4 (modifications for Northern Ireland) is amended as follows.

(2) In paragraph 15 after the substituted version of section 39(2) there is inserted –

    '(2A) But, for the purposes of this Part, a hearing of the kind mentioned in section 45(2)(b) of the Criminal Justice Act 2003 is not a pre-trial hearing.'

(3) In paragraph 15 in paragraph (b) of the substituted version of section 39(3) –

    (a) for 'when a jury is sworn' there is substituted 'at the time when a jury is sworn', and

    (b) for 'a jury is sworn' there is substituted 'the time when a jury is sworn'.

(4) After paragraph 15 there is inserted –

    '15A In section 39(4) for "(3)" substitute "(3)(b)".'

Crime and Disorder Act 1998 (c. 37)

73 In paragraph 2(2) of Schedule 3 to the Crime and Disorder Act 1998 (applications for dismissal) for 'a jury properly to convict him' there is substituted 'him to be properly convicted'.

Youth Justice and Criminal Evidence Act 1999 (c. 23)

74 The Youth Justice and Criminal Evidence Act 1999 is amended as follows.

75 In section 32 (warning to jury) after 'indictment' there is inserted 'with a jury'.

76 In section 39(1) (warning to jury) after 'indictment' there is inserted 'with a jury'.

Anti-terrorism, Crime and Security Act 2001 (c. 24)

77 In paragraph 19(6)(c) of Schedule 1 to the Anti-terrorism, Crime and Security Act 2001 (general interpretation) after 'finding' there is inserted 'otherwise than in circumstances where the proceedings are continued without a jury'.

Proceeds of Crime Act 2002 (c. 29)

78   In section 316(9)(c) of the Proceeds of Crime Act 2002 (general interpretation) after 'finding' there is inserted 'otherwise than in circumstances where the proceedings are continued without a jury'.

PART 5

EVIDENCE

Criminal Procedure Act 1865 (c. 18)

79   In section 6 of the Criminal Procedure Act 1865 (witness's conviction for offence may be proved if not admitted) –

(a)   for 'A witness may be' there is substituted 'If, upon a witness being lawfully';

(b)   the words 'and upon being so questioned, if' are omitted.

Criminal Evidence Act 1898 (c. 36)

80   In section 1 of the Criminal Evidence Act 1898 (defendant as witness) –

(a)   at the beginning of subsection (2) there is inserted 'Subject to section 101 of the Criminal Justice Act 2003 (admissibility of evidence of defendant's bad character),';

(b)   subsection (3) is omitted.

Army Act 1955 (c. 18)

81   In section 99(1) of the Army Act 1955 (rules of evidence) after 'courts-martial etc)' there is inserted 'to Schedules 6 and 7 to the Criminal Justice Act 2003'.

Air Force Act 1955 (c. 19)

82   In section 99(1) of the Air Force Act 1955 (rules of evidence) after 'courts-martial etc)' there is inserted 'to Schedules 6 and 7 to the Criminal Justice Act 2003'.

Naval Discipline Act 1957 (c. 53)

83   In section 64A(1) of the Naval Discipline Act 1957 (rules of evidence) after 'courts-martial etc)' there is inserted 'to Schedules 6 and 7 to the Criminal Justice Act 2003'.

Armed Forces Act 1976 (c. 52)

84   In paragraph 11(1) of Schedule 3 to the Armed Forces Act 1976 (rules of evidence) after 'paragraph 12 below' there is inserted 'to Schedules 6 and 7 to the Criminal Justice Act 2003'.

Police and Criminal Evidence Act 1984 (c. 60)

85   (1)   Section 74 of the Police and Criminal Evidence Act 1984 (conviction as evidence of commission of offence) is amended as follows.

(2) In subsection (1) (commission of offence by non-defendant) for the words from ', where to do so' to 'committed that offence' there is substituted 'that that person committed that offence, where evidence of his having done so is admissible'.

(3) In subsection (3) (commission of offence by defendant) the words from 'in so far' to 'he is charged,' are omitted.

PART 6

MISCELLANEOUS

Criminal Appeal Act 1968 (c. 19)

86 The Criminal Appeal Act 1968 is amended as follows.

87 In section 31(1) (powers of Court of Appeal exercisable by single judge) after paragraph (a) there is inserted –

'(aa) the power to give leave under section 14(4B) of the Criminal Appeal Act 1995;'.

88 In section 31A (powers of Court of Appeal exercisable by registrar) after subsection (4) there is inserted –

'(5) In this section "respondent" includes a person who will be a respondent if leave to appeal is granted.'

89 In section 45 (construction of references to Court of Appeal) –

(a) in subsection (1), for 'section 44A' there is substituted 'sections 44A and 51',

(b) in subsection (2) after 'sections' there is inserted '23A,'.

90 (1) Section 51 (interpretation) is amended as follows.

(2) In subsection (1) the definition of 'the defendant' is omitted.

(3) After that subsection there is inserted –

'(1A) In Part 2 of this Act "the defendant" –

(a) in relation to an appeal under section 33(1) of this Act against a decision of the Court of Appeal on an appeal under Part 1 of this Act, means the person who was the appellant before the Court of Appeal,

(b) in relation to an appeal under section 33(1) of this Act against any other decision, means a defendant in the proceedings before the Crown Court who was a party to the proceedings before the Court of Appeal, and

(c) in relation to an appeal under section 33(1B) of this Act, shall be construed in accordance with section 33(4) of this Act;

and, subject to section 33(1A) of this Act, "prosecutor" shall be construed accordingly.'

Criminal Appeal (Northern Ireland) Act 1980 (c. 47)

91 The Criminal Appeal (Northern Ireland) Act 1980 is amended as follows.

92 (1) Section 19 (legal aid) is amended as follows.

(2) In subsection (1) after 'an appeal' there is inserted 'under this Part of this Act'.

(3) In subsection (1A) for 'for the purpose' there is substituted 'in respect'.

(4) In subsection (1A)(a) –

(a) the words 'application for leave to' are omitted, and

(b) after 'hearings)' there is inserted 'or section 47 of the Criminal Justice Act 2003'.

(5)   For subsection (1A)(b) there is substituted –

'(b)   any other appeal to the Court of Appeal under any Northern Ireland legislation (whenever passed or made) from proceedings before the Crown Court; or

(c)   an application for leave to appeal in relation to an appeal mentioned in paragraph (a) or (b) above.'

(6)   After subsection (1A) there is inserted –

'(1B)   The Crown Court or the Court of Appeal may order that an acquitted person shall be given legal aid in respect of an application made in relation to him under section 76 of the Criminal Justice Act 2003.'

(7)   In subsection (3) for 'an appellant' there is substituted 'a person'.

93   (1)   Section 28 (costs) is amended as follows.

(2)   In subsection (2)(a) for 'this Part' there is substituted 'section 19(1)'.

(3)   After subsection (2) there is inserted –

'(2AA)   The expenses of any solicitor or counsel assigned to a person pursuant to a grant of legal aid under section 19(1A) or (1B) of this Act shall, up to an amount allowed by the Master (Taxing Office), be defrayed by the Lord Chancellor.'

(4)   In subsection (2A) after '(2)(a)' there is inserted 'or (2AA)'.

(5)   In subsection (2G) –

(a)   after '(2)(a)' there is inserted 'or (2AA)', and

(b)   for 'subsection (2)' there is substituted 'subsections (2) and (2AA)'.

94   For section 31(3) (definition of defendant and prosecutor) there is substituted –

'(3)   In this Part of this Act "the defendant" –

(a)   in relation to an appeal under subsection (1) above against a decision of the Court on an appeal under Part 1 of this Act, means the person who was the appellant before the Court;

(b)   in relation to an appeal under subsection (1) above against any other decision, means a defendant in the proceedings before the Crown Court who was a party to the proceedings before the Court;

(c)   in relation to an appeal under subsection (1B) above, shall be construed in accordance with subsection (4) below;

and, subject to subsection (1A) above, "prosecutor" shall be construed accordingly.'

95   In section 45 (powers of Court of Appeal exercisable by single judge) after subsection (3B) there is inserted –

'(3C)   Subject to section 44(4) above, the power of the Court of Appeal to give leave under section 14(4B) of the Criminal Appeal Act 1995 may be exercised by a single judge of the Court.'

Criminal Justice Act 1988 (c. 33)

96   In section 36 of the Criminal Justice Act 1988 (reviews of sentencing) –

(a)   in subsection (3), for '10' there is substituted '11',

(b)   in subsection (9)(b), for '10 and 35(1)' there is substituted '11 and 35(1)'.

Criminal Appeal Act 1995 (c. 35)

97   In section 15(2)(a) of the Criminal Appeal Act 1995 (investigations by Criminal Cases Review Commission for Court of Appeal) for 'case', in both places where it occurs, there is substituted 'appeal or application for leave to appeal'.

Powers of Criminal Courts (Sentencing) Act 2000 (c. 6)

98   In section 159 of the Powers of Criminal Courts (Sentencing) Act 2000 (execution of process between England and Wales and Scotland), for 'paragraph 3(2) of Schedule 1' there is substituted 'paragraph 3(2) or 9C(2) of Schedule 1'.

SCHEDULE 37   REPEALS   Section 332

PART 1

REPEALS RELATING TO AMENDMENTS OF POLICE AND CRIMINAL EVIDENCE ACT 1984

Short title and chapter	Extent of repeal
Police and Criminal Evidence Act 1984 (c. 60)	In section 1(8), the word 'and' at the end of paragraph (c). In section 54(1), the words 'and record or cause to be recorded'. In section 63(3)(a), the words 'is in police detention or'. In section 67 – (a) the word 'such' in subsections (9), (10)(a), (b) and (c) and in both places where it occurs in subsection (11), and (b) the words 'of practice to which this section applies' in subsection (9A). In section 113 – (a) in subsection (4), the words 'issued under that subsection', (b) in subsection (8), the words 'of practice issued under this section', and (c) in subsection (10), the word 'such' in both places where it occurs.
Criminal Justice and Public Order Act 1994 (c. 33)	Section 29(3).
Armed Forces Act 2001 (c. 19)	In section 2(9), the word 'and' at the end of paragraph (c).
Police Reform Act 2002 (c. 30)	In Schedule 7, paragraph 9(1) and (6).

PART 2

BAIL

Short title and chapter	Extent of repeal
Criminal Justice Act 1967 (c. 80)	In section 22, in subsection (1) the words 'subject to section 25 of the Criminal Justice and Public Order Act 1994' and in subsection (3) the words from 'except that' to the end.
Courts Act 1971 (c. 23)	In Schedule 8, in paragraph 48(b), the word '22(3)'.
Bail Act 1976 (c. 63)	In section 3(6), the words 'to secure that'. In section 3A(5), the words 'for the purpose of preventing that person from'. In section 5, in subsection (3), the words from 'with a view' to 'another court', and in subsection (6), in paragraph (a) the words 'to the High Court or' and paragraph (b). In section 5A(2), in the substituted version of section 5(3), the words from 'with a view' to 'vary the conditions'.
Supreme Court Act 1981 (c. 54)	In section 81(1)(g), the word 'or' at the end of sub-paragraph (ii).
Criminal Justice Act 1991 (c. 53)	In Schedule 11, in paragraph 22(2), the words 'and the words' onwards.
Criminal Justice and Public Order Act 1994 (c. 33)	Section 26. In Schedule 10, paragraphs 15 and 34.
Powers of Criminal Courts (Sentencing) Act 2000 (c. 6)	In Schedule 9, paragraph 87(b).

PART 3

DISCLOSURE

Short title and chapter	Extent of repeal
Criminal Justice Act 1987 (c. 38)	In section 9(5)(i) and (iii).
Criminal Justice (Serious Fraud) (Northern Ireland) Order 1988 (S.I. 1988/1846 (N.I. 16))	Article 8(5)(i) and (iii).
Criminal Procedure and Investigations Act 1996 (c. 25)	Section 5(6) to (9). Section 6(3). Section 7. Section 9. Section 20(2). Section 32(6)(a) and (c).

PART 4

ALLOCATION AND SENDING OF OFFENCES

Short title and chapter	Extent of repeal
Bankers' Books Evidence Act 1879 (c. 11)	In section 4, the paragraph beginning 'Where the proceedings'. In section 5, the paragraph beginning 'Where the proceedings'.
Explosive Substances Act 1883 (c. 3)	Section 6(3).
Criminal Justice Act 1925 (c. 86)	Section 49(2).
Administration of Justice (Miscellaneous Provisions) Act 1933 (c. 36)	In section 2(2), paragraphs (aa) to (ac), paragraphs (iA) and (iB), and the words from 'and in paragraph (iA)' to the end.
Criminal Justice Act 1948 (c. 58)	Section 41(5A). In section 80, the definition of 'Court of summary jurisdiction'.
Backing of Warrants (Republic of Ireland) Act 1965 (c. 45)	In the Schedule, in paragraph 4, the words 'and section 2 of the Poor Prisoners Defence Act 1930 (legal aid before examining justices)'.
Criminal Procedure (Attendance of Witnesses) Act 1965 (c. 69)	Section 2(5).
Criminal Justice Act 1967 (c. 80)	In section 9(1), the words ', other than committal proceedings'. In section 36(1), the definition of 'committal proceedings'.
Criminal Appeal Act 1968 (c. 19)	In section 9(2), the words from 'section 41' to 'either way offence'.
Firearms Act 1968 (c. 27)	In Schedule 6, in Part 2, paragraph 3.
Theft Act 1968 (c. 60)	Section 27(4A).
Criminal Justice Act 1972 (c. 71)	In section 46, subsections (1A) to (1C).
Bail Act 1976 (c. 63)	In section 3, subsections (8A) and (8B), and the sub-section (10) inserted by paragraph 12(b) of Schedule 9 to the Criminal Justice and Public Order Act 1994 (c. 33). Section 5(6A)(a)(i).
Criminal Law Act 1977 (c. 45)	In Schedule 12, the entry relating to the Firearms Act 1968 (c. 27).
Interpretation Act 1978 (c. 30)	In Schedule 1, in the definition of 'Committed for trial', paragraph (a).
Customs and Excise Management Act 1978 (c. 2)	Section 147(2).
Magistrates' Courts Act 1980 (c. 43)	Sections 4 to 8, and the cross-heading preceding section 4. In section 8B(6)(a), the words 'commits or' Section 24(1A) and (2). In section 25, subsections (3) to (8).

Short title and chapter	Extent of repeal
Magistrates' Courts Act 1980 (c. 43) – *cont.*	In section 33(1), paragraph (b) and the word 'and' immediately preceding it.
	Section 42.
	Section 97A.
	Section 103.
	Section 106.
	In section 128, in subsection (1)(b), the words 'inquiring into or', and in each of subsections (1A)(a), (3A), (3C)(a) and (3E)(a), the word '5,'.
	In section 130(1), the word '5,'.
	Section 145(1)(f).
	In section 150(1), the definition of 'committal proceedings'.
	In section 155(2)(a), the words '8 (except subsection (9))'.
	In Schedule 3, paragraph 2(a).
	In Schedule 5, paragraph 2.
	In Schedule 7, paragraph 73.
Criminal Justice (Amendment) Act 1981 (c. 27)	The whole Act.
Criminal Attempts Act 1981 (c. 47)	In section 2(2)(g), the words 'or committed for trial'.
Contempt of Court Act 1981 (c.49)	Section 4(4).
Supreme Court Act 1981 (c. 54)	Section 76(5).
	Section 77(4).
	In section 81 –
	(a) in subsection (1)(a), the words 'who has been committed in custody for appearance before the Crown Court or in relation to whose case a notice of transfer has been given under a relevant transfer provision or',
	(b) subsection (1)(g)(i),
	(c) subsection (7).
Criminal Justice Act 1982 (c. 48)	Section 61.
	In Schedule 9, paragraph 1(a).
Mental Health Act 1983 (c. 20)	In section 52(7)(b), the words 'where the court proceeds under subsection (1) of that section,'.
Police and Criminal Evidence Act 1984 (c. 60)	Section 62(10)(a)(i).
	In section 71, the paragraph beginning 'Where the proceedings'.
	Section 76(9).
	Section 78(3).
Prosecution of Offences Act 1985 (c. 23)	In section 16, subsections (1)(b), (2)(aa) and (12).
	In section 23A(1)(b), the words from 'under' to '1998'.
	In Schedule 1, paragraphs 2 and 3.
Criminal Justice Act 1987 (c. 38)	Sections 4 to 6.
	In section 11 –
	(a) subsection (2)(a),
	(b) subsection (3),
	(c) in subsection (7), the word '(3),',

Short title and chapter	Extent of repeal
Criminal Justice Act 1987 (c. 38) – cont.	(d) in subsection (8), the word '(3),', (e) subsections (9) and (10), (f) in subsection (11), paragraphs (a) and (d). In Schedule 2, paragraphs 1, 9 and 14.
Criminal Justice Act 1988 (c. 33)	Section 23(5). Section 24(5). In section 26, the paragraph beginning 'This section shall not apply'. In section 27, the paragraph beginning 'This section shall not apply'. Section 30(4A). Section 33. In section 40(1), the words 'were disclosed to a magistrates' court inquiring into the offence as examining justices or'. Section 41. Section 144. In Schedule 15, paragraphs 10, 66 and 104.
Road Traffic Offenders Act 1988 (c. 53)	Section 11(3A). Section 13(7). Section 16(6A). Section 20(8A).
Courts and Legal Services Act 1990 (c. 41)	In Schedule 18, paragraph 25(5).
Broadcasting Act 1990 (c. 42)	In Schedule 20, paragraph 29(1).
Criminal Justice Act 1991 (c. 53)	Section 53. Section 55(1). Schedule 6. In Schedule 11, paragraph 25.
Criminal Justice and Public Order Act 1994 (c. 33)	Section 34(2)(a). Section 36(2)(a). Section 37(2)(a). In Schedule 9, paragraphs 12, 17(c), 18(d), 25, 27, 29 and 49. In Schedule 10, paragraphs 40 and 71.
Criminal Procedure and Investigations Act 1996 (c. 25)	In section 1(2), paragraphs (a) to (c) and, in paragraph (cc), the words from 'under' to the end. In section 5, subsections (2) and (3). In section 13(1), paragraphs (a) to (c) of the modified section 3(8). Section 28(1)(b). Section 44(3). Section 45. Section 49(4). Section 68. In Schedule 1, paragraphs 2 to 5, 8, 10, 12, 13, 15 to 19, 22(3), 24 to 26, 28 to 32, and 34 to 38. Schedule 2.
Sexual Offences (Protected Material) Act 1997 (c. 39)	Section 9(1).

Short title and chapter	Extent of repeal
Crime and Disorder Act 1998 (c. 37)	Section 47(6). In section 50(1), the words 'unless the accused falls to be dealt with under section 51 below'. In Schedule 3, in paragraph 2, sub-paragraphs (4) and (5), paragraph 12, and in paragraph 13(2), the words from 'unless' to the end. In Schedule 8, paragraphs 8, 37, 40, 65 and 93.
Access to Justice Act 1999 (c. 22)	Section 67(3). In Schedule 4, paragraphs 16, 39 and 47. In Schedule 13, paragraphs 96, 111 and 137.
Youth Justice and Criminal Evidence Act 1999 (c. 23)	Section 27(10). In section 42(3), paragraphs (a) and (b).
Powers of Criminal Courts (Sentencing) Act 2000 (c. 6)	In section 89(2)(b), the words 'trial or'. In section 140(1)(b), the words 'was committed to the Crown Court to be tried or dealt with or by which he'. In Schedule 9, paragraphs 62, 63, 64(2), 65, 91 and 201. In Schedule 11, paragraph 9.

PART 5

EVIDENCE OF BAD CHARACTER

Short title and chapter	Extent of repeal
Criminal Procedure Act 1865 (c. 18)	In section 6, the words 'and upon being so questioned, if'.
Criminal Evidence Act 1898 (c. 36)	Section 1(3).
Children and Young Persons Act 1963 (c. 37)	Section 16(2) and (3).
Criminal Evidence Act 1979 (c. 16)	In section 1, the words from 'each of the following' to '1898, and'.
Police and Criminal Evidence Act 1984 (c. 60)	In section 74(3), the words from 'in so far' to 'he is charged,'.
Criminal Justice and Public Order Act 1994 (c. 33)	Section 31.
Crime (Sentences) Act 1997 (c. 43)	In Schedule 4, paragraph 4.
Youth Justice and Criminal Evidence Act 1999 (c. 23)	In Schedule 4, paragraph 1(5).
Powers of Criminal Courts (Sentencing) Act 2000 (c. 6)	In Schedule 9, paragraph 23.

PART 6

HEARSAY EVIDENCE

Short title and chapter	Extent of repeal
Registered Designs Act 1949 (c. 88)	In section 17, in subsection (8) the words 'Subject to subsection (11) below,' and in subsection (10) the words ', subject to subsection (11) below,'.
Patents Act 1977 (c. 37)	In section 32, in subsection (9) the words 'Subject to subsection (12) below,' and in subsection (11) the words ', subject to subsection (12) below,'.
Criminal Justice Act 1988 (c. 33)	Part 2. Schedule 2. In Schedule 13, paragraphs 2 to 5. In Schedule 15, paragraph 32. In Schedule 4, paragraph 6(2).
Finance Act 1994 (c. 9)	Section 22(2)(b). In Schedule 7, paragraph 1(6)(b).
Value Added Tax Act 1994 (c. 23)	In Schedule 11, paragraph 6(6)(b).
Criminal Justice and Public Order Act 1994 (c. 33)	In Schedule 9, paragraph 31.
Civil Evidence Act 1995 (c. 38)	In Schedule 1, paragraph 12.
Finance Act 1996 (c. 8)	In Schedule 5, paragraph 2(6)(a).
Criminal Procedure and Investigations Act 1996 (c. 25)	In Schedule 1, paragraphs 28 to 31.
Crime and Disorder Act 1998 (c. 37)	In Schedule 3, paragraph 5(4).
Youth Justice and Criminal Evidence Act 1999 (c. 23)	In Schedule 4, paragraph 16.
Finance Act 2000 (c. 17)	In Schedule 3, paragraph 126(2)(a).
Finance Act 2001 (c. 9)	In Schedule 7, paragraph 3(2)(a).
Crime (International Co-operation) Act 2003 (c. 32)	In section 9(4), the words 'section 25 of the Criminal Justice Act 1988 or'.

PART 7

SENTENCING: GENERAL

Short title and chapter	Extent of repeal
Piracy Act 1837 (c. 88)	Section 3.
Children and Young Persons Act 1933 (c. 12)	In section 16(3), the words 'mandatory and'.
Criminal Justice Act 1967 (c. 80)	In section 104, in subsection (1) the definition of 'suspended sentence' and subsection (2).
Criminal Appeal Act 1968 (c. 19)	In section 10 subsection (2)(c) and the word 'or' immediately preceding it. Section 11(4).
Social Work (Scotland) Act 1968 (c. 49)	In section 94(1), the definition of 'community rehabilitation order'.
Bail Act 1976 (c. 63)	In section 2(1)(d), the words 'placing the offender on probation or'.
Magistrates' Courts Act 1980 (c. 43)	In section 82(4A), paragraph (e) and the word 'or' immediately preceding it. Section 133(2). In Schedule 6A, the entry relating to section 123(3) of the Powers of Criminal Courts (Sentencing) Act 2000.
Forgery and Counterfeiting Act 1981 (c. 45)	Section 23(1)(b), (2)(b) and (3)(b).
Mental Health Act 1983 (c. 20)	In section 37(1B), the words '109(2),'. In section 45A(1)(b), the words from 'except' to '1997'.
Road Traffic Offenders Act 1988 (c. 53)	In section 46(1), paragraph (a) and the word 'or' following it.
Football Spectators Act 1989 (c. 37)	In section 7, subsection (9) and in subsection (10)(b) the words from '(or' to the end.
Children Act 1989 (c. 41)	In section 68(2)(d), the words 'a probation order has been made in respect of him or he has been'. In Schedule 9A, in paragraph 4(2)(g), the words 'placed on probation or'.

Criminal Justice Act 1991 (c. 53)	Sections 32 to 51.
	Section 65.
	Schedule 5.
	In Schedule 12 –
	  (a) in paragraph 8(8), paragraph (d), and
	  (b) in paragraph 9(3), paragraph (c).

Prisoners and Criminal Proceedings (Scotland) Act 1993 (c. 9)	In section 10(1)(a), sub-paragraph (i) and the succeeding 'or'.
Criminal Justice Act 1993 (c. 36)	Section 67(1).
Criminal Justice and Public Order Act 1994 (c. 33)	In section 25(3)(c), the words 'placing the offender on probation or'.

Short title and chapter	Extent of repeal
Criminal Procedure (Scotland) Act 1995 (c. 46)	In section 234 – (a) in subsection (1), the words after paragraph (b), (b) in subsection (3), the words from 'or to vary' to 'one hundred', and (c) subsection (11).
Crime (Sentences) Act 1997 (c. 43)	Sections 35 and 40. In Schedule 1, paragraph 15(5). In Schedule 2, paragraphs 2 and 3. In Schedule 4, paragraphs 6(2), 7, 10(1), 12(1), 13 and 15(10).
Crime and Disorder Act 1998 (c. 37)	In section 18, subsection (2). In section 38(4)(i), the words 'section 37(4A) or 65 of the 1991 Act or'. Sections 59 and 60. Sections 80 and 81. Sections 99 and 100. Section 101(1). Sections 103 to 105. In section 121(12), the words from the beginning to 'paragraphs 56 to 60 of Schedule 8 to this Act;'. In Schedule 7, paragraph 50. In Schedule 8, paragraphs 11, 13(2), 56, 58, 59, 79 to 84, 86 to 91, 94, 97, 132 and 135(3) and (4).
Criminal Justice (Children) (Northern Ireland) Order 1998 (S.I. 1998/1504 (N.I. 9))	In Schedule 5, paragraph 28(b).
Access to Justice Act 1999 (c. 22)	Section 58(5).
Powers of Criminal Courts (Sentencing) Act 2000 (c. 6)	Section 6(4)(d). Section 12(4). Sections 34 to 36A. In section 36B, subsections (4) and (8) and, in subsection (9), the words from 'a community punishment order' to 'a drug abstinence order'. In section 37, in subsection (9) the words 'who on conviction is under 16' and subsection (10). In section 40A, subsection (4), in subsection (9) the words 'who on conviction is under 16' and subsection (10). Sections 41 to 59. In section 60, in subsection (1), paragraph (c) and the word 'or' immediately preceding it. Section 62. Section 69(11). Section 73(7). Sections 78 to 82. Section 84. Section 85. Sections 87 and 88. Section 91(2). Section 100(4). Section 106(2) and (3).

Short title and chapter	Extent of repeal
Powers of Criminal Courts (Sentencing) Act 2000 (c. 6) – cont.	Section 109.

Section 110(3).

Section 111(3).

In section 112(1)(a), the words '109,'.

In section 113, in subsection (1)(a), the words 'a serious offence or' and in subsection (3), the words ' "serious offence",' and '109,'.

In section 114(1)(b), the words 'a serious offence,'.

In section 115, the word '109,'.

Sections 116 and 117.

Sections 118 to 125.

Sections 126 to 129.

Sections 151 to 153.

Sections 156 to 158.

In section 159, the words ', 121(1) or 123(1)' and 'paragraph 6(6) of Schedule 4 to this Act,'.

In section 160 –

(a) in subsection (2), in paragraph (a) the words from '42(2E)' to 'Schedule 2' and in paragraph (b) the words from '122(7)' to the end,

(b) in subsection (3), in paragraph (a) the words '45, 50, 58, 58A(4), 85(7)', paragraph (b) and the word 'or' immediately preceding it,

(c) subsection (4), and

(d) in subsection (5), in paragraph (a) the words from 'or paragraph 7' to the end, and in paragraph (b) the words from '42(2E)' to the end.

Section 161(2) to (4).

Section 162.

In section 163, in the definition of 'affected person', paragraphs (b) and (c), the definitions of 'the appropriate officer of the court', 'community punishment and rehabilitation order', 'community rehabilitation order', 'community rehabilitation period', 'community punishment order', the definitions of 'drug abstinence order', 'drug treatment and testing order', 'falling to be imposed under section 109(2), 110(2) or 111(2)', 'pre-sentence report', 'protecting the public from serious harm', in the definition of 'responsible officer', paragraphs (b) to (ee) and the words from 'except that' to 'that section;', the definitions of 'review hearing', 'sexual offence', 'specified Class A drug', 'suspended sentence supervision order', 'the testing requirement', 'the treatment provider', 'the treatment requirement', 'the treatment and testing period', 'trigger offence' and 'violent offence'.

In section 168 –

(a) in subsection (1), the words 'to subsection (2) below and', and

(b) subsections (2) and (3).

Schedule 2.

Schedule 4.

Short title and chapter	Extent of repeal
Powers of Criminal Courts (Sentencing) Act 2000 (c. 6) – cont.	In Schedule 7, paragraph 3(4). In Schedule 8, paragraph 3(4). In Schedule 9, paragraphs 7, 24(a), 26(2), 28, 29, 52, 54(3), 55, 61, 76, 81, 82, 89(2), 90(2), 94, 102, 137 to 145, 147(2) and (3)(a) to (d) and (e)(i), 151, 174, 176(2) to (5) and (7), 177(2) and (3), 184, 185, 186(3) and (4), 187(2), (3) and (5), 196 and 202.
Terrorism Act 2000 (c. 11)	In Schedule 15, paragraph 20.
Child Support, Pensions and Social Security Act 2000 (c. 19)	Section 62(10).
Criminal Justice and Court Services Act 2000 (c. 43)	Section 47 to 51. Sections 53 to 55. Section 63. Section 64(5)(e). In section 78(1), the definition of 'community order'. In Schedule 7, paragraphs 1 to 3, 104 to 107, 111(b), 123(a) and (c) to (f), 124(a) and (b), 133, 139, 140, 161, 162, 165 to 172, 177, 179, 189, 196(c)(ii) and (iii), 197(c) and (g)(ii), 198 to 200 and 206(a).
Anti-terrorism, Crime and Security Act 2001 (c. 24)	Section 39(7).
Proceeds of Crime Act 2002 (c. 29)	In Schedule 11, paragraph 32.

PART 8

LIFE SENTENCES

Short title and chapter	Extent of repeal
Murder (Abolition of Death Penalty) Act 1965 (c. 71)	Section 1(2).
Repatriation of Prisoners Act 1984 (c. 47)	In section 2(4)(b)(i), the words 'or 29(1)'. Section 3(9). Paragraph 3 of the Schedule.
Crime (Sentences) Act 1997 (c. 43)	Section 29. Section 31(4). Section 33. In section 34(3), the words from the beginning to 'advocate; and'.
Crime and Punishment (Scotland) Act 1977 (c. 48)	In Schedule 1, paragraph 10(3).
Crime and Disorder Act 1998 (c. 37)	In Schedule 8, paragraphs 57 and 60.
Powers of Criminal Courts (Sentencing) Act 2000 (c. 6)	In section 82A, in subsection (4) the words 'subject to subsection (5) below', and subsections (5) and (6).

PART 9

ALTERATION OF PENALITIES FOR SUMMARY OFFENCES

Short title and chapter	Extent of repeal
Vagrancy Act 1824 (c. 83)	Section 5. Section 10.
Railway Regulation Act 1842 (c. 55)	In section 17, the words from 'be imprisoned' (where first occurring) to 'discretion of such justice, shall'.
London Hackney Carriages Act 1843 (c. 86)	In section 28, the words from '; or it shall be lawful' to the end.
Town Police Clauses Act 1847 (c. 89)	In section 28, the words from ', or, in the discretion' to 'fourteen days'. In section 29, the words from ', or, in the discretion' to the end. In section 36, the words, from ', or, in the discretion' to 'one month'.
Ecclesiastical Courts Jurisdiction Act 1860 (c. 32)	In section 2, the words from ', or may, if the justices' to the end.
Town Gardens Protection Act 1863 (c. 13)	In section 5, the words ', or to imprisonment for any period not exceeding fourteen days'.
Public Stores Act 1875 (c. 25)	In section 8, the words from ', or, in the discretion' to the end.
North Sea Fisheries Act 1893 (c. 17)	In section 2 – (a) in paragraph (a), the words from ', or, in the discretion' to the end, and (b) in paragraph (b), the words from ', or in the discretion' to the end. In section 3(a), the words from ', or, in the discretion' to the end.
Children and Young Persons Act 1933 (c. 12)	In section 4(1), the words from ', or alternatively' to the end.
Protection of Animals Act 1934 (c. 21)	In section 2, the words from ', or, alternatively' to the end.
Public Health Act 1936 (c. 49)	In section 287(5), the words from 'or to imprisonment' to the end.
Essential Commodities Reserves Act 1938 (c. 51)	In section 4(2), the words from 'or to imprisonment' to the end.
London Building Acts (Amendment) Act 1939 (c. xcvii)	In section 142(5), the words from 'or to imprisonment' to the end.
Cancer Act 1939 (c. 13)	In section 4(2), the words from 'or to imprisonment' to the end.
Civil Defence Act 1939 (c. 31)	In section 77, the words from 'or to imprisonment' to the end.
Hill Farming Act 1946 (c. 73)	In section 19 – (a) in subsection (2), the words from ', or to imprisonment' to the end, and

Short title and chapter	Extent of repeal
Hill Farming Act 1946 (c. 73) – *cont.*	(b) in subsection (3), the words from 'or to imprisonment; to the end.
Agriculture Act 1947 (c. 48)	In section 14(7) (as remaining in force for the purposes of section 95), the words – (a) 'to imprisonment for a term not exceeding three months or', and (b) 'or to both such imprisonment and such fine'. In section 95(3), the words – (a) 'to imprisonment for a term not exceeding three months or', and (b) 'or to both such imprisonment and such fine'.
Civil Defence Act 1948 (c. 5)	In section 4(4), the words from 'or to imprisonment' to the end.
Agricultural Wages Act 1948 (c. 47)	In section 12(7), the words from 'or to imprisonment' to the end.
Wireless Telegraphy Act 1949 (c. 54)	In section 14(1B), the words – (a) 'to imprisonment for a term not exceeding three months or', and (b) ', or both'.
Prevention of Damage by Pests Act 1949 (c. 55)	In section 22(5), the words from 'or to imprisonment' to the end.
Coast Protection Act 1949 (c. 74)	In section 25(9), the words from 'or to imprisonment' to the end.
Pet Animals Act 1951 (c. 35)	In section 5 – (a) in subsection (1), the words 'other than the last foregoing section' and the words from 'or to imprisonment' to the end, and (b) subsection (2).
Cockfighting Act 1952 (c. 59)	In section 1(1), the words – (a) 'to imprisonment for a term not exceeding three months, or', and (b) ', or to both such imprisonment and such fine'.
Agricultural Land (Removal of Surface Soil) Act 1953 (c. 10)	In section 2(1) – (a) paragraph (a) of the proviso, (b) the word '; or' immediately preceding paragraph (b) of the provisio, and (c) the words 'or to both'.
Accommodation Agencies Act 1953 (c. 23)	In section 1(5), the words from 'or to imprisonment' to the end.
Army Act 1955 (3 & 4 Eliz. 2 c. 18)	In section 19(1), the words 'to imprisonment for a term not exceeding three months or'. In section 161, the words from ', or to imprisonment' to the end. In section 171(1), the words from ', or to imprisonment' to the end. In section 191, the words from 'or to imprisonment' to the end.

Short title and chapter	Extent of repeal
Army Act 1955 (3 & 4 Eliz. 2 c. 18) – *cont.*	In section 193, the words from 'or to imprisonment' to the end. In section 196(3), the words from 'or to imprisonment' to the end. In section 197(3), the words from 'or to imprisonment' to the end.
Air Force Act 1955 (3 & 4 Eliz. 2 c. 19)	In section 19(1), the words 'to imprisonment for a term not exceeding three months or'. In section 161, the words from ', or to imprisonment' to the end. In section 171(1), the words from ', or to imprisonment' to the end. In section 191, the words from 'or to imprisonment' to the end. In section 193, the words from 'or to imprisonment' to the end. In section 196(3), the words from 'or to imprisonment' to the end. In section 197(3), the words from 'or to imprisonment' to the end.
Naval Discipline Act 1957 (c. 53)	In section 96, the words from 'or to imprisonment' to the end. In section 99(3), the words from 'or to imprisonment' to the end.
Agricultural Marketing Act 1958 (c. 47)	In section 45(6), the words – (a) 'to imprisonment for a term not exceeding one month, or', and (b) ', or to both such imprisonment and such fine'.
Rivers (Prevention of Pollution) Act 1961 (c. 50)	In section 12(2), the words from 'or to imprisonment' to the end.
Betting, Gaming and Lotteries Act 1963 (c. 2)	In section 8(1), the words – (a) 'or to imprisonment for a term not exceeding three months, or to both', and (b) 'in any case'.
Children and Young Persons Act 1963 (c. 37)	In section 40 – (a) in subsection (1), the words from 'or imprisonment' to the end, and (b) in subsection (2), the words from 'or imprisonment' to the end.
Animal Boarding Establishments Act 1963 (c. 43)	In section 3 – (a) in subsection (1), the words 'other than the last foregoing section' and the words from 'or to imprisonment' to the end, and (b) subsection (2).
Agriculture and Horticulture Act 1964 (c. 28)	In section 20(2), the words from 'or to imprisonment' to the end.
Emergency Laws (Re-enactments and Repeals) Act 1964 (c. 60)	In Schedule 1 – (a) in paragraph 1(3), the words 'to imprisonment for a term not exceeding three months or' and ', or to both', and

Short title and chapter	Extent of repeal
Emergency Laws (Re-enactments and Repeals) Act 1964 (c. 60) – *cont.*	(b) in paragraph 2(4), the words 'to imprisonment for a term not exceeding three months or' and ', or to both'.
Riding Establishments Act 1964 (c. 70)	In section 4(1), the words from 'or to imprisonment' to the end.
Industrial and Provident Societies Act 1965 (c. 12)	In section 16(5), the words from 'or to imprisonment' to the end. In section 48(2), the words from 'or to imprisonment' to the end.
Cereals Marketing Act 1965 (c. 14)	In section 17(1), the words from 'or to imprisonment' to the end.
Gas Act 1965 (c. 36)	In Schedule 6, in paragraph 9, the words from 'or to imprisonment' to the end.
Armed Forces Act 1966 (c. 45)	In section 8, the words 'to imprisonment for a term not exceeding three months or'.
Agriculture Act 1967 (c. 22)	In section 6(9), the words from 'or to imprisonment' to the end. In section 14(2), the words from 'or to imprisonment' to the end. In section 69, the words from 'or imprisonment' to the end.
Criminal Justice Act 1967 (c. 80)	Section 20.
Sea Fisheries (Shellfish) Act 1967 (c. 83)	In section 14(2), the words from 'or to imprisonment' to the end.
Theatres Act 1968 (c. 54)	In section 13(3), the words from 'or to imprisonment' to the end.
Theft Act 1968 (c. 60)	In Schedule 1, in paragraph 2(1), the words – (a) 'to imprisonment for a term not exceeding three months or', and (b) 'or to both'.
Agriculture Act 1970 (c. 40)	In section 106(8), the words from 'or imprisonment' to the end.
Breeding of Dogs Act 1973 (c. 60)	In section 3(1) – (a) paragraph (a), (b) the word '; or' immediately preceding paragraph (b), and (c) the words 'or to both'.
Slaughterhouses Act 1974 (c. 3)	In section 38(5), the words 'or imprisonment for a term of three months or both'.
National Health Service Act 1977 (c. 49)	In Schedule 11 – (a) in paragraph 8(3), the words 'to imprisonment for a term not exceeding three months or' and ', or to both', and (b) in paragraph 9(4), the words 'to imprisonment for a term not exceeding three months or' and ', or to both'.

Short title and chapter	Extent of repeal
Magistrates' Courts Act 1980 (c. 43)	In section 84(3), the words – (a) 'imprisonment for a term not exceeding 4 months or', and (b) 'to both'.
Animal Health Act 1981 (c. 22)	In paragraph 6 of Schedule 1, the words – (a) 'or to imprisonment for a term not exceeding 2 months,', and (b) 'in either case'.
Fisheries Act 1981 (c. 29)	In section 5(4), the words from 'or to imprisonment' to the end.
Civil Aviation Act 1982 (c. 16)	In section 82(2), the words from 'or to imprisonment' to the end.
Criminal Justice Act 1982 (c. 48)	Section 70.
Mental Health Act 1983 (c. 20)	Section 43(5). In section 103(9), the words – (a) 'to imprisonment for a term not exceeding three months or', and (b) 'or both'. In section 129(3), the words – (a) 'to imprisonment for a term not exceeding three months or', and (b) 'or to both'.
Building Act 1984 (c. 55)	In section 96(3), the words 'or to imprisonment for a term not exceeding three months'.
Surrogacy Arrangements Act 1985 (c. 49)	In section 4(1) – (a) paragraph (a), and (b) in paragraph (b), the words 'in the case of an offence under section 3'.
Animals (Scientific Procedures) Act 1986 (c. 14)	In section 22(3), the words – (a) 'to imprisonment for a term not exceeding three months or', and (b) 'or to both'. In section 23(2), the words – (a) 'to imprisonment for a term not exceeding three months or', and (b) 'or to both'. In section 25(3), the words – (a) 'to imprisonment for a term not exceeding three months or', and (b) 'or to both'.
Motor Cycle Noise Act 1987 (c. 34)	In the Schedule, in paragraph 1(1), the words 'to imprisonment for a term not exceeding three months or'.
Human Organ Transplants Act 1989 (c. 31)	In section 2(5), the words – (a) 'imprisonment for a term not exceeding three months or', and (b) 'or both'.

Short title and chapter	Extent of repeal
Town and Country Planning Act 1990 (c. 8)	In Schedule 15, in paragraph 14(4), the words from 'or to imprisonment' to the end.
Environmental Protection Act 1990 (c. 43)	In section 118(7), the words from 'or to imprisonment' to the end.
Criminal Justice Act 1991 (c. 53)	Section 26(5).
Deer Act 1991 (c. 54)	In section 10(3), the words from 'or to imprisonment' to the end.
Water Industry Act 1991 (c. 56)	In section 206(9), the words – (a) 'to imprisonment for a term not exceeding three months or', and (b) 'or to both'. In Schedule 6, in paragraph 5(5), the words – (a) 'to imprisonment for a term not exceeding three months or', and (b) 'or to both'.
Social Security Administration Act 1992 (c.5)	In section 105(1), the words – (a) 'to imprisonment for a term not exceeding 3 months or', and (b) 'or to both'. In section 182(3), the words – (a) 'to imprisonment for a term not exceeding 3 months or', and (b) 'or to both'.
Local Government Finance Act 1992 (c. 14)	In section 27(5), the words – (a) 'imprisonment for a term not exceeding three months or', and (b) 'or both'.
Trade Union and Labour Relations (Consolidation) Act 1992 (c. 52)	In section 240(3), the words – (a) 'to imprisonment for a term not exceeding three months or', and (b) 'or both'.
Merchant Shipping Act 1995 (c. 21)	In section 57(2) – (a) in paragraph (a), the words 'except in a case falling within paragraph (b) below,', and (b) paragraph (b).
Reserve Forces Act 1996 (c. 14)	In section 75(5), the words – (a) 'imprisonment for a term not exceeding 3 months or', and (b) '(or both)'. In section 82(1), the words – (a) 'imprisonment for a term not exceeding 3 months', and (b) '(or both)'. In section 87(1), the words – (a) 'imprisonment for a term not exceeding 3 months or', and (b) '(or both)'.

Short title and chapter	Extent of repeal
Reserve Forces Act 1996 (c. 14) – *cont.*	In section 99, the words – (a) 'imprisonment for a term not exceeding 3 months', and (b) '(or both)'. In Schedule 1, in paragraph 5(2), the words – (a) 'imprisonment for a term not exceeding 3 months or', and (b) '(or both)'.
Housing Act 1996 (c. 52)	In Schedule 1 – (a) in paragraph 23(6), the words from 'or imprisonment' to 'or both', and (b) in paragraph 24(6), the words from 'or imprisonment' to 'or both'.
Broadcasting Act 1996 (c. 55)	In section 144(4), the words – (a) 'to imprisonment for a term not exceeding three months or', and (b) 'or to both'.
Breeding and Sale of Dogs (Welfare) Act 1999 (c. 11)	In section 9 – (a) in subsection (1), paragraph (a), the word ', or' immediately preceding paragraph (b) and the words 'or to both', and (b) in subsection (7), paragraph (a), the word ', or' immediately preceding paragraph (b) and the words 'or to both'.
Powers of Criminal Courts (Sentencing) Act 2000 (c. 6)	In section 6(4), paragraph (a).
Countryside and Rights of Way Act 2000 (c. 37)	In section 81, subsections (2) and (3).
Transport Act 2000 (c. 38)	In section 82, subsection (5).

PART 10

JURY SERVICE

Short title and chapter	Extent of repeal
Juries Act 1974 (c. 23)	In section 2(5)(a), the word '9(1),'. In section 9, subsection (1) and in subsection (2) the words from 'and' to the end.
Criminal Law Act 1977 (c. 45)	In Schedule 12, the entry relating to the Juries Act 1974.
Criminal Justice Act 1982 (c. 48)	In Schedule 14, paragraph 35.
Mental Health (Amendment) Act 1982 (c. 51)	In Schedule 3, paragraph 48.
Mental Health Act 1983 (c. 20)	In Schedule 4, paragraph 37.

Short title and chapter	Extent of repeal
Juries (Disqualification) Act 1984 (c. 34)	The whole Act.
Coroners Act 1988 (c. 13)	Section 9(2).
Criminal Justice Act 1988 (c. 33)	Section 119. In Schedule 8, paragraph 8.
Courts and Legal Services Act 1990 (c. 41)	In Schedule 17, paragraph 7. In Schedule 18, paragraph 5.
Criminal Justice Act 1991 (c. 53)	In Schedule 11, paragraph 18.
Probation Service Act 1993 (c. 47)	In Schedule 3, paragraph 5.
Police and Magistrates' Courts Act 1994 (c. 29)	In Schedule 8, paragraph 28.
Criminal Justice and Public Order Act 1994 (c. 33)	Section 40. Section 42. In Schedule 10, paragraph 29.
Criminal Appeal Act 1995 (c. 35)	In Schedule 2, paragraph 8.
Police Act 1996 (c. 16)	In Schedule 7, paragraph 23.
Police Act 1997 (c. 50)	In Schedule 9, paragraph 27.
Government of Wales Act 1998 (c. 38)	In Schedule 12, paragraph 18.
Scotland Act 1998 (c. 46)	Section 85(1).
Access to Justice Act 1999 (c. 22)	In Schedule 11, paragraph 22.
Criminal Justice and Court Services Act 2000 (c. 43)	In Schedule 7, paragraph 47.
European Parliamentary Elections Act 2002 (c. 24)	In Schedule 3, paragraph 2.

PART 11

REPEALS RELATING TO AMENDMENTS OF PART 5 OF POLICE ACT 1997

Short title and chapter	Extent of repeal
Police Act 1997 (c. 50)	In section 115, subsections (3) to (5) and subsections (6C) to (6E). Section 120(3). In section 125, subsection (3) and, in subsection (4), the words 'to which subsection (3) does not apply'.
Care Standards Act 2000 (c. 14)	Section 104(3)(a). In Schedule 4, paragraph 25(2)(a).
Private Security Industry Act 2001 (c. 12)	Section 21. Section 26(3)(a).

Short title and chapter	Extent of repeal
Health and Social Care Act 2001 (c. 15)	Section 19.
Criminal Justice and Police Act 2001 (c. 16)	Section 134(3) and (4).
National Health Service Reform and Health Care Professions Act 2002 (c. 17)	Section 42(7). In Schedule 2, paragraph 64.
Education Act 2002 (c. 32)	In Schedule 12, paragraph 15(2). In Schedule 13, paragraph 8(2).
Licensing Act 2003 (c. 17)	In Schedule 6, paragraph 116.

PART 12

MISCELLANEOUS

Short title and chapter	Extent of repeal
Criminal Appeal Act 1968 (c. 19)	Section 10(4). In section 11(2), the words from '(which expression' to 'purposes of section 10)'. In section 51(1), the definition of 'the defendant'.
Bail Act 1976 (c. 63)	In section 5(1)(c), the words 'a court or officer of a court appoints'.
Magistrates' Courts Act 1980 (c. 43)	In section 1(3), the words 'and substantiated on oath'. Section 12(1)(a)(i). In section 13(3)(a), the words 'the information has been substantiated on oath and'.
Criminal Appeal (Northern Ireland) Act 1980 (c. 47)	In section 19(1A)(a), the words 'application for leave to'.
Criminal Procedure and Investigations Act 1996 (c. 25)	In Schedule 4, paragraph 16.
Crime and Disorder Act 1998 (c. 37)	In section 8(2), the words from 'and to section 19(5)' to '2000'.
Youth Justice and Criminal Evidence Act 1999 (c. 23)	In Schedule 4, paragraphs 26 and 27.
Powers of Criminal Courts (Sentencing) Act 2000 (c. 6)	In section 19(5), paragraph (c) and the word 'or' immediately preceding it. In Schedule 9, paragraphs 194 and 195.
Criminal Justice and Court Services Act 2000 (c. 43)	Sections 67 and 68.

SCHEDULE 38   TRANSITORY, TRANSITIONAL
AND SAVING PROVISIONS   Section 333(6)

Sentencing of offenders aged 18 but under 21

1   If any provision of Part 12 ('the relevant provision') is to come into force before the day on which section 61 of the Criminal Justice and Court Services Act 2000 (abolition of sentences of detention in a young offender institution, custody for life, etc.) comes into force (or fully into force) the provision that may be made by order under section 333(1) includes provision modifying the relevant provision with respect to sentences passed, or other things done, at any time before section 61 of that Act comes into force (or fully into force).

Sentencing guidelines

2   The repeal by this Act of sections 80 and 81 of the Crime and Disorder Act 1998 does not affect the authority of any guidelines with respect to sentencing which have been included in any judgment of the Court of Appeal given before the commencement of that repeal ('existing guidelines'), but any existing guidelines may be superseded by sentencing guidelines published by the Sentencing Guidelines Council under section 170 of this Act as definitive guidelines.

3   (1)   Subject to sub-paragraph (2), the repeal by this Act of section 81 of the Crime and Disorder Act 1998 does not affect the operation of subsection (4) of that section in relation to any notification received by the Panel under subsection (2) of that section, or proposal made by the Panel under subsection (3) of that section, before the commencement of the repeal.

(2)   In its application by virtue of sub-paragraph (1) after the commencement of that repeal, section 81(4) of that Act is to have effect as if any reference to 'the Court' were a reference to the Sentencing Guidelines Council.

(3)   In this paragraph 'the Panel' means the Sentencing Advisory Panel.

Drug treatment and testing orders

4   A drug treatment and testing order made under section 52 of the Powers of Criminal Courts (Sentencing) Act 2000 before the repeal of that section by this Act is in force (or fully in force) need not include the provision referred to in subsection (6) of section 54 of that Act (periodic review by court) if the treatment and testing period (as defined by section 52(1) of that Act) is less than 12 months.

Drug testing as part of supervision of young offenders after release

5   (1)   Until the coming into force of the repeal by this Act of section 65 of the Criminal Justice Act 1991 (c. 53) (supervision of young offenders after release), that section has effect subject to the following modifications.

(2)   In subsection (5B) –

(a)   in paragraph (a), for '18 years' there is substituted '14 years',

(b)   for paragraph (b) there is substituted –

'(b)   a responsible officer is of the opinion –

(i)   that the offender has a propensity to misuse specified Class A drugs, and

       (ii)   that the misuse by the offender of any specified Class A drug caused or contributed to any offence of which he has been convicted, or is likely to cause or contribute to the commission by him of further offences; and'.

(3) After subsection (5D) there is inserted –

'(5E) A person under the age of 17 years may not be required by virtue of subsection (5A) to provide a sample otherwise than in the presence of an appropriate adult.'

(4) For subsection (10) there is substituted –

'(10) In this section –

"appropriate adult", in relation to a person aged under 17, means –

(a) his parent or guardian or, if he is in the care of a local authority or voluntary organisation, a person representing that authority or organisation,

(b) a social worker of a local authority social services department, or

(c) if no person falling within paragraph (a) or (b) is available, any responsible person aged 18 or over who is not a police officer or a person employed by the police;

"responsible officer" means –

(a) in relation to an offender aged under 18, an officer of a local probation board or a member of a youth offending team;

(b) in relation to an offender aged 18 or over, an officer of a local probation board;

"specified Class A drug" has the same meaning as in Part 3 of the Criminal Justice and Court Services Act 2000 (c. 43).'

Intermittent custody

6   If section 183 (intermittent custody) is to come into force for any purpose before the commencement of the repeal by this Act of section 78 of the Powers of Criminal Courts (Sentencing) Act 2000 (c. 6) (which imposes a general limit on the power of a magistrates' court to impose imprisonment), the provision that may be made by order under section 333(1) includes provision modifying any period or number of days specified in section 183 with respect to sentences passed by magistrates' courts before the commencement of that repeal.

Transfer to Scotland of community orders and suspended sentence orders

7   (1) Until the coming into force of the repeal by the Mental Health (Care and Treatment) (Scotland) Act 2003 of the Mental Health (Scotland) Act 1984 (c. 36), in the provisions mentioned in sub-paragraph (2) the reference to the Mental Health (Care and Treatment) (Scotland) Act 2003 has effect as a reference to the Mental Health (Scotland) Act 1984.

(2) Those provisions are –

(a) paragraph 2(4) of Schedule 9 (transfer of community orders to Scotland or Northern Ireland), and

(b) paragraph 4 of Schedule 13 (transfer of suspended sentence orders to Scotland or Northern Ireland).

INDEX

Sexual Offences Act 2003

A Guide to the New Law
Paul Lewis

The Sexual Offences Act is the most far-reaching and comprehensive legislative reform in the area for over 100 years. It aims to overhaul and consolidate all sexual offences into one major Act, and to introduce and define a number of new offences.

This authoritative guide provides detailed advice on the practical implications of these radical changes including:

- strengthening and modernising the law on sex offences, including consent, indecency, prostitution, trafficking, sexual assault and rape
- increased protection for children and vulnerable people
- the introduction of measures to tighten the requirements of the sex offender's register, improve monitoring of offenders and build in safeguards against evasion and retrials.

This book includes a copy of the Act reproduced in full.

Available from Marston Book Services:
Tel. 01235 465 656.

1 85328 965 5
256 pages
£34.95
Feb 2004

The Law Society

Understanding Legal Aid

A Practical Guide to Public Funding

Vicky Ling and Simon Pugh

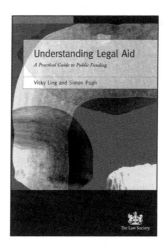

An indispensable quick reference guide to the various types of public funding available and the context in which they operate. The emphasis is on the practical implementation of the schemes and wherever possible tactical advice and checklists are provided.

- covers both civil and criminal legal aid schemes
- providing useful insights into other services performed by the Legal Services Commission, such as the Community Legal Service and Public Defender Service
- includes cross-references to official sources of information for other areas.

Written by a leading consultant and a specialist practitioner, *Understanding Legal Aid* is an easily comprehensible guide to doing publicly funded work, applicable equally to solicitors, the not-for-profit sector and the Bar.

Available from Marston Book Services:
Tel. 01235 465 656.

1 85328 895 0
256 pages
£29.95
2003

The Law Society

Forensic Practice in Criminal Cases

Lynne Townley and Roger Ede

This is a practical guide to understanding the uses, strengths and limitations of forensic practice.

Advised by experts and written by lawyers in a modern, accessible style, *Forensic Practice in Criminal Cases* takes readers through the nature and uses of forensic evidence and explores specific areas of expertise.

The book offers practical coverage of:

- the types of forensic investigation which should be carried out
- how investigations can go wrong
- what further investigations need to be carried out
- what documentary records of the investigation should be made
- how to instruct a forensic scientist to provide or challenge scientific evidence.

'At last a new and innovative book which brings together the theory and practice of criminal law and forensic science in an accessible way.'
Robert Brown, President of the London Criminal Courts Solicitors Association

Available from Marston Book Services:
Tel. 01235 465 656

1 85328 821 7
504 pages
£44.95
Dec 2003

The Law Society

Drinking and Driving Offences

Jonathan Black

This guide provides practitioners with a logical route through the maze of legislation, practice and case law that has developed around the subject of drink-driving.

The book:

- analyses relevant case law on the statutory provisions relating to drinking and driving
- examines all major challenges in courts to breathalyser law
- reviews statutory provisions relating to Human Rights Act '98
- includes details of Magistrates' Courts sentencing guidelines
- provides helpful checklists at the end of every chapter.

Contents: An overview of the procedure; The screening breath test; The arrest; Protection for hospital patients; Driving or in charge whilst under the influence; The 'in charge' statutory defence; Drinking whilst over the prescribed limit; Evidence of analysis; Using specimen evidence, post-accident consumption and back-calculation; Failure to provide a specimen; Causing death whilst under the influence of drink or drugs; Sentencing.

Available from Marston Book Services:
Tel. 01235 465 656.

1 85328 851 9
208 pages
£29.95
2002

The Law Society

CLSA Duty Solicitors' Handbook

2nd edition

Andrew Keogh

The only book to provide complete coverage of procedure in both the police station and magistrates' court.

This updated and extended 2nd edition incorporates the very latest legislative changes, including:

- Magistrates' Association sentencing guidelines
- key guideline cases including *Kefford*, *Ghafoor*, *Oliver* and *McInerney*
- new PACE Codes of Practice reproduced in full
- updated to reflect changes to the general criminal contract
- section on funding of criminal cases
- coverage of anti-social behaviour orders, youth court procedure, bail and magistrates' court procedures
- convention rights
- all the important cases of the last 12 months.

'Provides no-nonsense solutions in an easy-to-find, easy-to-follow handbook that covers the frequent and infrequent problems that arise with police station work.'
Independent Lawyer (of first edition)

Available from Marston Book Services:
Tel. 01235 465 656

1 85328 975 2
600 pages
£44.95
Nov 2003

The Law Society